BUSINESS APPLICATION DEVELOPMENT WITH EXCEL 2007

Marilyn T. Griffin

Virginia Polytechnic Institute and State University

KENDALL/HUNT PUBLISHING COMPANY

4050 Westmark Drive   Dubuque, Iowa   52002

Business Application Development with Excel 2007 is an independent publication and is not affiliated with, nor has it been authorized, sponsored, or otherwise approved by Microsoft Corporation. Excel is a registered trademark of Microsoft Corporation in the United States and/or other countries.

Cover image created by Klaus Shmidheiser

Printed in the United States of America
10 9 8 7 6 5 4 3 2 1

CONTENTS

Chapter 5   List Management   155

Chapter 6   Using Excel to Support Decisions   227

PART 2   DESIGNING PROJECT ENHANCEMENTS   277

Chapter 7   Introduction to Problem Solving and Programming Logic   279

Chapter 8   Modeling Problem Solutions with Pseudocode and Flowcharts   295

Chapter 9   Introduction to Programming Concepts and the Programming Process   319

Chapter 10   Modular Program Design & Event Programming   339

Chapter 11   Modeling Decisions for Programming   357

Chapter 12   Loop Design and Modeling   383

PART 3   ENHANCING EXCEL PROJECTS WITH VBA   407

Chapter 13   Introduction to Visual Basic for Applications   409

Chapter 16   Controlling Code Execution with Loops and Error Handling   529

PART ONE

Building Excel Projects

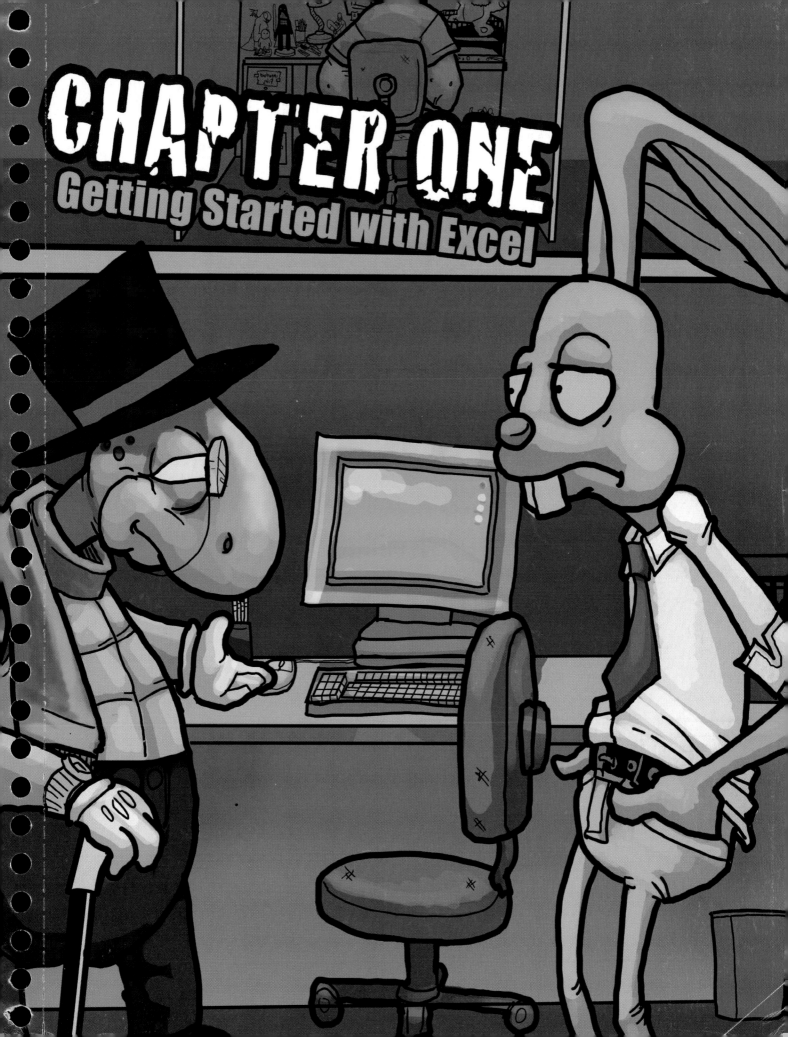

1. Create and save a new Excel workbook using an appropriate file extension
2. Explore and become familiar with the Excel ribbon, tabs, and menus
3. Access Offline and Online Excel *Help* topics
4. Enter and format worksheet data
5. Become familiar with the standard Excel data formats
6. Insert and delete rows and columns in a worksheet
7. Set up a worksheet for printing, including headers, footers, and page breaks

Introduction to Microsoft Excel 2007

Excel is a spreadsheet software program that is included in the Microsoft Office suite of applications. It is a powerful program that can be used to create and format spreadsheets for storing, analyzing, summarizing, presenting, and sharing data in order to provide decision makers the information needed to make informed decisions. Excel files are called *workbooks.* Workbooks represent the entire Excel project and may contain one or more *worksheets,* charts or graphs, macros, and other customizations.

A worksheet (also called a *spreadsheet*) is a two-dimensional table with a *cell* at the intersection of each column and row. The user may enter an item of data or a *formula* into each cell of the worksheet. A *formula* is a mathematical expression that uses other worksheet cell contents as inputs to the calculation or expression. The value of using formulas in Excel is that the formula will enable the cell content in which it is entered to stay up-to-date as the contents of the input cells change. Formulas that reference worksheet cell contents are the engines that drive the tremendous power, productivity, and flexibility supported by Excel.

Microsoft Office Fluent User Interface

With the Microsoft Office 2007 suite of applications, Microsoft introduces a new menu system that replaces most of the menu and toolbar systems found in previous versions of the Office applications. The new interface design is called the *Microsoft Office Fluent User Interface (UI).* The redesign from previous versions of Microsoft Office is an attempt to provide a navigation system to the user that focuses on *what* the user wants to do instead of *how* to do it. As more functionality has been added to each new version of Office, the menu paths have gradually grown more complex and difficult to recall by the user. Microsoft's goal in the new design is to make each application easier to use with less interface clutter and disruption. The Microsoft Fluent UI has nine key components as illustrated below in Excel 2007.

1. **The Ribbon:** The ribbon is the primary replacement for the menus and toolbars of the previous versions of Excel. Application tasks are grouped according to the type of activity and represented by task groups on named tabs on the ribbon. For example, tasks related to Page Layout are grouped together and tasks related to Data are grouped together. The user can select the tab that corresponds to the task he wants to perform and a ribbon appears with features to support the task type. Default tabs that appear on the ribbon for Excel are *Home, Insert, Page Layout, Formulas, Data, Review,* and *View.*

Figure 1-1: The Excel ribbon (*Home* tab).

2. **Contextual Tabs:** In addition to the default tabs that appear on the ribbon, context tabs appear automatically in response to a type of task performed by the user. For example, when the user inserts a chart onto a worksheet, additional *Chart Tools* tabs appear (*Design, Layout, and Format*).

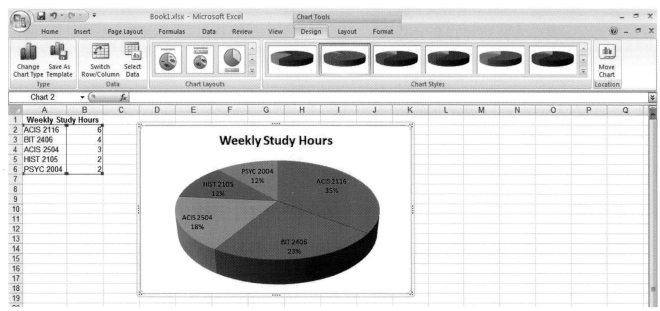

Figure 1-2: Contextual Tabs after inserting a chart.

3. **The Office Button** 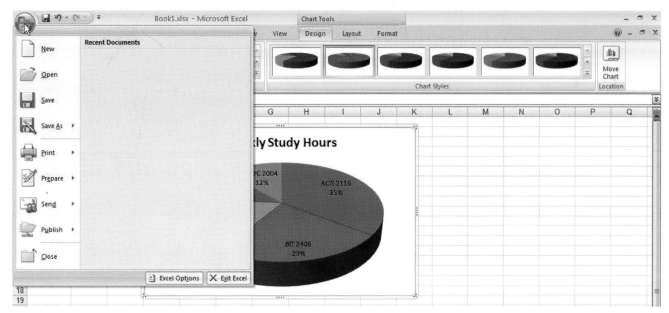**:** The Office Button provides options for file manipulation, such as creating, naming, saving, closing, converting, printing, publishing, sending, and preparing a file. It replaces the *File* menu in previous versions of Excel.

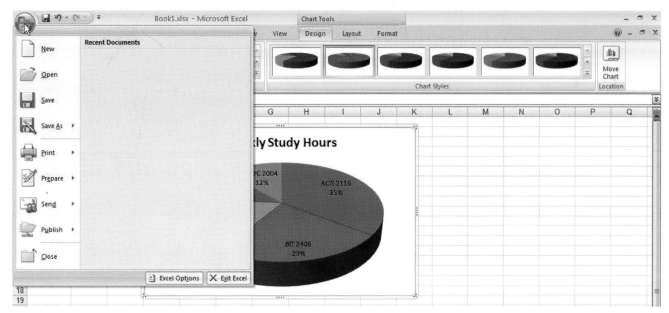

Figure 1-3: The Office Button provides features for manipulating Excel files.

4. **Galleries:** Galleries are visual sets of options available for a spreadsheet (Excel), document (Word), presentation (PowerPoint), or database (Access) that are accessed with a single click by the user. The purpose of the galleries is to streamline the process of producing professional-looking results without the use of complex dialog boxes which contain many different options to select.

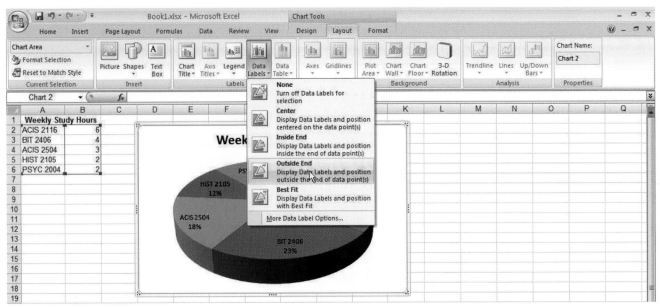

Figure 1-4: Chart Layout gallery feature.

5. **Live Preview:** This dynamic feature shows the result of a gallery selection within the spreadsheet or document before the gallery selection is actually applied. The effects can be viewed when the mouse rolls over a selection. For example, before changing a font type, the selected text in the document or worksheet changes to the font type as the mouse rolls over the selection in the font type list.

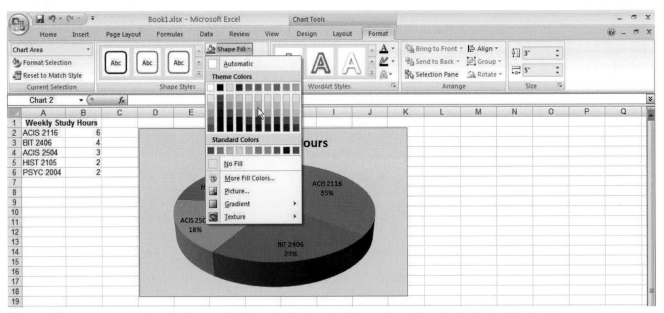

Figure 1-5: Note how the chart background changes as the mouse rolls over the color selection in the Live Preview.

6. **Mini Toolbar:** The Mini Toolbar provides easy access to the most often-used formatting commands. Instead of highlighting the text to edit, then applying the format from a menu item, the Mini Toolbar appears to the right of the selected text. The Mini Toolbar can be used to manipulate text font type, size, style, color, background color, indent, list type, and paragraph style.

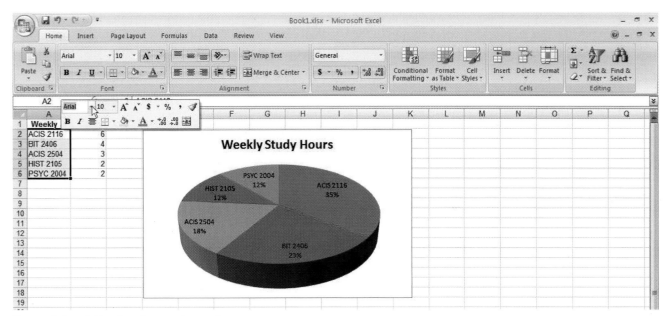

Figure 1-6: Mini Toolbar for text formatting.

7. **Enhanced Screen Tips:** Screen tips are pop-up boxes of text that explain a feature when the mouse rolls over the ribbon icon. The screen tips include a detailed explanation of the feature, keyboard shortcuts where applicable, and a link to associated entries in the Help feature.

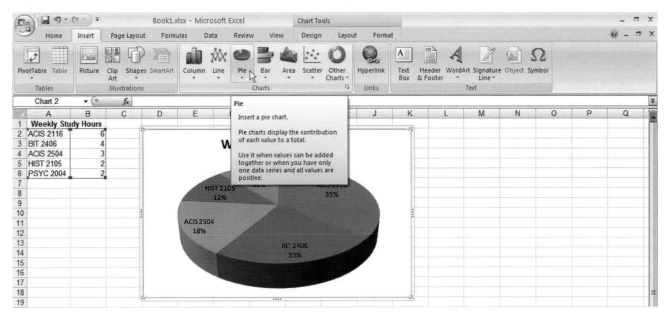

Figure 1-7: View Enhanced Screen Tips when the mouse rolls over a ribbon selection.

8. **Quick Access Toolbar:** The Quick Access Toolbar provides a single location for users to access the most often-used features with one click. The Quick Access Toolbar resides to the right of the Office Button. By default, the toolbar includes some core features such as *Save, Undo, and Redo.* Other feature shortcut icons may

Figure 1-8: Use the Quick Access Toolbar (to the right of the Office Button) to store frequently used feature shortcut icons.

be added to the toolbar by right-clicking on the feature icon on the ribbon and selecting **Add to the Quick Access Toolbar** from the context menu.

9. **Key Tips:** The same keyboard shortcuts are supported in Office 2007 as in previous versions. To further assist with keyboard shortcuts, Office 2007 displays the
keyboard shortcut keys above the ribbon tabs and Quick Access Toolbar items
when the *Alt* key is pressed.

Figure 1-9: Access Key Tips by pressing the *Alt* key.

Using Excel *Help* Features

In addition to the nine key components of the new ribbon and tab design is the universal Help icon 🔘 that appears on the far right side of the tab layout portion of the

Figure 1-10: Use the Help icon to launch the Help feature.

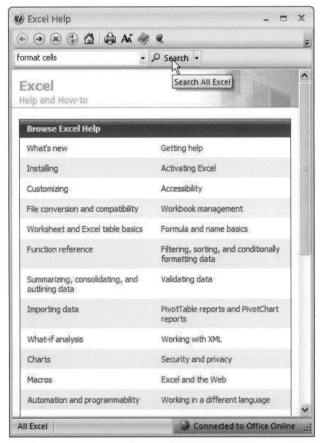

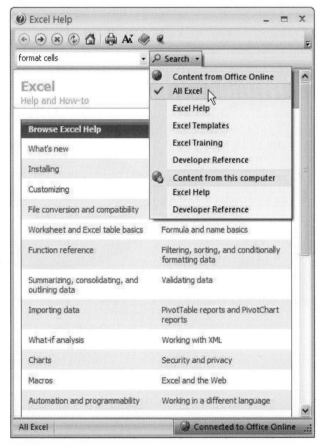

Figure 1-11: When the Excel Help feature opens, type a search
topic or question into the Search text box or select a topic from the
list of topics presented. The Help feature automatically connects to
the Web-based help files located on the Microsoft Web site.

Figure 1-12: After entering a topic in the Search text box, you
may select the Help location(s) to search for a topic.

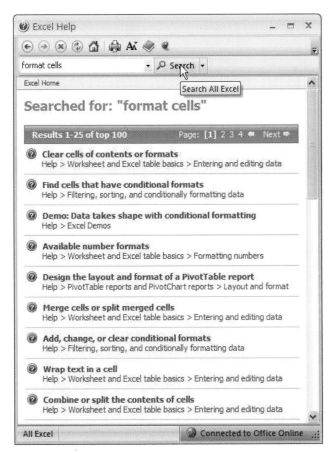

Figure 1-13: Search results for "format cells" topic. Each item in the result list is a link to an explanation of the topic in Excel Help.

Figure 1-14: You may also elect to search Offline Help files (those located on the same machine that is running the Excel application) by clicking on the link "Show me offline help from my computer."

Quick Tip!

ribbon. One click on the Help icon brings up the Help search utility and Help topics to browse.

Access the complete Excel Help feature quickly by using the keyboard shortcut F1 key.

Creating, Saving, and Closing a Workbook

When Excel opens, a new blank workbook is visible. To open a new workbook with Excel already open, select the **Office Button→New.** Select **Blank Workbook** from the *New Workbook* dialog box that appears.

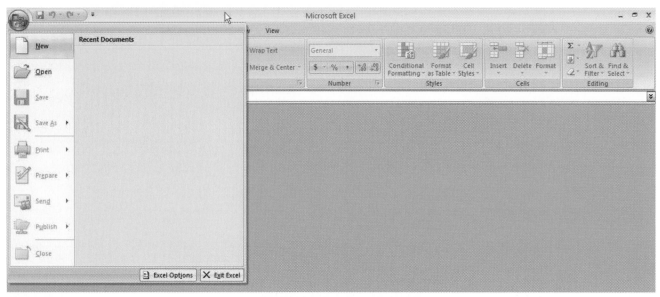

Figure 1-15: To open a new workbook, select *New* from the Office Button menu list.

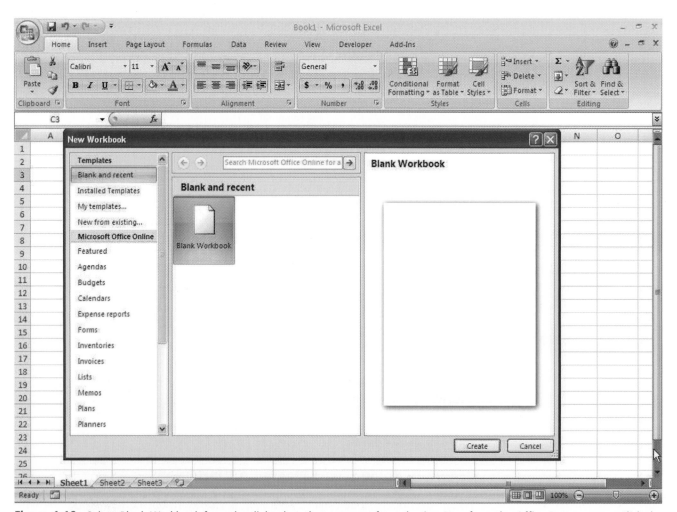

Figure 1-16: Select *Blank Workbook* from the dialog box that appears after selecting *New* from the Office Button menu. Click the *Create* button to begin using the new workbook.

By default, the new workbook file contains three blank worksheets. The new workbook is ready for the user to enter data or formulas into its worksheet cells.

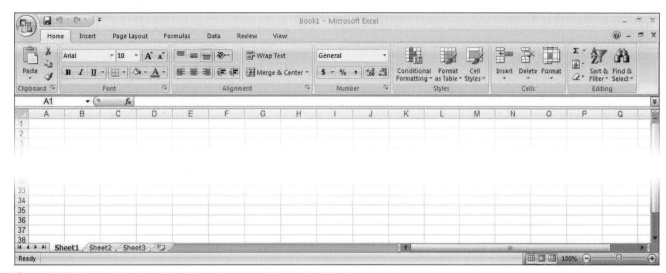

Figure 1-17: A new Excel workbook has three worksheets by default.

To save and name the new workbook, select the **Office Button→Save As.** A secondary menu will appear to allow the user to select the file format for the new workbook. Select the desired file format from the secondary menu. When the workbook is reopened after the last *Save* and *Close,* it will reopen to the worksheet that was active at the last *Save.* As each worksheet is activated, the last cell(s) selected will be the current active cell(s) upon reactivating the worksheet.

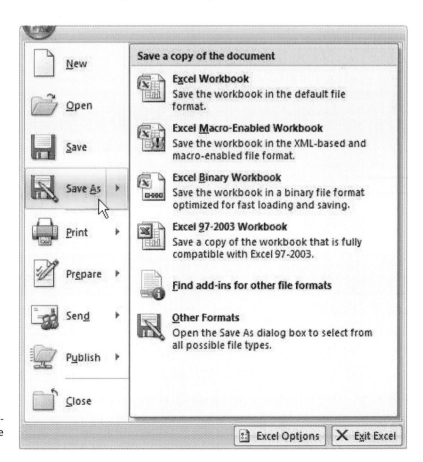

Figure 1-18: Options for file formats appear in response to the *Save As* command.

Each file format has an associated file extension that is included in the Excel file name. The file extension is based on file extensions from previous versions of Excel plus an additional character that differentiates between files that support VBA code (including macros) and files that are free of VBA code (and macros). Additionally, some file extensions support XML format and some do not.

VBA stands for Visual Basic for Applications and is a programming environment that is separate from but runs inside Excel. It is used to automate and customize Excel workbooks and other types of Microsoft Office files. VBA in Excel is the topic of Chapters 13, 14, 15, and 16 of this book.

XML stands for *eXtensible Markup Language* that is introduced in Office 2007 as a file format to facilitate the integration of data from Office applications with external data and also to improve data recovery and reduce file size. The file format is called *Office Open XML* format and is also used to format Excel workbooks for Web presentation.

Table 1-1: Excel 2007 file extensions and characteristics of each.

File Extension	File Type	Description
.xlsx	Excel 2007 XML workbook	The default file extension and format for an Excel workbook. Cannot store VBA (macro) code but does support XML.
.xlsm	Excel 2007 XML macro-enabled workbook	Differs from the default extension in that it supports both macros and XML.
.xltx	Excel 2007 XML template	The default file extension and format for an Excel template. Cannot store VBA (macro) code but does support XML.
.xltm	Excel 2007 XML macro-enabled template	Differs from the default template file extension in that it supports both VBA code and XML. Workbooks created from an .xltm template inherit the VBA project part of the template in addition to the basic components of the template workbook.
.xlsb	Excel 2007 binary workbook (BIFF 12)	A fast-loading binary file format that supports large complex workbooks and VBA projects but does not support XML. It can also be used to optimize performance and for backward compatibility.
.xlam	Excel 2007 XML macro-enabled add-in	An Excel "Add-in" which is a supplemental program that runs inside Excel. These add-ins support both VBA projects and XML.

To close the saved workbook, select the **Office Button→Close.** If changes have been made to the workbook since it was last saved, you will be prompted to save the file before closing. If you wish to close the Excel application select the **Office Button→Exit** or click the *Close Window* icon in the upper right corner of the application window.

Compatibility with Earlier Versions of Excel

In addition to file formats that are new for Excel 2007, the user has the option of saving the workbook in a format that is compatible with Excel 1997–2003 versions. In earlier versions of Excel, you can install updates and backward compatibility converters that help you open Excel 2007 workbooks for editing. The converters permit you to edit using a previous Excel version, then save back in Excel 2007 formats so it can be opened again in Excel 2007 without losing any previous Excel 2007 features. Find updates and converters for earlier Excel versions currently at www.microsoft.com and search for "office 2007 converters."

Accessing Excel Features

When Excel opens for the first time, the ribbon is displayed with the *Home* tab selected. Explore the ribbon features by rolling over the ribbon icons with the mouse and review the Screen Tips as they appear. Some screen tips will only appear when an appropriate object is selected, such as a worksheet cell, a chart, or a picture.

Figure 1-19: Feature icons on the *Home* tab of the ribbon.

Figure 1-20: Feature icons on the *Insert* tab of the ribbon.

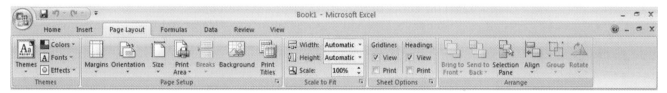

Figure 1-21: Feature icons on the *Page Layout* tab of the ribbon.

Figure 1-22: Feature icons on the *Formulas* tab of the ribbon.

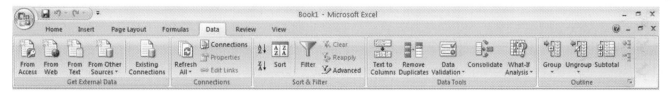

Figure 1-23: Feature icons on the *Data* tab of the ribbon.

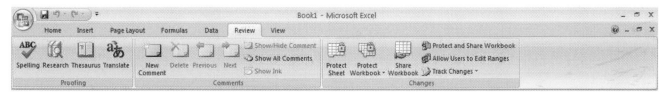

Figure 1-24: Feature icons on the *Review* tab of the ribbon.

Figure 1-25: Feature icons on the *View* tab of the ribbon.

Entering and Editing Cell Contents

To enter data or text into a worksheet cell, select the cell with the mouse or keyboard arrow keys. Once the cell is *active* (selected), begin typing to enter content into the cell. To leave the cell once the desired content has been entered, use the *Enter* key or an arrow key to move from the active cell.

There are three ways to select a cell for editing. (1) You may select the cell as described earlier and edit the content in the *formula bar*. (2) You may double-click the cell and edit the content directly in the cell. (3) With the cell selected, use the F2 key on the keyboard to enable editing directly within the cell.

Special Editing Features

Excel includes features that improve the ability to edit cell contents. These features are also found in Microsoft Word and other word processing applications. Such features include Spell Checking, Auto Correction, and Find and Replace.

To check spelling for the active worksheet, select **Review(tab)→Proofing (group)→Spelling.**

To set auto-correction options for correcting spelling as you type data into cells, select the **Office Button→Excel Options→Proofing.**

To use the Find and Replace feature select **Home (tab)→Editing (group)→Find and Replace.**

Copy and Paste Cell Contents

Excel offers many "smart" options for copying and pasting cell contents from one cell to another. Simple copy and paste may be completed using the Clipboard task group on the ribbon or by using the context menu which may be accessed by right-clicking on the selection to copy. Keyboard shortcuts used in other Microsoft Office applications may also be used to cut, copy, and paste. The following keyboard shortcuts used in Microsoft Office applications also work in Excel:

Table 1-2: These Microsoft Office keyboard shortcuts also work in Excel.

Keyboard Shortcut	Action
Ctrl + c	Copy
Ctrl + v	Paste
Ctrl + x	Cut
Ctrl + y	Repeat last action
Ctrl + z	Undo last action

Pasting a Series of Data

In many cases users label worksheet rows or columns with a series of data, such as a number sequence, or a date sequence. For example, a store manager may wish to number a list of inventory items sequentially so that each item will have a unique identification number. Excel's *Auto Fill* feature enables the user to fill contiguous cells with a series of numbers or dates. To use the Auto Fill feature, enter the first number or date in the series you wish to create. If you are numbering by one value for each row or column, only the initial number or date is needed. Select the cell with the initial value. Using the *fill handle*, drag the handle down or across to fill the desired range of cells. All the cells in the selected range will likely contain the original value at first. While the range is selected, the *Auto Fill Options* icon will appear at the bottom right corner of the selected range. From the drop-down list on the icon, select *Fill Series*. The range will then be filled with a sequence of numbers or dates beginning with the value entered into the initial cell of the range.

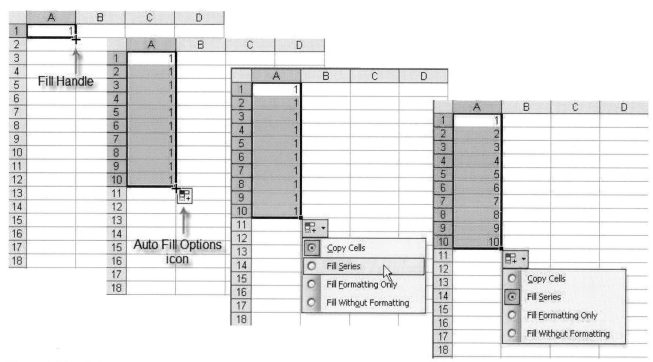

Figure 1-26: Fill down a numeric sequence with the *Auto Fill* feature.

Excel's *Auto Fill* feature also extends to data items containing a mixture of text and numbers. When portions of date/time data are used as the initial value, the item will be incremented by one in the fill series. For example, if the first entry is Monday, the next consecutive cells will be filled with Tuesday, Wednesday, etc.

Pasting a Repeating Pattern of Data

In some cases, it may be desirable to fill a range of cells with a sequence of values that change by a different value other than one, or it may be desirable to fill a range with another pattern of values or labels. To fill a range of worksheet cells with a specific pattern of values, enter the first two or more values into the first contiguous cells. You will need to enter enough values to establish the entire pattern. For example, if you are wishing to use a sequence of numbers that change by a value of 5, you will need to enter at least the first two values, such as 0 and 5, or 5 and 10, or 1 and 6. By doing so, you are showing Excel the pattern you wish to paste.

When using dates, users often wish to paste a particular series of dates, sometimes using only weekdays and sometimes having only month or year change for each contiguous cell. Excel offers additional options in the *Auto Fill* icon drop-down list for working

Table 1-3: Auto Fill results

Initial Value	Auto Fill Series
September 1, 2007	September 2, 2007; September 3, 2007, etc.
Monday	Tuesday, Wednesday, Thursday, etc.
January	February, March, April, etc.
January, 2004	January, 2005; January, 2006; January, 2007; etc.
1st Quarter	2nd Quarter, 3rd Quarter, 4th Quarter, 1st Quarter, 2nd Quarter, etc.
8:00 a.m.	9:00 a.m., 10:00 a.m., 11:00 a.m., etc.
Option 1	Option 2, Option 3, Option 4, etc.

with a series of dates. For example, if you would like to fill a column with only Tuesdays and Thursdays, enter the dates for the first Tuesday and the first Thursday in the first two cells of the range you wish to fill. Select the two cells and paste down the entire column using the fill handle. Note that the column is filled with the sequence of dates that represent every other day. We want to show only dates for Tuesdays and Thursdays. From the drop-down list on the *Auto Fill* icon, select *Fill Weekdays*. The sequence will change to only those dates that represent only a Tuesday or a Thursday instead of every other day.

Quick Tip!

When filling a column in an existing worksheet list (where the column to fill is beside another filled column), double-click on the *fill handle* to fill the entire column. This is particularly helpful when there are hundreds or thousands of cells in the column to fill.

Figure 1-27: Fill in a sequence of Tuesday and Thursday dates using the *Fill Weekdays* option.

Move Contents of a Cell

To move the contents of one cell or region to another, select the source cell(s) (those with the content you want to move) and select **Home(tab)→Clipboard (group)→ Cut** to remove the contents from the source cell or region. To paste the content into the target cell(s) select **Home(tab)→Clipboard(group)→Paste** or use the keyboard shortcut (Ctrl + V) to paste it into the target cell.

Quick Tip!

To move the contents of a cell to another cell, select the source cell then position the mouse pointer over an edge of the cell until the cursor changes to a "move" pointer. Using the left mouse button, drag the cell contents and drop it into the desired cell. (The program will alert you before allowing you to overwrite already existing data in the target cells.)

Formatting Cell Contents

When data is entered into a worksheet cell, it is formatted or presented in a particular style. Each cell contains a *value* (the data entered into the cell) and each cell also has a *format* (the presentation style). A value may appear different to the viewer as different formats are applied. For example, the value 9.6 may appear as 10 if the number of decimal places is changed from one to zero because it would automatically round the value to the closest whole number (with no decimal places). The format containing zero decimal places is simply the format or presentation style of the value and not the actual value itself.

The contents of a worksheet cell are values that are either text (alphanumeric characters) or numeric. Various format options are available for cell contents. For example, numeric data may be formatted with or without decimal places, comma separators, or dollar signs. Text and numeric data may be formatted with various font effects (bold, italic, underline, etc.) and may be aligned with the right or left side of the cell or centered in a cell or across a range of cells.

When a new worksheet is created, all cells are assigned the *General* format by default. The *General* format style is a "smart" style Excel uses that responds to the type of data entered into the cell and formats it in a style appropriate for the specific type of data. For example, the default alignment within a cell for text data is to the left side of the cell, so when a user enters text data into a cell, it is automatically aligned left. The default alignment for numeric or date values is the right side of the cell so when a number or date is entered into a cell, it is automatically aligned right. If there are leading zeros in numeric entries, Excel automatically removes the leading zeros from the display. Excel reads the data entered and figures out the type of data and formats it appropriately. Sometimes the automatic format is desirable to the user, but sometimes the user prefers to apply a different format to the cell or cell range. To select a specific format for a cell or cell range, first select the cell or cell range and select the desired format from the drop-down list on the **Home(tab)→Number(group)** of the ribbon. In addition to various number and currency formats, numbers may also be formatted as dates or text using the ribbon selection or by typing an apostrophe in front of the numeric entry. The apostrophe signals to Excel that a text entry follows so it aligns the entry left by default and will retain any leading zeros that may be present.

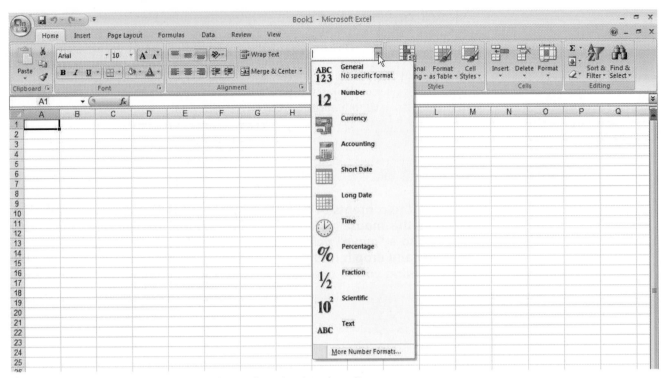

Figure 1-28: Select a predefined number format from the drop-down list.

Selecting Cells for Formatting

Cells may be selected using the mouse or keyboard. Using the mouse, hold down the left mouse button while dragging to select the desired contiguous range of cells. Using the keyboard, use the arrow keys to move to the desired single cell or to a cell at the corner of a range of cells you wish to select. While holding down the *Shift* key, use the arrow keys to move up, down, left, or right to select the desired cell range. Use the *Home* keyboard shortcut to move to the beginning of a row and the *End* key to move to the end of a row. Use the *Ctrl+Home* keyboard shortcut to move to the upper left cell of the filled region and *Ctrl+End* to move to the bottom right cell of the filled region. Once a range of cells has been selected, the same format may be applied to all cells in the selected range at once.

Non-contiguous cell ranges may also be selected and formatted at the same time. To select a non-contiguous range of cells, use the mouse to select the first contiguous range, then while holding down the *Ctrl* key, use the mouse to select additional ranges of cells.

	A	B	C	D	E	F	G	H	I
1	Employee ID	Last Name	First Name	Birth Date	Gender	Hire Date	Department	Job Title	Salary
2	1	Abner	David	11/15/1977	M	6/20/2006	Sales		$ 110,958
3	2	Butler	Susan	11/16/1967	F	8/13/1978	Marketing	Staff	$ 40,816
4	3	Conrad	Michael	9/14/1955	M	12/25/2001	Product Development	Engineer	$ 74,665
5	4	Davis	Randall	7/15/1947	M	5/25/1980	Finance		$ 140,712
6	5	Edwards	Minnie	3/8/1959	F	11/26/1991	Human Resources		$ 90,228
7	6	Franklin	Margaret	11/25/1979	F	3/15/1977	Product Development	Staff	$ 42,976
8	7	Gardner	William	11/15/1968	M	2/7/1999			$ 90,650
9	8	Hilton	Hillery	11/23/1949	F	11/8/2005	Sales	District Sales Manager	$ 128,845
10	9	Jameson	Jennifer	1/17/1959	F	11/28/1992			$ 110,496
11	10	Kelly	Chester	10/28/1968	M	1/3/1994			$ 98,538
12									

Figure 1-29: A non-contiguous range selected for formatting.

Selecting entire rows of the worksheet can be accomplished by clicking on the row number to the left of the worksheet. When the mouse pointer is positioned over the row number, an arrow points to the right indicating the entire row may be selected. Click on the row number to select the row. Multiple rows may be selected by dragging the mouse down to select multiple row numbers. Non-contiguous rows may be selected with the mouse while holding down the *Ctrl* key. One or more entire columns may be selected similarly by clicking on the column letter or number at the top of the column. When the mouse pointer is positioned over the column letter or number, an arrow that points down will appear. Non-contiguous columns may be selected with the mouse while holding down the *Ctrl* key.

If it is desirable to select all cells on the worksheet at once, such as to set a background color for the entire worksheet, use the mouse pointer to select the Select All button in the upper left corner of the worksheet border. Alternately, use the keyboard shortcut *Ctrl+a* to automatically select a contiguous range (first select a cell inside a range) and/or the entire worksheet (click outside all contiguous ranges on the worksheet in general).

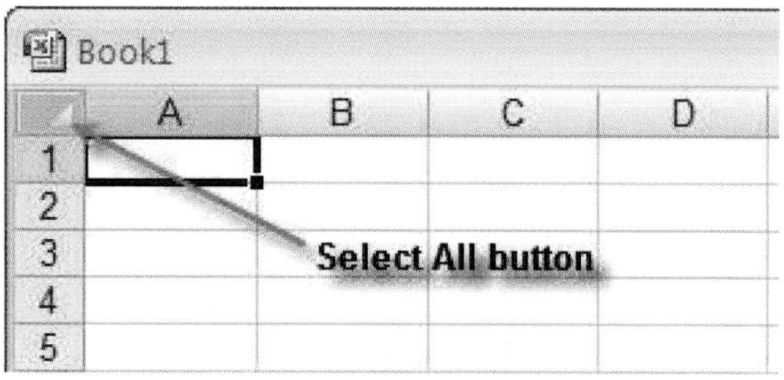

Figure 1-30: Use the *Select All* button to select all cells on the worksheet.

Formatting Numeric Data

Excel offers many standard numeric data formats that are readily available within the *Format* menu options. For numeric data, the user may choose the number of decimal places to display and whether or not to display the comma separator (for thousands). Excel also offers two types of predefined formats for monetary values, *Currency* and *Accounting*. The *Currency* format displays the dollar sign (or other monetary symbol) immediately to the left of the value. It offers a choice for the number of decimal places to be displayed and four options for displaying negative values. The *Accounting* format displays the dollar sign in the far left margin of the cell such that a column of values with the Accounting format will have all dollar signs aligned. It automatically displays negative numbers within a set of parentheses with the dollar sign outside the parentheses at the left cell margin.

"Currency" Format	"Accounting" Format
$15,650.00	$ 15,650.00
$17,526.00	$ 17,526.00
$25,869.00	$ 25,869.00
$24,789.26	$ 24,789.26
$11,085.25	$ 11,085.25

Figure 1-31: Examples of *Currency* and *Accounting* formats.

There may be special circumstances in which numeric data neither represents an actual number value or date nor is used in a calculation. In such cases, the numeric characters should be treated as text instead of numbers. Examples of such cases are social security numbers, phone numbers, and zip codes when these numbers are entered without separating characters such as hyphens. By treating such entries as text, Excel will not drop the leading zero when the value is entered. To apply a text format to numbers, be sure to apply the format to the cell range before the numeric characters are actually entered.

Formatting Percent Values

Fractional numeric values may be displayed in a percentage format by selecting the cells to format then select *Percentage* from the drop-down list on the **Home(tab)→Number (group)** (see Figure 1-28). The percentage format allows the user to specify the precision of the format by specifying the number of decimal places to the right of the decimal. The percent value is displayed as a whole number and the specified number of decimal places followed by the percent symbol (%). If percentage data is entered into a formatted cell by the user, it should be entered as a decimal value. For example, if the percentage you wish displayed is 70.52%, the value 0.7052 should be typed into the cell.

Quick Tip!

Icons in the Number group of the Home tab provide a quick way to apply *Accounting* and *Percentage* formats, to insert commas into numeric values and to increase or decrease the number of decimal places.

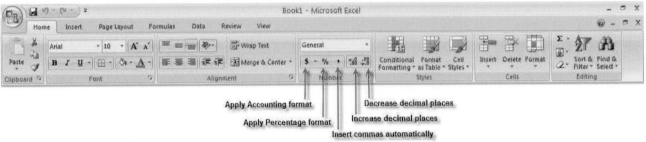

Figure 1-32: Use icons in the Number group of the Home tab to quickly apply Accounting and Percentage formats, insert commas, increase, or decrease decimal places.

Formatting Worksheet Text

To format worksheet text, select the cell(s) to format then select **Home(tab)→Font (group).** Use the task group icons to select the font type, size, characteristics (bold, italic, and underlined), color, background color, cell border placement, and style. Use the large or small "A" icon to make all mixed size text one size larger or smaller with each click.

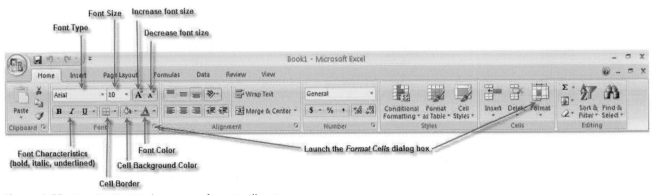

Figure 1-33: Use the *Font* task group to format cell text.

There are two additional ways to access most of the same cell formatting features. One is to click on the bottom right corner of the *Font* task group and the *Format Cells* dialog box will appear. Another way to view the same *Format Cells* dialog box is to select **Home(tab)→Cells(group)→Format→Format Cells.** The *Format Cells* dialog box contains six tabs; *Number, Alignment, Font, Border, Fill,* and *Protection.*

The *Number* tab is the same dialog tab as viewed when you select *More Number Formats* on the drop-down number formats list (see Figure 1-19). Formats for cell contents may be selected as well as number of decimal places and comma separators.

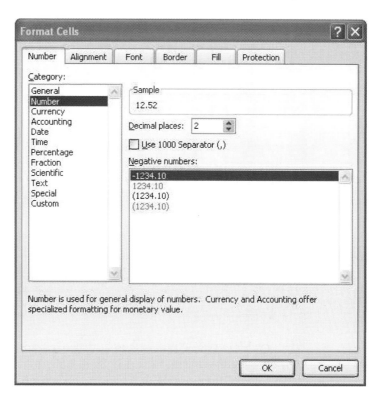

Figure 1-34: *Number* tab of *Format Cells* dialog box.

The *Font* tab of the *Format Cells* dialog box will likely look familiar as it is very similar to the *Font* dialog box in other Microsoft applications. Both the ribbon icons and the Font dialog box utilities permit the user to change font name, size, effect (bold, italic, underline), and color of the text.

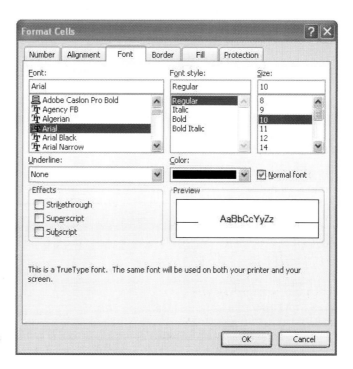

Figure 1-35: Select the font options for cell contents.

To change the color or pattern of the cell background, select the *Fill* tab on the *Format Cells* dialog box.

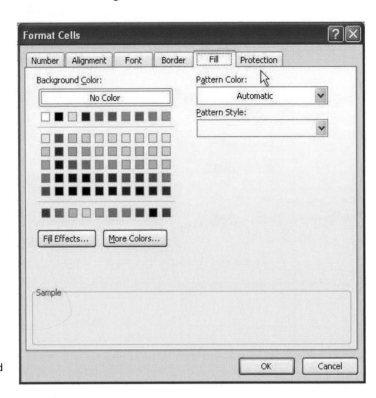

Figure 1-36: Select the background options for cell contents.

On a worksheet, the cells are visually separated by *Gridlines* which form a matrix of faint outlines for the cells that, by default, do not print (see the topic "Formatting Worksheets" for more about *Gridlines*). To add a border to certain cells for printing or emphasis, select the desired border position and style on the *Border* tab of the *Format Cells* dialog box.

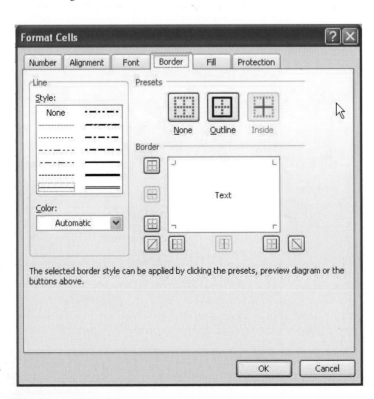

Figure 1-37: Select cell border options and style.

Borders may also be added by using the *Border* icon in the *Font* group of the *Home* tab.

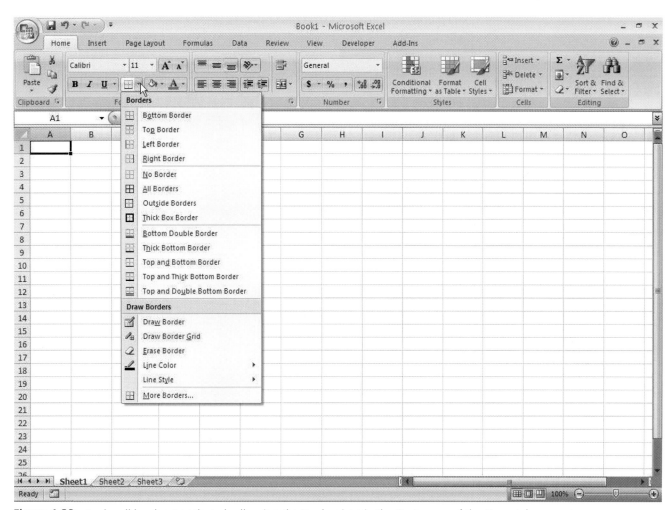

Figure 1-38: Apply cell borders to selected cells using the Borders icon in the *Font* group of the *Home* tab.

Aligning Cell Contents

The most efficient way to align cell contents horizontally or vertically is to select the cells to align and select **Home(tab)→Alignment(group)** and click on the appropriate alignment icon in the group. For example, to center column labels, select the column label row and click the *Center* horizontal alignment icon.

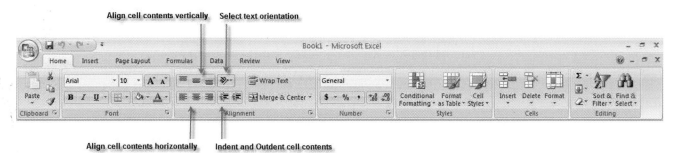

Figure 1-39: Select alignment options with the *Alignment* task group.

Titles or labels may be aligned over a number of columns or rows. To merge two or more cells while centering the contents across the merged cells, select **Home(tab)→**

Alignment(group)→**Merge & Center** icon. The *Merge Cells* feature is also available on the *Alignment* tab of the *Format Cells* dialog box.

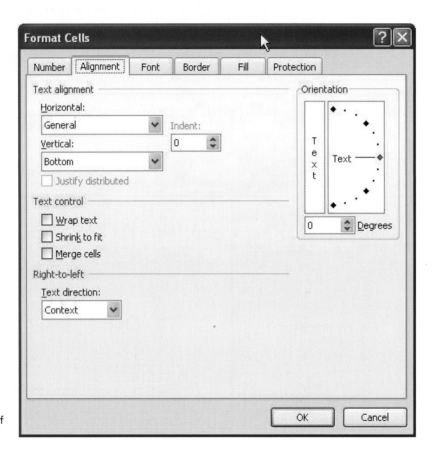

Figure 1-40: Format alignment of text within cells.

Cell titles or text may also be aligned at various angles by selecting the number of degrees to angle or by dragging the red tip of the *Orientation* line on the *Alignment* tab of the *Format Cells* dialog box. Text may also be formatted at an angle using the drop-down options on the *Orientation* icon in the *Alignment* task group of the *Home* tab (see Figure 1-19).

Conditional Formatting

In most cases, the same formatting is applied to a range of cells regardless of the value of the data item contained in the cells. In some cases, it is desirable to have the formatting draw attention to values that fall within a specific range of data. Special dynamic formatting can be applied to worksheet cells so that the format of a cell changes if the data value in the cell changes such that it becomes a value within a specified range. Consider a column of grade averages in a worksheet containing student grades. Special formatting can be applied such that if any student's average falls below 60, the student's grade average appears in a different color text, or with a different cell background. This type of formatting is called *conditional formatting*. If a cell meets one or more specified conditions, a specific format is applied.

To apply *conditional formatting*, select the range of cells to format and select **Home(tab)**→**Styles(group)**→**Conditional Formatting**→**New Rule** from the ribbon. The *New Formatting Rule* dialog box opens. There are six different types of rules from which to choose.

Many formats are available in the gallery for use in Conditional Formatting, but formats can be set manually by clicking on the Format button in the *New Formatting Rule* dialog box where applicable. Access the gallery formats by clicking on the drop-down list of other Conditional Formatting options (**Home(tab)→Styles(group)→ Conditional Formatting**).

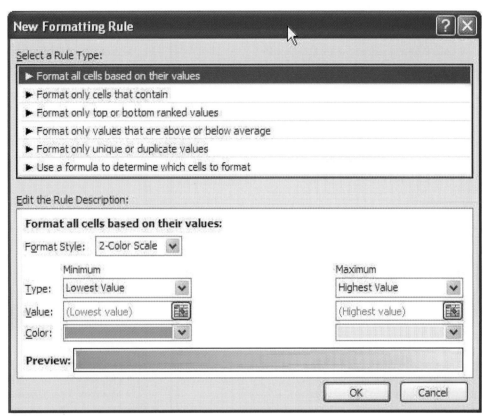

Figure 1-41: *Conditional Formatting* options based on actual cell values. Use the *Format Style* and the *Type* drop-down lists to select ways of evaluating the cell's value.

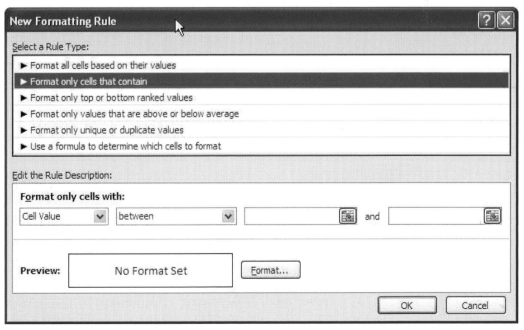

Figure 1-42: *Conditional Formatting* options based on cell values within a range.

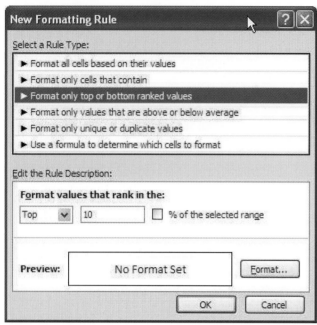

Figure 1-43: *Conditional Formatting* options based on rank of each cell value.

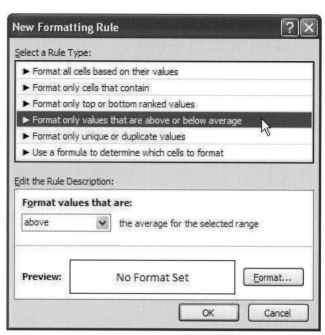

Figure 1-44: *Conditional Formatting* options based on values relative to other cells.

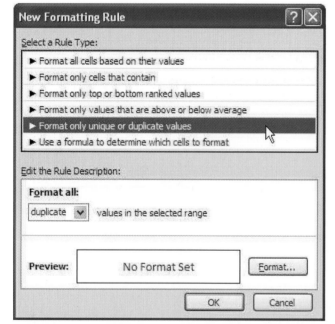

Figure 1-45: *Conditional Formatting* options for duplicate values in the formatted range.

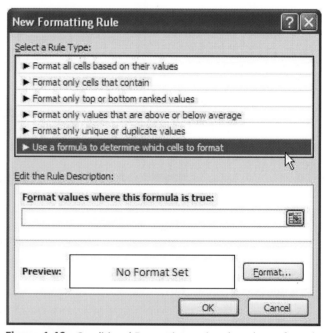

Figure 1-46: *Conditional Formatting* options based on a formula applied to each cell.

Conditional Formatting Example

If we would like to highlight the employees who earn the top salaries, we can apply conditional formatting so that the top three salaries are highlighted. Highlight the values in the "Salary" column. Select the rule type "Format only top or bottom ranked values." Select "Top" in the first drop-down list and enter "3" in the second text box. Leave the box beside "% of selected range" unchecked. Click the *Format* button to add the format for the conditional values. Set the font color to red.

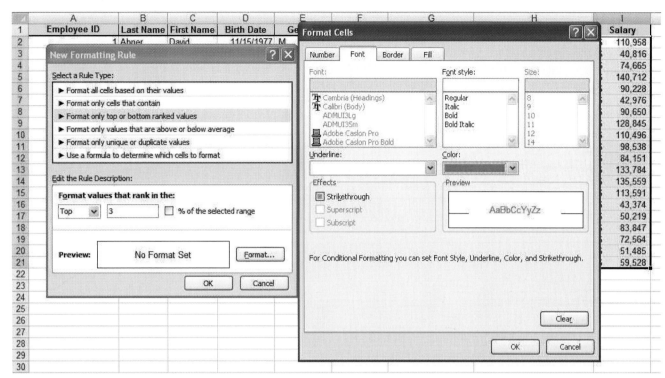

Figure 1-47: Set the conditional format for the top three salaries to display in red.

	A	B	C	D	E	F	G	H	I
1	Employee ID	Last Name	First Name	Birth Date	Gender	Hire Date	Department	Job Title	Salary
2	1	Abner	David	11/15/1977	M	6/20/2006	Sales		$ 110,958
3	2	Butler	Susan	11/16/1967	F	8/13/1978	Marketing	Staff	$ 40,816
4	3	Conrad	Michael	9/14/1955	M	12/25/2001	Product Development	Engineer	$ 74,665
5	4	Davis	Randall	7/15/1947	M	5/25/1980	Finance		$ 140,712
6	5	Edwards	Minnie	3/8/1959	F	11/26/1991	Human Resources		$ 90,228
7	6	Franklin	Margaret	11/25/1979	F	3/15/1977	Product Development	Staff	$ 42,976
8	7	Gardner	William	11/15/1968	M	2/7/1999			$ 90,650
9	8	Hilton	Hillery	11/23/1949	F	11/8/2005	Sales	District Sales Manager	$128,845
10	9	Jameson	Jennifer	1/17/1959	F	11/28/1992			$110,496
11	10	Kelly	Chester	10/28/1968	M	1/3/1994			$ 98,538
12	11	Zahn	Geoffrey	9/6/1952	M	3/4/1999			$ 84,151
13	12	Patel	Michael	4/20/1974	M	3/19/2003	Sales	District Sales Manager	$133,784
14	13	Schnider	Elizabeth	6/6/1958	F	6/27/1997			$135,559
15	14	Zulkowski	Mary	5/8/1967	F	9/1/1999			$113,591
16	15	Crockett	Carol	11/19/1953	F	12/3/1994	Sales	Staff	$ 43,374
17	16	Hancock	Christopher	4/30/1967	M	11/18/1999	Sales	Staff	$ 50,219
18	17	Bateman	Matthew	1/27/1956	M	8/3/1998			$ 83,847
19	18	Powell	Bruce	5/8/1966	M	12/29/1985	Product Development	Engineer	$ 72,564
20	19	Phillips	Wiley	11/17/1952	M	5/1/1987	Finance	Staff Accountant	$ 51,485
21	20	Howard	Emile	3/24/1985	M	4/3/1980			$ 59,528
22									

Figure 1-48: As a result of conditional formatting, the top three salaries are shown in red.

Wrapping Text within a Cell

Text that is too long to fit into a single cell will extend to the adjacent cell to its right if that cell is empty. If there is data or text in the adjacent cell, the text is *truncated* or cut off at the cell margin. In order to have the text wrap to the next line within a cell, select the cell to format and then select **Home(tab)→Alignment(group)→Wrap Text** from the ribbon. The Text Wrap feature may also be accessed by checking the box beside

Wrap text on the Alignment tab of the Format Cells dialog box (see Figure 1-19). With the *Wrap text* option selected, the text will automatically wrap to the next line as the user enters text into the cell

If you wish to break a line of text after a specific word, you may apply the line break manually. To break the line of text manually, type text into the cell and at the point you would like to insert a line break, use the keyboard keys **Alt+Enter,** then resume typing. You may apply multiple manual line breaks within one cell using this technique.

Annotating Cells

Since Excel workbooks are viewed and utilized extensively in the electronic version, it is often helpful to be able to add notes to special cells for which you would like to further explain to the viewer. For cells that you would like to add additional viewer information, cell *comments* may be added. Cell *comments* are viewed by positioning the mouse pointer over the cell containing the comment. With the mouse pointer over the cell, the comment box appears and the viewer can read the comment contained within the comment box.

Figure 1-49: Position the mouse pointer over a cell to read its comment.

To insert a cell comment, select the cell in which you would like to add the comment and select **Review(tab)→Comments(group)→NewComment** from the ribbon (see Figure 1-24). The comment box will appear and will perform as a text editor. You may add, edit, or delete text in the comment box. You may also add special text effects such as bold, italics, or underlines. The name of the computer's registered owner also appears automatically in the comment box when a new comment is inserted. You may remove the name if desired using the text editing features within the comment box.

Clearing Cell Contents, Formats, and Comments

To clear the cell contents only, select the cell or cell range to clear and use the Delete key to remove the values within the cell(s). You may clear contents, formats, comments or all by selecting **Home(tab)→Editing(group)→Eraser** icon from the ribbon. Select the item(s) you would like to clear from the icon's drop-down item list.

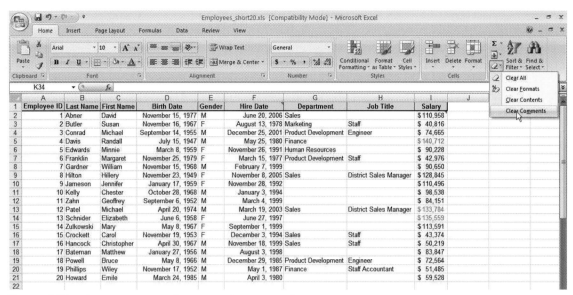

Figure 1-50: Clear comments, cell contents, formats or all.

You may also remove a comment by selecting **Review(tab)→Comments (group)→Delete** (see Delete icon in Figures 1-24).

Quick Tip!

Perform many useful tasks such as formatting, editing, and adding comments for a single cell or cell range by right-clicking on the selected cell(s) to access the context menu.

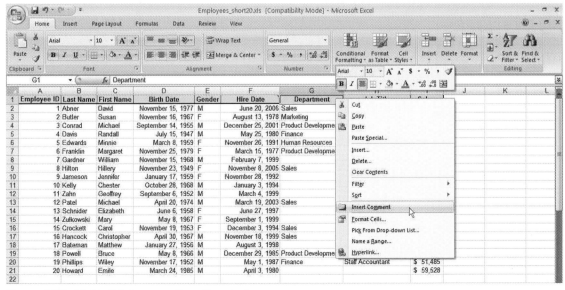

Figure 1-51: Right-click to access the cell context menu.

Formatting Dates in Excel

When date values are entered into cells that have the General format assigned, Excel will automatically assign a *Date* format to the entry if it recognizes a typical date format. It will try to match one of the pre-defined date formats to the format that is entered by the user. Dates are actually numeric data with a special format applied. The default date system in Excel is derived from the Julian date system. Each value of one represents a whole day. The first date value in the system (1) represents January 1, 1900. The date value 400 represents February 3, 1901, and so forth. Time is represented by a fractional portion of one such that a date value of 39380.75 represents 6:00 p.m. October 25, 2007. Each date value in Excel represents a specific date and time even though the time was never entered by the user. If only a date is entered, the default time associated with the date is midnight, or 12:00 a.m.

Formatting Errors

When an error occurs within a cell that prevents the proper cell value from displaying correctly, Excel displays an error value in the cell. The actual error value (text and/or symbols) depends on the type of error encountered. When Excel cannot display the entire numeric value in a cell in its specified format due to the column width being too narrow, it fills the entire cell with pound signs (#). To fix the problem, widen the column until the pound signs disappear and the number or date is displayed in the cell.

	A	B	C	D	E	F	G	H	I
1	Employee ID	Last Name	First Name	Birth Date	Gender	Hire Date	Department	Job Title	Salary
2	1	Abner	David	##############	M	June 20, 2006	Sales		$ 110,958
3	2	Butler	Susan	##############	F	August 13, 1978	Marketing	Staff	$ 40,816
4	3	Conrad	Michael	##############	M	December 25, 2001	Product Development	Engineer	$ 74,665
5	4	Davis	Randall	July 15, 1947	M	May 25, 1980	Finance		$ 140,712
6	5	Edwards	Minnie	March 8, 1959	F	November 26, 1991	Human Resources		$ 90,228
7	6	Franklin	Margaret	##############	F	March 15, 1977	Product Development	Staff	$ 42,976
8	7	Gardner	William	##############	M	February 7, 1999			$ 90,650
9	8	Hilton	Hillery	##############	F	November 8, 2005	Sales	District Sales Manager	$ 128,845
10	9	Jameson	Jennifer	January 17, 1959	F	November 28, 1992			$ 110,496
11	10	Kelly	Chester	October 28, 1968	M	January 3, 1994			$ 98,538
12	11	Zahn	Geoffrey	##############	M	March 4, 1999			$ 84,151
13	12	Patel	Michael	April 20, 1974	M	March 19, 2003	Sales	District Sales Manager	$ 133,784
14	13	Schnider	Elizabeth	June 6, 1958	F	June 27, 1997			$ 135,559
15	14	Zulkowski	Mary	May 8, 1967	F	September 1, 1999			$ 113,591
16	15	Crockett	Carol	##############	F	December 3, 1994	Sales	Staff	$ 43,374
17	16	Hancock	Christopher	April 30, 1967	M	November 18, 1999	Sales	Staff	$ 50,219
18	17	Bateman	Matthew	January 27, 1956	M	August 3, 1998			$ 83,847
19	18	Powell	Bruce	May 8, 1966	M	December 29, 1985	Product Development	Engineer	$ 72,564
20	19	Phillips	Wiley	##############	M	May 1, 1987	Finance	Staff Accountant	$ 51,485
21	20	Howard	Emile	March 24, 1985	M	April 3, 1980			$ 59,528
22									

Figure 1-52: The "Birth Date" column is not wide enough to show longer date formats. To correct the formatting error, widen the column until all the # signs disappear.

Formatting Worksheets

Editing Worksheet Names

There are special formatting considerations for the worksheet as a whole that will enhance the visual appeal of the electronic version and add detail to the printed copy. When a new workbook is created it contains three worksheets (specified by the default setting). The three worksheets are named Sheet1, Sheet2, and Sheet3, respectively. The worksheet name is displayed on the worksheet tab at the bottom of the worksheet. To change the name to something more meaningful, right-click on the worksheet tab and select *Rename* from the context menu. The old worksheet name will be highlighted and the new name can be typed onto the tab. After the new name is typed, use the *Enter* key to save the worksheet name. Alternately, the worksheet name can be edited by double-clicking on the worksheet tab. To change the background color of the worksheet tab, right-click on the tab and select *Tab Color* from the context menu, then select the desired color from the color palette that appears.

Additional worksheets may be added in front of any worksheet by right-clicking on the tab of the worksheet in front of which you want to insert a new sheet. Select *Insert* from the context menu. When the *Insert* dialog box appears, select *Worksheet.* The new worksheet will be inserted in front of the worksheet that was selected. Following the last worksheet tab in a workbook is an icon for inserting a new worksheet after the last worksheet with a single click on the icon. To remove unwanted worksheets, right-click on the tab of the worksheet to be removed and select *Delete* from the context menu.

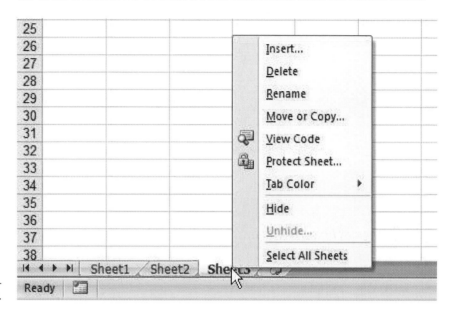

Figure 1-53: Right-click on a worksheet tab to access its context menu.

Formatting Columns and Rows

Inserting Cells, Columns, and Rows

When formatting a worksheet for presentation, adding, deleting, or resizing columns or rows may enhance the visual appeal or clarity of the worksheet content. To insert a new column, select the column in front of which you would like to place the new column and select **Home(tab)→Cells(group)→Insert(click the arrow)→Insert Sheet Columns** (or just click the **Insert** icon) from the ribbon. The Insert Cells command will also insert new columns if one or more entire columns have been selected. To insert multiple columns in one place, select the number of columns you would like to insert and apply the *Insert* command. For example, if three contiguous columns are selected before applying the *Insert* command, three new columns will be inserted in front of the three selected by the user. Rows may be inserted similarly by selecting one or more rows (the number or rows you wish to insert) and select **Home(tab)→Cells(group)→Insert(click the arrow)→Insert Sheet Rows** (or just click the **Insert** icon) from the ribbon.

To insert one or more cells without inserting an entire row or column, select the cell or block of cells in the location at which you would like to insert cells and select **Home (tab)→Cells(group)→Insert(click the arrow)→Cells** from the ribbon. The insert features provides the option of shifting existing (selected) cells to the right or down when the new cells are inserted in addition to enabling the addition of an entire row or column.

Quick Tip!

Columns or rows can be inserted quickly by selecting the column(s) or row(s) in front of which you would like to insert and right-click and select Insert from the context menu that appears.

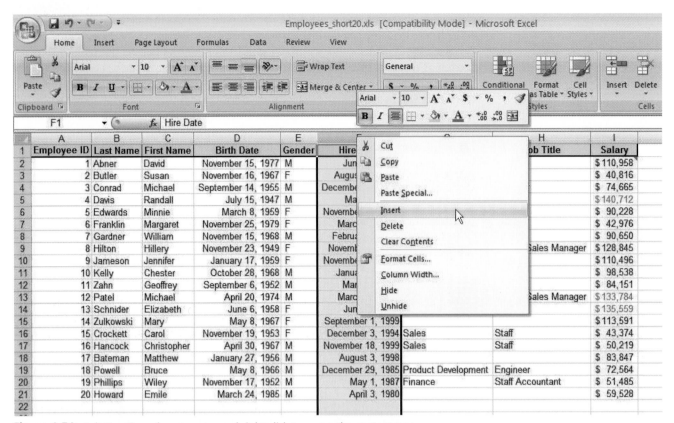

Figure 1-54: Select entire column or row and right-click to access the context menu.

Removing Columns and Rows

To delete one or more columns, select the column(s) you wish to delete and select **Home(tab)→Cells(group)→Insert(click the arrow)→Delete Sheet Columns** (or just click the **Delete** icon) from the ribbon (see Figure 1-19). Rows may be deleted similarly by selecting one or more rows (the number of rows you wish to delete) and select **Home(tab)→Cells(group)→Insert(click the arrow)→Delete Sheet Rows** (or just click the **Delete** icon) from the ribbon. Columns or rows can also be deleted using the context menu. Right-click on the selected column(s) or row(s) and select **Delete** from the context menu.

To remove one or more cells without removing an entire row or column, select the cell or block of cells to be removed and select **Home(tab)→Cells(group)→Delete (click the arrow)→Delete Cells** from the ribbon. The remove feature provides the option of closing the deleted area by shifting existing cells to the left or up when the selected cells are removed. It also includes the option of removing an entire row or column. Alternately, the context menu may be used to delete cells by right-clicking on the selected cells and selecting **Delete** from the context menu.

Resizing Columns and Rows

To change the width of a column or the height of a row, the column or row need not be selected prior to resizing. When the mouse pointer is positioned between two columns or rows in the row or column header margin of the worksheet, the cursor turns to a *Resize* cursor. By holding down the left mouse button the column or row boundary can be dragged to the desired width (for columns) or height (for rows). Multiple columns or rows may be resized together (making all the same width or height) by selecting the columns or rows to be resized before using the mouse to resize as described above. If you wish to set the column width or row height to an exact size in number of characters, select the column(s) or row(s) and select **Home(tab)→**

Cells(group)→Format(click the arrow)→Column Width from the ribbon for columns and **Home(tab)→Cells(group)→Format(click the arrow)→Row Height** for rows. Alternately, the context menu may be used by right clicking on the column or row headers (the row numbers or the column letters or numbers) for the columns or rows you wish to resize. The context menu will contain the option *Column Width* when a column is selected and the option *Row Height* when a row is selected.

Quick Tips!

To automatically resize a column to the correct width for its contents, double-click on the right margin of the column header. (Rows will automatically resize by double-clicking on the lower margin of the row header.)

To automatically resize all columns or rows to the correct size at once, select all cells on the worksheet (using the Select All button) and double-click on any column margin to automatically resize all columns and double-click on any row margin to automatically resize all rows to fit the contents of the particular column or row.

Format Worksheets for Printing

Worksheets that will be printed require some additional considerations for the appearance of the printed presentation. There are special formatting features in Excel that support worksheet printing.

To set up the worksheet for printing, select **Page Layout(tab)→Page Setup(group)** from the ribbon then **click on the bottom right corner of the *Page Setup* group** to launch the *Page Setup* dialog box. The worksheet formatting options are divided into four general categories as indicated by the tabs on the *Page Setup* dialog box. The first tab, the *Page* tab, allows the user to set the paper orientation to *Portrait* or *Landscape*, scale the worksheet to better fit the printed page, and set the paper size and quality. It also provides a way to set up color printing options by selecting the *Options* button.

Figure 1-55: *Page* tab of *Page Setup* menu option (Page Layout (tab)→Page Setup(group) and click on the bottom right corner of the *Page Setup* group to launch the *Page Setup* dialog box).

The second tab, the *Margins* tab of the *Page Setup* dialog box, provides features for setting top, bottom, and side margins and for centering the content on the page.

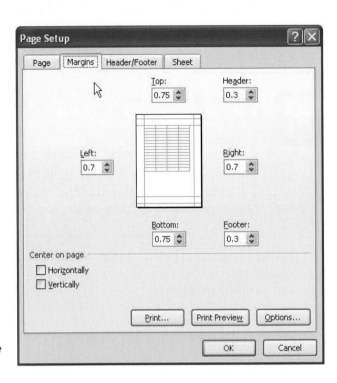

Figure 1-56: *Margins* tab of *Page Setup* dialog box.

The third tab, the *Header/Footer* tab, allows the user to set up *Headers* to print at the top of the paper page and *Footers* to print at the bottom of the page. There are a number of pre-formatted headers and footers that include such information as date and time of printing, file name, and page numbers. There is also an option available to create custom headers and footers for the printed worksheet.

The header and footer appear in the printed copy of the worksheet only so are a part of the print setup for the worksheets.

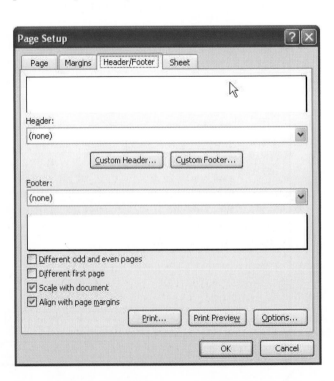

Figure 1-57: *Header/Footer* tab of *Page Setup* dialog box.

The last tab, the *Sheet* tab of the *Page Setup* dialog box, includes options for specifying which worksheet contents are to be included on the printed page. If the entire worksheet is not to be included in the printed page, the specific area to print can be specified with the *Print Area* option. Select the area to print each time the print command is issued by clicking on the *Select Cells* icon to the right of the text box and select the desired range of cells from the worksheet to print then click on the icon again to save the selected cell range reference in the associated text box. If specific rows should be printed as the first row of each worksheet, or a column that is to printed as the first column of each worksheet, select those rows or column in the same manner as setting the print area by clicking the *Select Cells* icon to the right of each respective text box. After selecting the rows or columns, click the icon once more to save the selection reference. Other printing options exist under the *Print* and *Page Order* sections of the *Sheet* tab that include printing gridlines, and column and row headings as well as the print order for printing multiple pages.

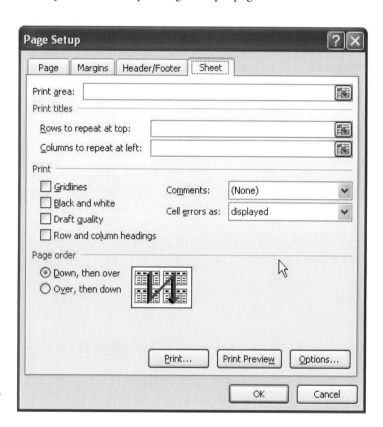

Figure 1-58: *Sheet* tab of *Page Setup* dialog box.

Two options exist for previewing the page breaks for the printed worksheet. To preview the printed pages, select the **Office Button→Print→Print Preview** from the ribbon. The *Page Break Preview* also offers a view of the page breaks for the worksheet and permits the user to change the page breaks by dragging the page breaks with the left mouse button to different locations within the worksheet. To access the *Page Break Preview,* select **View(tab)→Workbook Views(group)→Page Break Preview** icon from the ribbon. To exit the Page Break view, select **View(tab)→Workbook Views(group)→ Normal** from the ribbon.

AutoFormats for Worksheets

Several pre-defined formats are defined in the Excel Galleries. To select one of the pre-defined formats, select **Home(tab)→Styles(group)→Format as a Table** icon from the ribbon. A palette will appear with many design and color choices for auto-formatting an Excel table.

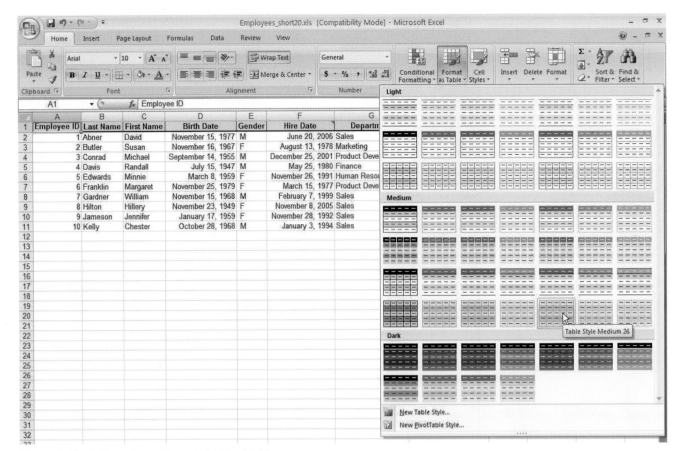

Figure 1-59: Gallery of auto-formats for Excel tables.

Review Questions

1. What file extensions are used for Microsoft Excel files?

   _____

   _____

   _____

2. Explain why Excel is described as "flexible."

   _____

   _____

   _____

3. What options are available for searching for Help topics in Excel?

   _____

   _____

   _____

4. What feature in Excel allows the user to automatically insert a series of sequential numbers, dates, or other specialized serial values?

   _____

   _____

   _____

5. Explain the difference between the value contained in a cell and the cell's format. Give an example of one cell's possible value and format.

   _____

   _____

   _____

6. How can a user select non-contiguous cell ranges on a worksheet?

   _____

   _____

   _____

7. Explain the difference between regular cell formatting and conditional formatting. Give an example of how conditional formatting might be used.

_____

_____

_____

8. How could a user break a line of text into two or more lines without using the *Wrap text* feature?

_____

_____

_____

9. How are dates stored in Excel? Give an example of an actual date value stored in Excel and a date format for the value.

_____

_____

_____

10. What does the error value ####### indicate when it fills a cell?

_____

_____

_____

11. How can rows and columns be resized automatically to fit the contents of the row or column?

_____

_____

_____

12. Explain the difference between gridlines and cell borders.

_____

_____

_____

Practice Problems

1. Create a new Excel workbook. Name the workbook *Employees.xlsx*.

   a. Enter the following column labels in the first row of the worksheet: *Employee ID, Last Name, First Name, Birth Date, Gender, Hire Date, Department,* (Job) *Title.*

   b. Select the entire column label row and make the font bold and center the labels in their respective cells. Apply a background color to the row.

   c. Enter five rows of sample data representative of employee data omitting the Employee ID.

   d. Enter employee identification numbers in the first column under the column label *Employee ID.* Make the employee numbers a sequence that increments by 100. The first value should be 1100. Use the Auto Fill feature to fill the column for the five rows of data you entered previously.

   e. Select the data cells only (not column label cell) in the *Birth Date* and the *Hire Date* columns simultaneously. Change the date format to *dd-mm-yy.*

   f. Insert two columns (at the same time) after the *Hire Date* column. Enter the column labels *Pay Rate,* and *Pay Type* into the two cells. Format the column label like the other column labels. (If you applied the previous column label format to the entire row, the inserted columns will automatically be formatted like the other columns.) Enter either the value *Salary* or *Hourly* in the *Pay Type* column for each of the five employees. In the *Pay Rate* column enter an appropriate rate of pay for the pay type you entered in the *Pay Type* column. For example, if an employee has a pay type of *Salary,* enter an annual salary amount. If the employee has a pay type of *Hourly,* enter an hourly pay rate. Format the pay rate values so that the dollar sign is aligned with the left cell margin and the comma separator is used to separate thousands.

   g. Select the column label cell *Employee ID.* Format the cell such that the two words in the column label are on separate lines. (There are two options for accomplishing this task.)

   h. Apply conditional formatting to the *Hire Date* column such that hire dates before January 1, 2006 are highlighted with red text. (If you have no dates that fall within that range, you may need to alter some values to test your conditional formatting.) Add a cell comment to the column label cell explaining the values highlighted in red.

   i. Name the worksheet *Employees.*

   j. Remove the blank worksheets from the workbook.

   k. Resize all columns so that there are no truncated text or formatting errors for numbers or dates (######).

2. Set up the worksheet you created in Problem 1 for printing. Apply formatting that will accomplish the following effects. Use the *Print Preview* feature to observe the effects of the formatting you applied. You are not required to actually print the final worksheet.

    a. Print the title "Employees" at the top of the sheet, before the column label row.
    b. Print the file name in the bottom left corner and print the date and time the worksheet is printed in the lower right corner.
    c. Print worksheet in portrait orientation.
    d. Repeat the employee ID numbers, last name and first name of employee on each consecutive page across.
    e. Repeat the column label row for each consecutive page down.
    f. Print gridlines.

3. Use Excel Offline and Online Help to find additional information on the following topics.

    a. *Conditional formatting:* List some specific examples of how conditional formatting may be used to enhance worksheets.
    b. *Paste Special:* How is this feature different from the other Paste feature in Excel?
    c. *Dates and date systems:* Could there be a problem when moving Excel documents from Excel for Windows and Excel for Macintosh? Why or why not?

Learning Objectives

1. Design a new workbook for maximum flexibility
2. Copy and paste worksheet formulas effectively using absolute, relative, and mixed cell references
3. Use named cell ranges in formulas
4. Remove formulas from calculated columns
5. Troubleshoot for formula errors using Excel troubleshooting tools
6. Protect worksheets and workbooks

Designing a New Workbook

There are many reasons people use spreadsheets. Some people use them to manage collections of data, especially for small businesses. Others use them to analyze large collections of data. Some companies use them to produce financial summary reports. Many people use them to create decision models that vary from the most simple to the extremely complex. Whatever the purpose of the spreadsheet, it is essential that it is designed for maximum flexibility. The flexibility of Excel is the reason people use spreadsheets at all. So what is meant by *flexibility*? It is the ability of the worksheet to adapt to changing inputs to readily view the related outputs with minimal effort to the user. In order to create a spreadsheet with maximum flexibility, consideration must be given to the design of the worksheet beforehand. A key part of the design process is the design of the worksheet *formulas*. Well-designed formulas are the key for maximizing the power Excel can lend to solving complex problems in many disciplines.

Spreadsheet Design Goals

As you prepare to create a spreadsheet solution, keep in mind the following design goals.

1. *Flexibility:* This is the most important design goal and the reason you are using the spreadsheet. The inputs should be easy to locate and change so that updated outputs recalculate automatically with minimal effort on the part of the user. Formulas should be used whenever possible to minimize manual changes when worksheet data changes.

2. *Accuracy:* Excel is capable of performing extremely complex calculations. The design of the formulas required for the calculations ensures accuracy of the results. To make sure results are accurate, test the spreadsheet using manual calculations for comparisons.

3. *Ease of Information Gathering:* The user should be able to quickly gather key information by glancing across the spreadsheet. Use of "white space," borders, background, font color, and other formatting that highlights key outputs (or inputs) enhances the ability to gather spreadsheet information quickly.

4. *Documentation:* A good spreadsheet is well-documented. Documentation includes such information as a purpose description for the workbook, its author, when it was created, information about key inputs or outputs. The actual values on the worksheet should be properly labeled so the intended user can easily understand the information conveyed by the spreadsheet. Examples of value labels are column and row headings. Adding comments to individual cells can add additional helpful information to the worksheet.

Workbook Design Steps

Excel provides an environment that supports the creation of well-designed spreadsheet solutions. An Excel workbook may contain as few as one worksheet or as many as the computer's available memory will handle. The support of multiple worksheets provides a way to organize spreadsheet content across multiple worksheets to improve clarity and differentiate results. For example, a small business may be storing data about its products, employees, customers, and sales in a workbook. A larger company may use a workbook to summarize sales for many different products. Excel worksheets allow the user to organize the data so that data about different types of entities may be stored on different worksheets. The worksheets may be named (visible on the worksheet tabs) so that it is easy to go directly to the specific type of data of interest. Deciding how to organize the spreadsheet data involves spending some effort designing the workbook. Several steps are involved in creating a good workbook design.

1. *Determine the overall purpose of the workbook:* What problem is the workbook intended to solve? Who will use the workbook and what is their level of spreadsheet expertise? Is it intended for data management in which users will enter new data on a daily basis or is it intended to analyze and summarize data on a periodic basis? The design of the workbook should be suitable for its intended use and intended users.

2. *Determine what data will be collected:* If the workbook will be used for data management, what types of data will be collected and stored. For example, a small business owner might wish to collect and store data about inventory items, employees, customers, sales to customers, and purchases from vendors. Will the data be collected directly into the workbook, or will it be imported from an outside source? Answers to these questions determine how the workbook is organized.

3. *Identify reports that will be needed:* If the workbook is used for summarizing and reporting summary results, the needed outputs (summary values) must be identified. Once the outputs are identified, the inputs necessary to produce the outputs must also be available to the workbook. What input values will remain constant and what values will change frequently? Values that change are sometimes called *decision variables* and should be well labeled so that the user can make necessary changes efficiently.

4. *Organize the data:* What worksheets are needed to properly organize the data? What will be on each sheet? It is best to place summary data on a separate worksheet from the detailed data inputs. Will you want a different worksheet for different months, quarters, years, or products? Will there be special data analysis in addition to summary data? If so, it should be placed on a separate worksheet. It is best to use multiple worksheets to organize workbook data so that only one type of data is on each worksheet and each can be easily identified and accessed.

5. *Design formulas:* What formulas are needed to produce the desired outputs? Formulas are the key component to producing the reports and calculations required for the workbook. Formulas define the relationships between the input and output values. Some relationships may be as simple as transferring one cell value to another, and some may be very complex. Some relationships may fit well into a *pattern* or known model which can be reused for similar problems. Whatever the relationship, it can be expressed in worksheet formulas. Formulas should be designed for maximum flexibility.

6. *Enter text, numeric data, and formulas:* Arrange numeric values and text labels in rows and/or columns. Enter formulas and output labels for the calculated values. For maximum flexibility of worksheet formulas, use cell references that contain the input values. (Specific techniques for using cell references will be discussed later in this chapter.)

7. *Test the formulas for correctness:* As an initial test, evaluate the calculated values for "reasonableness." Do a quick mental calculation to determine if the result is a reasonable answer for the formula. Use round values such as 1, 100, or 10% in testing worksheet formulas to make mental calculations practical for comparison to the worksheet results. Test the extreme values for the application (very highest to very lowest). The Excel *Formula Auditing* tools are also helpful in locating the source of an error once it is suspected. They are also helpful for troubleshooting formulas that fail to produce a result and display an error value.

8. *Format the workbook to enhance appearance:* Add titles and formatting to worksheets to enhance the visual appeal of the workbook. Adjust font size and appearance for better readability. Font smaller that 10 point is not recommended for general worksheet contents.

9. *Document the workbook:* Rows and calculated values should be clearly labeled and formatted to distinguish the labels from data cells. Add comments to individual cells to improve clarity and provide additional helpful information. It is a good practice to add a cover worksheet to the front of the workbook on which important information about the workbook can be displayed to the user. The following information should be included on this *Documentation* worksheet as it applies to each individual workbook:
    a. Workbook purpose and description
    b. Creator/Author of the workbook
    c. Date the workbook was created
    d. Date and description of any modifications
    e. Overall assumptions that are not common knowledge
    f. Location of input values that may be changed by the user
    g. Worksheet summary or a brief explanation of each worksheet and its purpose
    h. Any specific user instructions on how to use the workbook and its features

10. *Protect the workbook:* Creating complex workbooks requires considerable time and effort. To ensure that users change only the input values and not the formulas, selected cells may be made available to users for editing while the remainder of the worksheet is locked for selecting and/or editing. All cells containing formulas should be locked to ensure the continued accuracy of the worksheet calculations. Protection may be applied to individual worksheets or to the entire workbook.

11. *Set Printing Options (as needed):* Set up printing options for each worksheet, including page numbers, headers, footers, and data printing options.

Entering Worksheet Formulas

Formulas provide a means for entering calculated values into worksheet cells. A formula entered into an Excel cell always begins with an *equal sign* (=). The equal sign signals to Excel that a formula will follow. A formula may be entered by typing directly into the selected cell or by typing into the *formula bar.*

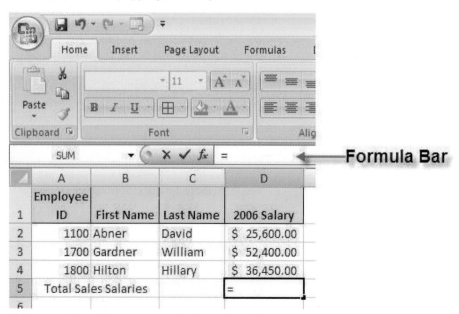

Figure 2-1: Enter formula into formula bar or directly into active cell.

All standard mathematical operations can be performed in Excel.

Table 2-1: Standard mathematical operators used in Excel.

Symbol	Mathematical Operation
^	Exponent (or "to the Power of")
*	Multiplication
/	Division
+	Addition
−	Subtraction
( )	To control the order of operations

Once a formula has been entered, edit it by first selecting the formula cell, then click on the formula bar to place the cursor in the desired location to begin editing the formula. The formula may also be edited by double-clicking on the formula cell and edit the formula directly in the cell. Once the cell is in the edit mode, use the keyboard backspace and delete keys to edit as much as you would in a standard text editor.

Entering Formulas Using Cell References

When designing formulas in Excel, it is important to differentiate inputs that are apt to change from inputs that will likely never change. Only values for inputs that are unlikely to change should be entered directly into a formula. For example, if a calculation is performed that involves multiplying by the number of months in a year. That number will always need to be 12. In workbooks, never-changing values are rare. More often a formula will perform a calculation based on values that are subject to change, such as the detailed sales data for a given period of time, or an employee's rate of pay. In these cases, a reference to the cell that contains the value should be used instead of typing the value directly into the formula. When cell references are used, the calculated result will remain accurate even though the input values in the referenced cells change. To insert a formula in the example worksheet that will calculate the total annual salaries of the sales employees, the detailed salary values should be referenced by their cell location or cell *address*. The cell *address* is expressed in terms of the *row* and *column* intersection where it is located. In the Figure 2-2 worksheet, the detailed salary values are located in cells D2, D3, and D4. All input values are located in column D, in rows 2, 3, and 4. To perform operations on values contained in cells, use mathematical operators between two cell references just as you would use the operator between two numeric values. In order to calculate the total salaries, the formula can be entered as =**D2+D3+D4.**

Quick Tip!

After typing in the operator (=, +, −, *, /, ^, etc.), you can quickly insert a cell or cell range reference into a formula by selecting the cell or cell range with the mouse pointer. The cell address of the selected range is automatically inserted into the formula.

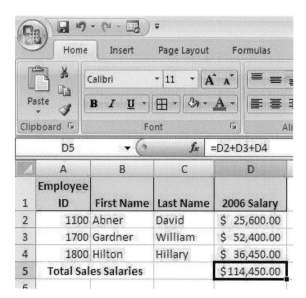

Figure 2-2: View the formula in cell D5 in the formula bar.

Copying and Pasting Formulas

A major strength of spreadsheets is their ability to easily copy and paste formulas from one cell to other cells. Formulas can be copied and pasted using the *Copy* and *Paste* options found in the *Clipboard* group of the *Home* tab of the ribbon. To paste formulas to adjacent cells, the *fill handle* provides a quick alternative to the ribbon command. Formulas are copied and pasted in the same manner as other worksheet values. When a column has data in an adjacent column, double-click on the fill handle to finish filling the column with the formula.

Suppose an employer wishes to give all employees a 5% raise. A formula may be entered into the "New Salary" column for the first employee listed, then copied down the column to fill the "New Salary" cells for all subsequent employees in the list. In this case, the calculation in subsequent rows differs only by the row of one of the input values, the old salary. The first-row formula for calculating the new salary may be entered as **=D2*1.05 or =D2*(1+0.05)**.

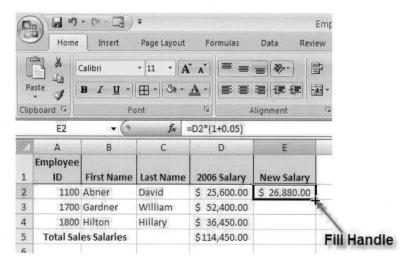

Figure 2-3: New salary raise amount (5%) is written into the formula in cell E2.

Once the formula is entered into the "New Salary" cell for the first employee, it can be copied and pasted to the subsequent rows of the same column. When formulas are copied and pasted in Excel, by default the row portion of the cell reference changes as the formula is pasted into subsequent rows such that the row referenced in the cell reference is in the same relative location to the formula cell as it was in the initial formula cell.

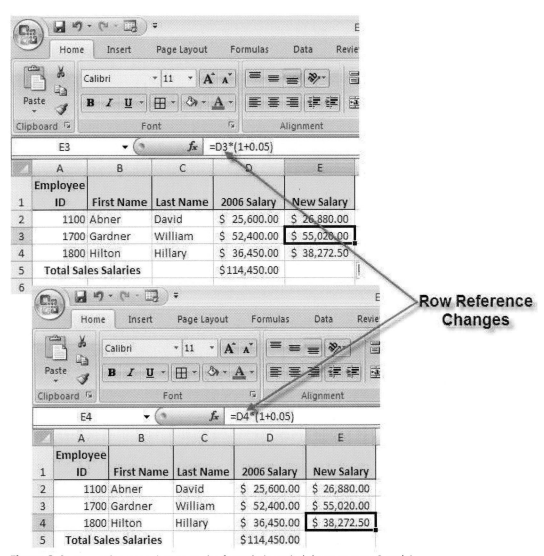

Figure 2-4: Row references change as the formula is copied down to rows 3 and 4.

What if the employer is not certain that the company can afford a 5% raise and he needs to experiment with the total salary budget for the sales department to see how much salary increase the company can afford? The current salary budget is $115,000. Suppose next year's salary budget is $120,000. Will the company be able to give the employees a 5% raise? In order to make the worksheet more flexible, let's remove the raise percentage from the formula and place it in a cell that can easily be changed if needed. This value is called an *assumption value* because the calculation is based on the assumption of a 5% raise. The cell where we place the assumption value is called an *assumption cell*. Let's revise the formula so that we can reference an assumption cell instead of entering the 5% directly into the formula. Place assumption cells in a location that the user can easily find and manipulate as needed. Label the assumption cells and enter an assumption value (0.05). Be sure to leave at least one column or one row between the list of data and the assumption cells. You may format the assumption value so that it displays the value followed by the % symbol. Once the assumption values have been removed from the formula and placed in an assumption cell, we can reference the assumption cells in our revised formula. It is acceptable to leave the value of one (1) in the formula rather than moving it to an assumption cell because that value is not likely to change in the future.

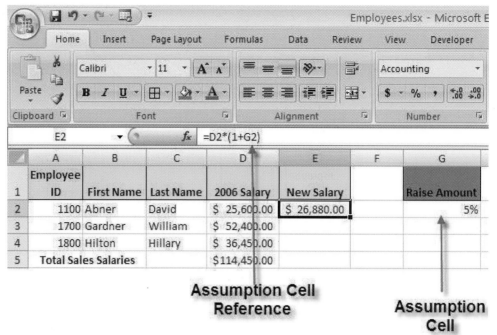

Figure 2-5: Revised formula using assumption cell reference.

When we copy the formula down to the remaining rows of the list, what happens? Why did the salaries in rows 3 and 4 not change?

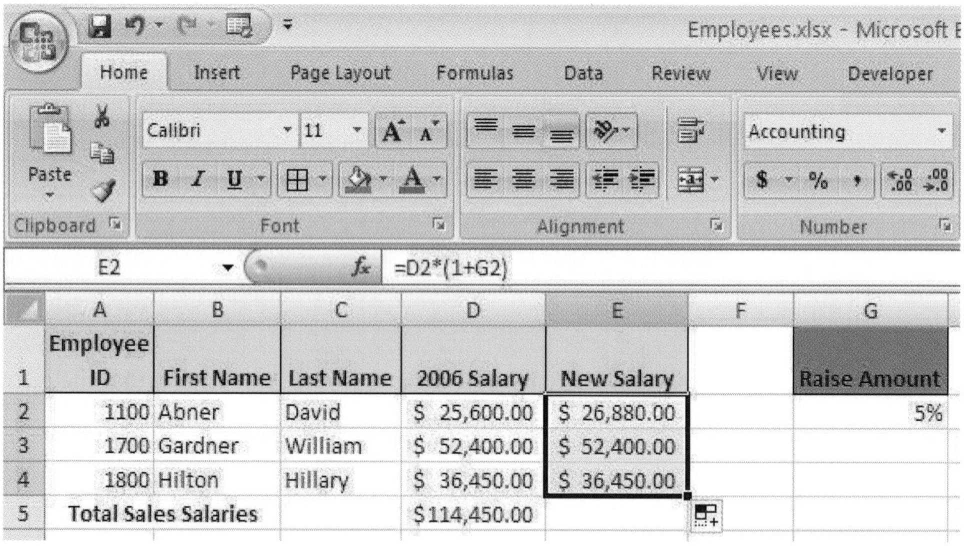

Figure 2-6: Note result errors in cells E3 and E4.

Viewing All Worksheet Formulas

In order to troubleshoot the formulas in cells E3 and E4, it is helpful to view all the formulas at once to easily compare formulas in different cells to observe cell reference changes when pasted. To help troubleshoot formulas containing cell references, Excel offers a *formula view* option. The *formula view* allows the user to see all the worksheet formulas at once instead of the formula result values in worksheet formula cells. To access the formula view option, select **Formulas(tab)→Formula Auditing(group)→Show Formulas** icon from the ribbon. When you select *Show Formulas*, formulas will replace the results in the formula cells of the worksheet.

Excel can be set to show all formulas on a worksheet routinely by setting the option to "Show formulas in cells instead of their calculated results." To set the formula view option, select the **Office Button→Advanced→Display options for this worksheet and check the box to the left of "Show formulas in cells instead of their calculated results."**

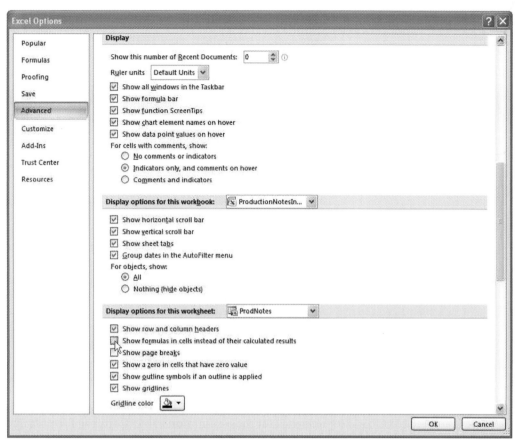

Figure 2-7: Set worksheet to the formula view.

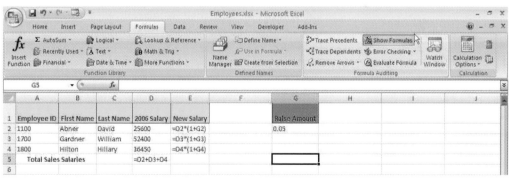

Figure 2-8: Formula view of worksheet. Note the incorrect references to the assumption cell in formulas in cells E3 and E3. The correct assumption cell reference is G2.

Worksheet formulas may also be printed while in the formula view. To remove the formula view and view the worksheet normally, select **Formulas(tab)→Formula Auditing(group)→deselect Show Formulas icon.**

Quick Tip!

To toggle between the normal view and the formula view, use the keyboard shortcut Ctrl + ` (the accent grave key).

Types of Cell References

Examine the cell references in the formula cells of our example worksheet. When formulas are copied and pasted in Excel, the row and column portions of the cell reference change or adjust as the formula is pasted into subsequent rows or columns. Note that in subsequent rows of the new salary column, the cell reference for the old salary changes so that the old salary is accurate for each subsequent employee's new salary calculation. Note the cell reference for the assumption value (the raise percentage) in the pasted rows. What happened to that cell reference? Since by default Excel adjusted the raise percentage cell reference to the next row down, the cell references in rows 3 and 4 are referencing empty cells (G3 and G4) which caused the result errors. The formula interpreted the empty cells as containing values of zero.

When Excel changes the cell reference in a pasted formula, it is referencing a cell in the same location relative to the pasted formula cell as was the copied cell to the original formula cell. That type of cell reference is called a *relative cell reference.* It is the default cell reference style when formulas are copied and pasted in Excel. Not all cell references need to change as a formula is pasted into a new location. A good example is the assumption cell containing the raise percentage in our example. Instead of the assumption cell adjusting its cell reference as the formula is copied down to subsequent rows, the reference should remain unchanged. A cell reference that does not change when a formula is pasted to other cells is called an *absolute cell reference.* Since the default reference style in Excel is *relative,* the user must explicitly set cell references to be *absolute.* To make a cell reference *absolute,* the $ symbol is inserted in front of the column and row values so that neither of them will change when the formula is pasted into new cells. To make the G2 cell reference absolute, insert the cell reference as **$G$2** instead of G2. Note that *relative cell references* include no symbols. The absence of symbols in the cell reference indicates that it is a *relative cell reference.* Let's rewrite the original formula in row 2 using an absolute reference for the assumption value. Copy the formula and paste it into the next two cells down. Note that the absolute reference (**$G$2**) for the raise percentage did not change. Now copy the formula for the 2006 "Total Sales Salaries" over to the same row in the new salary column so that the proposed increased salary total can be calculated. Note the change in the cell references. When the formula is copied to the new column, the column cell reference changes. Can the company afford the salary increase?

Formula View

	A	B	C	D	E	F	G
						F9	
1	Employee ID	First Name	Last Name	2006 Salary	New Salary		Raise Amount
2	1100	Abner	David	25600	=D2*(1+$G$2)		0.05
3	1700	Gardner	William	52400	=D3*(1+$G$2)		
4	1800	Hilton	Hillary	36450	=D4*(1+$G$2)		
5	Total Sales Salaries			=D2+D3+D4	=E2+E3+E4		

Normal View

	A	B	C	D	E	F	G
						J10	
1	Employee ID	First Name	Last Name	2006 Salary	New Salary		Raise Amount
2	1100	Abner	David	$ 25,600.00	$ 26,880.00		5%
3	1700	Gardner	William	$ 52,400.00	$ 55,020.00		
4	1800	Hilton	Hillary	$ 36,450.00	$ 38,272.50		
5	Total Sales Salaries			$ 114,450.00	$ 120,172.50		

Figure 2-9: Revised formula using absolute reference for assumption cell.

The employer discovers that a 5% raise to all employees will put the salary budget for next year over the $120,000 limit. Now the assumption value for the raise percentage can be easily manipulated to figure out how much the company can raise salaries. Change the value in the assumption cell to **0.045** and observe the change in the new salaries and in the total of the new salaries for next year. (You may need to adjust the decimal places in the assumption cell format to be able to view decimal percent values.) It seems that a raise of 4.5% instead of 5% is within the department's salary budget for next year. The worksheet and its formulas are now designed for maximum flexibility.

Formula View

	A	B	C	D	E	F	G
1	Employee ID	First Name	Last Name	2006 Salary	New Salary		Raise Amount
2	1100	Abner	David	25600	=D2*(1+$G$2)		0.05
3	1700	Gardner	William	52400	=D3*(1+$G$2)		
4	1800	Hilton	Hillary	36450	=D4*(1+$G$2)		
5	Total Sales Salaries			=D2+D3+D4	=E2+E3+E4		

Normal View

	A	B	C	D	E	F	G
1	Employee ID	First Name	Last Name	2006 Salary	New Salary		Raise Amount
2	1100	Abner	David	$ 25,600.00	$ 26,880.00		5%
3	1700	Gardner	William	$ 52,400.00	$ 55,020.00		
4	1800	Hilton	Hillary	$ 36,450.00	$ 38,272.50		
5	Total Sales Salaries			$ 114,450.00	$ 120,172.50		

Figure 2-10: Change the raise amount to 4.5% and note the changes in the new salaries and the total new salary amount.

Occasionally pasted formulas require that the row reference change but the column reference remains constant or *vice versa*. Consider the worksheet below. It represents an analysis of a mix of products produced by one manufacturer. Cells with assumption values are shaded yellow. Cells containing labels for the data items are shaded blue. Cells without background shading contain calculated values (formulas).

	A	B	C	D	E	F	G	H
1	**Product Mix Analysis for February, 2007**							
2								
3				Product 1		Product 2		Product 3
4		Units Produced		10		20		10
5		Unit Revenue		$ 1,200		$ 1,500		$ 2,200
6	Cost Category	Unit Cost	Cost Units	Total cost	Cost Units	Total cost	Cost Units	Total cost
7	Labor Hours	$ 15	15	$ 225	18	$ 270	10	$ 150
8	Material	$ 80	5	$ 400	7	$ 560	15	$ 1,200
9	Fixed	$ 125	1	$ 125	1	$ 125	1	$ 125
10	**Product Cost**			$ 7,500		$ 19,100		$ 14,750
11	**Product Profit**			$ 4,500		$ 10,900		$ 7,250
12	**Total Profit**							$ 22,650
13								

Figure 2-11: "Product Mix" worksheet.

The first formula cell, D7, contains a formula that multiplies the unit cost of labor times the number of labor hours required to produce one unit of Product 1. The formula is =**B7*C7**. When the formula is copied and pasted to the two cells below it (D8 and D9), the row references for both cell addresses in the formula change to supply the inputs from row 8 for the calculation in cell D8 and to row 9 for the calculation in cell D9.

Now think about the impact of copying the formula from D7 and pasting it into cell F7.

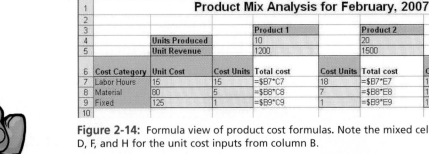

	A	B	C	D
1				Product Mix Analysis
2				
3				Product 1
4		Units Produced		10
5		Unit Revenue		1200
6	Cost Category	Unit Cost	Cost Units	Total cost
7	Labor Hours	15	15	=B7*C7
8	Material	80	5	=B8*C8
9	Fixed	125	1	=B9*C9
10				

Figure 2-12: Formulas in cells D8 and D9 will produce the correct results using a relative reference to input values in column B.

	A	B	C	D	E	F
1				Product Mix Analysis for February, 200
2						
3				Product 1		Product 2
4		Units Produced		10		20
5		Unit Revenue		1200		1500
6	Cost Category	Unit Cost	Cost Units	Total cost	Cost Units	Total cost
7	Labor Hours	15	15	=B7*C7	18	=D7*E7
8	Material	80	5	=B8*C8	7	
9	Fixed	125	1	=B9*C9	1	
10						

Figure 2-13: When the formula in cell D7 is copied to F7, the reference to input values in column B is incorrectly changed to column D.

The reference to the number of units of each cost category needed to produce one unit of Product 2 (C7) will paste with a relative reference of E7 which will work fine because that input value is still the cell in the same row and the first column to the left of the formula cell (F7). Now consider the other cell reference in the formula, B7. Cell address B7 references values in column B in the initial formula that is written in cell D7. When the formula is pasted from cell D7 into cell F7, the reference to the values in column B automatically change to column D. The formula in cell F7 should still reference the unit costs in column B. When the formula is copied down to rows 8 and 9, the row portion of cell reference B7 needs to change to produce the correct results. In order to make the column reference remain constant (absolute reference) and the row reference to change (relative reference), the $ symbol (to indicate absolute reference) should be placed in front of the column address, but not in front of the row address. The correct reference notation for B7 in the formula in cell D7 is $B7. A cell reference that is a combination of an absolute reference and a relative reference is called a *mixed cell reference*. Examine the formula view of the entire worksheet below. Note that the reference to column B in the original formula remains unchanged when pasted to columns F and H.

	A	B	C	D	E	F	G	H
1				Product Mix Analysis for February, 2007
2								
3				Product 1		Product 2		Product 3
4		Units Produced		10		20		10
5		Unit Revenue		1200		1500		2200
6	Cost Category	Unit Cost	Cost Units	Total cost	Cost Units	Total cost	Cost Units	Total cost
7	Labor Hours	15	15	=$B7*C7	18	=$B7*E7	10	=$B7*G7
8	Material	80	5	=$B8*C8	7	=$B8*E8	15	=$B8*G8
9	Fixed	125	1	=$B9*C9	1	=$B9*E9	1	=$B9*G9
10								

Figure 2-14: Formula view of product cost formulas. Note the mixed cell references in columns D, F, and H for the unit cost inputs from column B.

Quick Tip!

Use the keyboard shortcut F4 function key to quickly change a relative reference to an absolute reference. Place the cursor immediately before, after or in the center of the reference to edit. The key cycles the reference through four combinations of row and column references. If the cell reference is currently all relative (i.e., A1, the default cell reference style), the key changes it to an absolute reference, both row and column (i.e., $A$1)). The second toggle makes only the row reference absolute and changes

the column reference back to relative (A$1). The third toggle makes the column reference absolute and changes the row reference beck to relative (i.e., $A1). The fourth toggle makes both the column and row references relative (i.e., A1). The key repeats the cycle as many times as the F4 key is pressed. If a cell reference is already a mixed or absolute reference, the F4 key toggles to the next type of reference in the sequence.

Using Named Cell Ranges

Another way to use absolute cell references is to name an input cell range (one or more cells) with a descriptive name and use the range name in the calculation instead of the cell or range address. By default named ranges are absolute references since the name refers to one static range of cells, not a moving range. A named range of cells may contain one to any number of cells. Names for ranges must be one word and must not contain special characters. The underscore is the only special character allowed in a range name. Range names cannot begin with a numeric character, but numeric characters may be used within the name. Multi-word range names can be written as one word using an underscore to link all words together to form a one-word name.

To name a cell range, first select the cell or range of cells to name, then select **Formulas(tab)→Defined Names(group)→Define Name icon** from the ribbon. The *New Name* dialog box will appear with a suggested name for the cell range in the *Name* text box. If you would like a different name, type into the *Name* text box the name you wish to use for the cell range then click the *OK* button. If the cell range has not been selected prior to accessing the *New Name* dialog box, you may select the range with the dialog box open by using the *Select Cells* icon to the right of the *Refers to* text box at the bottom of the dialog box. After selecting the desired range of cells to name, click the icon to save the selection. After selecting the range to name, click the *OK* button to save the named range. Once the range has been named, it will appear in the *Name Box* of the worksheet.

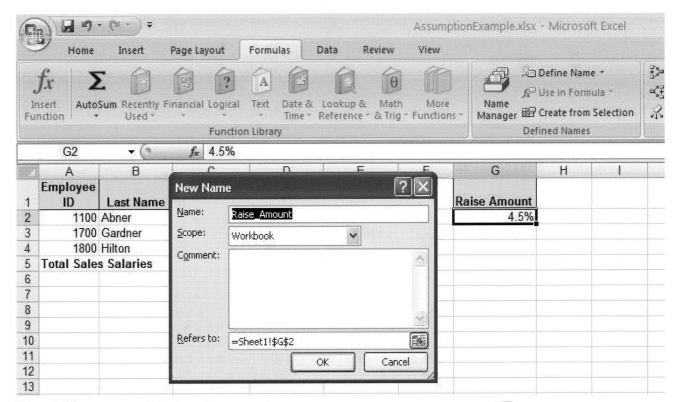

Figure 2-15: *New Name* dialog box with suggested range name.

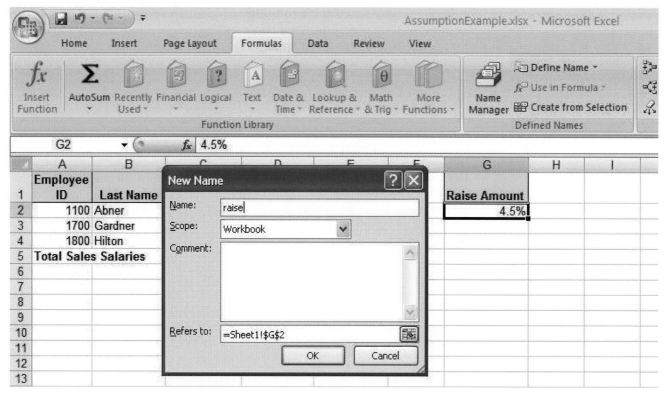

Figure 2-16: Type in the new range name.

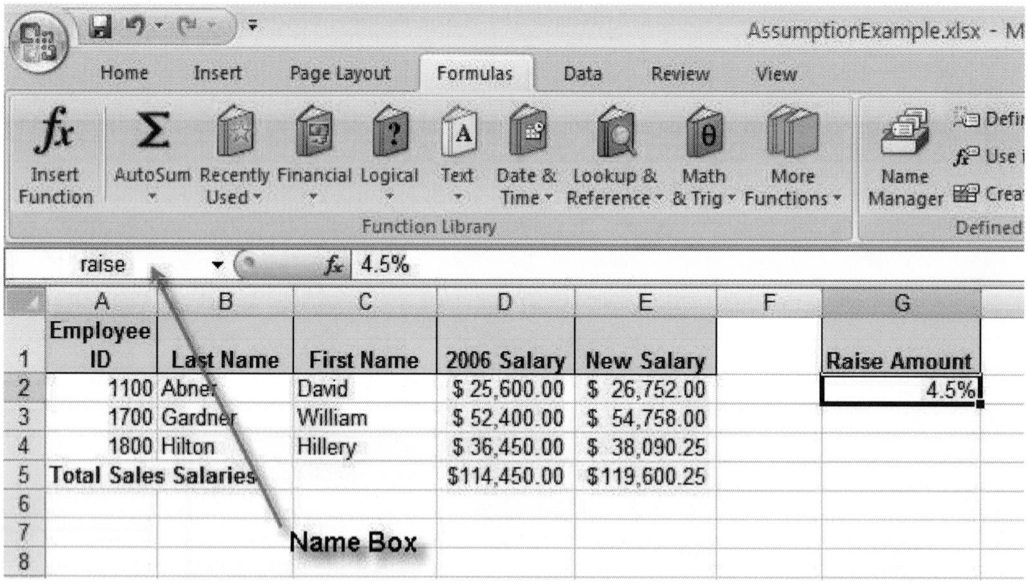

Figure 2-17: The new range name appears in the *Name Box*.

To edit the name or cell range of a named range, open the *Name Manager* dialog box by selecting **Formulas(tab)→Defined Names(group)→Name Manager icon** from the ribbon. Select the range name to edit from the list and click the *Edit* button at the top of the dialog box. The *Edit Name* dialog box will appear which mirrors the *New Name* dialog box. The name or cell range may be edited in the *Edit Name* dialog box in the same fashion as the range was named originally.

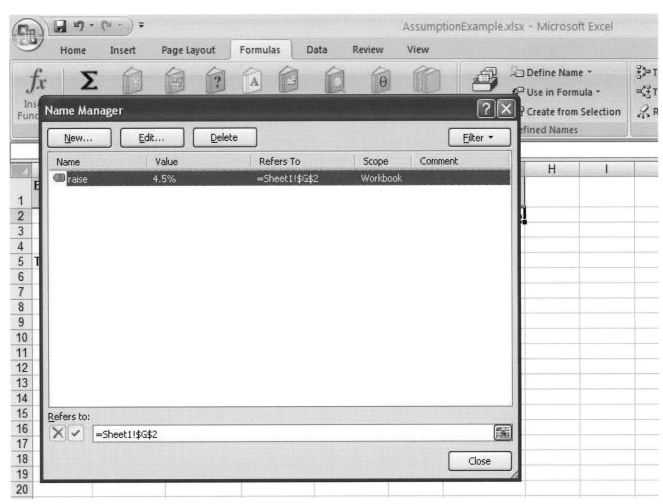

Figure 2-18: The range *Name Manager* dialog box.

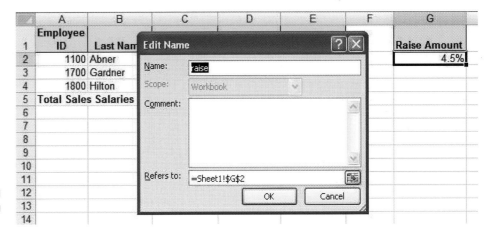

Figure 2-19: Edit names or cell references of named ranges using the *Edit Name* dialog box.

To remove a named range, select the range name in the *Name Manager* dialog box and click the *Delete* button (see Figure 2-18). Click the *Close* button or *Window Close* icon (upper right corner of dialog box) to close the dialog box.

Recall our previous example in which we placed the employee salary raise percentage into an assumption cell. Now let's name the assumption cell "raise." Once the cell is named, we can use the name of the assumption cell in our formula. By using the range name, both the column and row cell references of the named range will automatically be absolute.

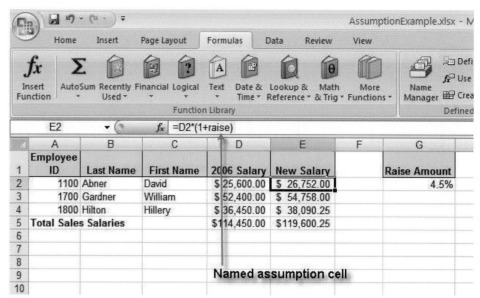

Figure 2-20: The revised formula using the name for the assumption cell G2.

Name a range of cells quickly by selecting the range to name and type the range name into the *Name Box* (see *Name Box* in Figure 2-17). Be sure to press the Enter key to save the name.

Removing Formulas from Calculated Cells

Occasionally a user may wish to remove the formula underlying a calculated value leaving only the result value in the cell. When worksheet data is exported to other programs, the new program may not support the formulas. In order to export only the data values resulting from calculations, formulas must be directly replaced by their corresponding result values. To remove the formulas from a cell range, the contents of the range may be copied and pasted back into the exact same range using a Paste Special option provided by Excel. To remove formulas from formula cells, select the range of cells and perform the *Copy* command (using ribbon command or keyboard shortcut). With the same range still selected select **Home(tab)→Clipboard(group)→Paste→Paste Values** from the drop down list on the ribbon. Select a cell in the range to observe its contents. The content of the cell is the result value from the calculation, not the formula itself as before. Be aware that once formulas have been removed and replaced with result values only, the calculated cells will no longer update when the input data changes.

To view other *Paste* options, select **Home(tab)→Clipboard(group)→Paste→Paste Special**. In the *Paste Special* dialog box, note the various options for pasting. To paste values without the formulas, select the *Paste Values* option. Click the *OK* button to execute the selection.

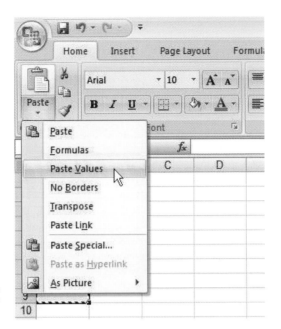

Figure 2-21: Select *Paste Values* to remove formulas from a range of cells.

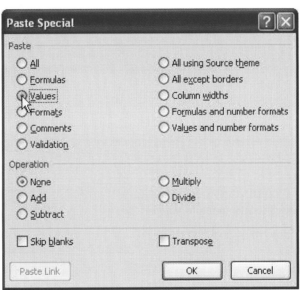

Figure 2-22: Access various Paste options through the Paste Special dialog box (Home(tab)→Clipboard (group)→Paste→Paste Special).

Date Calculations

Dates are actually numeric data with a special format applied. The default date system in Excel is derived from the *Julian* date system in which each value of one represents a whole day. The date system used in the Windows operating system environment assigns the first date value (1) to January 1, 1900. When calculating periods of time using dates in Excel, calculations are performed in units of days. If the output is desired in other units, such as years or months, the final result must be converted from days into the desired unit. Try using Excel to perform a date calculation. Enter a date into cell A1 and enter a later date into cell A2. Enter a formula into cell A3 that will calculate the number of days between the two dates. How does the result value look? It should be a number, but it may be in a date format because you entered dates in the two adjacent cells so Excel may think the result of the calculation should also be a date. Keep in mind that what you see on the worksheet represents only the format and not the actual value contained in the cell. If the result is in a date format, correct the format by selecting the formula cell and from the ribbon select **Home(tab)→Number (group)** and select *Number* from the drop-down format list. After the *Number* format is applied, the number of days should be displayed as the result value for the calculation.

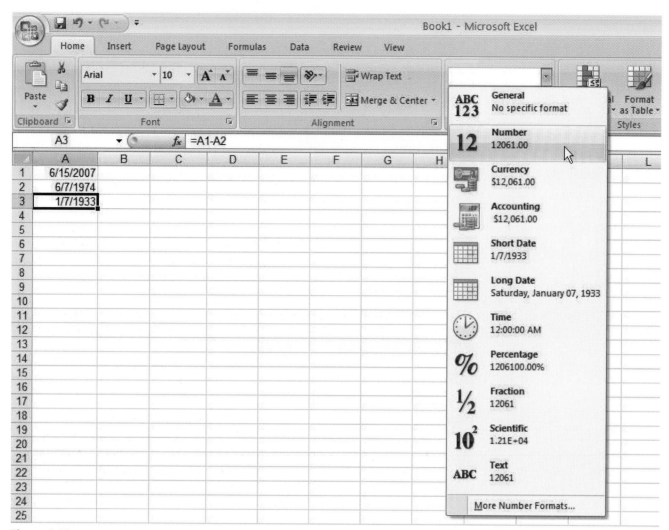

Figure 2-23: Change format of date calculation result to *Number*.

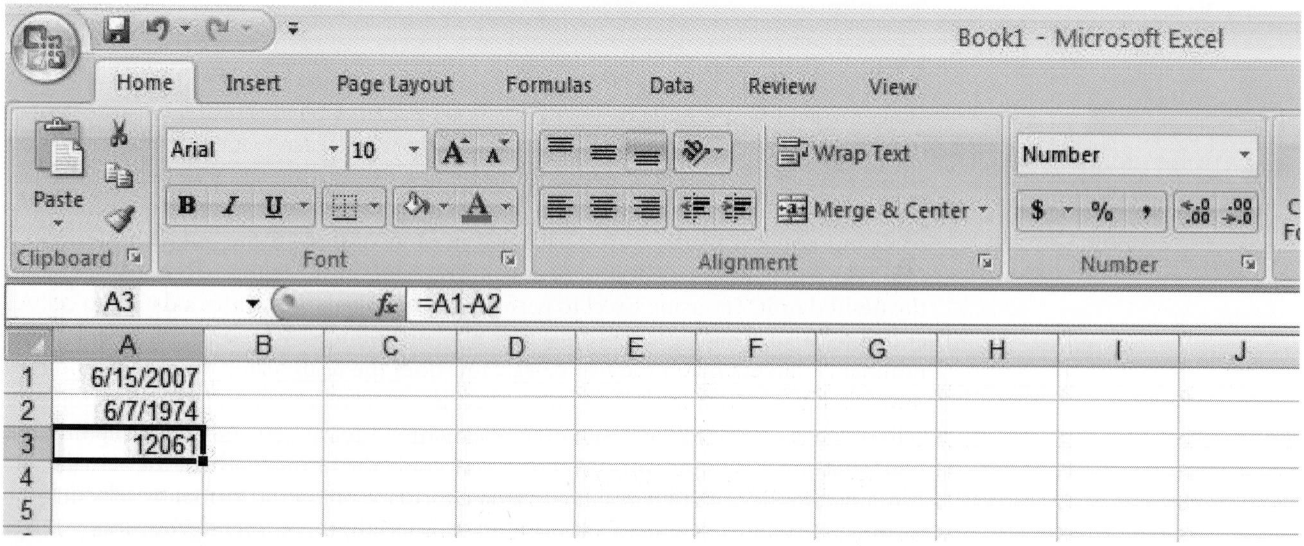

Figure 2-24: Calculation result in the *Number* format.

Troubleshooting Worksheet Formula Errors

Testing the worksheet formulas for accuracy is an important part of worksheet development. Three types of problems may occur when working with worksheet formulas.

1. *Formatting Error:* Formatting errors occur when an incorrect format is applied to a cell or cell range. The most common formatting error produces the error value ##### across the entire width of the cell. This error value indicates that a numeric (including date) format is wider than the current column width. To correct the error, increase the column width until all the # signs disappear from all the affected cells. Other formatting errors include inconsistent worksheet formats for currency, decimal places or percentages, and displaying numeric characters as numbers instead of text. For example, if a string of numeric characters is used as an identification number (such as a Social Security Number), it may include zeros at the beginning of the identifier. If a numeric format is applied, the leading zeros will be dropped. If a text format is applied, the leading zeros will be retained.

2. *Result or Logic Error:* An incorrect calculation result in a cell is caused by incorrect logic in the formula. Some common causes of result errors are incorrect order or operations, incorrect cell references, and missing or incorrect placements of parentheses in formulas. Result errors do not produce an error value (as shown in Table 2-2), so the only way a user can identify a result error is to test the results of calculations by other means.

3. *Syntax or Formula (Structure) Error:* Formula errors result from syntax errors which are errors in the construction of the formula. Syntax errors include such things as misspelled function and range names and omitting a closing parenthesis. When a formula contains a syntax or structural error, it will not produce a calculated result, but instead will produce an error value. Table 2-2 includes a list of error values that are returned as a result of formula syntax errors. The list also includes one formatting error value.

Troubleshooting Formula Syntax or Structure Errors

An error may occur when structuring a formula such that the formula fails to calculate a result. This type of error is called a *formula error* or a *syntax error. Syntax* is the set of rules for structuring formulas much like grammar rules dictate the correct structure for a human language. If a formula cannot calculate properly, it will display an error value in the formula cell. All error values start with a pound sign (#), and the error name is displayed in capital letters. Although the error value names might not seem entirely intuitive, each type of error is linked with a specific type of causation. The most difficult task in fixing a formula error is detecting the exact cause of the error. Becoming familiar with possible causes of each error type will enable you to proceed with identifying and correcting the error. Your ability to effectively troubleshoot formulas will significantly enhance your productivity in using Excel. The error names listed in Table 2-2 are designed to assist you in identifying the type of error in your formulas and some possible causes of each. (Many of the error values will be discussed in more detail in future chapters.)

Formula Auditing Tools

Excel provides a collection of special tools, called *Formula Auditing Tools,* to aid in locating the portion of the formula that is producing the formula's error value. To access

Table 2-2: Error values for formula errors.

Error Value	Common Causes
########	Column width is not wide enough to display a numeric or date format. It also occurs when a date format is assigned to a negative value. This error value is actually a formatting error rather than a formula error.
#VALUE!	An argument to a function is the wrong data type.
#DIV/0!	Results when a value is divided by zero or an empty cell.
#NAME?	Some text in the formula is not recognized by Excel, such as a misspelled range name, workbook name, worksheet name, or function name.
#N/A	An argument is missing from a function call. Also occurs if a lookup function does not find an exact match (when indicated) or if the lookup table is not sorted properly for a range match.
#REF!	A cell reference is invalid. Usually occurs when a cell is deleted that is referenced in a formula.
#NUM!	When text is entered for a function argument that should be a number.
#NULL!	Using an incorrect character (or space) in the place of a colon in a cell range address.

the *Formula Auditing Tools,* select **Formulas(tab)→Formula Auditing (group)** from the ribbon. The task group options include:

- *Trace Precedents:* Highlights all cells whose values impact the current formula cell's result

- *Trace Dependents:* Highlights all cells whose formula results are impacted by the current formula cell's value

- *Error Checking:* Checks all formulas on a worksheet for error values or inconsistency.

- *Trace Error* (on *Error Checking* drop-down list): Traces precedent cells for a cell that contains an error value result for a formula

- *Evaluate Formula:* Permits the user to watch the execution of each individual step of a formula with multiple operations or nested expressions

- *Watch Window:* Watch cell values and their formulas while working elsewhere on the worksheet

Figure 2-25: *Formula Auditing* options on the *Formulas* ribbon tab.

Error Checking Tool

Error Checking is a *Formula Auditing* tool that checks an entire worksheet at once for potential problems with formulas. Access to the feature is available in the *Formula Auditing* task group. *Error Checking* a worksheet is much like spell-checking or grammar-checking a text document. It checks each formula in the worksheet against a set of rules. The rules are designed to locate problems with formulas that either cause a current formula error or have the potential of causing future errors. *Error Checking* checks formulas that:

1. Evaluate to an error value (#VALUE!, #DIV/0!, #NAME?, #N/A, #REF!, #NUM!, #NULL!).

2. Contain dates represented as text (often as arguments to a function) that contain two-digit years that could be misinterpreted at some later time.

3. Contain numbers stored as text, often imported from other programs. If a number is to be used in a formula, it is generally best to change it to a numeric data type.

4. Are inconsistent with those in the same region, such as having inconsistent cell reference types.

5. Omit cells in a region. For example, if adjacent cells are omitted or skipped from a sum formula.

6. Contain unlocked cells that contain formulas when the worksheet is protected.

7. Contain cell references for empty cells.

To error check a worksheet, select the worksheet to check then click on the *Error Checking* icon in the *Formula Auditing* task group (see Figure 2-25). If no errors are found, a message box will appear to notify the user that no errors were found and the error check is complete. If an error is found, the *Error Checking* dialog box will appear. If a potential error is located, four options are offered for handling the formula.

1. One of the first two options (the first two options are not always presented in the same order) will be a solution to the problem based on the rule that was violated. For example, if the formula is inconsistent with others in the same region, a solution is offered to copy a formula from another cell in the same region to fill the cell in question. If a formula cell on a protected worksheet is unlocked, the solution offered is to lock the cell.

2. The other of the first two options is to get more help on the error from Excel *Help*. When this option is selected, a Help window should appear with information relating to the formula problem.

3. The third option is to ignore the error in the case that the omission or inconsistency is intentional.

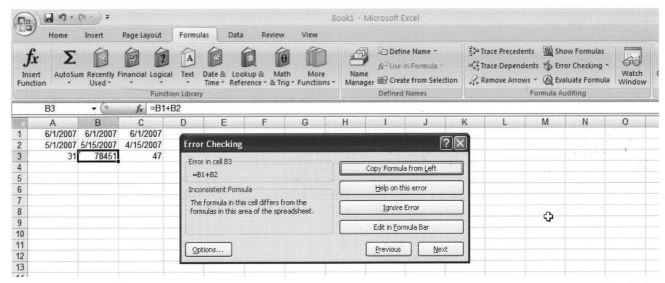

Figure 2-26: *Error Checking* dialog box showing four options for handling the identified error. Note that the formula error identified in column B adds the two dates together instead of subtracting the date in row 2 from the date in row 1 as performed in column A and C.

4. The fourth option is to edit the formula in the formula bar. When this option is selected, the cell will be highlighted and the cursor will appear in the formula bar ready for editing the formula.

An *Options* button is also on the *Error Checking* dialog box. Selecting it opens the *Formula* page of the *Excel Options* and allows the user to check or uncheck the error checking rules to apply when checking worksheet errors.

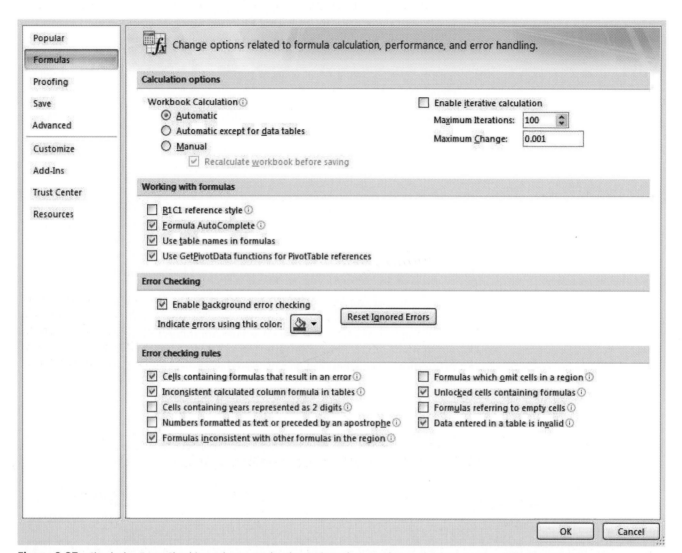

Figure 2-27: Check the *Error Checking* rules to apply. The options that are shown checked are the default options.

Troubleshooting Result Errors

Result errors are detected by thoroughly testing the results of the worksheet formulas. Formulas may be logically incorrect, yet not return an error value. *Result errors* are commonly called *logic errors* because they result from incorrect logic within the formula. To test formula results for accuracy, recalculate the formulas manually and compare the results. For doing mental calculation checks, it is helpful to replace input values with round numbers that are easy to calculate, such as 1, 100, or 10%. Another technique for checking formula results is the *reasonableness test*. The reasonableness test requires the user to make some mental calculations to determine whether or not the result is reasonable given the inputs. For example, if two decimal values are multiplied (such as 0.25×0.75), the result must be less than both of the input values (the actual result is 0.1875). A value greater than one of the input values would not be a "reasonable" result for this formula.

Once result errors are detected, the logic of the formula should be corrected so the formula will produce the correct results. A common cause of logic errors lies with the standard mathematical *order of operations*. The *order of operations* refers to the order in which Excel (or any calculator or programming language) executes the mathematical operations in a formula that includes multiple operations. Mistakes involving the order of operations can easily occur while formulating complex calculations that require multiple mathematical operations on multiple cell references.

Table 2-3: Correct order of operations.

First (^)	Excel executes all exponential calculations.
Second (* or /)	Excel executes multiplication and division simultaneously in the order that the operations occur from left to right.
Third (+ or −)	Excel executes addition and subtraction simultaneously in the order that the operations occur from left to right.

Parentheses can be used to change the order of operations. Formulas can be nested such that the output of an inner formula provides an input to an outer formula. Working from the inner-most set of parentheses to the outer-most, multiple operations within each set of parentheses are performed according to the standard order of operations. Note how parentheses affect the formula in cell D10 of the "Product Mix" worksheet.

	A	B	C	D	E	F	G	H
1				**Product Mix Analysis for February, 2007**				
2								
3				Product 1		Product 2		Product 3
4		Units Produced		10		20		10
5		Unit Revenue		1200		1500		2200
6	Cost Category	Unit Cost	Cost Units	Total cost	Cost Units	Total cost	Cost Units	Total cost
7	Labor Hours	15	15	=$B7*C7	18	=$B7*E7	10	=$B7*G7
8	Material	80	5	=$B8*C8	7	=$B8*E8	15	=$B8*G8
9	Fixed	125	1	=$B9*C9	1	=$B9*E9	1	=$B9*G9
10	Product Cost			=(D7+D8+D9)*D4		=(F7+F8+F9)*F4		=(H7+H8+H9)*H4
11	Product Profit			=D5*D4-D10		=F5*F4-F10		=H5*H4-H10
12	Total Profit							=D11+F11+H11
13								

Figure 2-28: *Formula view* of the "Product Mix" worksheet. Consider the impact of removing the parentheses from the formula in cell D10.

The correct result value for the formula in cell D10 is $7500 (see the normal view of the worksheet in Figure 2-11). Consider the impact of removing the parentheses from the formula in cell D10. The formula would then be **=D7+D8+D9*D4**. The revised (incorrect) result would then be $1,875. Understanding and controlling the mathematical order of operations is a vital step in designing formulas for accuracy.

Excel Tools for Troubleshooting Result Errors

The formula auditing tools of particular value for troubleshooting result errors are *Trace Precedents, Trace Dependents, Trace Error, Evaluate Formula,* and the *Watch Window.*

Trace Precedents

The *Trace Precedents* tool highlights all cells that contain immediate inputs for the current formula cell being evaluated. It aids the user in troubleshooting a result error by locating input cells that could potentially contain an error that leads to the error in the current formula cell of interest (the dependent cell). To trace precedents, make the formula cell the active cell and choose *Trace Precedents* from the *Formula Auditing* task group options. Precedent cells are marked with blue dots and all precedent cells are linked to the current cell (dependent cell) with blue arrows that begin with the precedent cells and end at the cell being evaluated (the dependent cell). In the figure below, note that D2 and G2 are precedent cells of the "New Salary" calculation. In the case of error values in the precedent cells, the dot and arrows will be red from the cell that contains the error value to the current formula cell (the one being traced).

	A	B	C	D	E	F	G
1	Employee ID	Last Name	First Name	2006 Salary	New Salary		Raise Amount
2	1100	Abner	David	$ 25,600.00	$ 26,752.00		4.5%
3	1700	Gardner	William	$ 52,400.00	$ 54,758.00		
4	1800	Hilton	Hillery	$ 36,450.00	$ 38,090.25		
5	Total Sales Salaries			$114,450.00	$119,600.25		
6							

Figure 2-29: *Trace Precedents* for "New Salary" formula.

Trace Dependents

Once a result error is discovered in a calculated cell, the user may wish to locate all cells that use that cell's calculated value in their own formulas. Cells that depend on the current cell's value are called *dependent cells* and can be highlighted using the *Trace Dependents* tool. To trace dependents, make the formula cell the active cell and choose *Trace Dependents* from the *Formula Auditing* task group options. The dependent cells will be marked in the same way as precedents are marked with a blue dot and blue arrows that link the current formula cell to all dependent cells. When tracing dependents, the arrows begin with the current cell and end at the dependent cell. The arrows always flow in the same direction as the dependency, always from precedents to dependents.

	A	B	C	D	E	F	G
1	Employee ID	Last Name	First Name	2006 Salary	New Salary		Raise Amount
2	1100	Abner	David	$ 25,600.00	$ 26,752.00		4.5%
3	1700	Gardner	William	$ 52,400.00	$ 54,758.00		
4	1800	Hilton	Hillery	$ 36,450.00	$ 38,090.25		
5	Total Sales Salaries			$114,450.00	$119,600.25		
6							

Figure 2-30: Tracing dependents with *Trace Dependents* formula auditing tool.

To remove all precedent and dependent tracing arrows, select *Remove Arrows* from the *Formula Auditing* task group.

Trace Error

If an error value in a precedent cell is responsible for an error value in a dependent cell, the problem cell can be located using the *Trace Error* tool. The *Trace Error* tool traces not only the precedent cells immediate to the current formula cell (as does the *Trace Precedents* tool), but also traces all precedents to the current formula cell. The advantage of using Trace Error over Trace Precedents is that the error can be traced all the way back to its origin through multiple precedent levels if necessary. The precedent cells back to the point of the error are marked with red dots and are linked with red arrows. The precedent cells immediate to the error cell are marked with blue dots and are linked to the error cell with blue arrows. The formula cell (the one being traced) must contain an error value in order for the *Trace Error* tool to be enabled for the cell.

	A	B	C
1		**Monthly Production Plan**	
2		*Hokie Furniture Manufacturing*	
3			
4	**Revenue**		
5		Units Produced	15
6		Price Per Unit	$ 1,800
7		Total Revenue	#NAME?
8			
9	**Variable Costs (per unit)**		
10		Direct Labor	$ 350
11		Direct Material (wood, hardware)	$ 250
12		Direct Supplies	$ 60
13		Sales Commissions	$ 125
14		Overhead	$ 175
15		Total Variable Costs (all units)	$ 14,400
16			
17	**Contribution Margin**		
18		Contribution Margin	#NAME?
19			
20	**Fixed Costs**		
21		Rent	$ 3,200
22		Utilities	$ 1,200
23		Supplies	$ 845
24		Equipment Leases	$ 850
25		Total Fixed Costs	$ 6,095
26			
27	**Profit**		
28		Revenue	#NAME?
29		Total Costs (fixed + variable)	$ 20,495
30		Net Income (profit)	#NAME?
31			

Figure 2-31: *Trace Error* tool marks precedent cells in red that contain error values.

Evaluate Formula

The *Evaluate Formula* tool allows the user to watch each step of a formula as it evaluates. In complex or nested formulas, the user can test a formula best by breaking it apart into its respective pieces or steps and testing the result of each part. The *Evaluate Formula* tool essentially does that for the user. The tools show the user each calculated step and its result in the order it is evaluated. The user can control the pace of the evaluation process by clicking the *Evaluate* button to move to each consecutive step. The following figure illustrates how the *Evaluate Formula* tool executes a formula one step at a time. Consider the "Product Mix" worksheet in which we removed the parentheses in the formula in cell D10. Select cell D7, then select *Evaluate Formula* from the *Formula Auditing* task group. The *Evaluate Formula* dialog box will appear. The portion of the formula that will execute first is underlined. Click the *Evaluate* button to evaluate the first step. Note that the second step is now underlined. The underlined portion of the formula is that part that will evaluate next. Continue to click the *Evaluate* button until the final result is calculated. When the final step is evaluated, the *Start* button appears to provide the opportunity to begin the evaluate process again.

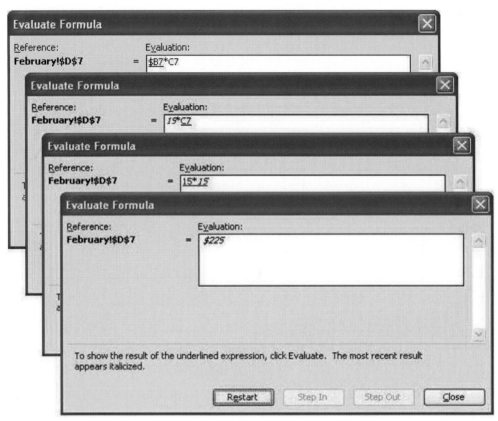

Figure 2-32: Steps to *Evaluate Formula* in cell D7 of "Product Mix" worksheet.

The *Watch Window* option can help you watch a cell to see what is happening to its value while you work elsewhere in the worksheet, even when you work out of view of the cell itself or on another worksheet or workbook. Any cell whose value or formula is an input to another cell's calculated result is called a *precedent cell*. Likewise, a cell whose formula depends on the output of the current cell's calculation is a *dependent cell*. A specific cell may be both a precedent cell (to some output cell) and a dependent cell (of some input cell). The *Watch Window* allows the user to watch the dependent cells while making changes to the values or formulas in their precedent cells. To view a cell's value or formula as it changes, the user must add the cell to the "watch" list in the *Watch Window*. To add a cell to the "watch" list, open the *Watch Window* by selecting *Watch Window* from the *Formula Auditing* task group. The window may be allowed to float over the worksheet or can be docked at the top of the worksheet below the ribbon.

To remove a "watch" from the list, highlight the item in the list and click the *Delete Watch* command at the top of the window. Close the Watch Window by either clicking on the Close Window icon (the red X) in the upper right corner of the window or by deselecting *Watch Window* in the *Formula Auditing* task group.

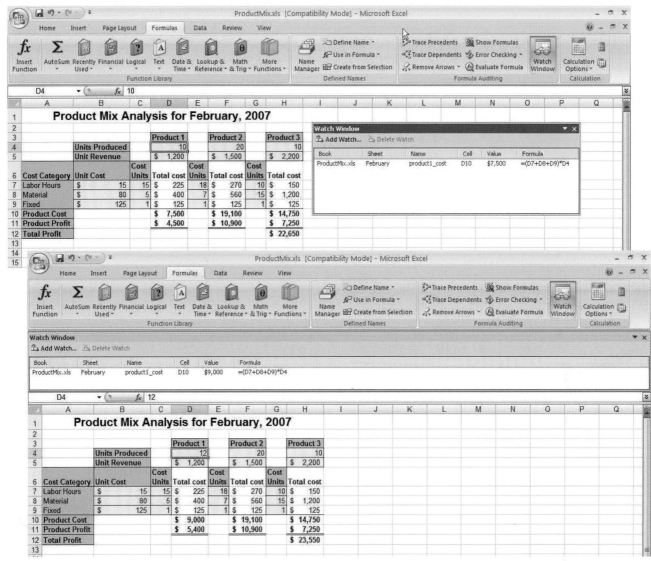

Figure 2-33: Cell D10 has been added to the *Watch Window*. Note the change in the value of D10 (in the *Watch Window*) as the value of an input, D4 is changed from 10 to 12. The name listed in the *Name* column of the *Watch Window* is the range name of cell D10. The *Watch Window* may float (above) or may be docked under the ribbon (below).

Protecting the Workbook

To protect formula cells, labels and any input cells that should not be changed by the user, Excel provides workbook protection options for protecting individual worksheets from being altered or the entire workbook from unauthorized users' access.

Worksheet Protection

The first step to protect a worksheet is to unlock the cells that you would like to permit the user to select and/or edit. By default all cells are "locked" so that when protection is applied to the worksheet, all cells of the worksheet are locked for editing. The user will be able to select any cell on the worksheet, but will not be permitted to alter it. To unlock cells to permit the user to alter, select the cell range(s) to unlock and select **Home(tab)→Cells(group)→Format→Lock Cell** from the drop-down menu. Note that the *Lock Cell* icon is selected when the drop-down list is accessed. Selecting

Lock Cell deselects the *Lock Cell* icon to indicate that the cells are now unlocked. Clicking the *Lock Cell* menu item once more will make the icon appear selected and the cells will again be locked.

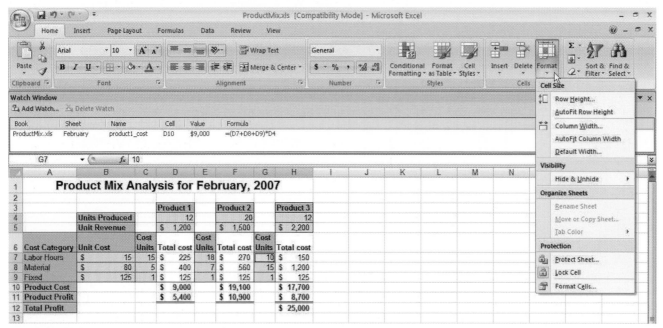

Figure 2-34: Unlock cells that users may change before adding worksheet protection.

Now you are ready to apply protection to the remainder of the worksheet. To apply protection to the worksheet, select **Review(tab)→Changes(group)→Protect Sheet** from the ribbon. A *Protect Sheet* dialog box will appear. Make any desired selections in the list box under *Allow all users of this worksheet to*. In some cases it may be

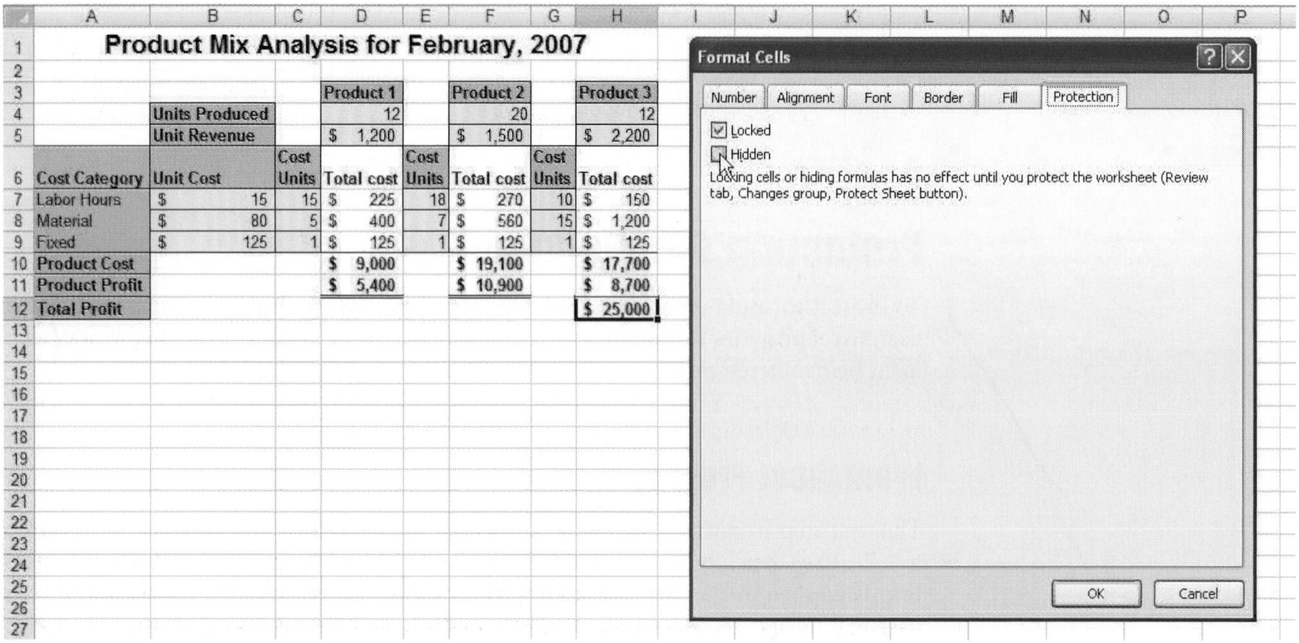

Figure 2-35: Use the "Hidden" feature on the *Protection* tab of the Format Cells dialog box to hide formulas from users. The formula cannot be viewed after worksheet protection has been applied.

confusing to permit users to select cells they cannot alter. You may choose to disallow users to select locked cells by removing the check from the *Select locked cells* check box. If you would like users to be able to view formulas although they are not permitted to change them, leave the *Select locked cells* check box checked and the user will be able to select any cell on the worksheet and view its formula in the formula bar. If you would like to allow users to select some cells to view formulas but do not wish for the users to view all formulas, you may hide the formula in specific cells. To hide a formula from user view, select the formula cell(s) to hide then select **Home(tab)→Font** from the ribbon **and click on the lower right corner of the task group**. The *Format Cells* dialog box will appear. The same dialog box can be accessed by selecting **Home(tab)→Cells→Format→Format Cells** from the ribbon. Keep in mind that the formulas will not be hidden until protection is applied to the worksheet.

Apply protection to the worksheet by selecting **Home(tab)→Cells(group)→Format→Protect Sheet** from the ribbon. Worksheet protection may also be applied using the path **Review(tab)→Changes(group)→Protect Sheet**.

Figure 2-36: The *Review* tab of the ribbon. To apply worksheet protection, select *Protect Sheet* from the *Changes* task group.

	H12			f_x				
	A	B	C	D	E	F	G	H
1	**Product Mix Analysis for February, 2007**							
2								
3				**Product 1**		**Product 2**		**Product 3**
4		**Units Produced**		12		20		12
5		**Unit Revenue**		$ 1,200		$ 1,500		$ 2,200
6	**Cost Category**	**Unit Cost**	**Cost Units**	**Total cost**	**Cost Units**	**Total cost**	**Cost Units**	**Total cost**
7	Labor Hours	$ 15	15	$ 225	18	$ 270	10	$ 150
8	Material	$ 80	5	$ 400	7	$ 560	15	$ 1,200
9	Fixed	$ 125	1	$ 125	1	$ 125	1	$ 125
10	**Product Cost**			$ 9,000		$ 19,100		$ 17,700
11	**Product Profit**			$ 5,400		$ 10,900		$ 8,700
12	**Total Profit**							$ 25,000
13								

Figure 2-37: After worksheet protection is applied, note that the formula in cell H12 is not displayed in the formula bar when the cell is selected by the user.

To keep unauthorized users from removing protection from a worksheet, set a password that will be required to unprotect the worksheet. Be sure to remember the password because it will be required for you to remove protection from the worksheet. When you provide a password, you will be prompted to enter it a second time for additional validation of the new password.

	A	B	C	D	E	F	G	H	I	J	K	L	M
1	**Product Mix Analysis for February, 2007**												
2													
3				**Product 1**		**Product 2**		**Product 3**					
4		Units Produced		12		20		12					
5		Unit Revenue		$ 1,200		$ 1,500		$ 2,200					
6	Cost Category	Unit Cost	Cost Units	Total cost	Cost Units	Total cost	Cost Units	Total cost					
7	Labor Hours	$ 15	15	$ 225	18	$ 270	10	$ 150					
8	Material	$ 80	5	$ 400	7	$ 560	15	$ 1,200					
9	Fixed	$ 125	1	$ 125	1	$ 125	1	$ 125					
10	Product Cost			$ 9,000		$ 19,100		$ 17,700					
11	Product Profit			$ 5,400		$ 10,900		$ 8,700					
12	Total Profit							$ 25,000					
13													
14													
15													
16													
17													
18													

Protect Sheet   [?][X]

☑ Protect worksheet and contents of locked cells

Password to unprotect sheet:
[   ]

Allow all users of this worksheet to:

☑ Select locked cells
☑ Select unlocked cells
☐ Format cells
☐ Format columns
☐ Format rows
☐ Insert columns
☐ Insert rows
☐ Insert hyperlinks
☐ Delete columns
☐ Delete rows

[OK]   [Cancel]

Figure 2-38:   Once input cells are unlocked and formulas hidden as desired, apply worksheet protection. Set a password (optional) that is required to unprotect worksheets.

Workbook Protection

To prevent an unauthorized user from changing the structure of a workbook, such as adding or removing worksheets, apply protection to the entire workbook by selecting **Review(tab)→Changes→Protect Workbook→Protect Structure and Windows** from the ribbon. The *Protect Structure and Windows* dialog box will appear. Two options exist for what elements of the workbook to protect. Protecting structures (adding or removing worksheets) is checked by default. If you would like to prevent the users from altering the window size and position when the workbook opens, check the *Windows* check box in addition to the *Structure* check box. To prevent users from removing workbook protection, set a password. When you provide a password, you will be prompted to enter it a second time for additional validation of the new password.

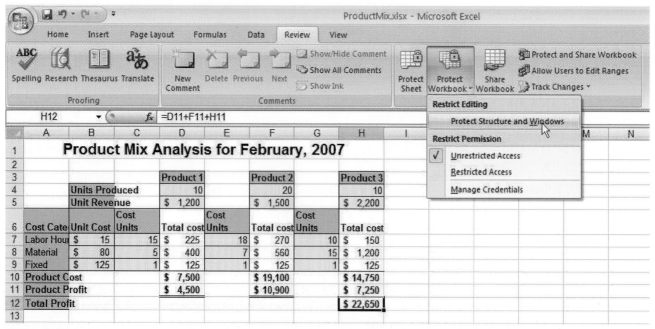

Figure 2-39: Add protection to workbook structure and windows.

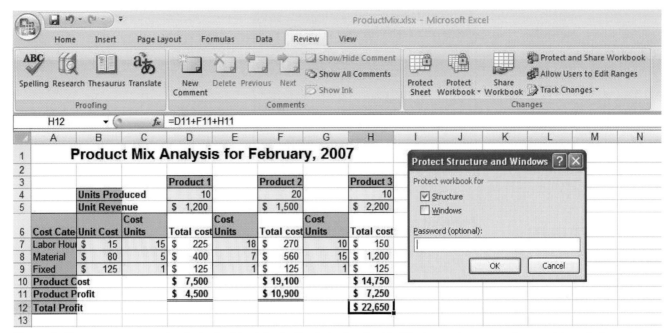

Figure 2-40: Structure protection is checked by default. Check the box beside *Windows* to keep users from resizing windows. A password may also be added that will be required to unprotect the workbook.

To prevent an unauthorized user from opening a workbook, you can specify a password for opening the workbook when the file is saved by selecting the **Office Button→Save As** from the ribbon. The *Save As* dialog box will appear. From the *Tools* drop-down list, select *General Options*. The *General Options* dialog box will appear. Enter a password for opening and/or modifying the workbook into the two respective text boxes.

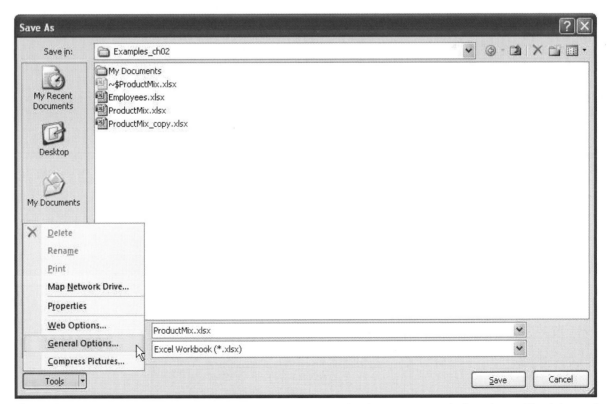

Figure 2-41: To prevent unauthorized users from opening a workbook, set a password when the workbook is saved (*Office Button→Save As→Tools→General Options*).

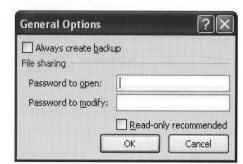

Figure 2-42: Set a password to open and/or modify the workbook. You will be prompted to confirm the password by retyping it into an addition dialog box.

Encrypt a Workbook

Along with password-protecting a workbook, the creator also has the option of encrypting the workbook file. Excel 2007 uses Office Open XML Formats that provide stronger encryption than is available in previous versions of Excel. To add encryption to a workbook, select the **Office Button→Prepare→Encrypt Document.** You will be prompted to provide a password for encryption which may be the same or different from the password to open or modify the workbook.

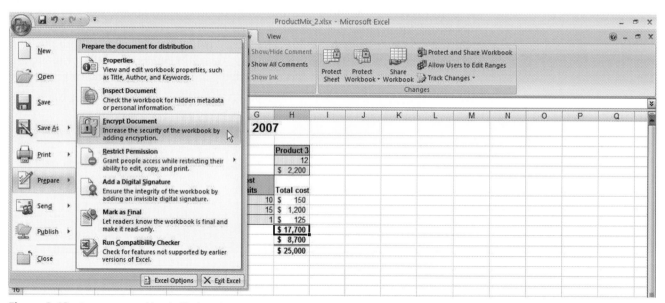

Figure 2-43: Encrypt a workbook file by selecting the *Office Button→Prepare→Encrypt Document.*

Encrypt Document

Encrypt the contents of this file

Password:

Caution: If you lose or forget the password, it cannot be recovered. It is advisable to keep a list of passwords and their corresponding document names in a safe place. (Remember that passwords are case-sensitive.)

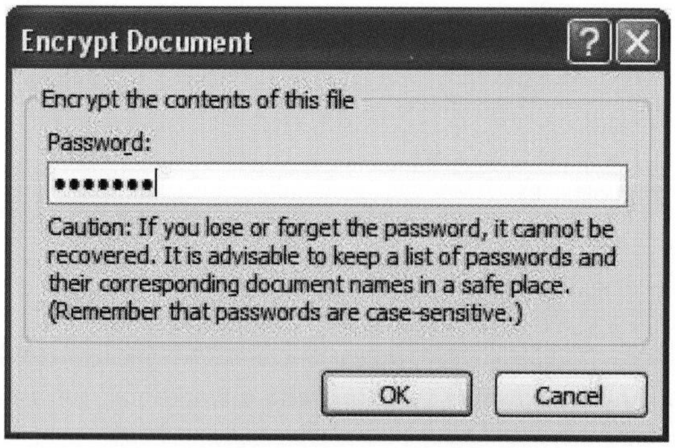

Figure 2-44: Set a password for workbook encryption.

Review Questions

1. What is meant by a flexible Excel workbook?

   _____

   _____

   _____

2. What role do formulas play in the design of a flexible worksheet?

   _____

   _____

   _____

3. List four goals of good spreadsheet design.

   _____

   _____

   _____

4. How does the type of user (experienced or inexperienced) impact the design of an Excel workbook?

   _____

   _____

   _____

5. What are three ways to add documentation to a workbook?

   _____

   _____

   _____

6. How does Excel know a formula has been entered into a worksheet cell?

   _____

   _____

7. How does the use of cell references as input values affect the flexibility of an Excel formula?

_____

_____

_____

8. Explain the difference among absolute, relative, and mixed cell references with regard to copying and pasting Excel formulas from one cell to other cells. What is the default cell reference type in Excel?

_____

_____

_____

9. What is an assumption cell and how is it used to support flexible formula design?

_____

_____

_____

10. When would it be helpful to be able to view all worksheet formulas?

_____

_____

_____

11. What is the purpose of a named range of cells in Excel and how might they be used in worksheet formulas?

_____

_____

_____

12. Give an example of a situation in which it would be advantageous to re-move a formula from a range of cells in Excel and replace the formula with the result value of the calculation. How does removing a formula

affect the flexibility of the workbook? What *Edit* feature is used to paste a formula result in the place of a formula?

_____

_____

_____

13. When date calculations are performed in Excel, what is the default unit of the calculated result value?

_____

_____

_____

14. Give three examples of specific errors that might be diagnosed by using the *Evaluate Formula* feature of the *Formula Auditing* tools.

_____

_____

_____

15. If the error value ##### is displayed in a worksheet cell, what are possible causes? How do you fix the problem?

_____

_____

_____

16. What is one possible cause of the *#NAME?* error value?

_____

_____

_____

17. What is the purpose of the *Watch Window*?

_____

_____

_____

18. What types of protection can be applied to a worksheet?

_____

_____

_____

19. What types of protection can be applied to a workbook?

_____

_____

_____

20. How might you tell if the incorrect result of a date calculation is negative?

_____

_____

_____

Practice Problems

1. Construct the following multiplication table in Excel. Using appropriate types of cell references (absolute, relative, and mixed), enter a formula into cell B2 such that when it is copied across and down to fill the table it will produce the correct results.

	A	B	C	D	E	F	G
1		0	1	2	3	4	5
2	0	0	0	0	0	0	0
3	1	0	1	2	3	4	5
4	2	0	2	4	6	8	10
5	3	0	3	6	9	12	15
6	4	0	4	8	12	16	20
7	5	0	5	10	15	20	25

2. Design a formula in Excel that calculates your age in years. Enter the inputs and the formula into an Excel worksheet.

3. Open the Excel file "ProductMix_ErrorCheck.xlsx". Use the Error Checking tool to find and correct the worksheet errors. What errors were identified?

4. Error values in formulas (especially the #N/A error) are sometimes expected in some cells. Use Excel *Help* (Offline or Online) to figure out how you might hide those error values in cells that you might not want the user to see if and only if there is an error value that will display in the cell.

1. Incorporate worksheet functions and their arguments into Excel formulas
2. Enter functions into worksheet cells using the *Function Library* task group and keyboard shortcut
3. Locate functions that are available for use in Excel workbooks
4. Design worksheet formulas to utilize a variety of functions from common categories of worksheet functions
5. Explore specific functions and categories of functions in Excel Help
6. Troubleshoot formula errors for formulas containing functions

Using Excel Functions

Functions are pre-defined formulas in Excel that are named and have a specific ordered list of inputs. An example of an Excel worksheet function is AVERAGE that calculates the average of a group of numeric values. The concept of a function is common to virtually all mathematics and quantitative sciences. A function relates each of its inputs to exactly one output. Excel worksheet functions work exactly the same way. Functions return exactly one value to the location from which they are "called."

The inputs to a function are referred to as its *arguments*. To "call" a function means to insert its name and its ordered argument list into a formula in a worksheet cell. A function may also be called from another function or from a programming module associated with an Excel workbook. A function may be used alone as a cell formula or it may be used within a formula to return some value to a component of the formula. Some functions perform calculations while others format values or text for display. Many functions are already defined in Excel and ready for use. There are over 330 Excel worksheet functions available in eleven different categories. There are over 50 financial functions alone and over 75 statistical functions included. In addition to Excel worksheet functions, the user may define custom functions in the programming environment associated with Excel. *Custom functions* or *user-defined functions* can also be used in Excel worksheet formulas. In this chapter, discussion of functions will be limited to those already defined for Excel worksheets.

Argument List

Associated with each function in Excel is a list of required and/or optional arguments. An argument is one data item a function uses as input to perform its operation. Some functions have one or more arguments that the user is required to enter. Some functions have optional user-supplied arguments. Still other functions require no argument at all to be entered by the user. The argument list is always enclosed in a set of parentheses that follows the name of the function. Each argument in the list is separated by a comma. If no user-supplied argument is required, we say the argument list is "empty." Although a function may require no arguments, the set of empty parentheses must still be entered immediately after the function name.

Entering Functions into Worksheet Cells

Since a function is a predefined formula, it is entered following an equal sign as are other formulas. If the function is used alone in the formula cell, the name of the function is entered immediately following the equal sign. Following the function name, the list of arguments must be specified inside a set of parentheses. Depending on the type of data required (or permitted) for an argument, arguments may be supplied by typing in a value, by typing in a cell reference, or by selecting a single cell or range of cells that contains the needed numeric or text value(s).

There are several methods for inserting a function into a worksheet cell or formula. Begin by selecting the worksheet cell in which you would like to insert the function then use one of the methods listed to insert the function and its arguments.

1. Select **Formulas(tab)→Function Library→Insert Function** from the ribbon. The *Insert Function* dialog box will appear and offer a guide for entering the function arguments.

2. Type the function name directly into the cell or into the formula bar immediately following the equal sign, or wherever the function is to be "called" within the formula. After the function name is recognized by Excel, an *argument tooltip* appears to show the name and order of the argument list. As arguments are entered by the user, the next argument to enter is shown in bold text. Tooltip arguments enclosed in square brackets indicate optional arguments.

   The order of the arguments the user supplies to a function is very important. In most cases, when the name of the function is typed directly into the cell, an *argument tooltip* will pop-up to prompt you to enter the arguments in the correct order. You may also click on the name of the function on the tooltip and a *Help* dialog box will appear that gives you more information about the function and its arguments.

Figure 3-1: Click on the function name on the *argument tooltip* to get Help on the function and its arguments. The argument shown in bold text is always the next argument to insert.

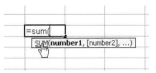

3. Click on the drop-down arrow on the Auto-Sum icon Σ in the *Function Library* task group on the ribbon and select *More Functions...* . The *Insert Function* dialog box will appear and offer a guide for entering the function arguments.

4. Click on the *fx* to the left of the formula bar. The *Insert Function* dialog box will appear and offer a guide for entering the function arguments.

Quick Tip!

The *Insert Function* dialog box may be accessed quickly by using the keyboard shortcut Shift+F3.

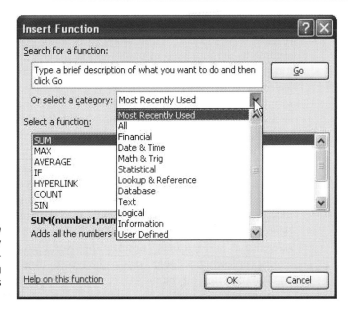

Figure 3-2: The *Insert Function* dialog box appears when any method is used for inserting a function with the exception of typing the function name and arguments directly into the cell.

When the *Insert Function* dialog box opens, it will show the most recently used functions listed in the *Select a function* list box. The functions are grouped by categories, including the *All* category that lists all the worksheet functions alphabetically. A function may be accessed by its category by using the drop-down list beside the caption *Or select a category*. If you know the name of the function but do not know its category, you may either select it from the *All* category or type the function name into the first text box labeled *Search for a function* then click the *Go* button to search for the function by name. Note that once a function name is selected and highlighted in the function list box, a brief description appears below the list box that includes the function's arguments and the nature of its return value. Select the function from the list box and click the *OK* button. The *Function Argument* dialog box will appear.

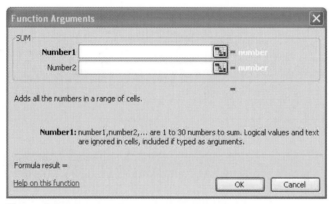

Figure 3-3: The *Function Arguments* dialog box.

Once a function has been selected, the user is prompted to enter its arguments into the *Function Argument* dialog box. For arguments that will use cell references, place the cursor (by using the mouse pointer) inside the text box for the specific argument then select the cell or cell range to reference using the mouse pointer and left mouse button. If the dialog box is covering the range of cells that you wish to select, drag the box by its title bar to a different location by using the left mouse button, or use the *Select Cells* icon to collapse the dialog box while selecting the cell range. To save the cell range reference in the argument text box, use the icon at the end of the text box (or the Enter key) to extend the dialog box and write the cell reference into the argument text box. Note that the text box labels for required arguments are indicated with bold text and optional arguments are indicated in plain text. There is a brief description of the nature of the function's return value under the argument text boxes. As each argument text box is selected for entry, a description of the argument appears beneath the function return description. After entering all the required arguments and the desired optional arguments, click the *OK* button to insert the function and its arguments into the selected cell on the worksheet.

In addition to supplying the correct number of required arguments and in the correct order, the functions require you to match the *type* of input data for each argument to the *type* of data (or data type) the function needs to perform its operation. For example, the mathematical function ROUND requires a *numeric type* of data. The numeric data item may be typed directly into the argument list, or it may be entered by referencing an Excel cell (by its cell address) which contains numeric data. Using a cell reference as an argument supports the overall goal of maximum flexibility for Excel worksheet formulas. Table 3-1 lists the type of inputs Excel functions use, and provides an example of each type.

Table 3-1: Types of input data for Excel functions

Data Type	Description	Examples
Numeric	Numbers that include decimal values and date values	1 1.25 39100
Text	Alphanumeric characters, including special characters	ACIS 2504 3070 Pamplin
Boolean	Only two values are permitted, one that represents *True* and one that represents *False*.	True or 1 False or 0
Cell reference	The address of one worksheet cell	C2 $C$2
Cell range	The address of a range of worksheet cells	A1:B6
Error	Error value returned by a worksheet formula	#NAME? #VALUE! #DIV/0!

Date and Time Functions

Dates are used extensively in all business disciplines including accounting, finance, management, marketing, and economics. Many financial calculations involve dates or time frames, such as calculating interest, determining payment due dates, or counting days since a customer placed an order or made a payment. Gaining experience with date and time functions will allow the user to perform many date-based tasks automatically in Excel.

There are date and time functions that return specific components of the serial date value. Recall that a date is stored in Excel as a serial number which begins with January 1, 1900 (in Windows operating environments) having a value of one. Date functions perform complex calculations on the serial date to return values for such components as year, month, day of the month, hour, minute, and second. Each function in this group

Table 3-2: Date functions that extract a date component value

Function & Argument	Description of Return Value
YEAR(serial_number)	Returns the year from the date value
MONTH(serial_number)	Returns the month of the year from the date value as an integer (1 through 12)
DAY(serial_number)	Returns the day of the month from the date value as an integer (date of month, 1 through 31)
HOUR(serial_number)	Returns the hour of the day from the date value
MINUTE(serial_number)	Returns the minute from the date value
SECOND(serial_number)	Returns the second from the date value

has only one input value or argument and that is the serial number representing the date value. Each of the functions in Table 3-2 returns a specific component from the date value.

"WEEK" Functions

The functions WEEKDAY and WEEKNUM involve the determination of how a serial date value relates to a week or day of the week. Both use an optional argument, *return-type*, in addition to the serial date value.

Table 3-3: Functions that calculate their results based on how a week is determined.

Function & Arguments	Description of Return Value
WEEKDAY(serial_number, [return_type]) (*Return_type* values 1, 2, or 3 are accepted. The default type is 1.)	Returns the non-weekend day of the week from the date value as a numeral
WEEKNUM(serial_number, [return_type]) (*Return_type* values 1 or 2 are accepted. The default type is 1.)	Returns the number of the week as it falls numerically within the year

In some domains, the first day of a week may be Sunday and in others it may be Monday. In order to extract a week value from a serial date value, the function must be told on what day to start the week. This information is provided in an optional argument called *return_type*. The following return types are defined:

> *Return_type 1:* The integers 1 through 7 represent days Sunday through Saturday.
> *Return_type 2:* The integers 1 through 7 represent days Monday through Sunday.
> *Return_type 3:* The integers 0 through 6 represent days Monday through Sunday.

Functions That Return a Date Value

The TODAY and NOW functions return the current system date. They differ only slightly in that the NOW function includes the date and time of day in its return value and TODAY returns only the date. Neither function requires a user-supplied argument. A special consideration when using the TODAY or NOW functions is that their calculations are dynamic in that they will update as the date (or time in the case of NOW) changes. If you want a calculation input to remain constant for some point in time, enter the current date and time directly into the formula or cell without using the TODAY or NOW functions.

A number of other date functions compose the serial date value from other cell references that are supplied as arguments. For example, the DATE function accepts input values that represent the year, the month and the day. From those values, a serial date value is calculated and displayed.

Another useful date and time function in accounting and finance domains is the DAYS360 function which calculates the number of days between two dates based on a 360-day year as is common practice in financial calculations. The DAYS360 function requires two arguments, the *start_date* and the *end_date*. An optional third argument indicates whether to use the United States method or the European method for dealing with months that have more than 30 days. With the U.S. method (a value of FALSE for the argument), if the start date is the 31st day of a month, it becomes equal to the 30th of the same month. If the end date is the 31st day of the month, and the start date

Table 3-4: Functions that return a serial date value

Function & Arguments	Description of Return Value
TODAY()	Returns today's date value without a time component
NOW()	Returns today's date value including a time component
DATE(year, month, day)	Returns a serial date value for a particular date
TIME(hour, minute, second)	Returns a fraction that represents particular time of day
EDATE(start_date, months)	Returns a serial date value that represents a given number of months before or after the *start_date*
EOMONTH(start_date, months) (Included in the Analysis Tookpak add-in)	Returns a serial date value that represents the last day of the month a given number of months before or after the *start_date*
WORKDAY(start_date, days, [holidays]) (Holidays is a list of holidays referenced by a range of cells.)	Returns a serial date value that represents an indicated number of work days before or after the *start_date*

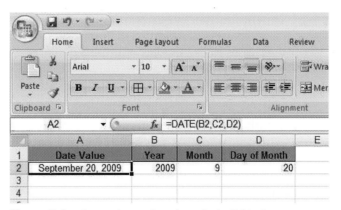

Figure 3-4: Composing a date from its individual components using the DATE function.

is earlier than the 30th day of a month, the end date becomes equal to the 1st day of the next month; otherwise the end date becomes the 30th day of the same month. With the European method (a value of TRUE for the argument), both start and end dates that occur on the 31st day of a month become equal to the 30th of the same month. The U.S. method is the default method if no input for the *method* argument. The DAYS360 function syntax:

=DAYS360(start_date, end_date, [method])

Logical Functions

A logical expression makes a comparison between two values or two expressions and evaluates to one of only two possible outcomes, TRUE or FALSE. The return type of data that permits only the values TRUE or FALSE is called *Boolean*. Logical comparisons are made between values or expressions using comparison operators.

Table 3-5: Comparison operators in Excel

Operator	Description
>	Greater than
<	Less than
>=	Greater than or equal to
<=	Less than or equal to
=	Equals
<>	Not equal to

Logical functions in Excel are used in conjunction with worksheet formulas to identify the outcome of one or more logical expressions and return a specified value or calculation result based on that outcome. The logical function AND evaluates to TRUE only if all logical comparisons in its argument list are evaluated to TRUE. The OR function evaluates to TRUE if any of the logical comparisons in its argument list are evaluated to TRUE. The NOT function reverses a Boolean value. In some cases it may simplify a formula design if the Boolean outcome of a comparison is reversed.

Table 3-6: Logical functions in Excel. The *logical* argument represents a logical comparison which will evaluate to either TRUE or FALSE

Function & Arguments	Description of Return Value
AND(logical1, [logical2, ...])	Returns TRUE if all arguments are TRUE, returns FALSE if any argument is FALSE
OR((logical1, [logical2, ...])	Returns TRUE if any argument is TRUE, returns FALSE only if no argument is TRUE
NOT(logical)	Reverses the logic of its argument
IF(logical_test, value_if_true, [value_if_false])	Specifies a logical test to perform and specifies the return value in the case that the logical test evaluates to TRUE, and (optionally) specifies the return value in the case that the logical test evaluates to FALSE

ID	Last Name	First Name	Birth Date	Gender	Hire Date	Department	Job Title	Salary	Sales Dept. and Staff Job Title
1	Abner	David	11/15/1977	M	6/20/2006	Sales	Manager	$110,958	FALSE
2	Butler	Susan	11/16/1967	F	8/13/1978	Marketing	Staff	$ 40,816	FALSE
3	Conrad	Michael	9/14/1955	M	12/25/2001	Product Development	Staff Engineer	$ 74,665	FALSE
4	Davis	Randall	7/15/1947	M	5/25/1980	Finance	Staff Accountant	$ 42,106	FALSE
5	Edwards	Minnie	3/8/1959	F	11/26/1991	Human Resources	Manager	$ 90,228	FALSE
6	Franklin	Margaret	11/25/1979	F	3/15/1977	Product Development	Staff	$ 42,976	FALSE
7	Gardner	William	11/15/1968	M	2/7/1999	Sales	Staff	$ 90,650	TRUE
8	Hilton	Hillery	11/23/1949	F	11/8/2005	Sales	District Sales Manager	$128,845	FALSE
9	Jameson	Jennifer	1/17/1959	F	11/28/1992	Sales	Manager	$110,496	FALSE
10	Kelly	Chester	10/28/1968	M	1/3/1994	Sales	Staff	$ 98,538	TRUE
11	Zahn	Geoffrey	9/6/1952	M	3/4/1999	Sales	Staff	$ 84,151	TRUE
12	Patel	Michael	4/20/1974	M	3/19/2003	Sales	District Sales Manager	$133,784	FALSE
13	Schnider	Elizabeth	6/6/1958	F	6/27/1997	Sales	Staff	$ 35,025	TRUE

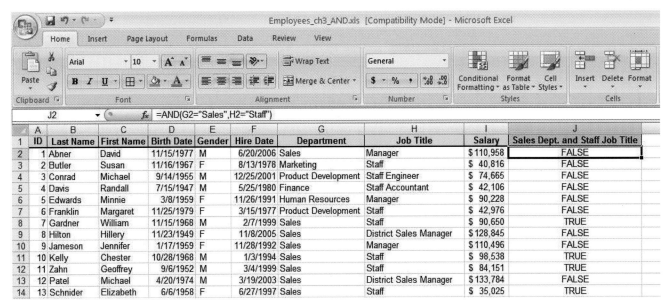

Figure 3-5: The AND function returns TRUE if both logical conditions are TRUE.

ID	Last Name	First Name	Birth Date	Gender	Hire Date	Department	Job Title	Salary	Sales Dept. and Staff Job Title
1	Abner	David	11/15/1977	M	6/20/2006	Sales	Manager	$110,958	TRUE
2	Butler	Susan	11/16/1967	F	8/13/1978	Marketing	Staff	$ 40,816	TRUE
3	Conrad	Michael	9/14/1955	M	12/25/2001	Product Development	Staff Engineer	$ 74,665	FALSE
4	Davis	Randall	7/15/1947	M	5/25/1980	Finance	Staff Accountant	$ 42,106	FALSE
5	Edwards	Minnie	3/8/1959	F	11/26/1991	Human Resources	Manager	$ 90,228	FALSE
6	Franklin	Margaret	11/25/1979	F	3/15/1977	Product Development	Staff	$ 42,976	TRUE
7	Gardner	William	11/15/1968	M	2/7/1999	Sales	Staff	$ 90,650	TRUE
8	Hilton	Hillery	11/23/1949	F	11/8/2005	Sales	District Sales Manager	$128,845	TRUE
9	Jameson	Jennifer	1/17/1959	F	11/28/1992	Sales	Manager	$110,496	TRUE
10	Kelly	Chester	10/28/1968	M	1/3/1994	Sales	Staff	$ 98,538	TRUE
11	Zahn	Geoffrey	9/6/1952	M	3/4/1999	Sales	Staff	$ 84,151	TRUE
12	Patel	Michael	4/20/1974	M	3/19/2003	Sales	District Sales Manager	$133,784	TRUE
13	Schnider	Elizabeth	6/6/1958	F	6/27/1997	Sales	Staff	$ 35,025	TRUE

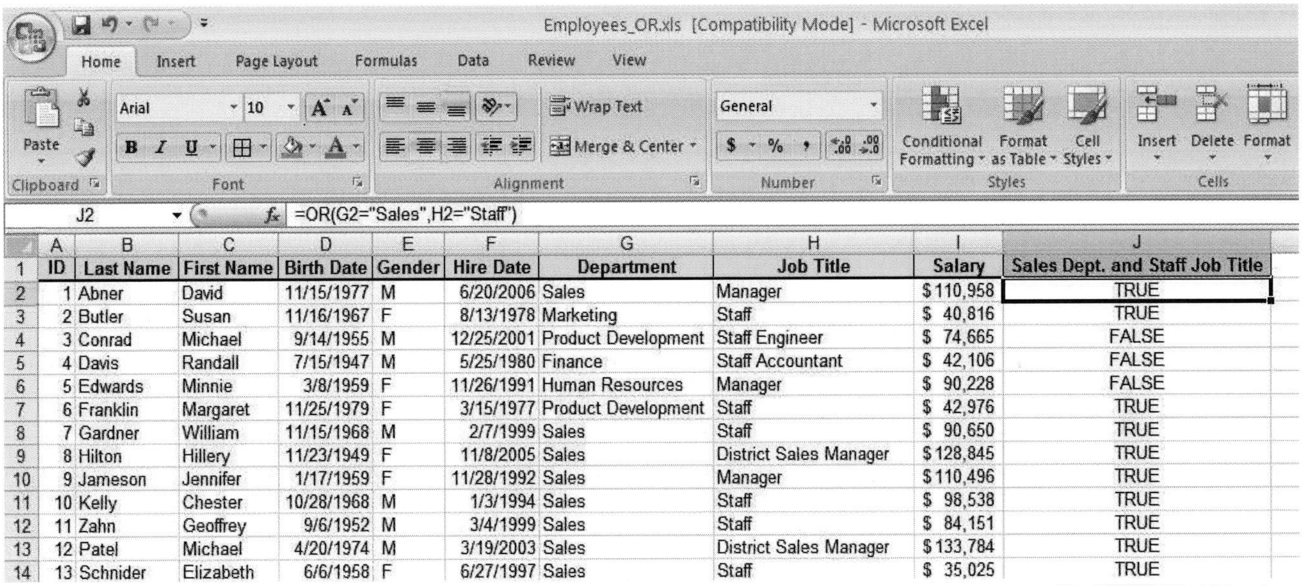

Figure 3-6: The OR function returns TRUE if either logical condition is TRUE. Compare the results with the use of the AND function in the previous figure.

The IF Function

The most commonly used function of Excel's logical functions is the IF function. Use the IF function to specify alternatives for a cell's contents. The general syntax of the IF formula:

=IF(logical_test, value_if_true, [value_if_false]).

Arguments of the IF Function

Logical_test is the comparison of two values which may be simple character or numeric values, or values represented by cell references or results of other functions or formulas.

Value_if_true is the value or formula that is returned to the cell if the *logical_test* specified in the first argument evaluates to TRUE. If this argument is omitted (after typing the comma after the *logical_test*), the function will return a value of 0(zero) if the *logical_test* evaluates to TRUE and will return a value of FALSE to the cell if the *logical_test* evaluates to FALSE. Note that this argument is required, therefore, a comma is required after the *logical_test* argument, but nothing is required past the comma that signals the beginning of the second argument.

Value_if_false is the value or formula that will be inserted into the cell if the *logical_test* evaluates to FALSE. This argument is optional. If this argument is omitted entirely (no comma inserted to signal its beginning), the logical value FALSE will be returned if the *logical_test* evaluates to FALSE. If only the comma argument separator is inserted after the second argument to signal the beginning of the *value_if_false* argument (nothing is entered after the comma), the return value is 0(zero) when the *logical_test* evaluates to FALSE.

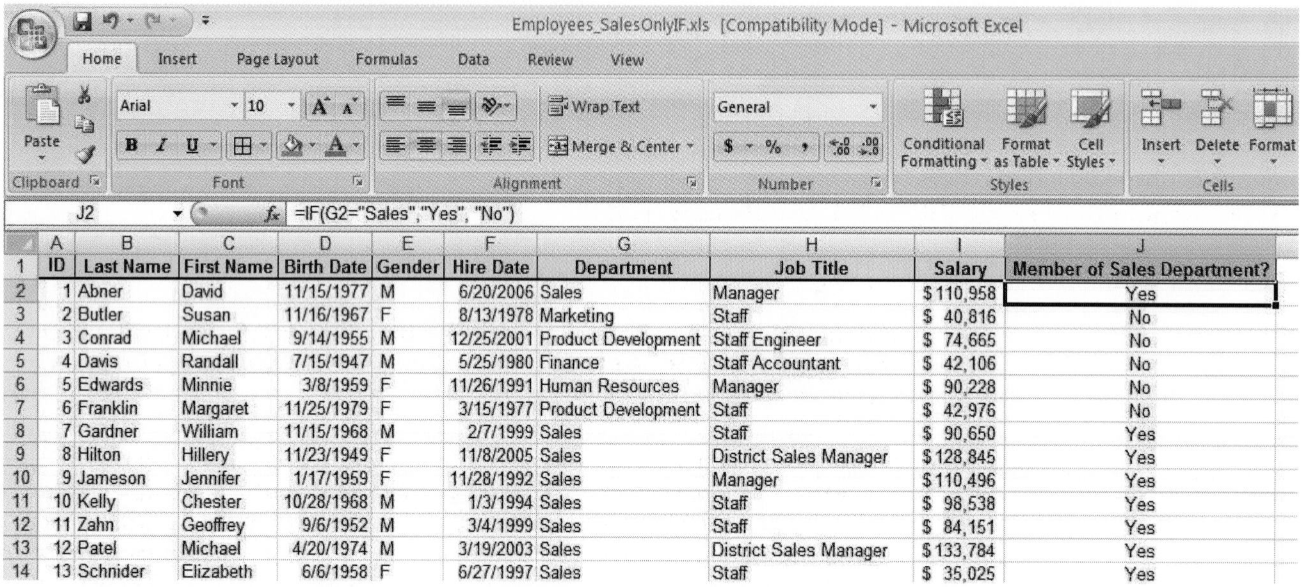

J2 =IF(G2="Sales","Yes", "No")

ID	Last Name	First Name	Birth Date	Gender	Hire Date	Department	Job Title	Salary	Member of Sales Department?
1	Abner	David	11/15/1977	M	6/20/2006	Sales	Manager	$110,958	Yes
2	Butler	Susan	11/16/1967	F	8/13/1978	Marketing	Staff	$ 40,816	No
3	Conrad	Michael	9/14/1955	M	12/25/2001	Product Development	Staff Engineer	$ 74,665	No
4	Davis	Randall	7/15/1947	M	5/25/1980	Finance	Staff Accountant	$ 42,106	No
5	Edwards	Minnie	3/8/1959	F	11/26/1991	Human Resources	Manager	$ 90,228	No
6	Franklin	Margaret	11/25/1979	F	3/15/1977	Product Development	Staff	$ 42,976	No
7	Gardner	William	11/15/1968	M	2/7/1999	Sales	Staff	$ 90,650	Yes
8	Hilton	Hillery	11/23/1949	F	11/8/2005	Sales	District Sales Manager	$128,845	Yes
9	Jameson	Jennifer	1/17/1959	F	11/28/1992	Sales	Manager	$110,496	Yes
10	Kelly	Chester	10/28/1968	M	1/3/1994	Sales	Staff	$ 98,538	Yes
11	Zahn	Geoffrey	9/6/1952	M	3/4/1999	Sales	Staff	$ 84,151	Yes
12	Patel	Michael	4/20/1974	M	3/19/2003	Sales	District Sales Manager	$133,784	Yes
13	Schnider	Elizabeth	6/6/1958	F	6/27/1997	Sales	Staff	$ 35,025	Yes

Figure 3-7: The IF function tests values in the "Department" column against the test value "Sales." If the value matches (returns TRUE), "Yes" is written into the cell, otherwise "No" is written into the cell.

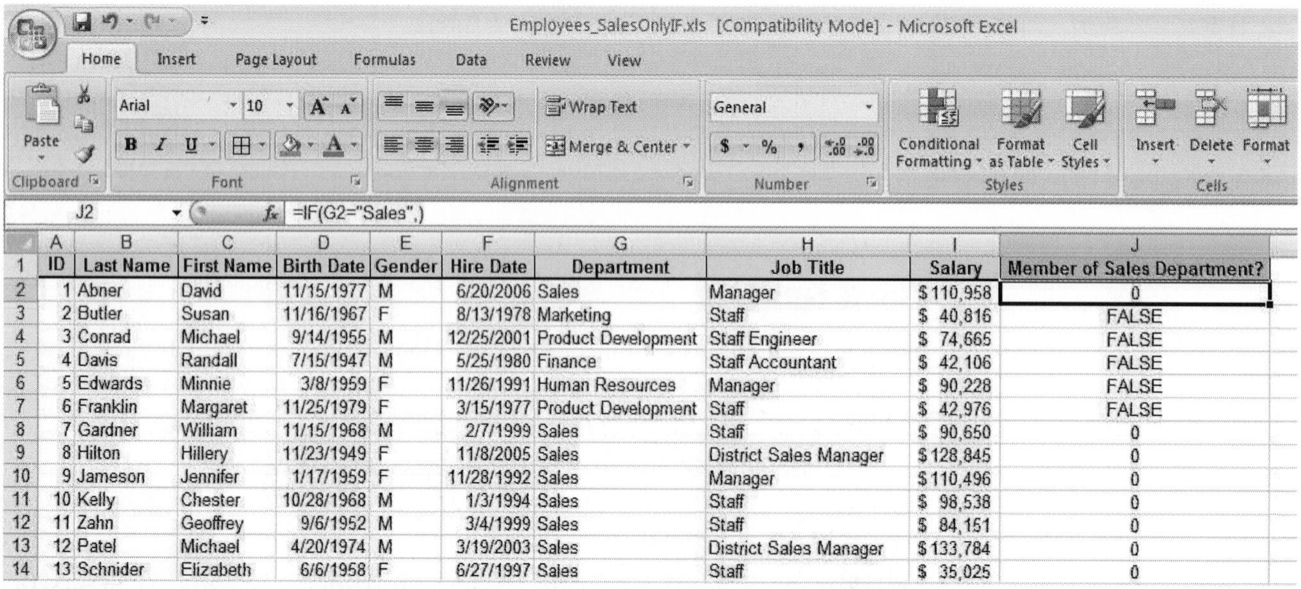

J2 =IF(G2="Sales",)

ID	Last Name	First Name	Birth Date	Gender	Hire Date	Department	Job Title	Salary	Member of Sales Department?
1	Abner	David	11/15/1977	M	6/20/2006	Sales	Manager	$110,958	0
2	Butler	Susan	11/16/1967	F	8/13/1978	Marketing	Staff	$ 40,816	FALSE
3	Conrad	Michael	9/14/1955	M	12/25/2001	Product Development	Staff Engineer	$ 74,665	FALSE
4	Davis	Randall	7/15/1947	M	5/25/1980	Finance	Staff Accountant	$ 42,106	FALSE
5	Edwards	Minnie	3/8/1959	F	11/26/1991	Human Resources	Manager	$ 90,228	FALSE
6	Franklin	Margaret	11/25/1979	F	3/15/1977	Product Development	Staff	$ 42,976	FALSE
7	Gardner	William	11/15/1968	M	2/7/1999	Sales	Staff	$ 90,650	0
8	Hilton	Hillery	11/23/1949	F	11/8/2005	Sales	District Sales Manager	$128,845	0
9	Jameson	Jennifer	1/17/1959	F	11/28/1992	Sales	Manager	$110,496	0
10	Kelly	Chester	10/28/1968	M	1/3/1994	Sales	Staff	$ 98,538	0
11	Zahn	Geoffrey	9/6/1952	M	3/4/1999	Sales	Staff	$ 84,151	0
12	Patel	Michael	4/20/1974	M	3/19/2003	Sales	District Sales Manager	$133,784	0
13	Schnider	Elizabeth	6/6/1958	F	6/27/1997	Sales	Staff	$ 35,025	0

Figure 3-8: If the *value_if_true* argument is omitted (but the comma argument separator is present), a value of 0(zero) will be returned if the logical test evaluates to TRUE. Since the *value_if_false* argument is omitted altogether (no comma separator to mark the place for the argument), a value of FALSE is returned if the logical test evaluates to FALSE. Note that the *value_if_true* is required so the comma (at least) must be placed after the first argument.

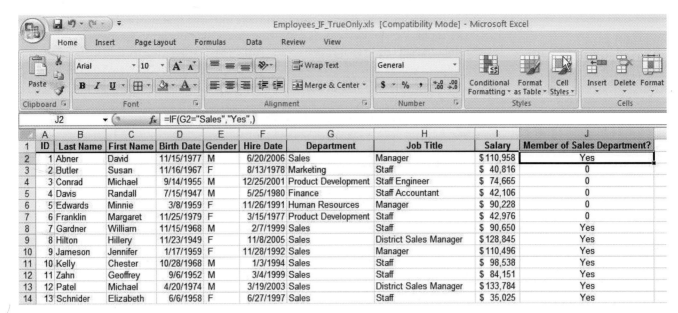

Figure 3-9: If the *value_if_false* argument is omitted (but the comma argument separator is present after the *value_if_true* argument), a value of 0(zero) will be returned if the logical test evaluates to FALSE.

Nesting Functions

It is common practice to nest functions so that the return value from one function becomes an input value to another. Let's look at the steps to calculate a person's age and determine if they are over 18.

1. First we must enter today's date. We can do that with the TODAY function or type in today's date value. Note that if you use the TODAY function, the age calculation will be dynamic and will always update as today's date changes. (Note that the NOW function is not a good choice because it contains a time component which can be a problem when doing comparisons of dates only. It too will update as the date and time change.) If you wish for the calculation to be locked as of today, enter today's date by typing the date value directly into a cell or formula bar.

2. Enter the birth date into another cell.

3. Enter a formula that subtracts the birth date from today's date. Include in the formula a conversion factor to convert days (always the result of date subtraction) to years.

4. Enter a formula to test the calculated age with the value 18 to determine if the person is of legal age.

The following figure offers a formula view of the calculation steps outlined above. The calculation is performed in three steps. The birth date is entered in the yellow cell.

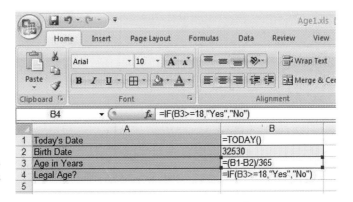

Figure 3-10: Three formulas are used to determine if the person is of legal age (formula view).

Let's combine the previous formula steps into one that uses only the birth date as a user input. We can nest the TODAY function inside of the IF function to create the formula =**IF((TODAY()-B2)/365>=18, "Yes", "No")** where the birth date is in cell B2.

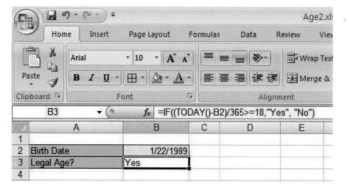

Figure 3-11: One formula used to determine legal age by nesting the TODAY function inside the IF function. The calculation result from subtracting the birth date from today's date is divided by 365 to convert the result units from days to years.

When nesting functions to perform very complex calculations, keep in mind that Excel will allow nesting of functions to only seven levels.

Nesting IF Functions

When using the IF function, the arguments for *value_if_true or value_if_false* may be literal strings (simple text data), numeric values (including dates), cell references, other calculations, or other functions, including other IF functions. IF functions can be nested in Excel such that two (or more) alternatives are available for each TRUE or FALSE value at each level of nesting. Consider that we would like to identify all employees of the sales department and also the marketing managers. The IF logic is represented by the following flowchart.

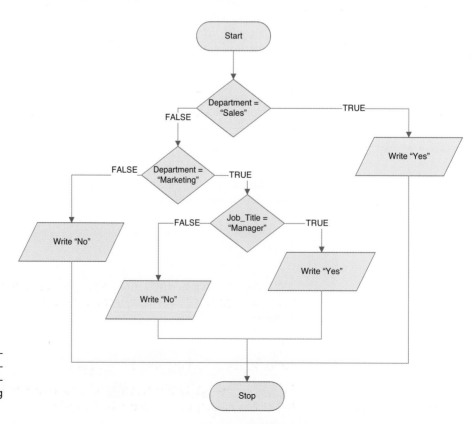

Figure 3-12: The flowchart represents the logic of selecting employees who either work in the sales department or who are marketing managers.

The Excel formula represented by the flowchart may be inserted into the "Employee" worksheet to identify the sales employees and marketing managers.

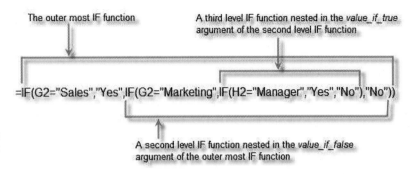

Figure 3-13: An Excel formula that utilizes IF functions nested at three levels.

	A	B	C	D	E	F	G	H	I	J
1	ID	Last Name	First Name	Birth Date	Gender	Hire Date	Department	Job Title	Salary	Sales Employee or Marketing Manager
2	1	Abner	David	11/15/1977	M	6/20/2006	Sales	Manager	$110,958	Yes
3	2	Butler	Susan	11/16/1967	F	8/13/1978	Marketing	Staff	$ 40,816	No
4	3	Conrad	Michael	9/14/1955	M	12/25/2001	Product Development	Staff Engineer	$ 74,665	No
5	4	Davis	Randall	7/15/1947	M	5/25/1980	Finance	Staff Accountant	$ 42,106	No
6	5	Edwards	Minnie	3/8/1959	F	11/26/1991	Human Resources	Manager	$ 90,228	No
7	6	Franklin	Margaret	11/25/1979	F	3/15/1977	Product Development	Staff	$ 42,976	No
8	7	Gardner	William	11/15/1968	M	2/7/1999	Sales	Staff	$ 90,650	Yes
9	8	Hilton	Hillery	11/23/1949	F	11/8/2005	Sales	District Sales Manager	$128,845	Yes
10	9	Jameson	Jennifer	1/17/1959	F	11/28/1992	Sales	Manager	$110,496	Yes
11	10	Kelly	Chester	10/28/1968	M	1/3/1994	Sales	Staff	$ 98,538	Yes
12	11	Zahn	Geoffrey	9/6/1952	M	3/4/1999	Sales	Staff	$ 84,151	Yes
13	12	Patel	Michael	4/20/1974	M	3/19/2003	Sales	District Sales Manager	$133,784	Yes
14	13	Schnider	Elizabeth	6/6/1958	F	6/27/1997	Sales	Staff	$ 35,025	Yes

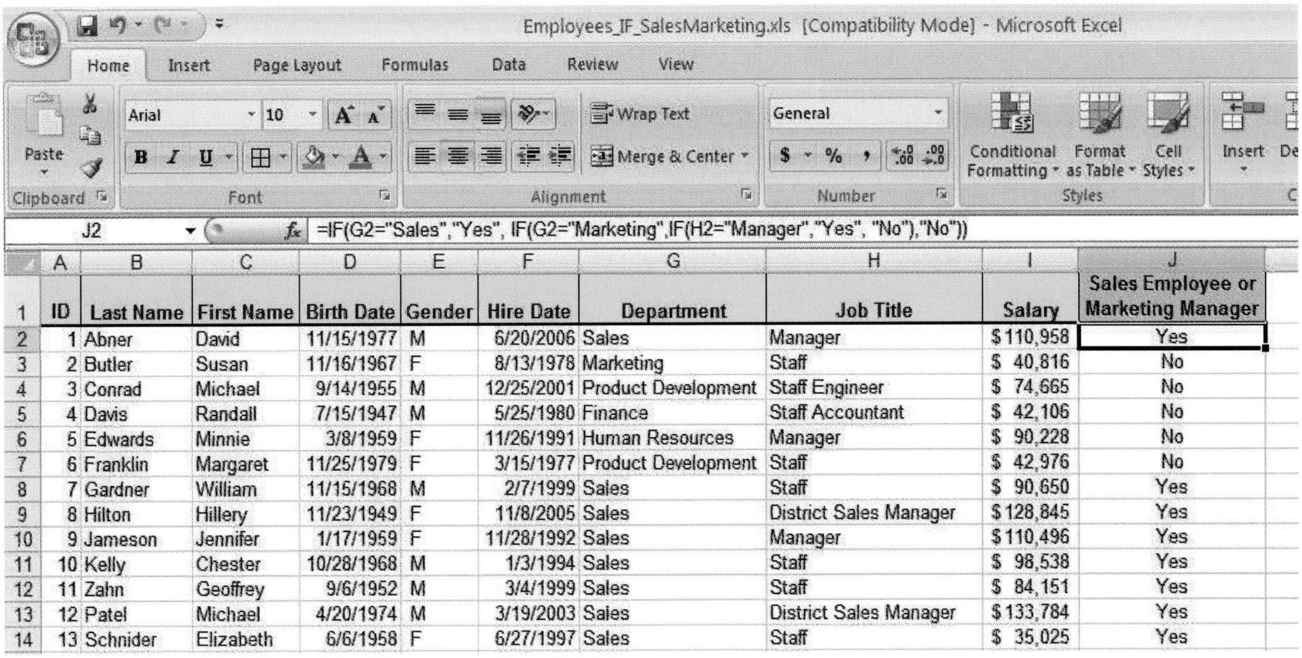

Figure 3-14: The nested IF formula is entered into cell J2.

Mathematical Functions

Adding Numbers

The most popular mathematical spreadsheet operation is adding numbers. There are many ways to add numbers in worksheets using common operators or special Excel features.

Add Values Using the Plus Sign

Insert the plus sign (addition arithmetic operator) between numbers or cell references to be added together. Example: =D2+D3+D4

AutoSum Feature

To add contiguous numbers in a row or column select the range to sum then click on the AutoSum icon Σ to insert the SUM function and its arguments automatically. Use the *Enter* key to save the formula.

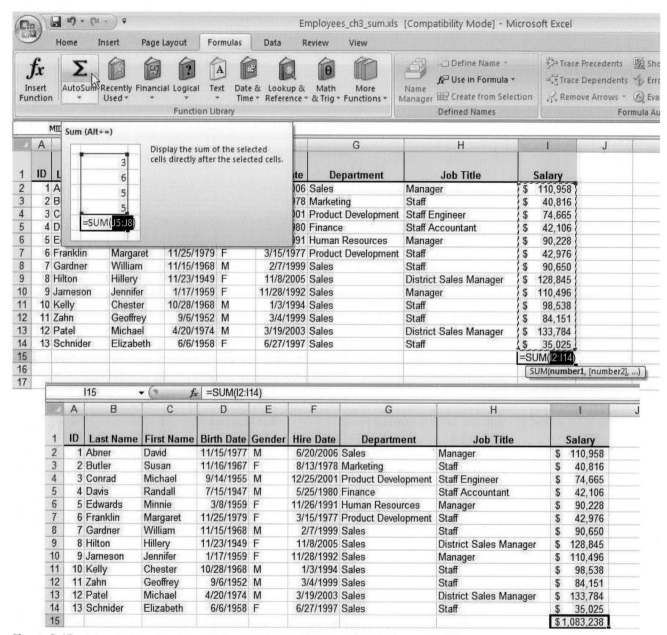

Figure 3-15: Select a range of cells you wish to sum then click the *AutoSum* icon (top). The *AutoSum* result is shows in the bottom worksheet.

SUM Function

To add non-contiguous numbers on a worksheet, type into the selected cell =**SUM**(then while holding down the Ctrl key, use the left mouse button to select each range to sum. After all ranges are selected, use the *Enter* key to save the formula. Each non-contiguous cell range selected will appear as a separate argument (separated by commas) for the SUM function. The SUM function may include up to 255 arguments including numbers, separate cells, or cell range references. Note the formula in cell F16 in Figure 3-16 for summing a non-contiguous range.

F16		f_x =SUM(B7,B15,B21,F6,F13)					
	A	B	C	D	E	F	G

Spring Dance Expenses

	A	B	C	D	E	F	G
2		Estimated	Actual			Estimated	Actual
3	Site				Program		
4	Hall rental	$350.00			Band	$425.00	
5	Equipment rental	$125.00			Vocalist	$125.00	
6	Cleaning service	$100.00			Totals	$550.00	$0.00
7	Totals	$575.00	$0.00				
8					Miscellaneous		
9	Decorations				Invitations	$35.00	
10	Table covering	$50.00			Postage	$40.00	
11	Centerpieces	$150.00			Printing	$40.00	
12	Plant rental	$25.00			Other		
13	Signs	$15.00			Totals	$115.00	$0.00
14	Napkins & paper supplies	$20.00					
15	Totals	$260.00	$0.00				
16					Total Expenses	$2,150.00	$0.00
17	Refreshments						
18	Food	$400.00					
19	Drinks	$250.00					
20	Ice						
21	Totals	$650.00	$0.00				
22							

Figure 3-16: Use the SUM function in cell F16 to add non-contiguous cell ranges.

SUMIF Function

Add numbers in one cell range based on one condition in another corresponding cell range using the SUMIF function. For example, you can sum salary values listed in the "Salary" column for all employees who work in the sales department by using "Sales" as the criterion value in the "Department" column. Arguments to the SUMIF function are *range, criteria,* and *sum_range* (optional). The general syntax for the SUMIF function:

=SUMIF(range, criteria, [sum_range])

If the range of cells to sum is the same as the range of cells containing the criteria for summing, the third argument is omitted. For example, if you wish to sum all salaries that are over $40,000, the criteria column ("Salary") is the same as the sum column ("Salary"). When summing salaries for the sales department, the first argument (*range*) is the range containing the criteria ("Department" column). The *criteria* argument is the value ("Sales") to identify in the criteria range, and the third argument, *sum_range,* is the ("Salary") range that is to be added. In this case, the third argument must be specified since the criteria range and the range to sum are different.

I15		f_x =SUMIF(G2:G14, "Sales",I2:I14)						
	A	B	C	D	E	F	G	H	I

	ID	Last Name	First Name	Birth Date	Gender	Hire Date	Department	Job Title	Salary
2	1	Abner	David	11/15/1977	M	6/20/2006	Sales	Manager	$ 110,958
3	2	Butler	Susan	11/16/1967	F	8/13/1978	Marketing	Staff	$ 40,816
4	3	Conrad	Michael	9/14/1955	M	12/25/2001	Product Development	Staff Engineer	$ 74,665
5	4	Davis	Randall	7/16/1947	M	5/25/1980	Finance	Staff Accountant	$ 42,106
6	5	Edwards	Minnie	3/8/1959	F	11/26/1991	Human Resources	Manager	$ 90,228
7	6	Franklin	Margaret	11/25/1979	F	3/15/1977	Product Development	Staff	$ 42,976
8	7	Gardner	William	11/15/1968	M	2/7/1999	Sales	Staff	$ 90,650
9	8	Hilton	Hillery	11/23/1949	F	11/8/2005	Sales	District Sales Manager	$ 128,845
10	9	Jameson	Jennifer	1/17/1959	F	11/28/1992	Sales	Manager	$ 110,496
11	10	Kelly	Chester	10/28/1968	M	1/3/1994	Sales	Staff	$ 98,538
12	11	Zahn	Geoffrey	9/6/1952	M	3/4/1999	Sales	Staff	$ 84,151
13	12	Patel	Michael	4/20/1974	M	3/19/2003	Sales	District Sales Manager	$ 133,784
14	13	Schnider	Elizabeth	6/6/1958	F	6/27/1997	Sales	Staff	$ 35,025
15									$ 792,447
16									

Figure 3-17: Use the SUMIF function to sum only the sales department salaries.

Conditional Sum Wizard

Add numbers based on multiple conditions using the *Conditional Sum Wizard* which is an Excel Add-in. In the preceding example using the SUMIF function, only one condition could be applied in a single range to determine the cells to include in the added range. The *Conditional Sum Wizard* will walk you through steps to add multiple criteria for selecting cells to add. In order for the data to be included in the sum, it must meet *all* of the conditions specified. The conditions specified with the Conditional Sum Wizard are considered to be logically connected with an "AND." For example, if conditions are set for *Department = Sales* AND *Job Title = Manager,* the employee must match both conditions at the same time in order for the salary to be included in the sum.

In order for the *Conditional Sum Wizard* to work, the criteria ranges and the range to sum must be part of a well-structured list in Excel in which columns contain attributes of the entities that are listed in rows. The columns must include a title at the top that is formatted differently from the column data.

To use the *Conditional Sum Wizard* feature, first select a cell within a list range. To launch the *Conditional Sum Wizard,* select **Formulas(tab)→Solutions(group)→ Conditional Sum** from the ribbon. The *Conditional Sum Wizard* will appear.

If you do not have the Solutions group or Conditional Sum task available on the ribbon, you will need to install the Add-In by selecting the **Office Button→Excel Options→Add-Ins**. The *Excel Options* dialog box will appear. At the bottom of the dialog box, select *Excel Add-Ins* in the drop-down list beside *Manage:* and click the *Go* button. The *Add-Ins* dialog box will appear. Check the box beside of *Conditional Sum Wizard* and click the *OK* button. Once the installation is complete, the *Conditional Sum* icon will appear in the *Solutions* task group.

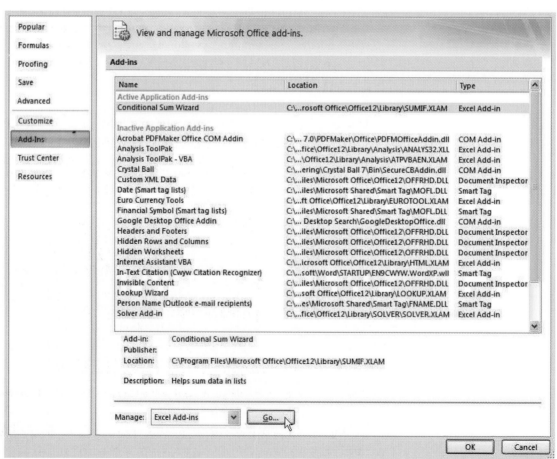

Figure 3-18: To install the *Conditional Sum Wizard* select the *Office Button→Add-Ins* and select *Excel Add-Ins* from the drop-down list.

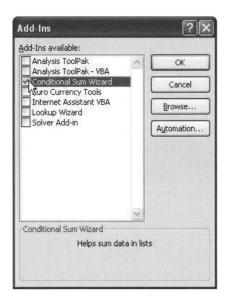

Figure 3-19: Check the box beside
Conditional Sum Wizard.

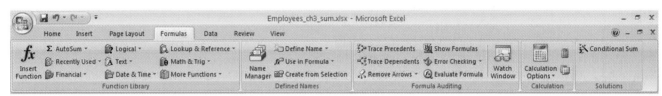

Figure 3-20: The *Solutions* group and *Conditional Sum Wizard* icon will appear on the ribbon.

The first screen of the Conditional Sum Wizard asks you to verify the list range
that contains the criteria ranges and the range to sum. (If a cell is selected within the
list before launching the *Conditional Sum Wizard*, Excel will automatically select the
list range.)

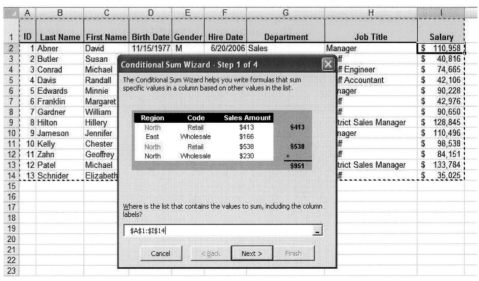

Figure 3-21: Verify the list range in the first screen of the *Conditional Sum Wizard*.

The second screen allows you to select the column to sum by choosing the column
title from the drop-down list. To add conditions to the criteria list box, select the column, the logical operator, and the criterion value then click the *Add Condition* button
to add each one.

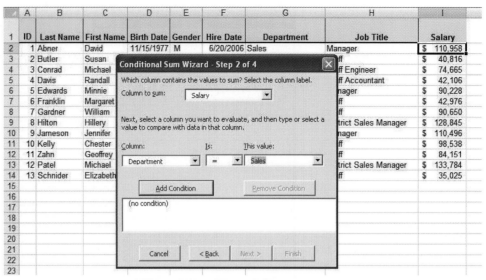

Figure 3-22: Using the drop-down lists for columns, logical operators, and values, add conditions in the second screen of the *Conditional Sum Wizard*.

The third screen offers options for selecting a cell to enter just the conditional sum formula or to select a location to which the actual *conditional values* are copied. The *conditional values* are those that meet the criteria and form the basis for the *conditional sum* calculation. If you choose the second option, you will be prompted for each cell location, one for the formula and another for pasting the conditional values. (See Figures 3-23 through 3-26.)

Quick Tip!

To sum a large range of cells quickly, select the cell below a column of numeric values and click the *AutoSum* icon. The SUM function will be inserted automatically into the cell with the adjacent contiguous cell range as its argument. The range is highlighted for the user to verify. Use the *Enter* key to enter the formula into the cell. (If empty cells occur within the range you intend to sum, you may need to adjust the range selected before saving the formula.)

Figure 3-23: Click the *Next* button after conditions have been added to the conditions box.

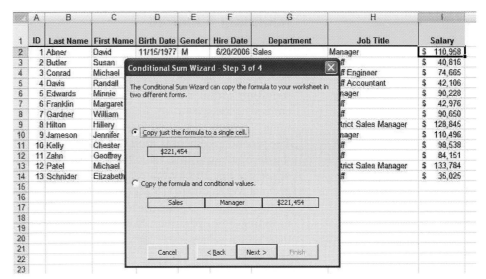

Figure 3-24: In step 3 choose whether to simply display the formula and result or to also display the conditional values.

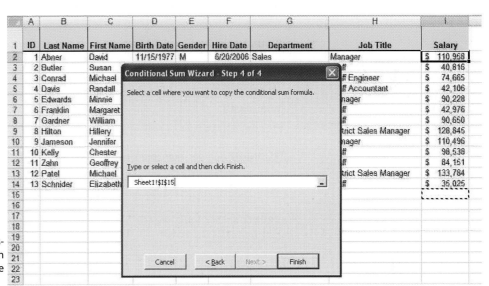

Figure 3-25: Select the cell to display the formula and result then click the *Finish* button to complete the operation.

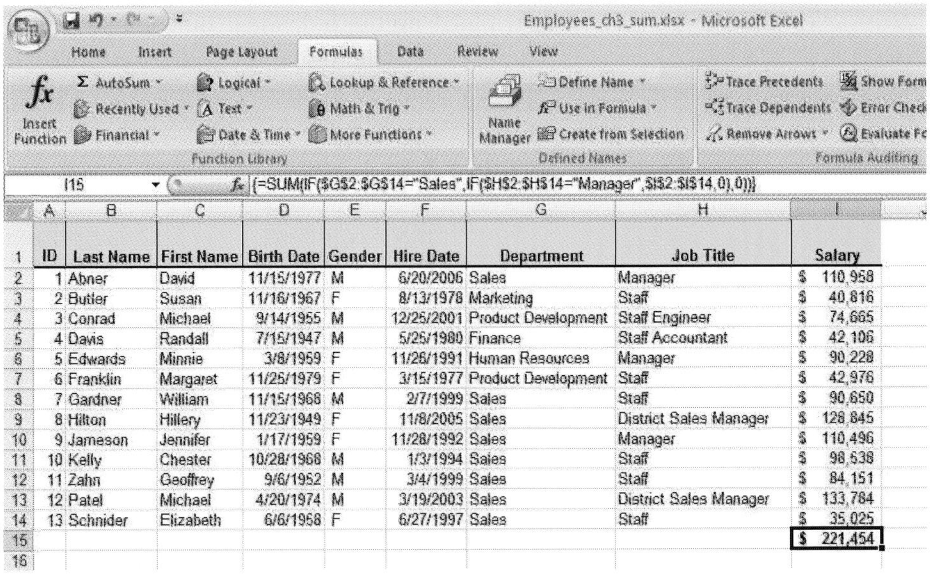

Figure 3-26: The formula is written into the selected cell and the result is displayed.

Rounding Numbers

Another common task that is performed with spreadsheet data is rounding numbers. Excel offers several functions for rounding with some variation among them in how they round. The ROUND, ROUNDDOWN, ROUNDUP, and TRUNC functions round up and/or down to a value length specified by the number of decimal places entered as the second argument. The argument list for this group of functions is the same. The first argument is *number* which represents the numeric value to round. The second argument is *num_digits* which represents the number of digits relative to the decimal. A positive value for *num_digits* indicates a number of places to the right of the decimal and a negative number indicates a number of places to the left of the decimal. When 0(zero) is entered for the *num_digits* argument, the return value will be a whole number. Explore the following list of functions in the table below that perform rounding-type operations. Note the differences in how they work and in the nature of their return values.

Table 3-7: Functions that round to a decimal value

Function & Arguments	Description of Return Value
ROUND(number, num_digits)	Rounds up or down to the closest specified number of decimal places
ROUNDDOWN(number, num_digits)	Rounds up or down toward zero to the closest specified number of decimal places. Positive values are rounded down and negative values are rounded up
ROUNDUP(number, num_digits)	Rounds up or down away from zero to the closest specified number of decimal places. Positive values are rounded up and negative values are rounded down
TRUNC(number, [num_digits])	Truncates a number to the specified number of decimal places. (In most cases the result is the same as with the ROUNDDOWN function.) If the optional *num_digits* argument is omitted, it will return a whole number

A number of functions round only to a whole number, but the whole number is determined by the individual function. Because the number of decimal places is zero(0) for all functions in this group, most need only one argument. The MROUND function requires a second argument to indicate the multiple for rounding.

Table 3-8: Functions that round to a whole number

Function & Arguments	Description of Return Value
INT(number)	Rounds down to the closest integer
EVEN(number)	Rounds up to the closest even integer
ODD(number)	Rounds up to the closest odd integer
MROUND(number, multiple)	Rounds up or down to the closest multiple specified

Statistical Functions

Closely related to the mathematical functions are the statistical functions. One of the most commonly used statistical functions is the AVERAGE function. Just as it implies, it returns the average (or mean) for a range of numeric values. The MIN returns the single minimum value for a range and the MAX returns the single maximum value for a range. The COUNT function returns the number of numeric values within a range. Each of these functions allows multiple arguments that may be literal numbers, or cell references or ranges.

In some cases, you may want to find the average or count of a range of values that contain other types of values besides numeric values. The COUNTA function counts all non-blank cells regardless of type of data that is in the cell. It counts a cell with an empty string of text (""), but does not count empty cells.

B11 | =COUNT(A1:H9)

	A	B	C	D	E	F	G	H
1	Product Mix Analysis for February, 2007							
2								
3				Product 1		Product 2		Product 3
4		Units Produced		10		20		10
5		Unit Revenue		$ 1,200		$ 1,500		$ 2,200
6	Cost Category	Unit Cost	Cost Units	Total cost	Cost Units	Total cost	Cost Units	Total cost
7	Labor Hours	$ 15	15	$ 225	18	$ 270	10	$ 150
8	Material	$ 80	5	$ 400	7	$ 560	15	$ 1,200
9	Fixed	$ 125	1	$ 125	1	$ 125	1	$ 125
10								
11	COUNT Function Result:	27						
12	COUNTA Function Result:	44						
13								

Figure 3-27: Note the results using the COUNT function in cell B11 and the COUNTA function in cell B12. The range being counted is A1:H9.

When using the AVERAGEA function, rules are applied for how the function handles cells that contain value types other then numeric. If a cell contains text values, including blank text ("", also called an empty string), it is evaluated to zero. If the cell contains logical values, TRUE is evaluated as 1 and FALSE is evaluated as zero. Empty cells are ignored. Note that empty cells are not the same as a cell with blank text ("").

The LARGE and SMALL functions work much like the MIN and MAX functions except you may select a value that is not just the highest or lowest, but some relative position to the highest or lowest. Arguments to the LARGE and SMALL functions are the same. The first argument, *array* represents the range of cells to evaluate and *k* represents the relative position to the highest (for the LARGE function) or the lowest (for the SMALL function). Syntaxes for the LARGE and SMALL functions:

=LARGE(array, k)

=SMALL(array, k)

In the following example, the LARGE function is used in three different cells to determine the top three salaries.

	B17	▾		f_x =LARGE($I$2:$I$14,1)					

	A	B	C	D	E	F	G	H	I
1	Employee ID	Last Name	First Name	Birth Date	Gender	Hire Date	Department	Job Title	Salary
2	1	Abner	David	11/15/1977	M	6/20/2006	Sales	Manager	$ 110,958
3	2	Butler	Susan	11/16/1967	F	8/13/1978	Marketing	Staff	$ 40,816
4	3	Conrad	Michael	9/14/1955	M	12/25/2001	Product Development	Staff Engineer	$ 74,665
5	4	Davis	Randall	7/15/1947	M	5/25/1980	Finance	Staff Accountant	$ 42,106
6	5	Edwards	Minnie	3/8/1959	F	11/26/1991	Human Resources	Manager	$ 90,228
7	6	Franklin	Margaret	11/25/1979	F	3/15/1977	Product Development	Staff	$ 42,976
8	7	Gardner	William	11/15/1968	M	2/7/1999	Sales	Staff	$ 90,650
9	8	Hilton	Hillery	11/23/1949	F	11/8/2005	Sales	District Sales Manager	$ 128,845
10	9	Jameson	Jennifer	1/17/1959	F	11/28/1992	Sales	Manager	$ 110,496
11	10	Kelly	Chester	10/28/1968	M	1/3/1994	Sales	Staff	$ 98,538
12	11	Zahn	Geoffrey	9/6/1952	M	3/4/1999	Sales	Staff	$ 84,151
13	12	Patel	Michael	4/20/1974	M	3/19/2003	Sales	District Sales Manager	$ 133,784
14	13	Schnider	Elizabeth	6/6/1958	F	6/27/1997	Sales	Staff	$ 35,025
15									
16	Top 3 Salaries:					Top 3 Salaries:			
17	1	$ 133,784.00				1	=LARGE($I$2:$I$14,1)	Formula view inset	
18	2	$ 128,845.00				2	=LARGE($I$2:$I$14,2)		
19	3	$ 110,958.00				3	=LARGE($I$2:$I$14,3)		
20									

Figure 3-28: Use the LARGE function to identify the top three salaries. The inset shows the formulas for the three results. Note the formulas differ only by the value for *k*, the final argument.

Financial Functions

Time Value of Money Functions

The number of financial functions in Excel is second only to the number of statistical functions. There are over 50 financial functions available. A common group of financial functions calculates various components for time value of money problems. The data variables for calculating the future value of a present sum of payments or the present value of a future sum of payments are the same. Excel provides a function that returns a value for each of these.

Table 3-9: Variables for *Time Value of Money* calculations

Common Variable Abbreviation	Description	Related Excel Function
PV	The value of an investment at time = 0	PV
FV	The value of an investment at time = n	FV
n	The number of periods of time in which you are operating (days, months, years, etc.)	NPER
r	The interest rate that will be compounded for each period	RATE
A	The value of each individual payment in compounding period	PMT
NPV	Net present value of future cash flows	NPV

Table 3-10: *Time Value of Money* functions and their arguments

Function & Arguments	Additional Notes
PV(rate, nper, pmt, [fv, type])	Type refers to payment timing; type=0 for payments at the end of the period, type=1 for payments at the beginning of the period.
FV(rate, nper, pmt, [pv, type])	
NPER(rate, pmt, pv, [fv, type])	
RATE(nper, pmt, pv, [fv, type, guess])	*Guess* is your guess for what the rate will be.
PMT(rate, nper, pv, [type])	
NPV(rate, value1, [value2...])	*Value1, value2...* refers to evenly spaced cash inflows or outflows.

Two additional *Time Value of Money* functions are helpful when constructing an amortization schedule for loans or investments. The IPMT calculates the interest portion of a single payment and the PPMT calculates the principal portion of a payment.

Table 3-11: Calculate interest and principal payments with IPMT and PPMT functions.

Function & Arguments	Additional Notes
IPMT(rate, per, nper, pv, [fv, type])	Type refers to payment timing; type=0 for payments at the end of the period, type=1 for payments at the beginning of the period.
PPMT(rate, per, nper, pv, [fv, type])	

Depreciation Functions

Another common group of financial functions used extensively in accounting practice are depreciation functions. Excel depreciation functions support standard ways to calculate depreciation; straight line, declining balance, and sum-of-years digits. Each function calculates one period of depreciation as indicated by the period number specified. Common arguments among the depreciation functions are *cost* which represents the initial cost of the asset, *salvage* which represents the salvage value at the end of the depreciation period, and *life* which represents the number of periods over which the asset is depreciated (usually in units of years). All except the straight-line depreciation function (SLN) also accept the argument *per* or *period* as the number of the specific period for which the depreciation is calculated. Since the straight-line method calculates all periods in the same way, the *period* argument is not needed for the SLN function.

PMT (86/12, 85 · 12, 84)

Table 3-12: Excel depreciation functions

Function & Arguments	Additional Notes
SLN(cost, salvage, life)	Straight line method for a number of years
DB(cost, salvage, life, per, [month])	*Month* is the number of months in the first year. If omitted, it is assumed to be 12.
DDB(cost, salvage, life, per, [factor])	*Factor* is the rate at which the balance declines. If omitted it is assumed to be 2 (for double-declining balance).
VDB(cost, salvage, life, start_per, end_per, factor, no_switch)	-Calculates depreciation for any period specified, in cluding partial periods -If the *Factor* argument is omitted, it is assumed to be 2 (same as DDB). -*No-switch* takes a value of TRUE or FALSE to indicate whether to switch to the straight line method if that method calculates the depreciation to be greater than the declining balance method. The default value is FALSE if the argument is omitted.
SYD(cost, salvage, life, per)	Sum-of-years' digits

Lookup & Reference Functions

Lookup Functions

Spreadsheets that are designed for efficient maintenance and flexibility store each item of data once then reference it from its single location. The goal of an efficient workbook design is to simplify maintenance by having to update each data item in only one place when the item value changes. Many spreadsheet projects use sets of related data multiple times, such as a zip code which references a specific city and state. Instead of typing in the city and state for each entry, the city and state may be referenced from a zip code table.

There are four function options that could be used to retrieve a city or state from a zip code table. The first two options use either the VLOOKUP or HLOOKUP function. VLOOKUP (V stands for vertical) and HLOOKUP (H stands for horizontal) work the same way except for the arrangement of the lookup table. Values are organized in columns for the VLOOKUP function and in rows for the HLOOKUP function. Both formulas always search for matching values in the first column or row. Syntaxes for these two functions:

VLOOKUP(lookup_value, table_array, column_index_num, [range_lookup])

HLOOKUP(lookup_value, table_array, row_index_num, [range_lookup])

These two functions search for a value (first argument, *lookup_value*) in the first column (for VLOOKUP) or row (for HLOOKUP) of the lookup table (second argument, *table_array*) and return a corresponding value in a different column or row as indicated by the index number (third argument, *column(row)_index_num*). The reference for the table_array (the lookup table) must be an absolute reference in order for it to work correctly when copied to a new cell. An easy way to use lookup tables in the lookup functions is to name the lookup table data range and refer to it by the range name for the *table_array* argument. Be sure to include only the data rows and omit column headers in the lookup table range.

Looking Up Exact Matches

The final argument, *range_lookup,* accepts either TRUE or FALSE to determine whether the function searches for a match within a range (TRUE or omitted), or searches for an exact match (FALSE). Consider retrieving a city or a state from a zip code table when a zip code is the *lookup_value.* You will want the function to return a city or a state that represents an exact match for the zip code.

ID	Last Name	First Name	Street	Zip	City	State		Zip	Town	State
			Employee List					**Lookup Table**		
1	Abner	David	102 Fifth St.	24324				24301	Pulaski	VA
2	Butler	Susan	5 Olander Ct.	24323				24311	Atkins	VA
3	Conrad	Michael	1556 Seaweed Ln.	24312				24312	Austinville	VA
4	Davis	Randall	4762 Newell Rd.	27262				24313	Barren	VA
5	Edwards	Minnie	952 Green St.	27289				24315	Bland	VA
6	Franklin	Margaret	58 Remington Ave.	24319				24317	Cana	VA
7	Gardner	William	16 Beulah Rd.	24313				24319	Chilhowie	VA
8	Hilton	Hillery	1114 Williams Rd.	24301				24323	Crockett	VA
9	Jameson	Jennifer	4262 Lane St.	27235				24324	Draper	VA
								27235	Colfax	NC
								27237	Cumnock	NC
								27239	Denton	NC
								27244	Elon	NC
								27249	Gibsonville	NC
								27262	Emerywood	NC
								27289	Eden	NC

Figure 3-29: The formula for the "City" and "State" columns will lookup the value of zip code that is in column E. An exact match is needed in this case.

The formula for the "City" column will look for the value of the zip code that is in column E and find a match in the lookup table and return the value in the second column of the lookup table. The lookup table range ($I$3:$K$18) referenced in the *table_array* argument excludes the column headers and table title, and is absolute. The optional *range_lookup* argument is set to FALSE so the function will find only an exact match. The zip code in cell E8 was not in the lookup table, so the function returned the error value #N/A.

F3   =VLOOKUP($E3,$I$3:$K$18,2,FALSE)

ID	Last Name	First Name	Street	Zip	City	State		Zip	Town	State
			Employee List					**Lookup Table**		
1	Abner	David	102 Fifth St.	24324	Draper	VA		24301	Pulaski	VA
2	Butler	Susan	5 Olander Ct.	24323	Crockett	VA		24311	Atkins	VA
3	Conrad	Michael	1556 Seaweed Ln.	24312	Austinville	VA		24312	Austinville	VA
4	Davis	Randall	4762 Newell Rd.	27262	Emerywood	NC		24313	Barren	VA
5	Edwards	Minnie	952 Green St.	27289	Eden	NC		24315	Bland	VA
6	Franklin	Margaret	58 Remington Ave.	27319	#N/A	#N/A		24317	Cana	VA
7	Gardner	William	16 Beulah Rd.	24313	Barren	VA		24319	Chilhowie	VA
8	Hilton	Hillery	1114 Williams Rd.	24301	Pulaski	VA		24323	Crockett	VA
9	Jameson	Jennifer	4262 Lane St.	27235	Colfax	NC		24324	Draper	VA
								27235	Colfax	NC
								27237	Cumnock	NC
								27239	Denton	NC
								27244	Elon	NC
								27249	Gibsonville	NC
								27262	Emerywood	NC
								27289	Eden	NC

Figure 3-30: The formula for the "City" column to find the zip code of column E in column I of the lookup table and return the city name from column J. The zip code found in cell E8 so an error value is returned.

G3			f_x =VLOOKUP($E3,$I$3:$K$18,3,FALSE)							
	A	B	C	D	E	F	G	H	I	J	K

Employee List (columns A–G) and **Lookup Table** (columns I–K)

	ID	Last Name	First Name	Street	Zip	City	State		Zip	Town	State
3	1	Abner	David	102 Fifth St.	24324	Draper	VA		24301	Pulaski	VA
4	2	Butler	Susan	5 Olander Ct.	24323	Crockett	VA		24311	Atkins	VA
5	3	Conrad	Michael	1556 Seaweed Ln.	24312	Austinville	VA		24312	Austinville	VA
6	4	Davis	Randall	4762 Newell Rd.	27262	Emerywood	NC		24313	Barren	VA
7	5	Edwards	Minnie	952 Green St.	27289	Eden	NC		24315	Bland	VA
8	6	Franklin	Margaret	58 Remington Ave.	27319	#N/A	#N/A		24317	Cana	VA
9	7	Gardner	William	16 Beulah Rd.	24313	Barren	VA		24319	Chilhowie	VA
10	8	Hilton	Hillery	1114 Williams Rd.	24301	Pulaski	VA		24323	Crockett	VA
11	9	Jameson	Jennifer	4262 Lane St.	27235	Colfax	NC		24324	Draper	VA
12									27235	Colfax	NC
13									27237	Cumnock	NC
14									27239	Denton	NC
15									27244	Elon	NC
16									27249	Gibsonville	NC
17									27262	Emerywood	NC
18									27289	Eden	NC
19											

Figure 3-31: The formula for the "State" column differs from the formula for the "City" column only by the column index (index 3 indicates column K) for the return value from the lookup table.

In most cases, we like to separate reference data from the business data in the workbook and place it on another worksheet. When referencing a lookup table from another worksheet, it simplifies the formula to name the lookup range and refer to the range name in the lookup formula. Let's move the zip code table to another worksheet and name the lookup data range "zips."

F3			f_x =VLOOKUP($E3,zips,2,FALSE)					
	A	B	C	D	E	F	G	H

Employee List

	ID	Last Name	First Name	Street	Zip	City	State
3	1	Abner	David	102 Fifth St.	24324	Draper	VA
4	2	Butler	Susan	5 Olander Ct.	24323	Crockett	VA
5	3	Conrad	Michael	1556 Seaweed Ln.	24312	Austinville	VA
6	4	Davis	Randall	4762 Newell Rd.	27262	Emerywood	NC
7	5	Edwards	Minnie	952 Green St.	27289	Eden	NC
8	6	Franklin	Margaret	58 Remington Ave.	27319	#N/A	#N/A
9	7	Gardner	William	16 Beulah Rd.	24313	Barren	VA
10	8	Hilton	Hillery	1114 Williams Rd.	24301	Pulaski	VA
11	9	Jameson	Jennifer	4262 Lane St.	27235	Colfax	NC
12							

Figure 3-32: The range name of the lookup table ("zips") replaces the previous lookup table cell range.

Looking Up Range Matches

Many uses of lookup tables involve finding a value within a given range and returning some corresponding value. Consider a shipping charge structure for an online order.

Table 3-13: Schedule of shipping charges

Order Amount	Shipping Charge
Less than $25	$ 5.95
$25, but less than $50	$ 8.95
$50, but less than $100	$11.95
$100, but less than $200	$14.96
$200, but less than $500	$25.95
$500 or more	$35.00

To set up the range lookup table in Excel, a single dollar value (without text) must be entered into the first column. To avoid an error value for values under $25 in our example problem, we will also include a 0(zero) range in the lookup table. This value range lookup is implemented using the VLOOKUP function in the example worksheet. The optional argument is omitted or set to TRUE for a range match.

	B2		f_x	=VLOOKUP(B1,D3:E8,2)		
	A	B	C	D	E	F
1	Enter the Order Total:	$159.95		**Schedule of Shipping Charges**		
2	Shipping Charge	$14.95		Order >=	Charge	
3				$0.00	$5.95	
4				$25.00	$8.95	
5				$50.00	$11.95	
6				$100.00	$14.95	
7				$200.00	$25.95	
8				$500.00	$35.00	
9						

Figure 3-33: A range match is performed using the VLOOKUP function.

Range matches or exact matches may also be accomplished by using the HLOOKUP. The lookup table must be arranged in rows rather than columns in order to use the HLOOKUP function. The HLOOKUP function searches the first row of the lookup table for the matching value or range and returns a corresponding value in another row that is indicated by the integer entered for the *row_index_num* argument.

	B2		f_x	=HLOOKUP(B1,E3:J4,2)						
	A	B	C	D	E	F	G	H	I	J
1	Enter the Order Total:	$159.95		**Schedule of Shipping Charges**						
2	Shipping Charge	$14.95								
3				Order >=	$0.00	$25.00	$50.00	$100.00	$200.00	$500.00
4				Charge	$5.95	$8.95	$11.95	$14.95	$25.95	$35.00
5										

Figure 3-34: A range match is performed using the HLOOKUP function.

Other Lookup Functions

The other two function options for retrieving data use the two versions of the LOOKUP function (no V or H precedes this function name). One version of the LOOKUP function uses two different one-dimensional arrays of data (vectors) for the search range and the return range. The other uses one two-dimensional array that includes both ranges. The two functions are named the same, but the arguments for the two functions differ, therefore they are really two different functions. A function is defined not only by its name, but additionally by its argument list. It is common for multiple functions in a program environment to have the same name, but different argument lists, thereby making them different functions which perform their operations differently.

The LOOKUP function that uses two vectors looks up the lookup value in one specified vector and returns a value from the same position (i.e., same row or same column) in a second specified vector. The syntax for this LOOKUP function:

=LOOKUP(*lookup_value, lookup_vector, result_vector***)**

The *result_vector* must be the same size (have same number of items) as the *lookup_vector*.

The other LOOKUP function, the one that uses only one two-dimensional array, looks up the *lookup_value* in the first row or column of the array and returns a related value from the last row or column of the array. Whether the function searches in rows or columns depends on the shape of the lookup table. If the table of values is wider than it is long (more columns than rows), it searches and returns row values. If it is longer than it is wide (more rows than columns), it searches and returns column values. The syntax for this LOOKUP function:

=LOOKUP(*lookup_value, array***)**

zips   Towns
↑   ↑

| F3 | | | ƒx =LOOKUP(E3,$I$3:$I$18,$J$3:$J$18) | | | | | | | |

	A	B	C	D	E	F	G	H	I	J	K
1	**Employee List**								**Lookup Table**		
2	ID	Last Name	First Name	Street	Zip	City	State		Zip	Town	State
3	1	Abner	David	102 Fifth St.	24324	Draper	VA		24301	Pulaski	VA
4	2	Butler	Susan	5 Olander Ct.	24323	Crockett	VA		24311	Atkins	VA
5	3	Conrad	Michael	1556 Seaweed Ln.	24312	Austinville	VA		24312	Austinville	VA
6	4	Davis	Randall	4762 Newell Rd.	27262	Emerywood	NC		24313	Barren	VA
7	5	Edwards	Minnie	952 Green St.	27289	Eden	NC		24315	Bland	VA
8	6	Franklin	Margaret	58 Remington Ave.	27319	Eden	NC		24317	Cana	VA
9	7	Gardner	William	16 Beulah Rd.	24313	Barren	VA		24319	Chilhowie	VA
10	8	Hilton	Hillery	1114 Williams Rd.	24301	Pulaski	VA		24323	Crockett	VA
11	9	Jameson	Jennifer	4262 Lane St.	27235	Colfax	NC		24324	Draper	VA
12									27235	Colfax	NC
13									27237	Cumnock	NC
14									27239	Denton	NC
15									27244	Elon	NC
16									27249	Gibsonville	NC
17									27262	Emerywood	NC
18									27289	Eden	NC
19											

Figure 3-35: An exact match is performed using the LOOKUP(*lookup_value, lookup_vector, result_vector*) function. This column returns the value in the *lookup_vector* in the same row as the *lookup_value*.

In the example below, the only two arguments that are accepted are the *lookup_value* and the *array* that represents the lookup table. With this LOOKUP function, the return value is from the last vector (row or column) of the array, so no argument is needed for the return column or row index.

| G3 | | | ƒx =LOOKUP(E3,$I$3:$K$18) | | | | | | | |

	A	B	C	D	E	F	G	H	I	J	K
1	**Employee List**								**Lookup Table**		
2	ID	Last Name	First Name	Street	Zip	City	State		Zip	Town	State
3	1	Abner	David	102 Fifth St.	24324	Draper	VA		24301	Pulaski	VA
4	2	Butler	Susan	5 Olander Ct.	24323	Crockett	VA		24311	Atkins	VA
5	3	Conrad	Michael	1556 Seaweed Ln.	24312	Austinville	VA		24312	Austinville	VA
6	4	Davis	Randall	4762 Newell Rd.	27262	Emerywood	NC		24313	Barren	VA
7	5	Edwards	Minnie	952 Green St.	27289	Eden	NC		24315	Bland	VA
8	6	Franklin	Margaret	58 Remington Ave.	27319	Eden	NC		24317	Cana	VA
9	7	Gardner	William	16 Beulah Rd.	24313	Barren	VA		24319	Chilhowie	VA
10	8	Hilton	Hillery	1114 Williams Rd.	24301	Pulaski	VA		24323	Crockett	VA
11	9	Jameson	Jennifer	4262 Lane St.	27235	Colfax	NC		24324	Draper	VA
12									27235	Colfax	NC
13									27237	Cumnock	NC
14									27239	Denton	NC
15									27244	Elon	NC
16									27249	Gibsonville	NC
17									27262	Emerywood	NC
18									27289	Eden	NC
19											

Figure 3-36: An exact match is performed using the LOOKUP (*lookup_value, array*) function. This LOOKUP function returns the corresponding value in the last column or row in the *array*.

Use Nested IF Functions or Lookup Functions?

By now you may be thinking that the lookup functions behave much like the IF function in that they test for a matching value, then return some value if the match is TRUE. In the case of the lookup functions, when no match is found, an error value will be returned. There are two things to consider when choosing between using a set of nested IF functions or a LOOKUP function. First, recall that functions can only be nested up to seven levels deep, so if there are more than seven values or ranges to compare, the IF function will not be sufficient. Also, when using LOOKUP functions, we are limited to comparing one variable, the *lookup_value* (such as zip code) against multiple possible values. When nesting IF functions, you may compare a different variable to some value in the *logical_test* of each nested IF function. For example, we can compare one value for "Department" in one IF function, and compare a value for "Job Title" in another nested IF function.

Reference Functions

The ADDRESS, COLUMN, and ROW functions are called reference functions because they return some part of the reference of a worksheet cell, such as the entire cell address, just the column, or just the row. These are rarely used alone on worksheets, but may be helpful to return information about a cells location to aid other functionality, such as programming a custom function or procedure in Visual Basic for Applications in conjunction with an Excel project. The COLUMNS function (pleural and differs from the COLUMN function) returns the number of columns in a range and the ROWS functions returns the number of rows in a cell range.

Information Functions

"IS" Functions

Closely related to reference functions are information functions. This group of functions returns information about the contents of a cell or cell range rather than information about its location or structure. Most of the functions begin with the word "IS" and the function name is designed to ask a question, such as ISBLANK or ISNUMBER. Collectively these functions are commonly called "IS" functions. In response to the "question" implied by the function name, functions in this group return a Boolean value. These functions are used to test to see if some condition exists in the cell so that further processing may occur based on the condition being TRUE or FALSE. All "IS" functions take only one argument, the value (or cell reference to the value) to evaluate. The "IS" functions and the descriptions of their returns values are listed in the table below.

Table 3-14 : Excel "IS" functions

Function	Description
ISBLANK(value)	Returns TRUE if the cell is empty (Note that a cell with an empty string ("") is not empty.)
ISERR(value)	Returns TRUE for any error value except #N/A
ISERROR(value)	Returns TRUE for any error value
ISLOGICAL(value)	Returns TRUE is the value or cell contents is TRUE or FALSE
ISNA(value)	Returns TRUE if the cell contains an #N/A error
ISNONTEX(value)	Returns TRUE for any value or cell that does not contain text including a blank cell
ISNUMBER(value)	Returns TRUE if the value is a number (Note that numbers stored as text are considered text, not numbers.)
ISREF(value)	Returns TRUE if value is a cell reference (address)
ISTEXT(value)	Returns TRUE if the value or cell contents is text (Note that numbers stored as text are considered text, not numbers.)
ISEVEN(number)	Evaluates only numbers and returns TRUE if the number is even
ISODD(number)	Evaluates only numbers and returns TRUE if the number is odd

Troubleshooting Errors in Formulas That Include Functions

As we increase the use of functions in our workbooks, the formulas naturally grow more complex. Many error values are directly associated with things that can go wrong with a function's structure, such as an argument of the wrong data type, or a missing argument. The *Evaluate Formula* feature of the *Formula Auditing* tools is extremely helpful for troubleshooting formula errors that include function errors. With the step-by-step evaluation of each formula step and each function execution, it is easy to see which part of the formula produces the error value. Below is a recap of error values that are often directly related to a problem with function syntax or inputs.

Table 3-15: Common error values from improper function syntax in Excel

Error Value	Common Causes
#VALUE!	An argument to a function is the wrong data type.
#NAME?	Some text in the formula is not recognized by Excel, such as a misspelled range name, workbook name, worksheet name, or function name. This is a common problem when using named ranges as function arguments.
#N/A	An argument is missing from a function call. Also occurs if a lookup function does not find an exact match (when indicated) or if the lookup table is not sorted properly for a range match.
#NUM!	When text is entered for a function argument that should be a number.

Additional functions will be discussed in future chapters. It is impossible to discuss all Excel worksheet functions, but experimenting with those discussed in this and future chapters will hopefully increase the user's awareness of the number and nature of functions available in Excel. To explore more Excel worksheet functions, open the *Insert Function* dialog box and type in the name of an operation or type of operation you wish to perform. Excel will search for a function or term that matches the phrase and will present a list of candidate functions for your review. You may also use Excel *Help* to search for specific functions or categories of functions. To find a list of all Excel worksheet functions, search in Excel *Help* for "Worksheet Functions Listed by Category." Use the hyperlinks in the list to learn more about functions within each category. Mastery of a few key Excel functions and awareness of others used in your particular discipline will tremendously enhance your worksheet productivity.

Review Questions

1. How do functions differ from formulas?

_____

_____

_____

2. How is a function defined?

_____

_____

_____

3. What are function arguments?

_____

_____

_____

4. What is the purpose of a *function tooltip*?

_____

_____

_____

5. What is the difference between the TODAY and the NOW functions?

_____

_____

_____

6. Give an example of when the use of the TODAY or NOW function would be inappropriate?

_____

_____

_____

7. Explain the three arguments of the IF function.

_____

_____

_____

8. What type of data is returned from logical functions?

_____

_____

_____

9. What is meant by "nesting" IF functions? What is the advantage of nesting IF functions?

_____

_____

_____

10. What is meant by rounding "toward zero" or "away from zero" for the ROUNDUP and ROUNDDOWN functions? Give an example of an input value and the related output value for each function.

_____

_____

_____

11. What is the difference between the VLOOKUP function and the HLOOKUP function?

_____

_____

_____

12. What is the importance of the *range_lookup* argument of the VLOOKUP (or HLOOKUP) function?

_____

_____

_____

13. When looking up an exact match in a lookup table with the VLOOKUP function, what value is returned when a match is not found?

_____

_____

_____

14. What type of value is returned from an "IS" function?

_____

_____

_____

Practice Problems

1. Open the workbook "Employees_Prob3-1.xlsx." Using the functions presented in this chapter, enter formulas for the following items. Properly label each formula cell.

   a. Enter a new column to the right of the "Birth Date" column. Enter a dynamic formula that calculates each employee's age and keeps it current.
   b. Calculate the number of employees who work in the sales department.
   c. Enter a formula that rounds the salaries to the next highest thousand dollars.
   d. Add a new column to the right of "Salary." Name it "Salary Grade." Use a lookup function to assign a salary grade based on the following scale:

      Grade 1: Under $30,000
      Grade 2: $30,000 to under $45.000
      Grade 3: $45,000 to under $60,000
      Grade 4: $60,000 to under $75,000
      Grade 5: $75,000 to under $90,000
      Grade 6: $90,000 to under $150,000
      Grade 7: $150,000 and over

2. Construct an amortization table for a car loan. Columns in the table should include *Payment Number*, *Beginning Balance*, *Principal Paid*, *Interest Paid*, *Principal Paid to Date*, *Interest Paid to Date*, *Ending Balance*. There should be one row in the table for each payment. Design the worksheet so that the input values for purchase price, down payment, interest rate, and loan period (in years) may be entered by the user. Be sure to label the input cells clearly for the user.

3. Using Excel *Help*, find a list of all worksheet functions listed by category. Click on the category links to explore specific functions within each category. Click a function name to learn more about the function.

4. **Challenge Problem**: Using Excel *Help*, find information about the MATCH Function. Open the workbook "DeliveryPlanner_Prob3-4.xlsx." Study the structure of the workbook. Use the information you learned about the MATCH function to design a formula for cell C4 on the Practice worksheet. Use the lookup table on the "DistanceChart" worksheet to return the distance between each set of two cities for each leg of the delivery route. Copy the formula to cells C5, C6, and C7. Enter a formula into cell C8 that totals the distances for all legs of the route.

CHAPTER FOUR
Charts

Learning Objectives

1. Distinguish between *series* and *categories* of source data for charts
2. Explore various chart types and subtypes and some appropriate uses of each
3. Understand the difference between charts with 3-D visual effects and true 3-D charts
4. Understand the appropriate data arrangement for each chart type
5. Create an embedded chart using Excel's *Chart* tools
6. Become familiar with the location of various chart tools on the chart-specific tabs of the ribbon
7. Apply custom formatting to various parts of a chart
8. Modify source data for an existing chart
9. Modify chart type for an existing chart
10. Save a chart design as a custom chart template
11. Access a custom chart template for a new chart creation
12. Change the order of series and categories of data on existing charts
13. Add error bars to data markers
14. Use object linking and embedding to add Excel charts to Microsoft Word documents and PowerPoint presentations

Chart Types and Uses

Excel *charts,* also called *graphs,* are used to communicate graphically a summary of spreadsheet data. Different chart types help to emphasize different aspects of the data. Charts can also be a powerful tool for analyzing raw data. Charts are relatively simple to create in Excel. The greater challenge is in producing a chart that is effective for the type of data presented.

Excel charts are graphed on a *plot area* that is bounded by an *x-* and *y-axis.* In most charts, the y-axis is the *value axis* and the x-axis is the *category axis.* A chart graphs one or more *series* of values for which each series includes one value for each *category.* Below is a summary of Microsoft Corporation's revenue and net income for fiscal years 1997–2006. The data has two *series* of data, Revenue and Net Income. The categories of data are the years, 1997 through 2006.

Microsoft Financial Performance 1997-2006										
Fiscal Year Ended June 30	1997	1998	1999	2000	2001	2002	2003	2004	2005	2006
Revenue	$11,936	$15,262	$19,747	$22,956	$25,296	$28,365	$32,187	$36,835	$39,788	$44,282
Net income	$ 3,454	$ 4,490	$ 7,785	$ 9,421	$ 7,346	$ 5,355	$ 7,531	$ 8,168	$12,254	$12,599

Figure 4-1: Chart source data with data series in rows and categories of data in columns (Data source: Microsoft Corporation Annual Report 2006 and 2001, http://www.microsoft.com/msft/reports/default.mspx, accessed 03/16/2007).

We can produce an Excel chart that shows how both revenue and net income have changed over time and also show how the relationship between revenue and net income has changed over the last ten fiscal years. The chart in Figure 4-2 shows the data for revenue and net income on a *line chart.* A *line chart* is used to show a trend over some continuum which most often is time.

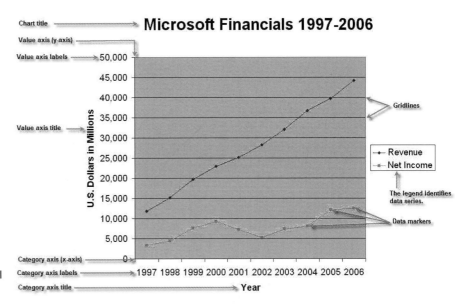

Figure 4-2: The anatomy of an Excel chart.

Chart Types

Many chart types and subtypes are available in Excel. The type of chart used depends on what type of relationship you wish to show for the summarized data. The choice of the appropriate chart type is vital to the effectiveness of the chart as a presentation tool. Chart types are chosen based on what you want to emphasize about the data. The same data may be presented effectively on different chart types when you wish to emphasize different aspects of the data.

Column and Bar Charts

The *column chart* is likely the most widely used chart type and the default chart type in Excel. Data markers are shown as columns on the plot area. Column charts are used to compare a small number of data series. Each "column" of the chart represents a value from a series of data. A separate column is produced for each data point in each series. If multiple series of data are graphed on a column chart, there will be multiple sets or clusters of columns on the graph. A cluster of columns along the x-axis represent one data value for each series of data within a category. Instead of clustering columns, the category of values may be stacked onto one column (a stacked column chart). The stacked column chart is more effective at emphasizing the cumulative effect of each data point within a category.

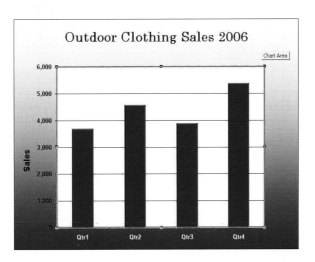

Figure 4-3: Column chart showing one series of data.

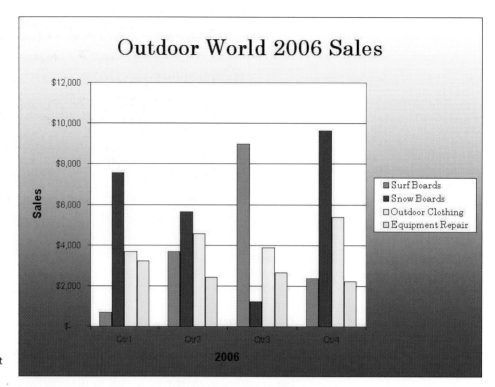

Figure 4-4: Clustered column chart showing four series of data.

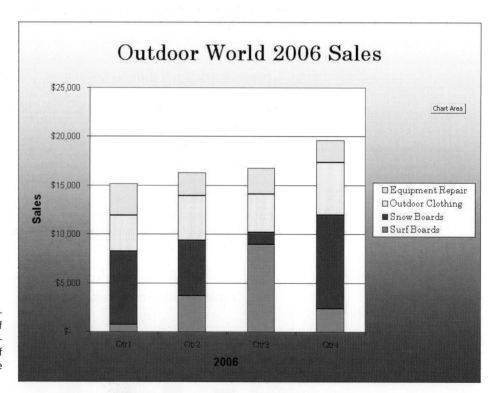

Figure 4-5: Stacked column (subtype) chart showing four series of data. The stacked column chart emphasizes the cumulative effect of each series value to the total value for the category.

The *bar chart* is sometimes incorrectly referred to as a horizontal column chart due to its arrangement. Like a column chart, a bar chart is also used to compare a small set of data items, but it differs from a column chart in that a bar chart represents some comparison for a progression over a continuum, such as points in time, or moving forward toward a goal. The chart emphasizes the idea of moving forward. Different from most chart types, a bar chart's value axis is horizontal and its category axis is vertical.

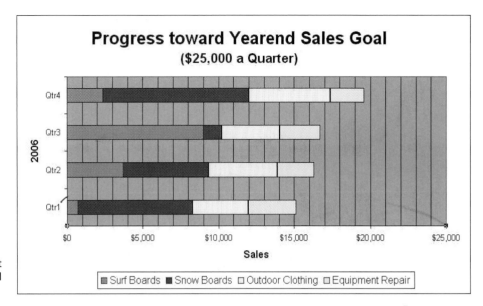

Figure 4-6: A stacked bar chart shows progress toward an overall sales goal of $25,000 a quarter.

Line Charts

Line charts are used to show trends, generally over time so the horizontal axis is usually a measure of time (year, quarter, month, etc.). Lines connect the data points for a series of data to create a visual sense of the trend. Each series of data markers is connected with a different line so there will be the same number of lines as series of data.

When more than one series of data is presented on a line chart, the relationship between the sets of data can also be a focus for the chart. For example, a line chart can represent sets of data for revenue and costs. The difference between the two sets of data (two lines on the chart) represents the profit trend. As costs decrease and/or revenues increase, the profit area between the two data series (between the two lines) will increase.

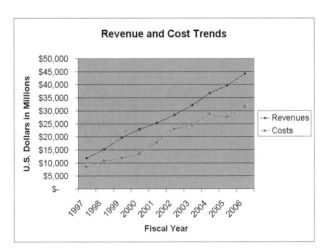

Figure 4-7: This line chart shows revenues and profits as data series. The distance between the two lines represents the profit trend.

Pie Charts

Pie charts are used to show proportional relationships of one series of data. For example, for a company's salary budget, a pie chart can show what proportion of the budget goes to each department's salaries. The pie chart is limited to displaying only one series of data. There are some additional limitations for pie charts. You cannot plot non-positive values, and all categories must represent parts of the whole pie.

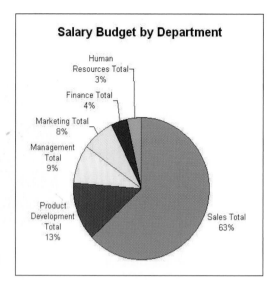

Figure 4-8: A pie chart shows only one series of data.

The data values in a pie chart should be arranged from highest to lowest beginning at the 12 o'clock position and moving clockwise so that the largest portion is in the right upper region of the pie and the smallest portion is in the left upper region. Data labels for the series name, category names, values, or percentages may be added to the pie slices. In the chart above, labels have been added for the category names and percentages.

One or more values of the pie data series can be emphasized by "exploding" the pie slices that represent the values of interest. The "exploded" pie chart is a simple modification of the regular pie chart. To explode a pie slice, click twice (two single clicks) on the pie slice with the mouse pointer, and drag the slice from the pie. Repeat the action for any slices you wish to emphasize.

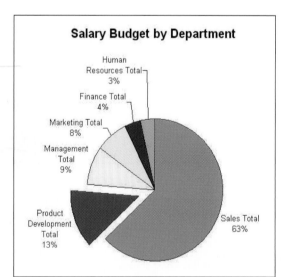

Figure 4-9: "Exploded" pie chart that emphasizes the Product Development portion of the company budget.

Pie Chart Subtypes

In some cases, the smaller slices of the pie represent such small values relative to the other pie slices that they are difficult to distinguish and difficult to label. For these cases, one of the two *extracted* subtypes of the pie chart can be used.

The *pie-of-pie* subtype moves the smallest pie slices out of the main pie chart and into a smaller pie chart that represents just those smallest data categories. The orientation of the pie slices are different from the regular pie chart in that the smallest slices must be at the center right region of the pie in order to be extracted from the main pie.

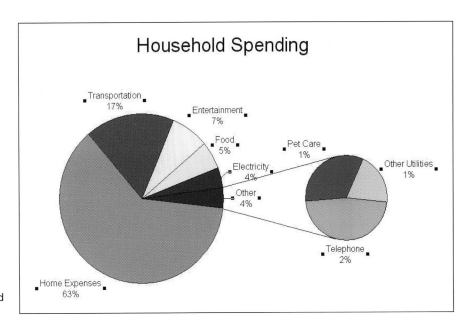

Figure 4-10: Pie-of-pie extracted chart subtype of the pie chart.

Another extracted subtype of the pie chart is the *bar-of-pie* chart. The bar-of-pie functions exactly as the pie-of-pie except that the smallest pie slices are extracted into a stacked bar rather than into a smaller pie.

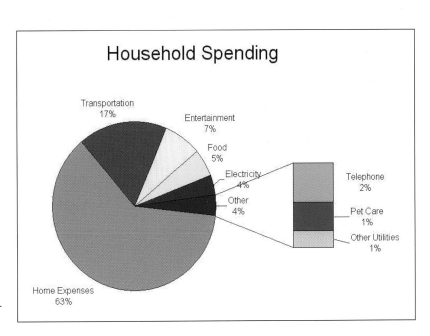

Figure 4-11: Bar-of-pie chart subtype of the pie chart.

Doughnut Charts

Doughnut charts serve the same purpose as the pie chart, to show a proportional relationship among values in one series of data. The difference between the pie chart and the doughnut chart is that the doughnut can represent multiple series of data whereas the pie chart can represent only one data series. The doughnut chart is most effective in comparing two series of data that differ only in their time component. For example, a doughnut chart may be used to show "before" and "after" values on the same chart. It may be used to show one year's data compared to another year.

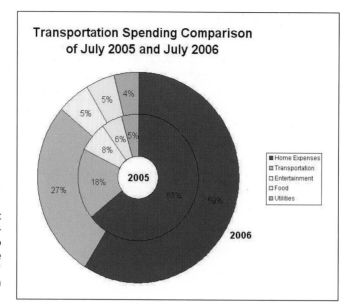

Figure 4-12: The doughnut chart shows that spending for transportation increased from 18% to 27% of the family budget in one year. The labels "2005" and "2006" were added to the chart area with text boxes.

XY (Scatter) Charts

Scatter charts, also know as scatter plots, are used most often to graph a set of values for a dependent variable as a function of a set of values for an independent variable. The thing that distinguishes the scatter chart from other chart types is that both the x and y axes are values axes as in the Cartesian coordinate system. The data marker is plotted in one graph quadrant where the x-value and the related y-value on each respective axis intersect. The data points may be connected with a line or a trend line may be added to the chart. Note that a scatter chart with lines is not the same as a line chart. A scatter chart represents the relationship between the independent variable values and the dependent variable values. XY scatter charts are used often to determine or show the correlation of two sets of variable values. The scatter chart is often used as a tool in regression analysis. Options exist for adding the trend line, r-squared value, and the trend line equation to the chart.

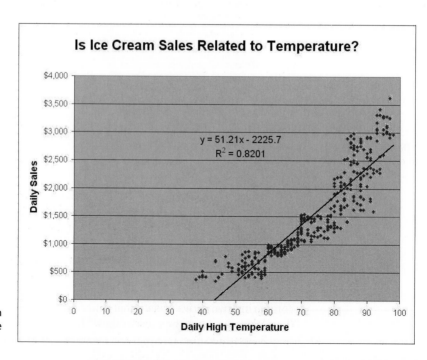

Figure 4-13: XY scatter chart with trend line, r-squared, and trend line equation added.

Area Charts

Area charts are used to emphasize the cumulative effect of changes for multiple categories over time. Each series of data is represented by a "layer" of the plot area. Each data series shows a trend for that series (the line) as well as its contribution to the cumulative total. For example, a company's sales may be graphed such that each product is a layer of the area chart showing each product's sales trend as well as its contribution to the overall total sales. The area chart below shows the first year's sales for a startup outdoor sports equipment retailer. The overall sales show a slight increase over the course of the year. The layers of the chart represent all product segments' contributions to total sales. Although sales of surf boards and snow boards have definite peaks and troughs over the course of the year, the chart shows that the two product segments together maintain steady sales and slight sales growth throughout the year.

Each product segment alone can also be evaluated visually with the area chart by noting the height of each layer over the time period. The area chart for Outdoor World sales shows that outdoor clothing sales increased slightly over the course of the year, but equipment repair shows little change or possibly a slight decrease in sales revenue over the year.

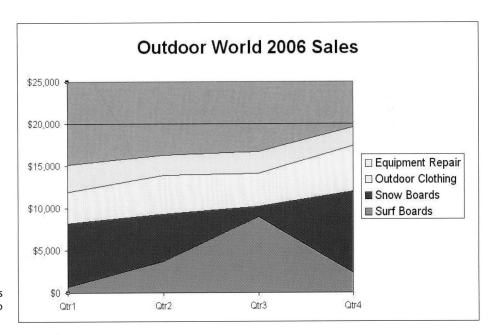

Figure 4-14: Area chart shows product segment contribution to total sales.

Stock Charts

Stock charts are most often used to show stock data over time, but may also be used in some scientific applications, such as those involving temperature highs and lows. Stock charts support data series for High, Low, Open, Close, and Volume.

- High: highest stock price for the day
- Low: lowest stock price for the day
- Open: stock price when the trading day opens
- Close: stock price at the close of trading for the day
- Volume: number of shares traded for the day

The four stock chart subtypes support various combinations of the five data series.

- High-Low-Close
- Open-High-Low-Close
- Volume-High-Low-Close
- Volume-Open-High-Low-Close

Stock charts differ from other Excel charts in that they have two y-axes, both of which are value axes. On the stock chart below, all five data series are represented. The primary y-axis (the left vertical axis) represents stock volume traded in millions of dollars and the secondary y-axis (the right vertical axis) represents the stock price. The columns represent volume traded and the data markers in the upper region of the chart represent the stock prices; open, high, low, and close. Each pair of high and low markers is connected by a thin vertical line. The open and close price pairs are connected by bars. If the close price is higher than the open price, the two are connected with an "up bar" as shown in blue on the chart below. If the close price is lower than the open price, the two are connected with a "down bar" as shown in red on the chart below. Trading dates are shown on the x-axis, the category axis.

When two y-axes are used, data markers sometimes overlap and are difficult to distinguish. The chart in Figure 4-16 shows the default scaling of the two y-axes for the stock data in the previous chart. Note that the data markers for the volume traded and the for the stock prices overlap in some areas.

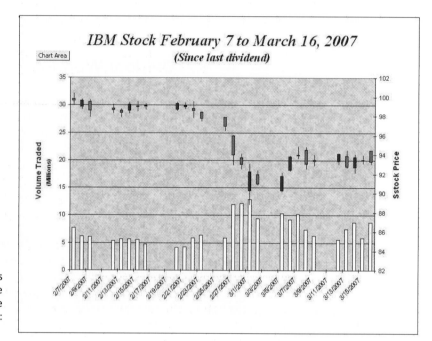

Figure 4-15: Stock chart shows Volume, Open, High, Low, and Close series of data. Stock prices use the secondary (right) y-axis. (Data source: www.finance.yahoo.com)

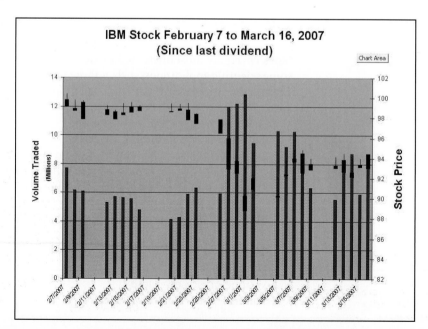

Figure 4-16: The default scales for the primary and secondary y axes.

The problem of overlapping data markers can usually be solved by changing the scales of one or both of the value axes. In the example in Figure 4-15 the primary (left) y-axis maximum value was changed from 14 million to 35 million in order to make the column data markers smaller. The secondary (right) y-axis scale was not changed in this example. If the data markers for the stock prices still overlap after changing the primary y-axis scale, the secondary y-axis scale can be changed in many cases to a lower maximum value in order to move the stock price markers to a higher position on the chart. Changes to the scale of the stock price axis are not always possible, depending on the highest stock value charted. The scale maximum cannot be lower than the highest stock price charted without losing data from the top of the chart.

Surface Charts

Surface charts are very complex charts that show a three-dimensional surface that looks much like a topographical map. In fact, a similar type of graph is used to construct topographical maps. Surface charts differ from most chart types in that they show relationships among three variables. When charting variables x, y, and z on a surface chart, the x and y values are actually numeric categories which are displayed on the horizontal and depth axes that form the *floor* of the surface chart. Both x and y are independent variables. The z-axis is the value axis. The value of z represents the dependent variable and height of the data point on the chart. Each z value is a function of a set of corresponding x and y values. Colors on surface charts do not represent data series as in many other chart types, but instead each color represents a range of values of z. In order for surface charts to be useful, many sets of data points are needed to smooth out the surface area.

Surface charts are commonly used for very complex mathematical, statistical and geographical applications, but they may also be used to visualize some types of complex financial data. In the case of option pricing models such as Black Scholes, a surface chart may be used to map volatility as it relates to specific combinations of years to maturity and expiry years.

One shortfall of surface charts is that although the categories are numeric values, they are not scaled but are spaced evenly across the axis regardless of the numeric interval between the two categories. For example, if the chart below included years to maturity of .25, .5, 1, 3, 5, and 10 instead of years 1 through 15, the physical interval on the chart between .25 and .5 (.25) would be the same as the physical interval between 5 and 10 (5), so the surface chart would not be useful for relative comparisons across a horizontal or depth axis (the two axes that form the floor of the chart).

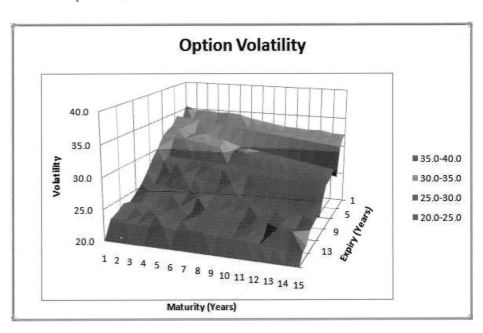

Figure 4-17: A surface chart that shows the relationship between years to maturity and expiry years.

Bubble Charts

A bubble chart is an extension of the XY (scatter) chart. A typical XY chart graphs two series of data, one each for x and y. The x (dependent variable) values are graphed on the horizontal axis while y values (independent variable) are graphed on the vertical axis as with an XY chart. A bubble chart can graph an additional series of data, one value for each pair of xy values. The data marker for the xy coordinate is a bubble. The size of the bubble is determined by the value of the data point it represents from the third series of data. For example, a bubble chart may show the number of products a company offers (x) and the related profit (y) while also showing the percent of the industry market share that corresponds to each pair of values for x and y. The size of the bubble indicates the relative percent of industry market share from one coordinate to another.

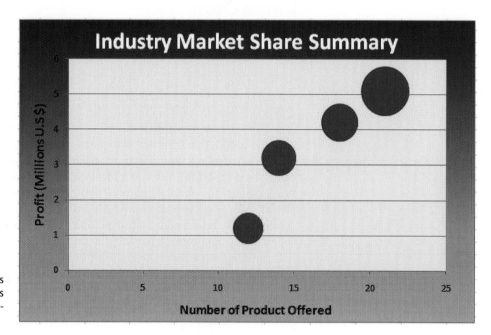

Figure 4-18: Bubble charts shows percent of industry market share as bubbles of relative size to one another.

Table 4-1: Data represented in the bubble chart above

Number Sport Products Offered	Profit (millions)	Market Share (%)
12	$1.2	14
21	$5.1	35
14	$3.2	18
18	$4.2	20

Radar Charts

Radar charts are used to compare the aggregate values of a number of data series as with types of "stacked" charts such as stacked columns, stacked bars, and area charts. A radar chart displays a separate axis for each category. The axes extend from the center of the chart outward to the perimeter increasing in value as they move toward the perimeter. The label for each category is displayed around the perimeter of the chart. The value of each data point (one series value for each category) is plotted on the corresponding axis. The larger the data value, the farther the marker extends from the center of the chart.

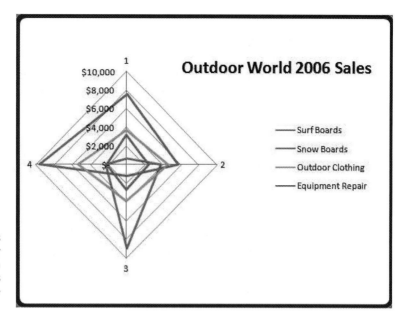

Figure 4-19: Radar chart that shows sales of each product segment by quarters. Each quarter is plotted on a separate category axis that extends from the center of the chart to the perimeter.

The filled radar chart below is one of the radar chart subtypes. In some cases filled radar charts offer a more concise view of the data, but in this particular case, some filled markers cover other markers which are visible in the standard version of the radar chart above.

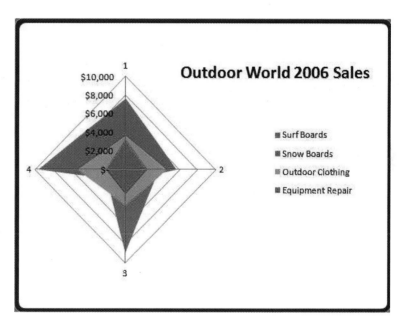

Figure 4-20: Filled radar chart that shows the same data as the previous chart. Note that some data markers (i.e., surf boards sales for Quarter 1) are covered by others (Equipment Repair) in the filled chart.

Since not many business professionals are familiar with the radar chart, it should be used sparingly and with caution. As with any chart, you want to be sure to use a chart type that the intended audience readily understands.

3-D Charts

Three-dimensional charts can add interesting visual appeal to charts and are perceived by most audiences to be more professional in appearance. Most chart types represent data in only two dimensions on two axes, a horizontal axis and a vertical axis. True 3-D charts use three axes to represent the data, a horizontal axis, a depth axis, and a vertical axis. On typical 2-dimensional charts, the horizontal axis is the x-axis or category axis, and the vertical axis is the y-axis or the value axis. In 3-D charts, there are two category axes, the horizontal axis (x) and the depth axis (y) and one value axis, the vertical z-axis.

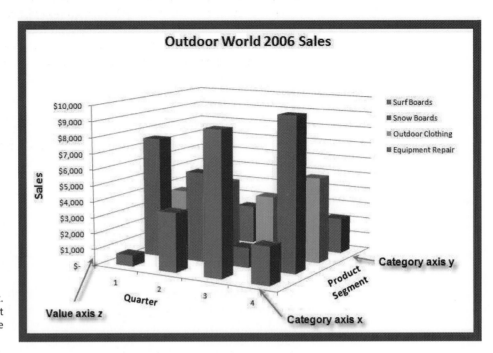

Figure 4-21: A 3-D column chart. Note the two category axes that form the floor of the chart and the one vertical (*z*) axis.

In the 3-D column chart, the data series are presented front to back instead of side-by-side as in the clustered column chart. One drawback of the 3-D column is that it may be difficult to see all the data markers when some data markers in a series are too small to be seen behind larger data markers. Sometimes rearranging the series along the y-axis will help to bring small markers to the front. In some cases the 3-D columns can be made more narrow and/or the space between them be increased to enable the user to view small data markers which are behind larger ones. In the chart above, each series has a small data marker so it is not feasible to move all the small markers to the front row, but we can try to help visualize the small markers in the back by narrowing the markers and increasing the gap between markers.

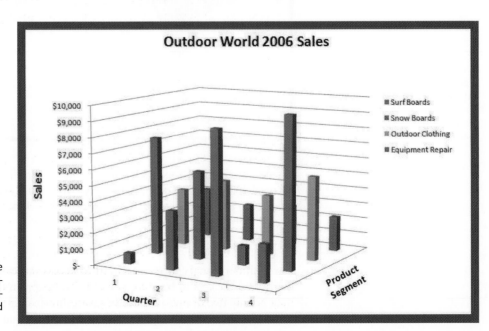

Figure 4-22: Data markers can be made narrower and the gap between markers increased to facilitate viewing small markers behind larger ones.

3-D Visual Effects

Many of the "3-D" charts frequently used in Excel are not true 3-D charts, but standard charts with 3-D visual effects. Those with 3-D visual effects use 3-D data markers to add the 3-D effect. Below is a clustered column chart with a 3-D visual effect. Compare it with the previous examples of 3-D column charts. Note that there is only one category axis. The category axis is simply thickened to make a chart floor to give the appearance of a 3-D graph.

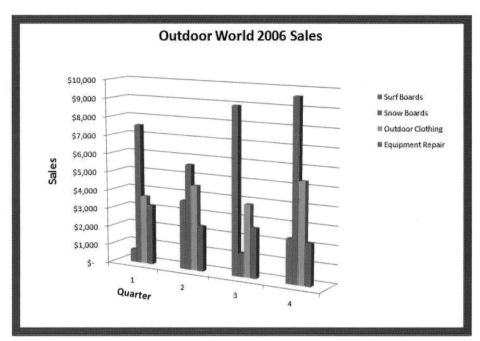

Figure 4-23: Clustered column chart with a 3-D effect.

In both types of 3-D charts the plot area is divided into two areas. The back and side of the plot area is collectively called the *walls*. The bottom of the plot area is called the *floor*. Special formatting and fill effects may be applied separately to each of these portions of the plot area.

Creating Excel Charts

To create a chart in Excel 2007, first enter on a worksheet the data and formulas needed for the chart. The arrangement of the data on the worksheet is dependent on the type of chart you wish to create. Table 4-2 provides some guidelines for arranging data optimally for each chart type.

Once the data is entered, select the data cells (and in some cases, the label cells also), and select from the ribbon **Insert(tab)→Charts(group)→the desired chart type from the drop-down list**. Once the chart is created, any aspect of the chart may be modified or formatted. When a chart is inserted into a workbook, three additional *Chart Tools* tabs are added to the ribbon, *Design, Layout,* and *Format.* Each tab has task groups which are used to access its features. For example, the Design tab includes a gallery of preformatted chart styles and chart layouts from which you may select. It also includes a task group for changing the chart type and changing the data selection.

Table 4-2: Guidelines for optimal data arrangement for various chart types.

Chart Type	Optimal Data Arrangement
Column Bar Line Area Surface Radar	In columns or rows such as: A B 1 2 3 4 Or: A 1 3 B 2 4
Pie Doughnut (with one series only)	One column (or row) of data and one column (or row) of data labels, such as: A 1 B 2 C 3 Or: A B C 1 2 3
Doughnut (with multiple series)	One column (or row) of data labels and any number of columns (or rows) of data, such as: A 1 2 B 3 4 C 5 6 Or: A B C 1 2 3 4 5 6
XY (scatter)	X values in one column and corresponding Y values in another column, such as: X Y 1 2 4 5
Bubble	X values in one column and corresponding Y values in another column, and bubble size values in an adjacent column, such as: X Y Bubble size 1 2 3 4 5 6
Stock	In columns or rows in the following order, using names or dates as labels, such as: Date Volume (millions) Open High Low Close 01/01/07 25.6 44.65 46.125 42 44.06 Or: Date 01/01/07 Open 44.65 High 46.125 Low 42 Close 44.06 Volume (millions) 25.6

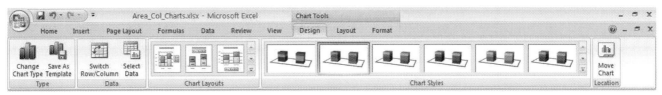

Figure 4-24: The *Design* tab of the special *Chart Tools* tabs.

Figure 4-25: The *Layout* tab of the special *Chart Tools* tabs.

Figure 4-26: The *Format* tab of the special *Chart Tools* tabs.

Once a chart is created, there are five major task categories that may include subcategories for chart modifications. For those users familiar with previous versions of Excel, these categories and subcategories somewhat parallel those included in the steps of the *Chart Wizard*. (The *Chart Wizard* itself is not utilized in Excel 2007).

1. *Chart Type*

   - Chart subtypes
   - Chart templates

2. *Data Selection*

   - Data range
   - Data series
   - Data categories
   - Legend entries

3. *Chart Layout*

   - Adding pictures, shapes and text boxes
   - Chart title
   - Axes titles & display preferences
   - Legend options
   - Gridline preferences
   - Data labels
   - Include table of data
   - Backgrounds
   - 3-D rotation
   - Chart name

4. *Chart Formatting*

   - Shape formatting
   - WordArt
   - Chart object arrangement

- Chart object sizing
- Fill (background options)
- Border color
- Border styles
- Shadow
- 3-D format
- 3-D rotation
- Placement and orientation of chart and axis titles

5. *Chart Placement*

- Embedded into worksheet
- Separate worksheet on a "chart sheet"

If you wish to make changes after the chart is finished, right-click on the chart area or chart object and select the desired task category from the context menu. A different context menu will appear based on the part of the chart selected before the right-click.

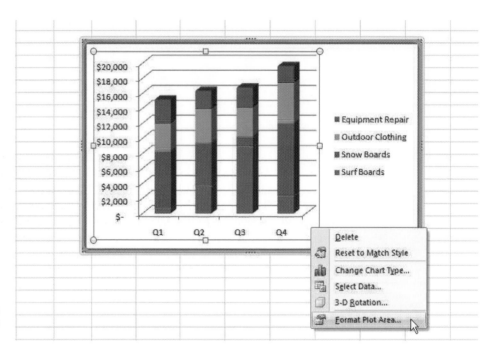

Figure 4-27: Access the plot area context menu by right-clicking on plot area of the completed chart.

Practice Creating a Chart in Excel 2007

Create a chart that shows the relative percent of the salary budget paid by each department. A pie chart will be the best chart for this presentation.

1. Open the practice file "EmployeesSalaryBudget_ch4".xlsx.

2. For a pie chart, the column headers and the grand total label and sum will not be needed. Select only the subtotal data and labels as shown below.

Figure 4-28: Select only the department labels and the salary subtotals, then select *Insert(tab)→ Charts(group)→Pie*.

	A	B
1	**Department**	**Salary Budget**
2	Finance	$ 315,220
3	Human Resources	$ 273,246
4	Management	$ 733,113
5	Marketing	$ 649,663
6	Product Development	$ 1,088,544
7	Sales	$ 5,156,788
8	**Grand Total**	$ 8,216,574
9		
10		
11		

3. **Select Insert(tab)→Charts(group)→Pie**. Select the first subtype which is the standard pie chart. The chart will be created using default colors and style for the standard pie chart.

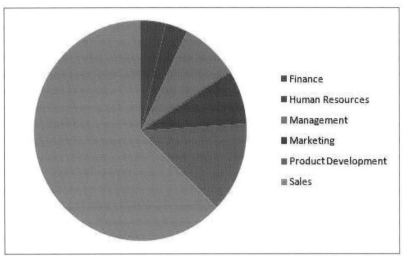

Figure 4-29: The default pie chart type.

4. Pie charts present data more clearly when the largest slice begins at the 12 o'clock position of the pie and extends clockwise. This chart displays the pie pieces in exactly the opposite order with the smallest pie piece beginning at the 12 o'clock position. Excel charts are dynamic so that correcting the problem does not require recreating the chart. Any changes made in the data are immediately reflected in the chart. Correct the order of the pie pieces by sorting the summary data from largest to smallest values in the "Salary Budget" column. To sort the chart data, select only the chart data (labels and values, omit column headers and "Grand Total" row). Select **Home(tab)→Editing(group)→Sort & Filter(drop-down list)→Custom Sort**. The *Sort* dialog box will appear.

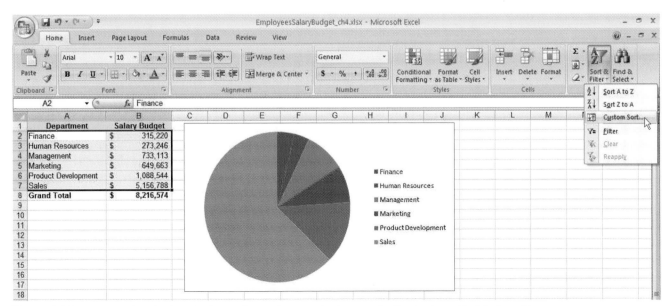

Figure 4-30: Sort data for pie chart in descending order to make largest pie slice begin at 12 o'clock position.

5. Select *Salary Budget* from the *Sort by* drop-down list and select *Largest to Smallest* in the *Order* drop-down list.

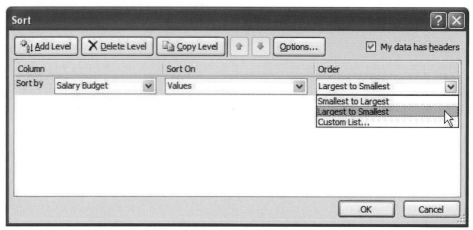

Figure 4-31: *Sort* dialog box.

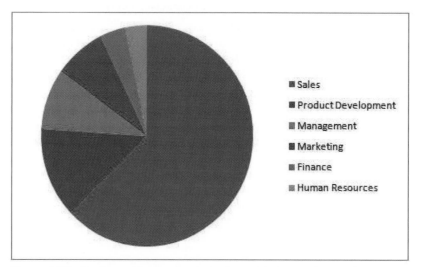

Figure 4-32: Pie chart with re-ordered pie slices with data in descending order.

6. Now that the pie chart data is in a good presentation order, additional formatting may be applied to the chart. Add a chart title by selecting the chart then select **Layout(tab)→Chart Title→Above Chart**. When the chart is selected, the *Chart Tools* tabs (*Design*, *Layout*, and *Format*) will appear. When the title is added above the chart, the plot area of the chart is resized to make room for the title at the top. The chart title may be added to overlay the chart so the plot area remains unchanged. Entitle the chart "Salary Budget by Department." To enter the title, select the chart title box and begin typing. The typed text will appear in the formula bar. The text will appear in the title box after the Enter key is pressed or after the cursor moves off the formula bar. Alternately, you can enter or modify the chart title directly in its title box by clicking twice (two single clicks) on the chart title box. (See Figure 4-33.)

7. Add labels to the markers that include the percentage of the total budget represented for each department. If there is room on the chart area, the category names may also be added so that the legend will not be necessary. With the chart selected,

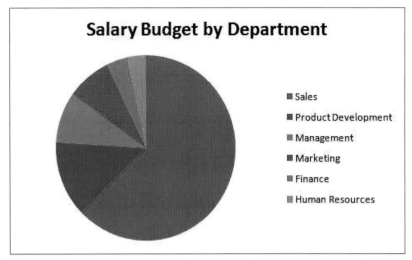

Figure 4-33: Chart title entered above the plot area.

select **Layout(tab)→Data Labels→More Data Label Options**. In the *Format Data Labels* dialog box, check the boxes beside *Percentage* and *Category Name*. Unselect any other checked boxes. Select *Label Position* option *Outside End*. Click the *Close* button to close the dialog box. On the pie chart, select individual data labels and move to the desired position around the outside edge of the pie. Remove the chart legend by selecting it and press the *Delete* key.

Figure 4-34: *Format Data Labels* dialog box.

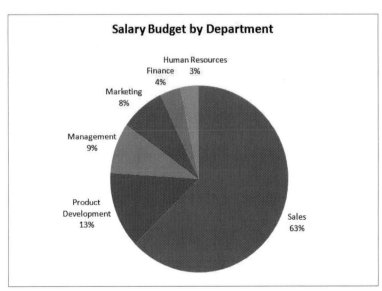

Figure 4-35: Pie chart with *Data Labels* added on outside of pie to replace the chart legend.

8. Change the pie chart to one with a 3-D visual effect. Select the chart and select **Design(tab)→Charts(group)→Change Chart Type→Pie→Pie in 3-D** (the second chart subtype for Pie charts). Change the 3-D rotation so that the pie appears three dimensional by selecting the general chart area (click on the chart outside all

chart objects) and right-click to access the context menu. Select *Format Chart Area* from the context menu. Change the *Rotation* for *Y* to 20°. Click the *Close* button to close the dialog box. Adjust the placement of data labels by selecting and dragging each one individually to the desired location. Add leader lines between the data labels and the pie slices by right-clicking on data labels and selecting *Format Data Labels* again from the context menu. Check the box beside *Show Leader Lines* in the *Format Data Labels* dialog box.

9. Draw attention to the pie slice that represents Sales by selecting the slice, then drag it away from the other slices using the left mouse button. (To select one pie slice, click once on a slice to select all slices then click a second time to select one slice.)

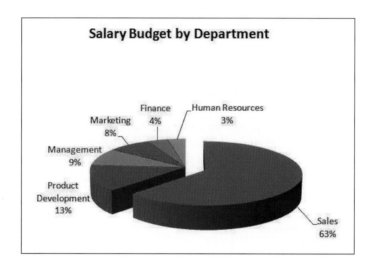

Figure 4-36: Exploded 3-D pie.

The appearance of the chart can be further enhanced by adjusting font sizes, size of plot area, and color of data markers (pie slides in this example). To format any part of the chart, select the chart area or object then select either the **Layout or Format Tab of the Chart Tools tabs→Current Selection(group)→Format Selection** from the ribbon. The *Format Selection* option is available on both of these tabs. The same menu options are available on the chart context menus that can be accessed by right-clicking on the chart area or any chart object. Experiment with making changes in various chart options and observe the results.

Formatting a Chart

Formatting the Chart Area

The *chart area* includes everything inside the chart boundaries. The chart area is the background for everything else on the chart. To add background color, textures, patterns, or images to the chart background, right-click on any blank part of the chart (between other chart items such as titles and labels). Select **Format Chart Area** from the context menu. The *Format Chart Area* dialog box will appear. Select *Fill* from the left frame of the dialog box to set background color and effects. For special background formatting such as color gradients, textures, patterns, or custom pictures, select the appropriate option button in the right frame of the dialog box. As each option is selected, additional options will appear such as color selector, transparency setting, gradient fill pattern selector, and picture and texture selector.

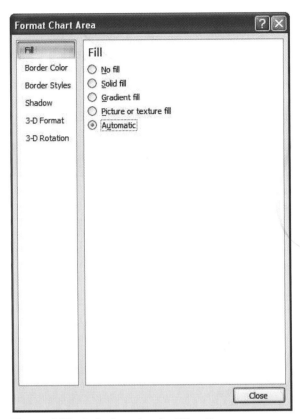

Figure 4-37: Default setting for Fill options.

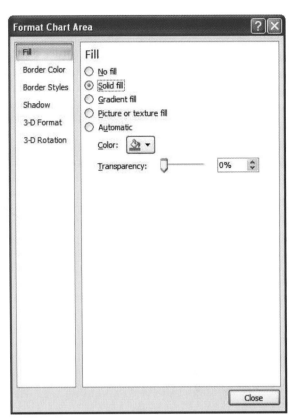

Figure 4-38: Color selector appears for adding fill color.

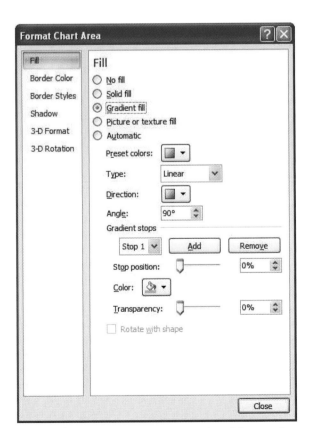

Figure 4-39: Gradient options appear for adding gradient color and pattern.

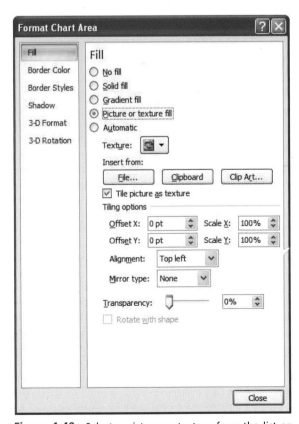

Figure 4-40: Select a picture or texture from the list or use a file to add a custom fill effect.

The "Format . . ." dialog box for each chart object mirrors the *Format Chart Area* dialog box. The *Border Color* group is used to set the color of the border or to remove the border. Several options exist for the *Border Style*, and *Shadow* effect for borders or background.

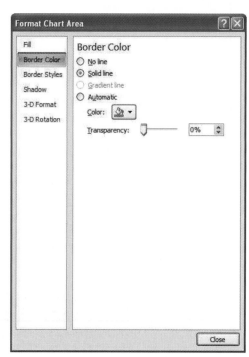

Figure 4-41: *Border Color* options for *Chart Area.*

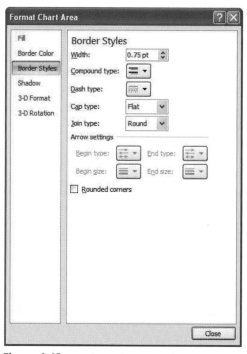

Figure 4-42: *Border Style* options for *Chart Area.*

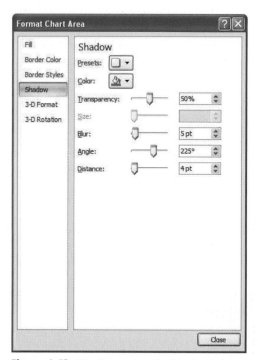

Figure 4-43: *Shadow* options for border and background.

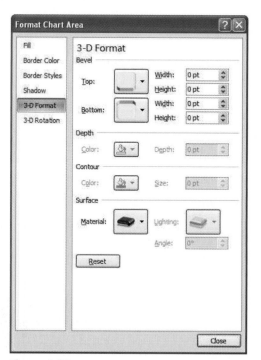

Figure 4-44: Change chart appearance with *3-D Format* options.

To format the font of chart labels or titles, select the chart area or object and select **Home(tab)→Font(group)** to choose the desired font size, color, or affects. A *Font*

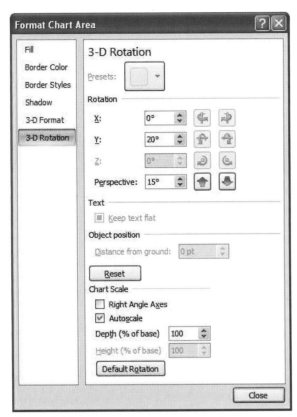

Figure 4-45: Modify chart orientation with *3-D Rotation* options.

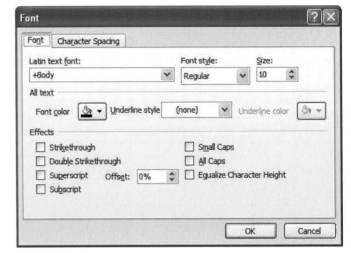

Figure 4-46: The Font dialog box accessed from the context menu.

dialog box with some font formatting options may also be accessed by right-clicking on a text object such as a chart title or axis labels and selecting *Font* from the context menu.

To name the chart select **Layout(tab)→Properties(group)** and type the name into the text box beneath *Chart Name*.

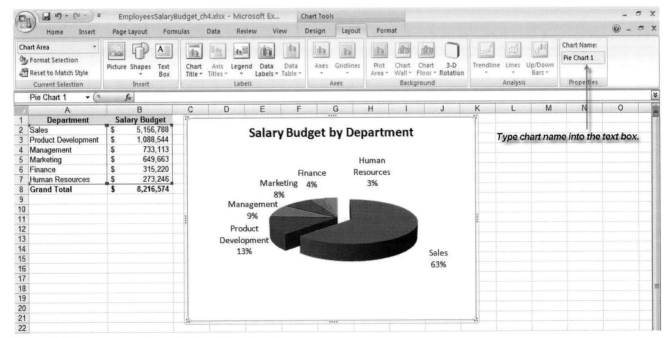

Figure 4-47: Type a name into the *Chart Name* text box.

Formatting the Plot Area

The *plot area* is a rectangular area bounded by the chart axes. In a pie or doughnut chart, the plot area is a rectangular area that encloses the data markers. To format the plot area, right-click anywhere within the chart axes where there is not another chart item (such as a data marker or gridline). Select **Format Plot Area** from the context menu. The *Format Plot Area* dialog box will appear. The same formatting options exist in the *Format Plot Area* dialog box and other "Format . . ." dialog boxes as those described for the *Format Chart Area* dialog box.

To format the plot area of a pie or doughnut chart, visualize a rectangular plot area around the circular arrangement of data markers. Click inside that imagined rectangle in one of the four corners outside the data markers. The rectangular plot area will become outlined and the *Format Plot Area* menu item will be available from the context menu. The same plot formatting options are available for the plot area of the pie and doughnut charts as for the other chart types.

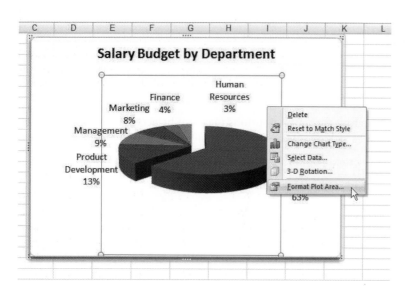

Figure 4-48: The plot area of a pie or doughnut chart is a rectangle around the data markers.

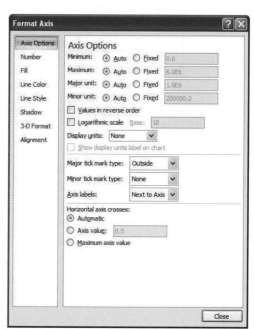

Figure 4-49: The *Format Axis* dialog includes special axis formatting options and other format options similar to those for other chart objects. The *Display units* drop-down list provides options for displaying unit values as Hundreds, Thousands, Millions, etc.

Formatting the X and Y Axes

Several options are available for formatting lines, axis scaling, font, text alignment, data types, and tick marks for each axis. To format an axis, right-click on the axis line or in the area of the axis value labels and click select **Format Axis . . .** from the context menu. The *Format Axis* dialog box will appear which includes formatting options similar to those for formatting other chart objects. Additional options are available for customizing the axis and its labels. (See Figure 4-49.)

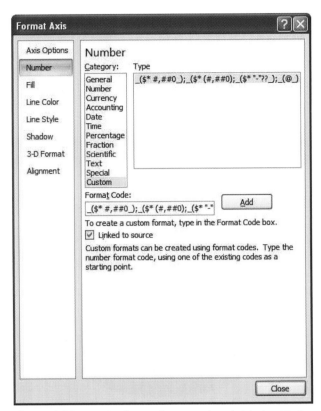

Figure 4-50: Set the format for numeric axis labels with the *Number* options.

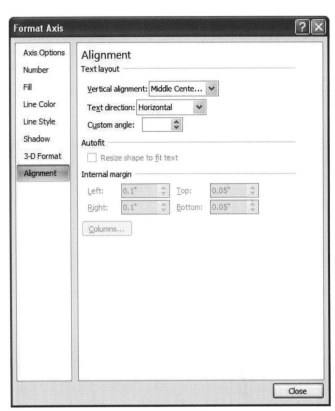

Figure 4-51: Change orientation of axis label text using the *Alignment* options so that labels can display in a smaller horizontal space.

Formatting Chart Gridlines

To make it easier to read the plotted values, Excel adds major *gridlines* for the value (y) axis on most chart types. *Gridlines* are extensions of the tick marks on either axis that extend across the plot area perpendicular to the axis. Minor gridlines can be added to charts with rectangular plot areas or gridlines may be removed altogether if desired. Gridline color and weight can be changed by right-clicking on a gridline and selecting *Format Gridlines*, or *Format Major Gridlines* from the context menu. Minor gridlines can be added by selecting *Add Minor Gridlines* from the context menu. Gridlines for each axis may be removed by selecting **Layout(tab)→Axes→Gridlines→(select axis)→None**.

Formatting Data Markers

In most chart types, the data markers for one series of data are formatted alike. In the pie and doughnut charts, various aspects of the data series may be formatted alike, but you have the option of formatting each data point separately with regard to fill color and effects and data labels. For each chart type, there is a default format for data markers for series and categories. Changes may be made to the series data marker formats by right-clicking on a data marker in the series you wish to format, and select **Format Data Series** from the context menu. The *Format Data Series* dialog box will appear. (See Figure 4-52.)

To format a single data marker, such as in the pie chart example, select the data marker by clicking once on the data series, and then click a second time to select the single data marker. Notice the "handles" are around all markers in a series on the first mouse click and are around only the selected marker on the second mouse click.

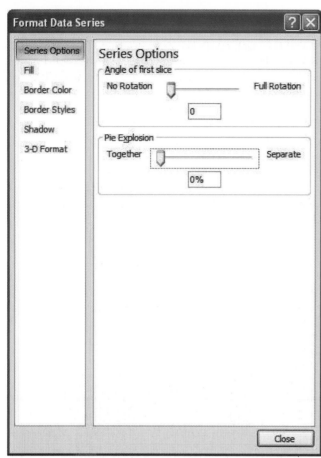

Figure 4-52: To access the *Format Data Series* dialog box, right-click on a data marker in the series you wish to format. Specific *Series Options* are available for each chart type.

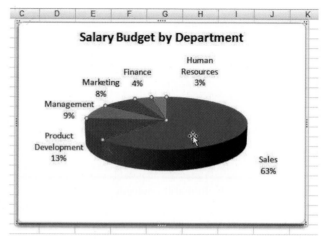

Figure 4-53: Note the "handles" around only all data markers in the series on the first mouse click.

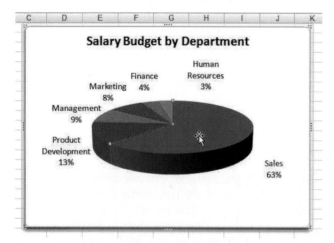

Figure 4-54: Note the "handles" around only the selected data marker on the second mouse click.

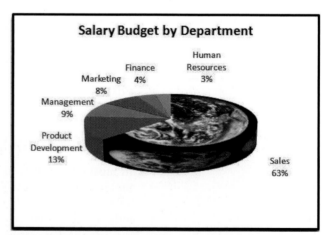

Figure 4-55: A single data marker may be filled with a clipart image or an image file.

Once the single data marker has been selected, it may be formatted separately by right-clicking and selecting **Format Data Point** from the context menu or by selecting **Format Selection** from the *Current Selection* group on either the *Layout* or the *Format* tab of the *Chart Tools* tabs. (See Figure 4-55 for the result.)

Rearranging Chart Data

When a chart is created, the data is presented in the same order as the source data. In some cases the data may make a better chart presentation in another order. For example, moving larger data series markers to the back of a 3-D chart will allow the smaller data markers to be viewed more easily. If you wish to change the order of the data series markers, you may do so by right-clicking on the chart and choose *Select Data* from the context menu. The *Select Data Source* dialog box will appear. The dialog box may be used to change the range of source data or to edit data series or categories. To rearrange the data series, select a series of data from the left list box and click the up or down arrow to more it before or after another data series. As data series are rearranged, the data markers on the chart will move accordingly. The Outdoor Clothing series is moved to the bottom of the list so it will appear at the back of the 3-D chart.

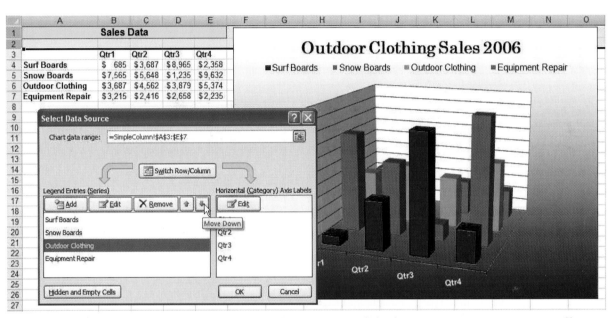

Figure 4-56: Change the order of data series on the *Select Data Source* dialog box.

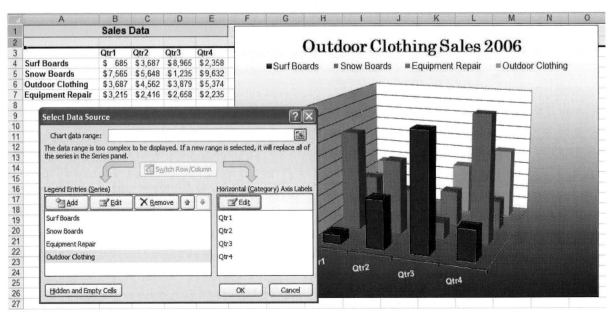

Figure 4-57: When a series of data is moved down on the list, it moves to the back of the 3-D chart.

Formatting the Legend

The background color and effects, font, and location of the legend may be changed using the *Format Legend* dialog box that may be accessed by selecting the chart and select **Layout(tab)→Labels(group)→Legend→More Legend Options** from the ribbon.

Figure 4-58: Use the Legend Options to relocate the legend on the chart area.

Custom Chart Types

The Excel 2007 chart tools allow the user to design a chart then save the chart as a design template that can be used as the starting point for other charts, just like the pre-defined chart types in Excel. To save a chart as a custom type, select the chart and select from the ribbon **Design(tab)→Type(group)→Save as Template**. To use a saved custom chart template, select the chart data and select from the ribbon **Insert(tab)→Charts(group)→Other Charts→All Chart Types**. The *Insert Chart* dialog will appear. Select the **Template** chart type group. User-defined custom charts will be displayed in the right frame.

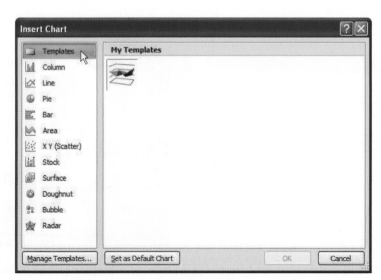

Figure 4-59: User-defined custom charts are included in the Templates chart type.

Modifying the Chart Location

A chart may be embedded into a worksheet or it may be placed on a new worksheet called a *chart sheet*. The default placement of the chart is on the active worksheet. To change the chart location select the chart and select **Design(tab)→ Location→Move Chart** from the ribbon. The *Move Chart* dialog box will appear so you may select the new placement of the chart on another worksheet or on a new worksheet.

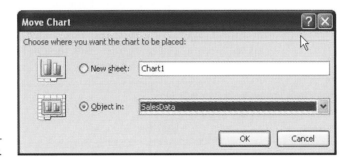

Figure 4-60: Change the chart location in the *Move Chart* dialog box.

Formatting Scientific Graphs

In some scientific applications, it may be desirable to mark potential error amounts graphically for each marker in a data series. Excel provides a *y error bar* option for marking potential errors. Potential errors may be plotted as a fixed value, a percentage of the data point value, a number of standard deviations, a standard error, or a custom amount. Potential error values may be plotted on the positive or negative side of the data point value, or on both sides. The default option is not to include y error bars on the data markers.

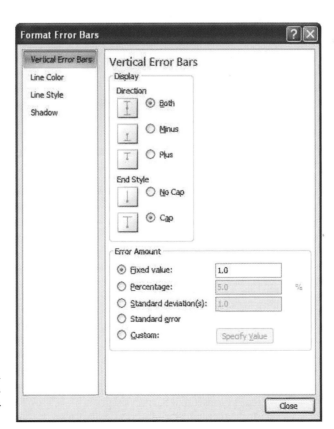

Figure 4-61: Add error bars to scientific or statistical charts by selecting *Layout(tab)→Analysis(group)→ Error Bars* from the ribbon.

Adding Error Bars to Scientific or Statistical Charts

Create a scatter chart that plots measures of weight and volume of a substance.

1. Open the practice file "Density_ch4.xlsx".

2. Select the data and column headers. Select **Insert(tab)→Charts(group)→Scatter (select the default type)**.

3. Right-click on the chart area and select **Select Data** from the context menu. The *Select Data* Source dialog box will appear. Select *Weight(grams)* in the left list box. Click the *Edit* button at the center top of the list box. The *Edit Series* dialog box will appear. Type in the first text box under *Series name* "Density Experiment." This will become the chart title. Click the *OK* button to close the *Edit Series* dialog box, then the *OK* button to close the *Select Data Source* dialog box.

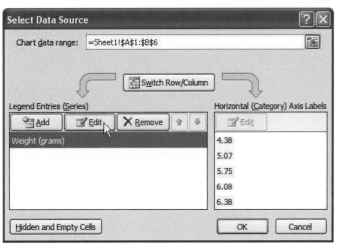

Figure 4-62: Select Data Source dialog box.

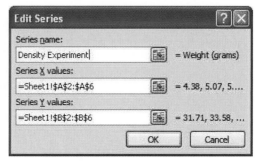

Figure 4-63: Edit Series dialog box.

4. Add a trend line to the plot area by right-clicking on a data marker and select **Add Trendline** from the context menu. Select the default trend line, the linear line.

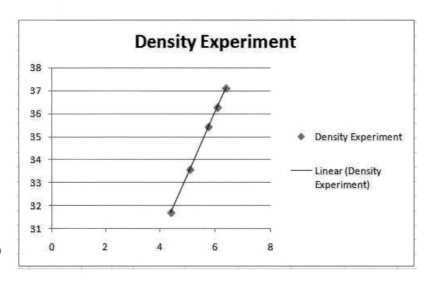

Figure 4-64: Density chart with a trend line.

5. Select the legend and use the *Delete* key to remove it.

6. Add error bars to the graph. Select the chart to activate the Chart Tools tabs and select Layout(tab)→Analysis(group)→Error Bars→More Error Bar Options. The *Format Error Bars* dialog box will appear (see Figure 4-61).

7. Select the *Error Amount* option button for *Percentage*. Enter 1.0 in the text box to the right of *Percentage*. The error bars are added to the data points.

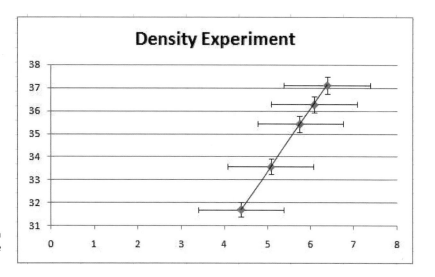

Figure 4-65: Error bars have been added to the data points of the "Density" chart.

Using Excel Charts in Other Applications

Charts created in Excel may be used in other applications such as Word documents and PowerPoint presentations. There are three ways a chart may be added to the external application. The chart may be:

- Pasted into the host application as an image object.
- Embedded into the host application.
- Added as a link to the original Excel workbook.

Pasting Charts as Image Objects

If you select a chart in Excel and use the *Copy* command, then paste it into Microsoft Word using the Paste command, it will be pasted as a static image object. Once it is in Word, changes cannot be made to the individual chart objects as could be done in Excel. Only formatting changes can be made that apply to any image object in Word.

Linking and Embedding Charts

If a chart is pasted into a PowerPoint presentation using simple *Copy* and *Paste* commands, the chart will be pasted as a chart object by default. Formatting changes can be made to the individual chart objects through the *Chart Tools* that are available in PowerPoint. For changes to the underlying data, the *Edit Data* or *Select Data* commands in PowerPoint will open the original data source (the worksheet data) in Excel.

Special pasting techniques can override the default *Paste* options. Charts may be either *embedded* in the new document or presentation or they may be *linked* with the Excel workbook where they were created. *Object Linking and Embedding* (OLE) is a technology used by Microsoft that enables objects created in one application to be linked or embedded into another application. Embedding a chart means a copy of the chart and its source data is embedded in the host document or presentation. The chart object and data can be modified without affecting the original chart or data. To embed a chart into a document or presentation, select the chart and copy it using the *Copy* command on the *Clipboard* task group of the *Home* tab of the ribbon. Paste it into the host file using the *Paste Special* command in the same task group. The *Paste Special* dialog box will appear. To embed, select the *Paste* option and select *Microsoft Office Excel Chart Object* for a Word document. Select *Microsoft Office Graphics Object* for a PowerPoint presentation.

When a chart is *linked* with a host document or presentation, the chart is actually pasted as a link to the original chart and its data in the Excel workbook. When changes are made to the linked chart, the changes are actually made in the original Excel workbook. To link a chart into a document or presentation, use the *Paste Special* command and select the *Paste Link* option and select *Microsoft Office Excel Chart Object* for both Word and PowerPoint. When the chart is accessed for modifications, the linked Excel workbook will open and the user will be directed to the chart and chart data in the workbook.

Review Questions

1. Explain the difference between a *series* of data and a *category* of data.

_____

_____

_____

2. How many series of data can be graphed with a pie chart?

_____

_____

_____

3. Explain the difference between the appropriate application of a pie chart and a doughnut chart.

_____

_____

_____

4. Explain the difference in the appropriate application of a column chart and a bar chart.

_____

_____

_____

5. Explain the difference between appropriate application of a line chart and an XY scatter chart that has a trend line.

_____

_____

_____

6. What aspects of the data are emphasized in a line chart?

_____

_____

_____

7. What is the advantage of using an area chart over a column chart for showing product sales for multiple product lines?

_____

_____

_____

8. What is unique about the structure of the plot area of a stock chart?

_____

_____

_____

9. Differentiate a true 3-D chart from a standard chart with 3-D visual effects.

_____

_____

_____

10. In a true 3-D chart what does the z-axis represent?

_____

_____

_____

11. Explain the difference between an exploded pie chart and an extracted pie chart.

_____

_____

_____

12. What can be done to help see small data markers that may be hidden by larger ones in a 3-D chart?

_____

_____

_____

13. What is a custom chart type and how is it created?

_____

_____

_____

14. How does linking an Excel chart into a Word document differ from embedding?

_____

_____

_____

Practice Problems

1. Create a chart that shows what portion of your study time goes to each course you are taking this semester.

2. Research to find historical stock prices for a stock of your choice. Create the appropriate type of stock chart for the data you find. Try to adjust the values scales so that the data markers for data represented on the two value axes do not overlap visually. (There are many Web sites that have links to historical stock data. Try using "historical stock data" as a search string.)

3. Select a publicly traded company and research its financial performance over the past 5 years. Create an Excel chart that shows the trend of revenue and costs over the 5-year period.

commonly uses the singular term to refer to an entire set of fields for one column, such as the Department field or Salary field.

In versions of Excel prior to the 2007 Office version, data management in columns and rows was referred to as "lists." In the 2003 version, Excel added some special list features that allowed a user to define a list by name and cell range, and once defined, special features and navigation techniques could be applied. In Excel 2007, the term "list" has been changed to "table" to be more consistent with other Microsoft Office applications. When looking for tools and commands to manage list data, look for "table" options and commands instead of those that apply to "lists" as in previous Excel versions. Be sure to use "table" as a help search term when you are requesting information about data management features and tools.

Designing an Excel List

Excel includes many features that support data management. In order for these features to work as intended, the list must be structured such that Excel recognizes the list, its columns, and its rows. The following guidelines will be helpful in designing a well-structured list in Excel.

1. Consider the reports that are required. Make sure all the data that is needed is included in the list.

2. Each field should store only one item of data and only one type of data (number or text). Separate mixed data items into separate fields.

    - Example 1: "25/hour" should be separated so that "25" is in one field and "hour" or "hourly" is in another field.
    - Example 2: Enter an address into separate fields, one each for the street address, city, state, and zip components of the address.

3. Each list should be about only one type of entity, such as customers, products, or orders.

4. Each list should be on a separate worksheet.

5. Column (attribute) labels should be in the first row of the list and should be formatted differently from the data rows in the list.

6. Column headers must be unique within one list.

7. There should be no blank columns or blank rows within the list.

8. There should be at least one blank row and one blank column around the list unless the boundary is the edge of the worksheet (such as left or top edge).

9. There should be no data stored in cells adjacent to the list. Always leave a row or column between the list and any other data on the worksheet.

10. Use one-word names for column headers of lists that may be shared with other programs. Use underscores to connect multiple words in an attribute (column header) name to make it more readable.

11. Column headers should fit in one cell. Wrap text within the cell if needed.

12. Enter data into the row directly below column headers. Do not skip rows after column headers or anywhere else in the list.

13. Use one-word worksheet names. Use underscores to connect multiple words in a worksheet name.

14. Do not indent within a cell using the space bar. Use the indent command to indent cell contents using **Home(tab)→Alignment(tab)→Increase Indent (icon)** or **Ctrl+Alt+Tab** for each indent step. (Decrease indent by using **Ctrl+Alt+ Shift+Tab**).

15. Be aware of how worksheets will look when printed. Wrap text in a column as needed to maintain more consistent column widths.

16. Enter data consistently. Avoid using various spellings or abbreviations for the same data value. Excel will consider different spellings as different values when sorting or filtering.

17. Test the design with a few rows of data and revise the design as needed before adding all the data.

Critical List Structure Guidelines

From the previous list of guidelines, there are a few that are critical to the automatic list management features in Excel. Excel must be able to clearly distinguish the boundaries of the list and the column header row in order for the list management features to work automatically and correctly. The critical guidelines are repeated here.

1. Column labels (the column header row) should be in the first row of the list and should be formatted differently to distinguish it from the data rows of the list.

2. There should be no blank columns or blank rows within the list.

3. There should be a blank row and column around the list unless the list boundary is the edge of the worksheet (such as left and/or top edge).

4. There should be no data stored in cells adjacent to the list (thus violating the previous guideline).

Entering List Data

Begin a list by entering a column header in the first row for each of the attributes you plan to store. Format the column header row differently from the data rows in the list, such as applying a background color or making the font bold. Distinct formatting allows Excel to know that the row is a header row and not part of the list data. Without distinctive formatting, the Excel sorting and filtering features will not work correctly. Note the formatted column header row in Figure 5-1.

Sometimes column labels are longer than the longest data item in the column. In those cases, you can wrap the text in the column header row in order to make the columns narrower so that more columns may be viewed on one screen.

	A	B	C	D	E	F	G	H	I	J	K	L	
1	Place	Position in Age Group/Number in Age Group	FirstName	MiddleInitial	LastName	Age	Gender	ParticipantCity	ParticipantState	GardenOfTheGods	SummerRoundupTrail	PikesPeakAscent	Tot
2	1	1/29	Scott		Lebo	39	M	Colo Springs	CO	0:58:01	0:50:27	2:32:25	
3	2	2/29	Cornelis	B	Guijt	39	M	Colo Springs	CO	1:00:37	0:52:04	2:35:20	
4	3	3/29	Paul	L	Kooh	38	M	Colo Springs	CO	1:02:11	0:53:24	2:32:51	
5	4	1/11	Gerald	B	Romero	34	M	Colo Springs	CO	1:02:14	0:57:34	2:31:49	
6	5	1/23	Steve		Moon	40	M	Colo Springs	CO	1:05:37	0:56:04	2:45:58	
7	6	4/29	Andrew	W	Subudhi	37	M	Colo Springs	CO	1:04:30	0:56:17	2:52:17	
8	7	2/23	Bill		Means	41	M	Monument	CO	1:05:14	0:56:49	2:51:45	
9	8	5/29	Kevin	S	Wilder	38	M	Colo Springs	CO	1:06:04	0:56:30	2:55:00	
10	9	2/11	Christopher	D	Borton	30	M	Golden	CO	1:02:10	0:57:19	2:58:18	

Figure 5-2: Long column labels.

To wrap the text within the column header cells, select the entire row for editing by clicking the row number on the worksheet margin to the left of the column header row then select **Home(tab)→Alignment(group)→Wrap Text** from the ribbon.

To format the column headers so that they take the minimum amount of horizontal space in the worksheet, change the orientation of the column headers so that they are presented at an angle to the first data row. This is especially helpful for worksheets with numerous narrow data fields. Select the entire row and change the alignment of the column header row in one of the following ways:

1. **Home(tab)→Alignment(group)→Orientation icon** . From the drop-down list select the direction in which you want the text to angle.

2. Access the *Format Cells* dialog box in one of three ways:

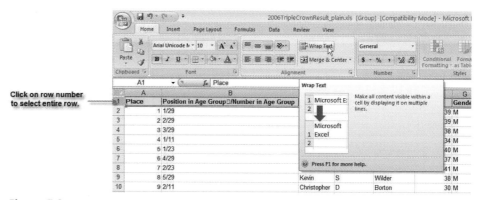

Figure 5-3: Select the entire row and format to wrap column headers within the cell.

	A	B	C	D	E	F	G	H	I	J	K	L	M
1	Place	Position in Age Group/Number in Age Group	FirstName	Middle Initial	LastName	Age	Gender	Participant City	Participant State	GardenOf TheGods	Summer Roundup Trail	PikesPeak Ascent	Total Time
2	1	1/29	Scott		Lebo	39	M	Colo Springs	CO	0:58:01	0:50:27	2:32:25	4:20:53
3	2	2/29	Cornelis	B	Guijt	39	M	Colo Springs	CO	1:00:37	0:52:04	2:35:20	4:28:01
4	3	3/29	Paul	L	Koch	38	M	Colo Springs	CO	1:02:11	0:53:24	2:32:51	4:28:26
5	4	1/11	Gerald	B	Romero	34	M	Colo Springs	CO	1:02:14	0:57:34	2:31:49	4:31:37
6	5	1/23	Steve		Moon	40	M	Colo Springs	CO	1:05:37	0:56:04	2:45:58	4:47:39
7	6	4/29	Andrew	W	Subudhi	37	M	Colo Springs	CO	1:04:30	0:56:17	2:52:17	4:53:04
8	7	2/23	Bill		Means	41	M	Monument	CO	1:05:14	0:56:49	2:51:45	4:53:48
9	8	5/29	Kevin	S	Wilder	38	M	Colo Springs	CO	1:06:04	0:56:30	2:55:00	4:57:34
10	9	2/11	Christopher	D	Borton	30	M	Golden	CO	1:02:10	0:57:19	2:58:18	4:57:47

Figure 5-4: Column headers with text wrapped.

2. Access the *Format Cells* dialog box in one of three ways:

a. **Home(tab)→Alignment(group)→Orientation icon** 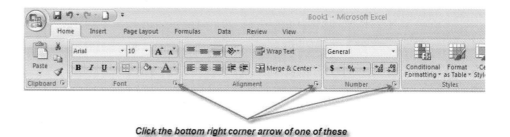**→Format Cell Alignment**.

b. **Click on the bottom right corner arrow of either of the *Font, Alignment,* or *Number* task groups on the *Home* tab** of the ribbon.

Figure 5-5: Access the *Format Cells* dialog box from the *Font, Alignment,* or *Number* task group.

c. Select **Home(tab)→Cells(group)→Format→Format Cells. Fomat→Cells→ Alignment (tab)** from the ribbon.

Select the *Alignment* tab of the *Format Cells* dialog box. In the *Orientation* (upper right) area of the tab, select the red diamond with the mouse pointer and drag the pointer to represent the angle at which you wish to display the column header text.

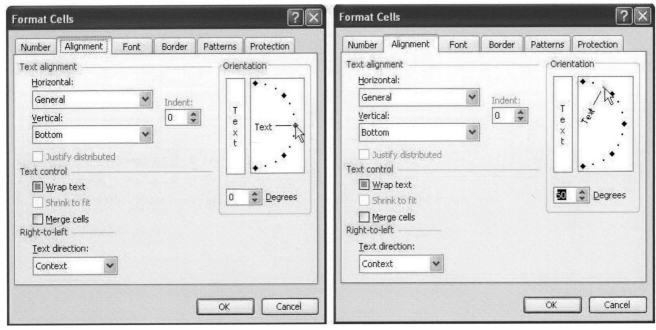

Figure 5-6: Drag the red diamond to the desired angle of text within the cells.

	A	B	C	D	E	F	G	H	I	J	K	L	M	N
1	Place	Position in Age Group /Number in Age Group	FirstName		MiddleInitial	LastName	Age	Gender	ParticipantCity		ParticipantState	GardenOfTheGods	SummerRoundupTrail	PikesPeakAscent	TotalTime
2	1	1/29	Scott		Lebo		39	M	Colo Springs	CO	0:58:01	0:50:27	2:32:25	4:20:53	
3	2	2/29	Cornelis	B	Guijt		39	M	Colo Springs	CO	1:00:37	0:52:04	2:35:20	4:28:01	
4	3	3/29	Paul	L	Koch		38	M	Colo Springs	CO	1:02:11	0:53:24	2:32:51	4:28:26	
5	4	1/11	Gerald	B	Romero		34	M	Colo Springs	CO	1:02:14	0:57:34	2:31:49	4:31:37	
6	5	1/23	Steve		Moon		40	M	Colo Springs	CO	1:05:37	0:56:04	2:45:58	4:47:39	
7	6	4/29	Andrew	W	Subudhi		37	M	Colo Springs	CO	1:04:30	0:56:17	2:52:17	4:53:04	
8	7	2/23	Bill		Means		41	M	Monument	CO	1:05:14	0:56:49	2:51:45	4:53:48	
9	8	5/29	Kevin	S	Wilder		38	M	Colo Springs	CO	1:06:04	0:56:30	2:55:00	4:57:34	
10	9	2/11	Christopher	D	Borton		30	M	Golden	CO	1:02:10	0:57:19	2:58:18	4:57:47	

Figure 5-7: Angled text in column labels enable more narrow columns.

Formatting List Data

All cells of new worksheets have the *General* Excel format by default. The *General* format allows the user to enter text, dates, or numeric data and Excel will adjust the format according to the type of data entered. Text entries are automatically aligned to the left cell margin. Dates and numeric data are aligned to the right cell margin. When leading zeros are entered in front of whole numbers, they are omitted automatically by Excel. In some cases, numeric characters are intended to represent non-numeric data such as identification numbers, social security numbers, and telephone numbers. In such cases these entries should be formatted as text rather than numbers. Formatting numbers as text will ensure that leading zeros in such identification numbers are not omitted. To override the automatic formatting of numeric data, format the column as *Text* instead of *General*. To change the format of a column, select the column to format then from the ribbon select **Home(tab)**→**Number(group)**→**select the desired format from the drop-down list** in the task group. In the example below, the employee identification numbers are required to be four digits including leading zeros. Note the green triangles in the left upper corners of the cells in the "EmployeeID" column. When numeric data is entered as *Text*, a green triangle *error indicator* will appear in the upper left corner of the cell. The *Trace Error* icon ⬧ appears to the left of the cell when the cell is selected. (If the column is against the left boundary of the worksheet, the icon will appear on the right side of the cell.) The green triangle alerts the user to a possible error in the cell.

	A	B	C	D	E	F	G	H	I
1	EmployeeID	LastName	FirstName	BirthDate	Gender	HireDate	Department	JobTitle	Salary
2	0001	Abner	David	11/15/1977	M	6/20/2006	Sales	Manager	$110,958
3	0002	Butler	Susan	11/16/1967	F	8/13/1978	Marketing	Staff	$ 40,816
4	0003	Conrad	Michael	9/14/1955	M	12/25/2001	Product Development	Staff Engineer	$ 74,665
5	0004	Davis	Randall	7/15/1947	M	5/25/1980	Finance	Staff Accountant	$ 42,106
6	0005	Edwards	Minnie	3/8/1959	F	11/26/1991	Human Resources	Manager	$ 90,228
7	0006	Franklin	Margaret	11/25/1979	F	3/15/1977	Product Development	Staff	$ 42,976
8	0007	Gardner	William	11/15/1968	M	2/7/1999	Sales	Staff	$ 90,650
9	0008	Hilton	Hillery	11/23/1949	F	11/8/2005	Sales	District Sales Manager	$128,845
10	0009	Jameson	Jennifer	1/17/1959	F	11/28/1992	Sales	Manager	$110,496

Figure 5-8: The employees' ID numbers are stored as text. Note the green triangles in the upper left corner of each cell in the 'EmployeeID' column.

To remove the green triangle indicator, click on the *Trace Error* icon and select *Ignore Error* from the drop-down list.

	A	B	C	D
1	EmployeeID	LastName	FirstName	BirthDate
2	0001	⬧ ▾	David	11/15/1977
3	0002			67
4	0003	Number Stored as Text		55
5	0004			47
6	0005	Convert to Number		59
7	0006	Help on this error		79
8	0007			68
9	0008	Ignore Error		49
10	0009			59
11	0010	Edit in Formula Bar		68
12	0011	Error Checking Options...		52
13	0012	Pater	Michael	4/20/1974

Figure 5-9: Remove green triangle error indicators by ignoring the error "Number stored as text".

To ignore the error and remove the green triangles from all cells on the worksheet that store numbers as text, select **Error Checking Options** from the same drop-down list. The *Excel Options* dialog box appears with the *Formulas* options visible. Uncheck the check box beside *Numbers stored as text or preceded by an apostrophe*. Click the *OK* button to close the dialog box. The best way to avoid the omission of leading zeros is to format the cells as text before entering or importing the numeric characters data whenever possible.

Quick Tip!

When entering data into a single cell, format numbers as *Text* by preceding the entry with an apostrophe ('). For example, the entry '0987654 will be stored as a *Text* value.

Using Conditional Formatting to Highlight Worksheet Rows

For large worksheet lists with numerous columns, it is often difficult for the human eye to follow a long row of data, especially on the printed copy. Applying a background color to every other row, or every third row, helps the eyes track a row of data more easily. *Conditional Formatting* includes an option that makes adding alternating shading or cell background colors simple. It utilizes the conditional format rule type *Use a Formula to determine which cells to format* for specifying a condition. A formula that can be applied to row shading uses the MOD function and the ROW function. The MOD function returns the modulus, or remainder, when some value is divided by another. The *number* argument represents the dividend portion of the calculation. The MOD function syntax:

> **=MOD(number, divisor)**

The ROW function was introduced in Chapter 3. It returns the row number of the current row. The ROW function syntax:

> **=ROW(row)**

To highlight every other row in the list, select the entire list or entire worksheet then select **Home(tab)→Styles(group)→Conditional Formatting→New Rule** from the ribbon. The *New Formatting Rule* dialog box will appear. In the formula box enter the nested MOD and ROW functions in the formula **=MOD(ROW(),2)=0**. Click the *Format . . .* button to specify the format to apply if the formula evaluates to TRUE. The *Format Cells* dialog box will appear. Use the *Fill* tab to apply gray background to the cells. The ROW function returns the row number to the *number* argument of the MOD function. The MOD function divides the row number by the *divisor* argument which is in this case 2. If the remainder from the calculation is zero (since the expression is set equal to zero in the formula), the specified format is applied. If you wish to apply the conditional format to every third or fourth row, replace the 2 in the formula with a 3 or 4, respectively. In the example below, the row divisor is 3, so every third row is shaded. When the entire list or worksheet is selected, the column header row is row 1 so the first shaded row is the second row of data (row 3).

	A	B	C	D	E	F	G	H	I
1	EmployeeID	LastName	FirstName	BirthDate	Gender	HireDate	Department	JobTitle	Salary
2	0001	Abner	David	11/15/1977	M	6/20/2006	Sales	Manager	$110,958
3	0002	Butler	Susan	11/16/1967	F	8/13/1978	Marketing	Staff	$ 40,816
4	0003	Conrad	Michael	9/14/1955	M	12/25/2001	Product Development	Staff Engineer	$ 74,665
5	0004	Davis	Randall	7/15/1947	M	5/25/1980	Finance	Staff Accountant	$ 42,106
6	0005	Edwards	Minnie	3/8/1959	F	11/26/1991	Human Resources	Manager	$ 90,228
7	0006	Franklin	Margaret	11/25/1979	F	3/15/1977	Product Development	Staff	$ 42,976
8	0007	Gardner	William	11/15/1968	M	2/7/1999	Sales	Staff	$ 90,650
9	0008	Hilton	Hillery	11/23/1949	F	11/8/2005	Sales	District Sales Manager	$128,845
10	0009	Jameson	Jennifer	1/17/1959	F	11/28/1992	Sales	Manager	$110,496
11	0010	Kelly	Chester	10/28/1968	M	1/3/1994	Sales	Staff	$ 98,538
12	0011	Zahn	Geoffrey	9/6/1952	M	3/4/1999	Sales	Staff	$ 84,151
13	0012	Patel	Michael	4/20/1974	M	3/19/2003	Sales	District Sales Manager	$133,784
14	0013	Schnider	Elizabeth	6/6/1958	F	6/27/1997	Sales	Staff	$ 35,025
15	0014	Zulkowski	Mary	5/8/1967	F	9/1/1999	Sales	Manager	$113,591
16	0015	Crockett	Carol	11/19/1953	F	12/3/1994	Sales	Staff	$ 43,374
17	0016	Hancock	Christopher	4/30/1967	M	11/18/1999	Sales	Staff	$ 50,219
18	0017	Bateman	Matthew	1/27/1956	M	8/3/1998	Sales	Staff	$ 83,847
19	0018	Powell	Bruce	5/8/1966	M	12/29/1985	Product Development	Staff Engineer	$ 72,564
20	0019	Phillips	Wiley	11/17/1952	M	5/1/1987	Finance	Staff Accountant	$ 51,485
21	0020	Howard	Emile	3/24/1985	M	4/3/1980	Sales	Staff	$ 59,528

Figure 5-10: Use *Conditional Formatting* to shade alternating rows of a worksheet. Gray fill color is the applied format.

Quick Tip!

To quickly shade alternating rows of a list, select a cell inside the list and select Insert(tab)→Table→(group)→Table from the ribbon. The list or the "table" of data will be formatted automatically using a default color scheme and row shading much like that accomplished with conditional formatting. To change the color scheme and row, column shading options, select a cell inside the table and select Design(tab)→Table Styles→select the desired table style. The Design tab is automatically added to the ribbon when a cell inside the table is selected.

An advantage of using conditional formatting to shade rows over automatic formats in the table style gallery is that more options are available for color choices and the particular rows or columns to shaded or highlight.

Validating Data Entry

In order to maintain good quality data in a list, it is important to control the type and quality of data that is entered. Excel includes a *Data Validation* feature that controls specific aspects of list data as it is entered by the user. Some options for validating data include allowing only entries that are limited to:

- Whole numbers within a specified range
- Decimal values within a specified range
- Values specified on a list
- Dates within a specified range
- Times within a specified range
- A minimum number of characters
- A maximum number of characters
- Data resulting from a specified formula

One of the most common applications of data validation is limiting entries to items specified in a list. The *List* type of data validation prevents typographical errors and unacceptable values in a range. For an organization's employee list, the values for the "Department" column should be limited since there are only a few specific departments that are valid for the organization.

To apply the *List* validation to the data cells in the "Department" column of the employee list, select the first cell in the range and select from the ribbon **Data(tab)→Data Tools(group)→Data Validation→Data Validation**. The *Data Validation* dialog box will appear. Select *List* from the drop-down list under *Allow*. In the *Source* text box, type in the names of the departments separated by commas. Click the *OK* button to save the validation selections. By default a drop-down list will appear in the cell to allow the user to select the desired input.

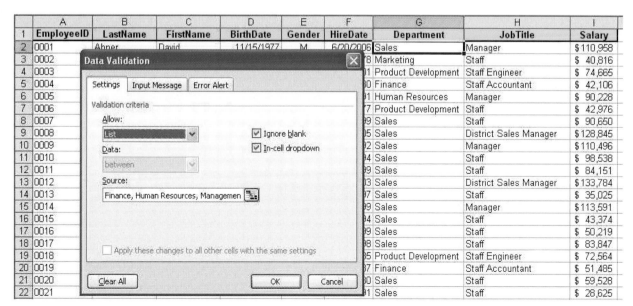

Figure 5-11: To restrict entry to a list of items, type the valid data items into the *Source* text box.

	A	B	C	D	E	F	G	H	I
1	**EmployeeID**	**LastName**	**FirstName**	**BirthDate**	**Gender**	**HireDate**	**Department**	**JobTitle**	**Salary**
2	0001	Abner	David	11/15/1977	M	6/20/2006	Sales	anager	$110,958
3	0002	Butler	Susan	11/16/1967	F	8/13/1978	Finance	aff	$ 40,816
4	0003	Conrad	Michael	9/14/1955	M	12/25/2001	Human Resources	aff Engineer	$ 74,665
5	0004	Davis	Randall	7/15/1947	M	5/25/1980	Management / Marketing	aff Accountant	$ 42,106
6	0005	Edwards	Minnie	3/8/1959	F	11/26/1991	Product Development	anager	$ 90,228
7	0006	Franklin	Margaret	11/25/1979	F	3/15/1977	Sales	aff	$ 42,976
8	0007	Gardner	William	11/15/1968	M	2/7/1999	Sales	Staff	$ 90,650
9	0008	Hilton	Hillery	11/23/1949	F	11/8/2005	Sales	District Sales Manager	$128,845
10	0009	Jameson	Jennifer	1/17/1959	F	11/28/1992	Sales	Manager	$110,496
11	0010	Kelly	Chester	10/28/1968	M	1/3/1994	Sales	Staff	$ 98,538
12	0011	Zahn	Geoffrey	9/6/1952	M	3/4/1999	Sales	Staff	$ 84,151

Figure 5-12: When data entries are restricted to a list, permitted values appear in a drop-down list.

Copy the data validation to the remaining cells in the column. Use the *Paste Special* option and select *Validation* from the *Paste Special* dialog box. Data validation can be pasted to all cells in the column, even rows that are blank below the last data row.

Quick Tip!

A more efficient way to apply data validation to a column, including blank rows, is to select the entire column before applying validation. After applying validation to the entire column, clear the validation from the column header cell.

Name a Data Validation List

In some cases, it may be necessary to add new acceptable values to a data validation list. For easier maintenance of the validation list, specify the list of valid values on a reference worksheet. In order to access a validation range of values on another worksheet,

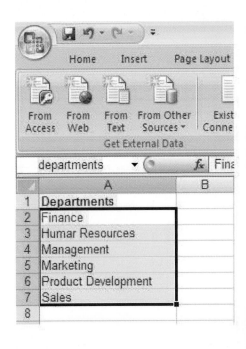
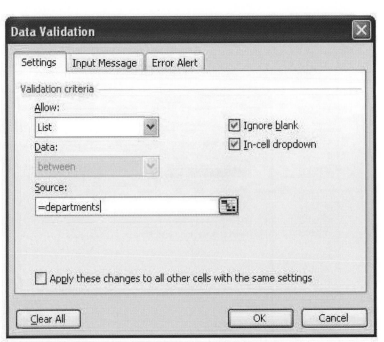

Figure 5-13: When data entries are restricted to a list, permitted values appear in a drop-down list.

you will need to define a name for the range of values (excluding any label cells). In the *Source* text box of the *Data Validation* dialog box, type "=range_name" (without quotes). For the Employee list, the list of department names may be named "departments". In that case, you would enter "=departments" (without quotes) in the *Source* text box. (See Figure 5-13.)

To add a new department to the list, insert a row between the top and bottom rows of data. Type the new department name into the inserted cell. Select the range name from the Name Box to be sure it includes the new department name in the list. When values are inserted within the named range, the range automatically adjusts to include the added cells. You can add the new department to the bottom row of the list, but you will need to edit the range definition in order to update the cell range reference. To edit the cell range of a named range, open the *Name Manager* dialog box by selecting **Formulas(tab)→Defined Names(group)→Name Manager** from the ribbon. Select the range name to edit from the list and click the *Edit* button at the top of the dialog box. The *Edit Name* dialog box will appear. The cell range may be edited in the *Edit Name* dialog box.

Displaying Records in a Data Form

Large lists of data in Excel are sometimes difficult to navigate because you constantly have to scroll up and down and back and forward to enter or review data. Excel offers a list management feature that allows the user to view one record at a time in a form that floats over the worksheet. The *Data Form* feature allows the user to view, enter, delete, or modify records in a list.

In Excel 2007 many commands do not appear on the ribbon in its default view. The *Data Form* is one of those commands. To access these commands, the user will need to add the command to the *Quick Access Toolbar*. To locate the *Data Form* tool, select the **Office Button→Excel Options→Customize**. Select the option to display the *Commands Not in the Ribbon* from the drop at the top of the left list box. Select *Form . . .* from the list and click the *Add* button to add it to the Quick Access Toolbar. Other common commands that don't appear on the ribbon, but can be added to the Quick Access Toolbar are *Undo, Repeat, Speech tool,* and *AutoCorrect* options.

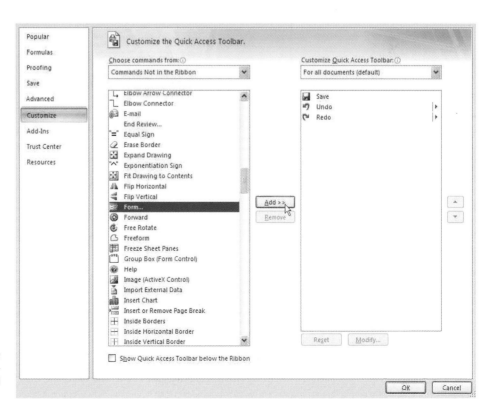

Figure 5-14: Add the *Data Form* to the *Quick Access Toolbar* by selecting the **Office Button→Excel Options→Customize**.

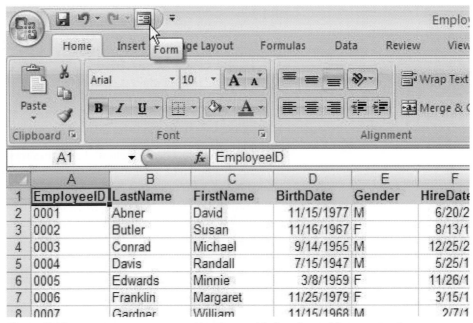

Figure 5-15: The *Data Form* command has been added to the *Quick Access Toolbar*.

To access the *Data Form*, select the *Form* icon on the *Quick Access Toolbar*.

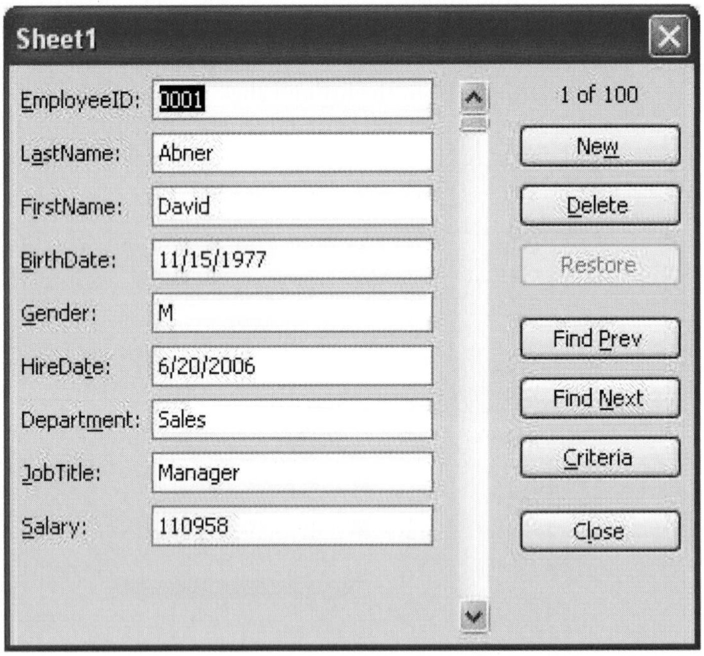

Figure 5-16: Use a *Data Form* for viewing, entering, modifying, or deleting records from a list.

Practice 5-1

Open practice file Employees_ch5-1.xlsx. Practice using the *Data Form* to perform the following actions:

1. *Enter a New Record:* Click the *New* button on the *Data Form*. Type a value into the form field. Use the Tab key to move to the next field. When all fields are filled, use

the Enter key to save the entry. The new record is written to the next blank row at the bottom of the list and the cursor is placed in the first form field to begin the next entry. The new record is also saved when the scroll bar is moved to the previous record (scrolled up). Note: When entering numbers to be stored as text using the *Data Form*, be sure to precede the number with an apostrophe when entering it into a *Data Form* field. Even if the column to which the data is added has already been formatted, the number will not appear as text unless it is preceded by an apostrophe in the *Data Form* field.

2. *Delete a Record:* Scroll or query (see the "Query Records" *Data Form* topic) to locate the record to delete then click the *Delete* button. The user is prompted to confirm the deletion before the record is permanently removed from the list.

3. *Modify a Record:* Scroll or query to select the record to modify. Modify the desired fields and use the Enter key to save the changes. The changes will be saved and the *Data Form* will move to the next record in the list. If multiple records are altered in one session, the scroll bar may be also be used to move off of the current record (scroll up or down) and save the changes.

4. *Query Records:* The *Data Form* offers a way to view only the records that match criteria specified by the user. The criteria may include text or numeric, or logical conditions. For example, you can view all employees whose last name begins with "s," all employees in the "Sales" department, or all employees whose salary is greater than $50,000. To filter the records to view, click the *Criteria* button on the Data Form. The fields will be cleared. Enter the criteria into the desired text boxes. Query criteria may be entered for multiple fields at once. For example, you can query for all employees whose last name begins with "s" AND all employees in the "Sales" department AND all employees whose salary is greater than $50,000. After the criteria have been entered, use the *Find Next* or *Find Prev* button to view records that match the criteria.

Navigating an Excel List

In addition to selecting single cells or cell ranges within a list using the mouse pointer, Excel provides several keyboard shortcuts for navigating a list of data. (See Table 5-1.)

Freezing Panes

In many cases, Excel lists are large and extend past the boundaries of the computer monitor screen. When scrolling down the list, the column header row may scroll off the top of the screen. When scrolling to the right to view more columns, row header columns, such as identification numbers, or customer names, may scroll off the screen to the left. The *Freeze Pane* feature allows you to keep column and row labels in place while scrolling through all columns and rows of data.

Freeze Pane Steps

1. Make the cell active that is immediately to the right of the row labels and immediately beneath the column labels. This is the first cell you would like to remain in place when scrolling.
2. From the ribbon, select **View(tab)→Window(group)→Freeze Panes**. The rows above and columns to the left of the active cell remain in place while the cursor is moved to other rows and columns.
3. To unfreeze the panes, select **View(tab)→Window(group)→Unfreeze Panes** from the ribbon.

Table 5-1: Keyboard shortcuts for navigating an Excel list

Key or Key Combination	Action
Enter	Moves to the next cell down (This direction option can be changed by selecting the **Office Button**→**Excel Options**→**Advanced**→**Editing options**. From the drop-down list for that option, select the direction for the Enter key action.)
Tab	(1) Move right to the next cell (2) If the last cell in a list row is the active cell, the *Tab* key will move the cursor to the first cell of the next row. The list must be defined as a "table" to activate this navigation feature.
Shift + Tab	(1) Move left to the next cell (2) If the first cell in a list row (other than in the first row) is the active cell, the key combination key will move the cursor to the last cell of the previous row. The list must be defined as a "table" to activate this navigation feature.
Home	Move to the beginning of a row
End	Move to the last filled cell in a row
Ctrl + Home	Move to the first cell (left upper) in the worksheet
Ctrl + End	Move to the intersection of the last row and last column (to the right) of the worksheet that currently contains data, or has contained data
Ctrl + arrow keys	Move to the edge (last cell) of the list in the direction of the arrow
Ctrl + a	Once to select the current list (when the active cell is inside the list), twice to select the current list and its summary rows, three times to select the entire worksheet. (If the active cell is not inside a list, the key combination will select the entire worksheet the first time it is selected. If the list contains no summary rows, the key combination will select the entire worksheet on the second click.)
Ctrl + *	Select the list surrounding the active cell. (Make a cell in the list the active cell before applying this shortcut.)
Ctrl + Shift + arrow keys	Select cells in a column from (and including) the active cell to the edge of the spreadsheet in the direction of the arrow
Ctrl + d	Copies a formula from the cell above to the selected cell(s) below in the same column
Ctrl + ; (semi-colon)	Insert the current date
Ctrl + : (colon)	Insert the current time only (no date)
Alt + arrow down	Display a drop-down list of values from a list box in the active cell
Ctrl + Shift + F3	Create named ranges from row and/or column labels
Ctrl + t	Converts the current region (around the active cell) to a table. It launches the Create Table dialog box.
Esc	Cancel a cell entry that is in progress

In the example Employee list, it would be helpful to freeze the column header row and the three columns on the left (that identify each employee record). To freeze those cells while others scroll, select the first cell (upper left) that you want to scroll then apply the *Freeze Panes* command.

Figure 5-17: To freeze the top row and first three columns, select cell D2 before applying the Freeze Panes feature. Lower records and columns right of the selected cell are scrolled into view while column and row header cells remain stationary.

	A	B	C	H	I	J
1	EmployeeID	LastName	FirstName	JobTitle	Salary	
95	0094	Powers	Jacob	Staff	$ 69,706	
96	0095	Walker	Vance	District Sales Manager	$ 133,856	
97	0096	Tidwell	Lorna	Manager	$ 128,552	
98	0097	Tripp	Lacey	Staff	$ 37,064	
99	0098	Wiggins	Janice	District Sales Manager	$ 132,215	
100	0099	Allen	Lance	Staff	$ 71,132	
101	0100	Lancaster	Jacqueline	Staff	$ 72,821	
102						
103						
104						
105						

Two automatic options exist for freezing panes, one for freezing the first column only and another for freezing the first row only. Only one of these two automatic options may be applied at once. For freezing both the first column and first row, use the first technique described above to freeze panes.

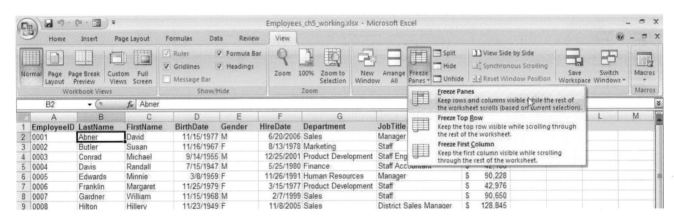

Figure 5-18: Three options exist for freezing worksheet panes for scrolling.

Splitting an Excel Window

If you want to view different parts of the same worksheet on the same screen, you may split the program window into two or four partitions and show each worksheet portion in a separate window partition. Although the window is split into sections, each section does not scroll vertically and horizontally entirely independently. When the split results in two horizontal partitions, the two window portions scroll independently vertically, but move together horizontally. When the split results in four partitions, each vertical pair (top and bottom on one side) of partitions scroll together horizontally, but scroll independently vertically. In a four-way split each horizontal pair of partitions (side by side on top or bottom) scroll together vertically, but scroll independently horizontally.

Practice 5-2

Split the window of the employee list into **two** horizontal partitions. Split the list so that the first six rows are in the top partition.

1. Open the Excel workbook "Employees_ch5-2.xlsx."
2. Select the cell where you would like the screen to split. It will split above and to the left of the active cell. To split the window into two partitions only, select the first cell in first column/row you wish to display in the right/bottom pane.

3. From the ribbon, select **View(tab)→Window(group)→Split**. Select the same command once more to remove the split window.

	A	B	C	D	E	F	G	H	
1	**EmployeeID**	**LastName**	**FirstName**	**BirthDate**	**Gender**	**HireDate**	**Department**	**JobTitle**	
2	1	Abner	David	11/15/1977	M	6/20/2006	Sales	Manager	
3	2	Butler	Susan	11/16/1967	F	8/13/1978	Marketing	Staff	
4	3	Conrad	Michael	9/14/1955	M	12/25/2001	Product Development	Staff Engineer	
5	4	Davis	Randall	7/15/1947	M	5/25/1980	Finance	Staff Accountant	
6	5	Edwards	Minnie	3/8/1959	F	11/26/1991	Human Resources	Manager	
98	97	Tripp	Lacey	10/14/1966	F	8/7/2001	Marketing	Staff	
99	98	Wiggins	Janice	5/4/1966	F	10/28/1982	Sales	District Sales Manager	
100	99	Allen	Lance	7/21/1971	M	4/30/1977	Sales	Staff	
101	100	Lancaster	Jacqueline	10/27/1965	F	12/6/1982	Sales	Staff	

Sheet1 / Sheet2 / Sheet3 /

Figure 5-19: Using the *Split Window* feature with two partitions, lower records are scrolled into view while column header cells remain stationary. Note that the cell selected for this split was A7.

Practice 5-3

Split the window of the employee list into **four** partitions. Split the list so that the first five rows are in the top partitions and the first four columns are in the left partitions.

1. Open the Excel workbook "Employees_ch5-3.xlsx." Make the cell active where you would like the screen to split. To split the window into four partitions, select the cell that is below row 6 and to the right of column 4 (cell E7).
2. From the ribbon, select **View(tab)→Window(group)→Split**. Select the same command once more to remove the split window.

	A	B	C	D	F	G	H	I	
1	**EmployeeID**	**LastName**	**FirstName**	**BirthDate**	**HireDate**	**Department**	**JobTitle**	**Salary**	
2	1	Abner	David	11/15/1977	6/20/2006	Sales	Manager	$ 110,958	
3	2	Butler	Susan	11/16/1967	8/13/1978	Marketing	Staff	$ 40,816	
4	3	Conrad	Michael	9/14/1955	12/25/2001	Product Development	Staff Engineer	$ 74,665	
5	4	Davis	Randall	7/15/1947	5/25/1980	Finance	Staff Accountant	$ 42,106	
97	96	Tidwell	Lorna	2/22/1966	6/21/1993	Sales	Manager	$ 128,552	
98	97	Tripp	Lacey	10/14/1966	8/7/2001	Marketing	Staff	$ 37,064	
99	98	Wiggins	Janice	5/4/1966	10/28/1982	Sales	District Sales Manager	$ 132,215	
100	99	Allen	Lance	7/21/1971	4/30/1977	Sales	Staff	$ 71,132	
101	100	Lancaster	Jacqueline	10/27/1965	12/6/1982	Sales	Staff	$ 72,821	

Sheet1 / Sheet2 / She

Figure 5-20: Using the *Split Window* feature with four partitions: Note that the cell selected for this split is E7.

Tiling Multiple Windows within One Workbook

For viewing different parts of a worksheet or workbook, new windows can be added to the program screen and each new window may view a different part of the workbook, including different worksheets. When multiple widows are used, each window can be navigated entirely independently of the others.

Practice 5-4

Add a new window that shows the same contents of the present window.

1. Open the Excel workbook "Employees_ch5-4.xlsx." From the ribbon, select **View(tab)→Window(group)→New Window**. A new window will open with the exact contents of the current window.

2. Repeat step one to add multiple windows. Each new window will be labeled with the file name, then a colon, then the window number. For example, the first new window added to a workbook named "Employees_ch5-4.xlsx" will be entitled "Employees_ch5-4.xlsx:2." The original window will be entitled "Employees_ch5-4.xlsx:1."

3. To select the newly added window select **View(tab)→Window(group)→Switch Windows→select new window title from the drop-down list** on the ribbon. Alternately, you can *Minimize* the current window and *Restore* the newly added window from the program screen.

4. Resize or tile the newly added windows manually or automatically using some of Excel's other *Window* menu options. (See Figure 5-21.)

5. To close newly added windows, use the same window close icon ⊠ used for closing any Excel window.

Additional Windows Options

Arranging Windows on the Screen

To automatically tile multiple windows on the program screen, select **Windows→ Arrange** from the ribbon. The *Arrange Windows* dialog box will appear. Use the option buttons in the dialog box to select the window arrangement options.

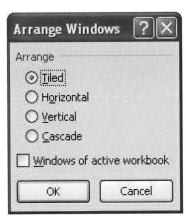

Figure 5-21: Window arrangement options in the Arrange Windows dialog box.

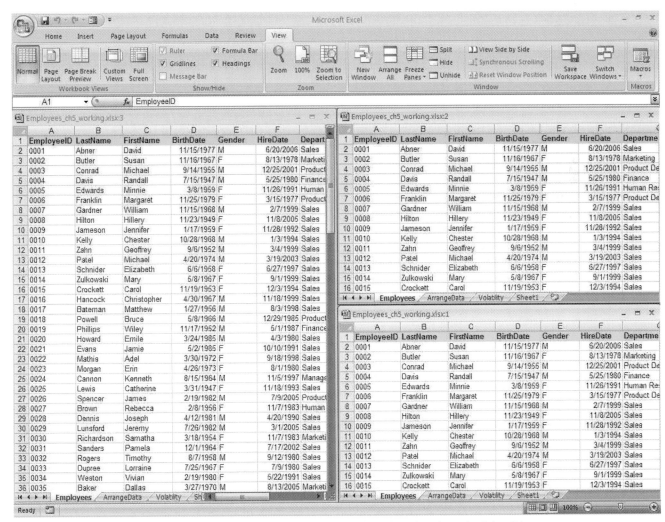

Figure 5-22: Windows arranged as *Tiled*. The *Window* task group is included on the *View* tab of the ribbon.

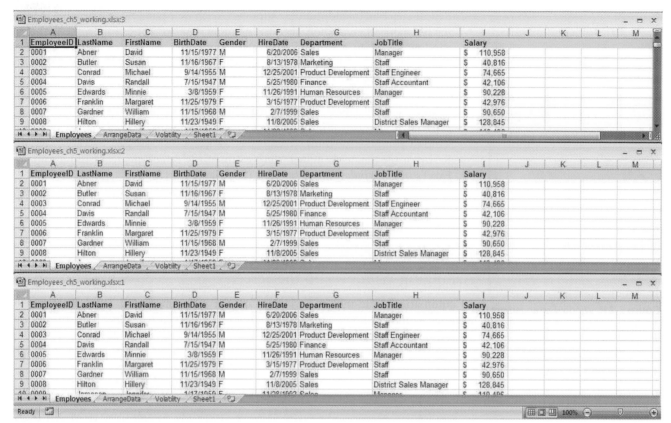

Figure 5-23: Windows arranged as *Horizontal*

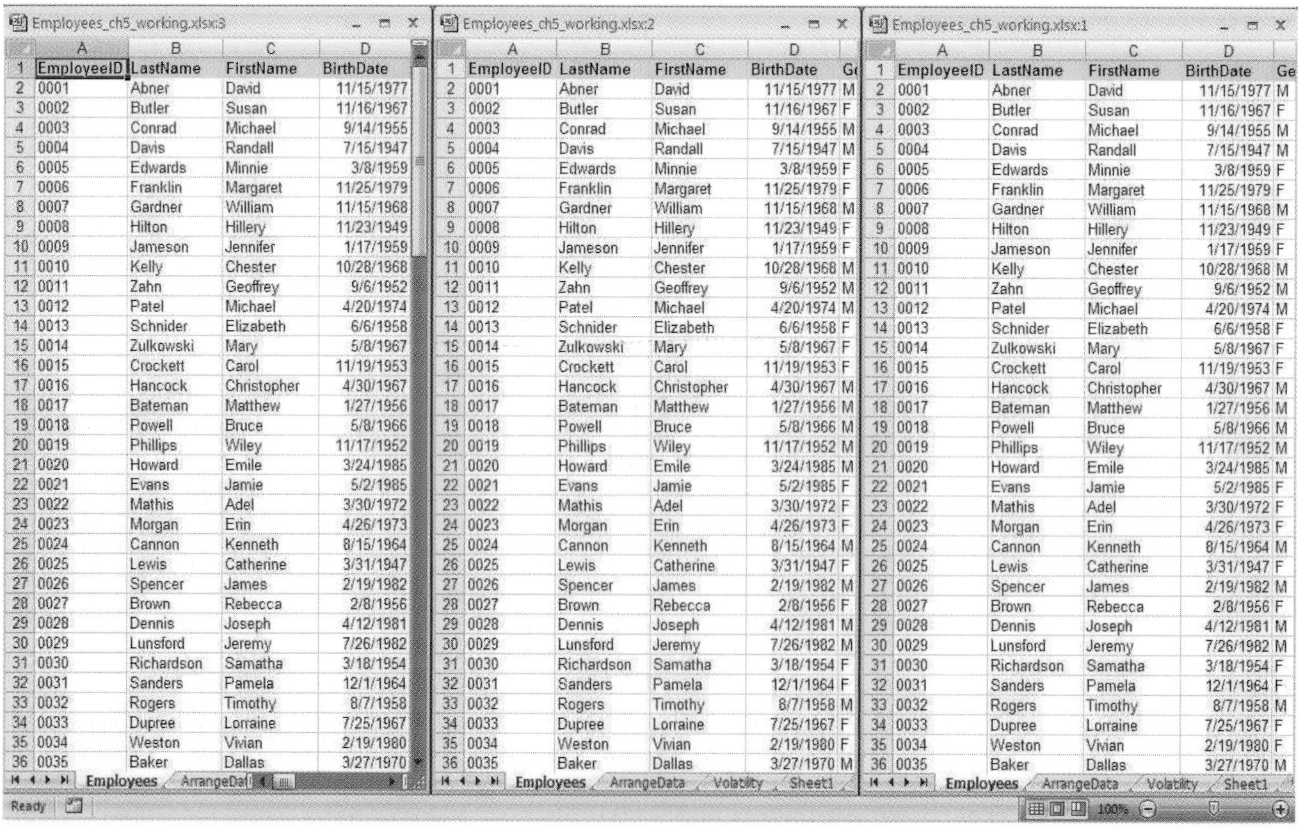

Figure 5-24: Windows arranged as *Vertical*

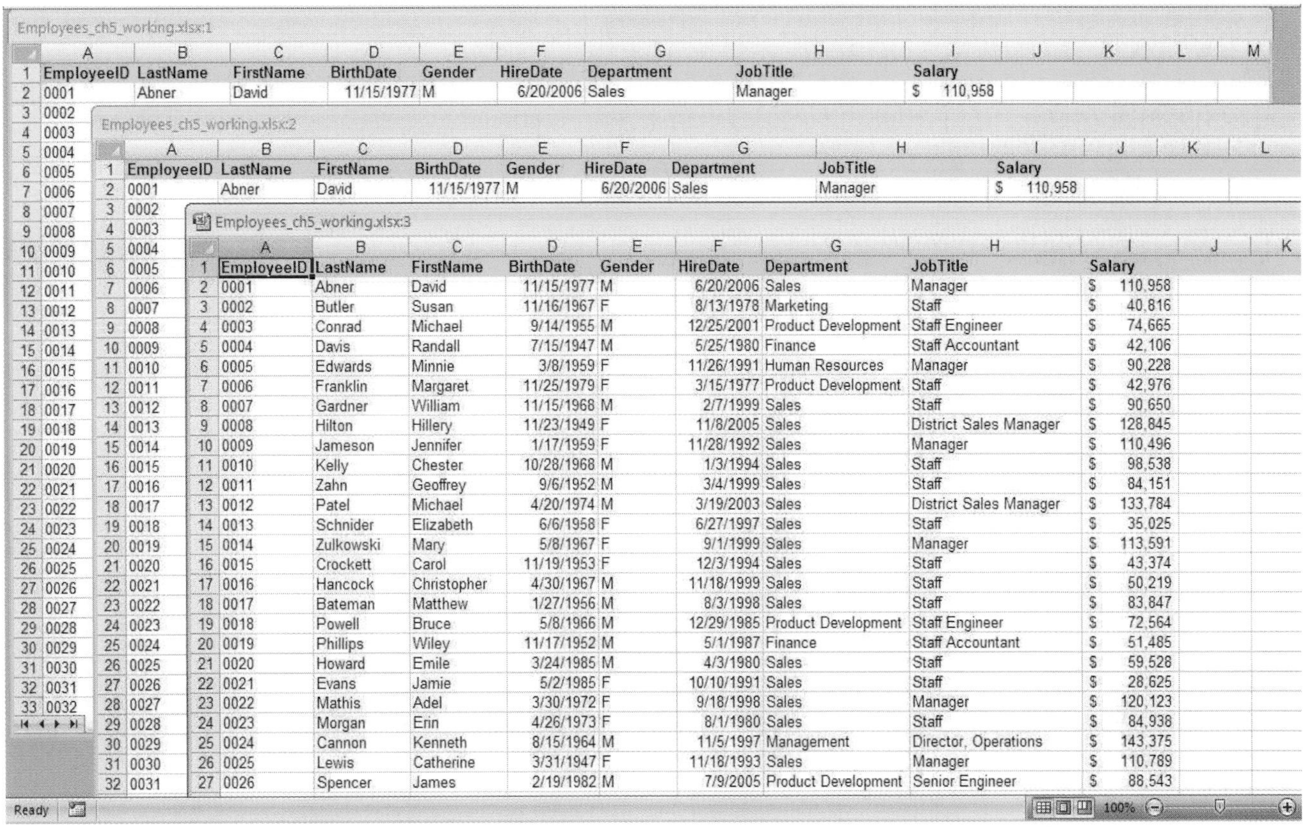

	EmployeeID	LastName	FirstName	BirthDate	Gender	HireDate	Department	JobTitle	Salary
2	0001	Abner	David	11/15/1977	M	6/20/2006	Sales	Manager	$ 110,958
3	0002	Butler	Susan	11/16/1967	F	8/13/1978	Marketing	Staff	$ 40,816
4	0003	Conrad	Michael	9/14/1955	M	12/25/2001	Product Development	Staff Engineer	$ 74,665
5	0004	Davis	Randall	7/15/1947	M	5/25/1980	Finance	Staff Accountant	$ 42,106
6	0005	Edwards	Minnie	3/8/1959	F	11/26/1991	Human Resources	Manager	$ 90,228
7	0006	Franklin	Margaret	11/25/1979	F	3/15/1977	Product Development	Staff	$ 42,976
8	0007	Gardner	William	11/15/1968	M	2/7/1999	Sales	Staff	$ 90,650
9	0008	Hilton	Hillery	11/23/1949	F	11/8/2005	Sales	District Sales Manager	$ 128,845
10	0009	Jameson	Jennifer	1/17/1959	F	11/28/1992	Sales	Manager	$ 110,496
11	0010	Kelly	Chester	10/28/1968	M	1/3/1994	Sales	Staff	$ 98,538
12	0011	Zahn	Geoffrey	9/6/1952	M	3/4/1999	Sales	Staff	$ 84,151
13	0012	Patel	Michael	4/20/1974	M	3/19/2003	Sales	District Sales Manager	$ 133,784
14	0013	Schnider	Elizabeth	6/6/1958	F	6/27/1997	Sales	Staff	$ 35,025
15	0014	Zulkowski	Mary	5/8/1967	F	9/1/1999	Sales	Manager	$ 113,591
16	0015	Crockett	Carol	11/19/1953	F	12/3/1994	Sales	Staff	$ 43,374
17	0016	Hancock	Christopher	4/30/1967	M	11/18/1999	Sales	Staff	$ 50,219
18	0017	Bateman	Matthew	1/27/1956	M	8/3/1998	Sales	Staff	$ 83,847
19	0018	Powell	Bruce	5/8/1966	M	12/29/1985	Product Development	Staff Engineer	$ 72,564
20	0019	Phillips	Wiley	11/17/1952	M	5/1/1987	Finance	Staff Accountant	$ 51,485
21	0020	Howard	Emile	3/24/1985	M	4/3/1980	Sales	Staff	$ 59,528
22	0021	Evans	Jamie	5/2/1985	F	10/10/1991	Sales	Staff	$ 28,625
23	0022	Mathis	Adel	3/30/1972	F	9/18/1998	Sales	Manager	$ 120,123
24	0023	Morgan	Erin	4/26/1973	F	8/1/1980	Sales	Staff	$ 84,938
25	0024	Cannon	Kenneth	8/15/1964	M	11/5/1997	Management	Director, Operations	$ 143,375
26	0025	Lewis	Catherine	3/31/1947	F	11/18/1993	Sales	Manager	$ 110,789
27	0026	Spencer	James	2/19/1982	M	7/9/2005	Product Development	Senior Engineer	$ 88,543

Figure 5-25: Windows arranged as *Cascade*

Comparing Two Windows Closely on One Screen

Steps to directly compare two windows of the same workbook on one screen:

1. Select one of the windows to compare.
2. Select View(tab)→**Windows**→**View Side by Side** from the ribbon. The *Compare Side by Side* dialog box will open.
3. Select the second window that you wish to compare to the current window. The two windows will tile horizontally unless they were tiled vertically before the *Compare Side by Side* feature was applied.
4. Once the *Compare Side-by-Side* command is executed, two additional options appear on the ribbon.
    a. *Synchronous Scrolling:* By default, when one window is scrolled, the other window scrolls synchronously horizontally or vertically. You can tell the synchronous scrolling is activated because it appears highlighted on the ribbon. To remove *Synchronous Scrolling,* elect *Synchronous Scrolling* again to toggle the feature off.
    b. *Reset Window Position:* If the windows are currently tiled vertically, clicking on the *Reset Window Position* command will change the comparison windows to horizontally tiling.
5. To remove the side-by-side comparison, toggle the View Side by Side command to inactivate it.

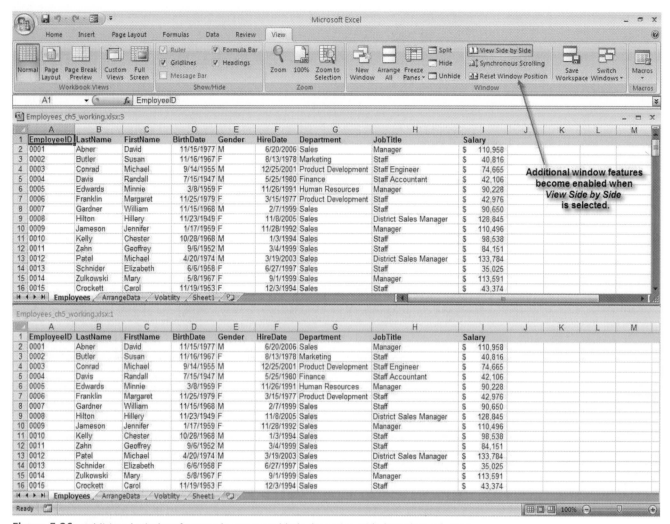

Figure 5-26: Additional window features become enabled when *View Side-by-Side* is selected.

Sorting an Excel List

To sort a list means to rearrange the rows or columns in the order specified by the user. *When a list is sorted, all rows and columns of the original data are included in the newly ordered list.* An Excel list may be sorted based on values in one or more columns or rows. Numeric and text data may be sorted in either ascending (A to Z for text values, low to high for numeric or date values) or descending (Z to A for text values, high to low for numeric or date values) order.

Sorting Rows of a List

Lists are sorted by rows, keeping all fields of each row intact. Rows are sorted based on the relative values in each row for the same column. For example, a list of students may be sorted by student identification numbers, or alternately by their last names. (See Figure 5-27.)

Lists can be sorted by multiple columns at once. Each column's set of values is evaluated in the order specified by the user. For example, a list may be sorted by department first, then by the employees' last names, then by the employees' first names. In this case, the "Department" column would be considered the first *sort key,* the "LastName" column is the second *sort key,* and the "FirstName" is the third *sort key.* In the results in Figure 5-28, all three columns are sorted in ascending order.

	A	B	C	D	E	F	G	H	I
1	EmployeeID	LastName	FirstName	BirthDate	Gender	HireDate	Department	JobTitle	Salary
2	0001	Abner	David	11/15/1977	M	6/20/2006	Sales	Manager	$ 110,958
3	0002	Butler	Susan	11/16/1967	F	8/13/1978	Marketing	Staff	$ 40,816
4	0003	Conrad	Michael	9/14/1955	M	12/25/2001	Product Development	Staff Engineer	$ 74,665
5	0004	Davis	Randall	7/15/1947	M	5/25/1980	Finance	Staff Accountant	$ 42,106
6	0005	Edwards	Minnie	3/8/1959	F	11/26/1991	Human Resources	Manager	$ 90,228
7	0006	Franklin	Margaret	11/25/1979	F	3/15/1977	Product Development	Staff	$ 42,976
8	0007	Gardner	William	11/15/1968	M	2/7/1999	Sales	Staff	$ 90,650
9	0008	Hilton	Hillery	11/23/1949	F	11/8/2005	Sales	District Sales Manager	$ 128,845
10	0009	Jameson	Jennifer	1/17/1959	F	11/28/1992	Sales	Manager	$ 110,496
11	0010	Kelly	Chester	10/28/1968	M	1/3/1994	Sales	Staff	$ 98,538
12	0011	Zahn	Geoffrey	9/6/1952	M	3/4/1999	Sales	Staff	$ 84,151
13	0012	Patel	Michael	4/20/1974	M	3/19/2003	Sales	District Sales Manager	$ 133,784
14	0013	Schnider	Elizabeth	6/6/1958	F	6/27/1997	Sales	Staff	$ 35,025
15	0014	Zulkowski	Mary	5/8/1967	F	9/1/1999	Sales	Manager	$ 113,591
16	0015	Crockett	Carol	11/19/1953	F	12/3/1994	Sales	Staff	$ 43,374
17	0016	Hancock	Christopher	4/30/1967	M	11/18/1999	Sales	Staff	$ 50,219

Figure 5-27: The employee records are sorted by the text values in the EmployeeID column.

	A	B	C	D	E	F	G	H	I
1	EmployeeID	LastName	FirstName	BirthDate	Gender	HireDate	Department	JobTitle	Salary
2	0069	Davis	Paul	4/19/1953	M	12/20/1986	Finance	Senior Accountant	$ 58,138
3	0004	Davis	Randall	7/15/1947	M	5/25/1980	Finance	Staff Accountant	$ 42,106
4	0086	Davis	Victor	5/4/1963	M	5/3/2000	Finance	Manager	$ 58,332
5	0052	Justice	Earlene	2/3/1953	F	12/7/1998	Finance	Senior Accountant	$ 54,902
6	0019	Phillips	Wiley	11/17/1952	M	5/1/1987	Finance	Staff Accountant	$ 51,485
7	0039	Thompson	Dupree	5/16/1966	F	4/13/1980	Finance	Staff Accountant	$ 50,257
8	0091	Brown	McCauley	10/18/1966	M	1/31/1994	Human Resources	Staff	$ 26,087
9	0027	Brown	Rebecca	2/8/1956	F	11/7/1983	Human Resources	Staff	$ 28,523
10	0047	Burnett	Kayla	3/27/1984	F	1/18/1977	Human Resources	Manager	$ 62,742
11	0005	Edwards	Minnie	3/8/1959	F	11/26/1991	Human Resources	Manager	$ 90,228
12	0081	Murray	Stephanie	10/13/1976	F	2/4/1992	Human Resources	Staff	$ 26,948
13	0067	Spears	Jeffrey	5/17/1972	M	9/13/1998	Human Resources	Staff	$ 38,718
14	0024	Cannon	Kenneth	8/15/1964	M	11/5/1997	Management	Director, Operations	$ 143,375
15	0044	Daye	Edmond	6/16/1975	M	9/18/1990	Management	Chief Operating Officer	$ 147,943
16	0060	Reaves	Matthew	1/12/1984	M	2/17/1981	Management	Chief Financial Officer	$ 146,357
17	0042	Walker	Aaron	7/15/1968	M	3/16/1989	Management	Chief Executive Officer	$ 149,278
18	0068	Walker	Marcia	3/14/1984	M	6/8/2006	Management	Chief Informations Officer	$ 146,160
19	0035	Baker	Dallas	3/27/1970	M	8/13/2005	Marketing	Staff	$ 45,005
20	0080	Bullard	Marci	2/1/1984	F	2/12/2002	Marketing	Director	$ 142,556

Figure 5-28: Records are sorted first by the values in the "Department" column, then by "LastName", then by "FirstName".

All columns of a list sort need not be sorted in the same order. For example, "HireDate" may be sorted in descending order (latest hire date first) while "LastName" and "FirstName" are both sorted in ascending order.

	A	B	C	D	E	F	G	H	I
1	EmployeeID	LastName	FirstName	BirthDate	Gender	HireDate	Department	JobTitle	Salary
2	0035	Baker	Dallas	3/27/1970	M	8/24/2006	Marketing	Staff	$ 45,005
3	0058	Baker	Frances	8/13/1952	F	8/24/2006	Sales	Staff	$ 28,242
4	0026	Spencer	James	2/19/1982	M	8/24/2006	Product Development	Senior Engineer	$ 88,543
5	0068	Walker	Marcia	3/14/1984	M	8/24/2006	Management	Chief Informations Officer	$ 146,160
6	0001	Abner	David	11/15/1977	M	6/20/2006	Sales	Manager	$ 110,958
7	0029	Lunsford	Jeremy	7/26/1982	M	5/25/2006	Sales	Manager	$ 110,210
8	0053	Palmer	Justin	4/14/1961	M	5/25/2006	Product Development	Staff	$ 63,310
9	0064	Parker	Nelson	5/1/1968	F	2/13/2006	Sales	Staff	$ 58,350
10	0008	Hilton	Hillery	11/23/1949	F	11/8/2005	Sales	District Sales Manager	$ 128,845
11	0070	Hester	Ralph	7/18/1953	M	10/11/2004	Sales	Staff	$ 74,423
12	0063	O'Connor	George	7/7/1966	F	2/5/2004	Sales	Staff	$ 77,622
13	0090	Milner	Carla	5/16/1952	F	5/11/2003	Sales	Staff	$ 44,649
14	0012	Patel	Michael	4/20/1974	M	3/19/2003	Sales	District Sales Manager	$ 133,784

Figure 5-29: Records are sorted first by the values in the "HireDate" column in descending order showing latest hire dates first. The second sort key is "LastName" (in ascending order), then by "FirstName" (in ascending order).

Steps to Sort Rows:

1. Select a cell in the list.
2. Select **Data(tab)**→**Sort & Filter(group)**→**Sort** from the ribbon. The *Sort* dialog box will appear.
3. If sorting by only one column, select it from the *Sort by* drop-down list. Leave *Values* in the *Sort on* drop-down list and select the desired sort order in the *Order* drop-down list. An appropriate list of options will be presented based on the type of data in the sort column. For example, text data will list options such as *A to Z* and date data will list options such as *Oldest to Newest.*
4. If other columns are desired as sort keys, define successive subordinate sort columns by clicking the *Add Level* button. Another row of drop-down lists will appear preceded by *Then by.* Select the column to sort in the left drop-down list and sort order in the *Order* drop-down list. In Excel 2007 up to 64 columns can be defined as sort fields.
5. If your list has a column header row, make sure the box is checked to the left of *My data has headers* in the Sort dialog box. (Excel most often selects the option automatically based on whether or not it detects a column header row.)
6. Click the *OK* button to close the dialog box and apply the sort options to the list.
7. Use the *Copy Level* button to quickly copy down the set of selections in the previous sort level entry. If all settings are the same except for the column to sort, you need only select the new column in the *Then by* drop-down list.
8. Click the *Delete Level* button to remove the selected sort level selections.

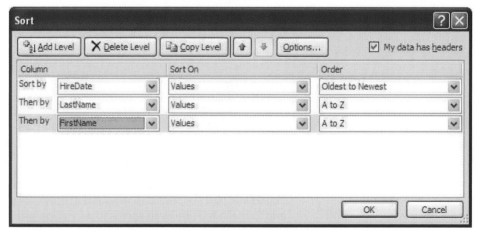

Figure 5-30: *Sort* dialog box shows three levels of sorting. Up to 64 sort levels may be defined.

Quick Tip!

To sort by only one column, select a cell within the column you wish to sort and click either the *Sort A to Z* or the *Sort Z to A* icon on the *Sort & Filter* task group of the *Data* tab of the ribbon. (Make sure the column header row is formatted differently from the data rows so it will not be included in the sorted rows.)

Custom Sort Order

When sorting list data by rows (or columns), the *Normal* sort order for text is alphabetical (ascending or descending) and for numbers is in numeric order (ascending or descending). In some cases, pure alphabetical or numeric order is not suitable for the particular list. For instance, suppose a list of maintenance tasks are to be performed on a weekly basis on a certain day of the week. One column will contain the day(s) of the week for the listed task. The users want to sort the list so that all tasks scheduled for Monday are listed first, then Tuesday's tasks, etc. If the list is sorted on the Weekday column using the *Normal* sort order, the days of the week will be sorted alphabetically since they are text values. The user can specify a custom order for the sort that will order the weekdays as they fall in the week (Monday, Tuesday, etc.).

The example below is a partial list of maintenance tasks required by OSHA for dry cleaning businesses. Some tasks are performed daily while others are performed weekly. It would be easier to make sure all tasks are performed on the correct day if the workers could view the tasks by the weekday on which the owner has assigned them.

	A	B	C
1	**Task**	**Weekday**	
2	Launder the lint bag.	Friday	
3	Measure PERC in the exhaust system.	Wednesday	
4	Measure the exhaust temperature of the refrigerated condenser.	Wednesday	
5	Perform leak checks on hose and pipe connections, fittings, couplings, and valves.	Tuesday	
6	Check the separator tank of the water seperator and perform leak checks.	Tuesday	
7	Check filters and filter housings seals and gaskets.	Thursday	
8	Check seals and gaskets muck cooker for liquid and vapor leaks.	Thursday	
9	Check seals and gaskets of the distallation unit.	Thursday	
10	Check door seatings and gaskets of machine cylinder for liquid and vapor leaks.	Monday	
11	Check door seatings and gaskets of machine cylinder for liquid and vapor leaks.	Tuesday	
12	Check door seatings and gaskets of machine cylinder for liquid and vapor leaks.	Wednesday	
13	Check door seatings and gaskets of machine cylinder for liquid and vapor leaks.	Thursday	
14	Check door seatings and gaskets of machine cylinder for liquid and vapor leaks.	Friday	
15	Check the button trap for lid leaks.	Monday	
16	Check the button trap for lid leaks.	Tuesday	
17	Check the button trap for lid leaks.	Wednesday	
18	Check the button trap for lid leaks.	Thursday	
19	Check the button trap for lid leaks.	Friday	
20	Clean button trap strainer and lint bag.	Monday	
21	Clean button trap strainer and lint bag.	Tuesday	
22	Clean button trap strainer and lint bag.	Wednesday	
23	Clean button trap strainer and lint bag.	Thursday	
24	Clean button trap strainer and lint bag.	Friday	
25	Desorb the carbon absorber.	Monday	

Figure 5-31: Maintenance tasks for a dry cleaning business. Some tasks must be performed daily, while others are performed weekly.

Steps to Apply a Custom Sort Order:

1. Select a cell in the list.
2. Select **Data(tab)**→**Sort & Filter(group)**→**Sort** from the ribbon. The *Sort* dialog box will appear.
3. Select column *Weekday* for the sort column. Leave *Values* in the *Sort on* box.
4. Select *Custom List . . .* from *Order* drop-down list. The *Custom Lists* dialog box will appear.
5. Select the list in the left list box by which you wish to sort (*Sunday, Monday, Tuesday,* etc.)
6. Click the *OK* button to close the *Custom Lists* dialog box.
7. Click the *OK* button to close the *Sort* dialog box.

	A	B
1	**Task**	**Weekday**
2	Check door seatings and gaskets of machine cylinder for liquid and vapor leaks.	Monday
3	Check the button trap for lid leaks.	Monday
4	Clean button trap strainer and lint bag.	Monday
5	Desorb the carbon absorber.	Monday
6	Dispose of contaminated water from the water seperator.	Monday
7	Rake out the still of the distallation unit.	Monday
8	Perform leak checks on hose and pipe connections, fittings, couplings, and valves.	Tuesday
9	Check the separator tank of the water seperator and perform leak checks.	Tuesday
10	Check door seatings and gaskets of machine cylinder for liquid and vapor leaks.	Tuesday
11	Check the button trap for lid leaks.	Tuesday
12	Clean button trap strainer and lint bag.	Tuesday
13	Desorb the carbon absorber.	Tuesday
14	Dispose of contaminated water from the water seperator.	Tuesday
15	Rake out the still of the distallation unit.	Tuesday
16	Measure PERC in the exhaust system.	Wednesday
17	Measure the exhaust temperature of the refrigerated condenser.	Wednesday
18	Check door seatings and gaskets of machine cylinder for liquid and vapor leaks.	Wednesday
19	Check the button trap for lid leaks.	Wednesday
20	Clean button trap strainer and lint bag.	Wednesday
21	Desorb the carbon absorber.	Wednesday
22	Dispose of contaminated water from the water seperator.	Wednesday
23	Rake out the still of the distallation unit.	Wednesday
24	Check filters and filter housings seals and gaskets.	Thursday
25	Check seals and gaskets muck cooker for liquid and vapor leaks.	Thursday
26	Check seals and gaskets of the distallation unit.	Thursday
27	Check door seatings and gaskets of machine cylinder for liquid and vapor leaks.	Thursday
28	Check the button trap for lid leaks.	Thursday
29	Clean button trap strainer and lint bag.	Thursday
30	Desorb the carbon absorber.	Thursday
31	Dispose of contaminated water from the water seperator.	Thursday
32	Rake out the still of the distallation unit.	Thursday
33	Launder the lint bag.	Friday
34	Check door seatings and gaskets of machine cylinder for liquid and vapor leaks.	Friday
35	Check the button trap for lid leaks.	Friday
36	Clean button trap strainer and lint bag.	Friday

Figure 5-32: Maintenance tasks sorted by Weekday which is a custom sort option.

The custom ordered list contains weekend days as well as weekdays. If no weekend days appear in the column to sort, the weekdays will still be sorted in the correct order.

Steps to Add a Custom Sort List:

a. With the *Custom List* dialog box open, make sure *NEW LIST* is selected in the left list box
b. Type the new list items into the right list box. Put each new list item on a separate line in the list box using the *Enter* key.
c. When all items are specified for the list, click the *Add* button.
d. Now you may select the new list for the sort order.

Sorting Columns of a List

It is less common to sort lists by columns, but there are applications in which that option is useful. For example, columns of financial performance data might be imported such that the columns are not in order as the months fall in a year. The columns may be rearranged in month order while keeping the row fields intact.

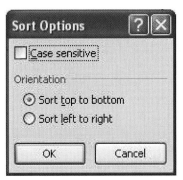

Figure 5-33: Change the sort orientation from rows to columns by selecting *Sort left to right* in the *Sort Options* dialog box.

Steps to Sort Columns in a List:

1. Select a cell within the list.
2. Select **Data(tab)**→**Sort & Filter(group)**→**Sort** from the ribbon. The *Sort* dialog box will appear.
3. Click the *Options* button. The *Sort Options* dialog box will appear.
4. In the *Orientation* section of the dialog box, select *Sort left to right*. (The default selection for this option is *Sort top to bottom*). Click the *OK* button to close the *Sort Options* dialog box.
5. Click the *OK* button to close the *Sort* dialog box and complete the sort operation.

Add Subtotals to List Data

One way to summarize data in an Excel list is to add subtotals to the list. "Subtotal" implies that an aggregate function is applied to a subset of the list's rows or columns. Aggregate functions perform a summary operation on a group of fields and return only one value. Examples of *aggregate functions* include SUM, AVERAGE, COUNT, COUNTA, MAX, and MIN. Some aggregate functions, such as SUM, and AVERAGE may be applied only to numeric values. Other aggregate functions, such as COUNTA, may be applied to either numeric or text values.

Subtotals are usually applied to a range of cells in one column (the calculated column) that have a common value in the same column or in a different column (the "group by" column). For example, you can average employees' salaries for each department by grouping the records by department and applying the subtotal function to the "Salary" column. For each unique value of department, a subtotal value will be returned.

Excel provides two options for calculating subtotals for a list column.

1. The SUBTOTAL function.
2. The *Subtotal* command on the *Data* tab.

The *Subtotal* command on the *Data* tab is the method of choice for most Excel users. It works automatically on a properly structured list. The SUBTOTAL function is applied manually giving the user more control over the summary calculation. The SUBTOTAL function does not restrict the display of subtotals to the list itself, but allows them to be displayed in a range outside the list, even on a different worksheet or workbook.

Using the SUBTOTAL Function

The SUBTOTAL function will apply one of 11 different summary operations to a range of cells. It is designed to work only on vertical ranges of cells (columns), not on horizontal ranges (rows). When the SUBTOTAL function is applied manually, it is generally entered into a cell outside the list range, perhaps even on another worksheet. The syntax of the SUBTOTAL function:

=SUBTOTAL(function_num, ref, [ref, ref, etc.])

The *function_num* argument is a constant that represents the aggregate function to apply to the cell range represented by the *ref* argument. The *function_num* constants are listed in the following table along with the function associated with each constant value.

Table 5-2: Argument value options for the SUBTOTAL function

Function_num Argument Value (includes hidden rows)	Aggregate Function Applied	Function_num Argument Value (ignores hidden rows)
1	AVERAGE	101
2	COUNT	102
3	COUNTA	103
4	MAX	104
5	MIN	105
6	PRODUCT	106
7	STDEV	107
8	STDDEVP	108
9	SUM	109
10	VAR	110
11	VARP	111

Up to 254 cell references may be included in the subtotal. The references may be single cells or multi-cell ranges. To apply the SUBTOTAL function, enter the function into a cell outside the list range. The cell ranges to include in the subtotal may be typed into the function argument list or selected using the mouse pointer. The cell ranges to include need not be contiguous.

When summarizing list data, the calculated column may or may not be the same column that is "grouped". For example, we can count the number of employees that have each job title. In this subtotal, we are grouping on the "JobTitle" column and also counting the occurrences within each unique job title in the same column, so the calculated column and the grouped column are the same.

If we want to calculate the average salary for each department, the "Department" column is grouped and the "Salary" column is calculated. For each unique department value (department name), the corresponding salary is included in the average subtotal calculation. In this example, the "Department" column is the grouped column and the "Salary" column is the calculated column.

Using the SUBTOTAL function is more efficient when the values in the grouping column are grouped together in consecutive rows. To group rows, sort the list (in any order) by the grouping column. By sorting the grouping column, you need only enter one range of cells as a *ref* argument to the SUBTOTAL function.

Practice 5-5

Calculate the average salary for employees who have the same job title.

1. Open the Excel workbook "Employees_ch5-5.xlsx."
2. Sort the records in the list by the "JobTitle" column (in any order).

3. Use the SUBTOTAL function to average the salaries for each job title.
  a. Enter a formula for each unique job title. Select the cells to include in each job title "group."
  b. Apply appropriate labels to the subtotals.

	C	D	E	F	G	H	I	J	K	L	M
1	FirstName	BirthDate	Gender	HireDate	Department	JobTitle	Salary				
2	Magan	4/10/1956	F	4/2/1994	Product Development	Chief Engineer	$135,493		Avearge Salary for	Chief Engineer	$135,493.00
3	Aaron	7/15/1968	M	3/16/1989	Management	Chief Executive Officer	$149,278				
4	Matthew	1/12/1984	M	2/17/1981	Management	Chief Financial Officer	$146,357		Avearge Salary for	Chief Financial Officer	$147,817.50
5	Marcia	3/14/1984	M	6/8/2006	Management	Chief Informations Officer	$146,160		Avearge Salary for	Chief Informations Officer	$146,160.00
6	Edmond	6/16/1975	M	9/18/1990	Management	Chief Operating Officer	$147,943		Avearge Salary for	Chief Operating Officer	$147,943.00
7	Mickey	5/8/1955	M	1/17/1995	Product Development	Director	$142,841				
8	Kevin	11/23/1958	M	5/25/1984	Sales	Director	$141,792				
9	Marci	2/1/1984	F	2/12/2002	Marketing	Director	$142,556		Avearge Salary for	Director	$142,396.33
10	Kenneth	8/15/1964	M	11/5/1997	Management	Director, Operations	$143,375		Avearge Salary for	Director, Operations	$143,375.00
11	Hillery	11/23/1949	F	11/8/2005	Sales	District Sales Manager	$128,845				
12	Michael	4/20/1974	M	3/19/2003	Sales	District Sales Manager	$133,784				
13	Ruffus	4/5/1959	M	12/18/1993	Sales	District Sales Manager	$132,470				
14	Raleigh	3/30/1952	M	6/19/1989	Sales	District Sales Manager	$134,092				
15	Vance	9/27/1957	M	3/28/1982	Sales	District Sales Manager	$133,856				
16	Janice	5/4/1966	F	10/28/1982	Sales	District Sales Manager	$132,215		Avearge Salary for	District Sales Manager	$132,543.67
17	David	11/15/1977	M	6/20/2006	Sales	Manager	$110,958				

Figure 5-34: Average salaries for each job title using the SUBTOTAL function.

Practice 5-6: (Continued from Practice 5-5)

Calculate the number of employees who work in each department.

4. Sort the "Department" column (in any order).
5. Use the SUBTOTAL function to count employees for each department.
  a. Enter a formula for each department
  b. Be sure to use the correct "count" function for counting non-numeric values.
  c. Apply appropriate labels to the subtotals

	C	D	E	F	G	H	I	J	K	L	M
1	FirstName	BirthDate	Gender	HireDate	Department	JobTitle	Salary				
2	Victor	5/4/1963	M	5/3/2000	Finance	Manager	$ 58,332				
3	Earlene	2/3/1953	F	12/7/1998	Finance	Senior Accountant	$ 54,902				
4	Paul	4/19/1953	M	12/20/1986	Finance	Senior Accountant	$ 58,138				
5	Randall	7/15/1947	M	5/25/1980	Finance	Staff Accountant	$ 42,106				
6	Wiley	11/17/1952	M	5/1/1987	Finance	Staff Accountant	$ 51,485				
7	Dupree	5/16/1966	F	4/13/1980	Finance	Staff Accountant	$ 50,257		Number of employee in	Finance	6
8	Minnie	3/8/1959	F	11/26/1991	Human Resources	Manager	$ 90,228				
9	Kayla	3/27/1984	F	1/18/1977	Human Resources	Manager	$ 62,742				
10	Rebecca	2/8/1956	F	11/7/1983	Human Resources	Staff	$ 28,523				
11	Jeffrey	5/17/1972	M	9/13/1998	Human Resources	Staff	$ 38,718				
12	Stephanie	10/13/1976	F	2/4/1992	Human Resources	Staff	$ 26,948				
13	McCauley	10/18/1966	M	1/31/1994	Human Resources	Staff	$ 26,087		Number of employee in	Human Resources	6
14	Aaron	7/15/1968	M	3/16/1989	Management	Chief Executive Officer	$149,278				
15	Matthew	1/12/1984	M	2/17/1981	Management	Chief Financial Officer	$146,357				
16	Marcia	3/14/1984	M	6/8/2006	Management	Chief Informations Officer	$146,160				
17	Edmond	6/16/1975	M	9/18/1990	Management	Chief Operating Officer	$147,943				
18	Kenneth	8/15/1964	M	11/5/1997	Management	Director, Operations	$143,375		Number of employee in	Management	6

Figure 5-35: Count employees in each department using the SUBTOTAL function.

Using the Subtotals Command

There are several drawbacks to applying using the SUBTOTAL function manually for summarizing list data:

1. The function must be entered once for each unique value in the "grouped" column.
2. In the previous example, one formula is needed for each unique value in the column to be summarized. Additionally, the cell references must be selected manually for each formula.

Excel's *Subtotal* command can automatically calculate subtotals and grand totals for a list of data. Before applying the *Subtotal* feature, sort the list to group rows together that are to be subtotaled. For example, if you want to subtotal salaries by department, sort by the "Department" column (in any order) to group rows by department. After the list is sorted to group rows, select a cell inside the list then select **Data(tab)→Outline(group)→Subtotal** from the ribbon. The *Subtotal* dialog box will appear. In the dialog box, select the column to group (top combo box), the aggregate function to apply (the *Use function* combo box), and the column to subtotal (*Add subtotal to* list box). Click the *OK* button to close the dialog box and insert the subtotals in the list.

Practice 5-7

Using the *Subtotals* command, add to the list the average salary for employees who have the same job title.

1. Open the Excel workbook "Employees_ch5-7.xlsx."
2. Sort the list (in any order) by the "JobTitle" column to group values.
3. Select a cell inside the list and select **Data(tab)→Outline(group)→Subtotal** from the ribbon. The *Subtotal* dialog box will appear.
4. In the *At each change in* text box, select *JobTitle* from the drop-down list.
5. Select *Average* from the drop-down list in the *Use function* text box.
6. Select "Salary" only in the *Add subtotal to* list box.
7. Accept the default selections at the bottom of the dialog box. Click the *OK* button to apply the subtotals.

Figure 5-36: *Subtotal* dialog box.

Figure 5-37 shows the subtotals that have been added to the employee list.

Hiding Detail Rows for Subtotals

When the *Subtotal* feature is applied, numbered brackets appear to the left of the worksheet in the window margin that represent three levels of detail, the grand total (#1), the subtotals(#2), and the detail rows(#3). Clicking on a "minus" box in level 2 will collapse rows of detail for a specific subtotal. To collapse all detail rows, click the box containing the number 2 at the top of the window margin. To collapse the subtotals and show only the grand total, click the box containing the 1. To return to the detail row view, click the box containing the number 3.

1 2 3	1	2	3	4	5	6	7	8	9
	EmployeeID	LastName	FirstName	BirthDate	Gender	HireDate	Department	JobTitle	Salary
2	46	Harris	Magan	4/10/1956	F	4/2/1994	Product Development	Chief Engineer	$135,493
3								**Chief Engineer Average**	$135,493
4	42	Walker	Aaron	7/15/1968	M	3/16/1989	Management	Chief Executive Officer	$149,278
5								**Chief Executive Officer Average**	$149,278
6	60	Reaves	Matthew	1/12/1984	M	2/17/1981	Management	Chief Financial Officer	$146,357
7								**Chief Financial Officer Average**	$146,357
8	68	Sheffield	Marcia	3/14/1984	M	6/8/2006	Management	Chief Informations Officer	$146,160
9								**Chief Informations Officer Average**	$146,160
10	44	Daye	Edmond	6/16/1975	M	9/18/1990	Management	Chief Operating Officer	$147,943
11								**Chief Operating Officer Average**	$147,943
12	51	Horne	Mickey	5/8/1955	M	1/17/1995	Product Development	Director	$142,841
13	61	Ross	Kevin	11/23/1958	M	5/25/1984	Sales	Director	$141,792
14	80	Bullard	Marci	2/1/1984	F	2/12/2002	Marketing	Director	$142,556
15								**Director Average**	$142,396
16	24	Cannon	Kenneth	8/15/1964	M	11/5/1997	Management	Director, Operations	$143,375
17								**Director, Operations Average**	$143,375
18	8	Hilton	Hillery	11/23/1949	F	11/8/2005	Sales	District Sales Manager	$128,845
19	12	Patel	Michael	4/20/1974	M	3/19/2003	Sales	District Sales Manager	$133,784
20	74	Coleman	Ruffus	4/5/1959	M	12/18/1993	Sales	District Sales Manager	$132,470
21	76	Warren	Raleigh	3/30/1952	M	6/19/1989	Sales	District Sales Manager	$134,092
22	95	Walker	Vance	9/27/1957	M	3/28/1982	Sales	District Sales Manager	$133,856
23	98	Wiggins	Janice	5/4/1966	F	10/28/1982	Sales	District Sales Manager	$132,215
24								**District Sales Manager Average**	$132,544
25	1	Abner	David	11/15/1977	M	6/20/2006	Sales	Manager	$110,958
26	5	Edwards	Minnie	3/8/1959	F	11/26/1991	Human Resources	Manager	$90,228
27	9	Jameson	Jennifer	1/17/1959	F	11/28/1992	Sales	Manager	$110,496
28	14	Zulkowski	Mary	5/8/1967	F	9/1/1999	Sales	Manager	$113,591
29	22	Mathis	Adel	3/30/1972	F	9/18/1998	Sales	Manager	$120,123

Figure 5-37: Subtotals applied using the **Subtotals** command on the *Data* menu.

Practice 5-8: (Continue from Practice 5-7)

Hide details rows and show only the salary averages for each job title.

8. Continue with the file from the previous Practice.
9. Click on the box at the top that contains the numeral 2 to collapse detail rows and show only subtotal averages and overall average.

1 2 3	A	B	C	D	E	F	G	H	I
	EmployeeID	LastName	FirstName	BirthDate	Gender	HireDate	Department	JobTitle	Salary
3								Chief Engineer Average	$135,493
5								Chief Executive Officer Average	$149,278
7								Chief Financial Officer Average	$146,357
9								Chief Informations Officer Average	$146,160
11								Chief Operating Officer Average	$147,943
15								Director Average	$142,396
17								Director, Operations Average	$143,375
24								District Sales Manager Average	$132,544
46								Manager Average	$105,775
49								Senior Accountant Average	$56,520
53								Senior Engineer Average	$88,062
106								Staff Average	$59,211
110								Staff Accountant Average	$47,949
115								Staff Engineer Average	$76,054
116								Grand Average	$82,166

Figure 5-38: Detail rows are hidden so that only the subtotals and overall total is displayed.

Filtering a List

To *filter* a list means to show only rows of data that meet specific criteria while hiding rows that do not. Another term for filter is *query*. In database terms, a *query* specifies which rows to "return" from the underlying data table(s) by stating which values of which columns to

select. Excel's filtering features execute background queries that determine which rows to
select. Excel offers two features for filtering a list, *AutoFilter* and *Advanced Filter*.

Selecting Rows with AutoFilter

The *AutoFilter* feature adds a drop-down list to each column header to allow the user to
quickly select the criteria for each column to include in the filter results. The *AutoFilter*
filters lists "in place" which means it merely hides the rows that do not meet the specified
criteria so that only the rows that do meet the criteria are visible. For rows that are
hidden, the row number (in the far left margin of the worksheet) will not be visible.

Apply the AutoFilter

To apply the *AutoFilter*, make a cell within the list the active cell then select **Data→(tab)→
Sort & Filter→Filter** from the ribbon. The *Filter* icon will become highlighted to indicate that the feature is active.

	A	B	C	D	E	F	G	H	I
1	EmployeeID	LastName	FirstName	BirthDate	Gender	HireDate	Department	JobTitle	Salary
2	1	Abner	David	11/15/1977	M	6/20/2006	Sales	Manager	$ 110,958
3	2	Butler	Susan	11/16/1967	F	8/13/1978	Marketing	Staff	$ 40,816
4	3	Conrad	Michael	9/14/1955	M	12/25/2001	Product Development	Staff Engineer	$ 74,665
5	4	Davis	Randall	7/15/1947	M	5/25/1980	Finance	Staff Accountant	$ 42,106
6	5	Edwards	Minnie	3/8/1959	F	11/26/1991	Human Resources	Manager	$ 90,228
7	6	Franklin	Margaret	11/25/1979	F	3/15/1977	Product Development	Staff	$ 42,976
8	7	Gardner	William	11/15/1968	M	2/7/1999	Sales	Staff	$ 90,650
9	8	Hilton	Hillery	11/23/1949	F	11/8/2005	Sales	District Sales Manager	$ 128,845
10	9	Jameson	Jennifer	1/17/1959	F	11/28/1992	Sales	Manager	$ 110,496
11	10	Kelly	Chester	10/28/1968	M	1/3/1994	Sales	Staff	$ 98,538
12	11	Zahn	Geoffrey	9/6/1952	M	3/4/1999	Sales	Staff	$ 84,151
13	12	Patel	Michael	4/20/1974	M	3/19/2003	Sales	District Sales Manager	$ 133,784
14	13	Schnider	Elizabeth	6/6/1958	F	6/27/1997	Sales	Staff	$ 35,025
15	14	Zulkowski	Mary	5/8/1967	F	9/1/1999	Sales	Manager	$ 113,591

Figure 5-39: When the *AutoFilter* is active, drop-down lists appear in the column headers. For the desired rows to be displayed, select
the criteria from the drop-down lists.

Using the arrow in the column header cell, leave a check mark in each box beside
the values you wish to include in the filtered result. (See also Figure 5-42 for the filter
options for the Salary column.)

Figure 5-40: Select the departments you wish to include in the filtered result.

Deactivating the AutoFilter

To deactivate the *AutoFilter* (remove the drop-down lists from column headers), select the same task as you did to apply the AutoFilter. The same ribbon command toggles the *AutoFilter* on and off.

Selecting the "Top 10" with AutoFilter

In addition to being able to select from the criteria list any single criteria for a particular column, you have the option of selecting the top n items or percent of items in a column. To select the top n items or percent, select **Number Filters→Top 10 from the** *AutoFilter* **drop-down list.**

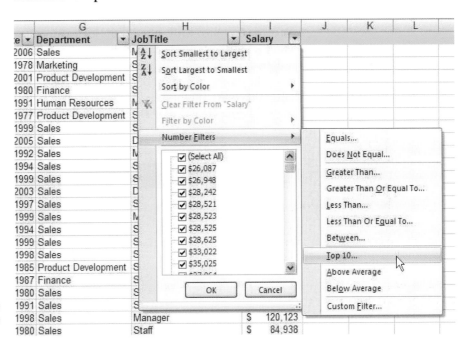

Figure 5-41: Select Top 10 from the *AutoFilter* from down list for the "Salary" column.

The *Top 10 AutoFilter* dialog box will open to allow you to select *Top* or *Bottom* from the drop-down list on the left and *Items* or *Percent* from the drop-down list on the right. Select or enter the number of items or percent into the center text box. Click the *OK* button to apply the filter.

Figure 5-42: Select bottom 5% of salaries in the Top 10 *AutoFilter* Dialog box.

	A	B	C	D	E	F	G	H	I
1	EmployeeID	LastName	FirstName	BirthDate	Gender	HireDate	Department	JobTitle	Salary
28	27 Brown		Rebecca	2/8/1956	F	11/7/1983	Human Resources	Staff	$ 28,523
32	31 Sanders		Pamela	12/1/1964	F	7/17/2002	Sales	Staff	$ 28,521
59	58 Black		Frances	8/13/1952	F	8/24/2006	Sales	Staff	$ 28,242
82	81 Murray		Stephanie	10/13/1976	F	2/4/1992	Human Resources	Staff	$ 26,948
92	91 Cantwell		McCauley	10/18/1966	M	1/31/1994	Human Resources	Staff	$ 26,087
102									
103									
104									
105									

Figure 5-43: Results of applying the Bottom 5% *AutoFilter* to the "Salary" column. Note that rows that do not meet the criteria are hidden as indicated by omitted row numbers.

Return to the Original List

There are two ways to remove the filter to make all list records visible. You may select *Clear Filter from "Salary"* from the drop-down list in the "Salary" column. If filters are applied to more than on column, disabling the *AutoFilter* feature will also remove all filters and show all rows. To deactivate the *AutoFilter* select the same command (*Filter*) as you did to activate it. The *Filter* command will toggle the *AutoFilter* on and off. The command icon appears highlighted only when the *AutoFilter* is active.

Applying Two Criteria for One Column with AutoFilter

You may also apply up to two logical comparisons in order to specify a range by which to filter values for one column. When two logical comparisons are used, the criteria may be combined with either of the logical operators AND or OR. To state logical conditions for filtering, select from the AutoFilter drop-down list **Number Filters (or Text Filters for text fields)→Custom Filter** (see Figure 5-41).

The *Custom AutoFilter* dialog box will appear. Select the logical comparison from the drop-down lists on the left and the comparison values from the drop-down lists on the right. Alternately, you may type the comparison value into the text boxes on the right.

Figure 5-44: Set two criteria in the Custom *AutoFilter* dialog box to filter salaries that are over $50,000 and under $80,000.

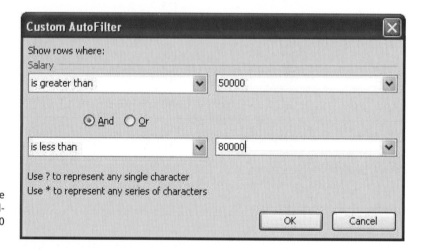

	A	B	C	D	E	F	G	H	I
1	EmployeeID	LastName	FirstName	BirthDate	Gender	HireDate	Department	JobTitle	Salary
4	3	Conrad	Michael	9/14/1955	M	12/25/2001	Product Development	Staff Engineer	$ 74,665
17	16	Hancock	Christopher	4/30/1967	M	11/18/1999	Sales	Staff	$ 50,219
19	18	Powell	Bruce	5/8/1966	M	12/29/1985	Product Development	Staff Engineer	$ 72,564
20	19	Phillips	Wiley	11/17/1952	M	5/1/1987	Finance	Staff Accountant	$ 51,485
21	20	Howard	Emile	3/24/1985	M	4/3/1980	Sales	Staff	$ 59,528
40	39	Thompson	Dupree	5/16/1966	F	4/13/1980	Finance	Staff Accountant	$ 50,257
41	40	Floyd	Howard	3/7/1972	F	7/13/1985	Sales	Staff	$ 77,291
48	47	Burnett	Kayla	3/27/1984	F	1/18/1977	Human Resources	Manager	$ 62,742
51	50	Bush	Daphne	6/11/1967	F	4/18/1979	Sales	Staff	$ 71,885
53	52	Justice	Earlene	2/3/1953	F	12/7/1998	Finance	Senior Accountant	$ 54,902
54	53	Palmer	Justin	4/14/1961	M	5/15/2006	Product Development	Staff	$ 53,310
57	56	Shaw	Alice	4/25/1964	F	4/22/1993	Product Development	Staff	$ 53,829
60	59	Raiford	Lucy	6/15/1949	F	10/31/1995	Marketing	Staff	$ 62,915
64	63	O'Connor	George	7/7/1966	F	2/5/2004	Sales	Staff	$ 77,622
65	64	Parker	Nelson	5/1/1968	F	2/13/2006	Sales	Staff	$ 58,350
66	65	Parks	Raymond	12/4/1985	F	6/15/1999	Sales	Staff	$ 77,203
70	69	Davis	Paul	4/19/1953	M	12/20/1986	Finance	Senior Accountant	$ 58,138
71	70	Hester	Ralph	7/18/1953	M	10/11/2004	Sales	Staff	$ 74,423
74	73	Rawlin	Pauline	4/30/1970	F	11/24/2001	Marketing	Staff	$ 69,546
80	79	Daniels	Ernest	7/12/1981	M	4/29/1991	Product Development	Staff Engineer	$ 76,963
87	86	Morris	Victor	5/4/1963	M	5/3/2000	Finance	Manager	$ 58,332
88	87	Hightower	Lawrence	8/21/1974	M	8/22/1984	Sales	Staff	$ 76,922
93	92	Burton	Manuel	3/23/1965	M	11/5/1990	Sales	Staff	$ 76,664
95	94	Powers	Jacob	8/3/1978	M	5/9/1979	Marketing	Staff	$ 69,706
100	99	Allen	Lance	7/21/1971	M	4/30/1977	Sales	Staff	$ 71,132
101	100	Lancaster	Jacqueline	10/27/1965	F	12/6/1982	Sales	Staff	$ 72,821
102									

Figure 5-45: *AutoFilter* results for Salaries that are between $50,000 and $80,000 (not inclusive).

The *AutoFilter* may be used to filter data in multiple columns. The list is first filtered by one column then additional filters may be applied, one column at a time to the already filtered list. With each new column that is filtered, the additional criteria further restrict rows from the filter result. When criteria in multiple columns are applied, the logical operator AND is assumed to combine the criteria. For example, if you would like to view employee records for those who work in the sales department and were hired after 1999, the "Department" column must be filtered first, then the "HireDate" column to select only records from the previous filter result that meet the criteria for the second (hire date) filter. To apply the *AutoFilter* for sales department employees whose salary is more than $50,000, select "Sales" from the drop-down *AutoFilter* list for the "Department" column and select **Number Filters**→*Custom Filter* from drop-down list in the "Salary" column. In the *Custom AutoFilter* dialog box, select *is greater than* from the drop-down list on the left and type "50000" (without quotes) into the value text box on the right. Click the *OK* button to close the dialog box and apply the filter.

	EmployeeID	LastName	FirstName	BirthDate	Gender	HireDate	Department	JobTitle	Salary
2	1	Abner	David	11/15/1977	M	6/20/2006	Sales	Manager	$ 110,958
8	7	Gardner	William	11/15/1968	M	2/7/1999	Sales	Staff	$ 90,650
9	8	Hilton	Hillery	11/23/1949	F	11/8/2005	Sales	District Sales Manager	$ 128,845
10	9	Jameson	Jennifer	1/17/1959	F	11/28/1992	Sales	Manager	$ 110,496
11	10	Kelly	Chester	10/28/1968	M	1/3/1994	Sales	Staff	$ 98,538
12	11	Zahn	Geoffrey	9/6/1952	M	3/4/1999	Sales	Staff	$ 84,151
13	12	Patel	Michael	4/20/1974	M	3/19/2003	Sales	District Sales Manager	$ 133,784
15	14	Zulkowski	Mary	5/8/1967	F	9/1/1999	Sales	Manager	$ 113,591
17	16	Hancock	Christopher	4/30/1967	M	11/18/1999	Sales	Staff	$ 50,219
18	17	Bateman	Matthew	1/27/1956	M	8/3/1998	Sales	Staff	$ 83,847
21	20	Howard	Emile	3/24/1985	M	4/3/1980	Sales	Staff	$ 59,528
23	22	Mathis	Adel	3/30/1972	F	9/18/1998	Sales	Manager	$ 120,123
24	23	Morgan	Erin	4/26/1973	F	8/1/1980	Sales	Staff	$ 84,938
26	25	Lewis	Catherine	3/31/1947	F	11/18/1993	Sales	Manager	$ 110,789
29	28	Dennis	Joseph	4/12/1981	M	4/20/1990	Sales	Manager	$ 102,407
30	29	Lunsford	Jeremy	7/26/1982	M	3/1/2005	Sales	Manager	$ 110,210
34	33	Dupree	Lorraine	7/25/1967	F	7/9/1980	Sales	Manager	$ 114,392
35	34	Weston	Vivian	2/19/1980	F	5/22/1991	Sales	Staff	$ 91,204
37	36	Southerland	Willis	11/16/1968	M	11/22/1982	Sales	Staff	$ 83,632
38	37	Clark	Alan	12/25/1950	M	11/13/1985	Sales	Staff	$ 83,588
39	38	Thomas	Burton	2/23/1984	F	5/10/2002	Sales	Manager	$ 105,386
41	40	Floyd	Howard	3/7/1972	F	7/13/1985	Sales	Staff	$ 77,291
49	48	Joyner	Julie	8/16/1979	F	8/16/1991	Sales	Manager	$ 121,181
50	49	Lambert	Charles	11/21/1985	M	6/10/1993	Sales	Manager	$ 107,689
51	50	Bush	Daphne	6/11/1967	F	4/18/1979	Sales	Staff	$ 71,885
55	54	Singleton	Marc	10/1/1956	M	3/17/1991	Sales	Manager	$ 124,497
56	55	Cooper	Nancy	4/25/1972	F	12/7/1979	Sales	Staff	$ 88,595
62	61	Ross	Kevin	11/23/1958	M	5/25/1984	Sales	Director	$ 141,792
63	62	Girssom	Mack	6/25/1982	M	10/22/2000	Sales	Manager	$ 120,787
64	63	O'Connor	George	7/7/1966	F	2/5/2004	Sales	Staff	$ 77,622
65	64	Parker	Nelson	5/1/1968	F	2/13/2006	Sales	Staff	$ 58,350
66	65	Parks	Raymond	12/4/1985	F	6/15/1999	Sales	Staff	$ 77,203
67	66	Shepherd	Lewis	12/21/1978	M	2/27/2002	Sales	Staff	$ 95,281
71	70	Hester	Ralph	7/18/1953	M	10/11/2004	Sales	Staff	$ 74,423
75	74	Coleman	Ruffus	4/5/1959	M	12/18/1993	Sales	District Sales Manager	$ 132,470
76	75	Clements	Nadia	8/31/1982	F	6/27/1993	Sales	Staff	$ 96,363
77	76	Warren	Raleigh	3/30/1952	M	6/19/1989	Sales	District Sales Manager	$ 134,092
78	77	Shrewsberry	Carol	10/3/1973	F	6/7/1983	Sales	Manager	$ 100,779
79	78	Holloway	Garret	4/12/1970	M	9/15/2000	Sales	Staff	$ 88,527
85	84	Holloman	Sally	6/1/1977	F	1/13/1993	Sales	Manager	$ 101,641
88	87	Hightower	Lawrence	8/21/1974	M	8/22/1984	Sales	Staff	$ 76,922
93	92	Burton	Manuel	3/23/1965	M	11/5/1990	Sales	Staff	$ 76,664
94	93	Shaw	Vincent	5/27/1985	M	6/28/1988	Sales	Manager	$ 107,433
96	95	Walker	Vance	9/27/1957	M	3/28/1982	Sales	District Sales Manager	$ 133,856
97	96	Tidwell	Lorna	2/22/1966	F	6/21/1993	Sales	Manager	$ 128,552
99	98	Wiggins	Janice	5/4/1966	F	10/28/1982	Sales	District Sales Manager	$ 132,215
100	99	Allen	Lance	7/21/1971	M	4/30/1977	Sales	Staff	$ 71,132
101	100	Lancaster	Jacqueline	10/27/1965	F	12/6/1982	Sales	Staff	$ 72,821

Figure 5-46: Filter result for employees in the Sales department whose salary is more than $50,000.

Selecting Rows with the Advanced Filter

The *Advanced Filter* feature provides another means for applying complex filers. In earlier versions of Excel (prior to Office 2007) the *AutoFilter* did not always support filtering on multiple criteria for one column so the *Advanced Filter* was available for such queries. In Excel 2007, the *AutoFilter* will allow filtering on any combination of values in each column in addition to custom filters for specifying range criteria. Although this added functionality of the *AutoFilter* in Excel 2007 reduces the need for the *Advanced Filter* for many complex queries, there are still situations in which the *Advanced Filter* adds some additional filtering capabilities. Using the *Advanced Filter* for complex queries is like being able to view custom filters for all columns at once. The *Advanced Filter* allows you to list the criteria in a special location of the worksheet so that all filter criteria can be viewed together and easily edited. In the next example, the particular filter criteria can be specified using either the *AutoFilter* or the *Advanced Filter*.

Applying the Advanced Filter

Applying the *Advanced Filter* is quite different from applying the *AutoFilter*. Before applying the Advanced Filter, you need to set up the filter criteria range.

1. Insert a few blank rows before the column header row.
2. Copy the column header row and paste it in the top row of the newly inserted rows.

	C	D	E	F	G	H	I
1	FirstName	BirthDate	Gender	HireDate	Department	JobTitle	Salary
2							
3							
4							
5							
6	FirstName	BirthDate	Gender	HireDate	Department	JobTitle	Salary
7	David	11/15/1977	M	6/20/2006	Sales	Manager	$ 110,958
8	Susan	11/16/1967	F	8/13/1978	Marketing	Staff	$ 40,816
9	Michael	9/14/1955	M	12/25/2001	Product Development	Staff Engineer	$ 74,665
10	Randall	7/15/1947	M	5/25/1980	Finance	Staff Accountant	$ 42,106
11	Minnie	3/8/1959	F	11/26/1991	Human Resources	Manager	$ 90,228
12	Margaret	11/25/1979	F	3/15/1977	Product Development	Staff	$ 42,976
13	William	11/15/1968	M	2/7/1999	Sales	Staff	$ 90,650
14	Hillery	11/23/1949	F	11/8/2005	Sales	District Sales Manager	$ 128,845
15	Jennifer	1/17/1959	F	11/28/1992	Sales	Manager	$ 110,496

Figure 5-47: To set up a criteria range insert blank rows at the top of the list and copy the column header row to the first blank row.

3. Use the blank rows beneath the pasted column header row for entering the filter criteria.
4. Enter the filter criteria into cells of the blank rows.
    a. Criteria in cells of the same row will be combined with AND logic.
    b. Criteria entered into cells of different rows will be combined with OR logic.
5. After all criteria are entered, make sure a blank row remains between the criteria range and the list range. Insert a new blank row if necessary.
6. Select **Data(tab)→Sort & Filter(group)→Advanced** from the ribbon. The *Advanced Filter* dialog box will appear.
7. Use the option buttons to select the location to display the filtered rows. The *Advanced Filter* may be performed "in place" as with the *AutoFilter*, or the filtered rows may be copied to another location.
8. Select the list range. If the active cell is inside the list when the *Advance Filter* menu option is selected, the list range will be selected automatically.
9. Select the criteria range. The criteria range includes the pasted column header row and all rows beneath it that contain filter criteria.
10. If the filter results are to be copied to another location, specify the location's first cell reference in the *Copy to* text box.
11. If only unique records (no duplicates) are to be displayed, check the *Unique records only* check box.
12. Click the *OK* button to execute the filter.

Practice 5-9: (Continued from Practice 5-8)

Using the *Advanced Filter* apply a filter that displays all rows for females who work in the "Product Development" department and make more than $50,000.

	A	B	C	D	E	F	G	H	I
1	EmployeeID	LastName	FirstName	BirthDate	Gender	HireDate	Department	JobTitle	Salary
2					F		Product Development		>50000
3									
4									
5									
6	EmployeeID	LastName	FirstName	BirthDate	Gender	HireDate	D	JobTitle	Salary
7	39	Thompson	Dupree	5/16/1966	F	4/13/1980	Finance	Staff Accountant	$ 50,257
8	52	Justice	Earlene	2/3/1953	F	12/7/1998	Finance	Senior Accountant	$ 54,902
9	4	Davis	Randall	7/15/1947	M	5/25/1980	Finance	Staff Accountant	$ 42,106
10	19	Phillips	Wiley	11/17/1952	M	5/1/1987	Finance	Staff Accountant	$ 51,485
11	69	Davis	Paul	4/19/1953	M	12/20/1986	Finance	Senior Accountant	$ 58,138
12	86	Morris	Victor	5/4/1963	M	5/3/2000	Finance	Manager	$ 58,332

Advanced Filter - Criteria range: Employees!$E$1:$I$2

Figure 5-48: When applying the *Advanced Filter*, include column headers in the criteria range selected. Criteria entered on the same row are interpreted using AND logic.

	A	B	C	D	E	F	G	H	I
1	EmployeeID	LastName	FirstName	BirthDate	Gender	HireDate	Department	JobTitle	Salary
2					F		Product Development		>50000
3									
4									
5									
6	EmployeeID	LastName	FirstName	BirthDate	Gender	HireDate	Department	JobTitle	Salary
35	46	Harris	Magan	4/10/1956	F	4/2/1994	Product Development	Chief Engineer	$135,493
36	56	Shaw	Alice	4/25/1964	F	4/22/1993	Product Development	Staff	$ 53,829
37	71	Nickolls	Mable	3/11/1973	F	10/2/1988	Product Development	Senior Engineer	$ 84,857
107									
108									
109									
110									

Figure 5-49: *Advanced Filter* results.

To enter criteria for filters using OR logic, enter the criteria for the OR logic in separate rows. AND and OR logic may be combined using AND logic on the same row and OR logic on different rows.

Practice 5-10: (Continued from Practice 5-9)

Apply a filter that shows the rows for employees who are females who work in the "Product Development" department and make over $50,000 OR are females who work in the "Finance" department (at any salary).

	A	B	C	D	E	F	G	H	I
1	EmployeeID	LastName	FirstName	BirthDate	Gender	HireDate	Department	JobTitle	Salary
2					F		Product Development		>50000
3					F		Finance		
4									
5									
6	EmployeeID	LastName	FirstName	BirthDate	Gender	HireDate	Department	JobTitle	Salary
7	39	Thompson	Dupree	5/16/1966	F	4/13/1980	Finance	Staff Accountant	$ 50,257
8	52	Justice	Earlene	2/3/1953	F	12/7/1998	Finance	Senior Accountant	$ 54,902
35	46	Harris	Magan	4/10/1956	F	4/2/1994	Product Development	Chief Engineer	$135,493
36	56	Shaw	Alice	4/25/1964	F	4/22/1993	Product Development	Staff	$ 53,829
37	71	Nickolls	Mable	3/11/1973	F	10/2/1988	Product Development	Senior Engineer	$ 84,857
107									
108									
109									

Figure 5-50: Note that AND criteria are on the same row and the OR criteria is on a different row.

In Practice 5-10, the minimum criteria range selected must be E2:I3 to include all the criteria. All criteria on row 2 is joined by AND logic. All criteria on row 3 is joined by AND logic. The combined criteria on line 2 is joined by OR logic to the combined criteria on row 3.

Unlike the *AutoFilter,* subsequent queries do not filter the previous filtered list. Each new *Advanced Filter* re-filters the original list.

To remove the *Advanced Filter* and return all rows to view, select **Data(tab)→Sort & Filter→Clear** from the ribbon.

Specifying Range Criteria for the Advanced Filter

The column criteria may be exact values or a range of values. Use logical operators < (less than) or > (greater than) to specify range bounds. A single-bounded range may be specified using only one logical comparison. A range between two bounds must include two logical comparisons, one for the lower bound and one for the upper bound. When two bounds are used for one column, an additional column must be inserted to provide a way to enter two criteria for the same column.

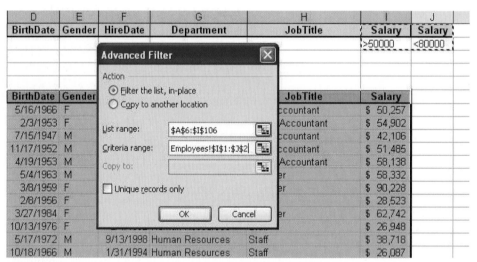

Figure 5-51: The "Salary" column header is duplicated to provide a way to set two criteria for one column. The criteria range includes both column headers and their criteria.

Using Wildcards in Advanced Filters

To include text values that share some common characters, the following wildcard characters may be used to substitute for the characters in the criteria that are different.

The **?** (question mark) substitutes any single character.
The ***** (asterisk) substitutes any number of characters.
The **~** (tilde) preceding a **?** (question mark), ***** (asterisk), or **~** (tilde) finds the specified symbol itself within text.

Filter Example Using the Question Mark (?)

The question mark is used when all characters of the filter range match the search criteria except one character. You may want to filter for the last name "Anderson," but you know there are many ways to spell similar last names that are all pronounced the same. If you are not certain of the exact spelling of the last name you want to find, you may design criteria that will return common spellings for the name. In the example, all spellings of the name are the same except for the last vowel. In the criteria field under the "Last Name" column header, enter the character string "Anders?n" (without quotes). When the filter is applied, the last names Andersen, Andersin, Anderson, and Andersun are included in the results.

	A	B	C	D	E	F	G	H	I
1	EmployeeID	LastName	FirstName	BirthDate	Gender	HireDate	Department	JobTitle	Salary
2		Anders?n							
3									
4									
5									
6	EmployeeID	LastName	FirstName	BirthDate	Gender	HireDate	Department	JobTitle	Salary
29	0023	Andersen	Erin	4/26/1973	F	8/1/1980	Sales	Staff	$ 84,938
34	0028	Anderson	Joseph	4/12/1981	M	4/20/1990	Sales	Manager	$102,407
51	0045	Andersun	Jackson	3/16/1982	M	9/5/1983	Sales	Staff	$ 42,568
54	0048	Andersin	Julie	8/16/1979	F	8/16/1991	Sales	Manager	$121,181
107									
108									

Figure 5-52: *Advanced Filter* results using a single character wildcard (?) in the criteria.

Filter Example Using the Asterisk (*)

When criteria are entered normally, the filter will return any rows that have a value in the criteria column that begins with the text string specified in the criteria field. The filter behaves as if there is an asterisk following the string entered into the criteria field. So if "Staff" (without quotes) is entered into the criteria field under the "Job Title" column header, the filter results will include any job titles that begin with "Staff."

	A	B	C	D	E	F	G	H	I
1	EmployeeID	LastName	FirstName	BirthDate	Gender	HireDate	Department	JobTitle	Salary
2								Staff	
3									
4									
5									
6	EmployeeID	LastName	FirstName	BirthDate	Gender	HireDate	Department	JobTitle	Salary
8	0002	Butler	Susan	11/16/1967	F	8/13/1978	Marketing	Staff	$ 40,816
9	0003	Conrad	Michael	9/14/1955	M	12/25/2001	Product Development	Staff Engineer	$ 74,665
10	0004	Davis	Randall	7/15/1947	M	5/25/1980	Finance	Staff Accountant	$ 42,106
12	0006	Franklin	Margaret	11/25/1979	F	3/15/1977	Product Development	Staff	$ 42,976
13	0007	Gardner	William	11/15/1968	M	2/7/1999	Sales	Staff	$ 90,650
16	0010	Kelly	Chester	10/28/1968	M	1/3/1994	Sales	Staff	$ 98,538
17	0011	Zahn	Geoffrey	9/6/1952	M	3/4/1999	Sales	Staff	$ 84,151
19	0013	Schnider	Elizabeth	6/6/1958	F	6/27/1997	Sales	Staff	$ 35,025
21	0015	Crockett	Carol	11/19/1953	F	12/3/1994	Sales	Staff	$ 43,374
22	0016	Hancock	Christopher	4/30/1967	M	11/18/1999	Sales	Staff	$ 50,219
23	0017	Bateman	Matthew	1/27/1956	M	8/3/1998	Sales	Staff	$ 83,847
24	0018	Powell	Bruce	5/8/1966	M	12/29/1985	Product Development	Staff Engineer	$ 72,564
25	0019	Phillips	Wiley	11/17/1952	M	5/1/1987	Finance	Staff Accountant	$ 51,485
26	0020	Howard	Emile	3/24/1985	M	4/3/1980	Sales	Staff	$ 59,528
27	0021	Evans	Jamie	5/2/1985	F	10/10/1991	Sales	Staff	$ 28,625
29	0023	Andersen	Erin	4/26/1973	F	8/1/1980	Sales	Staff	$ 84,938

Figure 5-53: Criteria entered normally return any data that begins with the text that is entered.

If the filter result is to include values that contain the criteria string in the middle of the text value, the asterisk wildcard is included before and after the criteria text. If we want our filter results to include all job titles that include Engineer, we would enter the criteria as "*Engineer*" (without quotes). (Since the filter automatically behaves as if there is an asterisk after the criteria entry, criteria entered as *Engineer* or *Engineer will return the same results.) Note that "Staff Engineer" and "Engineering Manager" job titles are included in the filter results in Figure 5-54.

	A	B	C	D	E	F	G	H	I
1	EmployeeID	LastName	FirstName	BirthDate	Gender	HireDate	Department	JobTitle	Salary
2								*Engineer*	
3									
4									
5									
6	EmployeeID	LastName	FirstName	BirthDate	Gender	HireDate	Department	JobTitle	Salary
39	0018	Powell	Bruce	5/8/1966	M	12/29/1985	Product Development	Staff Engineer	$ 72,564
40	0003	Conrad	Michael	9/14/1955	M	12/25/2001	Product Development	Staff Engineer	$ 74,665
41	0079	Daniels	Ernest	7/12/1981	M	4/29/1991	Product Development	Staff Engineer	$ 76,963
42	0085	Pike	Hadden	9/30/1963	M	4/23/1982	Product Development	Staff Engineer	$ 80,025
43	0071	Nickolls	Mable	3/11/1973	F	10/2/1988	Product Development	Senior Engineer	$ 84,857
44	0026	Spencer	James	2/19/1982	M	7/9/2005	Product Development	Senior Engineer	$ 88,543
45	0041	Shaw	Ian	4/12/1964	M	12/30/2000	Product Development	Engineering Manager	$ 90,785
46	0046	Harris	Magan	4/10/1956	F	4/2/1994	Product Development	Chief Engineer	$135,493
107									
108									
109									

Figure 5-54: Filter results for the criterion text string found anywhere in the data string.

Overriding the Automatic Trailing Asterisk

If we want to filter out all job titles that end in Manager, it is a reasonable assumption that the criteria would be entered as "*Manager" (without quotes). Note that not all values returned for the "*Manager" criteria end with "Manager."

	A	B	C	D	E	F	G	H	I
1	EmployeeID	LastName	FirstName	BirthDate	Gender	HireDate	Department	JobTitle	Salary
2								*Manager	
3									
4									
5									
6	EmployeeID	LastName	FirstName	BirthDate	Gender	HireDate	Department	JobTitle	Salary
12	0086	Morris	Victor	5/4/1963	M	5/3/2000	Finance	Manager	$ 58,332
17	0047	Burnett	Kayla	3/27/1984	F	1/18/1977	Human Resources	Manager	$ 62,742
18	0005	Edwards	Minnie	3/8/1959	F	11/26/1991	Human Resources	Manager	$ 90,228
32	0082	Durham	Gabriel	6/22/1981	M	11/29/1999	Marketing	Manager	$ 99,063
45	0041	Shaw	Ian	4/12/1964	M	12/30/2000	Product Development	Engineering Manager	$ 90,785
82	0010	Kelly	Chester	10/28/1968	M	1/3/1994	Sales	Manager, Softline Division	$ 98,538
83	0077	Shrewsberry	Carol	10/3/1973	F	6/7/1983	Sales	Manager	$100,779
84	0084	Holloman	Sally	6/1/1977	F	1/13/1993	Sales	Manager	$101,641
85	0028	Anderson	Joseph	4/12/1981	M	4/20/1990	Sales	Manager	$102,407
86	0038	Thomas	Burton	2/23/1984	F	5/10/2002	Sales	Manager	$105,386
87	0093	Shaw	Vincent	5/27/1985	M	6/28/1988	Sales	Manager	$107,433
88	0049	Lambert	Charles	11/21/1985	M	6/10/1993	Sales	Manager	$107,689
89	0029	Lunsford	Jeremy	7/26/1982	M	3/1/2005	Sales	Manager	$110,210
90	0009	Jameson	Jennifer	1/17/1959	F	11/28/1992	Sales	Manager	$110,496
91	0025	Lewis	Catherine	3/31/1947	F	11/18/1993	Sales	Manager	$110,789
92	0001	Abner	David	11/15/1977	M	6/20/2006	Sales	Manager, Hardware	$110,958
93	0014	Zulkowski	Mary	5/8/1967	F	9/1/1999	Sales	Manager	$113,591
94	0033	Dupree	Lorraine	7/25/1967	F	7/9/1980	Sales	Manager	$114,392
95	0022	Mathis	Adel	3/30/1972	F	9/18/1998	Sales	Manager	$120,123
96	0062	Girssom	Mack	6/25/1982	M	10/22/2000	Sales	Manager	$120,787
97	0048	Andersin	Julie	8/16/1979	F	8/16/1991	Sales	Manager	$121,181
98	0054	Singleton	Marc	10/1/1956	M	3/17/1991	Sales	Manager	$124,497
99	0096	Tidwell	Lorna	2/22/1966	F	6/21/1993	Sales	Manager	$128,552
100	0008	Hilton	Hillery	11/23/1949	F	11/8/2005	Sales	District Sales Manager	$128,845
101	0098	Wiggins	Janice	5/4/1966	F	10/28/1982	Sales	District Sales Manager	$132,215
102	0074	Coleman	Ruffus	4/5/1959	M	12/18/1993	Sales	District Sales Manager	$132,470
103	0012	Patel	Michael	4/20/1974	M	3/19/2003	Sales	District Sales Manager	$133,784
104	0095	Walker	Vance	9/27/1957	M	3/28/1982	Sales	District Sales Manager	$133,856
105	0076	Warren	Raleigh	3/30/1952	M	6/19/1989	Sales	District Sales Manager	$134,092
107									
108									

Figure 5-55: *Advanced Filter* results for criteria entered as ***Manager**.

Since Excel automatically treats the criteria entry as if an asterisk is at the end of the criteria string, it is necessary to enter the criteria text using a slightly different syntax. Using the equal sign in front of the criteria will force the filter to return only what is specified in the criteria field. When preceding the criteria with an equal sign, the wildcard characters are interpreted precisely as they are written. In addition to the equal sign, the entire entry for the criteria must be entered as text, so the entry must be preceded by an apostrophe ('). An entry for filtering all job titles that end with "Manager" would be entered:

'=*Manager

Enter an apostrophe at the beginning of the criteria to override the automatic trailing asterisk.

	A	B	C	D	E	F	G	H	I
1	EmployeeID	LastName	FirstName	BirthDate	Gender	HireDate	Department	JobTitle	Salary
2								=*Manager	
3									
4									
5									
6	EmployeeID	LastName	FirstName	BirthDate	Gender	HireDate	Department	JobTitle	Salary
12	0086	Morris	Victor	5/4/1963	M	5/3/2000	Finance	Manager	$ 58,332
17	0047	Burnett	Kayla	3/27/1984	F	1/18/1977	Human Resources	Manager	$ 62,742
18	0005	Edwards	Minnie	3/8/1959	F	11/26/1991	Human Resources	Manager	$ 90,228
32	0082	Durham	Gabriel	6/22/1981	M	11/29/1999	Marketing	Manager	$ 99,063
45	0041	Shaw	Ian	4/12/1964	M	12/30/2000	Product Development	Engineering Manager	$ 90,785
83	0077	Shrewsberry	Carol	10/3/1973	F	6/7/1983	Sales	Manager	$100,779
84	0084	Holloman	Sally	6/1/1977	F	1/13/1993	Sales	Manager	$101,641
85	0028	Anderson	Joseph	4/12/1981	M	4/20/1990	Sales	Manager	$102,407
86	0038	Thomas	Burton	2/23/1984	F	5/10/2002	Sales	Manager	$105,386
87	0093	Shaw	Vincent	5/27/1985	M	6/28/1988	Sales	Manager	$107,433
88	0049	Lambert	Charles	11/21/1985	M	6/10/1993	Sales	Manager	$107,689
89	0029	Lunsford	Jeremy	7/26/1982	M	3/1/2005	Sales	Manager	$110,210
90	0009	Jameson	Jennifer	1/17/1959	F	11/28/1992	Sales	Manager	$110,496
91	0025	Lewis	Catherine	3/31/1947	F	11/18/1993	Sales	Manager	$110,789
93	0014	Zulkowski	Mary	5/8/1967	F	9/1/1999	Sales	Manager	$113,591
94	0033	Dupree	Lorraine	7/25/1967	F	7/9/1980	Sales	Manager	$114,392
95	0022	Mathis	Adel	3/30/1972	F	9/18/1998	Sales	Manager	$120,123
96	0062	Girssom	Mack	6/25/1982	M	10/22/2000	Sales	Manager	$120,787
97	0048	Andersin	Julie	8/16/1979	F	8/16/1991	Sales	Manager	$121,181
98	0054	Singleton	Marc	10/1/1956	M	3/17/1991	Sales	Manager	$124,497
99	0096	Tidwell	Lorna	2/22/1966	F	6/21/1993	Sales	Manager	$128,552
100	0008	Hilton	Hillery	11/23/1949	F	11/8/2005	Sales	District Sales Manager	$128,845
101	0098	Wiggins	Janice	5/4/1966	F	10/28/1982	Sales	District Sales Manager	$132,215
102	0074	Coleman	Ruffus	4/5/1959	M	12/18/1993	Sales	District Sales Manager	$132,470
103	0012	Patel	Michael	4/20/1974	M	3/19/2003	Sales	District Sales Manager	$133,784
104	0095	Walker	Vance	9/27/1957	M	3/28/1982	Sales	District Sales Manager	$133,856
105	0076	Warren	Raleigh	3/30/1952	M	6/19/1989	Sales	District Sales Manager	$134,092
107									

Figure 5-56: *Advanced Filter* results for criteria entered as '**=*Manager**.

To force any filter to return an exact match to the criteria specified, use the syntax described above leaving out any wildcard characters. For example, if only job titles of just "Manager" are to be included in the filter results, the criteria would be specified as:

"'=Manager"

(Note there is no asterisk in this criterion.)

| | Arial | | ▾ | 10 | ▾ | **B** | *I* | U | ≡ | ≡ | ≡ | ▦ | $ | % | , | .00→.0 | .0→.00 | ▦ ▦ | ▦ ▾ | ♦ ▾ | **A** ▾ | |

| H2 | | ▾ | | *fx* | =Manager | |

	A	B	C	D	E	F	G	H	I
1	EmployeeID	LastName	FirstName	BirthDate	Gender	HireDate	Department	JobTitle	Salary
2								=Manager	
3									
4									
5									
6	EmployeeID	LastName	FirstName	BirthDate	Gender	HireDate	Department	JobTitle	Salary
12	0086	Morris	Victor	5/4/1963	M	5/3/2000	Finance	Manager	$ 58,332
17	0047	Burnett	Kayla	3/27/1984	F	1/18/1977	Human Resources	Manager	$ 62,742
18	0005	Edwards	Minnie	3/8/1959	F	11/26/1991	Human Resources	Manager	$ 90,228
32	0082	Durham	Gabriel	6/22/1981	M	11/29/1999	Marketing	Manager	$ 99,063
83	0077	Shrewsberry	Carol	10/3/1973	F	6/7/1983	Sales	Manager	$100,779
84	0084	Holloman	Sally	6/1/1977	F	1/13/1993	Sales	Manager	$101,641
85	0028	Anderson	Joseph	4/12/1981	M	4/20/1990	Sales	Manager	$102,407
86	0038	Thomas	Burton	2/23/1984	F	5/10/2002	Sales	Manager	$105,386
87	0093	Shaw	Vincent	5/27/1985	M	6/28/1988	Sales	Manager	$107,433
88	0049	Lambert	Charles	11/21/1985	M	6/10/1993	Sales	Manager	$107,689
89	0029	Lunsford	Jeremy	7/26/1982	M	3/1/2005	Sales	Manager	$110,210
90	0009	Jameson	Jennifer	1/17/1959	F	11/28/1992	Sales	Manager	$110,496
91	0025	Lewis	Catherine	3/31/1947	F	11/18/1993	Sales	Manager	$110,789
93	0014	Zulkowski	Mary	5/8/1967	F	9/1/1999	Sales	Manager	$113,591
94	0033	Dupree	Lorraine	7/25/1967	F	7/9/1980	Sales	Manager	$114,392
95	0022	Mathis	Adel	3/30/1972	F	9/18/1998	Sales	Manager	$120,123
96	0062	Girssom	Mack	6/25/1982	M	10/22/2000	Sales	Manager	$120,787
97	0048	Andersin	Julie	8/16/1979	F	8/16/1991	Sales	Manager	$121,181
98	0054	Singleton	Marc	10/1/1956	M	3/17/1991	Sales	Manager	$124,497
99	0096	Tidwell	Lorna	2/22/1966	F	6/21/1993	Sales	Manager	$128,552
107									

Figure 5-57: *Advanced Filter* results for criteria entered as '**=Manager** (without an asterisk).

Filtering Case-Sensitive Text

When using the filter criteria syntax discussed so far, Excel does not match case when filtering. To match the exact text, including case (upper or lower case), the criteria must be enclosed in the EXACT function and entered under a blank column header outside the criteria list columns. The EXACT function compares two text strings (its two arguments) and returns TRUE if the two strings match exactly and returns FALSE otherwise. It does match case, but disregards formatting. General syntax for the EXACT function:

=EXACT(text1,text2)

In order for a filter to return all values for "JobTitle" that match "Staff" exactly, enter a formula with the EXACT function into the row under the criteria column headers, but in the column to the right of the last criteria column header (where there is no column header). The column header for the formula cell may be left blank or you may enter a label for the additional criteria column.

To test the capability of the EXACT function to match case, three of the "Staff" positions in the example file have been changed to "staff" (all lower case). The formula entered into the criteria range is **=EXACT(H7,"staff")**. H7 is the cell reference for the first data cell of the "JobTitle" column. Note that the exact text to match is entered in double quotes.

J2 ▾ ƒx =EXACT(H7,"staff")

	A	B	C	D	E	F	G	H	I	J
1	EmployeeID	LastName	FirstName	BirthDate	Gender	HireDate	Department	JobTitle	Salary	
2										FALSE
3										
4										
5										
6	EmployeeID	LastName	FirstName	BirthDate	Gender	HireDate	Department	JobTitle	Salary	
7	0001	Abner	David	11/15/1977	M	6/20/2006	Sales	Manager, Hardware	$110,958	
8	0002	Butler	Susan	11/16/1967	F	8/13/1978	Marketing	staff	$ 40,816	
9	0003	Conrad	Michael	9/14/1955	M	12/25/2001	Product Development	Staff Engineer	$ 74,665	
10	0004	Davis	Randall	7/15/1947	M	5/25/1980	Finance	Staff Accountant	$ 42,106	
11	0005	Edwards	Minnie	3/8/1959	F	11/26/1991	Human Resources	Manager	$ 90,228	
12	0006	Franklin	Margaret	11/25/1979	F	3/15/1977	Product Development	staff	$ 42,976	
13	0007	Gardner	William	11/15/1968	M	2/7/1999	Sales	staff	$ 90,650	

Figure 5-58: The formula entered into the criteria cell returns the value of FALSE because the first record in the column does not match the criteria. For all entries that match (evaluate to TRUE), the row is selected by the filter.

When applying the filter, select both the new criteria column header (whether or not it is blank) as well as the criteria formula.

	A	B	C	D	E	F	G	H	I	J
1	EmployeeID	LastName	FirstName	BirthDate	Gender	HireDate	Department	JobTitle	Salary	
2										FALSE
3										
4										
5										
6	EmployeeID	LastName	FirstName	BirthDate	Gender	HireDate			Salary	
7	0001	Abner	David	11/15/1977	M	6/20/2006	S		$110,958	
8	0002	Butler	Susan	11/16/1967	F	8/13/1978	M		$ 40,816	
9	0003	Conrad	Michael	9/14/1955	M	12/25/2001	P		$ 74,665	
10	0004	Davis	Randall	7/15/1947	M	5/25/1980	F		$ 42,106	
11	0005	Edwards	Minnie	3/8/1959	F	11/26/1991	H		$ 90,228	
12	0006	Franklin	Margaret	11/25/1979	F	3/15/1977	P		$ 42,976	
13	0007	Gardner	William	11/15/1968	M	2/7/1999	S		$ 90,650	
14	0008	Hilton	Hillery	11/23/1949	F	11/8/2005	S		$128,845	
15	0009	Jameson	Jennifer	1/17/1959	F	11/28/1992	S		$110,496	
16	0010	Kelly	Chester	10/28/1968	M	1/3/1994	S		$ 98,538	
17	0011	Zahn	Geoffrey	9/6/1952	M	3/4/1999	Sales	Staff	$ 84,151	
18	0012	Patel	Michael	4/20/1974	M	3/19/2003	Sales	District Sales Manager	$133,784	

Advanced Filter dialog box:

Action
- ◉ Filter the list, in-place
- ○ Copy to another location

List range: $A$6:$I$106
Criteria range: Practice!$J$1:$J$2
Copy to:
☐ Unique records only

[OK]   [Cancel]

Figure 5-59: Be sure to select the blank column header cell along with the criteria for the exact match.

J2 ▾ ƒx =EXACT(H7,"staff")

	A	B	C	D	E	F	G	H	I	J
1	EmployeeID	LastName	FirstName	BirthDate	Gender	HireDate	Department	JobTitle	Salary	
2										FALSE
3										
4										
5										
6	EmployeeID	LastName	FirstName	BirthDate	Gender	HireDate	Department	JobTitle	Salary	
8	0002	Butler	Susan	11/16/1967	F	8/13/1978	Marketing	staff	$ 40,816	
12	0006	Franklin	Margaret	11/25/1979	F	3/15/1977	Product Development	staff	$ 42,976	
13	0007	Gardner	William	11/15/1968	M	2/7/1999	Sales	staff	$ 90,650	
107										
108										
109										

Figure 5-60: Results for the exact match criteria using all lower case letters for "staff."

Using Database Functions to Filter & Summarize

Database functions are used to summarize a filtered list of data. Database functions apply a calculation to a filtered subset of list data. Database functions filter records used for a calculation without hiding any rows of the list. All database functions have the same three arguments; *database, field, criteria*. All three arguments are cell ranges. Database functions differ from other spreadsheet functions in that they allow you to specify criteria for including records in the function calculation. The database functions parallel the worksheet functions and are named the same except that database functions are preceded with a "D." The general syntax for all database functions:

> =DFunctionName(database, field, criteria)

Database Function Arguments

*   *database* (the list): cell range (named or unnamed) for the list of data.

    Example: Employees or A6:I106

*   *field* (name of column): the column that the function will use for the calculation.

    Example: Column name such as "Salary."
    Note that field names must be inside double quotes in order for the database function to identify the field within the list.

*   *criteria* (column name(s) and column value(s) to include): determines the records within the list to include in the calculation. The criteria may include multiple values for one field or multiple fields. The criteria for the filter is defined in the same manner as for the *Advanced Filter*. Column headers of the list are duplicated in a row outside the list in a "criteria" range. The criteria values for each column are listed below the criteria column header(s) using AND logic for entries in the same row and OR logic for entries in different rows.

    Example 1: To include records for the Sales department only, enter the value "Sales" (without quotes) under the column header "Department."

    Example 2: To include records for Staff job title only in the Sales department, enter "Sales" (without quotes) under the criteria column header "Department" and enter "Staff" (without quotes) under the criteria column header "Job Title" in the same row.

Table 5-3: Common database functions

Function	Return Value
DSUM	Sum of values in the specified field whose records match the criteria values
DAVERAGE	Average of values in a specified field whose records match the criteria values
DCOUNT	Number of numeric values in a specified field whose records match the criteria values
DCOUNTA	Number of non-blank values in a specified field whose records match the criteria values
DMAX	Maximum value in a specified field whose records match the criteria values
DMIN	Minimum value in a specified field whose records match the criteria values

Practice 5-11

Calculate the average salary for "Staff" employees in the Sales department.

1. Open the workbook "Employees_ch5-11.xlsx."
2. Insert five new rows before the list rows.
3. Copy the column header row and paste it in the first of the inserted rows. The pasted column header row will become the criteria column header row.
4. Type the value "Sales" (without quotes) in the cell below the criteria column header "Department."
5. Type the value "Staff" (without quotes) in the cell below the criteria column header "Job Title" in the **same row** as the previous criteria entry.
6. Select the list of employee records, including the list column headers, and name the range "list."
7. Enter the appropriate database function in a cell to the right of the list.
   a. Use the DAVERAGE function.
   b. Use the range name for the *database* argument ("list").
   c. Be sure to put double quotes around the column name ("Salary") for the *field* argument.
   d. Select the *criteria* range that includes column headers "Department" and "JobTitle" and the values in the cells below the column headers (G1:H2). (You may select all column headers and criteria rows even though some cells within the range are blank. You may also name the entire criteria range "criteria" and use the named range for the *criteria* argument for the database function.)
8. Format the result as currency.

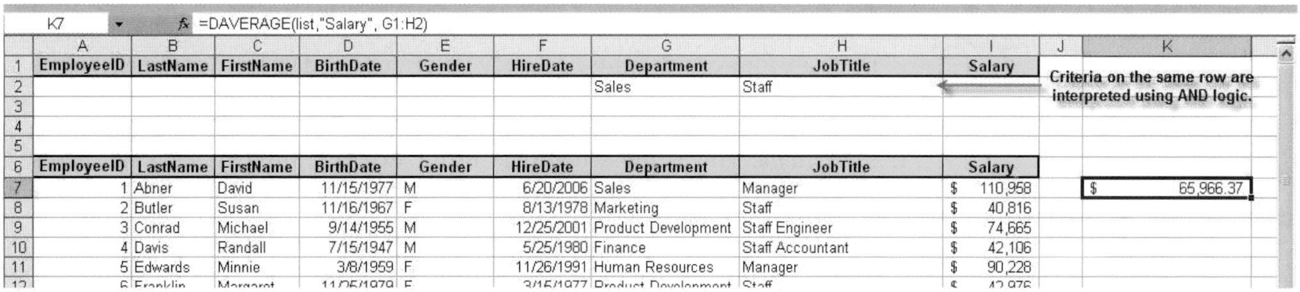

Figure 5-61: Database function using AND logic.

Practice 5-12: (Continue from Practice 11)

Calculate the average salary for all employees in the Sales department or Staff employees in any other department.

9. The value "Sales" (without quotes) should be in the cell below the criteria column header "Department."
10. Type the value "Staff" (without quotes) in the cell below the criteria column header "Job Title" in a **different row** from the previous criteria entry.
11. Enter the appropriate database function in a cell to the right of the list.
    a. Use the DAVERAGE function.
    b. Use the range name for the *database* argument ("list").
    c. Be sure to put double quotes around the column name ("Salary") for the *field* argument.
    d. Select the *criteria* range that includes column headers "Department" and "JobTitle" and the values in the cells below the column headers.
12. Format the result as currency.

	A	B	C	D	E	F	G	H	I	J	K	
K7	▼		*fx*	=DAVERAGE(list,"Salary", G1:H3)								
1	EmployeeID	LastName	FirstName	BirthDate	Gender	HireDate	Department	JobTitle	Salary			
2							Sales				Criteria in different rows are	
3								Staff			interpreted using OR logic.	
4												
5												
6	EmployeeID	LastName	FirstName	BirthDate	Gender	HireDate	Department	JobTitle	Salary			
7	1	Abner	David	11/15/1977	M	6/20/2006	Sales	Manager	$ 110,958		$ 76,807.00	
8	2	Butler	Susan	11/16/1967	F	8/13/1978	Marketing	Staff	$ 40,816			
9	3	Conrad	Michael	9/14/1955	M	12/25/2001	Product Development	Staff Engineer	$ 74,665			
10	4	Davis	Randall	7/15/1947	M	5/25/1980	Finance	Staff Accountant	$ 42,106			
11	5	Edwards	Minnie	3/8/1959	F	11/26/1991	Human Resources	Manager	$ 90,228			

Figure 5-62: Database function using OR logic.

Importing and Exporting Excel Data

Excel can be used not only to manage data within a workbook, but it may be used to import and analyze data from a source external to Excel. External data sources include files from other spreadsheet applications, text files, database files, and Online Analytical Processing (OLAP) cubes. Data that originates in a spreadsheet or database may be saved in a *delimited* file format so that a different spreadsheet or database program can read the fields of data. A *delimited* file is an intermediate file, such as a text file, in which the fields of data are separated by some character(s), such as commas or tabs, which determine the end of each data field and row. The sole purpose of this intermediate file is to transfer the data from one program to another. Once a file is in a delimited format, it can be imported into a different spreadsheet or database program.

In order for Excel to import data from an external source, it must establish a connection to the data source. The connection specifies how to locate, login, and access the external data source. Once the connection is made, the data can be refreshed periodically and automatically so that the data viewed in Excel reflects changes as they occur in the original data.

There are four components necessary for importing data from external sources to Excel.

1. *Source data:* This is the actual data in the external program such as Microsoft Access, SQL Server, Oracle, or delimited text files.

2. *Data Source Name (DSN):* The operating system or application import tools that are used to map a path to the external data. This path is specified in terms of one or both of two technologies; OLE DB (Object Linking and Embedding for Databases and ODBC (Open Database Connectivity). OLE DB is a Microsoft technology for connecting to databases and ODBC is an open source technology which means it is available for use with all database applications. Once the path to the external data is mapped, the path is named (the DSN) and can be accessed by referring to the DSN. The DSN forms an interface to the particular application such as Access, SQL Server, Oracle, dBASE, DB2, or Excel when it is accessed from an external program.

3. *Connection file:* All the information needed to access and retrieve the data items from a data source is stored in a file and is also stored in the target workbook. These files may be stored as a Micorsoft Office Data Connection (.odc) file or as a Data Source Name (.dsn) file.

4. *Excel workbook:* The connection information is copied from the connection file into an Excel workbook. Excel accesses the data source using the connection information. Once the data source is accessed, the data is copied into a workbook and can be used in the same ways as data originated in an Excel workbook.

Excel has specific tools for importing data from Microsoft Access, the Web, and text files. There is also a general import tool for importing data from additional program sources. The tools are accessed from the *Get External Data* task group on the *Data* tab of the ribbon.

Figure 5-63: *Data* tab of the ribbon.

Importing Data from Text Files

A true text file should contain only ASCII characters and no formatting. In a delimited text file, the delimiting character is also an ASCII character. Delimited text files may have one of many different file extensions. Some of the delimited file extensions hint at the delimiting character and some are more generic. A sample of delimited file extensions is listed below.

Table 5-4: Common delimited text file extensions

File Extension	Extension Letters Represent	File Characteristics
.csv	Comma-separated Values	Text file that is delimited with the comma character.
.txt	Text	Text file that may or may not be delimited. If delimited, may use any delimiting character(s).
.tsv	Tab-separated Values	Text file delimited with the tab character.
.scsv	Semicolon-separated Values	Text file delimited with the semicolon character.
.cas	Comma-delimited ASCII	A true ASCII text file that is delimited with the comma character.
.lst	List	A text file that may be delimited by any delimiting character.
.prn	Print	A delimited text file that is typically limited to sharing among print devices. When a command "prints to a file," the file generated may have a .prn extension.

To import a text file to Excel, select from the ribbon **Data(tab)→Get External Data(group)→From Text**. The *Import Text File* dialog box will open. Select the file to import and click the *Import* button. That action will launch the *Text Import Wizard*. In Step 1 of the wizard, select *Delimited* for the *Original data type* if you know the data is delimited with a specific character and select *Fixed width* if you know it is delimited by a fixed column width. (If you are not certain about which to select, open the text file first in a text editor such as Notepad to see how the file data is delimited.) Click the *Next* button to move to Step 2 of the wizard.

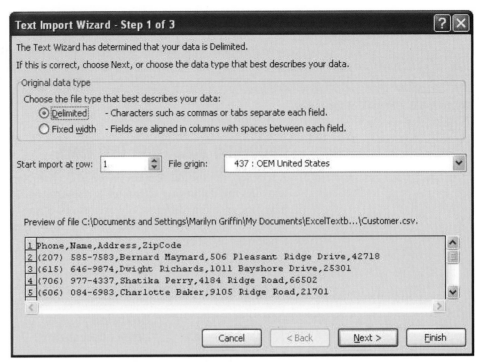

Figure 5-64: Step 1 of the *Import Text Wizard*.

In Step 2 select the delimiting character(s). You may experiment with different characters or combinations of characters and note the effect on the data in the *Data preview* box. Click the *Next* button to continue to Step 3.

Text Import Wizard - Step 2 of 3

This screen lets you set the delimiters your data contains. You can see how your text is affected in the preview below.

Delimiters
- ☑ Tab
- ☐ Semicolon
- ☑ Comma
- ☐ Space
- ☐ Other:

☐ Treat consecutive delimiters as one

Text qualifier: "

Data preview

Phone	Name	Address	ZipCode
(207) 585-7583	Bernard Maynard	506 Pleasant Ridge Drive	42718
(615) 646-9874	Dwight Richards	1011 Bayshore Drive	25301
(706) 977-4337	Shatika Perry	4184 Ridge Road	66502
(606) 084-6983	Charlotte Baker	9105 Ridge Road	21701

Cancel   < Back   Next >   Finish

Figure 5-65: Step 2 of the *Import Text Wizard*.

By default all columns are given the General data type when imported to Excel. The user has the option to select the data type for each column. In some cases, the user will want to override the default selection for columns that contain uncommon date formats and number columns that should be stored as text. Select the column by clicking on the data type name (*General*) at the top of the column. Select the desired data type from the *Column data format* option group. The selected data type will replace *General* at the top of the column. Select the *Finish* button to complete the import.

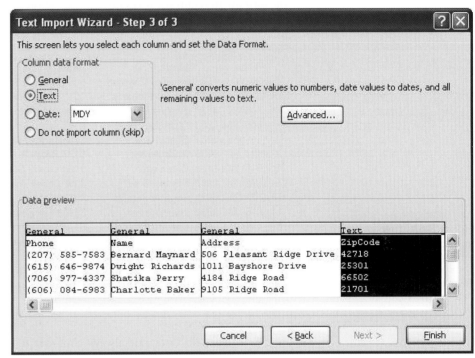

Figure 5-66: Step 3 of the *Import Text Wizard*.

The *Import Data* dialog will appear to give the user the option of importing the data to a range on the current worksheet or to a new worksheet.

Figure 5-67: The *Import Data* dialog box.

Quick Tip!

Text files with a .csv extension will open automatically in Excel when double-clicked because Excel is the application associated with that file type by default.

Caution: When the comma separated value file is opened automatically by double-clicking it or by using the *Open* file command, all columns will be formatted with a *General* format. To override the general format on any column, such as numbers that should be stored as text, or date formats unrecognized by Excel, you will need to use the *Text Import Wizard* to import these files.

The imported data will contain no special formats for column or row header cells. Add the desired formatting to the worksheet data. Keep in mind that any format added to the worksheet data will not be retained if the file is saved back to the delimited text file format. To retain the formatting, save the file as a type of Excel file.

	A	B	C	D	E
1	Phone	Name	Address	ZipCode	
2	(207) 585-7583	Bernard Maynard	506 Pleasant Ridge Drive	42718	
3	(615) 646-9874	Dwight Richards	1011 Bayshore Drive	25301	
4	(706) 977-4337	Shatika Perry	4184 Ridge Road	66502	
5	(606) 084-6983	Charlotte Baker	9105 Ridge Road	21701	
6	(615) 969-8901	Shara Kent	9286 Jacks Place	42420	
7	(808) 801-9830	Anita Hoker	9197 Hatch Road	96815	
8	(617) 843-6488	Cora Logan	1760 Cleary Street	02109	
9	(502) 007-0907	Elwood Gilbert	4407 Green Avenue	40342	
10	(701) 384-5623	Kaye Anderson	4333 Highland Road	58102	
11	(606) 740-3304	Lee Hopkins	3183 High Road	40330	
12	(408) 104-9807	Chris Robinson	8177 Horse Pen Lane	95035	
13	(606) 688-8141	Jolene Reid	8351 Oak Street	41073	
14	(702) 533-3419	Beth Henson	4042 West Bend Drive	89125	
15	(302) 701-7398	Connie Maynard	5095 Sugar Tree Road	19901	
16	(502) 444-1587	Rose Gentry	5744 High Street West	40342	
17	(608) 006-2256	Carly Haley	6087 Spring Street North	54601	

Figure 5-68: Unformatted data is imported to Excel from the delimited text file. Note that leading zeros are retained in the ZipCode column by selecting the Text data type for the imported column.

Imported data does not always conform to good list design in Excel. In the imported data in Figure 5-68, note that the first and last names of the customers are in the same column. Excel has a category of *Text and Data* functions that are very useful for manipulating data so that the user can get imported data into a proper format for analyzing in Excel. Table 5-5 includes some common text and data functions.

In the imported data above, we can use several text functions together to break apart, or *parse* the name into different columns for first and last names.

Practice 5-13

Use text functions to separate the first and last names from the name column and place each in a separate column.

1. You will need the data file "Customer_ch5-13.csv" for this exercise.
2. Open a new Excel file. Select **Data(tab)→Get External Data(tab)→From Text** from the ribbon.
3. Select the file "Customer.csv" and click the *Import* button.
4. In Step 1 of the *Text Import Wizard* make sure *Delimited* is selected as the *Original data type.* Click the *Next* button.
5. In Step 2 specify *Comma* as the delimiter and click the *Next* button.
6. In Step 2 select the "ZipCode" column and apply a *Text* format. Click the *Finish* button.
7. Click the *OK* button on the *Import Data* dialog box to import the data to the current worksheet.
8. Insert two new columns after the "Name" column. Add column headers of "FirstName" and "LastName."

Table 5-5: Some common text and data functions

Text/Data Function	Description
CONCATENATE(text1, text2, [text3 . . ., text255])	Joins multiple text items into one text item. The ampersand (&) may also be used to join text items.
DOLLAR(number, [decimals])	Converts a number to text, using the dollar ($) currency format. If the *decimals* argument is omitted, it is assumed to be 2.
EXACT(text1, text2)	Checks to see if two text values are identical.
FIND(find_text, within_text, [start_num])	Finds one text value within another (case-sensitive) and returns its start position. The *start_num* argument specifies the position to begin the search. If omitted, it is assumed to be 1.
LEFT(text, [num_chars])	Returns the leftmost characters (as specified by the *num_chars*) from a text value. If *num_chars* is omitted, it is assumed to be 1.
LEN(text)	Returns the number of characters in a text string
LOWER(text)	Converts text to lowercase
MID(text, start_num, num_chars)	Returns a specific number of characters from a text string starting at the position you specify by *start_num*.
PROPER(text)	Capitalizes the first letter in each word of a text value
REPLACE(old_text, start_num, num_chars, new_text)	Replaces characters within text with a different text based on the number of characters specified. *Start_num* specified the position within the *old_text* that you want to replace with *new_text*. Use REPLACE when you want to replace **any text** that occurs in a specific location in a string and use SUBSTITUTE when you want to replace **specific text** and.
RIGHT(text, [num_chars])	Returns a number of rightmost characters from a text value.
SEARCH(find_text, within_text, [start_num])	Finds one text value within another (not case-sensitive) and returns its start position. The start_num argument specifies the position to begin the search. If omitted, it is assumed to be 1.
SUBSTITUTE(text, old_text, new_text, [instance_num])	Substitutes new text for old text in a text string. Use SUBSTITUTE when you want to replace **specific text** and use REPLACE when you want to replace **any text** that occurs in a specific location in a string.
TEXT(value, format_text)	Formats a number and converts it to text. *Format_text* includes a numeric format enclosed in quotation marks using a 0 (zero) for the place holder. Example: "$0.00." View available formats in the formats drop in the Number task group of the Home ribbon tab.
TRIM(text)	Removes spaces from text except for single spaces between words.
UPPER(text)	Converts text to uppercase.

9. Enter a formula into the "FirstName" column that parses the first name from the text string in the "Name" column:

=LEFT(B2,FIND(" ",B2)-1).

10. Enter a formula into the "LastName" column that parses the last name from the text string in the "Name" column:

=RIGHT(B2,LEN(B2)-FIND(" ", B2))

11. Format the column header differently from the data rows of the list. Once the list is in an acceptable list format, Excel data management and data analysis tools may be applied.

Text Formulas Explained

When parsing the first name from the "Name" column, the FIND function locates the space between the two names in the original column and returns its character position in the data string to the num_chars argument of the LEFT function. Since the first name ends one position to the left of the space, we will need to subtract one from the space position number to get the exact number of characters needed for the first name. The LEFT function begins parsing at the first character in the original column and returns the number of characters determined by the return of the FIND function minus one.

When parsing the last name from the "Name" column, we want to begin at the right of the cell value and parse just to the right of the space to include all characters for the last name. The FIND function again locates the space between the two names in the original column and returns that position number but that alone is not adequate for parsing the last name. We need to know the length of the whole name string then parse from the right the length minus the position of the space between the first and last names. The LEN function returns the number of characters in the text string including any spaces or special characters. So the length minus the position of the space returns the number of characters in the last name which the RIGHT function needs to know.

Once the first and last names have been parsed into separate columns you may delete the original column. Since the values in the "FirstName" and "LastName" columns are dependent on the original column by way of formulas, we need to remove the formulas from the two new columns before deleting the original column. To remove the formulas, copy the two new columns and paste back to their same location using the *Paste Special* option. Select the option to *Paste Values* only. Once the formulas are removed from the new columns, the original column may be deleted.

	A	B	C	D	E	F
1	Phone	FirstName	LastName	Address	ZipCode	
2	(207) 585-7583	Bernard	Maynard	506 Pleasant Ridge Drive	42718	
3	(615) 646-9874	Dwight	Richards	1011 Bayshore Drive	25301	
4	(706) 977-4337	Shatika	Perry	4184 Ridge Road	66502	
5	(606) 084-6983	Charlotte	Baker	9105 Ridge Road	21701	
6	(615) 969-8901	Shara	Kent	9286 Jacks Place	42420	
7	(808) 801-9830	Anita	Hoker	9197 Hatch Road	96815	
8	(617) 843-6488	Cora	Logan	1760 Cleary Street	02109	
9	(502) 007-0907	Elwood	Gilbert	4407 Green Avenue	40342	
10	(701) 384-5623	Kaye	Anderson	4333 Highland Road	58102	
11	(606) 740-3304	Lee	Hopkins	3183 High Road	40330	
12	(408) 104-9807	Chris	Robinson	8177 Horse Pen Lane	95035	
13	(606) 688-8141	Jolene	Reid	8351 Oak Street	41073	
14	(702) 533-3419	Beth	Henson	4042 West Bend Drive	89125	
15	(302) 701-7398	Connie	Maynard	5095 Sugar Tree Road	19901	
16	(502) 444-1587	Rose	Gentry	5744 High Street West	40342	
17	(608) 006-2256	Carly	Haley	6087 Spring Street Noth	54601	
18	(304) 477-6629	David	Garrison	1830 Glenwood Drive	26261	
19	(614) 721-2870	Lisa	Patterson	3688 Longs Pike Road	43216	

Figure 5-69: Formatted customer data after parsing "Name" column into two separate columns for first and last name.

Importing Data from Microsoft Access

There are several ways to share data between Microsoft Excel and Microsoft Access. Data sharing may be initiated from either Excel or Access. Note that the word "import" has a different meaning depending on whether you are working from Excel or from Access. Working from Excel, import means to use a data connection to establish a permanent link between the imported data that can be viewed in Excel, and the original data. By linking to the original data source, the data in Excel may be refreshed when then original data changes. Working from Access, import means to bring a copy of the data into a database table but without using a data connection to maintain a permanent link to the original data.

Ways to bring data into Excel from Access

1. From Access copy data from a data sheet and paste it into an Excel worksheet.
   a. With the database open and a table selected in the data sheet view, click the *Select All* icon in the upper left corner of the data sheet (same location as the *Select All* icon on an Excel worksheet).
   b. Use the *Clipboard* copy and paste commands to copy from the Access data sheet and paste into an Excel worksheet.

2. From Excel, establish a connection to the Access database.
   a. From the Excel ribbon select **Data(tab)→Get External Data(group)→From Access**.
   b. Select the Access database file you wish to access. (The file extension may be *.accdb* for Access 2007 formats or *.mdb* for Access formats prior to the 2007 version.) The *Data Link Properties* dialog box will appear.
   c. Accept the default settings in the dialog box and click the *Test Connection* button to test the connection. (Note that the connection test will not be successful if the database file is open, but the actual connection should be successful.) Click the *OK* button to accept the settings.
   d. A dialog box will appear that shows the connection information. Verify the connection information and edit if necessary (for example, a username and/or password may be changed or added, then click the *OK* button to continue.
   e. A list of tables in the connected database will appear. Select the table to which you wish to connect and click the OK button.
   f. In the *Import Data* dialog box (see Figure 5-67) select the location and presentation options for the data. Click the *OK* button to complete the connection.
   g. To set refresh options for the linked data, select a cell inside the imported data list and from the ribbon select **Data(tab)→Connections(group)→Refresh All→Connection Properties**. Select as many of the refresh options as desired, then click the *OK* button to close the dialog box. (See Figure 5-70.)

3. From Access, export data from Access to Excel.
   a. Open the Access file from which you wish to export.
   b. Select the table you wish to export.
   c. Select **External Data(tab)→Export(group)→Excel**.
   d. Browse to save the file to the desired location. The file name may be changed from the default name which is the table name with the standard Excel file extension. Click the *Save* button to close the *File Save* dialog box.
   e. Select export options on the *Export* dialog box. Click the OK button to continue with the export. (See Figure 5-71.)

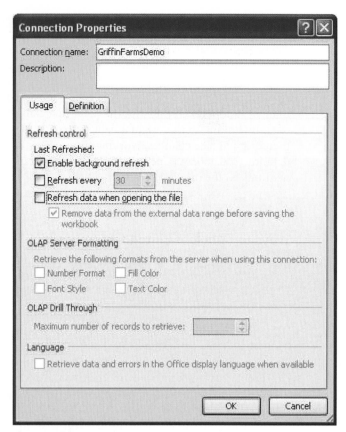

Figure 5-70: Set data refresh options in the *Connection Properties* dialog box.

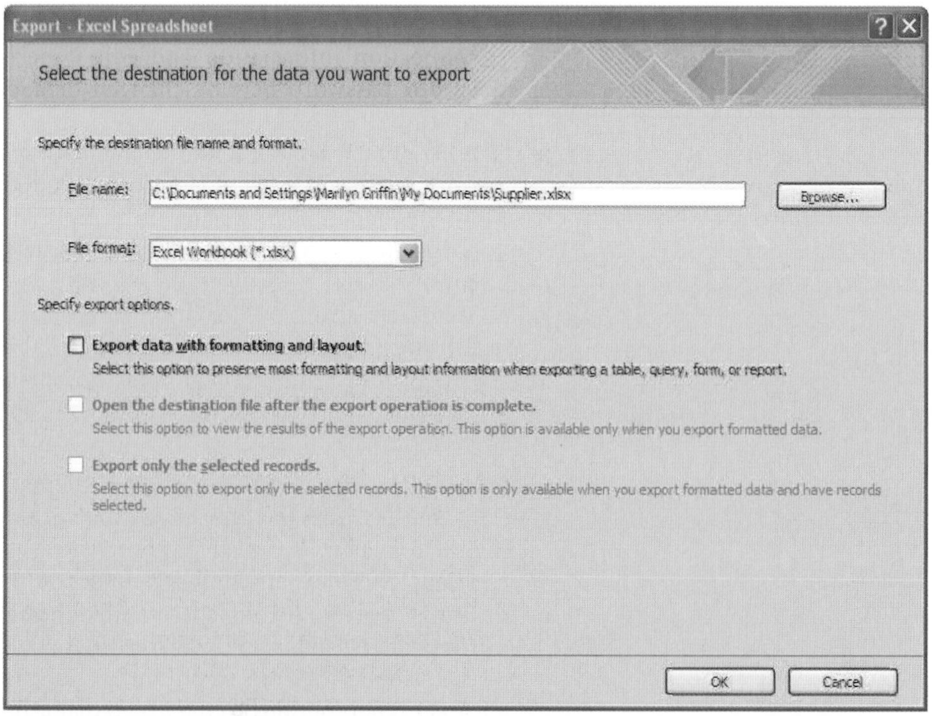

Figure 5-71: Select refresh options in the *Export* dialog box.

f. A dialog box will appear that gives you the option of saving the export steps in a separate file. Click *Save Export* to save and the *Cancel* button to bypass this step.

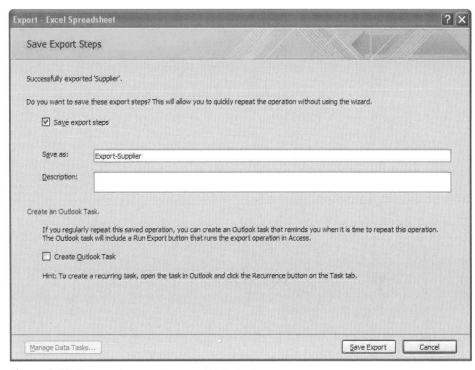

Figure 5-72: Export steps may be saved if desired.

You may now view the data in the Excel file. During the export process, you may select the export option to open the target Excel file after the export is complete.

Ways to bring data into Access from Excel

1. From Excel copy data from an Excel worksheet and paste it into an Access data sheet.
   a. With the Excel file open, copy the data to export from the Excel worksheet.
   b. Paste the copied data into an Access data sheet just as you would paste it into another worksheet. If you are exporting to a new table you will need to use the *Create* tab in Access to create the new table. You need not add any additional attributes (columns) to the table. Use the command **Home(tab)→Clipboard (group)→Paste→Paste Append** to complete the paste action.

2. From Access, import an Excel worksheet into an Access table.
   a. Open the Access database file into which you wish to import the Excel data. To begin the import, select **External Data(tab)→Import(group)→Excel** from the Access ribbon. The *Get External Data* dialog box will appear.
   b. Browse to select the Excel file and select the file to import.
   c. Select the option for importing into Access:
      i. Import into a new table.
      ii. Append an existing table (select the table)
      iii. Establish a link to the table.

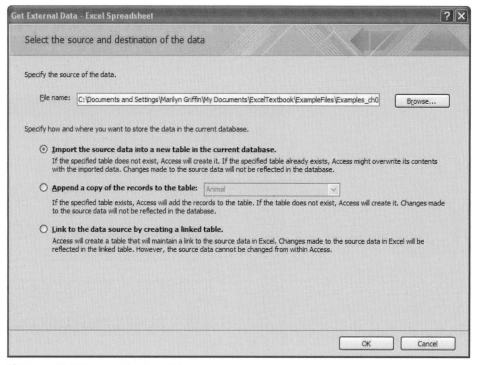

Figure 5-73: Import options for bringing Excel data into Access.

d. Click the *OK* button to continue with the import. The *Import Spreadsheet Wizard* dialog box will appear.
e. Select what you would like to import, a worksheet or a named range. Click the *Next* button to continue to the next step.

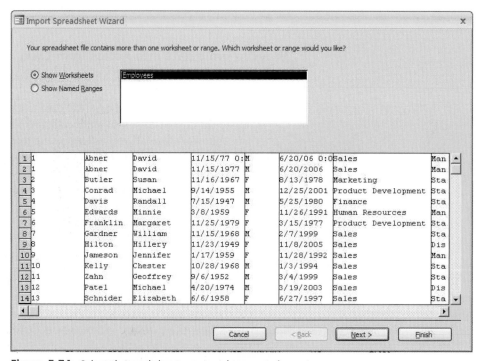

Figure 5-74: Select the worksheet or named range to import.

f. If the exported range has column headers, check the box beside *First Row Contains Column Headers*. Click the *Next* button to continue.

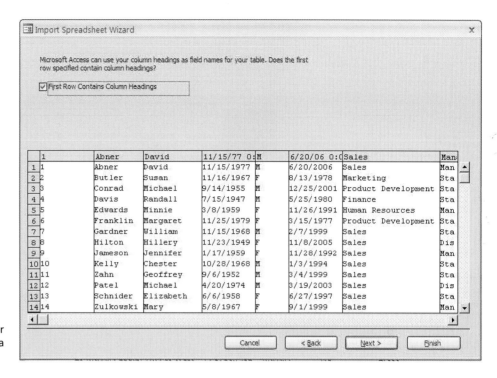

Figure 5-75: Verify whether or not the imported data contains a column header row.

g. In the next dialog box, select each field and review and edit the data type as needed for the imported data. Click the *Next* button to continue.

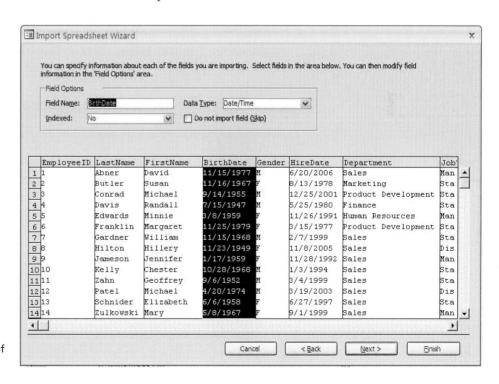

Figure 5-76: Edit the data type of each imported as needed.

h. In the next dialog box, select the option for a primary key. A database table must have a field that contains unique values for each record designated as a primary key. A current field that qualifies may be selected or the import wizard may add a primary key field.

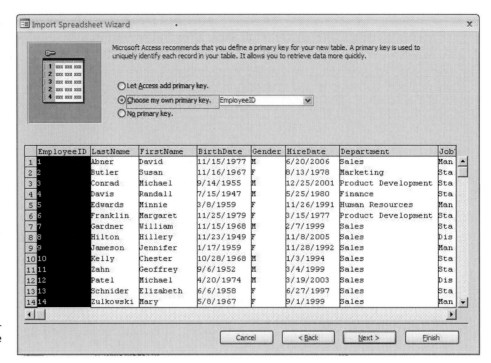

Figure 5-77: Select options for assigning a primary key field to the imported table.

   i. The next dialog box will ask you to name the new table (if the option was selected to import to a new table). Click the *Finish* button to complete the import. You will be prompted to save the import steps to a separate file if desired.

3. From Access, establish a connection to an Excel worksheet.
   a. From the Access ribbon, select **External Data(tab)→Import(group)→Excel**. The *Get External Data* dialog box will appear. Select the Excel file to link then select the option to *Link to the Date Source by Creating a Linked Table*.

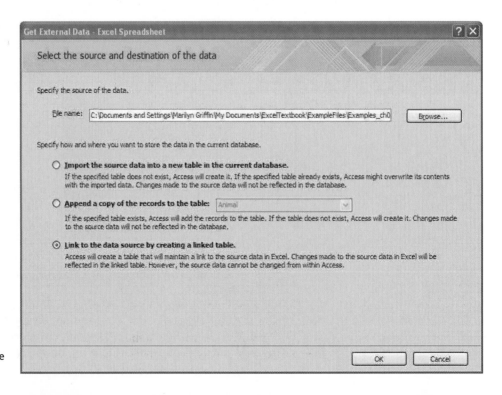

Figure 5-78: Select the Excel file to link with Access.

b. The remaining steps of establishing the link are the same as those for importing an Excel worksheet into Access.

c. When the data is changed in the Excel worksheet, the change is reflected immediately in the Access table.

Importing Data from the Web

Many Web pages contain delimited data that can be imported or linked directly to an Excel worksheet. Like other data brought into Excel, it may be used as a static set of data or it may be linked to the Web data making it refreshable. Data sets on the Web are brought into Excel by way of *Web Queries.*

Copy a Static Web Table into Excel

1. Open Internet Explorer. Navigate to the Web page from which you would like to download a table of data.
2. Right-click anywhere on the Web table and select **Export to Microsoft Excel** from the context menu.
3. A message such as ". . . Getting Data . . ." will appear while the data is downloading from the table.
4. Once the data appears on the Excel worksheet, it is no longer connected to the Web data source.

Figure 5-79: Use Internet Explorer to download static Web data into Excel.

Link Web Data to Excel Using a *Web Query*

1. Select from the Excel ribbon **Data(tab)→Get External Data(group)→From Web**. The *New Web Query* dialog box will appear. Enter the URL of the Web page into the *Address* box.
2. Navigate to the table on the Web page that you would like to import or link. Tables that are accessible from the Web page are indicated by a small arrow that points to the right. The arrow is in the upper left corner of the Web table. The arrow has a yellow background that changes to green when the mouse hovers over it. When the mouse hovers over the arrow, the table is outlined. Click the arrow to select the table

to import. Once the Web table is selected, the table is highlighted and the arrow turns into a check mark. Click the *Import* button to complete the import or link.

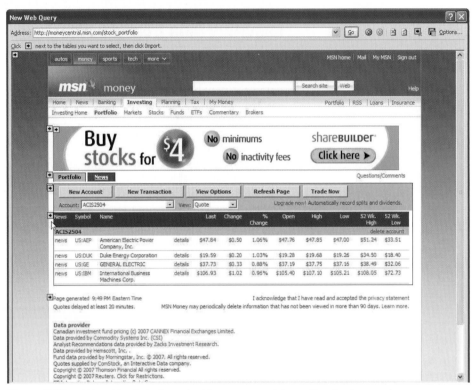

Figure 5-80: Web tables in indicated with an arrow with a yellow background.

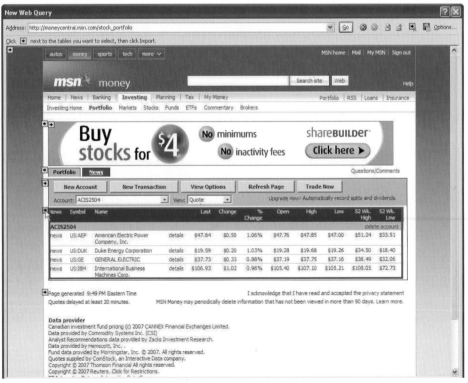

Figure 5-81: When the mouse hovers over the arrow, the background turns to green and the Web table is outlined.

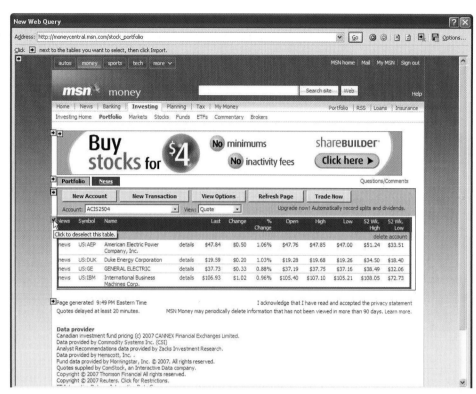

Figure 5-82: When the table is selected, it is highlighted and the arrow turns into a check mark.

After the import button is clicked, you will be prompted for the target location for the imported data. After the *Import Data* dialog box is closed, it may take a few seconds for the Web data to appear on the worksheet. A message such as ". . . Getting Data . . ." will appear on the worksheet until the Web data appears.

Once the Web data is present, it may be refreshed manually or set to refresh automatically by using the same commands as for refreshing other linked data.

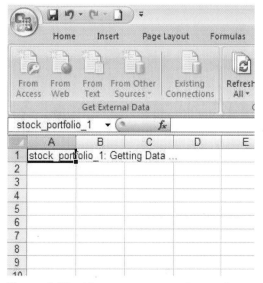

Figure 5-83: Message appears to let you know data is being accessed.

	A	B	C	D	E	F	G	H	I	J	K	L	M	N	O	P	Q	R	S	T	U	V	W
1	News		Symbol		Name				Last		Change		% Change		Open		High		Low		52 Wk. High		52 Wk. Low
2																							
3	ACIS2504																			delete account			
4	news		US:AEP		American Electric Power Company, Inc.		details		$47.84		$0.50		1.06%		$47.76		$47.85		$47.00		$51.24		$33.51
5																							
6	news		US:DUK		Duke Energy Corporation		details		$19.59		$0.20		1.03%		$19.28		$19.68		$19.26		$34.50		$18.40
7																							
8	news		US:GE		GENERAL ELECTRIC		details		$37.73		$0.33		0.88%		$37.19		$37.75		$37.16		$38.49		$32.06
9																							
10	news		US:IBM		International Business Machines Corp.		details		$106.93		$1.02		0.96%		$105.40		$107.10		$105.21		$108.05		$72.73
11																							

Figure 5-84: Web query result appears on Excel worksheet.

Importing Data to Excel from Other Sources

When linking to data from sources other than text files, Access, or the Web, the user will need to set up a data source name and a connection to the data source before being able to access the external data. For text files, Access data, and Web data, these steps are performed by the application (Excel, Access, or Internet Explorer) so the user need only use the import tools already provided by the Microsoft programs.

Add the Data Source Name (DSN)

Utilities for adding data sources are available in the Windows operating systems. The following steps are those needed to set up a data source in Windows XP Professional SP2. Similar steps are used in other Windows operating systems.

1. From the *Start* button of Windows, select **Control Panel→Administrative Tools→Data Sources (ODBC)→System DSN(tab)→Add** button. The *Create New Data Source* dialog box will appear.
2. Select the type of driver needed based on the type of database to which you wish to connect. For example, to connect to a database using Oracle XE (Express Edition) DBMS (database management system) select *Microsoft ODBC for Oracle* from the list.

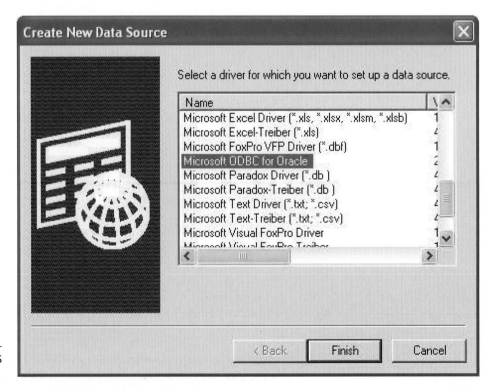

Figure 5-85: Select the appropriate driver for the type the DBMS you wish to access.

3. Click the *Finish* button to complete the driver selection. The dialog box will appear for specifying the login information for the data source. Login information includes the data source name, user name (and optional password), and the server machine name. Click the *OK* button to save the changes. The new data source name will appear in the *System DSN* list.

Figure 5-86: Specify the name and login information for the data source.

Create the Connection

Create the connection to the data source by using tools available in Excel.

1. Select from the Excel ribbon **Data(tab)→Get External Data(group)→From Other Sources→From Data Connection Wizard**. The *Data Connection Wizard* dialog box appears.
2. Select the type of data source. (Select ODBC DSN for Oracle data sources.) The next dialog box will display all data sources for the type selected.
3. Select the data source from the list. Click the *Next* button to continue.
4. The next dialog box asks for the login information (user name, password, and server name). Enter the login information and click the *OK* button to continue.
5. The next dialog box of the *Data Connection Wizard* lists the tables in the data source. Select the table you wish to import and click the *Next* button to continue.
6. In the next dialog box, enter a name and description for the new connection file. Click the *Finish* button to select the location for the imported data. Click the OK button to complete the import.
7. You may be asked to confirm the connection information or to supply a missing password before the data import is complete.

Data connections may also be created by selecting the *Connections* task from the *Connections* task group on the *Data* tab of the Excel ribbon. To create a connection using the Connections command:

1. Select **Data(tab)→Connections(group)→Connections**. The *Workbook Connections* dialog box will appear.
2. Click the *Add* button to add a new connection. The *Existing Connections* dialog box will appear.
3. If the connection is not already defined, click the *Browse for More* button on the dialog box.
4. Navigate to **My Documents→My Data Sources**. Select the data source for which you wish to create a new connection.
5. Click the *Close* button to close the *Workbook Connections* dialog box.
6. The new connection name will now appear in the list inside the *Existing Connections* dialog box.

The same *Data Connection Wizard* may also be accessed by selecting **My Documents→My Data Sources→Connect to a New Data Source**.

Excel 3D Formulas

Formulas that contain references to other worksheets or workbooks are commonly called "3D" formulas in Excel. In addition to the cell reference, a 3D reference must include the worksheet name for different worksheets and the workbook name for different workbooks. The best way to insert a reference to another worksheet into a formula is to click on the cell in the external worksheet. Using that technique, the worksheet and cell references will be inserted automatically in the proper syntax.

Referencing Another Worksheet

When referencing a different worksheet in a formula, the name of the worksheet is used in the formula followed by an exclamation point (!) to identify the text as a worksheet name. The cell reference is entered after the exclamation point. A reference to a worksheet named "Reference" that contains a lookup table would be written in the following format: **Reference!** A worksheet name that contains spaces will include single quotes around the worksheet name in the formula cell reference. For example, a reference to a worksheet named "Promotional Sales" would be referenced in the following syntax: **'Promotional Sales'!**

Referencing Another Workbook

When one workbook is referenced in a formula in another workbook, the two workbooks are said to be "linked." The referenced workbook's name is included in the formula inside a set of square brackets in the following format: **[Reference.xlsx]**. The workbook name appears first in the formula, followed by the worksheet name, and ending with the cell reference in the following format: **[Reference.xlsx] SalaryGrades!$A$1:$B$6.**

The best way to insert a reference to another workbook into a formula is to open the referenced workbook and use the mouse pointer to click on the desired cell in the external workbook. The reference, including the workbook name and cell reference will be inserted automatically with the proper syntax. The following formula is entered into the "SalaryGrade" column of the employee worksheet and it references a lookup table in an external workbook named "Reference_ch5.xlsx." The worksheet name is "SalaryGrades." The cell reference is the lookup table range.

=VLOOKUP(J2,[Reference_ch5.xlsx]SalaryGrades!$A$1:$B$6,2)

Note that the referenced or linked workbook filename reference is relative to the location of the current Excel file that references it. While all workbooks are open, Excel only inserts the filename and not the entire path to the file. After the workbook is saved and closed, the full file path will be displayed in the formula when the referencing workbook is reopened. Note that the file path is preceded by an apostrophe ('), the filename is in square brackets ([]), and the worksheet name is followed by an exclamation point (!). Note that single quotes are around the path and workbook name since some path folders contains spaces.

=VLOOKUP(J2, 'C:\Documents and Settings\Username\My Documents\ [Reference_ch5.xlsx]SalaryGrades'!$A$1:$B$6, 2)

Practice 5-14

1. Open the Excel workbooks "Employes_ch5-14.xlsx" and "SalaryGradesTable_ch5-14.xlsx."

2. Insert a formula in the "SalaryGrade" column that uses the unnamed lookup table in the "SalaryGradesTable_ch5-14.xlsx" workbook.

   a. To insert the table reference for the table_array argument of the lookup function, use the mouse pointer to select the lookup range on the "SalaryGrades" worksheet.

   b. Complete the formula by inserting 2 for the column index to return from the lookup table.

Excel maintains the link between the workbooks as long as neither workbook is moved to different location or folder. Sometimes Excel is able to track the referenced workbook and update the link to it automatically, but at times the user may need to update the link manually.

Practice moving the referenced workbook and editing the link to "point" to the new location if Excel does not track the moved workbook automatically. Select **Data(tab)→ Connections→Edit Links** from the ribbon and navigate to the new referenced workbook location.

Proactively, the link between the workbooks can be edited by selecting the same command from the ribbon. In the *Edit Links* dialog box, note the *Status* of the links listed. Those marked with error messages or "Unknown" should be updated. Select the link to update and click the *Update Values* button. Navigate through the file directory to locate the referenced workbook. Select the referenced workbook and click the *OK* button. By editing the link, you have "pointed" the referencing workbook to the new referenced workbook location. After clicking the *OK* button to update the link, you may be prompted to select the appropriate worksheet from a worksheet list associated with the referenced workbook. After the workbook link has been updated, select the formula cell to view the path to the new referenced workbook location.

If the referenced workbook is moved and the link not yet updated, you will be prompted to update the link when the referencing file is opened. You will be given the chance to update the link or not update the link and use the previous unchanged data.

Keep in mind that a referenced workbook must be stored or moved along the referencing workbook. For example, if a workbook file is copied onto an external storage device to take to a presentation, the referenced workbook must also be copied into the same relative location in order for the referencing workbook to remain up to date. You may need to update the link after moving both files to the new locations.

Working with Grouped Worksheets

Multiple worksheets with the same layout may be grouped so that formatting or formulas may be applied to all worksheets at once. When worksheets are grouped, actions performed on one worksheet are duplicated on all other worksheets in the group. For example, you may enter and format titles for worksheets such that each worksheet title may only need to be altered by some small detail, such as month, sales person, or quarter number. A formula may be entered into a cell on one sheet and will be duplicated for all other worksheets in the group. Note that automatic formats from the table design gallery cannot be applied to multiple worksheets at once.

To group worksheets, hold down the *Ctrl* key and click on each worksheet tab you wish to include in the group. To select a contiguous group of worksheets, click on the first worksheet tab to group and, while holding down the *Shift* key, click on the last worksheet tab to group. To ungroup worksheets, click on a worksheet tab that is not included in the group. If all worksheets in the workbook are included in the group, click on any worksheet tab to ungroup.

Practice 15

Add formatting and formulas to all worksheet in a group.

1. Open the Excel workbook "Roster_ch5-15.xlsx."
2. Group all worksheets in the workbook.
3. With all worksheets grouped, add a new column header to the right of the list. Enter the text "Average" into the column header.
4. In the first row of the new column, enter a formula that calculates the average for all exams for the first student.
5. Copy the formula to all remaining rows in the list.
6. In the row immediately under the list, enter a formula into the Exam1 column that will calculate the class average for that item.
7. Copy the formula to remaining columns for other exams.
8. In cell H27, enter a formula that calculates the overall average of all exams for all students. (This formula may be copied from the cell above or from the cell to the left.)
9. Add a label in cell B27 "Exam Averages."
10. Insert two new rows at the top of the worksheet.
11. In cell A1, enter the text "Class Roster 8:00 Class, Spring 2007."
12. Merge and center the text across all columns of the student list. Make the font bold and size 16 point. Add background and font color for the title.
13. Select the column headers. Change the font color and background to those of the title. Make the column header text bold.
14. Select all formula cells and format them to match column headers.
15. Ungroup the worksheets. Select worksheet "Class9." Change the "8" in the title to "9."
16. Select worksheet "Class10." Change the "8" in the title to "10."

	A	B	C	D	E	F	G	H
1		Class Roster 8:00 Class, Spring 2007						
2								
3	StudentID	LastName	FirstName	Exam1	Exam2	Exam3	Exam4	Average
4	1001	Akers	Joseph	75	75	83	82	78.75
5	1002	Allen	Robert	96	97	89	99	95.25
6	1003	Bayse	Frances	90	93	85	85	88.25
7	1004	Bridgen	Carol	78	82	81	80	80.25
8	1005	Crawford	Jerry	70	71	77	71	72.25
9	1006	Edmonds	Randal	91	93	87	91	90.5
10	1007	Durham	Ruby	100	92	97	88	94.25
11	1008	Fulford	Patricia	90	87	85	88	87.5
12	1009	Gresham	Lane	75	75	79	81	77.5
13	1010	Guffy	Barry	85	82	76	84	81.75
14	1011	Spencer	Jasmine	91	95	94	93	93.25
15	1012	Thomas	Regina	73	77	77	74	75.25
16	1013	Terrill	Gary	84	79	83	76	80.5
17	1014	Steele	Dean	87	99	98	89	93.25
18	1015	Shelton	Dennis	76	76	76	82	77.5
19	1016	Shockley	Frank	89	89	86	92	89
20	1017	Sauls	Mary	83	80	82	81	81.5
21	1018	Robertson	Darla	78	85	73	81	79.25
22	1019	Roman	Margie	85	81	80	85	82.75
23	1020	Reynolds	Beverly	99	95	88	86	92
24	1021	Powers	Douglas	78	82	81	85	81.5
25	1022	Prillaman	Arthur	88	92	86	86	88
26	1023	Palmerio	Barbara	72	81	73	76	75.5
27	1024	Noble	Rachel	99	89	94	96	94.5
28	1025	McRoy	Renee	92	93	85	91	90.25
29		Exam Averages		84.96	85.6	83.8	84.88	84.81

Class8 / Class9 / Class10 /

Figure 5-87: Format added to first sheet is applied to all worksheets in the group.

Documenting Excel Workbooks

Whether developing Excel workbooks for yourself or for other users, good workbook documentation helps to clearly state its purpose and guidelines for use. Documentation may also include user instructions and/or change history. Documentation is not only for the user's benefit, but it can also serve as a reminder to you as the workbook developer of development and maintenance issues.

The Documentation Worksheet

As soon as a workbook is opened the purpose and contents should be clear to the user. Adding a documentation worksheet as the first worksheet in the workbook is a good way to provide information that is helpful to both the user and developer. If the workbook is saved each time with the documentation workbook active, it will be active when the workbook is reopened. Documentation worksheets should contain at least the following basic information about the workbook.

1. Purpose of the workbook
2. Date created
3. Creator/Developer
4. Summary of worksheets

Additional information may include:

1. Workbook title
2. Changes or enhancements since the original development
3. Images or other visual enhancements

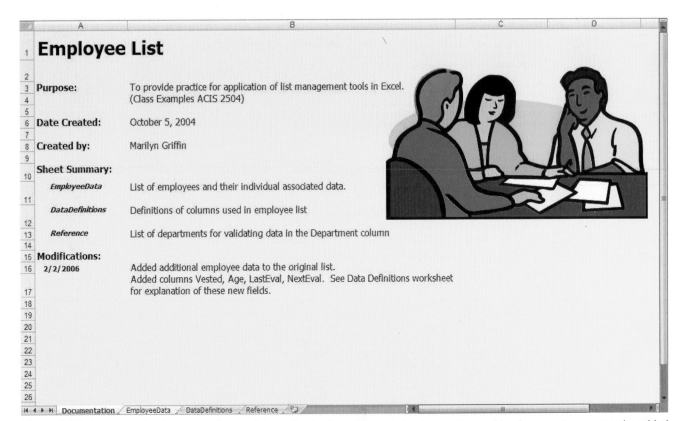

Figure 5-88: Example of a documentation worksheet that is the active worksheet when the workbook opens. Images may be added to worksheets by selecting **Insert(tab)→Illustrations(group)→(type of image)** from the ribbon.

Data Definitions for Workbook Data

In any application that presents and analyzes data, it should be clear what each data item represents and its characteristics so that data may be added or updated without compromising the integrity and flexibility of the workbook. To aid in communicating information about how the data is stored in a workbook, a list of data definitions is helpful. Data definitions should be documented on a worksheet separate from the data list(s). If there are several data items to define, you may want to dedicate an entire worksheet to the data definitions.

When defining the characteristics of stored data, the following information about each data item should be recorded.

1. Column (field) name
2. Data type of the field data
3. Description of the data item
4. Acceptable or restricted values (for purposes of data validation)
5. Formula in fields that contain calculated values

	ColumnName	Type	Description	Accepted Values	Formula
1	**Data Definitions**				
2					
3	ColumnName	Type	Description	Accepted Values	Formula
4	ID	Number	Company assigned identification number. Length is 4 digits.		
5	FirstName	Text	First name of the employee		
6	LastName	Text	Last name of the employee		
7	Department	Text	Employee's primary department in which he/she works		
8	Title	Text	Job title		
9	Salary	Currency	Annual salary		
10	HireDate	Date	Date employee was hired. If rehired, will list employee once for each employement period.		
11	Vested	Text	Up-to-date status of vesting in company retirement plan. Employee is vested after 5 years of employment.	Yes, No	=IF((TODAY()-G3)>5*365.35,"Yes", "No")
12	BirthDate	Date	Date of birth of employee		
13	Gender	Text	Gender of employee, M=Male, F=Female	M, F	
14	Age	Integer	Up-to-date age of employee in whole years.	Calculated field	=INT((TODAY()-I3)/365.25)
15	Clearance	Text	Level of security clearance. C=Basic clearance, S=Second level clearance, TS= Top level clearance, No value (blank cell)=No clearance	C, S, TS	
16	LastEval	Date	Date of last performance evaluation. Performance evaluations are done after 3 months of employments, then annally in month of employment thereafter. Date of last evaluation is entered manually by the evaluator.		
17	NextEval	Date	Date next performance evaluation is due. If last evaluation was 3-month initial evaluation, next evaluation is during month of hire one year after hiredate. Otherwise next evaluation is due one year after last evaluation.		=IF((M3-G3)>365,DATE(YEAR(M3)+1,MONTH(M3),DAY(M3)), DATE(YEAR(G3)+1,MONTH(G3),DAY(G3)))
18					
19					
20					
21					
22					
23					
24					
25					

Documentation / EmployeeData / **DataDefinitions** / Reference

Figure 5-89: Example of a data definition worksheet for the employee data stored in this workbook.

Review Questions

1. List or describe the characteristics of a list that allow Excel to readily recognize the list boundaries and column headers.

   _____

   _____

   _____

2. When using the *General* format in Excel, how is text aligned automatically in the cell? How are numeric data aligned in the cell? How are date values aligned in the cell?

   _____

   _____

   _____

3. How can *Conditional Formatting* be used to highlight alternating rows of a worksheet?

   _____

   _____

   _____

4. What is the purpose of *data validation*? To what range(s) of the list is *data validation* applied?

   _____

   _____

   _____

5. How can named ranges make *data validation* easier to implement?

   _____

   _____

   _____

6. What actions can be performed using a *Data Form*?

   _____

   _____

   _____

7. What is the purpose of *freezing panes* in a worksheet?

    _____

    _____

    _____

8. Give an example of how you would use a *custom sort order* (sorting by something other than alphabetical order or numeric order) in Excel.

    _____

    _____

    _____

9. Briefly describe two ways to apply subtotals to a list.

    _____

    _____

    _____

10. What does it mean to filter or query a list?

    _____

    _____

    _____

11. In what cases would you use the *Advanced Filter* feature rather than the *AutoFilter*?

    _____

    _____

    _____

12. What are *database functions* and how do they differ from their mathematical or statistical counterparts?

    _____

    _____

    _____

13. What are *wildcard characters* and what is the general purpose of them as they relate to the *Advanced Filter* and *database functions*?

_____

_____

_____

14. What is the syntax for entering a cell reference on a different worksheet?

_____

_____

_____

15. Using the correct syntax, write an example of a cell reference:

   a. To a different worksheet.
   b. To a different workbook (be sure to include the worksheet syntax also since is it also a different worksheet from the current worksheet).

_____

_____

_____

16. Briefly describe the return value of the following functions and give an example for each of a situation in which it might be applied.

   a. CONCATENATE
   b. FIND & SEARCH
   c. LEFT & RIGHT
   d. LEN

_____

_____

_____

17. What characteristic is common among all "delimited" files?

_____

_____

_____

18. List some common characters used as "delimiters" for delimited files.

_____

_____

_____

19. What is a *Web Query*? Give an example of how a *Web Query* might enhance an Excel workbook.

_____

_____

_____

20. Describe one advantage of using the *Data Import Wizard* in Excel to import a comma delimited file (.csv extension) rather than allowing Excel to open it automatically.

_____

_____

_____

21. How does importing data from text files, Access, or the Web differ from importing data from other sources into Excel? What are the general steps required to import data from a source other than Access, text files, or the Web?

_____

_____

_____

Practice Problems

1. Design a workbook to store information about your summer lawn service clients. Name and save the workbook. The workbook requirements are listed below.

   a. Store the following information:
      - Client's name
      - Client's physical address (street address only)
      - Client's complete mailing address (including city, state, and zip code)
      - Client's home telephone number and one alternate phone number
      - Day of the week preferred to have lawn serviced
      - Estimated amount of time it takes to service the lawn
      - Frequency of service (every week or every other week)
      - A record of each service performed to include the date, time required, amount collected (record tips separately), and date of next scheduled service based on the frequency requested by the client
   b. Add a documentation worksheet to the workbook to clearly state its purpose.
   c. Add a data definition table to clearly define the data items to be stored. Use the chapter example as a guide. Include formulas in the data definitions.
   d. You are not required to enter any data into the workbook, however you may include sample data as needed to test formulas.

2. Given the following imported data column, create a formula that will return the leading zeros to the zip code fields that have less than 5 numeric characters.

ZipCode
24061
24073
24358
2584
34585
256
25846
30358
6578

3. Create a sample data column in a new workbook that includes data validation that requires the user to enter exactly 5 numeric characters into a zip code field.

4. Open the Excel file Problem5-4.xlsx. Copy the list of data on Sheet1 to three additional worksheets (Sheet2, Sheet3, Sheet4). Using the *Subtotal* command from the Excel ribbon, enter the following subtotals for each set of data.

    a. Sheet1: The overall class average by section.
    b. Sheet2: The highest student overall average for each section.
    c. Sheet3: The average of each exam by section.
    d. Sheet4: The number of students receiving each final letter grade in all sections.

5. Open Microsoft Access 2007. Make sure the sample database "Northwinds 2007.accdb" is installed. Close Access. From Excel, practice importing Access tables and queries into Excel worksheets.

6. **Challenge Problem 1:**

    a. Import the text file "Employee.txt" into Excel using the *Text Import Wizard*. Select Fixed Width as the original data type. Be sure to import the data column as Text data type.
    b. In the first row of the column to the right of the imported column, use the CONCATENATE function to join into one cell the data in the first nine rows of the single data field. Include a comma between each of the data items in the cell.
    c. Select the first nine rows and copy the formula down to the remaining rows of the worksheet by dragging the fill handle.
    d. Remove the formulas in column B then delete column A.
    e. Format the first row differently from the remaining rows of data.
    f. Select the range of cells that includes all data rows and the blank rows between them. Do not include the first row of column headers in the selection. Sort the rows in any order.
    g. Select column B and using the *Text to Columns* feature, separate the delimited data in column B into separate columns for each data item. Be sure to select Text as the data type for the zip code field.
    h. Using text functions, parse the name into two columns, one for first name and one for last name.

7. **Challenge Problem 2:**

    a. Using Internet Explorer open the Web page http://www.pikespeak-marathon.org/race_results/2006_tcr_series.htm.
    b. Download the race results into an Excel worksheet.
    c. Insert three new columns to the right of the Name column.
    d. Look up the ISERROR function in Excel help. Study to understand the way the ISERROR function works and its return value.
    e. Combine the ISERROR function with the text and data functions presented in this chapter and create formulas to parse the Name column into three separate columns for first name, middle initial and last name.
    f. Remove the formulas from the three columns and delete the Name column.

- *Availability:* The model should have an interface that is intuitive and familiar to the user.

- *Auditability:* The model should make it possible to track the outputs back to valid input values in order to validate the outcomes of the model.

Subjective Decision Models

When making subjective decisions, it is often very difficult to decide which alternative to choose. If an organization is trying to decide among several locations for a regional distribution warehouse, it is difficult to compare subjective criteria that influence the project decision. The company may find that real estate prices, local tax incentives, and construction costs are more favorable in a more remote area, but those relative advantages of one alternative may be offset by lack of available workers, higher fuel consumption, and negative weather patterns that disrupt transportation. In order to pin down a decision, it helps to simplify the problem by breaking it into the various factors that impact the decision. Naturally, some criteria will influence the decision more than others. One spreadsheet model that is used frequently to support subjective decisions is the *decision matrix*.

Constructing a Decision Matrix

Subjective decisions can be modeled using a *decision matrix* which is also commonly sometimes called a *weighted criteria analysis.* The following steps serve as a guide for constructing and implementing a decision matrix.

1. *Identify the decision alternatives:* The purpose of the decision matrix is to help the user choose the best alternative among a group of acceptable solutions. In our warehouse location problem, the company already has a list of candidate locations for the facility, but it is not clear at this point which location will be best. For our example, we will assume the following cities are all acceptable locations for the warehouse.

   - Norfolk, VA
   - Valdosta, GA
   - Dallas, TX
   - Wichita, KS
   - Limon, CO
   - Cheyenne, WY
   - Billings, MT
   - Moab, UT
   - Pueblo, CO

2. *Identify the criteria:* Decide what factors influence the decision. For example, in trying to make a decision about where to locate a distribution warehouse, som factors that might affect the decision include:

   - Real estate prices
   - Local tax incentives
   - Construction costs
   - Available workers to staff the facility
   - The potential for disruptive weather patterns
   - Local fuel prices

3. *Rank each decision criterion:* Some criteria will naturally influer than others. Each criterion should be ranked according to its the overall decision by assigning it a relative *weight* factor influence will be weighted more by assigning a larger w portant criteria will be assigned a smaller weight fact ample, the most important factor may be the loca

main ongoing cost for the company over the long term. In that case, we would assign it the highest weight. The factor having the least impact may be the offer of local tax incentives. The decision makers may choose any range of numbers to represent the weight factors. The number of criteria and the closeness of importance among them will influence the actual range of numbers used for the weights. When there are many factors that are close in importance, a wider range of numbers might be useful. For our example, we will use a range of 1 to 5 to rank the decision factors. The list below represents one option for assigning weights for the decision criteria in our example.

- Real estate prices = 2
- Local tax incentives = 1
- Construction costs = 3
- Available workers to staff the facility = 4
- The potential for disruptive weather patterns = 3
- Local fuel prices = 5

4. *Define a scale for scoring the criteria:* A scoring scale must be clearly defined so that all criteria are rated consistently. One possible scoring scheme uses 10 for the most favorable score and 1 for the least favorable score. Be sure to use the scoring scale in the same way for all criteria, as an indicator of suitability for the project. For example, if one criterion is "price," you may consider entering a low score for a low price, but instead relate the lower price to project suitability. Since a lower price is more favorable, give it a higher score. If fuel costs are high, which is less favorable, give it a lower score.

5. *Score each criterion:* Using the scoring scale, evaluate each criterion according to its suitability for the project. Record its score.

6. *Calculate the weighted scores for each alternative:* To calculate the weighted overall score for each decision alternative, first calculate the weighted value for each criterion then sum all the weighted criteria values for each alternative.

7. *Evaluate the outcome:* In our example, the alternative with the highest overall score is the best alternative.

Below is a typical layout for a decision matrix. The decision alternatives (candidate cities) are listed as row labels in the first column. The criteria are listed in a row across the top of the matrix. The criteria weights are listed in the row below the criteria labels. The values in the cell range C6:H14 are the scores assigned by the user to each criterion for each city. The value in the "Weighted Score" column is calculated by multiplying each criteria weight by its score, then adding all the weighted criteria scores together for each city.

		Real Estate Prices	Local Tax Incentives	Construction Costs	Available Workers	Disruptive Weather	Local Fuel Prices	Weighted Score	Location Rank
Distribution Warehouse Location Decision Matrix									
Criteria:									
Weight:		2	1	3	4	3	5		
Site Location									
Norfolk, VA		2	8	1	10	2	2	71	
Valdosta, GA		6	4	4	7	10	8	154	
Dallas, TX		1	2	2	10	10	7	248	
Wichita, KS		5	5	4	7	8	8	229	
Limon, CO		9	9	5	6	4	7	240	
Cheyenne, WY	∗	8	8	7	4	3	10	285	1
Billings, MT		9	7	7	3	1	8	272	3
Moab, UT		7	7	8	6	6	7	248	
Pueblo, CO		8	6	4	9	7	7	275	2

Score Key:
10 = Most favorable
1 = Least favorable

Decision Matrix Formulas

The first formula in the "Weighted Score" column (cell I6) is designed so that it can be copied and pasted down to the remaining cells in the column. For that first formula, the weights in row 4 are multiplied by the scores in row 6 then the products of those calculations are added together to represent the overall weighted score for each alternative. Excel has a special function that allows us to perform both operations in one step; the SUMPRODUCT function. The SUMPRODUCT function multiplies the values in one *array* with the corresponding values in other *arrays* of the same dimensions then sums the resulting products to return one value. *Array* is a programming term used to represent either a vector or single list of like elements, or a two-dimensional matrix of like elements. When an Excel worksheet function requires an array type value, the array must be a rectangular range of cells of either one or two dimensions. The argument list for the SUMPRODUCT function is a list of up to 255 same-size arrays of worksheet cells to be multiplied then summed. The SUMPRODUCT syntax:

=SUMPRODUCT(array1, array2, [array3 . . .])

The formula for cell I6 is **=SUMPRODUCT($C$4:$H$4,C6:H6)**. The two arrays (ranges) to be multiplied are C4:H4 (the weights) and C6:H6 (the scores for the first alternative listed). Note that range C4:H4 uses an absolute reference so that the "Weight" array will not change as it is pasted down to the remaining cells in the column.

The "Location Rank" in column J is not required for the model, but was added to aid the user in quickly locating the top three weighted scores for comparison. The formula in column J utilizes the RANK function to rank the weighted scores in column I. The RANK function syntax:

=RANK(number, ref, [order])

The *number* argument is the value or cell to find in the reference list, *ref* is the reference list to rank, and *order* indicates whether to rank in ascending order or descending order. If order is 0(zero) or omitted, the rank is performed in descending order (high to low). If *order* is 1, rank is performed in ascending order (low to high).

The J6 formula also uses the IF and OR functions to specify that if the rank is one of the top three, the rank number should be written into the cell. (The OR and IF functions are introduced in Chapter 3.) The complete formula for cell J6 is explained below.

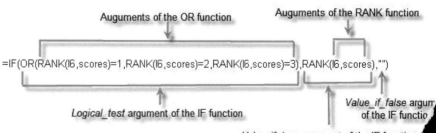

Figure 6-2: Arguments of the IF, OR, and RANK functions are identified.

Like the "Location Rank" in column J, column B is not required and mark the highest scoring alternative(s) as it is evaluated. The formula for ce ple IF function that tests the value in each row of column J to see if it is the values in that column (J). (Remember that the values in column J are ra est to lowest with the number 1 rank position being the highest rank.) given row in column J is the minimum value in the range specified $J$6:$J$14), an asterisk is entered into the cell in column B of the sar cell is not altered. Recall that the *value_if_false* argument of the IF that an IF function may address only one alternative (*value_if_true*) for the outcome of the condition (the *logical_test* argument). The MIN function is used to determine the minimum rank position (the highest rank) for the range. (The MIN function is introduced in Chapter 3.) The formula for cell B6 is **=IF(J6=MIN($J$6:$J$14),"*")**. Note that the range reference for the MIN function argument is absolute so it will not change as the formula is copied down to subsequent cells in the column.

It is important to consider that a decision matrix is very specific for not only the project decision, but specific to the person or team who designs the model. Different people or teams who have varying perspectives may choose different criteria altogether, or different weights for the same criteria which can significantly affect the decision analysis and outcome.

Objective Decision Models

Decision models that support objective decision-making are called *quantitative* models. Quantitative models are based on facts, particularly numbers that represent the reality of the decision domain. Examples of quantitative decision models include statistical analysis, multi-variable decision models, sensitivity analysis, financial analysis, and simulation models.

Estimator Model

Suppose you and a friend have decided to spend your summer painting the exterior of houses and other buildings. You have posted some flyers in the community and are beginning to get calls from people who would like you to provide estimates for painting their buildings. In order for you to provide an accurate estimate, you must first determine how much paint is required. After completing a few projects, you have figured out a formula for predicting how much paint is needed for each part of the project based on measures of square footage of the house, number of stories, number of windows, doors, shutters, and garage doors. Visiting customers in person takes quite a bit of time that you could be devoting to completing work already promised. Since you have a laptop computer and a mobile telephone that you can carry with you to each job, you have an idea that you could build a decision model in Excel that will perform the calculations automatically while you are on the phone with the customer. That way, you can give the customer an estimate while still on the phone with him. If the price is agreeable to the customer, you can go ahead and schedule the work immediately.

From your experience, you have learned the following:

1. Paint use can be estimated based on the adjusted square footage of floor space in a home. One gallon of paint is needed for each 200 square feet of floor space.
2. For homes more than one story, the number of stories is multiplied by the floor space on the main floor to calculate the total adjusted floor space.
3. One gallon of paint will paint four windows.
4. One quart of paint will paint four pairs of shutters.
5. One quart of paint will paint two exterior doors.
6. One quart of paint will paint one single garage door.
7. Two quarts of paint will paint one double garage door.
8. Exterior house paint can only be purchased in gallons and quarts.

Building the Decision Model

In order to build a decision model, the following components must be identified:

1. Inputs
2. Outputs

3. Formulas to produce the outputs in the appropriate units
4. How the user is to interact with the model

Model the Inputs

Inputs to the decision model are also called *decision variables*. The decision variables provide the answers to the following questions for our example model:

1. How many square feet are on the main floor?
2. How many stories is the house?
3. How many exterior doors must be painted?
4. How many windows must be painted?
5. How many pairs of shutters must be painted?
6. How many single garage doors must be painted?
7. How many double garage doors must be painted?

Model the Outputs

What outputs are needed from the model? The outputs are the items of information that are needed to make the decision, such as how much paint to buy. You need to know how many gallons and/or quarts of each kind and color of paint to purchase to paint all the different parts of the house:

1. Exterior wall paint
2. Door paint
3. Window and trim paint
4. Shutter paint
5. Garage door paint

Model the Formulas

What formulas are needed to produce the outputs from the inputs? A special consideration for this project is that you cannot buy partial gallons or quarts of paint. It is often helpful to write the formula logic in simple text before trying to enter the formulas in Excel. The following formulas will be needed to determine how many gallons and/or quarts of paint to purchase for each different category of house parts to be painted. Since it is easier to convert from quarts to gallons than *vice versa,* we will calculate the number of quarts first then calculate the number of gallons if the total amount needed is over four quarts.

1. Exterior wall paint
   a. Part 1: Multiply the number of square feet on the main floor by the number stories to get the adjusted total square feet.
   b. Part 2: Multiply the adjusted square feet by 1/50 (may multiply by 0.02 vide by 50) since one quart is needed for each 50 square feet (one ga each 200 square feet).
   c. Part 3: Finally, convert the number of quarts to the number of quarts to purchase.
   d. Additional considerations for all formulas for this problem:
      • Round up for the initial calculation since you cannot purchase of paint.
      • If more than four quarts are needed, calculate the number If a partial gallon is needed, calculate the number of qu stead of another whole gallon.

2. Door paint
   a. Part 1: Multiply the number of doors by 0.5 since it takes one half quart for each door (alternately you may divide by two) to get the number of quarts of paint needed.
   b. Part 2: Convert the number of quarts to gallons and quarts if the number of quarts to purchase is greater than four.

3. Window and trim paint
   a. Part 1: Multiply the number of windows by one. Since one gallon will paint four windows, one quart will be needed for each window.
   b. Part 2: Convert the number of quarts to gallons and quarts if the number of quarts to purchase is greater than four.

4. Shutter paint
   a. Part 1: Divide the number of shutter pairs by four (or multiply by 0.25) since one quart will paint four shutters.
   b. Part 2: Convert the number of quarts to gallons and quarts if the number of quarts to purchase is greater then four.

5. Garage door paint
   a. Part 1: Multiply the number of single garage doors by one since one quart will paint one single door.
   b. Part 2: Multiply the number of double garage doors by two since two quarts are needed for each double door. Add the two amounts together to get the total quarts to purchase.
   c. Part 3: Convert the number of quarts to gallons and quarts if the number of quarts to purchase is greater then four.

User Interface for the Model

Before actually constructing the model, think about how the user will need to interact with the model. In our example, we want the user to enter the decision variables. We need to give the user directions about how to enter the decision variables and how to interpret the outputs. We will clearly label the cells in which the user should input the variable values. The calculated outcomes will be clearly labeled with the gallons and quarts of each type of paint to purchase.

Building the Model

Now that all components of the model have been identified, construct the model. Below is one option for the paint estimator model. Note that user instructions are clear and output is clearly labeled.

	A	B	E	F	G
1	**Answer the following questions about your exterior paint project:**	*Enter Your Answers Here*	**Paint to Purchase**		
3		▼	*Gallons*	*Quarts*	
4	How many square feet on main floor?	1750	8	3	Exterior Wall Paint
5	How many exterior doors?	5	0	3	Door Paint
6	How many windows	15	3	3	Window and Trim Paint
7	How many pairs of shutters	20	1	1	Shutter Paint
8	How many single garage doors?	2	0	2	Garage Door Paint
9	How many double garage doors?	0			
10	How many stories is the house?	1			

mple of a deci-
stimating the
rchase for a

Let's examine the formulas used in the model. Getting to the whole numbers for Gallons and Quarts to purchase involves some interim calculations that are not apparent on first inspection of the model. In the model view in Figure 6-3, values in columns C and D represent the outcomes of those interim calculations and are hidden from the user's view since they are not needed for the decision model interpretation. In Figure 6-4, columns C, D, E, and F are expanded in the worksheet formula view to show the calculation steps involved. The formulas in hidden columns C and D are represented in white text in the figure.

B	C	D	E	F
Enter Your Answers Here				Paint to Purch
▼	(Qt)	(Gal)	Gallons	Quarts
1750	=B4/50*B10	=C4/4	=INT(D4)	=ROUNDUP((D4-E4)*4,0)
5	=B5/2	=C5/4	=INT(D5)	=ROUNDUP((D5-E5)*4,0)
15	=B6	=C6/4	=INT(D6)	=ROUNDUP((D6-E6)*4,0)
20	=B7/4	=C7/4	=INT(D7)	=ROUNDUP((D7-E7)*4,0)
2	=B8+B9*2	=C8/4		
0			=INT(D8)	=ROUNDUP((D8-E8)*4,0)
1				

Figure 6-4: Formula view of the paint estimator decision model.

Columns C and D are used as interim formulas to calculate the initial number of quarts needed (column C) then convert the number of quarts to the number of gallons, including fractional parts (column D). In column E, the whole gallons are extracted from the total gallon calculation in column D by using the INT function to capture only the integer portion of the calculated value. In column F, the partial gallons are derived by subtracting the whole gallons (column E) from the total gallons (column D). The partial gallon amount is then multiplied by four to convert it from partial gallons to quarts. The final value is rounded up using the ROUNDUP function since you cannot purchase partial quarts of paint. The functions INT and ROUNDUP are introduced in Chapter 3.

In order to hide the interim formulas in columns C and D, formatting is applied such that the text color is the same as the background color. The columns are narrowed so that they are not readily visible in the model, but they can be accessed by the developer for model modification when indicated.

Sensitivity (What-If) Analysis

For many business decisions, having the perfect information is rarely possible, especially with regard to costs that fluctuate frequently. Many decisions are based on assumption values for those fluctuating decision variables. In order for a manufactu of furniture to make decisions about how to price its products, the decision ma must understand the production cost impact of fluctuating costs of raw material labor. They must also price products and produce them at a level that allows t to meet its financial obligations and profitability goals. The firm needs a model that will support frequent changes in decision variables. This type process is called *what-if analysis,* or *sensitivity analysis* since it measures h the outputs are to changes in the decision variables (the inputs). The wh model removes all decision variables from the actual calculations and cells called *assumption cells* which are referenced by the decision form the decision variables from the formulas, it is easy to make chang variables without altering actual formulas. Examine the what-if de furniture factory that must make pricing and production level d products it manufacturers.

	A	B		C	D	E	F	G
1		**Revenue**		**Product 1**	**Product 2**		**Wood cost per board foot**	$ 3.00
2		Units Produced		30	15		**Average labor cost per hour**	$ 15.00
3		Price Per Unit	$	2,050	3200			
4		Total Revenue	$	61,500	$ 48,000			
5								
6		**Variable Costs (per unit)**						
7		Labor Hours Required		30	40			
8		Labor Costs	$	450	$ 600			
9		Board-feet Wood Required		240	320			
10		Wood Costs	$	720	$ 960			
11		Hardware Required	$	50	70			
12		Direct Supplies Required	$	20	60			
13		Sales Commissions	$	100	150			
14		Total Variable Costs (all units)	$	40,200	$ 27,600			
15								
16		**Contribution Margin**						
17		Contribution Margin	$	21,300	$ 20,400			
18								
19		**Fixed Costs**						
20		Rent	$	5,500				
21		Utilities	$	3,280				
22		Supplies	$	845				
23		Equipment Leases	$	1,968				
24		Total Fixed Costs	$	11,593				
25								
26		**Profit**						
27		Profit for Products 1 & 2			$ 30,107			

Figure 6-5: Example of a what-if decision model.

The decision variables for the model have been placed in assumption cells (C2, D2, C3, D3, G1, and G2) that are referenced by formulas in the model. The assumption cells are shaded to distinguish them from the other cells in the model. The shading will direct the user's attention to those cells for making changes in the assumption values. Examine the formulas in the formula view of the worksheet in Figure 6-6 to see how the assumption cells are referenced by the worksheet formulas. Note that the assumption cells for wood cost per board-foot (cell G1) and average labor per hour (cell G2) are referenced using absolute references.

B	C	D	E	F	G
	Product 1	**Product 2**		**Wood cost per board foot**	3
Units Produced	30	15		**Average labor cost per hour**	15
Price Per Unit	2050	3200			
Total Revenue	=C2*C3	=D2*D3			
Labor Hours Required	30	40			
Labor Costs	=C7*$G$2	=D7*$G$2			
Board-feet Wood Required	240	320			
Wood Costs	=C9*$G$1	=D9*$G$1			
Hardware Required	50	70			
Direct Supplies Required	20	60			
Sales Commissions	100	150			
Total Variable Costs (all units)	=SUM(C8,C10:C13)*C2	=SUM(D8,D10:D13)*D2			
Contribution Margin	=C4-C14	=D4-D14			
Rent	5500				
Utilities	3280				
Supplies	845				
Equipment Leases	1968				
Total Fixed Costs	=SUM(C20:C23)				
Profit for Products 1 & 2		=C17+D17-C24			

Formula view of the if model.

Scenario Manager

When multiple decision variables are used in a decision model, the user often wants to view the effects of specific scenarios that involve changes in multiple decision variables at once. It is cumbersome to change each input value individually each time the user would like to view a specific combination. Excel offers a feature called the *Scenario Manager* that allows the user to save a set of decision variable values as a scenario for later use. Access the *Scenario Manager* by selecting **Data(tab)→Data Tools(group)→What-If Analysis→Scenario Manager** from the ribbon. The *Scenario Manager* dialog box will appear. Click the *Add* button to add a new scenario. The *Add Scenario* dialog box will appear.

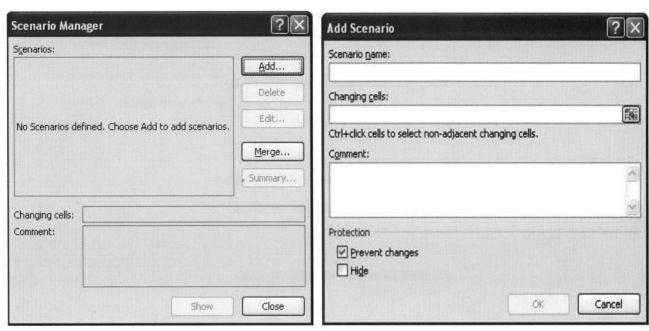

Figure 6-7: The *Scenario Manager* (left) and *Add Scenario* (right) dialog boxes.

To add a scenario, type a name for the scenario into the *Scenario name* text box, then select the cell range(s) that represents the set of assumption cells. You may select multiple non-contiguous ranges by holding down the *Ctrl* key while selecting cells with the mouse pointer or by typing the cell ranges into the *Changing cells* text box with a comma between ranges. You may add optional comments for each scenario. The *Prevent changes* box is checked by default to prevent a user from editing the scenario while worksheet protection is active. Removing the check allows any user to edit the scenarios while the worksheet is protected. Click the *OK* button to enter or edit values for the assumption cells in the *Scenario Values* dialog box. The values that appear in the *Scenario Values* dialog box are the current values in the assumption cells. Edit the values or save the current set of values for the new scenario by clicking the *OK* button to return to the *Scenario Manager* dialog box. To save another scenario with a new set of values for the same set of assumption cells, click the *Add* button on the *Scenario Values* dialog box and the *Add Scenario* dialog box will reappear allowing you to name the new scenario.

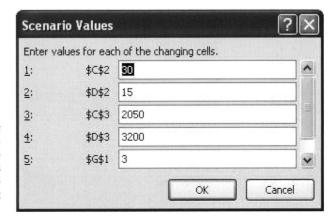

Figure 6-8: Use the *Scenario Values* dialog box to change assumption values for a new scenario. (Note that only 5 assumption cell values are visible in one view. Use the scroll bar to access additional input values.)

Once a scenario has been saved, it appears in the scenario list in the *Scenario Manager* dialog box. To show the particular scenario values in the actual model, select the scenario name in the list box and click the *Show* button. The assumption cells values will be replaced with the values stored in the scenario. The worksheet calculations will automatically reflect the changed inputs.

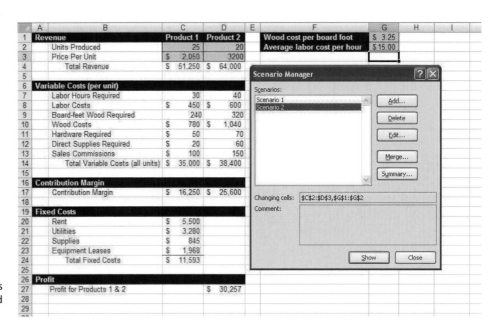

Figure 6-9: "Scenario 2" shows new values for units produced (C2:D2) and price of wood (G1).

A major limitation of the what-if analysis worksheet view is that you can only view one scenario of input values at a time. The *Scenario Manager* allows you to view all scenarios side-by-side for easier comparison. To show a summary of all scenarios plus the current set of values in the assumption cells, click the *Summary* button on the *Scenario Manager* dialog box. The scenario summary is written to a newly-inserted worksheet. In the example, current values were changed in assumption cells for units of products produced (C2:D2), and average labor cost (G2). Those values appear in the "Current Values" column of the summary.

		Current Values:	Scenario 1	Scenario 2
Changing Cells:				
$C$2		27	30	25
$D$2		18	15	20
$C$3	$	2,050	$ 2,050	$ 2,050
$D$3		3200	3200	3200
$G$1	$	3.25	$ 3.00	$ 3.25
$G$2	$	15.50	$ 15.00	$ 15.00
Result Cells:				
$C$17	$	17,145	$ 21,300	$ 16,250
$D$17	$	22,680	$ 20,400	$ 25,600
$D$27	$	28,232	$ 30,107	$ 30,257

Notes: Current Values column represents values of changing cells at time Scenario Summary Report was created. Changing cells for each scenario are highlighted in gray.

e scenario sum-
a newly-inserted
els are cell ref-
and output

In the scenario summary, the row labels are the cell references of the input and output cells of the what-if model. To make the summary easier to evaluate, change the row labels to something more meaningful for the model. The cell references are simply text so edit them by selecting the cell and typing in a new label.

	A	B	C	D	E	F
1						
2		**Scenario Summary**				
3				Current Values	Scenario 1	Scenario 2
5		**Changing Cells:**				
6			Units Product 1	27	30	25
7			Units Product 2	18	15	20
8			Revenue per unit Product 1	$ 2,050	$ 2,050	$ 2,050
9			Revenue per unit Product 2	3200	3200	3200
10			Wood cost per board-foot	$ 3.25	$ 3.00	$ 3.25
11			Average hourly labor cost	$ 15.50	$ 15.00	$ 15.00
12		**Result Cells:**				
13			Contribution Margin Product 1	$ 17,145	$ 21,300	$ 16,250
14			Contribution Margin Product 2	$ 22,680	$ 20,400	$ 25,600
15			Total Profit	$ 28,232	$ 30,107	$ 30,257
16		Notes: Current Values column represents values of changing cells at				
17		time Scenario Summary Report was created. Changing cells for each				
18		scenario are highlighted in gray.				

Figure 6-11: Cell reference row labels have been replaced with more meaning labels relating to the model.

One-Variable and Two-Variable Data Tables

Excel *data tables* provide another way to view multiple sets of inputs and resulting outputs of a model. A *data table* is a range of data that shows how changing values for formula inputs change the results of the formulas such as those in what-if analysis models. One advantage of data tables over scenario summaries is that the format of the input and output values is more compact so that more sets of input and output values may be viewed for comparison in a smaller area. The downside of data tables over scenario summaries is that only one or two input variables may be used. When one input variable is used in a data table, the number of outputs is virtually unlimited. When two variables are used in a data table, the output is limited to only one output from the model.

The calculations performed by the data table utility are based on a specific decision model. The data table setup asks what input(s) to the model you want to include in the summary and what output(s) from the model you want to produce. In the previous manufacturing example, we may want to see how the number of units of one or both products produced will affect the total costs, combined contribution margins and the overall profit of the firm.

One-Variable Data Table

To set up a one-variable data table, select a location for the table and decide whet' the input values will be arranged in a column or a row. For our example, we wa look at the effects on total costs, combined contribution margins, and profit f various units of "Product 2" produced while holding the units of "Product stant at 20 units. We will arrange the inputs in the first column of the table the column "Units Product 2." Under the column label, list the input valu uate. We will look at the effects of changes in Product 2 production uni unit increments. Our input variable values for units of Product 2 will ra 60 units.

Since values of the input variable are in the first column, we will columns for outputs. Enter formulas in the first row (beside the "Units Product 2") to reference the cell(s) for each output desired simple references to cells within the model or they may be a calculated value involving two or more cells in the model. For total costs, we will enter a formula that adds the total variable costs for both products and the total fixed costs in the formula **=SUM(C14:D14,C24)**. For the combined contribution margins, we will add together the margins for both products in the formula **=SUM(C17:D17)**. For the total profit we need only to reference cell D27 in the model so the formula for that column will be **=D27**.

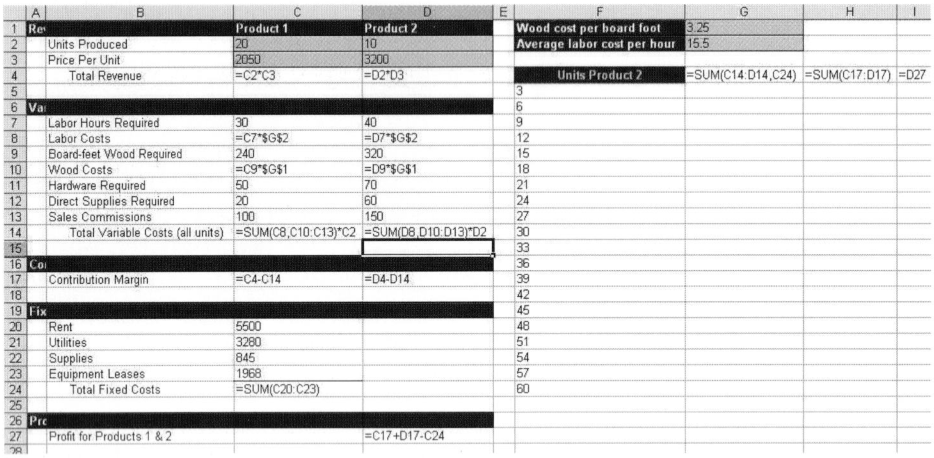

Figure 6-12: Formula view of one-variable data table formulas. Columns G, H, and I represent the outputs total costs, total contribution margins, and total profit respectively.

To fill the results into the data table, select the entire table, including column formulas (in the example F4:I24) and select **Data(tab)→Data Tools(group)→What-If Analysis→Data Table** from the ribbon. The *Data Table* dialog box appears to prompt for the input variables. If two variables are used, one variable will be the *Row input cell* and the other will be the *Column input cell*. If using only one variable, either the row or column input text box will be empty. For row or column input, indicate the cell in the actual model where the particular input values is used. For our example, we are using a column input only, so we will select cell D2 for the *Column input cell* argument and leave the text box empty for the *Row input cell* argument. Click the *OK* button to fill the data table outputs.

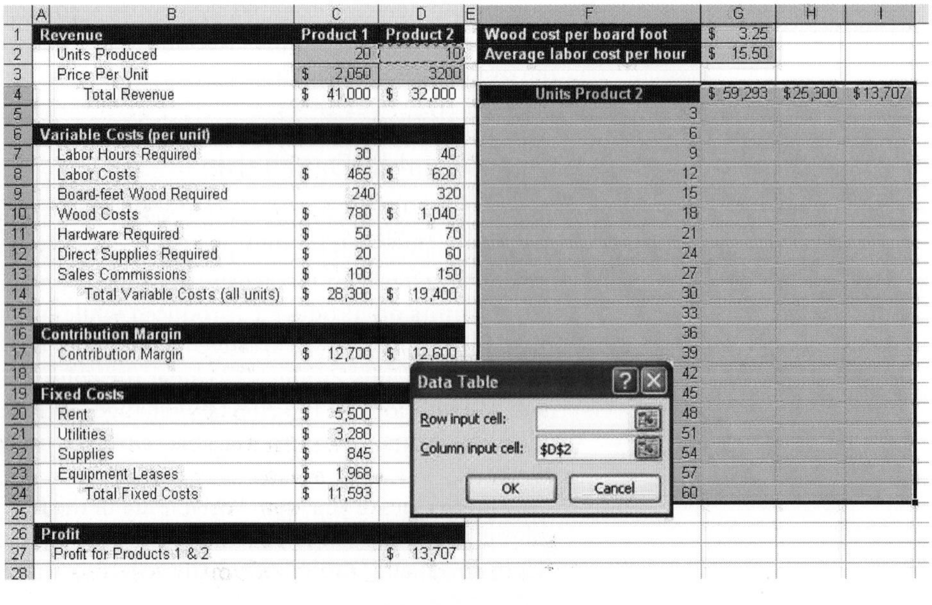

fill the outputs for
select the entire
lect **Data→Table**
Enter the cell
mn input.

	A	B	C	D	E	F	G	H	I
1		Revenue	Product 1	Product 2		Wood cost per board foot	$ 3.25		
2		Units Produced	20	10		Average labor cost per hour	$ 15.50		
3		Price Per Unit	$ 2,050	3200					
4		Total Revenue	$ 41,000	$ 32,000		Units Product 2	$ 59,293	$25,300	$13,707
5						3	45713	16480	4887
6		Variable Costs (per unit)				6	51533	20260	8667
7		Labor Hours Required	30	40		9	57353	24040	12447
8		Labor Costs	$ 465	$ 620		12	63173	27820	16227
9		Board-feet Wood Required	240	320		15	68993	31600	20007
10		Wood Costs	$ 780	$ 1,040		18	74813	35380	23787
11		Hardware Required	$ 50	$ 70		21	80633	39160	27567
12		Direct Supplies Required	$ 20	$ 60		24	86453	42940	31347
13		Sales Commissions	$ 100	$ 150		27	92273	46720	35127
14		Total Variable Costs (all units)	$ 28,300	$ 19,400		30	98093	50500	38907
15						33	103913	54280	42687
16		Contribution Margin				36	109733	58060	46467
17		Contribution Margin	$ 12,700	$ 12,600		39	115553	61840	50247
18						42	121373	65620	54027
19		Fixed Costs				45	127193	69400	57807
20		Rent	$ 5,500			48	133013	73180	61587
21		Utilities	$ 3,280			51	138833	76960	65367
22		Supplies	$ 845			54	144653	80740	69147
23		Equipment Leases	$ 1,968			57	150473	84520	72927
24		Total Fixed Costs	$ 11,593			60	156293	88300	76707
25									
26		Profit							
27		Profit for Products 1 & 2		$ 13,707					

Figure 6-14: Click the *OK* button to fill the data table outputs.

Apply Custom Formats

Select the output columns and apply one of the currency formats. The column labels (output formulas) are not very helpful to a user in interpreting the data table results. We can change those labels to make them more user-friendly without altering the underlying formulas by applying a custom format.

To apply a custom format to the output formula cells (G4, H4, I4), first select the column label for column G, the total costs column. Access the *Format Cells* dialog box by clicking on the bottom right corner arrow of the *Font, Alignment,* or *Number* group of the *Home* tab of the Excel ribbon. Select the *Number* tab of the dialog box and *Custom* for the category of format. In the *Type* text box type "Total Costs" (include the double quotes) and click the *OK* button. Change the label for column H to "Contribution Margins" in the same manner. For column I, enter the custom column label "Profit";"Profit" including all quotes and the semicolon. The second entry of "Profit" indicates the label for negative values. Should the value for the column label cell itself (the output formula) be negative, the text in the label would otherwise read "-Profit" (without the quotes). Since the totals costs and contribution margins will never be negative values, that additional label is not necessary for those columns. Background color and font characteristics may also be applied to the custom formats.

Now that the data table is filled, you can change the input values in the data table itself, or you can change any other assumption cell values in the model and the data table values will update automatically. Try changing the number of units of Product 1 to 5 and note the changes in the data table. Note how easy it is to see the break even point in the data table where the profit becomes positive. Changing the data table input value range from 3-60 to 1-20 will enable you to see exactly the number of units required to break even.

Two-Variable Data Table

If we wish to view the results on profit for various combinations of units of both products manufactured, we can use a *two-variable data table*. A *two-variable data table* is a matrix that includes one set of input values in the first column and the other set of input values in the first row. When using two input variables, we are able to view only one output value for each set of variable values. Each new value will appear at the intersection of the row and column input value.

	B	C	D		F	G	H	I
1	Revenue	Product 1	Product 2		Wood cost per board foot	$ 3.25		
2	Units Produced	5	10		Average labor cost per hour	$ 15.50		
3	Price Per Unit	$ 2,050	3200					
4	Total Revenue	$ 10,250	$ 32,000		Units Product 2	Total Costs	Contribution Margins	Profit
5					1	$ 20,608	$ 4,435	$ (7,158)
6	Variable Costs (per unit)				2	$ 22,548	$ 5,695	$ (5,898)
7	Labor Hours Required	30	40		3	$ 24,488	$ 6,955	$ (4,638)
8	Labor Costs	$ 465	$ 620		4	$ 26,428	$ 8,215	$ (3,378)
9	Board-feet Wood Required	240	320		5	$ 28,368	$ 9,475	$ (2,118)
10	Wood Costs	$ 780	$ 1,040		6	$ 30,308	$ 10,735	$ (858)
11	Hardware Required	$ 50	70		7	$ 32,248	$ 11,995	$ 402
12	Direct Supplies Required	$ 20	60		8	$ 34,188	$ 13,255	$ 1,662
13	Sales Commissions	$ 100	150		9	$ 36,128	$ 14,515	$ 2,922
14	Total Variable Costs (all units)	$ 7,075	$ 19,400		10	$ 38,068	$ 15,775	$ 4,182
15					11	$ 40,008	$ 17,035	$ 5,442
16	Contribution Margin				12	$ 41,948	$ 18,295	$ 6,702
17	Contribution Margin	$ 3,175	$ 12,600		13	$ 43,888	$ 19,555	$ 7,962
18					14	$ 45,828	$ 20,815	$ 9,222
19	Fixed Costs				15	$ 47,768	$ 22,075	$ 10,482
20	Rent	$ 5,500			16	$ 49,708	$ 23,335	$ 11,742
21	Utilities	$ 3,280			17	$ 51,648	$ 24,595	$ 13,002
22	Supplies	$ 845			18	$ 53,588	$ 25,855	$ 14,262
23	Equipment Leases	$ 1,968			19	$ 55,528	$ 27,115	$ 15,522
24	Total Fixed Costs	$ 11,593			20	$ 57,468	$ 28,375	$ 16,782
25								
26	Profit							
27	Profit for Products 1 & 2		$ 4,182					

Figure 6-15: Column labels are shown with a custom format. The break even point can be easily identified where the profit values become positive.

Set up a data table for units Product 2 in the first column and units of Product 1 in the first row. Enter units for product 2 in multiples of 3 and units of Product 1 in multiples of 5. The table must be laid out such that the first unit values for each respective product intersect at the first cell of the output range of the table (see Figure 6-16). Labels for the product units should be placed outside the actual data table.

The formula for the output value is entered into the cell located one column to the left and one row up from the intersection of the first two input values. In the example, we want to view total profit in this two-variable table, so the formula in cell J6 is a reference to cell D27, the profit calculation for our model.

	K	L	M	N	O	P	Q	R	S	T
1			Units Product 1							
2		=D27	5	10	15	20	25	30	35	40
3	Units Product 2	3								
4		6								
5		9								
6		12								
7		15								
8		18								
9		21								
10		24								
11		27								
12		30								
13		33								
14		36								
15		39								
16		42								
17		45								
18		48								
19		51								
20		54								
21		57								
22		60								

Figure 6-16: In a two-variable data table, the initial values of the column and row inputs must intersect at the first cell of the data table output range. Labels for the two input variables must be outside the actual data table range.

Fill the outputs for the table by selecting the entire table, including the formula for the output, and select **Data(tab)→Data Tools(group)→What-If Analysis→Data**

Table from the ribbon. This time we will select cell C2 of the model for the row input cell and cell D2 for the column input cell. Click the *OK* button to fill the table output values.

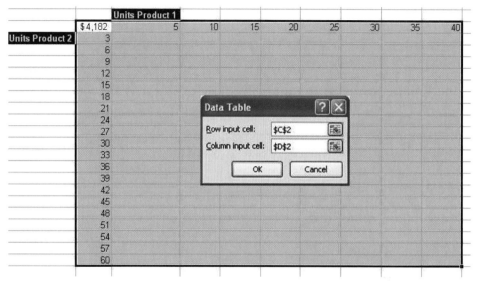

Figure 6-17: To fill the data table outputs, select the entire data table range and select **Data→Table** from the menu bar. Enter the cell reference for the row and column inputs. Click the *OK* button to fill the output range.

Apply a custom format for the formula cell to read "Profit" for both positive and negative values in the formula cell. Once a custom format is entered, it can be reused by selecting if from the list of custom formats available. Apply additional formats as desired.

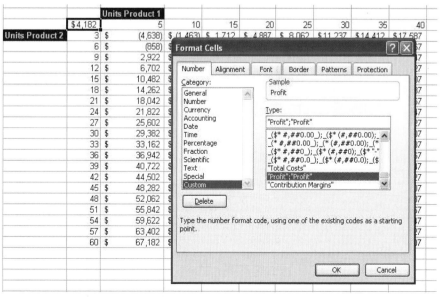

Figure 6-18: Apply a previously-defined custom format for the "Profit" label.

Units Product 2 \ Units Product 1 → Profit	5	10	15	20	25	30	35	40
3	$ (4,638)	$ (1,463)	$ 1,712	$ 4,887	$ 8,062	$11,237	$14,412	$17,587
6	$ (858)	$ 2,317	$ 5,492	$ 8,667	$11,842	$15,017	$18,192	$21,367
9	$ 2,922	$ 6,097	$ 9,272	$12,447	$15,622	$18,797	$21,972	$25,147
12	$ 6,702	$ 9,877	$13,052	$16,227	$19,402	$22,577	$25,752	$28,927
15	$ 10,482	$13,657	$16,832	$20,007	$23,182	$26,357	$29,532	$32,707
18	$ 14,262	$17,437	$20,612	$23,787	$26,962	$30,137	$33,312	$36,487
21	$ 18,042	$21,217	$24,392	$27,567	$30,742	$33,917	$37,092	$40,267
24	$ 21,822	$24,997	$28,172	$31,347	$34,522	$37,697	$40,872	$44,047
27	$ 25,602	$28,777	$31,952	$35,127	$38,302	$41,477	$44,652	$47,827
30	$ 29,382	$32,557	$35,732	$38,907	$42,082	$45,257	$48,432	$51,607
33	$ 33,162	$36,337	$39,512	$42,687	$45,862	$49,037	$52,212	$55,387
36	$ 36,942	$40,117	$43,292	$46,467	$49,642	$52,817	$55,992	$59,167
39	$ 40,722	$43,897	$47,072	$50,247	$53,422	$56,597	$59,772	$62,947
42	$ 44,502	$47,677	$50,852	$54,027	$57,202	$60,377	$63,552	$66,727
45	$ 48,282	$51,457	$54,632	$57,807	$60,982	$64,157	$67,332	$70,507
48	$ 52,062	$55,237	$58,412	$61,587	$64,762	$67,937	$71,112	$74,287
51	$ 55,842	$59,017	$62,192	$65,367	$68,542	$71,717	$74,892	$78,067
54	$ 59,622	$62,797	$65,972	$69,147	$72,322	$75,497	$78,672	$81,847
57	$ 63,402	$66,577	$69,752	$72,927	$76,102	$79,277	$82,452	$85,627
60	$ 67,182	$70,357	$73,532	$76,707	$79,882	$83,057	$86,232	$89,407

Figure 6-19: A custom format has been applied to the output formula cell ("Profit"). Other formatting may also be applied to row and column input values and labels.

Summarizing Data with PivotTable & PivotChart Reports

A *PivotTable* report is an interactive summary of an Excel list or an external data source. *PivotTables* are used to summarize data that has multiple perspectives. When a *PivotTable* is created, the data is summarized then filtered to show the results of interest. The user decides which summary data to show in the *PivotTable*. Typical ways Excel PivotTable reports are used include:

1. Grouping and summarizing numeric data, by categories and date groups.
2. Filtering summarized data in order to view specific categories of summary, such as a particular department or for a particular time period.
3. Changing levels of summary data interactively to higher (broader summaries) lower levels (more subcategories of summary data.
4. Change views of summary data by pivoting rows to columns and *vice versa* (categories to series and vice versa on PivotChart reports).
5. Viewing the detailed data rows for summary values of interest.
6. Summarizing very large quantities of data and presenting it in ways users can easily understand.
7. Presenting summary data that is professionally formatted through the use of automatic formats and styles available for both PivotTable and PivotChart reports.

A PivotChart report is a graphical representation of PivotTable data. Unlike the PivotTable, the PivotChart cannot entirely stand alone. It is based on a PivotTable report so that if a user wants to change the data or layout of a PivotChart, he must first make the necessary changes in the associated PivotTable.

Like other charts, a PivotChart report has series of data, categories of data, data makers, data axes, titles, labels, etc. And like other charts, you can add or change titles, legends and labels. A row label in a PivotTable corresponds to a category on a PivotChart. A column label on a PivotTable corresponds to a series of data on a PivotChart.

Think about how you record checks you have written from your checking account(s). The main data item for each check you write is the *amount*. Think about other attributes of a check:

- Check number
- Payee (to whom the check is written)
- Check date
- Expense category (i.e., rent, cell phone, entertainment, food)
- Account number (in case you have multiple checking accounts)

Each attribute represents a different perspective for summarizing check amounts. Consider ways you might summarize your check amounts.

- Examples of summarizing check amounts based on two perspectives:

    1. Sum check amounts for each expense category for each month.
    2. Average check amounts for each expense category for each year.

- Examples of summarizing check amounts based on three perspectives:

    1. Sum check amounts written to each payee for each expense category for each month.
    2. Count check each payee for each expense category for each month.

When viewing data (like the sum of check amounts) from only two perspectives, or *dimensions* as they are sometimes called, it might help to envision a logical layout of summary values in a two-dimensional table where columns represent values of one dimension (such as expense category) and the rows represent values for another dimension (such as date). The intersection of the rows and columns represent aggregate (summary) data for one value each of the row and column dimensions. For example, one table cell might represent the sum of check amounts for the "food" expense category and the month of March 2007. The PivotTable utility gives the user the ability to apply a filter to the summary results so that results can be viewed for only the categories of interest. For example, instead of viewing a sum of check amounts written for each expense category for each payee, you may be interested in viewing only summary data for checks to Kroger (one payee) for food (one expense category). Instead of viewing the sum of check amounts for each date, the user may prefer to group the dates by month or year and view only one year or only three particular months. Grouping and filtering data in these ways is the real strength of the PivotTable utility over calculating summary data by other means available in Excel.

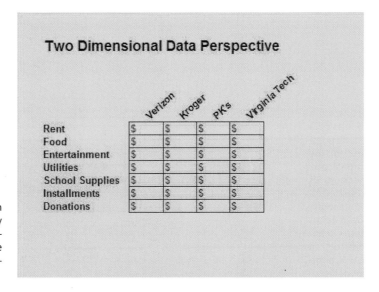

Figure 6-20: Summary data with two perspectives (expense category and payee) may be envisioned logically as a two-dimensional table with summary values in the intersections of columns and rows.

When data can be viewed from more than two perspectives, it is like adding one or more planes to the logical two-dimensional table we envisioned earlier for data with only two dimensions. The additional planes represent more dimensions added to the row and column dimensions. This logical three-dimensional (or multi-dimensional) perspective of data is often referred to by database professionals as a *data cube.* A multi-dimensional summary (such as sum, average, or count) of the data includes one value (also called a *measure*) from each dimension of interest (i.e., expense category = food; date = March, 2007; payee = Kroger).

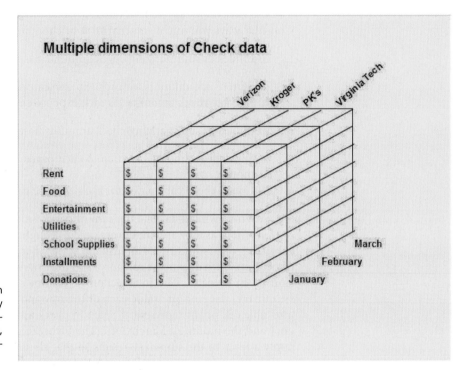

Figure 6-21: Summary data with more than two perspectives may be viewed logically as a multi-dimensional table, or *data cube*, with summary values in the intersections of columns, rows, and slices.

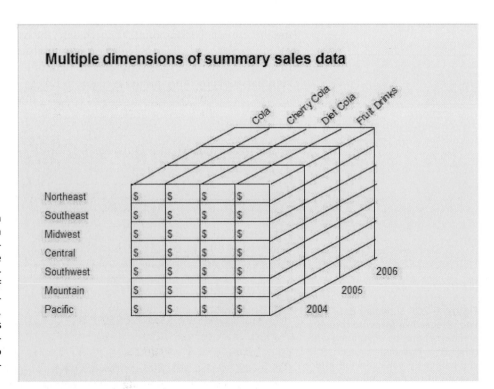

Figure 6-22: An example of a multi-dimensional view of sales data showing dimensions of region, product, and date. Each "slice" of the cube represents an additional perspective. Additional dimensions of sales data may include such variables as sales agent, sales manager, and wholesale outlet. (Data cubes may represent multiple data dimensions; however, it is difficult to model more than three logical dimensions on a physical model).

In a *PivotTable* report the dimensions of the data are placed in columns and rows such that the intersection of a column and a row displays a summary value where those two dimensions intersect. This type of report is also known as a *crosstab report* or *crosstab query* in other software environments.

The dimensions of data in a *PivotTable* can be nested to represent different levels of summary data, much like the additional dimensions of the *data cube* data. For example, you can summarize check amounts by summing those amounts written for food for one year (represented by grouped check dates). You can add an additional level of summary by further dividing the food category into the actual payees and by dividing (regrouping) the years into months so that the final summary result is the sum of checks written for food (filtered or restricted to one expense category) to each payee for each month of each year.

Sum of Amount			Category ▾	
Years ▾	Date ▾	Payee ▾	Food	Grand Total
2006	Jun	Annie Kay's	$ 35	$ 35
		Kroger	$ 165	$ 165
		Wade's	$ 23	$ 23
	Jun Total		$ 223	$ 223
	Jul	Annie Kay's	$ 18	$ 18
		Kroger	$ 116	$ 116
		Wade's	$ 18	$ 18
		Wal-Mart	$ 199	$ 199
	Jul Total		$ 351	$ 351
	Aug	Annie Kay's	$ 35	$ 35
		Kroger	$ 146	$ 146
		Wade's	$ 47	$ 47
	Aug Total		$ 228	$ 228
	Sep	Annie Kay's	$ 18	$ 18
		Kroger	$ 259	$ 259
		Wade's	$ 39	$ 39
		Wal-Mart	$ 60	$ 60
	Sep Total		$ 376	$ 376
	Oct	Annie Kay's	$ 35	$ 35
		Kroger	$ 123	$ 123
		Wade's	$ 16	$ 16
		Wal-Mart	$ 134	$ 134
	Oct Total		$ 308	$ 308
	Nov	Annie Kay's	$ 18	$ 18
		Kroger	$ 106	$ 106
		Wade's	$ 25	$ 25
		Wal-Mart	$ 23	$ 23
	Nov Total		$ 172	$ 172
	Dec	Kroger	$ 219	$ 219
		Wal-Mart	$ 98	$ 98
	Dec Total		$ 317	$ 317
2007	Jan	Annie Kay's	$ 41	$ 41
		Kroger	$ 172	$ 172
		Wade's	$ 25	$ 25
	Jan Total		$ 238	$ 238
	Feb	Annie Kay's	$ 55	$ 55
		Kroger	$ 105	$ 105
		Wade's	$ 36	$ 36
		Wal-Mart	$ 62	$ 62
	Feb Total		$ 258	$ 258
Grand Total			$ 2,471	$ 2,471

Figure 6-23: *PivotTable* that summarizes checks written for food by year, month, and payee.

PivotTables are named such because dimensions of the summarized data can be changed from column to row or from row to column areas easily, thus "pivoting" the table. That is *why PivotTables and PivotCharts are* said to be "interactive." Dimensions (list fields) can be added to or removed from the reports easily and the summary data is updated accordingly. Although PivotTables and PivotCharts are interactive in terms of adding or removing fields on the report, it is not dynamic in that it *does not update automatically when the underlying data or table structures change.* When data is changed or a column is added to the Excel list, the PivotTable must be refreshed manually using the *Refresh* option in the PivotTable utility.

Sources of PivotTable and PivotChart Data

A PivotTable or PivotChart may be created from any well-structured list of data in Excel, from an Excel "table", or from a named range in Excel. Also, a portion of a list may be selected for a PivotTable or PivotChart report. In addition to Excel data, data from external sources may also be imported or linked to Excel as a PivotTable or PivotChart report. External data sources include delimited text files, relational database tables, OLAP (Online Analytical Processing) data, and other source data accessed by way of Office Data Connection files. PivotTable or PivotChart reports can also be created from other PivotTable reports. (A PivotChart report may not be created directly from another PivotChart report, but rather from its underlying PivotTable report.)

For more information on accessing external data sources for PivotTable and PivotChart reports, see the topic "Importing and Exporting Excel Data" in Chapter 5 of this text. When importing or linking to external data sources from Excel, the last step of the import utility asks the user how the imported data is to be viewed in the Excel workbook. To view the imported data as a PivotTable report or PivotChart report or both, select the appropriate option in the *Import Data* dialog box.

Figure 6-24: PivotTable and PivotChart reports are options in Excel for viewing imported or linked data.

Creating a Pivot Table

Before creating the PivotTable report, identify the list of data to analyze and make certain it is structured according to list management guidelines for Excel. If subtotals have been added to a list by way of the *Subtotal* command, be sure to remove those from the list using the same *Subtotal* utility. When the list is ready select a cell inside the list. Alternately, just select the data you want to use in the report. To create the PivotTable select **Insert(tab)→Tables(group)→PivotTable** (icon). (To create a PivotChart, select *PivotChart* from the *PivotTable* drop-down list.) The *Create PivotTable* dialog box will appear.

Practice 6-1

Create a *PivotTable* that summarizes employees' salaries by showing an average salary for each department and for each gender within the department.

1. Open the Excel file "Employees_ch6-1.xlsx."
2. Select a cell inside the list.

3. Select **Insert(tab)→Tables(group)→PivotTable** (icon) from the ribbon. The *Create PivotTable* dialog box will appear.

4. In the dialog box, confirm the range for the Excel list to analyze. Click the *OK* button to continue.

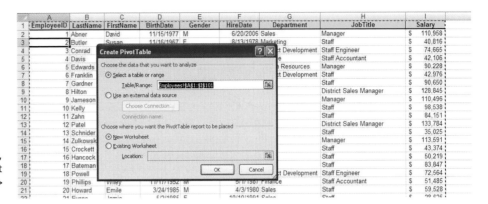

Figure 6-25: To create a PivotTable, select a cell inside the list and select **Insert(tab)→Tables(group)→ PivotTable** from the ribbon.

A blank PivotTable layout appears in the specified location. The PivotTable fields that are available for the table are listed in the PivotTable *Field List* window. The fields in the *Field List* represent column labels in the source data.

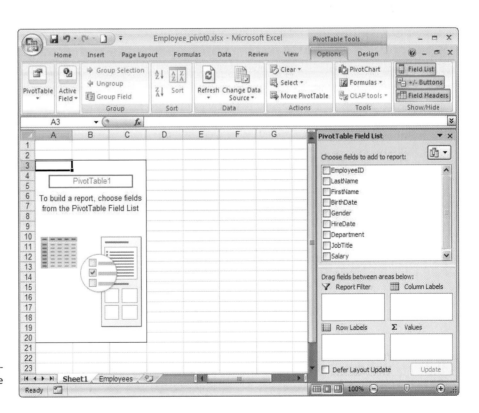

Figure 6-26: The PivotTable layout before fields are added to the table.

5. Check the fields in the *Field List* that you wish to add to the PivotTable. As each field is checked, it is added to a default area of the PivotTable. The field name is also added to the corresponding area box in the bottom of the *PivotTable Field List* window on the right. The first numeric field that is checked is added to the *Values* area (also called Data area) of the PivotTable. When numeric fields are added to the *Values* area, the SUM aggregate function is automatically applied. The field label appears in the PivotTable as "Sum of <field name>." When a text field is added

to the *Values* area, the COUNT aggregate function is automatically applied. The aggregate function may be changed by clicking on the down area of the value field name in the *Values* box of the *PivotTable Field List* window and selecting *Value field settings . . .* from the drop-down list. (The same command may be accessed by right-clicking on the value field label in the PivotTable layout.) The *Value Field Settings* dialog box will appear. Since we want to show average salaries, select *Average* in the list box.

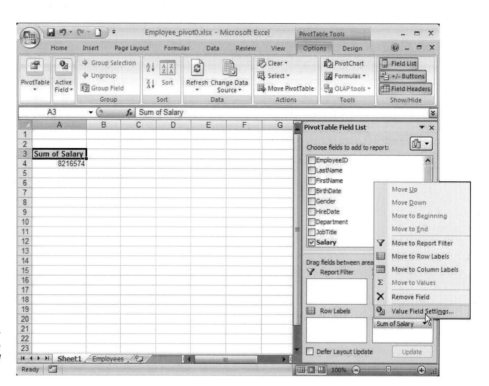

Figure 6-27: Change the aggregate function that is applied to the Value field with the *Value Field Settings . . .* command.

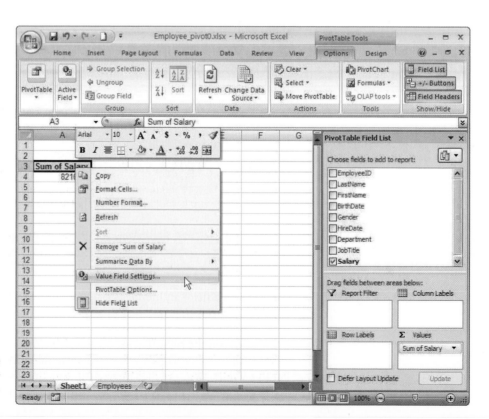

Figure 6-28: Right-click the value field label in the PivotTable to access the *Value Field Settings . . .* command from the context menu.

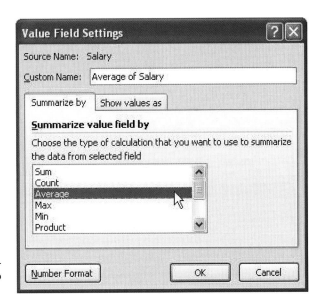

Figure 6-29: Change the aggregate function to apply from *Sum* to *Average*.

6. In the *Field List* window, check the "Department" and "Gender" fields. Both fields will be added to the *Row Labels* area of the PivotTable.
7. With the left mouse button, drag the "Gender" field into the *Column Labels* box of the *Field List* window or on the PivotTable itself.
8. Select and format the summarized data using a Currency format.

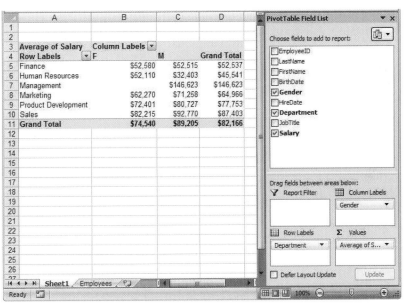

Figure 6-30: PivotTable result with the default automatic table format. Data cells have the Currency format applied (with no decimal places).

9. To close the *PivotTable Field List*, click on the close window icon in the far upper right corner of the window. To reopen the *Field List* window, right-click on the PivotTable and select *Show Field List* from the context menu.

Quick Tip!

Add special formats to any *PivotTable* cells just as you would any worksheet cells by selecting the cells to format then right-click and select *Format Cells* from the context menu to access the *Format Cells* dialog box.

Viewing Filtered Summary Results

Use the drop-down arrows in the row and column label areas to show any or all of the values in the respective field. If more than one field is in the column or row label area, first select the field from the drop-down list, then select the filter criteria for the selected field. The ability to filter the summary PivotTable results is one of the major strengths of the *PivotTable. The PivotTable displays filtered* **summarized** *data just as the AutoFilter and Advanced Filter display filtered* **detailed** *data.* PivotTables combine the capabilities of the *subtotaling* and *filtering* into one Excel tool.

Modifying a PivotTable

Refreshing a PivotTable

If the source data for the PivotTable changes, you will need to refresh the PivotTable data manually by selecting **Options(tab)→Data(group)→Refresh** from the ribbon. The *Options* tab and *Design* tab are context tabs added to the ribbon when a PivotTable is added to the Excel project. If the structure of the source data changes, such as the addition or deletion of a column, the *PivotTable Field List* must also be refreshed manually.

Practice 6-2

Add two new columns to the employees list.

1. Continue with the file from the previous Practice or open the Excel file "Employees_ch6-2.xlsx." In the employee list, insert a new column after the "BirthDate" column. Add the column header "Age" to the new column.
2. Insert a formula into the column for the first row that calculates age based on the birth date. Make the age always current.

   =INT((TODAY()-D2)/365)

3. Format the age in whole numbers without decimal places.
4. Copy the formula to the remaining rows of the column.

	A	B	C	D	E	F	G	H	I	J
	E2			f_x =INT((TODAY()-D2)/365)						
1	EmployeeID	LastName	FirstName	BirthDate	Age	Gender	HireDate	Department	JobTitle	Salary
2	1 Abner	David	11/15/1977	29	M	6/20/2006	Sales	Manager	$110,958	
3	2 Butler	Susan	11/16/1967	39	F	8/13/1978	Marketing	Staff	$40,816	
4	3 Conrad	Michael	9/14/1955	51	M	12/25/2001	Product Development	Staff Engineer	$74,665	
5	4 Davis	Randall	7/15/1947	59	M	5/25/1980	Finance	Staff Accountant	$42,106	
6	5 Edwards	Minnie	3/8/1959	48	F	11/26/1991	Human Resources	Manager	$90,228	
7	6 Franklin	Margaret	11/25/1979	27	F	3/15/1977	Product Development	Staff	$42,976	
8	7 Gardner	William	11/15/1968	38	M	2/7/1999	Sales	Staff	$90,650	
9	8 Hilton	Hillery	11/23/1949	57	F	11/8/2005	Sales	District Sales Manager	$128,845	
10	9 Jameson	Jennifer	1/17/1959	48	F	11/28/1992	Sales	Manager	$110,496	
11	10 Kelly	Chester	10/28/1968	38	M	1/3/1994	Sales	Staff	$98,538	
12	11 Zahn	Geoffrey	9/6/1952	54	M	3/4/1999	Sales	Staff	$84,151	
13	12 Patel	Michael	4/20/1974	33	M	3/19/2003	Sales	District Sales Manager	$133,784	
14	13 Schnider	Elizabeth	6/6/1958	49	F	6/27/1997	Sales	Staff	$35,025	
15	14 Zulkowski	Mary	5/8/1967	40	F	9/1/1999	Sales	Manager	$113,591	
16	15 Crockett	Carol	11/19/1953	53	F	12/3/1994	Sales	Staff	$43,374	
17	16 Hancock	Christopher	4/30/1967	40	M	11/18/1999	Sales	Staff	$50,219	
18	17 Bateman	Matthew	1/27/1956	51	M	8/3/1998	Sales	Staff	$83,847	

PivotTable1 **Employees**

Ready   100%

Figure 6-31: Age field is added to the employee list.

5. To the right of the list, make a new column and add the header "SalaryGrade."
6. Insert a new worksheet and name it "Reference." Set up a lookup table on the new sheet using the following values for determining the salary grade. Name the

	A	B	C
1	$0	A	
2	$30,000	B	
3	$50,000	C	
4	$70,000	D	
5	$100,000	E	
6	$125,000	F	
7			

Figure 6-32: Lookup table for salary grades.

lookup table "Grades." Remember that the lookup value (salary) must be in the first column. Be sure to include a "zero" range in the lookup table.

   a. $0 to below $30,000 = Salary Grade A
   b. $30,000 to below $50,000 = Salary Grade B
   c. $50,000 to below $70,000 = Salary Grade C
   d. $70,000 to below $100,000 = Salary Grade D
   e. $100,000 to below $125,000 = Salary Grade E
   f. $125,000 and over = Salary Grade F

7. Enter a formula into the first row of the "SalaryGrade" column that will return the salary grade letter from the lookup table.

   =VLOOKUP(J2, Grades, 2)

8. Copy the formula to remaining rows of the column.

K2   =VLOOKUP(J2,Grades,2)

	A	B	C	D	E	F	G	H	I	J	K
1	EmployeeID	LastName	FirstName	BirthDate	Age	Gender	HireDate	Department	JobTitle	Salary	SalaryGrade
2	1	Abner	David	11/15/1977	29	M	6/20/2006	Sales	Manager	$110,958	E
3	2	Butler	Susan	11/16/1967	39	F	8/13/1978	Marketing	Staff	$40,816	B
4	3	Conrad	Michael	9/14/1955	51	M	12/25/2001	Product Development	Staff Engineer	$74,665	D
5	4	Davis	Randall	7/15/1947	59	M	5/25/1980	Finance	Staff Accountant	$42,106	B
6	5	Edwards	Minnie	3/8/1959	48	F	11/26/1991	Human Resources	Manager	$90,228	D
7	6	Franklin	Margaret	11/25/1979	27	F	3/15/1977	Product Development	Staff	$42,976	B
8	7	Gardner	William	11/15/1968	38	M	2/7/1999	Sales	Staff	$90,650	D
9	8	Hilton	Hillery	11/23/1949	57	F	11/8/2005	Sales	District Sales Manager	$128,845	F
10	9	Jameson	Jennifer	1/17/1959	48	F	11/28/1992	Sales	Manager	$110,496	E
11	10	Kelly	Chester	10/28/1968	38	M	1/3/1994	Sales	Staff	$98,538	D
12	11	Zahn	Geoffrey	9/6/1952	54	M	3/4/1999	Sales	Staff	$84,151	D
13	12	Patel	Michael	4/20/1974	33	M	3/19/2003	Sales	District Sales Manager	$133,784	F
14	13	Schnider	Elizabeth	6/6/1958	49	F	6/27/1997	Sales	Staff	$35,025	B
15	14	Zulkowski	Mary	5/8/1967	40	F	9/1/1999	Sales	Manager	$113,591	E
16	15	Crockett	Carol	11/19/1953	53	F	12/3/1994	Sales	Staff	$43,374	B
17	16	Hancock	Christopher	4/30/1967	40	M	11/18/1999	Sales	Staff	$50,219	C
18	17	Bateman	Matthew	1/27/1956	51	M	8/3/1998	Sales	Staff	$83,847	D

PivotTable1   **Employees**   Reference

Ready   100%

Figure 6-33: SalaryGrade column is added to the right of the Employee list.

9. Select a cell in *the PivotTable you* created in the previous Practice. If the *Field List* window does not appear, select **Options(tab)→Show/Hide→Field List** from the ribbon or right-click on a PivotTable cell and select *Show Field List* from the context menu. Are the new fields visible in the *Field List*?

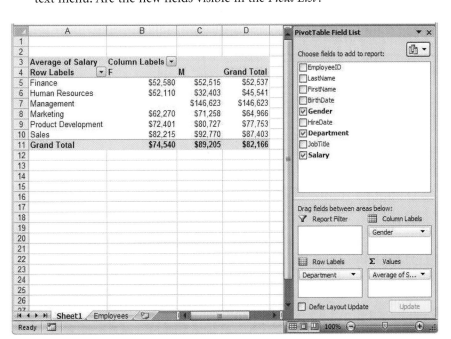

Figure 6-34: After adding two new columns to the source data, the column labels are not automatically included in the *Field List*.

10. Select the PivotTable and select **Options(tab)→Data(group)→Refresh** from the ribbon or right-click on the PivotTable and select *Refresh* from the context menu. Are both new fields now visible on the *Field List*? (Most likely the "Age" column will appear in the *Field List*, but not the "SalaryGrade" column.)

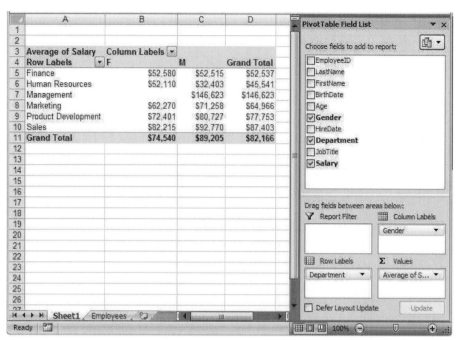

Figure 6-35: After the PivotTable is refreshed, the new "Age" column label appears in the *Field List* but the "SalaryGrade" field does not.

11. If the "SalaryGrade" column does not appear on the *Field List*, select **Options (tab)→Data(group)→Change Data Source** from the ribbon. Note that the current data source automatically selected does not include the "SalaryGrade" column.
12. Edit the data range to include the new "SalaryGrade" column. Click the *OK* button to close the dialog box.
13. The "SalaryGrade" column label should now be visible in the *Field List*. If it is not yet visible, refresh the PivotTable once more to view all column labels.

	EmployeeID	LastName	FirstName	BirthDate	Age	Gender	HireDate	Department	JobTitle	Salary	SalaryGrade	
1	EmployeeID	LastName	FirstName	BirthDate	Age	Gender	HireDate	Department	JobTitle	Salary	SalaryGrade	
2	1	Abner	David	11/15/1977	29	M	6/20/2006	Sales	Manager	$110,958	E	
3	2	Butler	Susan	11/16/1967	39	F	8/13/1978	Marketing	Staff	$40,816	B	
4	3							oduct Development	Staff Engineer	$74,665	D	
5	4	Da	Change PivotTable Data Source					ance	Staff Accountant	$42,106	B	
6	5	Ec						man Resources	Manager	$90,228	D	
7	6	Fr	Choose the data that you want to analyze					oduct Development	Staff	$42,976	B	
8	7	Ga	⊙ Select a table or range					les	Staff	$90,650	D	
9	8	Hi		Table/Range:	Employees!$A$1:$J$101			les	District Sales Manager	$128,845	F	
10	9	Ja	○ Use an external data source					les	Manager	$110,496	E	
11	10	Ke	Choose Connection...					les	Staff	$98,538	D	
12	11	Za	Connection name:					les	Staff	$84,151	D	
13	12	Pa						les	District Sales Manager	$133,784	F	
14	13	Sc			OK		Cancel	les	Staff	$35,025	B	
15	14	Zu						les	Manager	$113,591	E	
16	15	Crockett	Carol	11/19/1953	53	F	12/3/1994	Sales	Staff	$43,374	B	
17	16	Hancock	Christopher	4/30/1967	40	M	11/18/1999	Sales	Staff	$50,219	C	
18	17	Bateman	Matthew	1/27/1956	51	M	6/3/1998	Sales	Staff	$83,847	D	
19	18	Powell	Bruce	5/8/1966	41	M	12/29/1985	Product Development	Staff Engineer	$72,564	D	

◄ ◄ ► ► | PivotTable1 | **Employees** / Reference

Figure 6-36: Edit the list range to include the new "SalaryGrade" column.

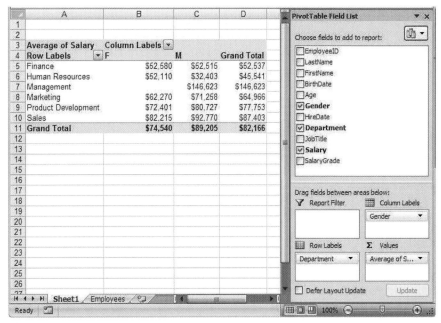

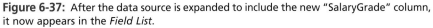

Figure 6-37: After the data source is expanded to include the new "SalaryGrade" column, it now appears in the *Field List*.

Quick Tip!

Use the keyboard shortcut Alt+F5 to refresh PivotTable data.

Applying Custom Calculations to PivotTable Data

In addition to sums, averages, counts, etc., PivotTable data may be displayed as percentages, differences from some base value, running totals or as an index of the total(s). To apply the optional custom calculation, open the *Value Field Settings* dialog box (use the PivotTable context menu or drop-down list in *Values* box of *Field List*). Select the *Show values as* tab of the dialog box. Select the display option from the *Show values as* drop-down list. For custom calculations that are based on other fields (i.e., showing values as *% Of* a base field) select the base field.

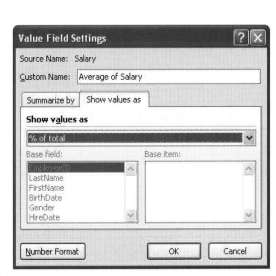

Figure 6-38: Customize the display of calculated values in the *Value Field Settings* dialog box.

Practice 6-3

Show all salary averages in terms of percent of total.

1. Continue with the previous Practice file or open the Excel file "Employees_ch6-3.xlsx" and select the "Pivot2" worksheet.
2. Right-click on the PivotTable label for the summarized data (*Average of Salary*) and select *Value Field Settings* from the context menu.
3. On the *Show value as* tab of the *Value Field Setting* dialog box, select *% of total* from the drop-down list. Click the *OK* button to close the dialog box.
4. Note that the index for the percent calculations is the "Grand Total." The percentages shown represent the percent of the overall average.

	A	B	C	D	E
1					
2					
3	Average of Salary	Column Labels ▼			
4	Row Labels ▼	F	M	Grand Total	
5	Finance	63.99%	63.91%	63.94%	
6	Human Resources	63.42%	39.44%	55.43%	
7	Management	0.00%	178.45%	178.45%	
8	Marketing	75.79%	86.72%	79.07%	
9	Product Development	88.12%	98.25%	94.63%	
10	Sales	100.06%	112.91%	106.37%	
11	Grand Total	90.72%	108.57%	100.00%	
12					

Figure 6-39: PivotTable result shows average salary by department and gender as percent of overall salary average.

The most common way users modify PivotTables is by "pivoting" the results, adding or removing fields from the column or row regions, and by applying advanced PivotTable features that enhance the data summary.

Advanced PivotTable Features

Grouping Summary Data

In many cases, the detailed data values for a field are too numerous to be of value in data analysis. For example, if you wish to view employee salary data by employee age, there are too many different age values which are not very useful in analyzing the data. If the ages could be grouped, say by decades, the salary summary will be of greater analytical value. The *PivotTable* feature provides a way to group numeric category values (including dates).

Practice 6-4

Alter the *PivotTable* in the previous Practice to include "Age" as a dimension and group ages by decades (20s, 30s, etc.). Remove the "Gender" dimension of the salary summaries.

1. Continue with the previous Practice file or open the Excel file "Employees_ch6-4.xlsx" and select the "Pivot2" worksheet.
2. Remove the "Gender" field from the PivotTable by removing the check from its box in the *Field List*. (It may also be removed by dragging the "Gender" field label from the *Column Label* box of the *PivotTable Field List* window or by right-clicking on the "Gender" field in the PivotTable and select *Remove "Gender"* from the context menu.)

3. Add the "Age" field to the *PivotTable* by placing a check beside it in the *Field List*. Move it to the *Column Labels* area of the PivotTable (drag to *Column Labels* box in *Field List*).

4. Select a cell in the "Age" column of the PivotTable. Select **Options(tab)→ Group(group)→Group Selection** from the ribbon. The *Grouping* dialog box will appear.

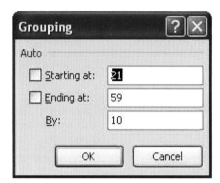

Figure 6-40: *Grouping* dialog box.

5. Change the *Starting at* value to 20 and the *Ending at* value to 60. Click the *OK* button to close the *Grouping* dialog box and show the grouped salaries.

	A	B	C	D	E	F
1						
2						
3	Average of Salary	Age				
4	Department	20-29	30-39	40-49	50-60	Grand Total
5	Finance	0.00%	0.00%	66.08%	62.87%	63.94%
6	Human Resources	76.36%	39.96%	70.78%	34.71%	55.43%
7	Management	178.00%	180.87%	174.49%	0.00%	178.45%
8	Marketing	106.31%	63.03%	45.11%	65.63%	79.07%
9	Product Development	77.69%	78.93%	85.32%	143.21%	94.63%
10	Sales	108.54%	109.06%	105.94%	99.97%	106.37%
11	Grand Total	107.63%	101.64%	95.71%	93.03%	100.00%
12						

Figure 6-41: Modified *PivotTable* showing ages grouped by decades.

Practice 6-5

Alter the previous *PivotTable* report to show average salaries by department and by year of hire.

1. Continue with the workbook from the previous Practice session or open the Excel workbook "Employee_ch6-5.xlsx" and select the "Pivot3" worksheet.
2. Remove "Age" from the PivotTable.
3. Move the "Department" field to the column region of the PivotTable.
4. Add the "HireDate" field to the row region of the PivotTable.
6. Select a cell in the "HireDate" column of the PivotTable and select **Options(tab)→ Group(group)→Group Selection** from the ribbon. The *Grouping* dialog box will appear.
7. Select *Years* in the *By* list box and unselect *Months*. Click the *OK* button to close the dialog box and display the grouped hire dates.

Figure 6-42: Select *Years* and un-select *Months* to group hire dates by year only.

	A	B	C	D	E	F	G	H
1								
2								
3	Average of Salary	Department						
4	HireDate	Finance	Human Resources	Management	Marketing	Product Development	Sales	Grand Total
5	1977	0.00%	76.36%	0.00%	0.00%	53.44%	86.57%	67.46%
6	1978	0.00%	0.00%	0.00%	49.68%	0.00%	0.00%	49.68%
7	1979	0.00%	0.00%	0.00%	84.84%	0.00%	97.66%	93.38%
8	1980	56.21%	0.00%	0.00%	0.00%	0.00%	88.81%	77.94%
9	1981	0.00%	0.00%	178.12%	0.00%	0.00%	0.00%	178.12%
10	1982	0.00%	0.00%	0.00%	0.00%	97.39%	112.02%	109.58%
11	1983	0.00%	34.71%	0.00%	54.68%	0.00%	87.23%	65.96%
12	1984	0.00%	0.00%	0.00%	0.00%	0.00%	100.30%	100.30%
13	1985	0.00%	0.00%	0.00%	0.00%	88.31%	97.90%	94.70%
14	1986	70.76%	0.00%	0.00%	0.00%	0.00%	0.00%	70.76%
15	1987	62.66%	0.00%	0.00%	0.00%	0.00%	0.00%	62.66%
16	1988	0.00%	0.00%	0.00%	0.00%	103.28%	130.75%	117.01%
17	1989	0.00%	0.00%	181.68%	0.00%	0.00%	163.20%	172.44%
18	1990	0.00%	0.00%	180.05%	0.00%	0.00%	108.97%	132.66%
19	1991	0.00%	109.81%	0.00%	0.00%	93.67%	111.21%	108.05%
20	1992	0.00%	32.80%	0.00%	0.00%	0.00%	134.48%	83.64%
21	1993	0.00%	0.00%	0.00%	0.00%	65.51%	137.43%	127.15%
22	1994	0.00%	31.75%	0.00%	0.00%	164.90%	86.36%	92.34%
23	1995	0.00%	0.00%	0.00%	76.57%	173.84%	0.00%	125.21%
24	1996	0.00%	0.00%	0.00%	0.00%	57.01%	0.00%	57.01%
25	1997	0.00%	0.00%	174.49%	0.00%	0.00%	42.63%	108.56%
26	1998	66.82%	47.12%	0.00%	0.00%	0.00%	124.12%	90.55%
27	1999	0.00%	0.00%	0.00%	83.44%	0.00%	101.21%	96.14%
28	2000	70.99%	0.00%	0.00%	0.00%	110.49%	127.37%	109.06%
29	2001	0.00%	0.00%	0.00%	64.87%	90.87%	55.04%	68.91%
30	2002	0.00%	0.00%	0.00%	173.50%	0.00%	92.98%	113.11%
31	2003	0.00%	0.00%	0.00%	0.00%	0.00%	108.58%	108.58%
32	2004	0.00%	0.00%	0.00%	0.00%	0.00%	92.52%	92.52%
33	2005	0.00%	0.00%	0.00%	54.77%	107.76%	145.47%	113.37%
34	2006	0.00%	0.00%	177.88%	0.00%	64.88%	80.14%	96.64%
35	Grand Total	63.94%	55.43%	178.45%	79.07%	94.63%	106.37%	100.00%
36								

Figure 6-43: PivotTable result for "HireDate" grouped by *Year*.

The PivotTable Page Field

An additional filter may be applied to the summarized PivotTable data by adding a field to the *Page* region of the PivotTable. As with the other PivotTable fields, use the drop-down list to select the value(s) you wish to represent in the summary data. Unlike adding fields to column or row regions of the PivotTable, adding a field to the *Page* region does not initially change the summary results. The table results are not altered until the additional filter is applied by selecting one or more *Page* values (but less than all the values) from the *Page* drop-down list. Note that if all *Page* values are selected, the list will remain the same as without the *Page* field.

Practice 6-6

Add a *Page* (*Report Filter*) field so that the data in the previous Practice PivotTable (average salaries by department, then by year of hire) may be viewed for each gender, one at a time.

1. Continue with the workbook from the previous Practice session or open the Excel workbook "Employee_ch6-6.xlsx" and select worksheet "Pivot4."
2. Add the "Gender" field back to the PivotTable by checking its box in the *Field List*. Move the "Gender" field onto the *Page* region of the *PivotTable* by dragging it to the *Report Filter* box in the *Field List* window.
3. Experiment with selecting first "M", then "F" from the "Gender" field drop-down list in the *Page* region of the PivotTable.

	A	B	C	D	E	F	G	H
1	Gender	(All)						
2								
3	Average of Salary	Department						
4	HireDate	Finance	Human Resources	Management	Marketing	Product Development	Sales	Grand Total
5	1977	0.00%	76.36%	0.00%	0.00%	53.44%	86.57%	67.46%
6	1978	0.00%	0.00%	0.00%	49.68%	0.00%	0.00%	49.68%
7	1979	0.00%	0.00%	0.00%	84.84%	0.00%	97.66%	93.38%
8	1980	56.21%	0.00%	0.00%	0.00%	0.00%	88.81%	77.94%
9	1981	0.00%	0.00%	178.12%	0.00%	0.00%	0.00%	178.12%
10	1982	0.00%	0.00%	0.00%	0.00%	97.39%	112.02%	109.58%

Page region of the PivotTable report

Figure 6-44: The "Gender" field is added to the *Page* region.

Changing PivotTable Options

Many options are available for displaying the summary data in the PivotTable. To view the various options, select the PivotTable and select **Options(tab)→ PivotTable(group)→Options** from the ribbon. PivotTable options may also be accessed from the context menu by right-clicking on the PivotTable and select *PivotTable Options*. The *PivotTable Options* dialog box will appear. Note the various groups of options available as represented on the dialog box tabs.

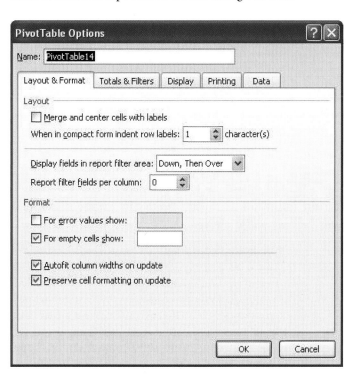

Figure 6-45: Many options are available for customizing PivotTable reports.

Practice 6-7

Instead of having the data summary show blank cells when there is no data to calculate for an intersection of row and column values, enter a default value to display. Either text or numeric default values may be displayed in blank cells.

1. Open the Excel file "Employees_ch6-7.xlsx" and select the worksheet "Pivot5." The PivotTable report shows the number of employees hired each year in each department.
2. Right-click on the PivotTable and select *PivotTable Options* from the context menu.
3. On the *Layout & Format* tab of the *PivotTable Options* dialog box enter the value "None" (without quotes) in the text box beside the *For empty cells, show:* in the *Format* section of the tab. (There should already by a check mark in the box in front of the option. The box must be checked before a value can be entered in the text box.) Click the *OK* button to close the dialog box and apply the change.

Count of EmployeeID	Department						
HireDate	Finance	Human Resources	Management	Marketing	Product Development	Sales	Grand Total
1977	None	1	None	None	2	1	4
1978	None	None	None	1	None	None	1
1979	None	None	None	1	None	2	3
1980	2	None	None	None	None	4	6
1981	None	None	1	None	None	None	1
1982	None	None	None	None	1	5	6
1983	None	1	None	1	None	2	4
1984	None	None	None	None	None	3	3
1985	None	None	None	None	1	2	3
1986	1	None	None	None	None	None	1
1987	1	None	None	None	None	None	1
1988	None	None	None	None	1	1	2
1989	None	None	1	None	None	1	2
1990	None	None	1	None	None	2	3
1991	None	1	None	None	1	4	6
1992	None	1	None	None	None	1	2
1993	None	None	None	None	1	6	7
1994	None	1	None	None	1	2	4
1995	None	None	None	1	1	None	2
1996	None	None	None	None	1	None	1
1997	None	None	1	None	None	1	2
1998	1	1	None	None	None	2	4
1999	None	None	None	2	None	5	7
2000	1	None	None	None	1	2	4
2001	None	None	None	2	1	1	4
2002	None	None	None	1	None	3	4
2003	None	None	None	None	None	2	2
2004	None	None	None	None	None	2	2
2005	None	None	None	1	1	2	4
2006	None	None	1	None	1	3	5
Grand Total	6	6	5	10	14	59	100

Figure 6-46: User may choose to display a default text or numeric value in empty cells.

Applying AutoFormat to PivotTables

As with an Excel list, you can apply a pre-formatted style to a *PivotTable*. To access the PivotTable style gallery, select **Design(tab)→PivotTable Styles** from the ribbon. Select the desired style from the gallery. To return to the default format style, select the first style in the design gallery list.

Creating PivotChart Reports

PivotTable summary data may be displayed in chart format instead of (or in addition to) a table format. To create a PivotChart report, select **Insert(tab)→Tables(group)→ PivotTable→PivotChart** from the ribbon. The same dialog box is presented as for the PivotTable to allow the user to verify the list range and select the PivotChart location (see Figure 6-24). A blank PivotChart and PivotTable layout are added to the workbook. A background PivotTable will be created for each PivotChart.

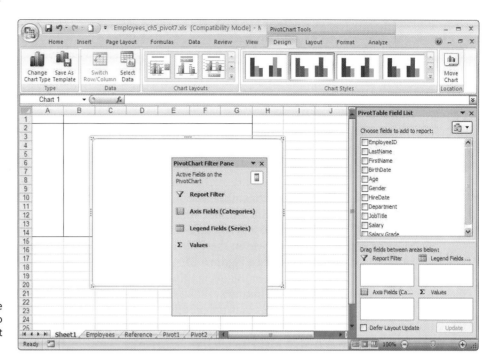

Figure 6-47: A blank PivotTable and PivotChart layout is added to the workbook when the PivotChart option is selected.

Instead of *Column Labels* and *Row Labels* areas of the PivotTable, the *Field List* has boxes for *Legend Fields* and *Axes Fields*. Fields are selected and positioned in the *Field List* in the same way as for the PivotTable report. The PivotTable column fields correspond with the chart series (Legend Fields area) and the PivotTable row fields correspond to the PivotChart categories (Axis Fields). A *Page* field (*Report Filter* box in the *Field List*) may be added to the PivotChart just as for the PivotTable report by adding the field to the *Report Filter* box in the *Field List*. Just as for the PivotTable, the PivotChart is interactive. Fields can be added, removed, or "pivoted" (moved between *Axis* and *Legend* areas) to change the view of the summary data.

A PivotChart report is initially created in the default Excel chart type which is a clustered column chart. To change the chart type or formatting, select the PivotChart and use the tasks on the PivotChart *Design* context tab of the Excel ribbon.

Figure 6-48: The *Design* context tab for PivotCharts.

Use the options on the *Layout* context tab to format various areas of the PivotChart just as you would for other chart types in Excel.

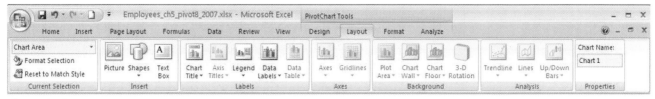

Figure 6-49: The *Layout* context tab for PivotCharts.

Practice 6-8

Create a PivotChart Report that shows the relative percent of salaries for each department compared to the total of all salaries.

1. Continue with the file from the previous Practice or open Excel file "Employees_ch6-8.xlsx" and select the "Employee" worksheet.
2. Select a cell within the employee list and select from the ribbon **Insert(tab)→ Tables(group)→PivotTable→PivotChart**.
3. Confirm the list range and location for new PivotChart in the *Create PivotTable with PivotChart* dialog box. Click the *OK* button to continue.
4. Select the "Salary" and "Department" fields in the *Field List*.
5. Change the *Sum of Salary* value field so that each department's salary total displays as a percentage of the total salary budget. Click on the arrow on the *Sum of Salary* field in the *Values* box of the *Field List*. Select *Value Field Settings* from the menu (see Figure 6-27).
6. On the *Show values as* tab, select *% of total* from the list. Click the *OK* button to continue.
7. So that the pie slices display from largest to smallest beginning at the 12 o'clock position, sort the PivotTable data in descending order. Select a cell in the "Total" column of the PivotTable and use the *Sort Z to A* icon from the ribbon to sort the percentages from largest to smallest (**Data(tab)→Sort & Filter(group)→Sort Z to A**).
8. Change the default chart title text by right-clicking on the title text box and select *Edit Text* from the context menu. Make the title "Salary Budget by Department."
9. Delete the chart legend (right-click and use the delete key).
10. Add data labels to the pie slices. Right-click on the data markers (click once to select all markers at once) and select *Add Data Labels* from the context menu.
11. On the *Label Options* tab of the *Format Data Labels* dialog box, check the boxes beside *Value* and *Category Name*. (Since the PivotTable data is already shown as a percent value, select *Value* instead of *Percentage*.) Select *Outside End* for the *Label Position*. Click the *Close* button to apply the changes.
12. Make the percentages appear as whole percentage amounts by formatting the percentage data in the PivotTable to whole numbers using the *Number* formatting options on the *Home* tab of the ribbon.
13. Change the text for the "Human Resources" data label. Click twice (two single clicks) on the data label then right-click and select *Edit Text* from the context menu. Change the text "Human Resources" to "HR" in the data label.
14. Resize the chart so that the data label texts do not overlap.

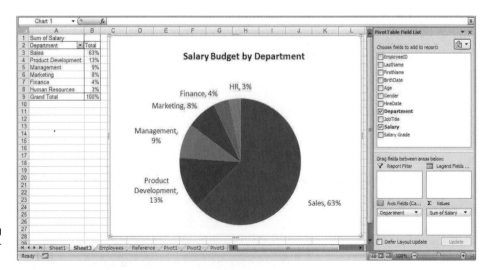

Figure 6-50: *PivotChart* showing percentage of salary budget allocated to each department.

Predictive Decision Models

Predictive models are based on statistical analysis of sets of known data to try to discover the relationships between an input value (also called independent variable or predictor) and the resulting output value (also called dependent variable or response variable). Independent variables are commonly referred to as "*x*" and dependent variables as "*y*." A retailer may be interested in seeing whether or not the amount of advertising funds spent on special promotions seems to affect sales revenue. Simple linear regression analysis is commonly used in business to determine if a particular input variable can be used to predict the value of an output variable. Special tools for performing statistical analysis of data are available as an add-in to Excel and are packaged with the program.

To install the data analysis tools, select the **Office Button→Excel Options→Add-Ins**. From the drop-down list at the bottom left area of the *Excel Options* dialog box, select *Excel Add-in* and click the *Go* button. Check the box beside *Analysis Tookpak* and click the *OK* button to complete the add-in installation.

Once the *Analysis Toolpak* is installed, a new *Analysis* task group is added to the *Data* tab of the ribbon. Access the data analysis tools by selecting the *Data Analysis* task from the new task group.

To use the regression analysis tool, select **Data(tab)→Analysis(group)→Data Analysis** and the *Data Analysis* dialog box will appear. Select *Regression* from the list box and click the *OK* button to close the dialog box. The *Regression* dialog appears to prompt the user for the input range (*known_x's*) and output range (*known_y's*) and other options for the data analysis.

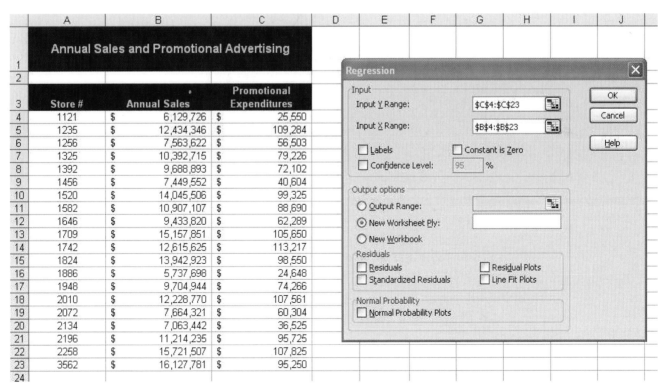

Figure 6-51: The Regression dialog box prompts the user to enter the input cell ranges for known *y*'s and related known *x*'s.

After clicking the *OK* button of the *Regression* dialog box, the summary of the analysis appears in the designated output cell range.

	A	B	C	D	E	F	G	H	I
1	SUMMARY OUTPUT								
2									
3	*Regression Statistics*								
4	Multiple R	0.901984595							
5	R Square	0.81357621							
6	Adjusted R Square	0.803219332							
7	Standard Error	12927.40732							
8	Observations	20							
9									
10	ANOVA								
11		*df*	*SS*	*MS*	*F*	*Significance F*			
12	Regression	1	13127809846	13127809846	78.55420028	5.53011E-08			
13	Residual	18	3008121480	167117860					
14	Total	19	16135931326						
15									
16		*Coefficients*	*Standard Error*	*t Stat*	*P-value*	*Lower 95%*	*Upper 95%*	*Lower 95.0%*	*Upper 95.0%*
17	Intercept	-10065.22702	10310.72288	-0.976190237	0.341908232	-31727.25194	11596.79791	-31727.25194	11596.79791
18	X Variable 1	0.008151486	0.000919712	8.863080744	5.53011E-08	0.006219242	0.01008373	0.006219242	0.01008373
19									

Figure 6-52: Output of the regression analysis is summarized on a newly-inserted worksheet as indicated by the user in the *Regression* dialog box.

Once a company has analyzed the input and output data and determined that a strong correlation exists between the independent and dependent variables, the model can be used to predict future values of *y* for new values of *x*.

Two worksheet functions that can be used for predictive decision-making are FORECAST and TREND. Both functions calculate their return values based on the underlying linear regression model. The FORECAST function uses linear regression analysis of known values for a related set of *x*'s and *y*'s to calculate a future value of *y*. The TREND function returns one or more values along an extended trend line produced by the underlying regression equation. The syntax for the FORECAST function:

=**FORECAST**(**x, known_y's, known_x's**)

The *known_y's* argument is the set of dependent variable values that corresponds to the set of *known_x's* (argument), the set of independent variable values. The argument *x* represents the new *x* value for which the output is forecasted.

The syntax for the TREND function:

=**TREND**(**known_y's, [known_x's], [new_x's], [const]**)

In addition to the *known_y's* and *known_x's* arguments, the *new_x's* argument is the new range of input values for which an output trend is predicted. The *const* argument indicates whether or not the constant (*b*, the y-intercept) is set to 0(zero). If the argument is TRUE or omitted, *b* is calculated normally. If it is set to FALSE, *b* is set equal to 0(zero).

Predicting with the FORECAST Function

If the retailer would like to predict the results of a given amount of promotional spending, the FORECAST function can be used without actually performing the regression analysis first in Excel. To set up the worksheet for using the FORECAST function, set up two columns, one for the independent variable (x) and one for the predicted values of the dependent variable (y). In the first row of the *x* column, enter a value within the range of known *x* values. In the first row of the *y* column, enter the FORECAST function. To access the *Function Arguments* dialog box for the FORECAST function, use *Shift+F3* or another insertion method that accesses the dialog box for input of arguments. (Review the various ways to insert functions in Chapter 3.)

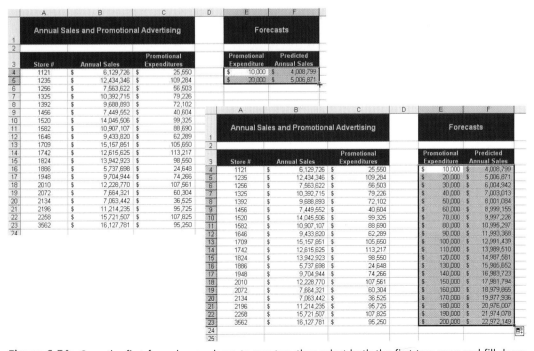

	A	B	C	D	E	F	G	H	I
1	**Annual Sales and Promotional Advertising**				**Forecasts**				
2									
3	Store #	Annual Sales	Promotional Expenditures		Promotional Expenditure	Predicted Annual Sales			
4	1121	$ 6,129,726	$ 25,550		$ 80,000	=FORECAST(E4,$B$4:$B$23,$C$4:$C$23)			
5	1235	$ 12,434,346	$ 109,284						
6	1256	$ 7,563,622	$ 56,503						
7	1325	$ 10,392,715	$ 79,226						
8	1392	$ 9,688,893	$ 72,102						
9	1456	$ 7,449,552	$ 40,604						
10	1520	$ 14,045,506	$ 99,325						
11	1582	$ 10,907,107	$ 88,690						
12	1646	$ 9,433,820	$ 62,289						
13	1709	$ 15,157,851	$ 105,650						
14	1742	$ 12,615,625	$ 113,217						
15	1824	$ 13,942,923	$ 98,550						
16	1886	$ 5,737,698	$ 24,648						
17	1948	$ 9,704,944	$ 74,266						
18	2010	$ 12,228,770	$ 107,561						
19	2072	$ 7,664,321	$ 60,304						
20	2134	$ 7,063,442	$ 36,525						
21	2196	$ 11,214,235	$ 95,725						
22	2258	$ 15,721,507	$ 107,825						
23	3562	$ 16,127,781	$ 95,250						

Function Arguments dialog box:

FORECAST
- X: E4 = 80000
- Known_y's: $B$4:$B$23 = {6129726;12434346
- Known_x's: $C$4:$C$23 = {25550;109284;565

= 10995296.8

Calculates, or predicts, a future value along a linear trend by using existing values.

X is the data point for which you want to predict a value and must be a numeric value.

Formula result = $ 10,995,297

Help on this function   [OK]   [Cancel]

Figure 6-53: Use the *Functions Arguments* dialog box to enter the arguments for the FORECAST function.

To enter the *x* argument for the FORECAST function, select the first cell in the independent variable column for the *x* input. Select the ranges of known *y* values and the corresponding set of known *x* values to enter for the next two arguments. Click the *OK* button to enter the formula and its arguments. Be sure to make the cell references to all the range arguments (*known_x's* and *known_y's*) absolute either when they are entered into the *Function Arguments* dialog box or by editing the formula after it is inserted.

To fill the remainder of the prediction table, replace the first *x* value in the independent variable column with a new *x* value for which you would like an output calculated. The value may be within the range of known *x's* or outside that range. Enter a second value for *x* in the second row of the column indicating the pattern by which to increment the *x* value as you copy down the values in the column. (Note that you do

Figure 6-54: Copy the first formula row down to row two then select both the first two rows and fill down to the last value of *x* desired.

not have to enter a range of values for proposed values of *x*. Random values of *x* may be entered into that column.) Copy down the formula from the first row of the dependent variable column to the second row. Now select rows 1 and 2 of both columns and using the fill handle, fill the formulas down to the desired number of rows. If you get a #DIV/0! error value in any of the cells, check to make sure the references for the *known_x's* and *known_y's* arguments are absolute.

The FORECAST function fills the *y* column with predicted values based on the correlation of the known *x*'s with the known *y*'s.

Predicting with the TREND Function

Like the FORECAST function, the TREND function returns values based on the linear regression analysis method. The TREND function specifically returns one or more values from along the trend line formed by the regression analysis equation. Businesses generally want to predict a trend over some continuum which is, in most cases, time. Consider the following sales history by quarter for years 2002–2007. To predict the sales for future quarters, use the TREND function to analyze the known set of independent variables (period numbers), and the known set of dependent variables (quarterly sales). (Note that period numbers are added to this model to represent the quarter number in a series because Excel does not recognize the text in the "Quarter" column as a series of data.)

To set up the worksheet for the trend prediction, structure a table similar to the original set of data. Enter quarters in the first column for which you would like to predict a sales value. Suppose you would like to predict sales for each quarter of the next 3 years. The first value in the "Quarters" column will be "2008 Q1" and the last value in the column will be "2010 Q4". Enter the period number (45) that corresponds with the next quarter (extended from the original data). Enter the next quarter period number (46) in the second row of the period number column to establish an incrementation pattern for filling the column. Select the first two cells in the period number column and copy down to fill in remaining period numbers for the quarters listed (to period number 56).

Using the *Function Arguments* dialog box, enter the TREND function into the first row of the predicted sales column. Be sure to make the cell references to all the range arguments (*known_x's*, *known_y's*, and *new_x's*) absolute either when they are entered into the *Function Arguments* dialog box or by editing the formula after it is inserted. Click the *OK* button to complete the formula entry.

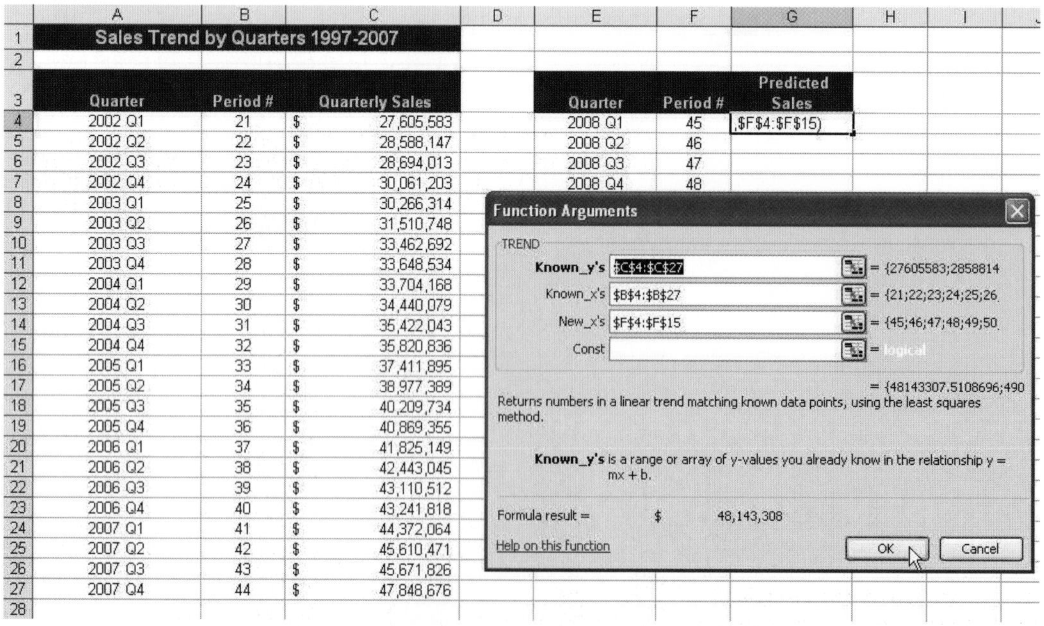

Figure 6-55: Enter the arguments to the TREND function using the *Function Argument* dialog box.

	A	B	C	D	E	F	G
1	Sales Trend by Quarters 1997-2007						
2							
3	Quarter	Period #	Quarterly Sales		Quarter	Period #	Predicted Sales
4	2002 Q1	21	$ 27,605,583		2008 Q1	45	$ 48,143,308
5	2002 Q2	22	$ 28,588,147		2008 Q2	46	
6	2002 Q3	23	$ 28,694,013		2008 Q3	47	
7	2002 Q4	24	$ 30,061,203		2008 Q4	48	
8	2003 Q1	25	$ 30,266,314		2009 Q1	49	
9	2003 Q2	26	$ 31,510,748		2009 Q2	50	
10	2003 Q3	27	$ 33,462,692		2009 Q3	51	
11	2003 Q4	28	$ 33,648,534		2009 Q4	52	
12	2004 Q1	29	$ 33,704,168		2010 Q1	53	
13	2004 Q2	30	$ 34,440,079		2010 Q2	54	
14	2004 Q3	31	$ 35,422,043		2010 Q3	55	
15	2004 Q4	32	$ 35,820,836		2010 Q4	56	
16	2005 Q1	33	$ 37,411,895				
17	2005 Q2	34	$ 38,977,389				
18	2005 Q3	35	$ 40,209,734				
19	2005 Q4	36	$ 40,869,355				
20	2006 Q1	37	$ 41,825,149				
21	2006 Q2	38	$ 42,443,045				
22	2006 Q3	39	$ 43,110,512				
23	2006 Q4	40	$ 43,241,818				
24	2007 Q1	41	$ 44,372,064				
25	2007 Q2	42	$ 45,610,471				
26	2007 Q3	43	$ 45,671,826				
27	2007 Q4	44	$ 47,848,676				

Figure 6-56: The return from the TREND function is visible in cell G4.

Inserting an Array Function

The TREND function operates differently from the FORECAST function in that it cannot be copied down to fill the remaining cells of the column and return the correct result. Recall that the FORECAST function accepts a single value for the new *x*, so it returns a separate value for each new *x*. Unlike the FORECAST function, the argument for the new value of *x* is an unchanging range in the TREND function and not a single *x* value. In order to fill the new range for y, we will need to enter the TREND formula as an *array formula*. *Array formulas* in Excel calculate and return results to a range of cells at once rather than to one single cell. To enter an array formula, the output or return range must be selected, then the formula must be entered using the *Ctrl+Shift+Enter* keys simultaneously rather than using just the *Enter* key as with non-array type functions.

To re-enter the TREND function for the entire array of predicted sales values, select the range G4:G15 and place the cursor at the end of the formula in the formula bar. Using the keyboard combination *Ctrl+Shift+Enter*, enter the formula into the selected array.

FORECAST =TREND($C$4:$C$27,$B$4:$B$27,$F$4:$F$15) ◄————— Cursor

	A	B	C	D	E	F	G
1	Sales Trend by Quarters 1997-2007						
2							
3	Quarter	Period #	Quarterly Sales		Quarter	Period #	Predicted Sales
4	2002 Q1	21	$ 27,605,583		2008 Q1	45	=TREND($C$4:$C
5	2002 Q2	22	$ 28,588,147		2008 Q2	46	
6	2002 Q3	23	$ 28,694,013		2008 Q3	47	
7	2002 Q4	24	$ 30,061,203		2008 Q4	48	
8	2003 Q1	25	$ 30,266,314		2009 Q1	49	
9	2003 Q2	26	$ 31,510,748		2009 Q2	50	
10	2003 Q3	27	$ 33,462,692		2009 Q3	51	
11	2003 Q4	28	$ 33,648,534		2009 Q4	52	
12	2004 Q1	29	$ 33,704,168		2010 Q1	53	
13	2004 Q2	30	$ 34,440,079		2010 Q2	54	
14	2004 Q3	31	$ 35,422,043		2010 Q3	55	
15	2004 Q4	32	$ 35,820,836		2010 Q4	56	
16	2005 Q1	33	$ 37,411,895				
17	2005 Q2	34	$ 38,977,389				
18	2005 Q3	35	$ 40,209,734				
19	2005 Q4	36	$ 40,869,355				
20	2006 Q1	37	$ 41,825,149				
21	2006 Q2	38	$ 42,443,045				
22	2006 Q3	39	$ 43,110,512				
23	2006 Q4	40	$ 43,241,818				
24	2007 Q1	41	$ 44,372,064				
25	2007 Q2	42	$ 45,610,471				
26	2007 Q3	43	$ 45,671,826				
27	2007 Q4	44	$ 47,848,676				

Figure 6-57: To enter the formula into the entire range, select the range and place the cursor at the end of the formula in the formula bar then press the key combination *Ctrl+Shift+Enter*.

Once an array formula has been entered, it appears in the formula bar with curly braces around the entire formula.

	A	B	C	D	E	F	G
	Arial		10		B I U		
	G4		fx {=TREND($C$4:$C$27,$B$4:$B$27,$F$4:$F$15)}				
1	Sales Trend by Quarters 1997-2007						
2							
3	Quarter	Period #	Quarterly Sales		Quarter	Period #	Predicted Sales
4	2002 Q1	21	$ 27,605,583		2008 Q1	45	$ 48,143,308
5	2002 Q2	22	$ 28,588,147		2008 Q2	46	$ 49,012,051
6	2002 Q3	23	$ 28,694,013		2008 Q3	47	$ 49,880,795
7	2002 Q4	24	$ 30,061,203		2008 Q4	48	$ 50,749,538
8	2003 Q1	25	$ 30,266,314		2009 Q1	49	$ 51,618,282
9	2003 Q2	26	$ 31,510,748		2009 Q2	50	$ 52,487,026
10	2003 Q3	27	$ 33,462,692		2009 Q3	51	$ 53,355,769
11	2003 Q4	28	$ 33,648,534		2009 Q4	52	$ 54,224,513
12	2004 Q1	29	$ 33,704,168		2010 Q1	53	$ 55,093,256
13	2004 Q2	30	$ 34,440,079		2010 Q2	54	$ 55,962,000
14	2004 Q3	31	$ 35,422,043		2010 Q3	55	$ 56,830,744
15	2004 Q4	32	$ 35,820,836		2010 Q4	56	$ 57,699,487
16	2005 Q1	33	$ 37,411,895				
17	2005 Q2	34	$ 38,977,389				
18	2005 Q3	35	$ 40,209,734				
19	2005 Q4	36	$ 40,869,355				
20	2006 Q1	37	$ 41,825,149				
21	2006 Q2	38	$ 42,443,045				
22	2006 Q3	39	$ 43,110,512				
23	2006 Q4	40	$ 43,241,818				
24	2007 Q1	41	$ 44,372,064				
25	2007 Q2	42	$ 45,610,471				
26	2007 Q3	43	$ 45,671,826				
27	2007 Q4	44	$ 47,848,676				
28							

Figure 6-58: The array is filled with new values for the predicted sales using the array function TREND. Note the curly braces around the array formula in the formula bar.

Decision Model Quality

Decision models are especially prone to errors since errors become more prevalent as formula size increases and formula structures get more complex. The quality of decision models can be defined on three different levels:

- *Level 1:* The model runs free of error values. It is also logically correct without result errors.
- *Level 2:* The model supports the decision process as intended.
- *Level 3:* The model adheres to best practices with regard to its design.

Guidelines to Minimize Decision Model Errors

1. *Separate data values and value labels into different cells.*
   For example, if a cell content represents cost per machine hour, instead of entering "$150/machine hour" into one cell, enter "150" into one cell and enter the label "Per machine hour" into the adjacent cell to the right. Format the "150" using a currency format rather than typing the $ symbol into the cell along with the value. Excel cannot distinguish numeric values from text when numbers and non-numeric characters are mixed in one cell.

2. *Adhere to good formula design.*
   Each input should be designed as a single value or formula. No literal values should be included in formulas. All assumption values should be removed from formulas to assumption cells and clearly labeled.

3. *Each input should be defined in only one location.*
   Maintenance problems are minimized when an input value need only be altered in one cell.

4. *Make a clear distinction between input values and calculated results.*
   Use formatting and labels to direct users to assumption cells that may be changed. Lock cells that contain formulas and apply worksheet protection to the individual worksheets to safeguard the formulas and model structure. Include specific user instructions on a documentation worksheet.

5. *Make sure all data cells are referenced.*
   Models are a combination of data cells and label cells. All the data cells in the model should be referenced in some area of the decision model.

6. *For very large or complex models, separate into multiple smaller models.*
   Using a divide-and-conquer strategy, divide large complex models into smaller models on separate worksheets, then connect them using formulas and references.

   Spreadsheets are likely the most widely-used decision support tool in business because spreadsheet software is so widely available to business users. Assuring the quality of the decision model is extremely important. A poor design can cost an organization thousands or millions of dollars.

   There are many Excel add-ins on the market that are available for data analysis and decision support. Some are relatively simple and inexpensive and some are very powerful and are used by many large organizations to support all types of business decisions. Also, many templates are available for common decision models. Explore Microsoft's Excel support Web site for an up-to-date list of Excel templates at www.microsoft.com.

Review Questions

1. What is a spreadsheet *decision model*?

_____

_____

_____

2. List the characteristics of a good decision model.

_____

_____

_____

3. What decision model is useful in making subjective decisions?

_____

_____

_____

4. What are the three elements required to construct a decision matrix or weighted criteria analysis?

_____

_____

_____

5. How does the RANK function work?

_____

_____

_____

6. What is a scenario with regard to the what-if model?

_____

_____

_____

7. How does the *Scenario Manager* support the what-if decision model?

    _____

    _____

    _____

8. How do *data tables* relate to the what-if decision model?

    _____

    _____

    _____

9. With regard to inputs and outputs, describe the difference in one- and two-variable *data tables*. What are the relative advantages and disadvantages of each?

    _____

    _____

    _____

10. How do *PivotTable Reports* differ from subtotals that are produced using the *Subtotal* ribbon command (topic from Chapter 5)?

    _____

    _____

    _____

11. What is a *custom* format? What is its purpose?

    _____

    _____

    _____

12. What is the major difference between the FORECAST and the TREND functions with regard to their return values?

    _____

    _____

    _____

13. What is meant by an *array* function? What does the user need to know about entering an array function?

_____

_____

_____

14. Describe the three levels of decision model quality.

_____

_____

_____

15. List the six guidelines for minimizing decision model errors.

_____

_____

_____

Practice Problems

1. Following the steps described in this chapter, construct a decision matrix to help you make an upcoming personal or business decision. Make certain the decision type is appropriate for the decision matrix model.

2. Develop a decision model that will help a health club manager quote *annual* and *monthly* membership rates to potential members who call on the telephone. The model will calculate two outputs, the annual membership fee and the monthly membership fee. The manager will need to enter the following information into the model as he receives it from the caller:

   • Number of people in the family
   • Age group of the primary member (<60, 60–69, >69)
   • Whether or not the potential member works for an employer who subsidizes the employee membership fee.

   The membership fee is calculated based on the following rules.

   • There is a base fee for a single member (no other family members).
   • A two-member family is charged 150% of the base rate.
   • For a family of three or more, the base fee is doubled.
   • A primary member having a corporate affiliation that subsidizes membership fees is given a 10% discount off the single or family fee.
   • Primary members over 60 receive a 10% discount off the single or family fee.
   • Primary members over 70 receive a 30% discount off the single or family fee.
   • Most members pay annually, but a few prefer to pay monthly. There is a 5% service charge for members who wish to pay the fee on a monthly basis.

3. Each year a large manufacturing firm must decide what health insurance package to purchase for its employees. Each year the cost of each of the components (medical, dental, vision) of the package increase. Each component has several levels of coverage from which to choose for the package. Each level has a different price tag and is priced per covered employee. The firm allocates a set percentage of its net operating income each year for employee benefit expense. That percentage may vary slightly from year to year. The company must decide each year which level of coverage to purchase for each component based on whether or not the entire health benefit package cost will be within the company's health benefit budget. Alternately, the company may choose to increase the employee's portion of the benefit payment to offset some increases rather than reduce the level of coverage. Currently employees pay 20% of the total premium.
   Construct a what-if analysis model that will help the firm decide which benefits to purchase. The benefits managers are interested in seeing the difference in the health benefit budget and the estimated cost of the benefit.
   Inputs to the model will be:

   • Number of employees
   • Cost of medical coverage per employee

- Cost of dental coverage per employee
- Cost of vision coverage per employee
- Percent of benefit paid by employee
- Net operating income
- Percent of net operating income budgeted to employee health benefits.

Outputs from the model will be:

- Total annual employee health benefit budget
- Total annual employee health benefit expense
- Budget remainder (the difference between employee health benefit budget and estimated annual cost of the employee health benefit package)

Clearly differentiate between the user inputs and the calculated outputs of the model. Provide appropriate data labels and user instructions for the model.

4. Using the *Scenario Manager*, practice saving various scenarios of the what-if analysis you performed in Problem 3.

5. Create a data table that shows the three related outputs for the what-if model you produced in Problem 3 when values are changed for the number of employees.

6. Create a data table that shows the budget remainder output for the what-if model you produced in Problem 3 when values are changed for the number of employees and employee contribution (%) toward the benefit payment.

7. Create a multiplication table using a two-variable data. The data table should produce the output visible in the shaded cells below.

Product	0	1	2	3	4	5
0	0	0	0	0	0	0
1	0	1	2	3	4	5
2	0	2	4	6	8	10
3	0	3	6	9	12	15
4	0	4	8	12	16	20
5	0	5	10	15	20	25

PART TWO

Designing Project Enhancements

CHAPTER SEVEN

Introduction to Problem Solving and Programming Logic

1. Understand the difference between heuristic and algorithmic problem solutions
2. Name and describe the steps required to solve a general problem that has an algorithmic solution
3. Describe how general problem-solving techniques relate to computer solutions
4. Name and explain the major phases in the systems development life cycle and the tasks involved in each phase
5. Understand the concept of *iterative* and *incremental* system development
6. Explain the meaning of structured program design
7. Name the three basic program control structures
8. Define two techniques for modeling algorithms

Introduction to Application Development with Excel

In Part 1 of this text you learned what a powerful tool Excel can be for storing, analyzing, and presenting data. Excel workbooks that are developed to support business tasks tend to be used extensively and repeatedly. Excel's capabilities extend far beyond those covered so far in this text. Excel also supports the automation of worksheet tasks, the creation of user-defined worksheet functions and procedures, and user-friendly graphical user interfaces that make an Excel workbook perform like a standalone software application.

Excel and other Microsoft Office applications are bundled with a programming environment that allows the user to develop the additional features that enhance an Excel workbook so that it can be used as an actual software application. Visual Basic for Applications (VBA) is a subset of the Visual Basic programming language and is packaged with some Microsoft Office products such as Excel, Word, Outlook, and PowerPoint as well as with other applications that are not a part of the Microsoft Office suite. Unlike Visual Basic, VBA is not a standalone programming environment. It functions only inside a host application such as Excel.

Today's business environments use spreadsheets more than ever. The complexity of spreadsheets in use has also increased significantly in recent years. Many end users are able to add automation, custom functions, and user interfaces to Excel workbooks after learning a few basic programming skills within the VBA programming environment. You don't have to be a "programmer" to develop complex business applications with Excel.

Because this text is written for business professionals who are non-programmers, it assumes the reader has no prior programming knowledge or experience. Before jumping straight into the VBA programming environment, the Excel project developer must figure out which enhancements would add significant value and usability to the project, and exactly what each of those enhancements must do. In order to develop quality enhancements with VBA, the intended functionality of the enhancements must be clearly understood and the solution must be carefully designed to produce the desired results. To make sure a software application (i.e., Excel project) will perform as it should, the developer should apply a proven problem-solving approach. Particular system development methods for producing software application have been developed that parallel good problem-solving approaches for any type of problem.

General Problem-Solving Concepts

We make decisions every day that affect our lives in some way. Some problems are simple, such as what we will have for dinner tonight, but others are more complex, such as choosing the right graduate school. Bad decisions cost time and resources, so we try to make the best decision possible from the outset. Here are six steps that can aid in finding the best solution to any type of problem.

1. *Identify the problem:* Most of the time in the classroom, the problem students are to solve is identified for them. But in our personal or professional lives, problems present themselves in many ways. It is important to identify the underlying problem rather than just the symptoms that may be apparent. You must correctly identify the problem before you can find a suitable solution.

2. *Understand the problem:* Once the problem is identified, you must analyze the problem to thoroughly understand it. You might be having a problem with a new employee that you supervise who is not performing satisfactorily. The unsatisfactory performance is a symptom of a problem. It is important to figure out why the employee is not performing as expected before the problem can be corrected. Does the employee simply lack the motivation to do the job well, or does he not understand the job tasks being performed due to inadequate training? Maybe the employee is not productive because he comes in to work late and takes long lunch breaks. There may be any number of factors that affect the employee's productivity that should be considered before the problem can be solved. Understanding the problem also includes understanding the knowledge base of the person (or machine) for whom (or which) you are solving the problem. Once the problem is thoroughly understood, steps can be taken to develop a solution.

3. *Identify alternative ways to solve the problem:* Make a list of all feasible solutions to the problem. The list should be as complete as possible. Maybe you determine that the employee who is not performing well did not get adequate training to perform his job. Possible solution alternatives might include (1) one-on-one training with an experienced employee, (2) reading the procedure manual for the tasks he is to perform, (3) using tutorial-type computer-based training that is available through the company's educational services department, (4) providing adequate work time for the employee to read the procedure manual as he encounters new tasks and assigning a specific experienced employee as a resource person to answer questions about the procedures. Any of the alternative solutions are feasible and are acceptable ways to solve the problem.

4. *Select the best way to solve the problem from the list of alternative solutions:* You must identify the pros and cons of each of the alternative solutions and apply some type of evaluation criteria in order to rate the solutions. Applying an appropriate decision support model, such as a weighted criteria analysis or decision matrix, is helpful to evaluate alternatives. It might be that all factors to be considered do not have equal impact on the solution. You may need to figure out a way to weight the important factors more heavily than the others. If you select the correct criteria for evaluating the alternatives, you will be able to arrive at the best possible solution.

5. *List instructions that enable you to solve the problem using the selected solution:* Recall from Step 2 that you must understand the knowledge base of the person or machine for which the solution is sought. The knowledge base will determine how detailed or on what level the instructions should be supplied. The instruction set must fall within that knowledge base. For the employee who needs more training, it is important to understand what he already knows about the training topic so that the instructions will be on a level he will understand.

6. *Make preparations for applying the solution:* Gather the necessary people, information, and materials to the required location for applying the solution.

7. *Apply the solution:* Using the resources gathered in Step 5, carry out the instructions that were specified in Step 5.

8. *Evaluate the solution:* Is the solution correct? Does it solve the problem? Is the solution satisfactory? If all of these questions cannot be answered "Yes," you must restart the process of solving the problem. Sometimes a minimal solution is correct and

solves the problem on a basic level, but it may not be completely satisfactory to the person with the problem. Satisfaction with the solution reflects the quality of the solution. Our goal should always be to provide the best solutions possible.

Using Computers to Solve Problems

The main focus of the remainder of this text will be developing solutions that computers can implement. The term *solution* applies to the set of instructions required to solve the problem. These instructions are listed in a step-by-step fashion that can be understood by the computer. These instructions will produce the most satisfactory *result* for the problem. *Result* refers to the outcome after the application of the solution, or the computer-assisted answer. A *program* is the set of instructions that have been written (or *coded*) in a particular programming language. There are many different programming languages. Each language has its own programming environment, which is also a type of software program that translates the programming language code (what the programmer writes) into computer machine language that the computer hardware understands (ones and zeros). Computer programs are also called *software, applications,* and *systems.* The term *system* is usually applied to the entire computer environment which includes both software and hardware. Computer *hardware* includes the machinery that is a part of a computer system, like the processing unit, monitor, and printer.

When developing computer programs to solve problems, a step-by-step decision process is followed much like the one outlined at the beginning of this chapter. This process is called the *system development life cycle (SDLC)* or more recently the *information systems life cycle.* The SDLC provides a broad general framework with which a computer system can be developed. Rather than steps, the framework is viewed as five phases that may overlap somewhat. One phase may begin before the previous phase has clearly ended. The five major phases of the SDLC are Analysis, Design, Development, Implementation, and Evaluation.

Divide and Conquer

The development of any size computer system can be complex and difficult to manage as a whole. Instead of trying to develop an entire computer system at once with one pass through the SDLC, the system should be broken into smaller more manageable pieces, or *modules.* A program *module* is any portion of the software solution that is self-contained and has minimal dependence on other modules. Modules may be very small, one that performs only one complex calculation, or they may be very large and composed of multiple smaller modules. (Strategies for dividing a system into modules are presented in Chapter 10 of this text.)

The phases in the SDLC are typically applied to each of the modules separately in an iterative fashion. This type of development is sometimes called *modular development.* As an iteration of the development cycle is applied to a module, additional functionality is added to the module. It may take multiple iterations of the development process to achieve a fully functional program module.

Being able to break the system into smaller, less complex pieces is certainly a big advantage with modular development, but there are additional advantages. Breaking the program apart allows different people or teams to work on different portions of the program simultaneously thus speeding the development process.

Since by definition a module is developed to be independent of other modules, a well-designed module may be reused in other software programs to perform similar or like functionality. For example, if a module is designed to calculate tax, it may be applied to any type of software application in which any type of tax is calculated with little or no changes to the module.

Modular system development in which the phases of the SDLC are applied in a cycles or iterations is also known as *iterative* and *incremental* development. *Iterative* refers to the cyclic approach and *incremental* refers to the idea that a small working part of the system is completed with each iteration.

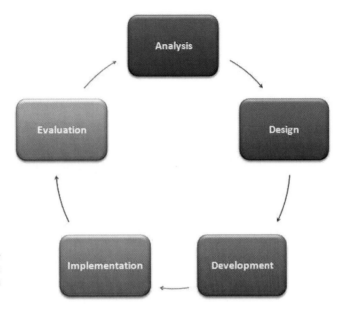

Figure 7-1: Phases of the SDLC are applied in cycles which result in added module functionality with each iteration.

Phases of the System Development Life Cycle

The phases of the SDLC mirror the steps involved in general problem solving. Similar activities are required in solving computer problems to those needed for general problem solving.

Table 7-1: Phases of the SDLC compared to steps in general problem solving

Comparable Phase of the SDLC	Steps in General Problem Solving
Analysis	Identify the problem Understand the problem Identify alternative ways to solve the problem Select the best from the list of alternative solutions
Design	List instructions for the selected solution alternative
Development	Make preparations for applying the solution
Implementation	Apply the solution
Evaluation	Evaluate the solution

There are many activities involved in satisfying each phase of the development cycle.

Analysis Phase

Like with any problem, the most important step, and often the most challenging one, is to figure out *what* the solution must do to satisfy the problem. The analysis phase is about analyzing the problem and developing a clear understanding of the problem and what is required of the solution. During this phase a list of unambiguous system requirements is produced. That means everyone who has a stake in the system must agree on the requirements. It is helpful to document the requirements clearly so those involved will be able to review and revise as needed to finalize a list of requirements agreed upon by all.

Determining the system requirements is the most important step in developing a new system, but is often the most neglected. It is impossible to develop a solution to a problem that is not clearly understood and whose requirements are unclear. You must determine *what* the system must do before you can design *how* the system will work. The analysis phase focuses on *what* the system should do whereas the design phase focuses on *how* the system will solve the problem.

The primary source for discovering the requirements is every user of the current and new system. All users who will use the system should be consulted when gathering system requirements. Other sources for requirements discovery are the current systems themselves and company documents. Even though the current system may be manual and paper-based, it is still the best source of information about what the new system should do. Understanding when the current system does gives insight into what the requirements of the new system should be. Company policies and procedures are another excellent source of requirements since those are likely to govern what the new system must be able to do. The outcome of the analysis phase is a detailed list of requirements for the new system.

Design Phase

Once the requirements are understood, we can begin designing the solution. The design phase involves specifying the steps needed to instruct the computer how to satisfy each requirement. The first task in the design phase is to separate the system requirements into manageable pieces, or *modules*. A *module* is a portion of a system that is self-contained and can function as a complete unit. Larger modules may contain smaller modules. For example, a Worksheet module in Excel can contain a smaller module that is a single procedure. A UserForm module may contain many smaller modules such as procedures for processing the form data and functions that may be used by the form procedures. Modular design is the most common way to break a computer system into manageable portions.

Once the system has been broken into modules, each module can be designed separately. Each module may even be designed by different people.

The very nature of good module design makes each module independent of other modules. (Modular program design is discussed in greater detail in Chapter 10.) Once the logic of each module is designed it should be tested with a variety of realistic data for *logic errors* (also called *result errors*). The outcome of the design phase of development is a detailed set of instructions for each of the lowest level program modules and a diagram called a *structure chart* that shows which modules interact with each other.

Development Phase

With the set of instructions for each module in hand, the program is written (or coded) in a programming language. During the development phase, each line of instruction is translated into computer code much like translating one human language to another. The programmer is the person who knows the programming language and can translate the design to program code. Once the program code is written it is tested extensively and *debugged* as needed. *Debugging* computer code is the process of testing, correcting, re-testing, correcting, etc. until the program is free of program errors.

An important part of the development phase is documenting the new system. Good documentation of the program code is critical for troubleshooting, maintaining, and upgrading the system. Good code documentation helps programmers quickly locate sections of the program code that may need revision. Even if all the program code is written by the same person, it can be difficult to locate problematic sections of code without good documentation.

User instructions should also be written during the development phase. They should be ready for users when the system is implemented and ready to use.

Implementation Phase

Implementation is the process of actually putting the completed system or system component into production. This phase involves not only launching the new system, but also training users, revising documentation as needed, and refining operating procedures and user instructions. The implementation of a new system may be done all at once or may be incremental in that different parts of the system are implemented at different times. There are many different strategies for implementing systems especially if they are quite large and will affect many users.

Evaluation Phase

An important outcome of a new system implementation is a formal evaluation to determine if it meets the users' requirements. Any deficiencies discovered during the post implementation evaluation period should be analyzed, redesigned, and reprogrammed as needed iterating through the phases of the development cycle until all deficiencies are corrected. Once deficiencies are corrected, the system is formally accepted by the users. In large system development projects, user acceptance marks the end of the project.

Table 7-2: Major tasks involved in each major phase of the SDLC

Phase of the SDLC	Goal	Examples of Tasks Involved	Outcome
Analysis	To document clearly WHAT the solution must do	Identify the problem Consult all stakeholders Examine the current system to understand what it does. Review documents to help understand current and future system requirements	Unambiguous list of solution requirements
Design	Specify steps needed to instruct the computer HOW to satisfy each requirement	Divide the system into modules Design the logic for each module Test the logic for each module	Set of detailed instructions for each module A structure chart that shows how modules interact
Development	To put the instructions into computer language	Code the instructions for each module Test and debug the computer code Document the computer code Write user instructions Write operating procedures	The working "program" User/Operator manual Developer manual
Implementation	Put the new system into production	Install the new system Train users Update system documentation Refine user instructions and operating procedures	The installed system
Evaluation	To gain user acceptance and project completion	Users use and evaluate the installed system Developers correct deficiencies	User acceptance of all parts of the system

Types of Solutions

Solutions that are a series of step-by-step instructions are called *algorithmic* solutions. The instruction steps for the solution form an algorithm. An *algorithm* is a set of ordered instructions defined to accomplish a specific task. An algorithm has a clear beginning and a clear end.

An algorithm may have steps that repeat and steps that require a decision. All decisions in an algorithm are formatted as comparisons that can be answered with either TRUE or FALSE. Multiple algorithms may be connected together to compose larger algorithms. An algorithm is like a recipe that is followed each time for a specific task. Examples of real life problems requiring algorithmic solutions include baking a cake or balancing a checkbook. Both problems can be solved with a finite set of instructions.

Other problems can not be solved by an ordered set of instructions. Problems such as deciding which stock to add to your portfolio, or what graduate school to attend, or which job to accept upon graduation are examples of complex problems that cannot be solved by the direct application of a standard set of instructions. These problems require reasoning that is based on knowledge and experience, and sometimes a process of trial and error. These problems require *heuristic* solutions.

Heuristic solutions are reproducible methods for arriving at a solution or outcome that involves more than just the evaluation of whether something is TRUE or FALSE. It involves being able to apply a different approach to a solution if the first solution does not satisfy the problem. When a solution cannot be found, a solution assumption can be made and heuristics will support working backwards to see if the solution is a reasonable one. Heuristics mimic the way a human experienced in the specific knowledge field would approach a problem solution. In solving problems with heuristic solutions, the same SDLC is required, but the design requires many more decisions and the last step, evaluating the solution, is more difficult. It is more difficult to assess whether you have chosen the best stock for your portfolio than it is to determine that your check book balanced. Many problems require a combination of the two kinds of solutions. Further discussion of software solutions in this text will be limited to algorithmic solutions.

Designing Algorithmic Solutions

The logic or algorithm of each module is designed using a *structured* approach. In the early days of programming, program design was unstructured in that the sequence of instructions flowed from top to bottom of a program module (or the entire program) and anywhere along the way the instructions could redirect the sequence to any other line of instruction and continue from there until it was again redirected. This type of unstructured program design was difficult to follow logically and was extremely difficult to troubleshoot or upgrade. Today's modern program design techniques use a *structured* approach to design the instructions within a module. The structure of the instructions dictates how the program instructions are executed by the computer, so they are also commonly called *control structures*. The term *structured* as it pertains to modular program design means that the module's instructions must be formatted in one of only three different types of logic control structures, a *sequence,* a *decision,* or a *loop.*

The advantage in troubleshooting and maintaining structured program code is derived from the ease in which the structured instructions created during the design process can be translated into actual program control structures. All programming languages include counterparts to the same types of logic control structures that vary only slightly from one programming language to another. Once the instructions are structured into one of the universal types of control structures during program design, the programming process is reduced to simply translating from one notation or language to another.

Most algorithmic solutions are composed of many individual instructions or steps. Each instruction represents an action that must be performed to complete the solution correctly. Different types of instructions must be formatted differently to be recognized by the computer. Some instructions may be simple steps that just follow one another in sequence. Other steps require the answer (TRUE or FALSE) to some question before the next step can be determined. Other steps in an algorithm may need to be repeated a number of times in order to complete the solution.

A single algorithm may be composed of a combination of all of these types of instruction steps. A *sequence* logic structure describes sequential steps without branching or repeating. A *decision* logic structure describes a step that requires a TRUE or FALSE answer to a question before it can proceed. A *loop* (also called *iteration* or *repetition*) logic structure requires that one or more actions be completed a number of times before the algorithm is permitted to proceed to a new instruction.

Sequence Control Structures

A *sequence* is a number of steps in an algorithm that follow each other in a specific order, one after the other without variations such as branching (decisions) or repeating. Each step in a sequence is a single action. In some cases, the actual order of the steps may not be critical and a number of steps may in fact be occurring at the same time. For example, if you must obtain the price of an item to be purchased and the appropriate tax rate for calculating the total sale price of an item, it does not really matter whether you obtain the price of the item or the tax rate first since both pieces of information will be utilized at the exact same time in calculating the total sale price of the purchase. If each step is a single action, you would list the instruction to get the item price as one step and to get the tax rate as another step. The decision regarding which action to list first is inconsequential to the final solution.

A good example of a sequence structure for a set of instructions is a recipe. In the following recipe instructions, one step follows another with no branching or repeating.

Sequence for making green chile sauce:
1. Add oil to pan.
2. Brown pork.
3. Remove browned pork from oil.
4. Cook onions and garlic in oil until tender.
5. Add broth, canned tomatoes, canned chiles, and salt
6. Return pork to sauce.
7. Simmer one hour.
8. Serve sauce.

Although the recipe sequence above is very clear and simple to follow, it does not provide for any unknowns along the way. For example, what if the spiciness of the green chiles vary from one brand to another or from one batch to another? What if sometimes the canned tomatoes you use contain salt and sometimes they do not? What if the pork is not tender after simmering one hour? The recipe does not allow for any deviations from the standard instructions. In order for solutions to deal with deviations from the standard routine, they must include some decisions that allow the solution to choose between one of two possible sets of instructions.

Decision Control Structures

The decision structure is the most powerful logic structure. Computers can only understand two commands, 0(zero) or 1(one). To computer hardware 0 is off and 1 is on. A decision structure is the only solution in which the computer can choose between two actions. It is relatively easy to understand because it works in the same way as most people think.

The center of the decision structure is a question that must be answered before the solution instructions can proceed. The answer to the question can only be TRUE or

FALSE. In primitive computer terms, FALSE evaluates to a value of 0(zero) and TRUE evaluates to a value of 1(one). For example, in order to balance your checkbook when you receive your bank statement, you must ask whether or not each check you have listed in your checkbook has been paid from your account before you will know how to proceed with the solution.

For some complex decisions, multiple questions may be asked, each of which can be answered either TRUE or FALSE. For example, in order for a cashier to complete a sales transaction, the payment method must be determined. With simple decision structures, the only option is to ask the customer multiple questions, of which each response will lead to the next question. For example, to determine the payment method for the customer, the cashier could ask the customer "Cash payment?" If the customer answers "Yes" (or TRUE), then the cashier can then follow the steps for completing a cash transaction. If the customer's answer is "No" (or FALSE), then the cashier will need to ask a second question, "Credit Card Payment?" If the answer to this question is TRUE, the cashier can then follow the steps for completing a credit card sale. If the customer answers "No," then the cashier will need to ask another question, such as "Check Payment?" and so on.

Consider our recipe sequence earlier. What if we could include some decisions that would add some flexibility to our instruction set? Let's revise the recipe to take some possible variations into consideration.

Decisions added to the **Sequence** for making green chile sauce:
 1. Add oil to pan.
 2. Brown pork.
 3. Remove browned pork from oil.
 4. Cook onions and garlic in oil until tender.
 5. Taste chiles before adding to sauce.
 6. If chiles taste mild, add two cans of chiles, otherwise add one can of chiles.
 7. Add broth, tomatoes, and salt.
 8. Return pork to sauce.
 9. Simmer one hour.
10. Taste sauce.
11. If sauce tastes bland, add salt.
12. Test pork for doneness.
13. If pork is not tender, simmer 10 more minutes.
14. Serve sauce

This revised instruction set is likely to product a better-tasting sauce than the previous sequence with no decision steps. But the instruction set still lacks some flexibility that would be desirable. For example, what is the sauce still tastes bland after more salt is added? What if the pork is still not tender after an addition 10 minutes of cooking time? In order for the sauce to taste the best, it may take multiple tries to get the salt right and to get the pork tender.

Loop Control Structures

The *loop* structure is also called the *repetition* structure or *iteration* structure. Most problems in business involve doing some action over and over multiple times. For example, if a bank system is posting transactions to accounts, the system will repeat the action as long as there are transactions to post. In Excel, a user may want to update the value of the same field in each row as long as there are more rows of data on the worksheet.

A *loop* is a set of instructions in a solution that will be repeated a number of times. Sometimes the number of times the set of instructions will repeat is known before the program runs and sometimes it is unknown until the solution is under way. For example, if you are printing time cards for each employee for the month and the pay periods are semi-monthly, the program knows to print two time cards for each employee so the loop will iterate twice. If you are processing payroll and printing pay checks, you will do the same action once for each employee as long as there are employees who earned wages for the pay period. In this case, the number of employees to process is unknown until the program evaluates each employee to see if they are due a pay check.

There is a decision structure at or near the beginning or end of the set of loop instructions that the loop uses to determine whether or not the set of instructions should keep repeating. For example, at the end of the payroll process for the first employee, the solution might ask the question "More employees to pay?" which requires a simple TRUE or FALSE response. If the response is TRUE, the loop will repeat one more time then ask the question again at the end until the answer to the question is FALSE. At that time, the set of instructions in the loop will not repeat another time and the next step following the loop will be performed. This question could easily be asked at the beginning of the loop to see if the set of loop instructions should be processed at all.

Consider our previous recipe sequence to which we added some decisions. What if we could also repeat some steps to try to make the sauce the best it can be? Let's revise the recipe again to add even more flexibility to the instruction set.

Revised recipe steps that now include **Iteration, Sequence,** and **Decision** instructions:
1. Add oil to pan.
2. Brown pork.
3. Remove browned pork from oil.
4. Cook onions and garlic in oil until tender.
5. Taste chiles before adding to sauce.
6. If chiles taste mild, add two cans of chiles, otherwise add one can of chiles.
7. Add broth, tomatoes, and salt.
8. Return pork to sauce.
9. Simmer one hour.
10. Taste sauce.
11. If sauce tastes bland, add salt.
12. Repeat steps 10 and 11 until sauce is not longer bland.
13. Test pork for doneness.
14. If pork not tender, simmer 10 more minutes.
15. Repeat steps 13 and 14 until pork is tender.
16. Serve sauce.

Sequence instructions alone are rarely sufficient for a complete and flexible solution. Program modules typically contain many different structures that are connected and/or nested in many different ways. But no matter how complex the solution may be, it can be accomplished through the use of only three types of logic control structures, sequences, decisions, and loops.

Modeling Logical Design

To aid in planning, documenting, and communicating module design, there are two standard notations used for modeling program logic; *pseudocode* and *flowcharts*. *Pseudocode* is a textual notation whereby native language is used to explain what action is to be taken. Pseudocode, of course, means "false code." Pseudocode instructions are written in the format of one of the three logic structures, sequence, decision, or loop, just as the programming code would be written. The difference between pseudocode and programming code is that the words and symbols used in pseudocode are natural language or common symbols. Because the text is written in a natural language and in a structured format, it is also *structured English.*

Flowcharts are graphical representations of module logic. Different shapes on the flowchart represent different types of instructions. The shapes on the flowchart are connected by flowlines to indicate the sequence of actions. Module logic may be modeled using either pseudocode or flowcharts. In some cases one notation may used to supplement the other. Specific pseudocode and flowchart notation are topics in future chapters of this text.

Review Questions

1. Briefly describe the difference between heuristic and algorithmic system solutions.

2. Name and describe the steps required to solve a problem that has an algorithmic solution.

3. Describe how general problem-solving techniques relate to the steps in developing a computer system.

4. Name the phases of the system development life cycle and briefly describe the major tasks in each phase.

5. What is meant by iterative system development?

6. What is meant by incremental system development?

7. What is meant by a *structured* module design? What is the advantage of specifying instructions in the three logic control structures?

_____

_____

_____

8. What is meant by *modular* program development?

_____

_____

_____

9. What are the three basic logic *control structures*?

_____

_____

_____

10. Which logic *control structure* would you consider to be the most important and why?

_____

_____

_____

11. Name and briefly describe two techniques for modeling solution algorithms.

_____

_____

_____

Practice Problems

1. Using the general problem solving steps discussed in this chapter, list the steps and the activities you would perform in each major step in order to solve the following problems:

   a. What will you do for an evening to entertain your out-of-town friend who is visiting for the weekend?
   b. You are chairman of the social committee of your fraternity. The social committee is responsible for providing a club social event at the end of the semester. What type of event will you provide and what activities will be provided in conjunction with the event (i.e., meal, dancing, games, etc.)?

2. Use a sequence control structure to describe to a friend the steps required to:

   a. Get a glass of water in your room, house, or apartment.
   b. Draw a two-inch square on a piece of paper.
   c. Draw a circle on a piece of paper.

3. Use sequence and/or decision control structures to define the instructions to:

   a. Prepare to go to school in the mornings.
   b. Prepare for bed in the evenings.
   c. Find the largest of three numbers.
   d. Calculate your paycheck at the end of the pay period.

4. Use sequence, decision, and/or loop control structures to:

   a. For three items you wish to purchase, calculate the subtotal, tax, and total for the order.
   b. Find a parking space in the student parking lots on campus.

CHAPTER EIGHT

Modeling Problem Solutions with Pseudocode and Flowcharts

Learning Objectives

1. Identify the four basic computer operations and how they relate to computer solution instructions
2. Use pseudocode keywords to model computer solution logic
3. Use standard programming control structures to model logic with pseudocode and flowcharts
   a. Sequence structure
   b. Decision structures
   c. Repetition structures (Loops)
4. Use common mathematical symbols to model logic with pseudocode and flowcharts
5. Select the appropriate flowchart symbol to match the type of instruction
6. Model single-alternative and dual-alternative decisions with pseudocode and flowcharts

Basic Computer Operations

Computer hardware and software work together to perform four types of operations.

1. *Input* operations get external data into an application through the use of computer hardware. Devices for input include keyboards, mice, touch pads, joysticks, document and image scanners, bar code scanners, light pens, microphones, and digital cameras. Input operations may also get external data from data storage such as a database. Software applications provide an interface for requesting and accepting the inputs from the hardware devices.

2. *Process* operations manipulate the inputs in some way, such as validating or calculating. Processes require the central processing unit (CPU) hardware to perform such tasks.

3. *Outputs* are performed by hardware output devices, such as monitors, printers, fax machines, and speakers. Sometimes the output operations stores the data outside the program for later use. Software applications provide an interface for interactions with the hardware.

4. *Storage* of data is performed by computer disks or tapes. Software programs provide the instructions for accepting inputs, processing data, sending outputs, and storing data.

All problem solutions in which some action is performed involve a process that performs the action. For example, if you are a cashier at a retail store, you perform the process of selling merchandise to customers every day. The process itself involves a number of steps:

1. Get the price for the merchandise
2. Calculate the tax for the merchandise
3. Total the merchandise plus tax
4. Collect payment from the customer
5. Give customer change if indicated
6. Give the customer a receipt and the merchandise

Think of a process as a transformer. It takes something and performs some action on it, and usually returns something. In the sales example above, we might call the process "Complete Sale." Something that the process requires in order to perform the process is an input. Inputs to the "Complete Sale" process include merchandise price, tax rate, and customer payment.

Each item of information that is generated by the process is an output of the process. Outputs from the "Complete Sale" process might include customer's change, and the sales receipt. In the sales example, the inputs to the process were data. One output was a tangible item, cash, if the customer required change. The other output was a tangible item (the receipt) that represented a report of the sale (data), which included the inputs which were processed in some way. In this case, the merchandise price was multiplied by the tax rate, then that sum was added to the merchandise price to generate the amount of payment due from the customer. In modeling a solution, we are primarily interested in data and information flows rather than in the flow of tangible items. There may be some cases in which a tangible output is important enough to be included in our solution model.

To design a computer solution, the logic of each operation (input, process, output, or storage) must be specified as a list of instructions. The list of instructions is called an *algorithm*. An algorithm is an explicit step-by-step set of instructions that solve a problem. The algorithm may be specified using one of two standard notations; *pseudocode* or *flowcharts*. *Pseudocode* is a textual notation written in human language that specifies each instruction step required to perform a task. Each line of pseudocode represents one instruction. *Flowcharts* are graphical representations of the solution algorithm. Each instruction is noted by a particular shape that represents a specific instruction type such as an input, output, process, or storage.

Modeling Program Logic with Pseudocode

Pseudocode is a way of writing computer instructions in a human language that mirrors the basic structures of computer programming languages. It allows the solution designer to focus on just the logic of the solution without having to deal with the syntax of the actual programming language at the same time. The vocabulary of pseudocode is that of the *problem domain* instead of that of the programming language. The problem domain refers to the business environment of the problem. If a program is written to process bank transactions, the problem domain is the bank and therefore terms from that environment are used in the pseudocode. The idea is that you can specify the instructions for the solution without knowing or using any of the actual programming language syntax. Once the instructions are written, a programmer can easily translate the instructions into a specific programming language. Pseudocode is independent of any particular programming language. Pseudocode is also called *structured English* because basic programming control structures are used to format the natural language instructions. (Programming logic control structures are introduced in Chapter 7 of this text.)

Pseudocode Keywords

There are some common keywords that are used in pseudocode to indicate input, output, process, and storage operations. The keywords are shown here in all upper case for emphasis, but upper case is not required for pseudocode keywords.

Input Keywords

GET: Receives input from some input device.
  Example: "GET price of first item"

READ: Retrieves data from a stored source outside the current program, such as an external file or database.
  Example: "READ customer name"

Output Keywords

PRINT: Print data to a printer
  Example: "PRINT payroll report"

WRITE: Store the data to external file or database.
  Example: "WRITE customer record to database"

PUT, DISPLAY, OUTPUT: Display data on the monitor screen.
  Example: "DISPLAY name, address, city, state, zip"

Process Keywords

COMPUTE: Perform some computation.
  Examples: "COMPUTE tax as subtotal times taxrate"

CALCULATE: Perform some computation
  Example: "CALCULATE tax as subtotal times taxrate"

INITIALIZE: Assign a value to a variable for the first time, or to restart something in the program.
  Example: "INITIALIZE taxrate to .05"

INIT: (1) Same as INITIALIZE. (2) Also the name given to a program startup routine or module, the top-level parent process.
  Examples: (1) Name a startup module "INIT"
           (2) "Call INIT", "RUN INIT"

INCREMENT: Add one to the value of a variable.
  Example 1: "INCREMENT rowNumber"
  Incrementing can also be specified using mathematical symbols.
  Example 2: rowNumber = rowNumber + 1
  (DECREMENT may be used when reducing a value by one.)

SET: Assign a value to a variable.
  Example: "SET total = subtotal + tax"

BEGIN: Marks the beginning of the pseudocode algorithm. The name of the algorithm follows the keyword.
  Example: "BEGIN Complete Sale"

END: Marks the end of a pseudocode algorithm.
  Example: "END" is the last line in a pseudocode algorithm

CALL, RUN: Invokes another procedure or function module.
  Examples: "CALL CalculateTax returning tax", "RUN INIT"

RETURNS or RETURNING: Precedes the variable that represents the return value from a "call" to another function or procedure module.
  Example: "Call getAcctBalance returning balance"
  (Also see example for "CALL".)

EXCEPTION: Signals the beginning of a block of instructions for handling program exceptions (another word for runtime errors). The keyword WHEN follows the EXCEPTION keyword. (See "EXCEPTION" example with "WHEN" below.)

WHEN: Precedes the exception type name in an exception handling block of pseudocode. Follows the keyword EXCEPTION. The line following the "WHEN" line are the instructions to execute if the named exception occurs.
  Example: "EXCEPTION
              WHEN divideByZero
                DISPLAY "Cannot divide by zero." "

Storage Keywords

STORE: Stores a current value for later use in the program.
  Example: "STORE count_of_items"

SAVE: Assign a value to a variable to be used later in the program.
    Example: "SAVE customer_number in last_customer_number"

In addition to keywords, common mathematical and logical operators can be used in pseudocode. For example, the same process may be written either way:
    "COMPUTE tax as subtotal times taxrate"
    "tax = subtotal * taxrate"

Table 8-1: Logical and mathematical operators may also be used in pseudocode

Symbol	Operation
+	Add
-	Subtract
*	Multiply
/	Divide
^	Exponent
= ==	Logical comparison (is equal to)
= :=	Assign a value to a variable. (Value on right side of symbol is assigned to the variable on the left side of the symbol.)
>	Logical comparison (greater than)
<	Logical comparison (less than)
>=	Logical comparison (greater than or equal to)
<=	Logical comparison (less than or equal to)
<>	Logical comparison (not equal to)
AND	Logical operator that links two logical expressions
OR	Logical operator that links two logical expressions
NOT	Logical operator that reverses an expression
&	Concatenation operator (used to connect literal or variable text strings)

Order of Precedence

When using mathematical formulas involving multiple types of operations, the standard order of precedence applies.

1. Parentheses: Operations in the inner most set of parentheses are executed first. Multiple operations inside one set of parentheses are executed in the standard order of precedence.

2. Exponents

3. Multiplication and Division: These operations are executed at the same level of precedence from left to right in the order that they appear.

4. Addition and Subtraction: These operations are executed at the same level of precedence from left to right in the order that they appear.

Pseudocode Examples

Let's look at a simple, though complete pseudocode algorithm of a retail sales transaction called "Complete Sale." Since this is a complete algorithm it starts with the keyword "BEGIN" and ends with the keyword "END." The only control structure used in this example is a sequence.

Pseudocode Algorithm Example: Complete Sale

```
BEGIN Complete Sale
    GET price
    READ taxrate
    COMPUTE tax as price * taxrate
    COMPUTE total as price + tax
    PRINT receipt (price, tax, total)
END
```

Programming Control Structures

There are three basic types of programming control structures; *sequence, decision,* and *repetition (loop)* structures. Within the decision and repetition types, there are subtypes of these structures that are used for more specialized types of decisions and loops (more on subtypes of decision and loop control structures in Chapters 11 and 12 of this text). In each structure-modeling example keep in mind that the structure shown is not a complete algorithm, but only one of the structures within an algorithm. For complete algorithms, the boundaries are defined using the keywords BEGIN and END for pseudocode algorithms and START and STOP for flowcharts.

Sequence Structures

The pseudocode algorithm example above includes just one programming control structure, a *sequence*. A *sequence* is a progression of instructions where one task is followed by another in a linear fashion. Each instruction is written on a line by itself. Instructions are performed in the order in which they are written. All lines of a sequence are written with the same left indention. Here is another example of a sequence structure that is a part of an algorithm.

Sequence Example

```
GET width of rectangle
GET height of rectangle
COMPUTE area as height times width
DISPLAY area
```

Decision Structures

IF-THEN-ELSE Structures

IF-THEN-ELSE is the structure most often used for decision instructions. The structure consists of a logical comparison (the IF clause) for which alternative actions are specified for the TRUE outcome (the THEN clause) and optionally for the FALSE outcome (the ELSE clause). The keywords IF, ELSE, and ENDIF are indented at the same level for the same decision structure. The keyword THEN is written at the end of the line after the IF expression. The instructions for the TRUE condition (THEN clause) are written on the next line. The instructions within the THEN clause and the ELSE clause are indented one level further than the IF, ELSE, and ENDIF keywords. The structure is terminated in pseudocode with the ENDIF keyword.

The general pseudocode syntax for the IF-THEN-ELSE structure:

> IF <some condition exists> THEN
>> Actions to perform (may be a single instruction, a sequence or any other control structure(s).
> ELSE (the "ELSE" keyword and actions that follow are optional)
>> Actions to perform (may be a single instruction, a sequence or any other control structure(s).
> ENDIF

The "ELSE" clause of the IF-THEN-ELSE structure is optional. When instructions are included for both alternatives, it is called a *dual-alternative* decision. The syntax above represents a dual-alternative decision. When the ELSE clause is omitted, the solution is called a *single-alternative* decision.

Single-alternative decision pseudocode structure:

> IF <some condition exists> THEN
>> Actions to perform (may be a single instruction, a sequence or any other control structure(s).
> ENDIF

IF-THEN-ELSE Examples

(Dual-alternative)

> IF employee status is "part-time" THEN
>> Add one to part-time count
> ELSE
>> Add one to full-time count
> ENDIF

(Single-alternative)

> IF checkAmount greater than accountBalance THEN
>> Print overdraftNotice
>> Subtract overdraftFee from accountBalance
> ENDIF

Repetition Structures (Loops)

A *repetition* control structure, commonly called a *loop*, allows instructions to be written once, then executed as many times as needed by enclosing the instructions inside a loop structures. In order for a set of instructions to repeat, the loop must perform a test for each iteration to determine whether or not the loop should execute again.

The WHILE loop structure tests the loop condition at or near the top or beginning of the loop. This loop structure begins with the keyword WHILE and ends with the keyword ENDWHILE. The instructions between the keywords WHILE and END-WHILE form the loop *body*. The loop body may be any combination of sequence, decision, or other loop structures. The loop condition tested at the top of the loop must evaluate to TRUE for the loop to iterate. Once the loop condition evaluates to FALSE, the loop terminates immediately after the test. It skips over the loop body and goes to the ENDWHILE. Something to keep in mind with the WHILE loop is that if the loop condition evaluates to FALSE on the first iteration, the loop body will never execute.

The general pseudocode syntax for the WHILE loop structures:

> WHILE <condition exists>
>> Actions to perform
> ENDWHILE

WHILE Loop Example 1

```
WHILE transactionNumber<numberOfTransactions
    Subtract transactionAmount from accountBalance
    Increment transactionNumber
    Read next transaction
ENDWHILE
```

The following example includes a decision structure in the loop body. The first logical expression (transactionNumber<numberOfTransactions) is the loop condition. As long as the condition is TRUE, the loop body will continue to iterate. The second logical expression (transactionType = "deposit") is the logical test for the IF decision structure.

WHILE Loop Example 2

```
WHILE transactionNumber < numberOfTransactions
    IF transactionType = "deposit" THEN
            Add transactionAmount to accountBalance
    ELSE
            Subtract transactionAmount from accountBalance
    ENDIF
    Increment transactionNumber
    Read next transaction
ENDWHILE
```

Modeling Program Logic with Flowcharts

You can describe the instructions for a solution using pseudocode, but at times visual representations can be more effective. *Flowcharts* can be used to design and structure a solution to a problem. Showing the problem solution in a visual model has several advantages over textual descriptions:

1. It conveys information more efficiently and takes less time for people to process. There is a high rate of information transfer through the eye. Verbal models or descriptions require sequential processing of the information before one can visualize the solution whereas graphic models permit simultaneous perception of the solution through the eye.

2. More visual information is retained by human users than textual information.

3. It communicates more clearly and is less ambiguous since everyone uses a standard set of symbols.

A *flowchart* is a visual way of presenting an algorithm that uses symbols to represent the various types of instructions in the algorithm. The symbols are connected with arrows to show the flow of the logic for the solution. The instruction represented by each symbol is written on the symbol using the same keywords that are used in pseudocode.

Flowchart Symbols

Figure 8-1: The input/output symbol with one entrance flowline and one exit flowline.

The *parallelogram* symbol represents either an input or an output instruction. Those instructions involve getting data into or out of the system. The input instructions generally precede a process and output instructions generally follow a process. The name of the input or output activity is written on the parallelogram.

Flowlines are arrows that connect the flowchart symbols to show the proper sequence of instructions for the solution. The input/output symbol has one flowline entering it from a previous symbol and one flowline exiting it that connects to another symbol.

A *rectangle* is the flowchart symbol used to represent a process instruction. A process instruction calculates, assigns a value, or transforms data in any way. Just as with pseudocode, process instructions may be written out or represented using mathematical operators.

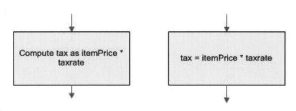

Figure 8-2: A rectangle is used to represent a process instruction on a flowchart. Instructions may be written out or expressed using mathematical symbols.

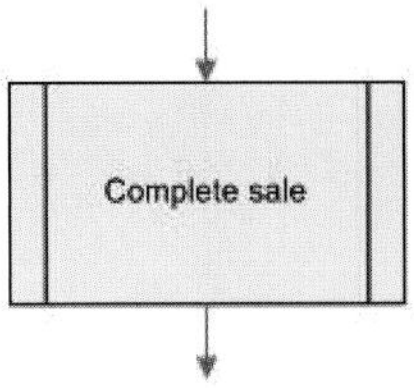

Figure 8-3: The module symbol represents an entire algorithm whose details are specified outside the current algorithm.

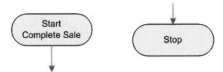

Figure 8-4: The diamond represents the decision question. The two flowlines exiting it represent the two alternatives for the decision evaluation.

A special rectangle is designated to represent an entire algorithm whose instructions are specified outside the current flowchart. The separate algorithm is called a *module* in that it represents a block of instructions that is complete for one independent process. The module symbol is a rectangle that has double lines on the sides. It has one entrance flowline and one exit flowline. The module symbol in a flowchart implies that the instructions jump from the current algorithm to another algorithm where it executes those instructions from beginning to end, then returns to the current algorithm and executes the next instruction following the module symbol.

The *diamond* is used to represent decision conditions (also called logical comparisons, or logical tests) on flowcharts. The decision symbol always has one flowline entering it, but two flowlines exiting it to represent the two alternative branches the instructions may take. One flowline or branch represents the path of the logic when the answer to the decision question is evaluated to TRUE and the other flowline or branch represents the path of logic if the decision question is evaluated to FALSE. The decision test condition is written on the symbol. Even if the decision is a single alternative decision, there is still a flowline for the FALSE response that connects to the shape that represents the next instruction after the decision structure (see Figure 8-12).

A *flattened ellipse* (also called *lozenge* or *racetrack*) shape is used for marking both the beginning and end of the flowchart algorithm. The label on the ellipse at the beginning of an algorithm should include the word "Start" or "Begin" and optionally the name of the algorithm, for example, "Start Complete Sale." The label for the ellipse at the end of the algorithm should simply be "Stop", "End," or "Exit." For an algorithm that is in a separate module (represented by the module shape), and used or "called" by the current algorithm, the word "Return" should be included on its label. "Return" implies that the control of the program returns back to the next instruction after the module was "called." If a value is returned from the module, that value should also be noted, as in "Return tax" from a module that calculates tax. If no value is returned from the external module, simply "Return" is sufficient for the shape label.

The ellipse marking the beginning of the algorithm has no entrance flowline and one exit flowline, the first flowline of the algorithm. Likewise, the ellipse marking the end of the algorithm has one entrance flowline and no exit flowline.

Figure 8-5: Ellipse, lozenge, or racetrack shape is used to mark the beginning and end of a flowchart algorithm.

Flowcharts are drawn so that the main logic flows from top to bottom, or in some cases left to right. Flowlines for loops may flow in different directions to represent the looping back of the logic to a previous algorithm step, but the main logic flow is from top to bottom or left to right. When a flowchart extends past one column on a sheet of paper, screen, or other drawing medium, two columns on the same page are connected using an *on-page* connector. The *on-page* connector is a pair of circles, one of which is placed at the bottom of the previous column and the second is placed at the top of the next column. The connector label consists of a letter (A, B, C, etc.) indicating the connector order. The same letter is used for both connectors in a pair. So the pair of connectors connecting the first column to the second will be labeled "A" and those connecting the second column with the third will be labeled "B", and so on. The first connector in the pair has one entrance flowline and no exit flowline. The second in the pair has no entrance flowline and one exit flowline.

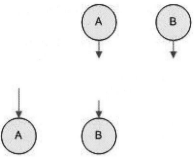

Figure 8-6: Pairs of *on-page* connectors. The "A" connectors connect the end of the first column with the beginning of the second column. The "B" connectors connect the end of the second column with the beginning of the third column.

A second connector shape is available for connecting flowchart pages or screens. It is called the *off-page* connector. It is shaped like a home plate on a baseball field. They are also used in pairs, but instead of letter labels, they are labeled with numbers to represent the order of the pages that are connected. The number "1" is the label of the connector pair connecting page one with page two and the number "2" labels the connector pair from page two to page three.

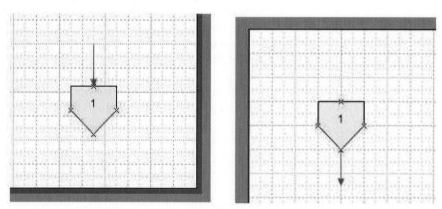

Figure 8-7: A pair of *off-page* connectors connecting the algorithm on the bottom right of page 1 to the algorithm on the upper left region of page 2.

For adding comments to any shape or any portion of the flowchart, an *annotation* is used. The textual comment is written inside the annotation bracket. A connector is attached to the annotation that can connect it to a shape or it can point to an area of the flowchart.

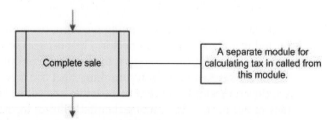

Figure 8-8: An *annotation* is attached to the "Complete sale" module with additional comments.

Use the summary below for a quick reference to flowchart symbols and notation.

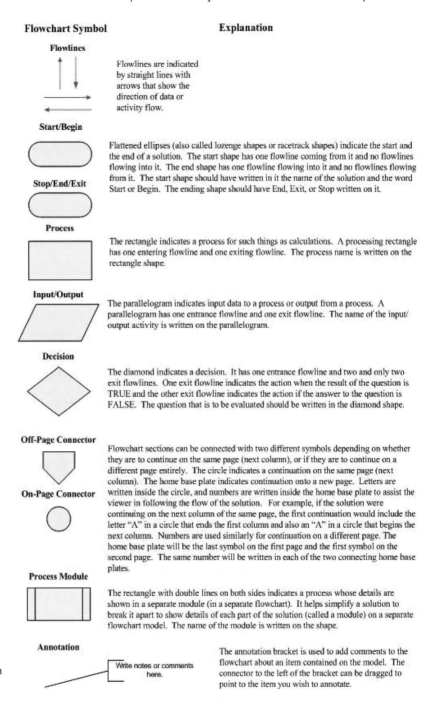

Figure 8-9:   Flowchart notation summary.

Flowchart Examples

Sequence Structure Flowchart Example

Figure 8-10 shows the complete flowchart of a retail sale transaction called "Complete Sale" that was introduced previously. Notice the specific shapes that are used for the various types of instructions. The ellipses are used for the start and stop instructions. Parallelograms are used for inputs to and outputs from the process. A rectangle is used for the process instruction that performs the calculation. The "Complete Sale" algorithm accepts the sale item price and the tax rate inputs and generates a receipt output that includes the item price, tax and total sale amount. The only control structure used in this example is the sequence.

Flowchart Algorithm Example: Complete Sale

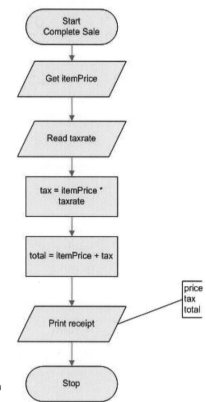

Figure 8-10: Flowchart algorithm example.

Decision Structure Flowchart Example

Flowcharts may include either dual-alternative and/or single-alternative decision structures. The instructions for each decision structure may be a single instruction (as in the example below), a sequence of instructions, or any number of other control structures. Note that the single-alternative decision structure (Figure 8-12) has no instructions for the FALSE alternative. The flowline goes from the FALSE side of the decision diamond to the next instruction after the decision structure.

Dual-alternative Decision Structure

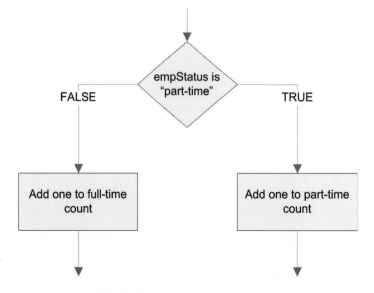

Figure 8-11: Dual-alternative decision structure.

Single-alternative Decision Structure

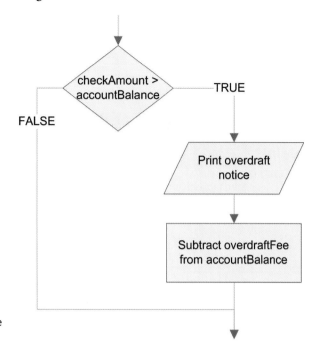

Figure 8-12: Single-alternative decision structure.

Repetition Structure Flowchart Examples

WHILE Loop Example 1

Recall that the WHILE loop tests the loop condition at or near the beginning of the loop. The loop condition is a logical test, a decision, that must evaluate to either TRUE or FALSE so a decision symbol (diamond) and a decision structure is used for the test.

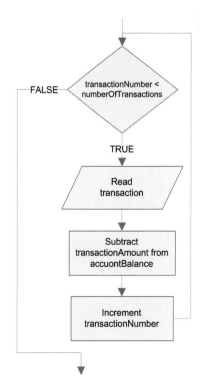

Figure 8-13: WHILE loop with a sequence of instructions in the loop body.

WHILE Loop Example 2

This WHILE loop includes a decision structure in the loop body. Do not confuse this second decision structure with the loop condition test which is the first decision structure in this loop.

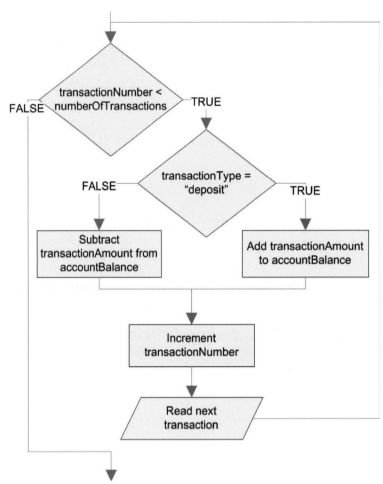

Figure 8-14: WHILE loop that includes a decision structure in the loop body.

Software Tools for Creating Flowcharts

Many software applications such as word processors and presentation software include utilities for drawing shapes and lines that make it possible to create flowchart diagrams. Some even have a special set of "flowchart" symbols and lines available. In most of these applications, flowchart symbols can be added to a document or presentation and connected with lines that have arrows on the leading end. Text can be written on the shapes to specify the instruction it represents. Although acceptable flowcharts may be created with such applications, they lack an important characteristic that makes flowchart modeling much more efficient and that is the ability to attach or anchor the flowlines onto the symbols. When flowlines are actually attached to the two symbols it connects, the flowlines remain attached when the symbol is moved.

There are many software programs available that allow you to create flowcharts that anchor the lines to the shapes and make it simple to create, move, or modify flowchart segments. Many integrated software development environments (IDEs) include utilities for producing models (including flowcharts) associated with system development but many are extremely complex to use and cost prohibitive for most end user developers. Microsoft Office Visio 2007 is an intermediate level modeling program that can be used to create many types of business and software development models such as business process models, network models, timelines, organization charts, and flowcharts. The product is user-friendly and relatively affordable for most small businesses and business professionals. The product is widely used in companies of all sizes and disciplines. A good alternative for students or professionals who want the experiment with Visio before purchasing it is a free trial that is available for downloading on the Microsoft Office Web site. Microsoft typically offers a 30- to 60-day trial of the most current version of Visio. At the time of this publication, the Visio 2007 trial download link is http://office.microsoft.com/en-us/visio/default.aspx. If the site should change, a Web search for "visio trial" should return a valid link.

Figure 8-15: A free trial version of Visio is usually available on Microsoft's Web site.

For those who want to produce simple flowcharts without installing special programs, Excel offers a variety of modeling tools, including flowcharting shapes and connectors, to support the Excel end user developer. To begin producing a flowchart, select **Insert(tab)→Illustrations(group)→Shapes→Flowchart** and select the desired shape from the *Flowchart* palette of shapes. Draw the desired size for the shape on the worksheet with the left mouse button.

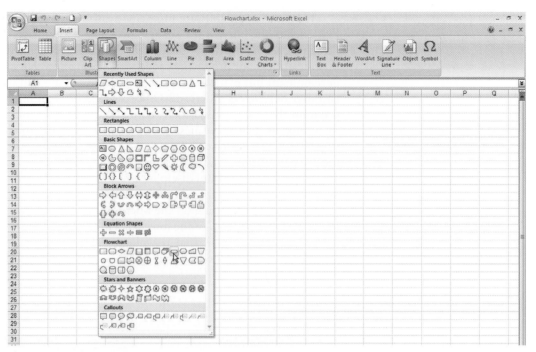

Figure 8-16: Begin a flowchart by selecting a shape from the *Flowchart* palette.

Once a flowchart shape has been added to the worksheet, the *Format* context tab appears on the ribbon and the flowchart symbols are added to the *Insert Shapes* task group on the far left side of the *Format* tab. When any object on the flowchart is selected, the *Format* context tab will be available.

To connect most shapes with flowlines, select the straight connector tool with an arrow on the bottom from the flowchart palette on the *Format* ribbon tab. With the mouse pointer, hover over the first shape to show the small red square "handles" that are available around the edge of the shape for anchoring the connector.

When the red handles are visible, hold down the left mouse button over one of the handles and draw the connector line to the next shape. When the mouse drags the connector over the edge of the second shape, its handles will appear. Release the mouse button over a handle on the second shape to anchor the arrow end of the connector.

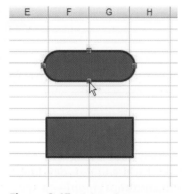

Figure 8-17: Select the connector line from the shape palette now visible on the Format context tab and hover the mouse over the shape to locate the anchor "handles."

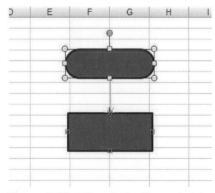

Figure 8-18: When the leading end of the connector is dragged over the edge of the next shape, the anchor handles become visible.

Use the elbow arrow connector to make right-angle connections. The connector will make one or more right angles as needed to connect two shapes.

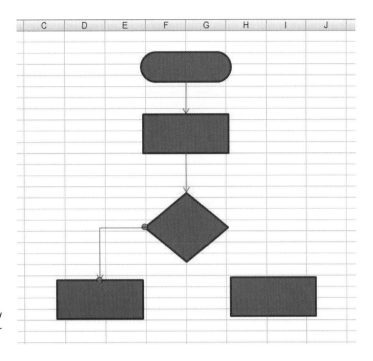

Figure 8-19: The elbow arrow connector makes right-angle connections.

To add text to a shape, select the shape and begin typing. To edit the text inside the shape, click on the text area of the shape to select the text. To format the text inside the shape, right-click on the text and select a formatting option from the context menu.

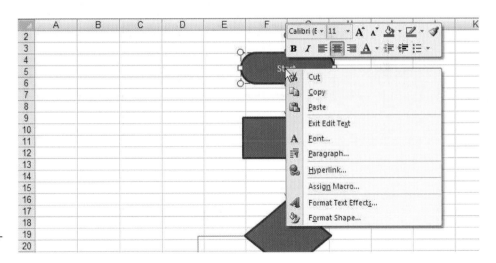

Figure 8-20: Shape text formatting options on the context menu.

The gridlines on Excel worksheets make good guides for aligning shapes vertically or horizontally on the flowchart. Once the flowchart is complete, the guidelines can be removed from the worksheet by selecting **Page Layout(tab)→Sheet Options(group)→ Gridlines** and uncheck the box beside *View*. Other worksheet formatting options, such as background color or patterns may be applied to the flowchart area. To apply a background color to the flowchart worksheet, select the entire worksheet using the Select All icon in the upper left corner of the worksheet margin and select **Home(tab)→ Font(group)→select the fill color from the drop list of the *Fill Color* icon.**

To select multiple objects on the flowchart or the entire flowchart for formatting or copying, use the selector tool that can be accessed from the ribbon by selecting **Home(tab)→Editing(group)→Find & Select→Select Objects.**

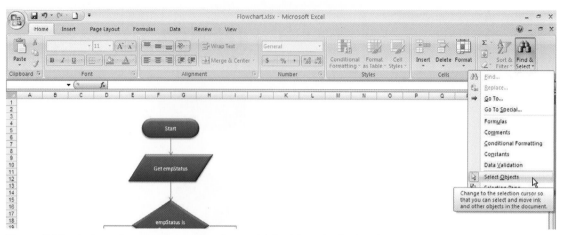

Figure 8-21: Activate the selector tool to select multiple objects for formatting.

Apply preformatted styles to all shapes on the model by selecting a style from the *Shape Style* gallery on the *Format* context tab of the ribbon.

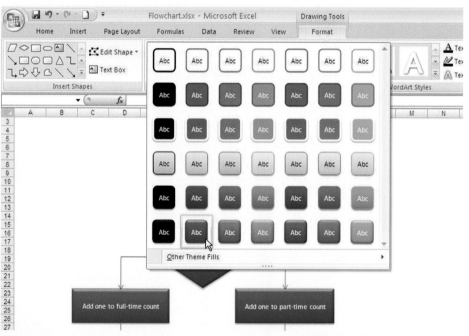

Figure 8-22: Many pre-defined formats are available in the *Shape Style* gallery on the *Format* context tab.

To add text to flowlines, such as those used to connect decision shapes, you may type into an Excel cell in the background or a text box may be added to the model and placed near the flowline. To add a text box to a flowline, select an object on the flowchart, then select the text box tool from the shape pallet. Draw the text box over the line and enter the text. Select the text box to format by removing borders (**Format(tab)→Shape Styles(group)→Shape Outline→No Outline**) or adding background color to match the background color of the remainder of the worksheet (**Format(tab)→Shape Styles(group)→Shape Fill→select a color or other fill option**).

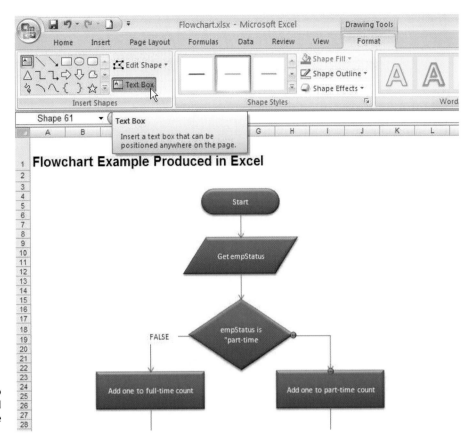

Figure 8-23: To add a text box to a flowline, select the text box tool from the shape pallet and draw the text box over the line.

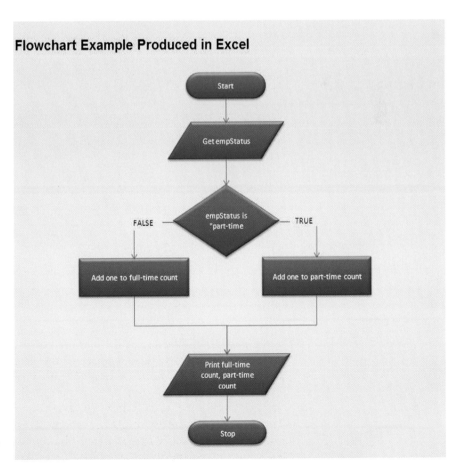

Figure 8-24: A formatted flow-chart model created in Excel.

Review Questions

1. Identify the four basic computer operations and give an example of each.

2. How do the pseudocode keywords GET and READ differ in the way they are used?

3. How do the pseudocode keywords PUT and WRITE differ in the way they are used?

4. How is the logical operator & (ampersand) used in logic modeling? Give an example of an appropriate use of the symbol.

5. What is the correct order of operations for computer instructions that include mathematical operations?

6. Name the three parts of a decision structure. Which part is optional?

7. What is a single-alternative decision structure?

_____

_____

_____

8. Differentiate between the two rectangle shapes that are used on flow-charts, the simple rectangle and the rectangle with double lines on the sides.

_____

_____

_____

9. Describe the difference between the two types of connectors used on flowcharts and specify how each are used.

_____

_____

_____

10. How are comments added to a flowchart?

_____

_____

_____

Practice Problems

1. Create an algorithm with pseudocode and flowchart that specifies the solution steps for a complete system that accepts exactly three sale item prices and gets a sales tax rate from a database. It calculates a subtotal of the three sale item prices, calculates sales tax, and finally calculates and prints a sales receipt that includes the three item prices, the subtotal, and the total. (Use a simple sequence for this solution.)

2. Create a new algorithm and modify the pseudocode and flowchart model produced in Problem 1 so that the system checks to see if each sale item is taxable before applying a sales tax. Print a receipt that includes item prices, subtotal, tax, and total. (Add decision structure(s).)

3. Create a new algorithm and modify the pseudocode and flowchart model produced in Problem 2 so that the system accepts any number of sale items. Print a receipt that includes item prices, subtotal, tax and total. (Add loop structure(s).)

4. Create an algorithm with pseudocode and flowchart that specifies the solution steps for a complete system that opens a customer file and prints four mailing labels for each club member in a file, then closes the file. The labels include the customer's first and last name, street address, city, state, and zip code.

CHAPTER NINE

Introduction to Programming Concepts and the Programing Process

LEARNING

General Problem-solving Steps

TYPES OF PROBLEM SOLUTIONS

str

Using computers to solve problems

Creating algorithms

PROGRAMMING
Using computers to solve problems

List the solution instructions

Creating al

1. Understand the characteristics of three programming paradigms; *procedural, object-oriented,* and *event-driven*
2. Recognize characteristics of the three programming paradigms found in VBA
3. Understand how a program is coded, compiled, and debugged
4. Understand how a computer program is developed from models such as flow-charts and pseudocode
5. Identify three types of programming errors, their causes, and corrective actions
6. Understand the role of variables, constants, and data types in a computer program
7. Understand levels of variable and constant scope as they apply to program modules
8. Write program instructions that declare variables and constants using valid identifiers and data types for both
9. Write program instructions that assign values to variables and constants
10. Identify how variables and constants are alike and how they differ
11. Become familiar with the general data types used in pseudocode and flowchart algorithms
12. Recognize specific data types used in VBA
13. Understand how to handle multiple data items in an array

Types of Programming Languages

There are literally thousands of programming languages and more are continually being developed. The languages are classified into more than 40 different categories. Most categories are not entirely distinct from the others. Most categories combine characteristics of a number of others. The programming languages used in programming modern business applications typically follow one or more of the following programming paradigms:

- *Procedural* programming is characterized by the specification of instructions step-by-step in procedures or short modules that may be "called" at any point in the program. A procedure may even be called by another procedure. The procedures may or may not accept data, and may or may not return data to the point of the program from which it was called.

- *Object-Oriented* programming uses *objects* that interact to specify the solution rather than a list of instructions. Each object is an independent package that can send messages to other objects, receive messages from other objects, and process data. An object is created from a *class* which provides the specifications for the characteristics and responsibilities of all objects of its particular type or class.

- *Event-Driven* programming allows the program flow to be determined by user actions. For any *event* such as a click on a form button, the programmer can write an *event procedure* to respond to the event. In event-driven systems, the operating system (OS) software captures the user interactions and processes them in a first-in-first-out order. The OS captures all user events, but responds only to those for which a procedure has been specified.

The programming language that is used with Excel is Visual Basic for Applications (VBA), (the topic of Chapters 13–16 of this text). It has characteristics of all three programming paradigms. It is event-driven in that the program does nothing until the user initiates an operation. It supports procedures that may be "called" from other program modules or that may respond to user actions. VBA is object-oriented in that program solutions involve the interaction of objects such as those representing workbooks, worksheets, cells, ranges, and user input forms. Programmers may even create domain classes in VBA to represent objects in the business domain, such as customers, employees, and products.

The Programming Process

Once solution steps have been developed into algorithms during the Design phase of the system development life cycle (SDLC), the program modules can be developed. The Development phase of the SDLC includes the following activities:

1. Begin with structured instructions in pseudocode or flowcharts.
2. Identify variables and constants needed for the solution.
3. Translate the design instructions into the specific programming language code.
4. Correct any syntax errors and compile the program.
5. Test the program for logic or result errors. Use debugging tools to help with result error testing.
6. Test the program for runtime errors.
7. Add error-handling routines as needed for runtime errors.
8. Document the program code for developers
9. Write user instructions.

This process of translating the instruction algorithms into a specific programming language is called *coding, writing, constructing,* or *programming* the computer solution. The programming language represents the knowledge base available to the programmer for constructing the program. Any program instructions that are written are restricted to just the *syntax* available in the particular programming language. *Syntax* is programming terminology that refers to the vocabulary, punctuation, line breaks, and other formatting of a particular programming environment. The syntax varies from one programming language to another in much the same way human languages vary. When translating from one human language to another, we can use only the words, symbols, and punctuation available in the target language. Each programming language has one or more proprietary software programs that support the programming efforts for the language. Some programming environments provide only a simple *code editor* and some have *debugging* tools. Other programming environments provide a more elaborate and comprehensive set of tools for developing software programs that may include design and modeling support. These more elaborate software development environments are generally referred to as *integrated development environments,* or *IDEs.*

Once a computer program is coded, it must be *compiled* before the computing machinery can run or *execute* the program. The *compiler* is the most important part of the programming environment. The compiler is the program that translates what the programmer writes, called the *source code,* into a language called *machine language* that the computing machinery can understand. The source code looks much like a human language, and the machine language consists of ones and zeros which operate the millions of on–off switches in the computer circuitry. The computer hardware can only understand machine language.

There are two ways a program can be translated from source code into machine language. Many languages are compiled as they are executed, which means the translation occurs immediately prior to what the user sees on his computer screen when the program runs. Other languages are compiled into an *intermediate language,* which is not source code and is not yet machine language. When the program runs, the intermediate language code is then translated into machine language by an *interpreter.* This two-step process is used when the programming language's compilation process is very resource-intensive and would result in poor system performance if it was compiled in a one-step process. Java is an example of a programming language in which programs are compiled when put into production, then when executed they are *interpreted* by a special *runtime environment.* Such programs will run only on machines that are equipped with the language-specific runtime environment. That runtime environment is typically much less resource-intensive than the IDE which is not required on the machines that actually runs the program.

Types of Programming Errors

During the development process the programmer will encounter three distinct types of programming errors; *syntax errors, result errors,* and *runtime errors.* Each type results from specific causes and each requires specific techniques to remedy.

Syntax Errors

Computer program code can actually be written using any text editing software such as Notepad or WordPad. During the actual "coding" of the computer program, the programmer may create errors as he attempts to enter the instructions in the programming language. Errors in the code vocabulary or punctuation are called *syntax errors.* Syntax errors will prevent the program from compiling because the compiler cannot "read" the syntax. *Code editors* are text editors that are especially designed for a specific programming language. A code editor works much more like word processors than like text editors in that they give the programmer information about the code as it is typed. It may correct some minor errors, just as a word processor might do using an auto-correct feature. It may use colored text or underlines to draw the programmer's attention to special text, such as *keywords* (words or phrases with special meaning in the programming language) or syntax errors. Drawing attention to syntax errors as code is typed is one way that the programming environment assists the programmer in preventing future compiling problems caused by syntax errors.

Before the compiler can actually compile the code, the code must be free of syntax errors. When the programmer attempts to compile the program, the compiler highlights syntax errors one at a time. Each time an error is located by the compiler, the programmer corrects the syntax and attempts to compile the code again. This process continues until all syntax errors are corrected. The process of locating and correcting program errors is called *debugging* the program. Programming IDEs provide multiple tools to assist with debugging program code. Once the program compiles successfully, the programmer knows the syntax is correct.

Some common syntax errors:

- Misspelling keywords of the programming language
- Attempting to assign values to variables without first declaring them (in some languages)
- Attempting to assign a value of an incorrect data type to a constant or variable
- Misspelling a variable name after it is declared
- Lines of code not started or ended as expected
- Missing punctuation such as commas, colons, parentheses, and quotation marks
- Misspelled data types in variable or constant declarations

Result Errors

The computer program may compile successfully (without syntax errors), however the program may not be entirely free of other types of errors. A program calculation may produce an incorrect result. This type of error is called a *result error,* and is caused by a *logic error* that can occur at design time or when translating the program instructions into the program code. Result errors are discovered when the program code is tested in the same way a user will use the program. The programming environment cannot find the logic errors for the programmer. The programmer must test the program extensively before placing it into production to assure that it performs its operations accurately.

Some common causes of result errors:

- Using an incorrect variable name in a calculation, such as "subtotal" instead of "total"
- Incorrect order of precedence specified by error or omission
- Missing or incorrect placement of parentheses

Runtime Errors

When the programmer designs the computer program he must try to anticipate things outside the program itself that may affect its successful operation. For example, if a program is designed to perform a calculation that allows the user to enter all the values to be used in the calculation, what happens if the user enters a zero for a value that will be used as a divisor? We know that dividing by zero produces an undetermined value, in other words, a calculation error. If a computer programmer does not anticipate that the user might enter a zero for a value used as a divisor, he will not write the program so that it will "handle" the potential error. Without coding instructions that allow the program to gracefully handle the error and resume normal operation, the program will halt and cease to function. This type of error is called a *runtime error*. Correctly so, the term implies that the error does not make itself evident until the program is running and attempting to perform a feature for which it was designed. When a program encounters a runtime error, it must be restarted before it will function again. Such unplanned shutdowns can cause serious loss of data and productivity. *Error-handling* is the technique of including program instructions that gives the program the ability to handle any event that has the potential to cause an unplanned system shut-down. Error-handling is an essential part of coding any size or type of computer program.

One of the main ways errors are handled in computer programs is actually by preventing them from occurring. In the example above, the programmer can prevent the entry of a zero as a divisor by testing the data when it is entered by the user. This process is called *data validation*. The program can alert the user when invalid data has been entered and give the user a chance to correct the entry to prevent a runtime error at a later time.

A second way to handle runtime errors is to "catch" the error as it occurs and "handle" it according to the type of error produced. Most modern programming languages have features and vocabulary included in the language to handle runtime errors. Since "error" is a human term, the computer just knows that an "exception" has occurred to the normal operation of the program. For this reason, some programming languages refer to runtime errors as "exceptions" and therefore the programming language vocabulary is in terms of "exception handling" instead of "error handling." Both terms refer to the same process of testing the program for runtime errors and writing special code to keep the program running in case runtime errors do occur.

Table 9-1: Summary of error types, causes and corrective actions

Error Type	Cause	Example	Corrective Action
Syntax	Error in programming code entry	Misspelling a language keyword	Use compiler to locate each error and the programmer corrects the syntax.
Result	Error in logic	Tax = (subtotal + taxrate) * subtotal (parentheses incorrectly placed)	Test logic at design time and test all program results at runtime to locate error. Correct the logic that caused the error.
Runtime	Unanticipated problem encountered while program runs	Program refers to an item in an array by using an index that exceeds the limit of the array	Test the program by using it as a user would, including making the type of mistakes a user is likely to make when using the program.

Variables & Constants

While a computer program runs, data must be captured, calculated, and presented by the program. Data is handled in a computer program by using *variables* and *constants* to hold the data values while the program runs. Variable and constant values are stored in volatile computer memory so their values are not retained after the program terminates. A *variable* is a location in volatile computer memory where space is reserved and named to store an item of data while the computer program or module is running or executing. The value of a variable may change multiple times while the program or module is running.

A *constant* is used much the same way as a variable except that its value remains constant and does not change while the program or module executes. Examples of constants include those that represent a tax rate or discount rate which will not change during the execution of the procedure or module. The only way a constant can be changed is by the programmer in the actual program code.

For a program that accepts input from the user for two numbers then sums the numbers, we need to specify three memory locations. We want to choose names for the locations that have meaning to the program, such as "number1", "number2," and "total." The value of the number the user enters first will be stored in location named "number1." The value of the second number entered by the user is stored in the location named "number2." The sum is calculated and stored in the location named "total." Now that the three values are stored, the program can use the values by calling the name of the storage location (the variable name). If the program is to print the calculated result, instructions are written by the programmer to print "total." The current value in "total" will print.

The main idea behind the use of variables is for the named memory location to be reused multiple times throughout the execution of the program. In the above example, after entering the two numbers the user might click a button labeled "Calculate" to display the sum that results from adding the two numbers together. After the sum is calculated and displayed, the three variables may be reused by the program for the next user action. Now the user can enter two new numbers then click the Calculate button again. That action will cause the two new numbers to be stored in the two respective memory locations named "number1" and "number2." A new calculated value will be stored in the memory location named "total." The previous values are no longer stored as each memory location can store only one data value at a time. Once a new value is assigned to the memory location, the previous value is no longer accessible.

Before the program can use the variable or constant, its memory location must be named and defined in the program code. Every programming language provides a keyword or phrase for defining variables. A variable definition requires, at a minimum, the *name* of the variable (name for the memory location), and the type of data to be stored in that variable. The type of data is generally referred to as the *data type*. The data type indicates how much memory to allocate to the variable. The variable name is also called its *identifier* since it is unique and used to identify or refer to the memory location. The process of defining a variable is called *variable declaration* since you are declaring the name and data type before actually assigning any value to the variable.

Naming Conventions for Variables and Constants

Each programming language has specific rules (acceptable syntax) for naming variables. In most languages you cannot begin a variable name with a numeric character, an underscore, or other special characters (such as @, #, $,), (, %, ^, *). In most languages, it is not acceptable to use any special character in the variable name other than the underscore. The underscore is often used to connect words in a variable phrase to make the name more readable, such as "tax_rate", or "order_quantity." Another technique for naming variables that are made up of multiple words is to use camel casing in which the first word in the variable is not capitalized, but the initial letter of each subsequent word is capitalized. In camel casing, no spaces or underscores are used to separate the words. Camel casing would result in variable names such as "taxRate" and "orderTotal." Spaces are never permitted in variables names as they must always be one continuous string of characters. The compiler begins looking for the variable name once it reads the variable declaration keyword or command syntax. It reads the name until it reads a space, so if a space is used in a variable name, any part of the name after the space is not considered a part of the variable and results in a syntax error.

Variables and constants should be declared at the beginning of the module in which they will be used. In addition to the naming requirements of the language, other naming *conventions* may be adopted. Naming *conventions* are not required characteristics of the variable or constant name, but rather a set of uniform naming rules on which one or more programmers agree. Once a naming convention is adopted, it is used consistently throughout a program. Some naming conventions include a prefix to the variable or constant name that indicates the data type assigned. For example, a variable that holds an integer type of data that holds the sum of a group of numbers might be named "intTotal." A variable holding a character string representing a customer's last name might be named "strLastName."

When declaring both variables and constants within the same module, all constants should be declared first so that they are easy to locate for efficient program maintenance when they need to be updated, such as when tax rates change. A common naming convention for constants uses all capital letters. The purpose of all capital letters is to be able to quickly distinguish constants from variables in the declaration area of the program module and in the program syntax. A constant that stores a decimal data type of single precision (called "single") may be named sngTAXRATE or sngDISCOUNT_RATE.

Table 9-2: Common variable prefixes that indicate data type

Data Type	Prefix	Example
Byte	byt	bytAge
Integer	int	intOrderQuantity
Long	lng	lngSalary
Single (precision decimal)	sng	sngItemPrice
Double (precision decimal)	dbl	dblDISCOUNT_RATE
Currency	cur	curOrderTotal
Character (single character)	chr	chrGender
String (fixed or variable)	str	strLastName
Date	date	dateBirthDate
Time	time	timeOrderTime
Date and Time combined	dt	dtOrderDateTime
Boolean	bln	blnShipped
Object	obj	objCustomer

Variable and Constant Scope

In modular program design, the same variables may be used and changed within one procedure or function, within one module (which might contain multiple procedures and/or functions), or within the entire programming project. The level of use of a variable is called its *scope*. The *scope* of a variable is set by where and how it is declared. The *declaration* of a variable is the specification of the name and data type of a variable or constant before it is used by the program.

Variable and Constant Scopes:

1. *Local scope:* When a variable or constant is declared inside a procedure or function, it is actually created by the program when that procedure or function executes. Once created, it is recognized throughout that procedure or function and throughout all code structures inside that procedure or function. It is said to be *local* to that procedure or function.

2. *Module-level scope:* When a variable or constant is declared at the module level, it is created when that module executes and is recognized throughout the entire module which may consist of several procedures and/or functions. A module-level variable is recognized in all procedures, functions, and code structures inside the module in which it is declared and is called a *module-level* variable, or *private* variable.

3. *Global scope:* A variable declaration that is preceded by the keyword "Public" is called a *global* variable and is recognized throughout the entire program, in all modules, in all procedures and functions, and in all code structures. Global variables are rarely, if ever, used in modern computer programs. Sharing the same variable in a global fashion allows any procedure, function, or module to change the value of the variable which gives rise to troubleshooting and maintenance problems. If one module needs the variable value from another module, the value can be easily "passed" from one module-level variable to another.

Data Types

When a variable or constant is declared, its data type must also be defined. The most common data types are numeric and character. Other types include date types and Boolean types. *Boolean* types also called *logical* types of data which can hold only one of two different values, TRUE or FALSE. There may be multiple data types in a programming language that represent character or numeric data. In some programming languages the *character* data type holds only one single alphanumeric character. For a string of alphanumeric characters, most modern programming languages have a special *String* data type. Specialized types of numeric data include *integer, decimal, double* (precision decimal), *single* (precision decimal), and *float* (floating point decimal). The actual data type available to the programmer varies with each programming language. For example, Visual Basic for Applications (VBA) does not have a "decimal" or "float" data type, so *single* or *double* must be used when decimal data types are needed. *String* is the common data type used in VBA for any number of alphanumeric characters.

Note that in the above explanations of data types, we refer to character or text data as alphanumeric data. That is because numbers can also be considered text or character data based on how the data are used. For example, a Social Security Number is composed of numbers, but it is considered character (or String) data because the numbers are not used to perform any calculations or other numeric operations. So it would be appropriate to store a Social Security Number as String type data. This is especially true if numbers are mixed with formatting characters such as Social Security Numbers and telephone numbers that may include dashes or parentheses. A zip code may be stored as String or numeric data depending on how it will be used. There are cases in which a zip code might need to be a numeric value, such as in programs that may require numeric values in order to develop a bar code for the value. The following table provides examples of some general data types that are used in pseudocode or flowchart algorithms.

Table 9-3: General data types used in pseudocode and flowcharts

Sample Data	Data Type	Explanation
Prices: 5.95, 10.29	Decimal or Currency	Some programming languages have a special format for currency, otherwise a decimal type is used.
Account numbers: "A2453" "1005869"	String	May consist of either alpha or numeric characters and it not used in calculations
A quantity: 5698	Integer	A whole number that may be used in calculations
An institution name: "Virginia Tech"	String	String of alphanumeric characters
Credit available for a customer: TRUE or FALSE	Logical (or Boolean)	Stores the value that results from a comparison expression, such as accountBalance < creditLimit
A gender value: "M" or "F"	Character	Represents only a single alphanumeric character that is not used in a calculation
A date: 01/26/05	Date	When the Date data type is available, programs recognize the underlying number value for a date and are able to perform date calculations for this data type.
A date: "01/26/05"	String	When date type is not available, dates are handled as text. Calculations cannot be performed using this data type.
A Julian date: 38376.25	Decimal	Can be used for calculations. In most programming languages a date type is converted (implicitly or explicitly) to a Julian date type before calculations can be performed.

Table 9-4: Specific data types used in VBA

Data Type	Storage Space (in Bytes)	Range of Values
Byte	1	0-255
Boolean	2	True, False
Integer	2	-32,768 to 32,767
Long	4	-2,147,483,648 to 2,147,483,647
Single	4	-3.402823E38 to -1.401298E-45 for negative numbers 1.401298E-48 to 3.402823E38 for positive numbers
Double	8	-1.79769313486231E308 to -4.94065645841247E-324 for negative numbers; 4.94065645841247E-324 to 1.79769313486232E308 to for positive numbers
Currency	8	-922,337,203,685,477.5808 to 922,337,203,685,477.5807
Date	8	January 1, 1900 to December 31, 9999
Object	4	Any object
String (variable length)	10 + string length	0 to approximately 2,000,000,000
String (fixed length)	String length	0 to approximately 65,400
Variant (numeric)	16	Same range as Double
Variant (String)	22 + string length	Same range as variable length String

Assigning Values to Variables and Constants

The instruction that stores a data value in a variable or constant is called *assignment*. We say a value is *assigned* to the variable or constant.

Assigning Values to Variables

Values are assigned to variables using an assignment operator specific to the programming language. The most common assignment operator is the equal sign (=). In this context, the symbol does not represent equality as we have been accustomed to using it in mathematics, but rather it represents "assignment." In an assignment statement, the variable name is always on the left of the assignment operator (=) and the value to be assigned is on the right of the operator. For example, if we want to store the value 5 in a variable named "number1," we use the pseudocode statement:

number1 = 5

The logic of the previous statement is "number1 is assigned the value of 5." Another common assignment operator is the combination of the colon and the equal sign in the syntax :=. The value on the right side is assigned to the variable on the left side of the assignment operator.

Assigned variable values for numeric data types can be real numeric values, such as 5, or they may be a value resulting from a calculation, formula, function (its return value), or from another variable. The following statements are valid variable assignment statements.

itemPrice = 12.50
itemPrice = listPrice
itemPrice = listPrice * (1-0.1)
totalPrice = price * taxRate
age = (currentDate() − birthDate)/365

Once the variable has been declared, it can then accept a value of the appropriate data type. The *assignment* of the initial value for the variable or constant is called *initialization*. The programmer may initialize the variable either in the declaration instruction (permitted by some programming languages) or in a statement following the declaration statement. The programmer is not required to initialize a variable. A variable is actually initialized by the program when the declaration instruction is executed. Most programming languages have a default initial value that is assigned to a variable. For example, a numeric data type is initialized to zero and a character data type is initialized to blank (an empty string).

Since variables are stored in the volatile memory of the computer, their names and memory allocations exist only as long as the program runs. With each execution of the program, the variables are declared and initialized. If variable values from one execution of the program are needed in a subsequent program execution, the variable values must be stored in some *persistent* storage format and on a non-volatile storage medium (like a hard disk drive). *Persistent* data is data that exists past one execution of the program. Persistent data is stored in some file format from which the data can be retrieved by the program. In most information systems today, persistent data is typically stored in a *relational database*. Persistent data may also be written to and read from an Excel worksheet using VBA and other programming languages and utilities.

Each programming language has special keywords for declaring variables. In the program design process with pseudocode and flowcharts, the keyword "Declare" is used to indicate variable or constant declaration.

The general pseudocode syntax for variable declarations:

Declare <*variableName*> as <*dataType*>

The scope of the variable is determined by where the declaration statement appears in the program. If it appears inside a procedure or function, it is procedure level. If is appears in a module outside of all procedures and functions, it has a module level scope.

Variable Declaration Examples:

Declare strFirstName as String
Declare intItemNumber as Integer
Declare blnValid as Boolean
Declare sngItemPrice as Single

Assigning Values to Constants

Constants are like variables in that they are named locations in volatile computer memory and are used for storing program data. They differ from variables in that once they are initialized, their value will not change during the current execution of the program. Many programming languages require initialization of constants in the declaration statement. Other languages permit initialization at runtime, but will not allow the value to change after that. Constants are used differently from variables. They are typically used for values that are not expected to change until the programmer changes the values. In an accounting system in which a discount rate is applied, a constant can be used to store the value of the discount. When the discount changes, the programmer changes the discount rate in the program code. If there is a multi-level discount structure, a constant can be used for each discount applied. For example, constants might be named LOW_DISCOUNT, MED_DISCOUNT, and MAX_DISCOUNT. Note that the example constant names are all upper case. Using all upper case characters for naming constants is the convention used in most programming environments. The idea is to draw attention to the constant declaration and initialization statements so that they will be easy to find when the programmer needs to change their values. For the same reason, constants are usually declared before variables so that they will appear near the beginning of the program code for each program module, procedure or function. Assignment of values for constants is done the same way as assignment of values to variables using an assignment operator.

A constant is declared with a special keyword to let the program know that its value should not be allowed to change. The initial value should be included in the declaration instruction in pseudocode and flowchart algorithms. In the program design process with pseudocode and flowcharts, the keyword "Constant" is included in the constant declaration instruction.

The general pseudocode syntax for constant declarations:

Declare Constant *<CONSTANT_NAME>* as *<dataType>* = *<initialValue>*

Constant Declaration Example

Declare Constant sngTAX_RATE as Single = .05

Arrays

Data structure implies how the data item is stored in volatile memory. Variables and constants represent a single data item that is stored in one memory location. Many business solutions involve the manipulation of collections of like data items. Programming languages provide an efficient data structure for handling multiple related data items. These complex data structures are called *arrays*. An *array* is a collection of related data items of the same data type. A one-dimensional array is represented logically by a row or list of single like items. A two-dimensional array is represented by a table or matrix. Arrays may also have more than two dimensions.

An array provides a way of referring to a collection of data by one variable name. When an array is declared, it is assigned an identifier (name). When the name is used in the program, it refers to the entire collection, not just one single data item. The array subscripts can be used in addition to the array name to refer to one single data item in the array. The subscript represents the index number of the position of the data item in the array. *The first index number is always zero so the last index number will be one less than the actual size of the array dimension.*

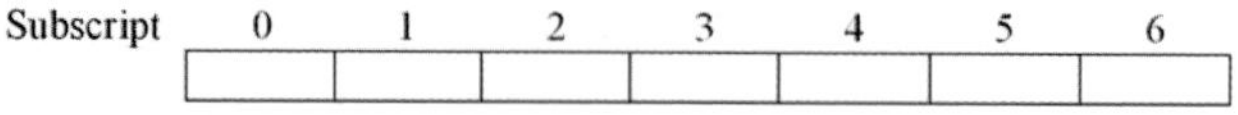

Figure 9-1: Logical representation of a one-dimensional array "days(6)."

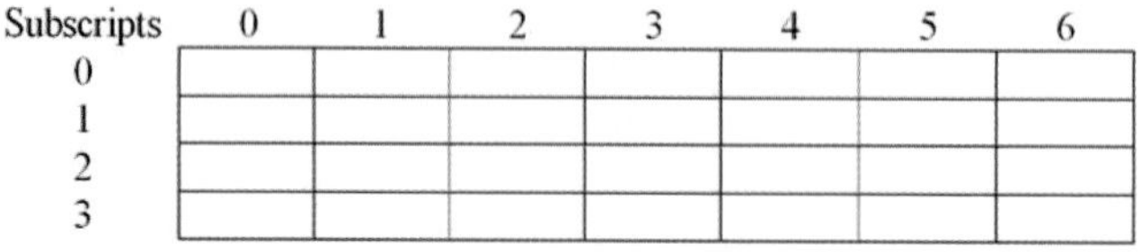

Figure 9-2: Logical representation of a one-dimensional array "table (6, 3)."

To declare an array in pseudocode, use parentheses after the array variable name to indicate the last index number that can be used. Keep in mind that position one has an index of zero so if you want an array that holds three items, the maximum position index in parentheses is two. Some programming language use parentheses to enclose the array dimensions and some use square brackets ([ ]). Arrays can be declared with a fixed size or they can be declared as *dynamic* arrays in some programming languages so that the array may expand as more items are added. A fixed size array is called a *static* array. There are advantages and disadvantages of both types of arrays. A fixed size array conserves memory space, but it cannot be expanded if needed. It must be re-declared to a larger size. When an array is re-declared, it typically loses its contents. Some programming languages provide special keywords to be used along with the re-declaration statement that will preserve the contents of the previous array of the same name. The down side of dynamic arrays is that while they offer flexibility, they may consume an enormous amount of memory due to the way they expand. The way a dynamic array expands is not simply to grow to fit the data that is added to it, but it usually expands by a percentage each time. At any given time, a large dynamic array may have much unused memory allocated to it.

Array Declaration

An array is declared by stating its identifier (name), its size (if static), and its data type. Like variables and constants, the scope of the array depends on where it is declared. Just like other variables, its scope may be local, module level, or global (not recommended). An array that holds the seven days of the week could be declared using the following pseudocode statement.

Declare days(6) as String

The "days" array is a one-dimensional array. That is indicated by only one number present inside the parentheses. When a multidimensional array is declared, the dimensions inside the parentheses are separated by commas. A two-dimensional array that has four by seven positions is declared using the following pseudocode statement.

Declare table(6, 3) as Integer

Some programming languages allow the declaration of a dynamic array. To declare a dynamic array, no size information is provided when it is declared.

Declare days() as String

Managing size changes in dynamic arrays is done differently in different programming languages. VBA does not support the automatic expansion of dynamic arrays. It requires the array to be re-declared with a new size in order for the array to accept its first item. The following pseudocode simulates the re-declaration statement for languages that require it.

Re-declare days(3) as String

Once the array is full and more size is needed, care must be taken with the re-declaration statement. Typically when the array is re-declared, its current data is deleted. Some programming languages offer a keyword like "PRESERVE" to prevent the current array data from begin deleted and places it is the newly dimensioned array. The following pseudocode represents the re-declaration of an array size while preserving its current contents.

Re-declare preserve days(6) as String

Adding Items to an Array

The positions in an array are reference by index numbers called *subscripts*. The index numbers begin at 0 for the first position in the array. For example, our "days(6)" array will hold 7 string data items. To add an item to the array, indicate the position to fill using its subscript (position index) in parentheses following the array name in the assignment statement.

days(0) = "Sunday"

Arrays do not require us to fill the positions in order. We can add an item to any index by referencing its subscript.

days(3) = "Wednesday"

Figure 9-3: Logical representation of writing data to positions (0) and (3).

Subscript:	0	1	2	3	4	5	6
Values:	Sunday			Wednesday			

When adding data to a multi-dimensional array subscripts of each dimension must be included.

table(2, 2) = "Virginia"
table(3, 2) = "Tech"

Subscripts	0	1	2	3	4	5	6
0							
1							
2			Virginia	Tech			
3							

Figure 9-4: Logical representation of writing to positions (2, 2) and (3, 2).

Accessing Items in an Array

Items in an array are accessed just as they are added, by referencing the item's position.

```
Dim days(6) as String
Dim firstDay as String
Dim fourthDay as String
FirstDay = days(0)
FourthDay = days(4)
```

Referencing the Whole Array

The biggest advantage in using the array structure is being able to pass the entire array through the program as one named package instead of having to reference each item individually. Consider the array declared earlier to hold the days of the week. To reference all the days in the week, we need only to reference the array name. The following example includes one procedure that declares and fills the array and another procedure that prints the array contents. The array itself is passed from one procedure to the other by using the array name. In the procedure that receives the array, its argument definition must include a set of parentheses following the array argument name to indicate it is an array.

```
BEGIN DaysArray
    Declare days(6) as String
    Days(0) = "Sunday"
    Days(1) = "Monday"
    Days(2) = "Tuesday"
    Days(3) = "Wednesday"
    Days(4) = "Thursday"
    Days(5) = "Friday"
    Days(6) = "Saturday"
    Call PrintDays(days)
END

BEGIN PrintDays(d() as String)
    Print d(0)
    Print d(1)
    Print d(2)
    Print d(3)
    Print d(4)
    Print d(5)
    Print d(6)
END
```

The value in "days" is passed from the first procedure into the "d()" argument of the second procedure. Once the array is received by the second procedure, it individual items are accessed for printing by referring to their subscripts.

Review Questions

1. What are three modern programming paradigms and what are the main characteristics of each?

   _____

   _____

   _____

2. How do the three programming paradigms you listed in the previous questions relate to VBA in Excel?

   _____

   _____

   _____

3. List the steps involved in transferring design models into a working system.

   _____

   _____

   _____

4. What is the purpose of a *compiler*?

   _____

   _____

   _____

5. What is the purpose of an interpreter? How is a program compiled and executed that uses an interpreter?

   _____

   _____

   _____

6. What is meant by *debugging* a computer program?

   _____

   _____

   _____

7. List three types of programming errors, some causes of each, and general remedies for the error type.

_____

_____

_____

8. Evaluate the error description in first column of the following table. For each description, enter in the second column the type of error (Syntax, Result, Runtime, or None if you do not think an error will occur). In the last column, describe how you, the programmer, would go about resolving the error, if any.

	Error Description	Type of Error	How to Resolve the Error
a.	Programmer misspells a keyword when declaring a variable.		
b.	Programmer misspells a variable name when declaring a variable.		
c.	User enters an employ's time card information as timeIn is 8:00 a.m. and timeOut is 4:00 p.m. The program calculates hours worked to be 4.0.		
d.	An on-line mail order program captures the customer's information, but the customer leaves the Zip Code field blank.		
e.	The programmer writes a series of loops that collectively update credit card balances. The program first adds all purchases then subtracts all payments and credits. The logical comparison (the condition that is tested) that checks to see if the customer has made any purchases is written at the end of the loop that adds customer purchases.		

_____

_____

_____

9. What is a variable? Compare and contrast variables and constants.

_____

_____

_____

10. For each of the following sample data items listed in the table below, de-
    cide whether they should be a variable or constant, and decide what data
    type would be most appropriate. Fill in the table with your responses.

	Data to Represent	Variable or Constant?	Data Type
a.	Last name of a person		
b.	Street address of a person		
c.	Zip code		
d.	State abbreviation		
e.	Name of an organization		
f.	Product description		
g.	Product ID		
h.	Colors available for a product (collectively)		
i.	Quantity on hand		
j.	Cost		
k.	Order date		
l.	Item still available from vendor?		
m.	A person's age		
n.	Sales tax rates for multiple localities		
o.	Should more product be ordered?		

_____

_____

_____

11. What are the naming rules for variables and constants? What is the dif-
    ference in a naming rule and a naming convention?

_____

_____

_____

12. In what portions of the program are local variables valid?

_____

_____

_____

13. In what portions of the program can module-level variables be used?

_____

_____

_____

14. In what portions of the program can global variables be used?

_____

_____

_____

15. What is the syntax for assigning a value to a variable?

_____

_____

_____

16. What does initialization mean with regard to variables and constants?

_____

_____

_____

17. What is an array? What is the advantage is using an array in a program?

_____

_____

_____

Practice Problems

1. Make a list of variables and constants and their respective data types that are needed to support a conference registration system that accepts user input for registrant's:

   a. Name
   b. Mailing address
   c. Member status (active/inactive)
   d. Credit card number
   e. Credit card expiration date (month and year only)

2. Make a list of variables and constants and their respective data types that are needed to support an order entry system that allows a user to:

   a. Select up to 10 items to order and place them in a shopping cart.
   b. Enter zip code to calculate shipping.
   c. Check out and have order total added to your account with the company.

3. For the algorithm you created in Practice Problem 3 of Chapter 8, write pseudocode to declare all variables and constants. Select appropriate data types for the variables and constants. Include initialization in any constant declarations.

4. For the algorithm you created in Practice Problem 4 of Chapter 8, write pseudocode to declare all variables and constants. Select appropriate data types for the variables and constants. Include initialization in the constant declaration.

1. Understand the advantages of modular program design
2. Use a procedural or event approach to break a system into manageable pieces for design purposes
3. Apply guidelines for designing the internal instructions of a module
4. Design modules using the lowest level of coupling possible
5. Design modules using a high level of cohesion possible
6. Pass data between two modules using *parameters, arguments,* and *return values*
7. Differentiate arguments passed *by value* and *by reference*
8. Use *factoring* to identify lower level modules

Modular Program Design

Before you can effectively design a solution, you must be able to identify the specific tasks the system must perform. Many of us are overwhelmed when presented with a large problem because it is difficult to envision each detailed task required for the solution. In order to develop a solution, it is necessary to adopt some kind of "divide and conquer" strategy that breaks the problem into manageable pieces. One such strategy that is used widely in software development is *modular program design*.

A program *module* is a named set of executable instructions with a single point of entry and a single point of exit. A module is designed to perform its functionality independent of other modules. Modular design utilizes modules at various levels of the program design. One module may perform all of one specific task, or may call on a number of other modules, each of which performs a part of the task or a subtask. Coordinated modules control the flow of the program. One module may be designed as the *control* module which actually starts the program and calls the next module(s) as needed.

Advantages of Modular Program Design

1. *Provides the ability to "divide and conquer":* It provides a way to break the larger problem into smaller pieces that are easier to understand, easier to program, and easier to maintain and upgrade.

2. *Provides a way to model the solution design by abstracting out the required system functionality:* It provides a way for the system designers to focus on what is important to the system without getting distracted by the details. You can design the specific instructions for each module later, after the overall system design has been completed.

3. *Allows multiple designers or programmers to work on one program since the modules function independently of each other:* When multiple project team members work on one program, it results in a significant decrease in the time it takes to develop a system. If only one programmer worked on a software program, it may take years to complete the product. It also supports specialization among programmers in that modules can be assigned to a programmer based on his/her area of programming expertise.

4. *Allows reuse of program modules:* One of the design goals for each individual module is reusability. If the functionality of a single module is restricted to one specialized task, it may be reused in subsequent programs that may need some similar functionality. For example, a module called "CalculateTax" might be used in multiple programs, such as a retail sales application, an income tax calculator, or property tax billing application. All tax calculations require a tax rate and a taxable amount in order to compute a tax, and they all require the result to be the tax amount itself.

5. *It makes it easier to properly structure a program for implementation:* By breaking a program design into modules, it allows the designer to focus on just one module at a time which requires a small number of instructions. Since pseudocode and modular design align so closely with how computer language code is written, implementation is merely a translation of pseudocode modules into coded program modules.

Types of Program Modules

We have already mentioned one type of module, the *control module* that drives the flow of the overall program. Other types of modules are designed to perform specific types of functions. Some modules can be designed to "initialize" the program, that is, perform startup procedures that are needed only when the program loads. Such procedures might include opening data files, or showing the main menu interface for the program. Each program will have only one *initialization module* and one *control module.*

Some modules are designed to perform some type of data processing. They are called *process modules.* Process modules include specialized modules that get input, validate input, perform calculations, and print output. These modules are called *read modules, data validation modules, calculation modules,* and *print modules,* respectively.

A final type of module processes instructions for application shutdown. These are called *clean-up, wrap-up,* or *shutdown* modules. They perform such tasks as closing data files and printing results. Like the initialization module, instructions in the shutdown module are executed only once each time the application runs.

Depending on the type of functionality a module has and its scope relative to the program, it may be called different things in different programming languages. Other names for modules include procedures, sub-procedures, sub-routines, subroutine procedures, subs, functions, methods, forms, classes, and components.

Procedure versus Function

Two of the most common types of module structures are *procedures* and *functions. Procedures* are used to perform some action. They may accept inputs but inputs are optional. Procedures may produce an output, but more typically they do not. In contrast, *functions* accept inputs and always return exactly one value to the point of the program from which it was called. Functions perform some type of transformation of the inputs to formulate the output. Functions are typically called from a procedure or from another function. A procedure may call another procedure, but a function does not typically call a procedure.

Organizing the Computer Solution

The first step in modular program design is identifying the modules that are needed for the solution. There are different approaches that can be used to break the system into modules, depending on system characteristics and the programming paradigm(s) used. Solutions that are primarily procedural, meaning that they perform some comprehensive process from beginning to end, are best approached from the top-down by dividing each process into smaller ones until each small process or module does only one task. Solutions that are driven by user actions are called *event-driven* programs. The best approach for identifying modules required for event-driven systems is to identify the ways users interact with the system then identify the modules needed to support each user interaction.

Procedural Approach to Identifying Modules

A procedural approach to modular program design follows a similar pattern to that of a company that is organized by functions, each with its own manager. In order for the company to solve an important problem, it must be brought to the attention of the company's chief executive (CEO). The CEO is the overall control agent for the entire organization. The company's CEO would then delegate responsibility to subordinate executive managers based on the functionality for which they are responsible. The executive managers will call on middle managers as needed to enlist their help in designing a solution that can be implemented by the line supervisors and their employees. In order to visually model such a structure in an organization, we use a hierarchical organizational structure chart.

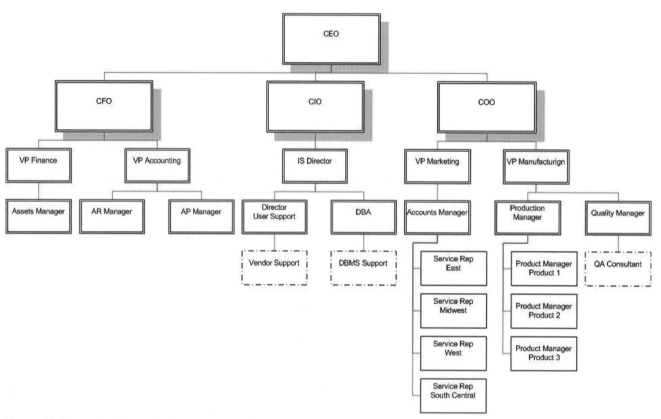

Figure 10-1: A typical hierarchical organizational structure chart.

The company is organized from a top-down approach that is called *functional decomposition* in program design terms. *Functional decomposition* is the process of breaking a larger functional piece (of an organization or a computer program) into smaller parts that each have a specific purpose. In the structure chart in Figure 10-1 the first level of subordinate organizational roles are divided according to the function each one oversees. The next level of subordinate roles further divides the superior role into smaller functional units. The process is continued until the smaller modules are *atomic,* meaning they cannot be broken down into smaller units that still have meaning. In programming we sometimes refer to these smallest modules as *primitive* units or processes. In response to a major manufacturing defect, the CEO would delegate the correction of the problem to the COO, who would in turn delegate to the VP of Manufacturing, who would delegate to the Production Manager for the specific product involved. The Production Manager would use the workers under his supervision to provide the detailed solution required to correct the defect. If each worker represents a specific task, such as a machine adjustment, he represents the lowest module in the solution, the one that actually does the work required for the solution.

Modules of a computer program may be broken down, organized, and modeled in a manner that is similar to an organization's management structure. The main module, or control module is at the top of the hierarchy. The modules called by the control module are modeled as the first level of subordinate modules. The modules in the second level of subordinate modules are called by the first level modules, and so on. Modules at the lowest level include the modules that actually perform the tasks which entail executing the instructions required for the solution. This hierarchical model of organized modules is called a *structure chart*. The organizational structure model in Figure 10-1 is a type of structure chart. A structure chart for a simple computer program that gets two inputs, calculates an answer, and prints the results, (we will call it the "Calculate" program) may be modeled in a structure chart such as the one in Figure 10-2.

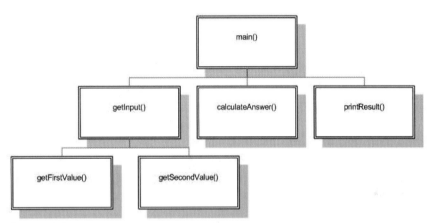

Figure 10-2: Structure chart for the calculation program.

Program control for the Calculate program would flow as follows:

1. The main() module calls the getInput() module.
2. The getInput() module calls the getFirstValue() module.
3. The getInput() module then calls the getSecondValue() module.
4. The getFirstValue() module and the getSecondValue() module each return the value and control back to the getInput module.
5. The getInput() module sends both the input values and control back to the main() module which then calls the calculateAnswer() module.
6. The calcualteAnswer() module sends the answer and control back to the main() module.
7. The main() module then calls the printResult() module.
8. The program control goes back to the main() module which waits for a signal that another calculation is desired.

Event Approach to Identifying Modules

Today's high level object-oriented programming languages are event-driven which means the program execution is initiated by some event. There are three types of system events than can drive the program execution; *external* events, *internal* events, and *temporal* events.

Types of Events

- *External events* are most often initiated by a user. An example of a user event is the selection of a menu option on a navigation screen or a button click on a form. An external event may also originate from another system that interfaces with the current system in some way.

- *Internal events* are initiated from within the current system. An example of an internal event is in an inventory system in which the quantity on hand falls below the reorder point for an inventory item.

- *Temporal events* are related to time. A specific date and/or time may trigger a temporal event. For example, midnight each night is an event that may trigger a batch update to run. A temporal event may be the result of a simulated clock that tracks passing time. Examples of simulated clock events are a monitor's screen saver or a user form becoming unavailable after 30 minutes of inactivity.

All graphical user interface (GUI) programs are event-driven. Event-driven programs simply wait for something to happen. A program action is performed based on the particular event that occurred. Types of events include mouse events, keyboard events, menu events, and window events. Sources of events include form controls, such as buttons, text boxes, list boxes, and check boxes. Program designers must design a procedure to respond to each user event of interest to the program. The user event will trigger the associated procedure to run.

How Events Are Handled

System events are detected by the operating system. The operating system puts the events in a queue and processes them in a first-in-first-out order. "Processing" the event means that the operating system searches applications to see if an *event procedure* exists for the particular event. If one exists, it is executed. If no associated event procedure is found, the next event in the queue is processed.

Module identification for an event-driven system should begin during system analysis. During analysis, the developer should indentify every business task that users will need to perform with the system. These business tasks are often called *use cases*. Use cases are named based on what the user accomplishes with the particular system feature. In a company payroll system, possible use cases are:

- EnterNewEmployee
- EnterPayPeriodData
- UpdateEmployeeData
- PrintPayrollChecks

For each use case, the GUIs must be designed according to the feature requirements and the user events must be identified. For each user event of interest, an event procedure is designed. Additional sub-procedures and/or functions may be needed to support the main event procedure. Just as with modules in a procedural program, the modules in an event-driven program also form a hierarchy. The GUIs, are the higher level modules and the event procedures are the next level modules that support the GUI events. The additional sub-procedures and functions become lower level modules that support the event procedures. The following structure chart models modules that might be used by the "PrintPayrollChecks" use case. The highest level module represents the menu GUI for the payroll system. The second level module represents the event procedure for the button click event of the menu button indicated for printing checks. The third level modules represent functions the support the general check printing process. All the fourth level modules represent functions that support the one broader function "CalculateWithholdings."

Although an event-driven system design begins with a user interaction and its associated events, it still uses the basic technique of functional decomposition to identify lower level modules. Note in Figure 10-3 that the event procedure "btnPrintChecks_Click" event is broken into smaller modules that do only one specialized task. The "CalculateWithholdings" function is then broken into multiple smaller functions that are focused on only one particular aspect of the withholding calculation.

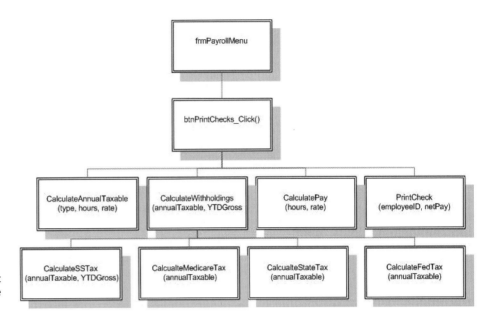

Figure 10-3: Structure chart model for modules related to the *PrintPayrollChecks* use case.

Factoring to Identify Modules

It is possible that modules can be identified from a *bottom-up approach* as well. If two modules within a program design are found to have some common instructions, such as calculating sales tax or printing a receipt, these sets of instructions can be *factored* out into separate modules. These modules can be written once and called on by multiple modules within the program, and in many cases be reused by other programs that are written in the same programming language. Simplifying program design by factoring out subordinate modules is much like factoring in mathematics to reduce fractions, or in algebra to simplify an equation.

Internal Module Design

By now you might be asking, "How do you know what to put in which module?" There are some guidelines and techniques that are helpful in making decisions for internal module design.

Module Cohesion

Cohesion is a relative measure of how closely a module's instructions adhere to the one task for which the module is designed. We say cohesion is high (desirable) when a module focuses only on one single task. We say cohesion is low (undesirable) when a module includes instructions extraneous to the main task for which it is designed. A module that reads a payroll record, calculates gross pay, and calculates deductions is a poorly designed module and not at all cohesive to one purpose. When the description of the task a module performs uses the word "and" to explain its function, it usually lacks adequate cohesion.

As you decide how much instruction and which instructions to include in each module, keep in mind that one module should only serve one purpose, or should do only one thing. For example, the main() (control) module only provides the overall control for the program. The calculateTax() module should only calculate tax and should not be used to calculate an order total or any other related process. Instructions within a single module may be related in different ways depending on the purpose of the module.

Functional Cohesion

When decomposing the system functionally, the goal of each module is *functional cohesion* in which all instructions strictly support the module's one functional task. In high functional cohesion, there are no instructions included that do not support that one specific task. Functional cohesion is considered the highest level of cohesion.

Temporal Cohesion

Not all modules result from functional decomposition of a larger process, but instead result from a need to group a set of instructions in some other useful way. Instructions that are time-related such as those instructions needed to initialize a system may be included in the same module. This type of module is referred to by the timing of its execution, such as initialization modules or shutdown modules. Cohesion in this type of module is described as *temporal cohesion,* since they are related by timing. Temporal cohesion is not considered a high level of cohesion, but it is an acceptable way to organize instructions that are related only by their timing.

Procedural Cohesion

Modules may be designed to include instructions related by the sequence in which they occur. For example a mainline or control module may include instructions that indicate the order in which other modules are called. These instructions are related only because they follow in sequence one after another. The instructions tend to be very general in nature and not related to the detailed activity that occurs in the system. Procedural cohesion is considered a medium level of cohesion relative to other ways of grouping module instructions.

Module Coupling

Each module should hide its internal data and processes from other modules. The module should compile alone without the necessity of compiling other modules. It should be able to execute from beginning to end with a minimal amount of dependence upon other modules. It is impossible for a module to be entirely independent of other modules because it must be called upon by some other program module to perform its function. The number of modules that are related to a single module and the nature of the relationship is a measure of the module's *coupling*. Coupling is defined as the extent to which two or more program modules are interdependent. It is most desirable for coupling among modules to be very low. The more modules that are interdependent, the more difficult the program is to write, debug, and maintain.

The measure of coupling is described in terms of tight coupling or loose coupling. There are many "levels" of coupling defined in current programming practice. The list below represents the most common types of module interdependency but is not all inclusive. The dependency levels are listed from loosest coupling (more desirable) to tightest coupling (least desirable).

1. *One module passes a local data variable value to another module.* This is the most desirable level of coupling. Neither module must know anything about the inner workings of the other module. Also known as *data coupling*.

2. *One module passes a local data structure to another.* A data structure is a complex data item such as an array, record, or object that is composed of multiple data

items in a specific structure. This type of coupling is still fairly loose and represents good module design. The only thing one module must know about the other is the structure of the complex data item passed between them so that the called module can access the data effectively. The disadvantage of this level of coupling is that two different modules are accessing and/or modifying data in the same object. Also known as *stamp coupling*.

3. *One module passes a variable value that controls the logic or sequence of execution of another module.* The two modules are coupled in that each must know something about the inner workings of the other. This type of coupling is not desirable and can be eliminated by using an intermediate module or command that maps each possible control variable value to a module whose logic specifically matches the requirement for that value. Also known as *control coupling*.

4. *A module is dependent on something outside the system, such as specific hardware or another software system.* This type of coupling is very undesirable and can be avoided by using an intermediate interface that simplifies access to both systems. Also known as *external coupling*.

5. *Two modules access and share the same global data variable, data structure, or process.* This type of coupling in extremely undesirable and the most easily remedied. Data sharing should be done through local variables which can be passed between modules. Certain processes (such as procedures or functions) that you wish to make available to all modules; they may be grouped into one "public" module where they can be accessed by all other modules. This arrangement creates only one module that has public access which makes the program maintenance simpler. Also known as *common coupling*.

In order for a program called "CompleteSale" to calculate the sales tax, the main program module, CompleteSale, should call the calculateTotal() module, which should in turn call the calcuateTax() module. It would be inappropriate coupling for the main module to call upon the calcuateTax() module directly. It is appropriate for the calculateTotal() module and the calculateTax() module to be coupled since their functions are also coupled in that the calcuateTotal() module depends on the calcuateTax() module to perform part of its functionality.

The modules represented on a program or module structure chart are usually numbered with an outline-type convention that relates the subordinate modules to their superior modules. The main program or highest level module is numbered 1.0. Each of its immediate subordinate modules begins with the number 1 and is followed by a different number for each module, such as 1.1, 1.2, 1.3. As modules are added that are subordinate to the second level modules, another digit is added to the right of the superior module number such as 1.1.1, 1.1.2, 1.1.3. Keep in mind that a structure chart may be for an entire program, in which case it would likely model only the first level of subordinate modules. Each subordinate module would then have its own structure chart to model all of its subordinate levels of modules. So a structure chart may be a model of the program itself or of any module within the program. When a structure chart models one module, it typically represents *all* related subordinate module, not just the first level subordinate modules.

In an ideal system design, the hierarchy of modules follows a strict tree structure (albeit an upside one). In the ideal system, lower level modules may be accessed only through the tree branch pathway. A module can be called directly by only one other module, its immediate superior. That means no upper level modules "share" any lower level modules. In practical applications of modular program design this "pure tree structure" is usually violated somewhat, especially in environments made to work within other host applications as VBA does within Excel. It is quite common to develop a custom function using VBA in Excel that may be called from more than one event procedure and may also be called from a worksheet cell. Remember that one of the goals for internal module design is reusability. If a module is well-designed with reusability in mind, it is more likely to be "shared" or called from more than one other module in the project.

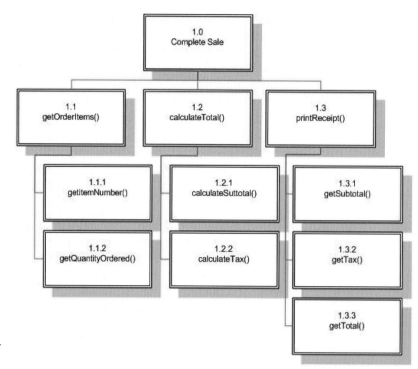

Figure 10-4: Structure Chart for *CompleteSale* Module.

Internal Module Design Checklist

1. Each module should be a complete instruction. There is only one entry point and one exit point. It should execute from beginning to end and not jump out of the middle of one module or into the middle of another module.

2. All instructions within one module should be closely related (strong cohesion) from either a functional, temporal, or procedural perspective.

3. Each module should be short enough to be easily understood and modified.

4. The length of the module is determined by its task and the number of instructions required to perform that task.

5. Each module should be as independent as possible with minimal dependency (loose coupling) on other modules.

Communication between Modules

So much has been said in this chapter about designing modules to be as independent as possible of each other. The fact is that if all modules were completely independent of other modules, they may not always be able to work together. As one module is called from another, sometimes the called module requires some program data in order for it to do its task. For example, if we pass control to a module that calculates tax, the module must know the taxable amount and also the tax rate or tax code of some sort before the tax can be calculated. When the calculation is complete, the calculated tax value must be passed back to the calling module. In such cases it is necessary to pass data from one module to another. If the variable holding a data value is only valid inside one variable, how is this transfer of data accomplished?

Parameters and Arguments

The module that requires data from a calling module must define those data requirements in the module header by naming each data item and defining its data type (much like a usual variable declaration). These data definitions in the called module are referred to as its *parameter list*. Each datum needed by the called module is a *parameter*. Once values have been received into the parameters, they are manipulated by the called module. The order in which the data are listed in the parameter list indicates the order in which they must be received to be recognized by the called module. The parameter list for the CalcualteTax module might include parameters that represent the taxable amount and the tax rate.

CalculateTax (amt as Single, taxRate as Integer)

Once the parameters are defined in the called module, the calling module can pass values to be received into those parameters. The values sent from the calling module are called *arguments*. *Arguments* are the actual values that are used to perform the task in the called module. They are passed from the calling module to the called module in variables local to the calling module (variables may be local or module level). The arguments are sent from the calling module by way of the *argument list*. Following the module "call" keyword and the name of the called module the arguments are enclosed in parentheses and separated by commas. The arguments must be listed in the same order as the parameters are listed in the called module.

salesTax = Call CalcualteTax(taxableAmount, rate)

Note that the argument name and the parameter name need not be the same. Data types are not included in the module call because they were defined earlier in a declaration statement for use in the called module.

The argument list must match both the position and the data type for each variable in the parameter list. For example, if the CalculateTax() module includes a parameter list of amt and taxRate, both decimal data types, then the calling module must send two variables, both decimal types to represent the amt and the taxRate. The first value listed in the argument list will be assigned to the first parameter (amt) and the second value listed will be assigned to the last parameter (taxRate). Care must be taken to send the arguments in the proper order. In the previous example, reversing the arguments would not result in a syntax error, but would cause a result error. Since both data types are decimal types, the program would not reject them based on their improper order. The error would only be found by manually testing the calculations performed by the program. If the reversed arguments were of different types (such as character and Boolean) the data type mismatch between the parameter list item and the argument list would result in a runtime error.

A Word about Semantics

Many people use the terms *parameter* and *argument* interchangeably. For that reason, another term often used for parameter is *formal parameter*. Another term often used for argument is *actual parameter* since it is the actual value of the parameter received and manipulated.

Pass Arguments by Value or by Reference

There are two ways arguments may be passed to called modules, *by value* or *by reference*. If a variable value is passed *by value* as an argument, logically a copy of the argument variable is passed to the memory location allocated to hold its matching parameter. If the variable is altered in the called module, the original variable value is not altered.

Passing *by reference* means that the actual memory reference to the variable is passed to the called module. The parameter in the called module is like an alias to the original variable. Any alteration to the argument in the called module alters the original variable value.

When given a choice, passing by value is considered the safer practice because it minimizes the exposure of the arguments to permanent change. Passing by reference is more efficient than passing by value because only a small pointer (the reference) is passed which takes very little memory to define. The pointer "points" directly to the variable data without duplications in memory requirements. In some cases where complex data structures are used, such as arrays or objects, passing by reference is required in some programming languages.

Module Outputs

The communication between two modules is bi-directional. One module passes control to another and the called module passes control back to the calling module. So far we have discussed only data (arguments) that are passed *to* the called module. The called module may simply perform its task and return the program control back to the calling module or it may also return data to the calling module. When an item of data is returned back to the calling module, it is called a *return value* or more simply the *return* from the module. The return variable is generally defined in pseudocode alongside the input parameters in the module header. The return variable name and data type are defined.

CalculateTax (amt as Single, taxRate as Integer) RETURNS tax as Single

The module returning a value to a calling module uses an instruction that includes only the pseudocode keyword RETURN followed by the return variable name. For example, a module that calculates tax would return its output data back to the calling module with the instruction "RETURN tax."

Review Questions

1. What is a *module* in terms of information system design?

   _____

   _____

   _____

2. What is meant by *modular program design*?

   _____

   _____

   _____

3. Briefly describe five advantages of modular program design.

   _____

   _____

   _____

4. List at least five types of system tasks that are suitable for a single module.

   _____

   _____

   _____

5. How do functions differ from procedures in terms of program modules?

   _____

   _____

   _____

6. Describe two approaches to breaking the complete information system into manageable pieces for design purposes.

   _____

   _____

   _____

7. What is meant by *factoring* to identify lower level modules?

   _____

   _____

   _____

8. In event-driven systems, what is an *event*?

   _____

   _____

   _____

9. What types of events might occur in event-driven systems?

   _____

   _____

   _____

10. How are system events connected to the action that should take place when they occur?

   _____

   _____

   _____

11. What is module *cohesion*?

   _____

   _____

   _____

12. What criteria might be used to group instructions into one module?

   _____

   _____

   _____

13. Describe five ways in which two modules might be interdependent.

   _____

   _____

   _____

14. What is a structure chart and what is its purpose in modular program design?

_____

_____

_____

15. What is module *coupling*?

_____

_____

_____

16. How is program control passed from one module to another?

_____

_____

_____

17. How is data passed from one module to another?

_____

_____

_____

18. What is a *parameter*? How do *arguments* differ from *parameters*?

_____

_____

_____

19. What does it mean to pass a value to a called module *by value* and *by reference*?

_____

_____

_____

Practice Problems

1. For a use case called "CalculateGrossPay", use functional decomposition to identify the modules that might be needed to support the following business rules.

   a. Hourly employees are paid a base hourly rate for the first 100 hours worked in a pay period and two times the base rate for every hour worked in excess of 100 in a pay period.
   b. Salaried employees are paid 1/26 of their base annual rate every pay period.

      • If the salaried employee is "exempt" they do not earn any extra pay for more than 100 hours worked in a pay period.
      • If the salaried employee is "non-exempt", he will earn .001 times his annual salary for every hour worked more than 100 in a pay period.

   c. Commissioned sales employees are paid a base hourly rate and 10% of their sales volume for the pay period. Commissioned employees are paid the same base hourly rate for all hours worked in a pay period.
   d. Each employee pays an insurance premium based on how many members of his family are insured. The insurance levels are "none", "single", "two", or "family." The insurance rates for the three insured levels are set for one year at a time. Insurance premiums are withheld from the employee's pay.
   e. Employee records including social security number, base pay rate, pay type (salaried/exempt, salaried/non-exempt, hourly, commissioned), and insurance level will be read from the employee database.

2. For a use case called "GenerateReorderList", use functional decomposition to identify the modules that might be needed to support the following business rules.

   a. Update the order quantity on hand for each inventory item by subtracting the day's sales quantities from the quantity on hand. Write the new quantity on hand back to persistent storage (a.k.a. the database).
   b. Generate a list of all inventory items in which the quantity on hand is lower than the reorder point. Use the backorder list to add back-ordered quantities to the difference between the reorder point and the quantity on hand. Generate a reorder list of those items that should be order after applying the backorder quantity. Items should be included on the reorder list whose quantity on hand plus the backorder quantity is lower than the reorder point.

3. For a use case called "EstimateMembershipFee" in an event-driven system, identify the modules that might be needed to support the following business rules.

   a. A form is used to calculate estimated health club membership fees when a prospective member phones. The user should be able to launch a form from an Excel worksheet that will help calculate membership dues based on user input on the same form.

b. The user should be able to enter the following data using the form:

- Family size as an integer
- Age group (under 60, 60–69, >69) for primary member
- Whether or not the caller works for a company that subsidizes 10% of membership fee.
- Month to begin the membership (the first year's membership fee is prorated)

c. The form should have a button that validates data entered and calculate the annual membership fee when the button is clicked.
d. The form should have two output fields, one for annual membership fee and one for monthly fee.
e. The form should have a button that clears all data entry fields when the button is clicked.

4. From the modules identified in Problem 1, select 2 modules that are coupled (interdependent in some way) and design the internal instructions for each. Make realistic assumptions about the actual variables and constants required for the modules. Be sure to include instructions for how the two modules will communicate.

5. Design the internal instructions of a function that may be called from another module. The function should accept input for hire date and should return (output) whether or not an employee is vested in the company's retirement program. An employee is vested after 5 years of continuous employment. Design the function parameters (input and output). Outside of the function module, give an example of an instruction in pseudocode that could be used to call the function module.

CHAPTER ELEVEN

Modeling Decisions for Programming

1. Use Boolean expressions to make comparisons
2. Use the logical comparison operators for decision comparisons
3. Apply nested IF-THEN-ELSE decision structures to problem solutions
4. Understand how to structure AND logic and OR logic for nested decision structures in pseudocode and flowcharts
5. Understand the order of precedence when combining AND and OR comparisons
6. Recognize when to use straight-line, positive, and negative logic
7. Be able to reverse the logic of a give decision structure
8. Model the CASE structure in pseudocode and flowcharts

Introduction to Decision Logic

Chapters 7 and 8 introduced the basic decision control structure and the notation for modeling it in pseudocode and flowcharts. Decision structures are the most powerful programming structures because the only way a computer can choose between two sets of actions is through a Boolean response to a logical comparison. Every decision that is made in a computer program involves evaluating a Boolean expression. Possible comparisons between two values are:

Are the two values equal?
Is the first value greater than the second?
Is the first value less than the second?
Is the first value greater than or equal to the second?
Is the first value less than or equal to than the second?
Are the two values not equal?

A Boolean expression is a logical comparison that uses logical operators to compare two values or expressions that can only be evaluated to one of two Boolean responses, TRUE or FALSE. For VBA the logical operators are:

$=$ Equal to
$>$ Greater than
$<$ Less than
$>=$ Greater than or equal to
$<=$ Less than or equal to
$<>$ Not equal to

In addition to the specific VBA logical operators listed, there are additional operators commonly used in pseudocode. The combined symbols $!=$ mean "not equal to." The keyword NOT is used to reverse a condition, for example "orderAmt NOT $>$ 1000." In pseudocode it is acceptable to write out the logical expression (i.e., hours are at least 40) or to use an appropriate logical expression that employs a logical operator symbol (i.e., hours $>=$ 40).

The decision structure is the most difficult to program because decision logic can be arranged in many different ways. Compare two ways the same decision logic may be written. Both arrangements accomplish the same final result.

Decision structure 1:
```
IF userInput is numeric THEN
    Process data
ELSE
    Display error message
ENDIF
```

Decision structure 2:

    IF userInput is not numeric THEN
        Display error message
    ELSE
        Process data
    ENDIF

Most decisions in programming solutions can be structured into one of the basic IF-THEN-ELSE structures. Recall that the basic IF-THEN-ELSE structure has three parts.

1. *IF:* Begins with the IF keyword in pseudocode. The keyword is followed on the same line in pseudocode by the logical condition to test. The IF clause ends after the decision condition(s). The keyword THEN is entered at the end of the last line of the IF clause, immediately after the comparison expression. In flowchart notation, the IF condition is written on the diamond shape that represents the decision.
2. *THEN:* Begins with the THEN keyword in pseudocode which is entered on the end of the last line containing the IF clause (condition to test). The instructions to be processed if the decision condition evaluates to TRUE are written on the next lines which are indented one step inside the IF keyword. In flowchart notation, the THEN clause is represented by the instruction steps shown on the TRUE side of the decision diamond.
3. *ELSE:* (optional) Begins with the ELSE keyword in pseudocode and includes the instructions to process if the decision condition is evaluated to FALSE. The ELSE keyword is entered on a line by itself at the same level of indention as the IF keyword. The instructions for the FALSE value follow in the next lines which are indented one step inside the IF and ELSE keywords. The ELSE clause ends with the keyword ENDIF on a new line following the ELSE instructions. ENDIF is indented at the same level as the IF and ELSE keywords. In flowchart notation, the ELSE clause, if present, is represented by the instruction steps on the FALSE side of the decision diamond.

The general pseudocode syntax for the IF-THEN-ELSE structure:

    IF <some condition exists> THEN
        Actions to perform (may be a single instruction,
        a sequence or any other control structure(s)).
    ELSE (the "ELSE" keyword and actions that follow are optional)
        Actions to perform (may be a single instruction, a sequence,
        or any other control structure(s)).
    ENDIF

When the optional ELSE clause is used so that instructions are included for both alternatives, it is called a *dual-alternative* decision. The syntax above represents a dual-alternative decision. When the ELSE clause is omitted, the solution is called a *single-alternative* decision. The single-alternative decision is interpreted such that if the decision condition test evaluates to FALSE, the action to perform is to "do nothing." Other names for the single-alternative IF structure include *null FALSE branch* and *null ELSE*. The word "null" in this case means "absent."

Single-alternative decision pseudocode structure:

    IF <some condition exists> THEN
        Actions to perform (may be a single instruction, a sequence,
        or any other control structure(s)).
    ENDIF

Simple IF-THEN-ELSE Examples

Dual-Alternative Pseudocode Example

```
IF employee status is "part-time" THEN
    Add one to part-time count
ELSE
    Add one to full-time count
ENDIF
```

Dual-Alternative Decision Flowchart Example

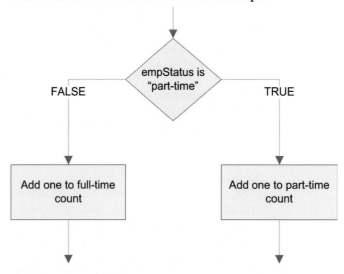

Figure 11-1: Dual-alternative decision structure.

Single-Alternative Decision Pseudocode Example

```
IF checkAmount greater than accountBalance THEN
    Print overdraftNotice
    Subtract overdraftFee from accountBalance
ENDIF
```

Single-Alternative Decision Flowchart Example

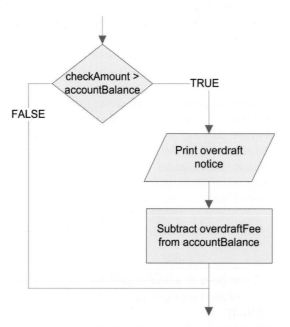

Figure 11-2: Single-alternative decision structure.

IF-THEN-ELSE Logic Applied Three Ways

So far the decision structure examples have involved simple decision logic. In each example, only one condition was tested and the instructions for the TRUE and FALSE branches of the structure have been relatively simple. Most decisions in programming are not this simple. Most often computer programs will require the testing of multiple conditions before an action is taken and some involve many complex instructions for each branch of the decision outcome.

The basic decision structure is easy to understand because it mirrors the way humans make decisions and perform actions. In spite of the simplicity of the basic decision structure, decision structures are the most difficult structures to implement because they can be written in so many different ways. For complex decisions, many beginning programmers often do not realize that complex decisions really boil down to answering multiple simple questions, each with a Boolean response. It is the arrangement of the multiple simple questions that achieve the results for complex decisions in programming.

There are three ways to arrange the IF structures when multiple logical comparisons are required for a solution. The arrangement that is chosen is usually based in part on the relationship of the individual decision structures to one another and in part on the program designer's or programmer's preference.

Structuring Decisions Using Straight-Through Logic

One way multiple IF structures may be arranged is to allow each independent IF structure to follow another in a sequence. Structures are *not* nested so all structures are processed because each decision structure is independent of the others. There is no ELSE clause in any of the decision structures. Each question is answered sequentially taking an action if the response is TRUE and taking no action if the response is FALSE. This way of processing multiple IF structures is the least efficient in that all instructions are processed, but in some cases it may be required when all questions are required for the solution.

Straight-Through Logic Example

If a program prompts a user to enter a zip code into a form text box, the data entered by the user in this solution must meet at least three requirements; the text box must not be blank, the data must be all numeric characters, the data must be exactly five characters in length. If we use straight-through logic to model the required decisions, it would require that at least one decision structure be processed for each criterion.

(Before these decision structures process, the value of validated = TRUE)

```
IF input is blank THEN
      validated = FALSE
ENDIF

IF input is not numeric THEN
      validated = FALSE
ENDIF

IF input length is not 5 THEN
      validated =FALSE
ENDIF

IF validated = TRUE THEN
      Process input
ENDIF
```

```
IF validated = FALSE THEN
      Display generic error message
      Return to input prompt
ENDIF
```

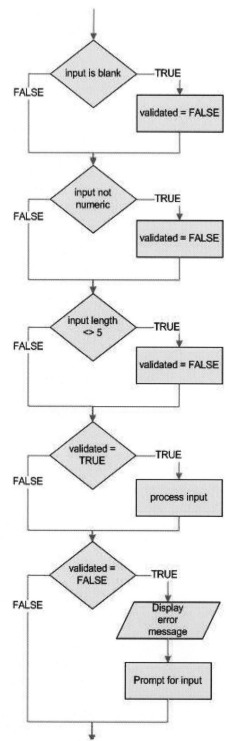

Figure 11-3: Flowchart showing straight-through processing of multiple decision structures.

Without ELSE clauses, the sequence of structures make it difficult to tailor the error message to the specific criterion violation. Also, if a criterion is violated, the remaining decisions process anyway unnecessarily. In order to display a specific message to the user, the decision structures will need modification and more decisions will be needed. In the following example, the data type of the variable "Validated" will need to change from Boolean to a string.

(Before these decision structures process, the value of Validated = "yes")

```
IF input is blank THEN
    validated = "blank"
ENDIF

IF input is not numeric THEN
    validated = "not numeric"
ENDIF

IF input length is not 5 THEN
    validated = "wrong length"
ENDIF

IF validated = "yes" THEN
    Process input
ENDIF

IF validated = "blank" THEN
    Display error message for blank
    Return to input prompt
ENDIF

IF validated = "not numeric" THEN
    Display error message for numeric
    Return to input prompt
ENDIF

IF validated = "wrong length" THEN
    Display error message for length
    Return to input prompt
ENDIF
```

This is a lot of logic to process one input item! Structuring the decision logic as nested decisions will be a more efficient use of processing resources. In the preceding example, if the text box was blank, there was no need to ask whether it was numeric or to ask about the length, but those decisions were processed anyway. In this case, if one data validation rule was violated, the user will need to re-enter the data item before further processing can occur. Consider rearranging the straight-through decision structures into nested decisions so that all instructions will not always need to execute.

Structuring Decisions Using Positive Logic

Decisions structured using positive logic are related in that only one of the multiple decisions is needed to evaluate to TRUE in order for processing to continue. Since they are related in this way, they are nested and include instructions for both the THEN and the ELSE clause for each IF structure. Each subsequent decision is nested in the ELSE clause of the previous decision. If the first decision result is TRUE, the THEN instructions are processed and no more questions are asked. If the first decision result is FALSE, the next question is asked. If the second question response is TRUE, the THEN instructions for that decision are processed. If the response to the second question is FALSE, the next question is asked and so on until either a TRUE response is obtained or there are no more questions to ask. If there is no TRUE response for any question, the final ELSE instructions are processed. This way of arranging multiple decision structures is very efficient in that not all instructions always need to execute. Once a

TRUE response is obtained and the associated instruction(s) processed, the nested structured is exited so no more decision structures are processed. Positive logic tends to be the easiest for most people to understand because it is the way most people think.

In the preceding example, if only one of the input criteria was violated, an error message should be displayed and the item re-entered by the user. Once one of the three criteria is violated, there is no need to ask the remaining validation questions. The straight-through logic can be revised to nest the decision structures such that once one decision test is true, no other decisions need to be processed.

```
IF input is blank THEN
      Display error message for blank
      Return to input prompt
ELSE
      IF input is not numeric THEN
            Display error message for numeric
            Return to input prompt
      ELSE
            IF input length is not 5 THEN
                  Display error message for length
                  Return to input prompt
            ELSE
                  Process input
            ENDIF
      ENDIF
ENDIF
```

Note that in decisions structured with positive logic, each ELSE clause comes immediately after its associated THEN clause. All the ENDIFs are isolated from the IF and THEN clauses and are all at the end of the nested structures.

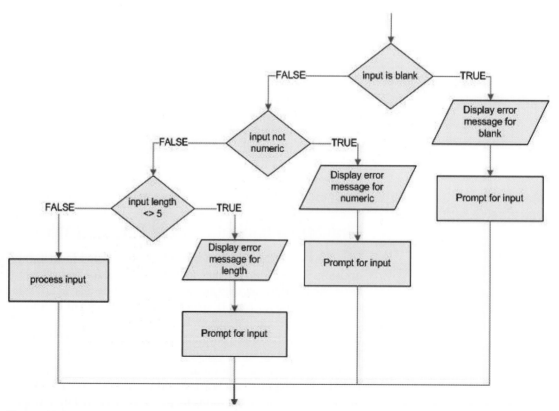

Figure 11-4: Flowchart showing positive logic.

Structuring Decisions Using Negative Logic

As you might imagine, the nesting arrangement of multiple IF structures using negative logic is the opposite of that for positive logic. With negative logic, the flow of processing will continue once one decision evaluates to FALSE. As long as decision questions evaluate to TRUE, another question will be asked. Once all questions have been asked and there is no FALSE result, the THEN instructions of the final decision structure will be processed and the nested decision structured exited.

```
IF input is not blank THEN
        IF input is numeric THEN
                IF input length is 5 THEN
                        Process input
                ELSE
                        Display error message for length
                        Return to input prompt
                ENDIF
        ELSE
                Display error message for numeric
                Return to input prompt
        ENDIF
ELSE
        Display error message for blank
        Return to input prompt
ENDIF
```

Note that in decisions structured with negative logic, the IF clauses are isolated and the ELSE and ENDIF clauses are together.

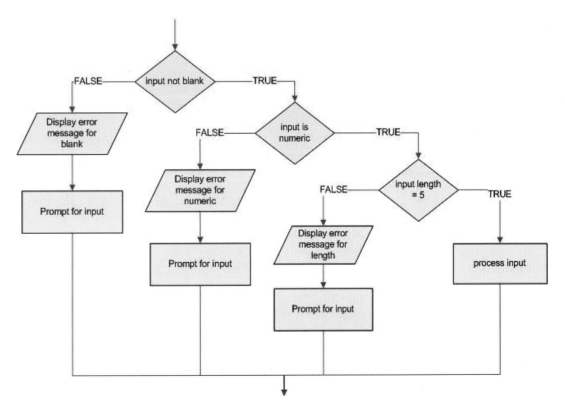

Figure 11-5: Flowchart showing negative logic.

Note that the flowchart showing negative logic is a reverse model of the flowchart showing the same processing in a positive logic arrangement.

Nested decisions may be structured using a combination of positive and negative logic, but they are much more difficult to structure, more difficult to follow and troubleshoot, and equally difficult to maintain or update. It is recommended that nested decision structures stick to either positive or negative logic for the entire nested structure. That way all the main line logic for the group of decisions is performed on either the FALSE branches of the decisions or all on the TRUE branches. Below is an example of the validation logic structured in a nested decision structure that uses positive logic for some decisions and negative logic for others. Note how difficult it is to follow the main line of processing through the nested structure.

```
IF input is blank THEN
        Display error message
        Return to input prompt
ELSE
        IF input is numeric THEN
                IF input length is 5 THEN
                        Process input
                ELSE
                        Display error message for length
                        Return to input prompt
                ENDIF
        ELSE
                Display error message for numeric
                Return to input prompt
        ENDIF
ENDIF
```

Deciding Which Logic to Use

The decision regarding which type of logic to use for a set of program decisions is based on factors that relate to the specific solution, such as:

- Which type would make the solution most readable?
- Which type would make the solution easiest to program and maintain?
- Which type would require the fewest tests when you don't know anything about the data?
- Which would require the fewest tests when you have information about the data?

If you have some knowledge of the data the program will be handling, you can choose a type of logic and structure that can handle the data most efficiently. Consider the following solution requirement. An application processes a large number of current subscriber records for a health club and for each member it updates the fee for basic health club membership. If the subscriber is 75 years of age or over (age is >75), a discount applies. If the subscriber is currently between age 65 and 75 (age >=65 and age <75), a lower discount applies. No discount is offered for those members who are less than 65 yeras of age. If you have knowledge about the data and know that more subscribers are less than age 65 than are over 75, you would want to place the "age <65" decision first in the nested decision structures such that if the subscriber is less than 65, the other age questions are not asked. If you know that there are more subscribers over 75 than are under 65, then it is best to ask the "age >=75" question first.

In the previous example, either positive or negative logic can accomplish the same final result. If positive logic is used, the most expected response will be a TRUE response to the first question. After that first question is evaluated to TRUE, the one line of instruction for the THEN clause of that IF structure will be processed and no other decision structures in the group will be processed.

```
IF age < 65 THEN
    DiscountRate = 0
ELSE
    IF age < 75 THEN
        DiscountRate = LOWER
    ELSE
        DiscountRate = HGHER
    ENDIF
ENDIF
```

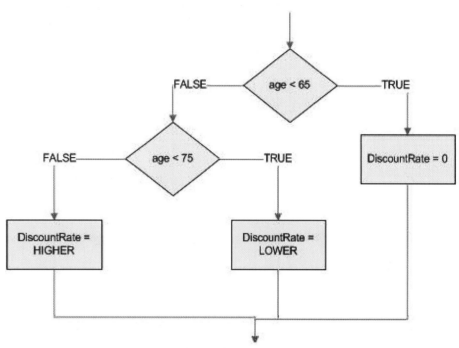

Figure 11-6: Positive logic flow-chart.

To apply negative logic to accomplish the same result, some changes are required to the nested decision structure. Recall that negative logic processes the main line of logic on the FALSE branch of the IF structure. To switch nested structures from one type of logic to another (positive to negative or *vice vesa*), here are some conversion tips to follow as you reverse the logic.

- Change all < to >=.
- Change all <= to >.
- Change all > to <=.
- Change all >= to <.
- Change all = to <>.
- Change all <> to =.
- Interchange all of the THEN sets of instructions with the ELSE sets of instructions.

The previous example may be switched to negative using the following arrangement of the nested decision structures.

```
IF age >=65 THEN
    IF age >=75 THEN
        DiscountRate = HIGHER
    ELSE
        DiscountRate = LOWER
    ENDIF
ELSE
    DiscountRate = 0
ENDIF
```

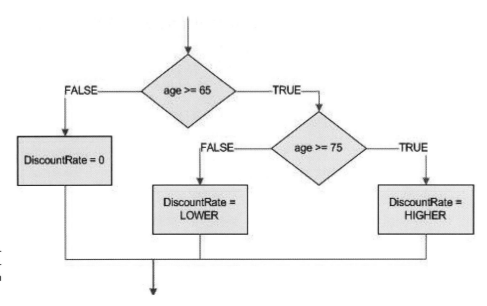

Figure 11-7: Positive logic flow-chart. Note that the flowchart decision structures are reversed from the model in Figure 11-6.

In many cases where efficiency is not a significant issue, the choice between using positive or negative logic is a matter of programmer expertise and habit. Programmers and program designers tend to prefer one arrangement of logic to another; therefore, they gain experience and expertise in structuring one type over another

Complex Decision Logic

AND Logic

Sometimes it takes more than one decision to determine if an action should be taken. Consider a program that determines acceptance of applicants to a graduate program of study in business. The values for undergraduate GPA and GMAT score must both be tested before admission can be offered. For the applicant to be accepted the undergraduate GPA must be over 3.5 AND the GMAT score must be over 600. When two or more conditions must be tested in order to determine if some action is performed, nested decisions are used. Multiple decisions can be nested such that the actions performed for one decision alternative can actually be another decision structure. Decisions can be nested in the THEN clause (TRUE branch of the flowchart) or the ELSE clause (FALSE branch of the flowchart) of the decision structure. When both conditions must be TRUE for some action to be performed, the second decision is nested in the THEN clause of the first decision. If in our example only one of the two conditions need to be TRUE for acceptance, if the GPA is over 3.5 OR the GMAT is over 600, the second decision is nested in the ELSE clause of the first decision. To summarize, *conditions joined with AND logic are modeled with decisions nested in the THEN clause. Conditions joined with OR logic are modeled with decisions nested in the ELSE clause.*

In the following example, **both** conditions (GPA > 3.5 **AND** GMAT > 600) must be evaluated to TRUE in order to print the acceptance letter. If the first condition is evaluated to FALSE, the inner decision structure will never execute but the ELSE clause of the outer decision will execute. If the first condition evaluates to TRUE, the second condition is tested. If the second test evaluates to FALSE, the ELSE clause of the inner decision will execute and the ELSE clause of the outer decision will never execute. If both conditions evaluate to TRUE, neither of the ELSE clauses will execute.

Decision Structure with AND Logic

```
IF GPA > 3.5 THEN
        IF GMAT > 600 THEN
                Print acceptance letter
        ELSE
                Print denial letter
        ENDIF
ELSE
        Print denial letter
ENDIF
```

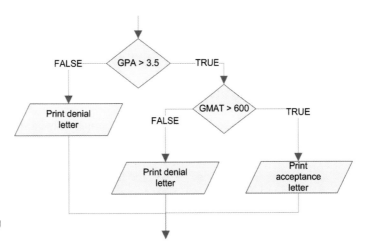

Figure 11-8: Flowchart showing decisions structured for AND logic.

Since most modern computer languages support combining multiple conditions to test in one IF clause, the decisions using AND logic may be structured in pseudocode by using the AND keyword to join conditions.

```
IF GPA > 3.5 AND GMAT > 600 THEN
        Print acceptance letter
    ELSE
        Print denial letter
    ENDIF
```

Although not entirely prohibited, it is less common to combine two decisions conditions in flowcharts since they represent more closely how the computer processes the solution instructions. A flowchart representing the combined condition in the example above would more often be structured without using condition combinations (see Figure 11-8). If the designer chooses to combine conditions into one decision in a flowchart, it might be represented in the following notation.

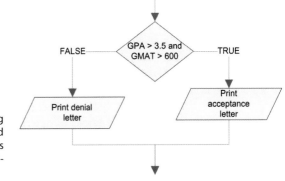

Figure 11-9: Flowchart showing both conditions on one diamond for AND logic. In flowcharts, it is more common to show each decision separately (see Figure 11-8).

OR Logic

What if the rules are changed in the example so that the acceptance letter will print if **either** condition (GPA > 3.5 **OR** GMAT > 600) is TRUE. Both conditions must be FALSE for the denial letter to print. Note that in this example if the first condition is TRUE, the second condition is not tested.

Decision Structure with OR Logic

```
IF GPA is greater than 3.5 THEN
        Print acceptance letter
    ELSE
        IF GMAT is greater than 600 THEN
            Print acceptance letter
        ELSE
            Print denial letter
        ENDIF
    ENDIF
```

Alternately, pseudocode for this example may be structured as:

```
IF GPA > 3.5 OR GMAT > 600 THEN
    Print acceptance letter
ELSE
    Print denial letter
ENDIF
```

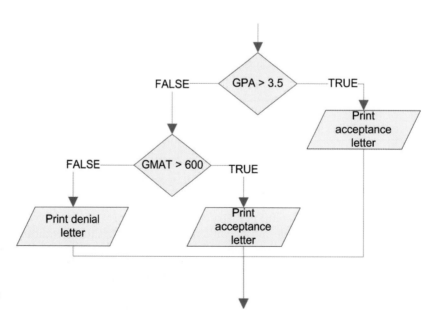

Figure 11-10: Flowchart decisions structured for OR logic.

Combining AND and OR Logic

Some decisions may involve conditions such that if one condition is true some action is taken, or if the condition is false, then two other conditions collectively must be true before an action is taken. Consider a system that processes thousands of employee records to determine which employees are eligible to begin receiving company retirement benefits. Two factors are evaluated, the employee's age and his number of years service to the employer. One of the following pairs of criteria must be met in order for the employee to be eligible to retire.

Age > 70 and at least 5 years of service
OR
Age > 65 and at least 10 years of service
OR
Age > 55 and at least 20 years of service
OR
Age > 50 and at least 25 years of service

The combination AND/OR logic can be modeled as a nested set of decision structures in pseudocode but most programming languages are able to process multiple conditions joined by multiple ANDs and ORs in the same decision structure. When using AND and OR together, each programming language gives precedence to either AND or OR. Most programming languages give precedence to the conditions joined by AND. That means the pairs of conditions joined by AND are evaluated first from left to right then the resulting pairs of conditions joined by OR are evaluated left to right. To make certain that the order of precedence is clearly understood, it is recommended that parentheses be used in pseudocode. Parentheses will help avoid mistakes in the interpretation of the order in which the conditions should be evaluated. Pseudocode that uses the keywords AND and OR might be structured like the following example. Parentheses are used for added clarity.

```
IF (age > 70 AND service >5) OR
    (age > 65 AND service > 10) OR
    (age > 55 AND service > 20) OR
    (age > 50 AND service > 25) THEN
    eligible = TRUE
ELSE
    eligible = FALSE
ENDIF
```

If you wish to override the programming language default order in which conditions joined with AND and OR logic are processed, change the placement of the parentheses to control the order of operations.

Using Decision Structures for Value or Range Checks

A common use of decision structures in programming is to locate the correct value range in which a given value falls. This is commonly called a *range check* or *range lookup* or, for a single value match, a *value check* or *lookup*. A range check may be performed using a wide variety of decision structure arrangements. In some cases, lookups can be performed by using straight-through decision sequences, but more often nested decisions are more efficient since most range checks (all except the highest and lowest ranges) involve checking both the upper and lower bounds of the range in some way. Use the following rules for applying an order discount and experiment with different ways the range lookup may be performed using decision structures.

Discount rate schedule:

- For order amounts less than $1000, no discount is given (discount level 0)
- For order amounts of $1000 or more and less than $3000, 5% discount is given (discount level 1)
- For order amounts of $3000 or more and less than $5000, 10% discount is given (discount level 2)
- For order amounts of $5000 or more and less than $10,000, 15% discount is given (discount level 3)
- For order amounts of $10,000 or more, 20% discount is given (discount level 4)

Using Straight-Through Logic for Range Checks

Straight-through logic will work for this solution, but it is terribly inefficient in that many processes must be carried out in order to achieve the correct final result. And as with all types of range checks, the order of the comparisons is very important. Begin with either the lowest range or the highest range and check each range in order (low to high or high to low). In this pseudocode example below, if the order amount is >$10,000, the DiscountRate variable will have to be reassigned four times! Remember that every IF structure in this group will be processed regardless of the result of another.

```
IF orderAmt <1000 THEN
    DiscountRate = LEVEL0
ENDIF

IF orderAmt >=1000 THEN
    DiscountRate = LEVEL1
ENDIF

IF orderAmt >=3000 THEN
    DiscountRate = LEVEL2
ENDIF

IF orderAmt >=5000 THEN
    DiscountRate = LEVEL3
ENDIF

IF orderAmt >=10000 THEN
    DiscountRate = LEVEL4
ENDIF
```

Using Positive Logic for Range Check

Positive logic may be used for this range lookup but for maximum efficiency the nature of the data must be known. If you know that most orders are less than $1000 or less than $3000, then most orders will be eliminated with the first or second comparison and the other two comparisons will never be performed. For orders that are over $10,000, nested positive logic is no more efficient that using straight-through logic. When it is known that more orders will be over $5000 or over $10,000 than in the lower ranges, positive logic may be used more efficiently by beginning with the highest range (>10000).

```
IF orderAmt <1000 THEN
    DiscountRate = LEVEL0
ELSE
    IF orderAmt <3000 THEN
        DiscountRate = LEVEL1
    ELSE
        IF orderAmt <5000 THEN
            DiscountRate = LEVEL2
        ELSE
            IF orderAmt <10000 THEN
                DiscountRate = LEVEL3
            ELSE
                DiscountRate = LEVEL4
            ENDIF
        ENDIF
    ENDIF
ENDIF
```

As each range maximum is checked, it eliminates that range for the next comparison. For example, in the first decision structure, order amounts less than 1000 are processed, so when the next range check is executed, it will only identify values less than 3000 and those greater than or equal to 1000 which is the maximum of the first range check decision.

Using Negative Logic for Range Check

There is little difference if any between the efficiency of performing range check using negative logic over using positive logic. It is still best to begin at the end of the range (high or low) where more order amounts are likely to occur. Whether you begin the range check on the high end or the low end is not determined by the type of logic used (positive or negative) but by which range(s) will prevent more decisions from being processed.

```
IF orderAmt <10000 THEN
    IF orderAmt <5000 THEN
        IF orderAmt <3000 THEN
            IF orderAmt <1000 THEN
                DiscountRate = LEVEL0
            ELSE
                DiscountRate = LEVEL1
            ENDIF
        ELSE
            DiscountRate = LEVEL2
        ENDIF
    ELSE
        DiscountRate = LEVEL3
    ENDIF
ELSE
    DiscountRate = LEVEL4
ENDIF
```

A Special Case of ELSE-IF Logic

Decisions nested using positive logic create what can be called an ELSE-IF pattern because the IF clause of the next decision is nested in the ELSE clause of the previous decision. The pattern is so common, most programming languages have a special keyword that combines ELSE with IF to eliminate the extra line of code for the ELSE keyword or they permit the two words ELSE IF to be written on the same line. Most languages use ELSEIF or ELSIF as the combination keyword. Compare the following ELSE-IF (positive logic) pattern with the positive logic range check example repeated below. In the following solution rules, only one of the three conditions must exist before an acceptance letter will be printed. A college applicant must have either a strong GPA (>3.5), a high class standing (top 10%), or have previously earned an undergraduate degree.

```
IF GPA > 3.5 THEN
    Print acceptance letter that mentions GPA
ELSE
    IF classStanding < 10% THEN
        Print acceptance letter that mentions class standing
    ELSE
        IF previousDegree = TRUE THEN
            Print acceptance letter that mentions degree
        ELSE
            Print denial letter
        ENDIF
    ENDIF
ENDIF
```

Range Lookup Example Repeated

```
IF orderAmt <1000 THEN
    DiscountRate = LEVEL0
ELSE
    IF orderAmt <3000 THEN
        DiscountRate = LEVEL1
    ELSE
        IF orderAmt <5000 THEN
            DiscountRate = LEVEL2
        ELSE
            IF orderAmt <10000 THEN
                DiscountRate = LEVEL3
            ELSE
                DiscountRate = LEVEL4
            ENDIF
        ENDIF
    ENDIF
ENDIF
```

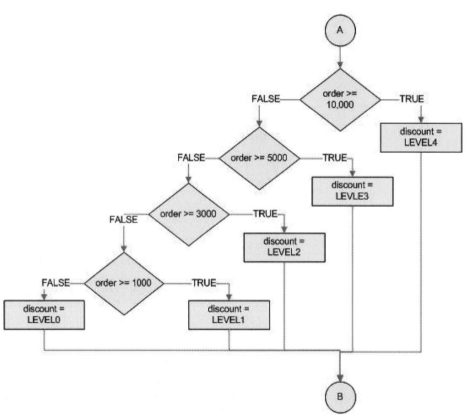

Figure 11-11: ELSE-IF pattern for a range check.

Examine the two previous examples closely. In the college admission example, a *different condition is tested in each of the decision structures.* In the range check example, *the same condition is tested (the order amount) against different values or ranges.* This differentiation is very important! When each decision structure in the ELSE-IF pattern tests the same variable or expression, but tests it against different values, a more efficient control structure exists. The CASE structure is a special type of decision structure to handle solutions that test one variable or expression against multiple mutually exclusive values.

CASE Structures

The CASE structure is another type of decision structure that is an extension of the IF-THEN-ELSE structure. The CASE structure represents a decision that has multiple alternatives depending on the value of a single expression. The multiple alternatives are mutually exclusive. It is a substitute for long nested IF-THEN-ELSE structures when there are multiple conditions to test and only one can be TRUE. Because the CASE structure supports selecting one of several alternatives, it is often called a *selection* structure.

The general pseudocode syntax for the CASE structures:

CASE <value to test>
value1: Actions to perform
value2: Actions to perform
value3: Actions to perform
value4: Actions to perform
ELSE: Actions to perform if the *value to test* does not match any of the other values
ENDCASE

CASE Pseudocode Example

(*The values 1, 2, 3 and 4 represent possible values for taxcode.*)

CASE taxcode
1: taxrate = .03
2: taxrate = .04
3: taxrate = .05
4: taxrate = .06
ELSE: taxrate = .07
ENDCASE

In the example above, the interpretation is as follows:

In the case that taxcode is 1, the taxrate is .03.
In the case that taxcode is 2, the taxrate is .04.
In the case that taxcode is 3, the taxrate is .05.
In the case that taxcode is 4, the taxrate is .06.
In the cast that taxcode is not 1, 2, 3, OR 4, the taxrate is .07.

Note that the choices for taxcode are mutually exclusive. Only one case can be selected. Once one case matches the *value to test,* the flow of logic goes to the ENDCASE then moves to the next instruction following the CASE structure. If no values for any case match taxcode, the case ELSE will execute. The case ELSE is optional, but is a very good idea to include to avoid a runtime error in the event that no matching value is found in the other "cases."

CASE Structure Flowchart Example

In the following CASE structure, taxcode is the *value to test*. The *value to test* is always the label for the decision symbol (the diamond). The numbers outside the rectangles are the values of taxcode that are tested, the "cases." The rectangles represent the operation that takes place for each case of the value of taxcode. Note that the operations are not connected together directly. The cases are mutually exclusive. Only one case will be executed. Once a case value is matched to the taxcode value, that case instruction set is executed and the others are ignored. If no values (1, 2, 3, 4) match the value of taxcode, the ELSE case executes. Once one of the case processes has executed, the logic flow continues to the next instruction following the end of the case structure.

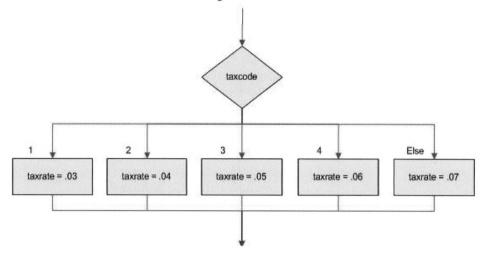

Figure 11-12: Flowchart of CASE structure for tax code lookup.

Now apply the CASE structure to the range check example for the order discount problem. You will see that the solution using the CASE structure in both pseudocode and flowchart notation is much more concise and easier to follow.

```
CASE orderAmt
  <1000: discountRate = LEVEL0
  <3000: discountRate = LEVEL1
  <5000: discountRate = LEVEL2
  <10000: discountRate = LEVEL3
  ELSE: discountRate = LEVEL4
ENDCASE
```

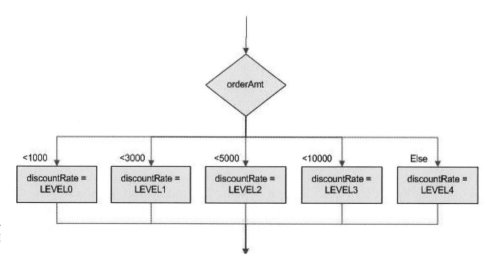

Figure 11-13: Flowchart of discount solution structured as a CASE structure.

In a CASE structure the ranges must be tested from high to low or from low to high. If the ranges are not tested in numeric order, the CASE structure will not always return the correct result. The same considerations applied to the nested decision structures apply to the structuring of a CASE structure with regard to which range to check first. If more tested values are likely to fall in the upper ranges, begin checking at the highest range. If more tested values are likely to fall into the lower ranges, begin checking at the lowest range. The idea is to eliminate as many instructions from executing as possible. Remember that once the CASE structure's test value matches a range or single value, the remainder of the CASE structure is skipped.

Review Questions

1. Explain the three parts of the decision structure in pseudocode and the purpose of each part.

2. What part of the IF-THEN-ELSE structure is optional? What does it mean when that part is omitted?

3. What does Boolean mean?

4. What is the difference between *dual-alternative* decision structures and *single-alternative* decision structures?

5. Describe a disadvantage to using the *straight-through* logic for structuring a group of decisions.

6. Name two advantages of using *positive logic* over *straight-through logic* to structure a set of decisions.

7. Briefly state the difference between *positive logic* and *negative logic* for structuring a group of decisions.

_____

_____

_____

8. What is taken into consideration for determining whether to use *positive logic* or *negative logic* for a group of decision structures?

_____

_____

_____

9. List six logical operators and what each represents.

_____

_____

_____

10. How can you make certain that decisions joined by AND or OR are processed in the correct order?

_____

_____

_____

11. How many expressions joined by OR must evaluate to TRUE in order for the TRUE branch of the decision structure to execute?

_____

_____

_____

12. How many expressions joined by AND must evaluate to TRUE in order for the TRUE branch of the decision structure to execute?

_____

_____

_____

13. When performing range checks with nested decisions or CASE statements, in what order should the ranges be compared to the value to test?

_____

_____

_____

14. When nesting decision structures, in which clause is the decision structure nested when both the decision conditions must be met (TRUE) in order for some action to be performed?

_____

_____

_____

15. When nesting decision structures, in which clause is the decision structure nested when only one decision condition must be met (TRUE) in order for some action to be performed?

_____

_____

_____

16. How does a CASE structure differ from a simple decision structure?

_____

_____

_____

Practice Problems

1. A plant nursery's customers have specific criteria that must be met for plants they wish to grow in their yards. Create an algorithm with pseudocode and flowchart that allows a customer to select a plant name from a list then reads the conditions from a database for that plant with regard to soil pH, winter temperature tolerance, light condition, and deer resistance (those that deer will not eat). The system must compare the selected plant to the following set of values selected by the customer as her criteria for her plants.

    - pH must be 6.5 (0.5 more or less)
    - Winter temperature tolerance must be −20 degrees Fahrenheit or less.
    - Light condition must be full sun.
    - Plants must be deer resistant.

    The system should return "Yes" if the selected plant matches the customer's criteria and "No" if it does not. (The system is not required to indicate which criteria the plant does not meet.)

2. Create **5 different algorithms** with pseudocode and flowchart that perform the following tasks. Each algorithm should produce the same result. Do not use straight-through logic for one of the algorithms.

    a. Prompts a user to enter a student's identification number and final grade average as a percent
    b. Matches the percent value to a range of values for a final letter grade
    c. Displays the student's identification number and final letter grade.

    The rules for assigning a letter grade are:

    - Averages of 90% and above receive an A.
    - Averages of 80% or above and less than 90% receive a B.
    - Averages of 70% or above and less than 80% receive a C.
    - Averages of 60% or above and less than 70% receive a D.
    - Averages less than 60% receive an F.

3. Create an algorithm with pseudocode and flowchart that specifies the solution steps for a complete system that accepts an order subtotal and a zip code then calculates sales tax based on the sales tax rate for the given zip code. After the sales tax is computed, the system calculates and displays the order total on the computer monitor. (Use a CASE structure to assign tax rates based on zip codes.)

    For zip code 27409 the sales tax rate is 6.5%.
    For zip code 24060 the sales tax rate is 5.0%.
    For zip code 24343 the sales tax rate is 4.5%.
    For zip code 28149 the sales tax rate is 5.5%.

4. In return for handling the legal matters for settling estates, a legal practice charges according to the following schedule:

    - 10% of the first $500,000 of the estate value
    - 8% of the next $700,000 of the estate value
    - 5% of the remaining estate value

    Create an algorithm with pseudocode and flowchart that specifies the solution steps for a complete system that accepts a value amount for an estate amount and returns a value for the legal fee.

5. Create an algorithm with pseudocode and flowchart that specifies the solution steps for a complete system that accepts a value for taxable income and returns the state income tax owed according to the following tax schedule.

    - 2% of the first $3000 of taxable income
    - 3% on income over $3000 but not over $5000
    - 5% on income over $5000 but not over $17,000
    - 5.75% on income over $17,000

CHAPTER TWELVE
Loop Design and Modeling

1. Recognize the advantages of using loops in programming
2. Recognize the logical parts of a loop structure
3. Use WHILE, UNTIL, and FOR loop structures to model repetitive instructions
4. Distinguish between WHILE loops and UNTIL loops
5. Recognize the advantages of using a FOR loop
6. Distinguish between count controlled loops and event controlled loops
7. Use accumulator and counter variables in loop structures
8. Create pseudocode and flowchart algorithms using nested loop structures
9. Match loop types with solution requirements

Advantages of Using Loops in Programming

Most problems in business involve doing the same task repeatedly for different sets of data. Loops provide computers with an amazing power to repeat a set of operations hundreds, thousands, or millions of times. Another name for the loop structure is *repetition structure* or *iterative structure*. Loops can process many sets of employee data, update value of all inventory items, or accumulate a running total. Loop instructions need only be written once. They can be executed an unlimited number of times, based on the particular solution. Programmers can write loops that repeat an operation until some target is reached, or while some condition is true or until some condition becomes true. Think about the tasks that are required in a typical payroll processing program. These are some of the tasks that may need to be performed for each employee.

1. Calculate regular pay for salaried employees.
2. Calculate regular pay for hourly employees.
3. Calculate overtime pay for hourly employees.
4. Calculate commission for sales employees.
5. Calculate vacation pay earned.
6. Calculate vacation pay used.
7. Calculate vacation time available.
8. Calculate total gross pay.
9. Calculate current federal income taxes to withhold.
10. Calculate current state income taxes to withhold.
11. Current local payroll taxes to withhold.
12. Calculate Social Security to withhold.
13. Calculate Medicare premium to withhold.
14. Calculate current payroll deductions for insurance and other benefits.
15. Calculate union dues to withhold.
16. Calculate charitable contributions to withhold.
17. Calculate year-to-date federal taxes withheld.
18. Calculate year-to-date state taxes withheld.
19. Calculate year-to-date local taxes withheld.
20. Calculate year-to-date benefit deductions.
21. Calculate net pay.
22. Print pay voucher.
23. Transfer pay funds to employee bank account.

You get the idea. And the list could be even longer. As you can imagine, payroll programs can be quite complex. Once the complex instructions are written, they may be executed an unlimited number of times.

The Anatomy of a Loop

There are five logical components of every loop. Some components are actually instructions that occur outside the loop, either preceding the loop or following it, but are related to the logical structure of the loop.

1. Loop initialization
2. Loop condition
3. Loop advancement
4. Loop body
5. Loop cleanup

Loop Initialization

Most loops require some preparation before actually starting the loop. Some input may be required, such as getting a record set or opening a file. By the very nature of loops, we usually need to locate the data and get it ready for loop processing. In Excel we usually need to locate the list range on a worksheet when the loop processes rows of a list. For loops that use a counter, the counter must be declared and in most cases initialized before the loop begins.

Loop Condition

Most loops evaluate a Boolean comparison to determine whether or not the loop should repeat. This comparison expression is commonly called the *loop condition* or *loop test*. Loop conditions may be tested at or near the beginning of the loop, or at or near the end of the loop structure. Loop conditions tested at the beginning of the loop are called *leading decisions* and those tested at the end of the loop are sometimes called *trailing decisions*. Other names given to leading and trailing loop decisions are *pretests* and *posttests*, respectively. When a leading decision (or pretest) loop is used, the test determines whether or not the loop is *entered*, so if the loop condition is not met, the loop may never execute. When using a trailing decision (posttest) loop, the loop condition determines whether or not the loop is *exited*. A trailing decision loop will always execute at least once.

The loop condition may be a comparison of a variable counter to an integer such as "count < 10" or may compare a loop control variable to a value that is determined at runtime, such as "transactionNumber < numberOfTransactions." The comparison may use any of the logical operators including AND, OR, and NOT and may use positive or negative logic.

Loop Advancement

In order for the loop to move to the next iteration, something inside the loop body must advance the loop to the next record, row, data item, or count. It may be a process instruction such as incrementing or decrementing a counter variable. It may be an input instruction such as "Get next record." Once a loop is entered, the loop must be advanced so that eventually it will meet the exit condition.

Body of the Loop

The body of the loop is the set of instructions that will repeat. The body of the loop is bounded on one end by the loop condition test and on the other by the keyword that either begins or ends the loop. Most of the instructions in the loop are there to carry out the intended purpose of the loop, the business processing. In addition to the business instructions, the loop also includes the loop advancement instruction.

Loop Cleanup

After the loop is exited, there may be instructions to process in order to get the program back in order after the loop processing. For example, if a file has been opened, it should be closed. There may be a counter or Boolean variable that should be reset to its pre-loop value. Further processing may be determined by whether or not the loop executed, so an instruction may be needed to supply that information to the next part of the program. Anything at all that is needed to follow up loop processing is included in the loop cleanup. In some cases, there may be nothing further required so loop cleanup may not be necessary. All loop cleanup instructions are following the end of the loop.

Types of Loop Structures

WHILE Loops

WHILE loops include a loop condition to test to see whether or not the loop should be entered or exited. *The WHILE loop will continue to repeat as long as the loop condition evaluates to TRUE.* Most WHILE loops test the loop condition at the beginning of the loop, but a WHILE condition may also be tested at the end of the loop. The logic of a WHILE loop can be described as "WHILE some condition exists (is TRUE), perform some actions." In the first loop example presented in Chapter 8 (repeated below), there is a leading decision that compares transactionNumber to numberOfTransactions. WHILE transactionNumber is less than numberOfTransactions, the loop will be entered and the entire body of the loop will execute. This WHILE loop uses a leading loop decision.

```
WHILE transactionNumber < numberOfTransactions
    Read transaction
    Subtract transactionAmount from accountBalance
    Increment transactionNumber
ENDWHILE
```

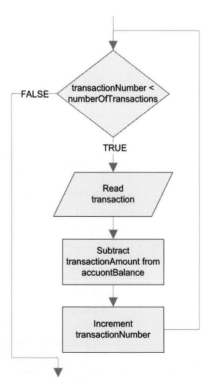

Figure 12-1: A WHILE loop that uses a leading decision to determine whether or not the loop should be entered.

A WHILE loop may also be structured with a trailing decision. The TRUE value of the decision test still indicates that the loop will repeat and a FALSE value indicates the loop will be exited. The trailing decision WHILE loop differs from the leading decision WHILE loop in that it tests the condition at the end of the loop so the loop will always execute at least once. The type of WHILE loop that uses the trailing decision is called a DO-WHILE loop. The logic of the DO-WHILE loop can be described as "Do these actions WHILE some condition exists (is TRUE). It begins with the keyword DO and ends with the keyword WHILE followed by the loop condition.

```
DO
    Read transaction
    Subtract transactionAmount from accountBalance
    Increment transactionNumber
WHILE transactionNumber < numberOfTransactions
```

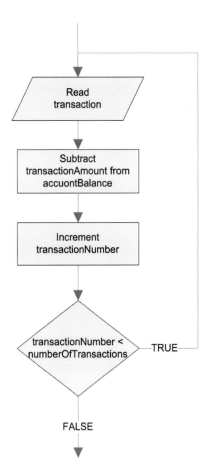

Figure 12-2: A WHILE loop that uses a trailing decision to determine whether or not the loop should be exited.

UNTIL Loop

The UNTIL loop continues to repeat a set of instructions as long as the loop condition is FALSE. Once the loop condition becomes TRUE, the loop terminates. The UNTIL loop typically uses a trailing decision, but like the WHILE loop, the UNTIL loop condition may be leading or trailing. The logic of a trailing decision UNTIL loop can be described as "Perform some actions UNTIL some condition exists (becomes

TRUE)." This type of UNTIL loop is commonly called a DO-UNTIL loop. The logic of a leading decision UNTIL loop can be described as "UNTIL some conditions exists (becomes TRUE), perform some actions". This loop is usually just called an UNTIL loop. The keyword DO signals the beginning of the loop. For a leading condition loop the keyword, "UNTIL" and the loop condition is entered immediately after the DO keyword on the same line. When a leading decision is used, the keyword LOOP is used to indicate the end of the loop. When a trailing decision is used, the opening keyword is simply DO and the keyword UNTIL followed by the loop exit condition marks the end of the loop.

The previous WHILE loop examples are revised to UNTIL loops. Note that when the loop condition is changed to exit on TRUE for the UNTIL loop (rather than exit on FALSE with the WHILE loop), the logic of the loop condition is reversed. The loop exit condition will become "transactionNumber = numberOfTransactions". So the logic of the UNTIL loop is to execute the loop body UNTIL "transactionNumber = numberOfTransactions." When the transactionNumber reaches a value equal to the numberOfTransactions, the loop will terminate.

```
DO
    Read transaction
    Subtract transactionAmount from accountBalance
    Increment transactionNumber
UNTIL transactionNumber = numberOfTransactions
```

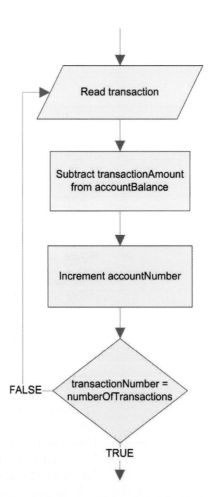

Figure 12-3: An UNTIL loop that uses a trailing loop decision to see whether or not the loop should be exited.

```
DO UNTIL transactionNumber = numberOfTransactions
    Read transaction
    Subtract transactionAmount from accountBalance
    Increment transactionNumber
LOOP
```

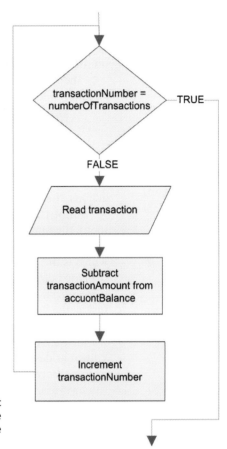

Figure 12-4: An UNTIL loop that uses a leading loop decision to see whether or not the loop should be entered.

In the previous examples the two loops, WHILE and UNTIL, carry out the same instructions the same number of times. So why have two different loop structures that do the same thing? The two types of loop provide several options for matching loop structures with business requirements. Loop conditions may be tested at the beginning or the end of the loop, whichever is more suitable for the type of data processed. When you know the loop needs to iterate at least once, use a trailing loop condition. When the loop may not need to execute at all, use a leading loop condition. The keywords WHILE and UNTIL offer the option of entering or exiting the loop on a value of TRUE or FALSE which makes the loop more flexible for the types of processing needed.

Ways to Control Loop Execution

There are two main ways to control the number of times a loop iterates. The loop may be controlled by a *loop control variable* (also called a counter) that represents the number or iterations, or it may be controlled by a program event.

Count Controlled Loops

Count controlled loops are used when the number of iterations is either known at design time or can be determined by the program before the loop begins. Another name for a count controlled loop is a *definite* loop. A *definite* loop is one whose number of repetitions is known before the loop begins. A variable called a *loop control variable* is initialized outside the loop and altered in some way inside the loop body until it reaches a value that causes the loop to terminate. Count controlled loop may use leading or trailing loop decisions. There are three actions always associated with counter-controlled loops.

1. The loop control variable is declared and initialized outside the loop.
2. The loop control value is tested inside the loop as a condition for repeating the loop body.
   a. May be tested at or near the beginning of loop.
   b. May be tested at or near the end of loop.
3. The value of the loop control variable is altered inside the loop body.

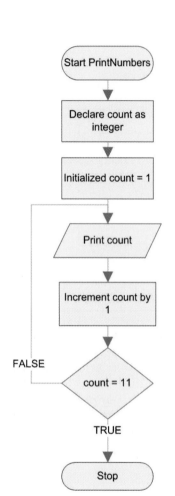

Figure 12-5: Flowchart for an UNTIL count controlled loop that repeats a fixed number of times.

Both the testing and altering of the loop control variable is critical. Without those actions, the loop would never terminate.

All of the loop examples presented so far are count controlled loops. For those loops, the number of iterations is not known at the time the program is designed and written, but is known before the loop begins. The value of numberOfTransactions, which is the value that terminates the loop, is determined by some process outside of the loop before the loop begins. The loop control variable is "transactionNumber" and is initialized to one before the loop begins. The loop control variable is incremented inside the loop body. Once the loop control variable reaches its terminal value (numberOfTransactions), the loop terminates.

In the following two examples, the number of times the loop will repeat is known at design time. The number of times to repeat is indicated by the difference in value between the initial value of the loop control variable (1) and its terminal value (<11).

UNTIL Count Controlled Loop Example

```
BEGIN PrintNumbers
Declare count as integer
count = 1
    DO
        Print count
        Increment count by 1
    UNTIL count = 11
END
```

WHILE Count Controlled Loop Example

```
BEGIN PrintNumbers
Declare count as integer
count = 1
    WHILE count < 11
        Print count
        Increment count by 1
    ENDWHILE
END
```

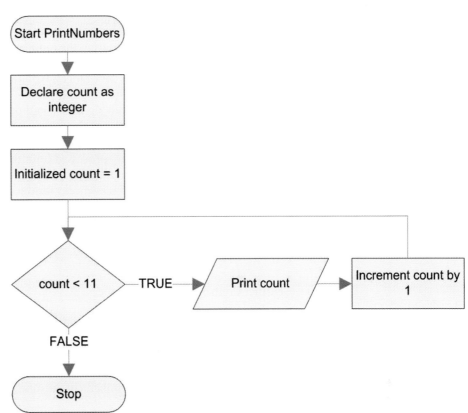

Figure 12-6: Flowchart for a WHILE count controlled loop that repeats a fixed number of times.

When using loop control variables to control the number of loop iterations, the typical logic is to initialize the loop control variable to zero or one and increment it by one during the loop body execution. The loop control variable may actually be initialized to any value, including negative values. The loop control variable value may be changed in the loop body by incrementing by any number or decrementing by any number. The previous UNTIL loop pseudocode has been altered so that the loop control variable is initialized to the number of iterations desired and its value is decremented in the loop body to the value that terminates the loop.

```
BEGIN PrintNumbers
    Declare count as integer
    count = 10
    DO
        Print count
        Decrement count by 1
    UNTIL count = 0
END
```

Event Controlled Loops

Event-controlled loops repeat until some condition inside the loop body changes that causes the loop to stop repeating. Since the number of loop iterations cannot be known before the program runs, event controlled loops are also called *indefinite* loops. *Indefinite* loops are any whose number of iterations is not known before the loop begins. There are three types of event controlled loops; *sentinel controlled*, *end-of-file controlled*, and *flag controlled*.

Sentinel Controlled Loops

Sentinel controlled loops keep repeating the loop body until a *sentinel* value is encountered or entered that stops the loop's repetitions. A sentinel value is a chosen value that is not a legitimate value in the data range for the tested values. For example, a bank batch processing system may enter a "dummy" check number of −1 at the end of each business day for every account to signal the end of checks and deposits for that day. The sentinel value −1 is not a valid check number so it signals the end of the day's transactions for a given account record. When the batch program runs to update the accounts, checks and deposits are processed until the check number −1 is reached for each account, then the program moves to the next account record. The following example includes a loop that processes checks for one bank account. Each check transaction is read and the check number is tested for the sentinel value before the loop iterates the first time. The WHILE loop works best for this problem because if the account has no checks to process for the day's update, the program control will not need to enter the loop at all.

Sentinel Controlled Loop Example

```
Begin UpdateBalance
    Read first checkNumber, checkAmount
    WHILE checkNumber NOT −1
        Update accountBalance = accountBalance − checkAmount
        Read next checkNumber, checkAmount
    ENDWHILE
END
```

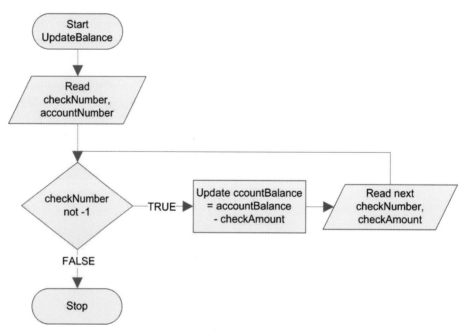

Figure 12-7: Flowchart for a sentinel controlled loop. Note the priming read before the loop begins.

A special requirement for the sentinel controlled loop is that it requires a *priming read* before the loop. *Priming read* means that the first record or data item is read outside the loop before the loop begins. Each successive record of data is read as the last step in the loop body.

End-of-File Controlled Loops

End-of-file controlled loops keep repeating the loop body as long as there are more records in the file. For example, in a payroll processing system, the system may fetch a batch of employee records, the number of which is unknown. This batch of records may be the result of a database query or the opening of another type of data file. The loop would move through each record, using some type of "next record" command to advance to the next record until there were no more records to process. The last "next record" would be null (absent). The loop stops when the program attempts to read a record that is null (not present) and registers the specific type of error that relates to a failed read attempt. The pseudocode abbreviation *eof* is used to represent *end-of-file*.

End-of-File Controlled Loop Example

```
BEGIN UpdateInventory
    Open inventory file
    WHILE NOT eof
        Read cost, qoh
        Update currentValue = cost * qoh
    ENDWHILE
    Commit updates
    Close inventory file
END
```

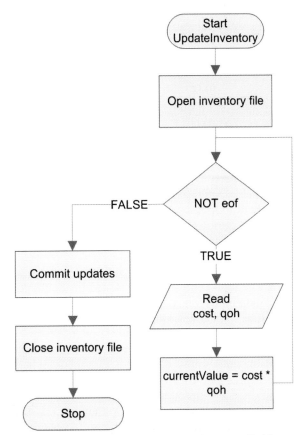

Figure 12-8: Flowchart for an end-of-file controlled loop.

Other ways in pseudocode of signaling that the end-of-file has not been reached is by using phrases such as "WHILE more data," "WHILE more records," or "WHILE records exist."

Flag Controlled Loops

Flag controlled loops use a Boolean variable as a *flag* that stops the loop. More commonly the initial value of the flag is set to TRUE, but it may also be set to FALSE. The loop body keeps repeating until some condition inside the loop body changes the value the flag to its opposite Boolean value. The condition that changes the flag is usually a nested decision structure that is not related to the loop decision. Flag controlled loops require four things of the designer and programmer.

1. Select a meaningful name for the flag.
2. Declare and initialize the flag to TRUE or FALSE. (The values of 1 and 0 may also be used with 1 representing TRUE and 0 representing FALSE).
3. Include a condition that changes the flag value.
4. Test the flag value inside the loop body.

Flag Controlled Loop Example

In the following example, the loop calculates a running total of the data items it reads. Once it reads an item that is not numeric the loop flag is set to TRUE and the loop terminates. A decision structure is needed to change a flag's value.

```
BEGIN AddNumbers
    Declare sum as number
    Declare quit as Boolean
    sum = 0
    quit = FALSE
    WHILE quit = FALSE        (or WHILE quit)
        Read n
        IF n is number THEN
            Sum = sum + n
        ELSE
            quit = TRUE
    ENDWHILE
END
```

FOR Loops

The FOR loop is a special loop type that can replace leading condition WHILE loops that are count controlled. Recall that count control loops require three action be performed on the loop control variable.

1. The loop control variable is declared and initialized outside the loop.
2. The loop control value is tested inside the loop as a condition for repeating the loop body.
3. The value of the loop control variable is altered inside the loop body.

The FOR loop provides a shortcut for count controlled loops. The loop control variable must still be declared before the loop begins, but the FOR loop performs the other three loop control variable actions automatically. The FOR loop automatically:

1. Initializes the loop control variable.
2. Tests the loop control variable.
3. Alters the loop control variable.

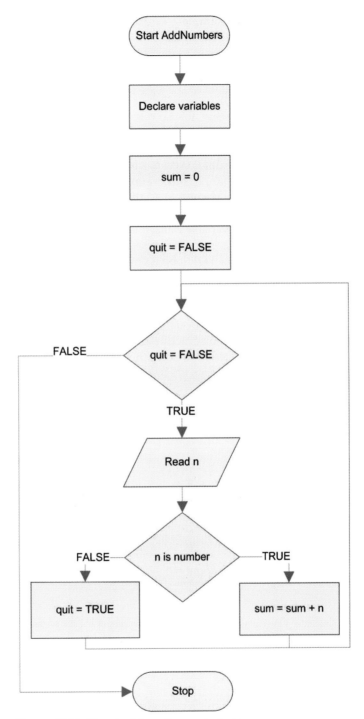

Figure 12-9: Flowchart for a flag controlled loop.

For example, a loop may iterate an exact number of times specified at design time. To iterate three times, the loop variable ("count" in the example below) is set to iterate for values of count from 1 to 3 inclusive. The general pseudocode syntax for the FOR loop structures:

FOR <iteration bounds>
    Actions to perform
ENDFOR

FOR Loop Example

> Declare count as integer
> FOR count 1 to 3
>   Print count
> ENDFOR

Notice that there are no statements for altering the loop control variable or incrementing the loop in the loop body. Count is actually initialized to zero when the declaration statement is executed, but it is set to the first value in the "iteration bounds" once the loop begins. In our example count is set to one when the loop begins. If the FOR condition is "count 4 to 7," the loop control variable will be set to four when the loop begins. Because the designer and programmer do not have to explicitly initialize and set the counter variable value, it is said that the counter is automatically "initialized" by the FOR loop.

Using the FOR loop is entirely optional. The same thing that a FOR loop does can be accomplished using the leading condition WHILE count controlled loop. The three advantages of using the FOR loop over the WHILE loop are that it initializes, tests, and alters the loop control variable automatically.

There is no special flowchart notation for a FOR loop. The flowchart for a FOR loop would look exactly like a WHILE loop that performs the same actions. There is a leading decision to begin the loop and the loop control variable is altered in the loop body.

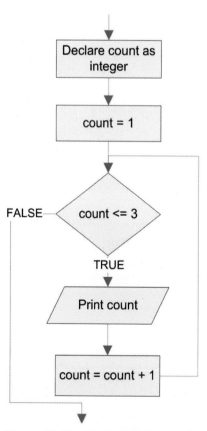

Figure 12-10: The flowchart for a FOR loop is exactly like the WHILE count controlled loop.

Counter and Accumulator Variables in Loops

Two common tasks that are performed in loops are *incrementing* a value and *accumulating* some value throughout the multiple iterations of the loop.

Incrementing a Value

The most common application of incrementing a value inside a loop is when we increment the loop control variable. Each time a loop iterates, one is added to the loop control variable to advance it toward its terminal value. Incrementing a variable is a special type of assignment operation. The variable name appears on both sides of the assignment operator. The assignment statement that increments a loop control variable by one would be **counter = counter + 1** with "counter" being the loop control variable.

Incrementing is a general term that applies to altering a variable value in either direction. An example of a statement that decrements a counter is **counter = counter − 1**.

Accumulating a Value

Suppose a loop scans a customer's items to purchase until there are no more items to scan. As each item is scanned, a running subtotal is calculated. Accumulating values in a variable is performed as a special type of assignment instruction, much like incrementing a variable. The accumulator variable appears on both sides of the assignment operator. For an assignment statement that accumulates a subtotal, the assignment statement would be **subtotal = subtotal + itemPrice**. As each new item is scanned, the new price becomes the itemPrice. That itemPrice is added to the previous value of subtotal to create the new value of subtotal.

Nesting Loops

Suppose you would like to print a number of time cards for each employee in your company each month. Since each month may have a different number of pay periods beginning in it, you would like to enter the number of time cards to print and have the system print that number for each employee. It is easy enough to print one timecard for each employee. We can use an end-of-file controlled loop to process each employee record. It is also a cinch to print a fixed number of timecards for one employee with a FOR loop, but how can we combine the two requirements? We can nest one loop inside another to accomplish the task. The outer loop will process each employee record and the inner loop will print each time card. Since printing the timecard involves special formatting depending on the type of card material, we will assume the timecard printing will actually be performed by another module.

The Inner Loop

```
FOR cards < numberCards
    Call PrintTimecard module
    cards = cards + 1
ENDFOR
```

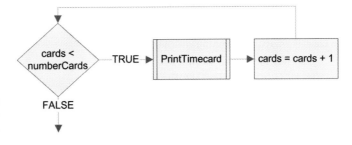

Figure 12-11: Flowchart for the inner loop. The PrintTimecard module will actually print each timecard.

The Outer Loop

```
WHILE NOT eof
     Read lastname, firstname, employeeID
     Print timecards (inner loop)
ENDWHILE
```

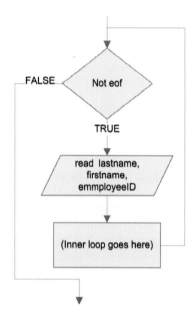

Figure 12-12: Flowchart for the outer loop.

Putting It Together

Below is a sample algorithm for a program that prints the monthly timecards. It accepts input from the user for the number of cards to print for the month. It loops through each employee record and prints the number of timecards indicated by the user for each employee. Note that when the inner loop terminates, the control goes back to the outer loop. The outer loop must also terminate to end the algorithm.

```
Begin PrintMonthlyCards
     Declare cards as integer
     Declare numberCards as integer
     GET numberCards
     numberCards = input numberCards
     WHILE NOT eof
          Read lastname, firstname, employeeID
          FOR cards 1 to numberCards
               Call PrintTimecard
               cards = cards + 1
          ENDFOR
     ENDWHILE
END
```

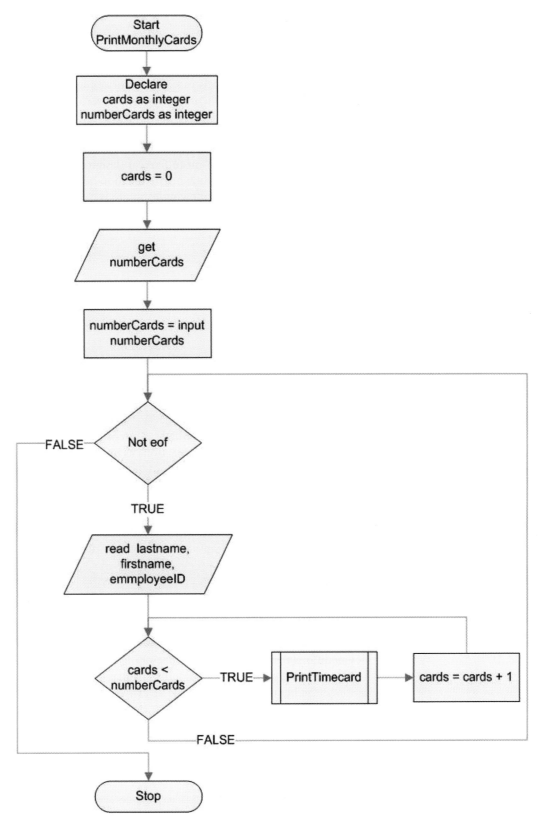

Figure 12-13: Complete flowchart for the nested loop.

Loop Summary

After seeing many loop examples, it still might be still a little confusing to figure out how loops are categorized and how to select the best type of loop structure for your solution. The fact is that loops may be categorized by several different things. Consider the following questions when deciding how to structure a particular loop.

Does the Loop Need to Iterate a Fixed Number of Times?

Remember that "fixed" can mean fixed at design time or it can mean that a terminal value is determined at runtime before the loop begins. Use count controlled loops for these definite loops. The following example is a loop whose number of iterations is fixed at design time.

```
BEGIN Print_a
    Declare a as integer
    FOR a 1 to 4
        Print a
    ENDWHILE
END
```

Compare the previous example to the next one where the numberOfTransactions is determined at runtime. It is still considered a "fixed" number of iterations because the number of iterations is known before the loop begins.

```
Begin UpdateAccounts
    Declare transactionNumber as integer
    Declare numberOfTransactions as integer
    transactionNumber = 0
    numberOfTransactions = Get count of transactions
    WHILE transactionNumber < numberOfTransactions
        Read transaction
        Subtract transactionAmount from accountBalance
        Increment transactionNumber by one
    ENDWHILE
END
```

Should the Loop Condition Be Tested at the Beginning or End of the Loop?

Conditions that are tested at the beginning of the loop determine whether or not the loop should be *entered*. Loop conditions that are tested at the end of the loop determine whether or not a loop should be *exited*. If you need a loop to iterate at least once, use a trailing decision. If you want an efficient loop that may not need to iterate at all in some cases, use the leading decision.

Should the Loop Enter/Exit Based on a TRUE or FALSE Value for the Loop Condition?

If you need the loop to be entered on a TRUE value of the loop decision and exit on a FALSE value, use any version of the WHILE loop. If you need to enter the loop when the loop decision is FALSE and exit when the loop condition becomes TRUE, use any version of the UNTIL loop.

Review Questions

1. What is the advantage of using loops in program design?

_____

_____

_____

2. Name the five logical parts of a loop and briefly state the purpose of each.

_____

_____

_____

3. What is the difference between WHILE loops and UNTIL loops?

_____

_____

_____

4. Explain the difference between loops that use a leading decision and those that use a trailing decision.

_____

_____

_____

5. How are *count controlled* loops terminated?

_____

_____

_____

6. What is a *loop control variable*?

_____

_____

_____

7. What are *definite* loops and *indefinite* loops?

_____

_____

_____

8. List and describe three ways an event controlled loop can be terminated.

_____

_____

_____

9. What special requirement is needed for the sentinel controlled loop that must be performed before the loop begins?

_____

_____

_____

10. What is the advantage of using a FOR loop instead of a WHILE loop for definite loops?

_____

_____

_____

11. Describe a business situation (other than the chapter example) in which a nested loop might be useful.

_____

_____

_____

12. What is the pseudocode syntax for incrementing a loop control variable?

_____

_____

_____

13. What is the syntax for accumulating a running sum over multiple iterations of a loop?

_____

_____

_____

14. List three ways in which loop structures might be categorized.

_____

_____

_____

Practice Problems

1. Create an algorithm with pseudocode and flowchart that will calculate the average of exactly four exam scores.

2. Create an algorithm with pseudocode and flowchart that will calculate the average of a list of exam scores of which the number of scores is not known.

3. Create an algorithm with pseudocode and flowchart that will total three items to purchase, calculate the tax and print a receipt that includes the subtotal, tax, and total. Assume the tax rate is read from a data source rather than entered by the user.

4. Create an algorithm with pseudocode and flowchart that will process a set of class exam grades, calculate an average and print the average, minimum and maximum grade. Assume the exam grader has entered a score of −1 as the last score in the list.

5. Create an algorithm with pseudocode and flowchart that will calculate the average miles per gallon of fuel used after 10 fill-ups. Recorded data includes starting odometer reading, odometer reading at each fill-up, and number of gallons of gas purchased at each fill-up. (Recorded data can be read by the program.)

6. **Challenge Problem:** Suppose a friend needs to borrow $1500 to purchase a new laptop. She can afford to make payments of $75 each month. She would like your help in creating a solution that will print an amortization table in Excel that shows her payment number, payment amount, interest paid each month, and current balance after each payment. The interest rate is 1% a month. Create an algorithm with pseudocode and flowchart that will

   a. Print column headers Payment Number, Payment Amount, Interest, and Balance in the first row of a worksheet.
   b. Print each payment number, payment amount, interest paid, and current balance for each payment on the next row each time.
   c. Adjust the balance and last payment amount so that the last payment will be the exact balance and the ending balance will be zero. (Hint: test the balance inside the loop for a negative value each time.)

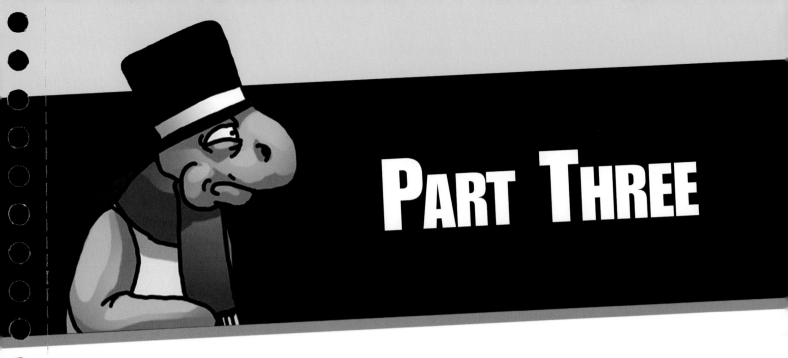

PART THREE

Enhancing Excel Projects with VBA

CHAPTER THIRTEEN

Introduction to Visual Basic for Applications

Learning Objectives

1. Name, record, and save a macro in the current workbook
2. Save a macro in a global workbook
3. Run a macro from the Excel ribbon command, a keyboard shortcut, the Quick Access Menu, a worksheet form control, a graphic object, and another macro in Visual Basic for Applications (VBA)
4. Use the *Visual Basic Editor* to view program code generated by the macro recorder
5. Alter macro code using the *Visual Basic Editor*
6. Become familiar with general object-oriented syntax in VBA
7. Document VBA code with comments
8. Understand how macro security level affects the performance of macros in Excel
9. Practice navigating the VBA programming environment in Excel

Macros

A macro in Excel is a sequence of instructions that are coded in Visual Basic for Applications (VBA) and stored so that they can be executed repeatedly with a simple user action. The program instructions may be written directly by the user or may be captured using the macro recorder in Excel. When a macro is recorded, all user actions are recorded until the macro recorder is stopped. Actions that are recorded include mouse clicks, keystrokes, worksheet selection, scrolling, entering cell contents, entering worksheet formulas, formatting cells, selecting ribbon tasks, etc. Once a macro is recorded, it can be executed again and again.

There is no limit to how macros can be used in host applications. In Excel, macros may be used to perform such repetitive tasks as:

- Applying a specific format to a range of cells
- Creating templates for new workbooks or worksheets in Excel
- Updating data in an Excel list
- Creating complex periodic reports

Once the macro instructions are saved, they can be recalled with simple user actions. When macros are saved, they are given a name to coincide with their purpose. For example, a macro that creates a template for a monthly budget worksheet might be called "CreateBudgetTemplate." A macro name must be one word. If a short action phrase is used to name a macro, underscores or camel casing can be used to make the name more readable. There are many ways to execute a macro's instructions. The common term used to mean execute the macro code is to "run" the macro. Excel macros may run from a variety of locations within the host application and project file. Some ways of running macros include:

- Run a macro from the Excel ribbon.
- Run a macro using a keyboard shortcut.
- Run a macro from an icon on the Quick Access Toolbar.
- Run a macro from a worksheet button.
- Run a macro from a graphic object on a worksheet.
- Run a macro from another macro.
- Run a macro in response to an event.

Macros are event procedures. Some event is required to trigger the macro to execute. In addition to user events such as mouse clicks and keyboard strokes, macros can be triggered by internal events such as a procedure call from another module.

Recording Macros

In order to record and store macros in a workbook, the workbook will need to be saved with an extension that supports macros. Both the *.xlsb* and *.xlsm* extensions support macros (more information on Excel 2007 file extensions is available in Chapter 1).

Before you can record a macro in Excel, you will need to access the macro utility. In Excel 2007 the macro utility is included in the "Developer" package of tools. In order to access those tools, you will need to select the *Developer* tab on the Excel ribbon. By default, the *Developer* tab is not visible when Excel is installed. To make the *Developer* tab visible, select the **Office Button→Excel Options→Popular→Top options for working with Excel→check the box beside** *Show Developer tab in the Ribbon.*

Figure 13-1: *Develop* tab of Excel ribbon.

To record a macro, select *Record Macro* from the *Code* task group on the *Developer* ribbon. The *Record Macro* dialog box will appear.

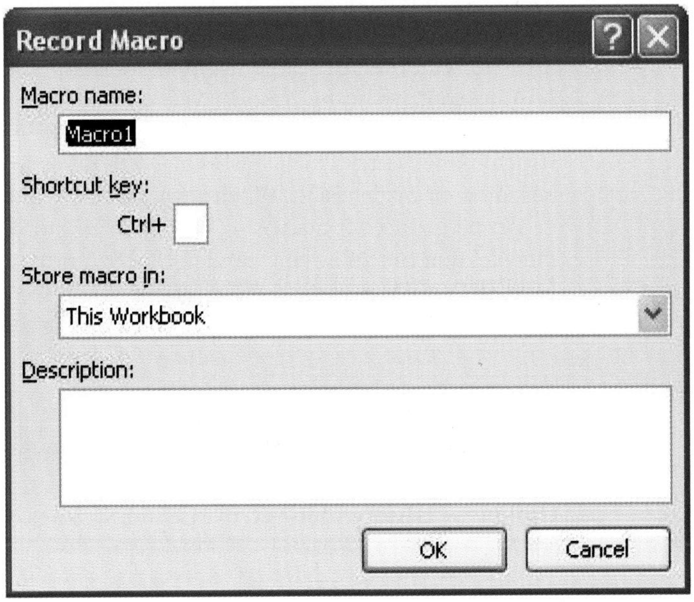

Figure 13-2: Record Macro dialog box.

Enter a name for the new macro in the *Macro name* text box. Select the storage location for the macro in the drop list under *Store macro in.* Options for storing recorded macros include:

- *This Workbook:* the current Excel workbook.
- *New Workbook:* a new Excel workbook.
- *Personal Macro Workbook:* a global workbook available to all Excel files.

Click the OK button to begin recording the macro. Perform the action you wish to record then select the *Stop Recording* (that replaces the *Record Macro* task while recording) task on the ribbon.

Personal Macro Workbook

The most common option for macro storage is the current workbook, but in some cases it is desirable to store macros in a workbook that can be accessed from all Excel projects. The *Personal Macro Workbook* is an actual workbook that opens every time Excel opens. It is created the first time a user selects the *Personal Macro Workbook* storage location option for a recorded macro. It contains only one worksheet (a minimum for Excel workbooks). The workbook file name for the Personal Macro Workbook is personal.xlsb. In earlier versions of Excel, it was named personal.xls. If you upgraded from an earlier version of Excel to Excel 2007, your system would likely load the older version, personal.xls, and would not create a new Personal Macro Workbook file. The personal.xls file may be renamed to personal.xlsb to make it compatible with all features of Excel 2007. If the file is renamed and contains macros called by macros from other workbooks, some small modification may be required for those macros in the older workbooks to redirect them to the new Personal Macro Workbook file name.

The personal.xlsb (or personal.xls) opens each time Excel opens because when it is created by Excel, it is automatically stored in a folder named XLSTART that is in a special location. Any files placed in the XLSTART folder will open each time Excel starts. There are two options for storing the Personal Macro Workbook in an XLSTART folder. The default location is in the user workspace on the machine. In Windows XP Professional the default path to the user's XLSTART folder is **My Computer→C:\Documents and Settings\User name\Application Data\Microsoft\Excel\XLSTART**. "User name" is replaced by the Windows user and "C" is the local hard drive. Whenever the specific user starts Excel, the workbook(s) stored in this location will open automatically.

The second option for storing the Personal Macro Workbook is a location that will allow it to open whenever any user of the machine starts Excel. The folder is still named XLSTART, but in Windows XP Professional is located at **C:\Program Files\Microsoft Office\Office 12\XLSTART**. (If you forget where these XLSTART folders are located, user the Windows file search utility to locate the folders named XLSTART.)

The contents of the Personal Macro Workbook are hidden by default from the Excel user. By hiding the global workbook, users are not likely to modify its contents or structure inadvertently while working with other Excel workbooks. Any workbook may be hidden or made visible. When a worksheet is "hidden" it means its worksheets cannot be viewed in Excel. If macros or VBA code are stored in the hidden workbook, the VBA modules and code may be viewed in the VBA programming application that runs inside Excel. To unhide a worksheet, select **View(tab)→Window(group)→Unhide** from the ribbon. A list of hidden workbooks will be displayed. Select the workbook to unhide.

Macro Security

In order to successfully run macros in Excel, an appropriate macro security level must be set. To view and alter the macro security level settings select the **Office Button→Excel Options→Trust Center→Trust Center Settings button→Macro Settings**.

Quick Tip!

From the *Developer* ribbon tab, select the *Macro Security* task from the **Code** task group.

Macros can be created to do just about anything, even bad things. Because malicious macros can be detrimental to your system, Excel includes tools for managing macros to help protect your system from harmful macros. Excel 2007 includes a *Trust Center* security system that allows you to choose what happens when you open a workbook that includes macros. There are four macro security settings available in Excel 2007 ranging from the highest to lowest level of security.

1. *Disable all macros without notification:* This setting will disable all macros and the security alerts about macros. If there are selected macros you would like to enable,

put the workbooks containing the macros in a *trusted location* and they will be permitted to run without begin checked each time by the *Trust Center* security system (more about *trusted locations* a little later).

2. *Disable all macros with notification:* This is the default setting when Excel 2007 is installed. Using this setting will let you choose one-by-one the macros you wish to enable. When a macro is encountered, a security alert will appear and ask for a user response with regard to allowing the macro to execute one time or every time.

3. *Disable all macros except digitally signed macros:* Macros created by trusted developers may be signed using a digital certificate of authenticity. All commercial software developers should obtain digital certificates to verify that macros in their products are safe and created by a reputable firm. An individual user may also create a digital signature to use on a personal machine to *self-sign* macro projects.

4. *Enable all macros:* This setting enables all macros regardless of their origin or authenticity. This setting does not allow the system to screen out malicious macros and is not recommended.

To apply changes in macro security levels, the Excel application must be closed and reopened to apply new security settings.

Trusted Locations

Additional options exist for the treatment of macros on a personal computer. The *Trust Center* includes a utility for setting *trusted locations* (folders) on a computer or network in which specific files containing macros can be stored so they will run every time without further scrutiny by the *Trust Center*. For Excel users, this option enables them to access all macros stored in trusted locations while disabling macros located elsewhere. To view the trusted locations identified on a machine, select the **Office Button→Excel Options→Trust Center→Trust Center Settings button→Trusted Locations**. By default, macros in files located in trusted locations are enabled whether or not they are signed. Some trusted locations are automatically added when Excel is installed. Others may be added later (such as C:\oracle\oradata\XE in the list below).

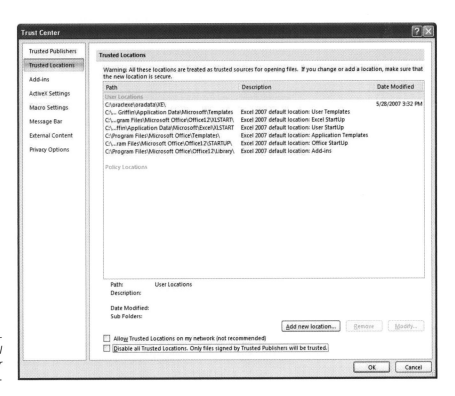

Figure 13-3: To view trusted locations select the *Office Button→Excel Options→Trust Center→Trust Center Settings button→Trusted Locations*.

If you wish to enable only signed macros, check the box at the bottom of the *Trusted Locations* screen beside *Disable all Trusted Locations. Only files signed by Trusted Publishers will be trusted.* An option also exists to add trusted locations on a network by checking the applicable check box at the bottom of the same screen.

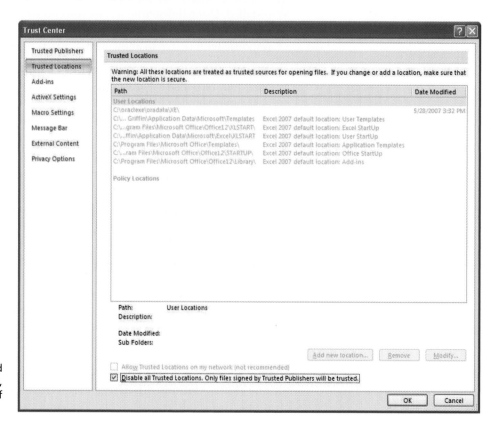

Figure 13-4: To enable only signed macros from trusted publishers, check the last box at the bottom of the *Trusted Locations* screen.

In order to add a trusted location, the check box disabling trusted location will need to be unchecked. To add a trusted location, click the *Add new location* button on the *Trusted Locations* screen and the *Microsoft Office Trusted Locations* dialog box will appear. Click the *Browse* button to navigate to the new trusted location. If the new location is not on the local machine, you will need to check the box beside *Allow Trusted Locations on my network.*

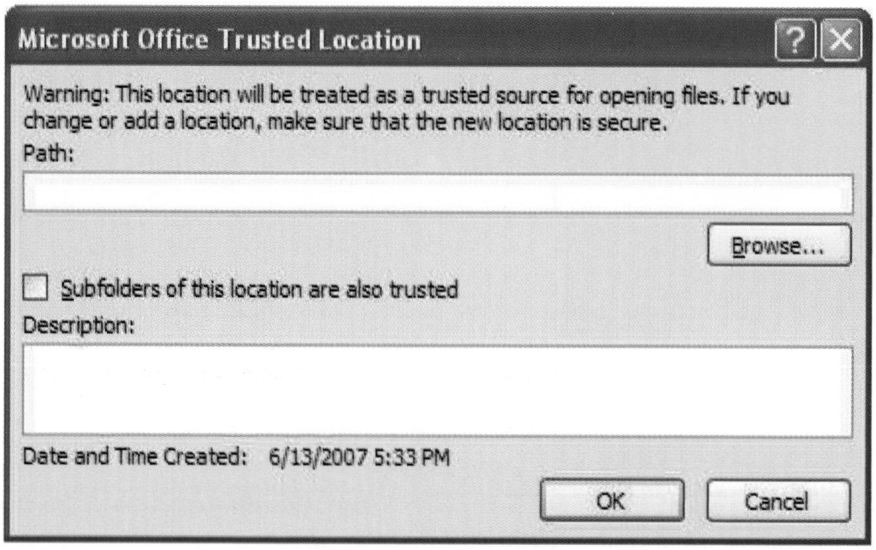

Figure 13-5: Click the *Browse* button to navigate to the new trusted location folder.

To remove a trusted location, select the location to remove and click the *Remove* button on the *Trusted Locations* screen of the *Trust Center* options.

Trusted Publishers

Another option for trusting macros automatically is adding the macro publisher to the *Trusted Publishers* list. To view the trusted publishers, select the **Office Button**→**Excel Options**→**Trust Center**→**Trust Center Settings button**→**Trusted Publishers**. The list of trusted publishers will vary from one machine to another depending on that actual publishers previously accepted.

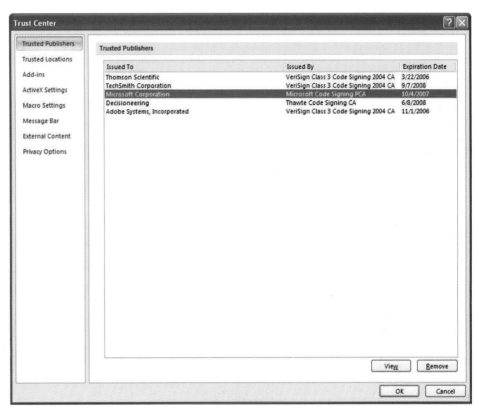

Figure 13-6: View a list of accepted trusted publishers.

To view the actual certificate information for publisher, select the trusted publisher and click the *View* button. The *Certificate* dialog box will appear with details of the publisher's digital certificate (see Figure 13-7).

When macros are encountered from a publisher not listed on the *Trusted Publishers* list, a macro security alert appears that prompts the user to accept the macro content. The publisher's content may be accepted for the one instance or the publisher can be added to the *Trusted Publishers* list by selecting the option to *Trust all documents from this publisher*. To accept only the current macro, select the option *Enable this content*.

To remove a publisher from the *Trusted Publisher* list, select the publisher and click the *Remove* button.

Figure 13-7: The digital certificate details for trusted publisher Microsoft Corporation.

Digitally Signed Macros

Microsoft Office 2007 products implement a technology called *Microsoft Authenticode* that provides a way for developers to "sign" a macro project or file containing macros to validate its authenticity. The "signature" is a *digital certificate* that is attached to the file to communicate to the person or program who receives the file that it is from a reputable source. A *digital certificate* is an electronic tag that represents an individual or organization. Software developers must apply for the digital certificate from a certificate authority such as VeriSign, DigiCert, or Comodo. There are many different certificate authorities. The authority certifies that the individual or organization is authentic (who they say they are) and issues a certification to that affect by way of the digital certificate. Users who receive notice of the signed file or program can choose to accept or reject the file based on the digital certificate information. When Excel users choose to accept all products bearing a specific digital certificate, the software organization is added to the *Trusted Publisher* list in Excel.

In order to use the macro security level that accepts only signed macros, you may wish to create a digital signature for yourself so you can "self-sign" your macro projects. The digital signature is not certified by any authority, but serves as a tag for your own system and programs to know the files are authentic and are without malicious content. Microsoft Office includes a program that allows a user to create a digital certificate for an Excel user. To create your own digital certificate, select **Start**→**All Programs**→**Microsoft Office**→**Microsoft Office Tools**→**Digital Signature for VBA Projects**. The *Create Digital Certificate* dialog box will appear. Enter your name in the text box and click the *OK* button to create the digital signature.

Signing VBA Projects

When a VBA project is signed, the digital certificate is issued for the entire project file. Before signing a VBA project, make certain the project is complete. If changes are made to the VBA code after the digital signature is applied, the digital certificate will be automatically revoked. Follow these steps to apply the digital signature to a VBA project:

1. Select *Visual Basic* from the *Code* task group of the *Developer* ribbon tab.

2. In the Project Explorer select the project to sign.

3. Select **Tools→Digital Signature** from the VBA menu bar. The *Digital Signature* dialog box will appear.

Figure 13-8: Select the *Choose* button to assign a digital certificate.

4. Click the *Choose* button to view a list of available certificates.

Figure 13-9: The certificate list shows all available digital certificates for a local machine.

5. Select the certificate to apply. The *Digital Signature* dialog box will be updated to show the digital signature applied to the project. Click the *OK* button to complete the signature.

Figure 13-10: The project is "signed" with the selected digital certificate.

Running Macros

Run a Macro from the Macro Utility

Macros may be executed in many ways within Excel and VBA. A macro may be executed by running it from the same macro utility that was used to record it. To run a macro from the macro utility, select **Develper(tab)→Code(group)→Macros**. The *Macro* dialog box will appear. Select the macro from the list and click the *Run* button. The list will include all macros available to the current workbook. If there are many macros in the list you may wish to limit the selection to those in a specific workbook to make locating the desired macro easier. To limit the macros in the list to those in one open workbook, select the open workbook file name from the drop list beside *Macros in*.

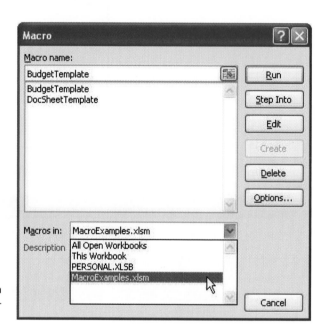

Figure 13-11: Limit the macros in the list to the one workbook selected.

Run a Macro Using a Keyboard Shortcut

A common way to execute a macro is by using a keyboard shortcut. When a macro is recorded, the user is given the option to set a key combination shortcut for executing the macro (the shortcut may also be added later). All macro shortcut key combinations must begin with the *Ctrl* key. One or more keys may be added to the *Ctrl* key for the shortcut. Since many keyboard shortcuts that are already assigned in software programs begin with the *Ctrl* key, it is helpful to include the *Shift* key in the combination. To specify the key combination shortcut, place the cursor in the box beside *Ctrl+* and simply press the additional keys on the keyboard. In Excel versions prior to 2007, if a keyboard shortcut assignment is attempted and the combination is already assigned, the user was prompted to select another key combination. In Excel 2007 the key combination assigned to the macro overrides keyboard shortcuts already used in Excel (such as *Ctrl+c* and *Ctrl+v*) while the affected workbook is open. Before assigning a shortcut key combination to a macro, you may want to be sure the key combination is not already assigned in Excel so it will not be overwritten. To view a list of keyboard shortcut combination already assigned for Excel, search Excel *Help* for "keyboard shortcuts" and select *Excel shortcut and function keys*.

To add a shortcut key combination after the macro is created, select **Developer (tab)→Code(group)→Macros→select the macro to alter and click the *Options* button.** The *Macro Options* dialog box will appear. Shortcut key combinations and/or macro descriptions may be added for the macro selected.

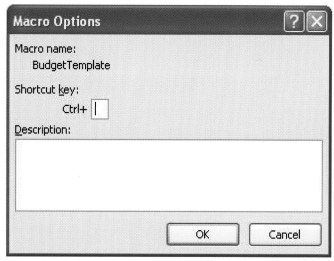

Figure 13-12: Use the *Macro Options* dialog box to add shortcut key combinations and descriptions for macros that have been created previously.

Run a Macro from the Quick Access Toolbar

Macros may be executed from an icon on the *Quick Access Toolbar*. This option may be especially convenient for frequently-used macros stored in a global macro workbook. To add a macro icon to the toolbar select the **Office Button→Excel Options→Customize**. Select Macros from the drop list at the top of the left list box. All available macros will be listed in the left list box. Select the macro to add to the toolbar and click the Add button.

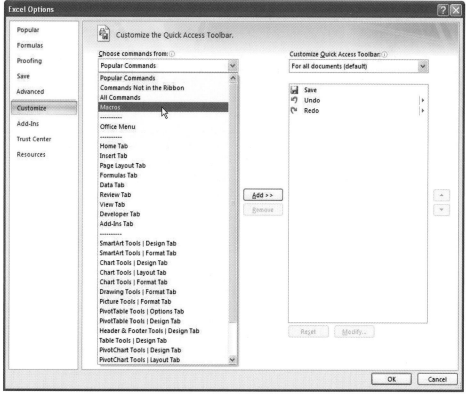

Figure 13-13: View the list of macros by selecting *Macros* from the drop list.

To modify the icon for the macro, select the macro from the right list box and click the *Modify* button. Select the desired icon from the icon list and click the *OK* button to save the selection.

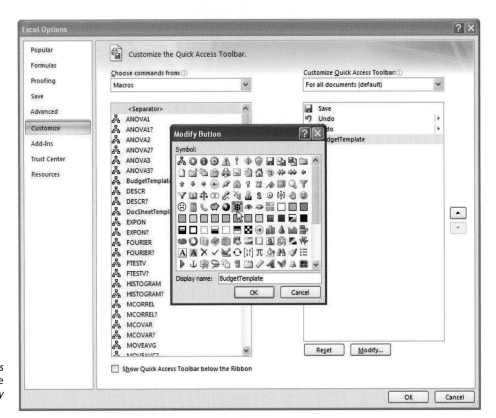

Figure 13-14: The *Quick Access Toolbar* icon for the macro may be changed by clicking the *Modify* button.

Figure 13-15: Select the icon on the *Quick Access Toolbar* to execute the macro. The macro name is displayed in the tooltip when the mouse hovers over the toolbar.

Quick Tip!

To add a command to the *Quick Access Toolbar*, right-click on the toolbar and select customize *Quick Access Toolbar*.

Run a Macro from a Graphic Object

Any graphic object in a workbook can be used to execute a macro. Insert the graphic object by selecting **Insert(tab)→Illustrations(group)**. Select the type of graphic object to add to the worksheet.

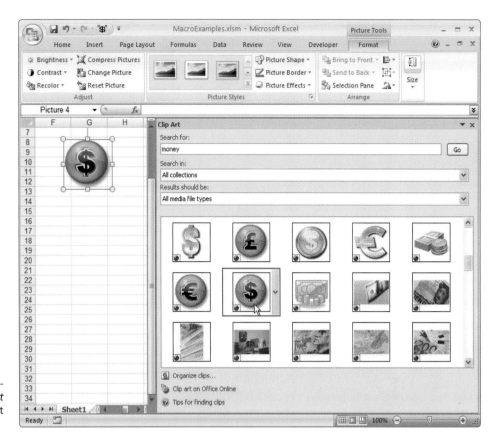

Figure 13-16: To add a graphic object to the worksheet select *Insert (tab)→Illustrations(group)* and select the type of image to add.

Once the object is added to the worksheet, assign a macro to it by right-clicking the image and select *Assign Macro* from the context menu. The *Assign Macro* dialog box will appear. Select the macro from the list and click the *OK* button to assign the macro. When the image is clicked, the macro will execute.

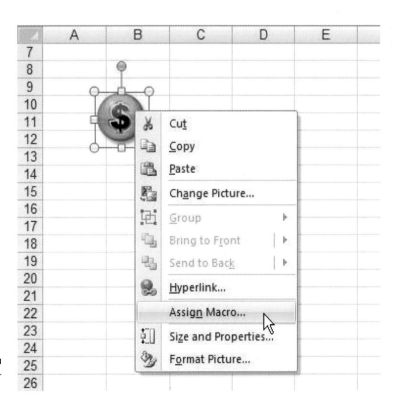

Figure 13-17: Use the context menu to assign a macro to the graphic object.

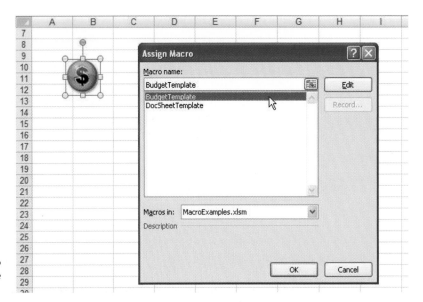

Figure 13-18: Select the macro to assign from the list of available macros.

Run a Macro from a Worksheet Form Control

Included in the *Developer* tools in Excel are two sets of worksheet controls. One set, the *Form Controls,* require no VBA programming to use them on a worksheet. The other set, *ActiveX Controls,* do require at least minimal VBA programming to implement. The *ActiveX Controls* mirror the controls that can be added to user forms that are developed in the VBA programming environment. The current discussion of form controls will be limited to non-ActiveX controls. In further discussion of these two form control types, the term "form control" will refer to controls from the non-ActiveX group. The term "ActiveX" will be included to note controls from that group.

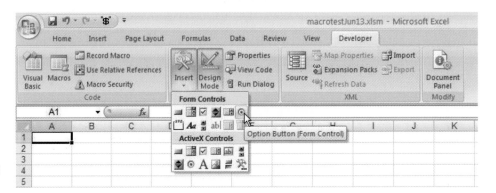

Figure 13-19: Select a form control to add to the worksheet.

To add a form control to a worksheet select **Developer(tab)→Controls(group)→ Insert→select the desired control from one of the two control groups.** Click on the worksheet to add the control. When a form control (a non-ActiveX control) is added to the worksheet, the *Assign Macro* dialog box appears to prompt the user to assign a macro. A macro may be assigned immediately or at a later time (or not at all). The control may be formatted by right-clicking on the control and select *Format Control* from the context menu. The *Format Control* dialog box will appear. Double-click on the form control to change the visible text. When there are no working form controls on a worksheet, the worksheet *Design Mode* is enabled as indicated by the selected *Design Mode* ribbon task (see Figure 13-19). Once a macro has been assigned to the control, the user may toggle *Design Mode* on and off. When *Design Mode* is enabled, modifications can be made to the form controls. When the *Design Mode* is off, the worksheet is in "run" mode and any user interaction with the form controls will execute assigned macros.

Configuring Worksheet (Non-ActiveX) Form Controls

When the *Format Control* dialog box is accessed from the particular control's context menu, a *Control* tab is available for controls that have more than one behavior option. The *Control* tab allows the user to set form properties such as, worksheet cell input range, output cell range, minimum value, incremental value, etc. Since only one option exists each for Button and Label controls, they do not have a *Control* tab available.

The following form controls (non-ActiveX controls) are available to Excel 2007 worksheets.

- *Button*
  Allows a user to assign a macro to its *Click* event to perform some action.

- *Combo Box*
  Allows a user to select from options in a drop-down list. The list may be populated from a worksheet range of cells (the input range). The output is the index number of the list item selected (beginning with 1) and is displayed in the designated output worksheet cell. A macro may be assigned to the *Change* event so that a new combo box selection may be reevaluated in formulas or other worksheet operations.

- *Check Box*
  Allows a user to toggle between the checked and unchecked states of the check box. A worksheet cell contains the value of TRUE when the box is checked and FALSE when the box is unchecked. When the check box or its associated text is clicked, the checked status is reversed. A macro may be assigned to the *Click* event of the check box so any change in checked status can update any associated worksheet values or operations.

- *Spin Button*
  Allows the user to change the value of a cell by clicking the up or down arrow. The spin button value is displayed in a designated worksheet cell. The current (default) value, minimum, maximum, and increment change can be set in on the *Control* tab of the *Format Control* dialog box. A macro may be assigned to the *Change* event of a spin button.

- *List Box*
  Allows the user to select from a list of options. The list may be populated from a worksheet cell range. Like the combo box, the index of the selected item appears in the worksheet output cell. A macro may be assigned to the *Change* event of a list box.

- *Group Box*
  Provides a container for grouping controls on worksheets for formatting and/or functionality. One specific use is for grouping option buttons that represent mutually exclusive selection options (option buttons are discussed next). A macro may be assigned to the *Click* event of a group box.

- *Option Button*
  Option buttons are designed to be used in a group for selecting mutually exclusive options. Multiple option buttons should be placed inside a *Group Box* to indicate that they are one group of mutually exclusive options. The group box placement will allow only one option button to be selected at any given time. All option buttons in one group are assigned the same worksheet output cell. The index number associated with the option that is selected is displayed in the worksheet cell. A different macro may be assigned to the *Click* event of each option button in the group.

- *Label*
  Text is displayed to a user in a label control. Although user interaction with a label is not typical, a macro may be assigned to its *Click* event.

- *Scroll Bar*
  Allows the user to drag a slider button in order to select a value. The current value, minimum value, maximum value, incremental change and page change values

may be set on the *Control* tab of the *Format Control* dialog box. The resulting value is displayed in a worksheet cell as the slider button is moved. A macro may be assigned to the *Change* event of a scroll bar.

ActiveX Form Controls

A great advantage of non-ActiveX worksheet form controls is that they can add flexibility to a workbook project without the user needing any programming skills at all. Their limitation is that their flexibility is very limited. Each one has just one "programmable" event, meaning only one event to which a macro may be assigned. The basic form controls originated with earlier versions of Excel which offered the capability of recording macros and assigning them to a worksheet form control, but did not include a fully integrated development environment (IDE) as do more recent versions. It is the opinion of some developers that the non-ActiveX controls are included in Excel 2007 for backward compatibility only and that they not be used for new development.

The ActiveX controls mirror the control set used for developing user forms in VBA. They provide a great deal more flexibility than the basic form controls, but required at least a minimal level of VBA programming skill. ActiveX controls have multiple events for which event procedures or macros may be executed. Once you learn to use the VBA form controls (the topic of Chapter 15), the same properties and event programming may be applied to the ActiveX worksheet form controls.

ActiveX controls are software components that must run within a host application such as a Web browser or a Microsoft Office application. They may be very simple, like a single form control, or they can be a very complex software component. They are commonly used to add functionality to Web sites and existing software applications. When the software components execute, they have unrestricted access to your computer system. They can change registry settings and access files on the machine. ActiveX components are frequently used by computer hackers to inflict damage to unsuspecting target machines.

If carefully designed with security in mind and by using proper *Trust Center* settings, ActiveX controls can be used safely in VBA projects. The following settings are available in the *Trust Center* for ActiveX controls.

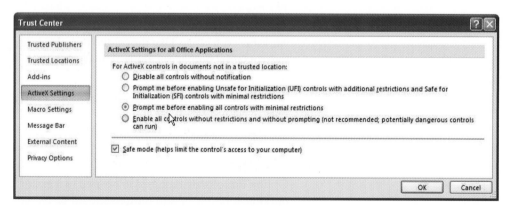

Figure 13-20: The *Trust Center* options for ActiveX controls.

When restricted settings are selected, the *Trust Center* applies many automatic checks on ActiveX controls before allowing them to execute. It can check for controls with known exploits and other characteristics that may make them unsafe to execute on the local machine.

Characteristics of Visual Basic for Applications

Visual Basic for Application (VBA) is not only a fully integrated program development environment used in conjunction primarily with Microsoft Office products (including Excel, Access, Word, Outlook), but is also used in other compatible software applications such as *Great Plains* (now known as *Microsoft Dynamics GP*). VBA is not a standalone programming environment, but is an extensive subset of the standalone Visual Basic versions prior to 2001. VBA must run inside a host application such as Excel. The purpose of including VBA in such host applications is to provide a way users can automate tasks and provide enhanced features to the underlying application with little programming knowledge or skill. VBA enhancements range from very simple, such as a recorded macro, to very complex. VBA was first included in Excel in 1993. Since then VBA enhancements have been added to subsequent versions such that VBA can now be used to add interfaces and functionality to Excel to make Excel projects sophisticated software applications.

VBA is used to add event-driven features to the Excel project file. VBA procedures are written to respond to user actions such a button click or the selection of a worksheet. The VBA program code is stored along with the application file (i.e., the Excel file or Word file). When user-created VBA enhancements are included in the application file, it is usually called a "project" rather than simply a workbook or document.

VBA is not only procedural in nature, but also has some object-oriented characteristics. In following the procedural programming paradigm, VBA code is recorded or written in short modules that are called by other modules or program events. Most users who include VBA code in Excel projects use only the procedural aspect of VBA. Most user-generated VBA enhancements are generally limited to VBA procedures, custom functions, and user forms which implement event programming.

VBA in Excel can also be used in an object-oriented manner to create and manipulate user-defined objects. Very few developers of Excel VBA projects utilize that extended object-oriented programming capability of VBA. VBA also follows the object-oriented paradigm in that its syntax is generally in terms of objects, properties, and methods.

VBA Object-Oriented Terminology

So what does it mean to be object-oriented? It means that a computer system is viewed entirely as a set of interacting objects. Objects in a computer system are viewed as "things", like things in the real world. The objects have certain features or characteristics and exhibit certain behaviors. Objects in a computer system are classified much like real-world objects might be. For example, in human terms a car is a type of object. A specific car, such as a specific Honda Civic with a unique vehicle identification number, is an object of the car type. The features of objects are called its *properties*. All objects of one type have the same properties, but different actual values for each property. For example, each car type object may have model name, model year, manufacturer name, vehicle identification number, color, number of doors, etc. Each car object will have a different set of values for the set of properties. One car object may be a 2007 Honda Civic which is blue and has two doors and another car object may be a 2005 Toyota Camry which is red and has four doors. Excel object types include worksheets, cell ranges, and form controls. Another term for type in object-oriented programming is "class." Individual objects are created from an object class. A class definition specifies all properties and behaviors available for all objects of the class.

In addition to properties, objects also have behaviors that are implemented as *methods*. A *method* is a specific action that an object of a given class can perform. For example, a car object can move, idle, accelerate, etc. All objects of the same class can do the same things, therefore have the same behaviors. For example, a worksheet object named "September 2007 Budget" can be visible or invisible and it is be able to recalculate itself. Both are examples of available worksheet behaviors.

An important aspect of object-oriented programming is that is employs a modular design. Examples of modules in VBA include an individual worksheet, a macro, a custom function, a user form and a class definition. These modules interact in some way. As is typical in procedural programming languages, one module will request the services of another. In object-oriented projects, modules may also be grouped together to form reusable program components. In VBA smaller modules such as procedures and functions can be grouped into larger modules. In VBA the larger module is simply referred to as a "module."

Object Properties

Properties of objects are in effect variables. They may be assigned values and their values may be captured and manipulated in the same way as other variables. To assign a value to a property, use the assignment operator after the object and property name followed by the value to assign in the following syntax. Objects and their properties and behaviors are noted using a period between the object name and the property or method.

General Assignment Syntax for Properties

ObjectName.PropertyName = value or expression to assign

Assignment Examples

```
ActiveCell.Value = "Virginia Tech"
ActiveCell.Value = 25
ActiveCell.Value = saleAmount * taxRate
```

In the previous examples, ActiveCell is the object, value is the property. "Virginia Tech" is a text value and 25 is a numeric value. Text values (also called "strings") must always be enclosed in double quotes in VBA. Variables may also be used in expressions in property assignment statements.

To capture a value from an object property, use a variable on the left side of the assignment operator and the object and property name on the right side in the following syntax.

General Syntax to Access a Property

Variable = ObjectName.PropertyName

Property Capture Examples

```
lastName = txtLastName.Text
tax = txtSaleAmount.Value * txtTaxRate.Value
```

In a text box, the text entered or displayed in the box is the value of the Text property. In the first example, the value of the Text property (the contents) of a text box is captured into a variable named lastName. In the second example two text box input values are used in a calculation just as you would use other variables.

Object Methods

Methods of objects are the actions they perform. An object can be invoked to perform as action by calling its name and its method name together in the syntax.

Method Call Syntax

ObjectName.MethodName

An example of a method "call" is requesting a cell range object to select or the current workbook object to update its links to other workbooks.

Method Call Examples

```
Range("A1:C10").Select
ThisWorkbook.UpdateLinks
```

Although VBA follows the general object-oriented syntax rules, its syntax frequently varies from the strict object-oriented paradigm. Visual Basic (not VBA) versions from 2001 forward more strictly follow object-oriented syntax rules so syntax in those newer versions is less like that of VBA.

The VBA Programming Environment

VBA runs as a separate program from Excel but runs inside Excel or another host application. VBA cannot run outside of a host application. To access the VBA programming utility (called the *Visual Basic Editor* in previous versions of Excel), select **Developer (tab)**→**Code(group)**→**Visual Basic.** (If the Developer tab is not visible, select *Office Button*→*Excel Options*→*Popular*→*Top options for working with Excel*→*check the box beside Show Developer tab in the Ribbon.*) The VBA programming environment will open in a window entitled *Microsoft Visual Basic.* Your view may be somewhat different from the example depending on the programs running on your machine.

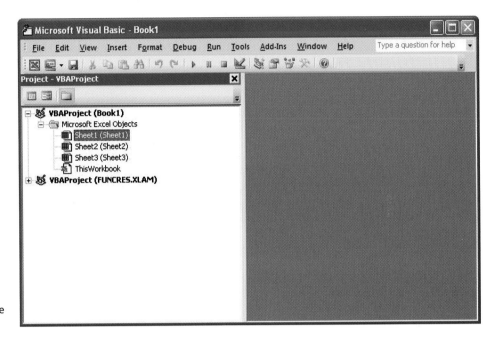

Figure 13-21: Initial view of the VBA programming environment.

The *Help* features for Excel and VBA are separate. To access help on Excel topics, return to the Excel workbook *Help* feature by clicking on the Excel icon on the far left side of the VBA toolbar and click on the *Help* icon (the blue question mark in the upper right corner of main Excel window). By using the Excel icon, VBA remains open and the Excel workbook window is shown in front of the VBA window. If you exit VBA by selecting *File*→*Close and Return to Microsoft Excel,* the entire VBA program will be closed. To toggle back to VBA from Excel, use the same ribbon task that you used to access VBA originally. For help on VBA topics, you will need to launch the *Help* feature from the VBA application (Use the *Help* menu or the *Help* icon on the toolbar).

Quick Tip!

To access help quickly for an object in VBA, select the object and press the F1 key. Select VBA code and press F1 to view an explanation and/or example of the object, property, or method used.

The frame on the left is called the *Project Explorer* window. It shows all open Excel projects. In addition to user projects, projects may also be visible that have a file extension beginning with ".xla." These files are add-in components of other programs that may be running on your machine. In Figure 13-21 "Book1" in the *Project Explorer* window represents the new Excel unnamed project. New files can only be opened from Excel, not from VBA. The *File* menu is very limited in VBA. You may only use it to save a file, import, export, or print a module or exit VBA and return to Excel (see Figure 13-22).

The *Project Explorer* window shows all project modules of each project which include all Excel objects and any objects added using VBA. Each worksheet object in a workbook is actually a program module that may contain any number of other smaller modules such as macros that relate to the worksheet's functionality. Code to implement any type of worksheet form control would be entered into the applicable worksheet module. The workbook itself is a module that may be used as a container for macros or other types of smaller modules that affect the workbook's behavior. Modules may be added by selecting **Insert→(type of module to insert)** from the menu bar. A blank module may be inserted or one of two specialized module may be added to the project. A *Class Module* is a special module used for defining a new class of objects. A *UserForm* module is a module that provides a drag and drop interface for creating custom forms to augment the Excel project (the topic of Chapter 15).

The properties of each project object may be viewed in the *Properties* window by selecting **View→Properties Window** from the menu bar. The *Properties* window appears in its default position underneath the *Project Explorer* window and shows all applicable object properties and the current values for each. Property values may be modified by selecting the property name in the left column of the properties list and begin typing the new value. The typed value will be entered into the corresponding property value box in the right column. You may also click directly in the value box to alter the value. Some values are altered by making selections from a list or in a dialog box. Try changing the name of the worksheet "Sheet1" to "MySheet" and note the change in the object's name in the *Project Explorer* window.

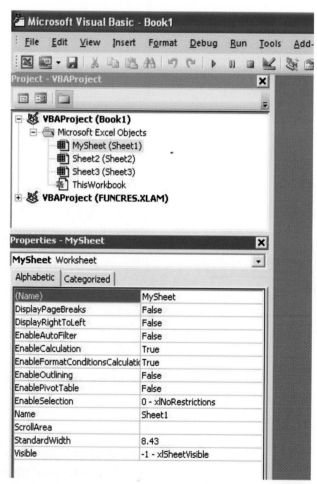

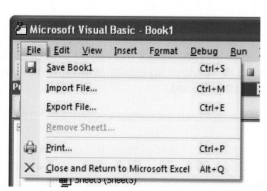

Figure 13-22: VBA's limited *File* menu.

Figure 13-23: Change property values by selecting the property name in the left column and enter new value in the right column.

When the first macro is recorded in an Excel project, a new module is added. The default names for new modules are "Module1", "Module2", etc. The same module is used to group all macros recorded in one session. When the project is closed and reopened, newly recorded macros are stored in another new module that is added automatically. All general modules are stored in a folder called "Modules" in the Project Explorer. Separate folders are used to store groups of *Class* modules and *UserForm* modules. The Excel objects are also stored in a special folder.

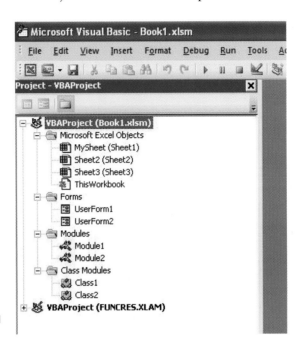

Figure 13-24: Modules are grouped folders by module type.

Individual modules can be renamed by selecting the item and entering the new name in the *Name* property box in the *Properties* window. (If the *Properties* window is not visible, open it by selecting **View→Properties Window**.)

Use VBA to View Macro Code

When a macro is recorded, VBA code is written into a module. The code module begins with the keyword *Sub* followed by the macro name. A set of empty parentheses follows the macro name to indicate an empty parameter list (no data is needed to perform the procedure). The macro ends with the keywords *End Sub*. Practice recording macro and view the code produced by the VBA programming environment.

Practice 13-1: Record and Modify Simple Macros

Record a macro that creates a template for a documentation worksheet that you can add to each of your new Excel workbooks. Store it in the Personal Macro Workbook so it will be available for each new workbook you create in Excel. Record as you enter the template labels (i.e., "Purpose," "Date created," "Developer," "Worksheet Summary"). Add formatting to the worksheet while recording the macro. Change the name of the worksheet on the worksheet tab to "Documentation." Enter your name in the cell beside the "Developer" label. Select the cell beside the "Purpose" label so that when the macro finishes executing the appropriate cell will be selected for you to begin entering information about the particular workbook.

1. Open a new Excel workbook. Make sure the *Developer* tab is visible.

2. Select **Developer(tab)→Record Macro** from the Excel ribbon. Name the macro "DocumentationTemplate." Assign the keyboard shortcut *Ctrl+Shift+D*. Add a descriptive note about the macro in the *Description* box of the *Record Macro* dialog box.

3. Select the first worksheet in the workbook. (Be sure to select the worksheet after the macro recorder is started even though it may already be selected.)

4. Type in template labels for a documentation worksheet.

5. Apply any desired formatting to the worksheet.

6. Rename "Sheet1" to "Documentation." Below is an example of a completed documentation worksheet template.

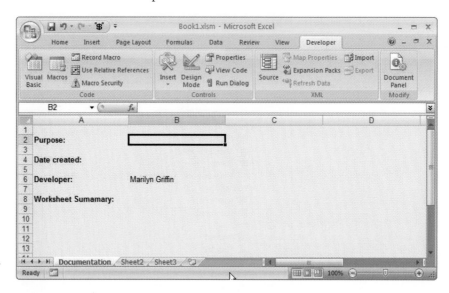

Figure 13-25: Example of the complete practice template.

7. When the worksheet is completed, stop the macro recorder.

8. Test the macro. If the macro does not perform as you wish, record the macro again to overwrite the original macro. (Naming a new macro the same as a previous macro will overwrite the code in the previous one.)

9. Use the *Visual Basic* command on the *Developer* ribbon tab to open the VBA application so you can view the macro code. If this is the first time a macro has been added to the Personal Macro Workbook, a new project named "PERSONAL. XLSB" will be listed in the *Project Explorer* window. If a macro has been stored in the Personal Macro Workbook previously, it is already listed among the project files.

10. Double-click on the "PERSONAL.XLSB" (or "PERSONAL.XLS" from earlier Excel versions) to view its objects. Double-click on the "Modules" folder. Select "Module1" and rename it to "DocTemplateModule".

11. Double-click on the new module name. The code window for the module will appear in the large frame on the right side of the VBA window. The code window is called the *Visual Basic Editor* and is the code editor for the VBA programming environment.

The program code shown in blue text in the Visual Basic Editor represents VBA keywords. Lines of code shown in green are comments that do not execute. Comments are used to include information about the programming code without interfering with the execution of the code. Preceding the comment with an apostrophe makes the compiler ignore the remainder of the line of code. Lines that may appear in red text indicate a syntax error that must be corrected before attempting to compile the code.

If you wish to make changes to the VBA code, the changes may be made directly into the VBA code window. For example, perhaps we would really like to make column B wider and wrap the text in that column. We can make changes directly, such as changing the width of column B (in the fifth line from the bottom of the macro code) to a higher number, or we can record another macro to help us alter the original one.

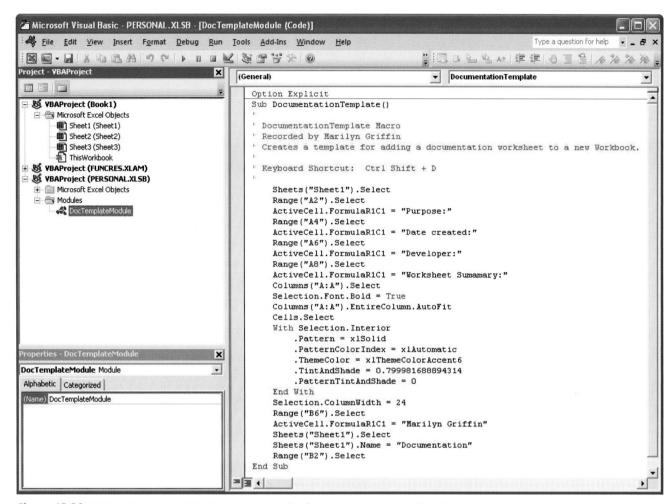

Figure 13-26: VBA code generated by the macro recorder for the DocumentationTemplate macro.

12. Record a second macro that widens column B and formats the text to wrap in the column. Name the macro "SetColumnB."

13. After the macro is recorded, open the DocTemplateModule to view the new macro code. (In the example below, green comments have been removed so that all lines of code for both macros may be view on the same screen.)

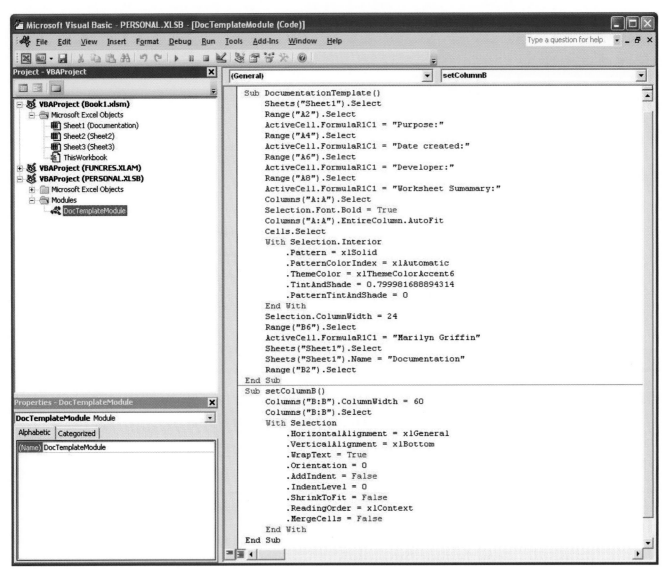

Figure 13-27: The new macro has been added to "DocTemplate-Module."

To execute all the recorded code at once, there are two options.

Option 1:

"Call" the second macro from the first. Be sure to place the "call" statement before the statement that selects cell B2 so that the macro will end with cell B2 selected and ready for user input. Test the revised macros by running the "DocumentationTemplate" macro.

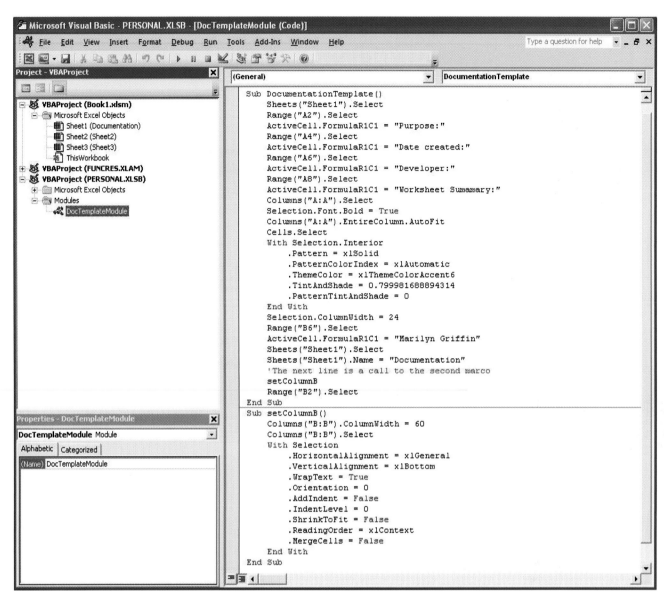

Figure 13-28: Second macro "called" from the original macro (see comments in green text).

Option 2:

Add the new macro code to the original macro. Move the new macro code and insert it before the last line of code of the first module. The Visual Basic Editor works just like a text editor permitting you to cut, copy, and paste using common menu commands or keyboard shortcuts. Again, you want cell B2 to be selected when the macro ends. Test the revised macro (run the "DocumentationTemplate" macro).

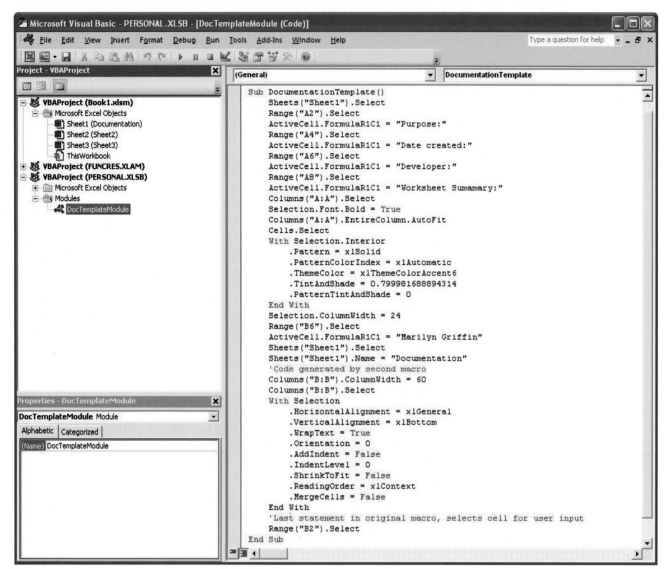

```
Sub DocumentationTemplate()
    Sheets("Sheet1").Select
    Range("A2").Select
    ActiveCell.FormulaR1C1 = "Purpose:"
    Range("A4").Select
    ActiveCell.FormulaR1C1 = "Date created:"
    Range("A6").Select
    ActiveCell.FormulaR1C1 = "Developer:"
    Range("A8").Select
    ActiveCell.FormulaR1C1 = "Worksheet Sumamary:"
    Columns("A:A").Select
    Selection.Font.Bold = True
    Columns("A:A").EntireColumn.AutoFit
    Cells.Select
    With Selection.Interior
        .Pattern = xlSolid
        .PatternColorIndex = xlAutomatic
        .ThemeColor = xlThemeColorAccent6
        .TintAndShade = 0.799981688894314
        .PatternTintAndShade = 0
    End With
    Selection.ColumnWidth = 24
    Range("B6").Select
    ActiveCell.FormulaR1C1 = "Marilyn Griffin"
    Sheets("Sheet1").Select
    Sheets("Sheet1").Name = "Documentation"
    'Code generated by second macro
    Columns("B:B").ColumnWidth = 60
    Columns("B:B").Select
    With Selection
        .HorizontalAlignment = xlGeneral
        .VerticalAlignment = xlBottom
        .WrapText = True
        .Orientation = 0
        .AddIndent = False
        .IndentLevel = 0
        .ShrinkToFit = False
        .ReadingOrder = xlContext
        .MergeCells = False
    End With
    'Last statement in original macro, selects cell for user input
    Range("B2").Select
End Sub
```

Figure 13-29: The code from the second macro is added to the code of the original macro (see comments in green text).

Move or Copy a Module

Modules may be copied to any other Excel/VBA project. To copy the module to another project, select the module name and drag the module name with the left mouse button and drop it onto the target project name in the *Project Explorer*. A copy of the module will be placed in the target project, but the original module will remain in the original project file. If you wish to move the module without leaving a copy in the original project, just remove the module from the original project after placing a copy in the target project.

Remove a Macro

Remove a macro by deleting the macro code from the VBA module. Be sure to remove all the macro code statements as well as the macro name header and the final "End Sub" statement. To delete an entire macro module, or other module type, right-click on the module name and select *Remove (module name)* from the context menu. You will be prompted to export the module if you wish. The exported module is saved into a separate file and can be imported into any other Excel/VBA project.

Practice 13-2: Record a Macro and Modify with VBA Code

Objective: To record a complex macro and edit the code in the Visual Basic Editor. Further customize the macro using VBA code to provide functionality that is not possible with the macro recorded utility. We want to ultimately create a macro that adds a new budget template to a new worksheet, and names the worksheet with an appropriate name for the upcoming month.

1. Open the Excel workbook "PersonalMonthlyBudget.xlsm." (This budget workbook was created using template 01023341.cab from the Microsoft Web side Office Templates at http://office.microsoft.com/en-us/templates/TC010233411033.aspx? CategoryID=CT101172321033.)

2. Save the workbook as "MyBudget.xlsm."

3. Rename the budget worksheet "Jan2008."

4. Record a macro named "BudgetTemplate" and store it in the current workbook. It should perform the following actions:
   a. Select all worksheet cells and copy contents.
   b. Add a new worksheet.
   c. Paste the copied contents to the new worksheet.
   d. On the new worksheet, select all non-shaded cells that are formatted to display currency values and delete their contents. (Those cells are in columns C, D, H, and I. Select all the applicable cells even if they are already empty.)
   e. Change the worksheet name to "Feb2008."
   f. Select the cell E6 (the first "income" cell).
   (You will not be able to test this macro without getting a run time error.)

5. Open the VBA programming application and open the macro module Module1 in the Visual Basic Editor.

6. Make the following modifications to the VBA code of the macro.
   a. Add comments to the VBA code to explain what the macro does. Be sure to precede each comment with an apostrophe. The comment should turn green when the cursor advances to the next line of text.
   b. Delete any lines of code that begin with "ActiveWindow.Scroll." These instructions were captured if you scrolled down or across on the Excel worksheet. Those instructions are not necessary for the macro to perform as we would like.

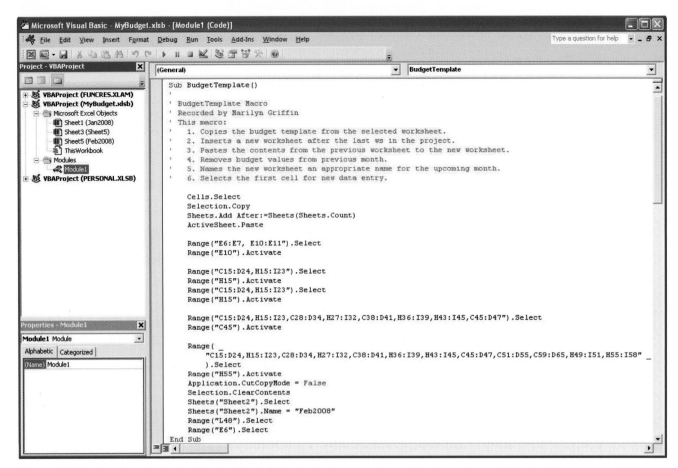

Figure 13-30: Sample code for the "BudgetTemplate" recorded macro with scrolling instructions deleted and comments added.

7. If your macro does not look similar to the example, copy and paste the macro code from the text file "BudgetTemplate.txt" provided for this exercise and paste to replace your macro code in the Visual Basic Editor.

8. Identify what each line of VBA code does so that you can alter some lines of code to customize the macro.

In the next part of the practice, you will be altering VBA code to customize the macro. When testing the macro, if a runtime error is encountered, the program goes into *break* mode (*Run* mode stops). *Break* mode is enabled when the program encounters a runtime error so the compiler can highlight the line of code that caused the program to halt. Before attempting to alter the VBA code, you should know how to take the VBA program out of *break* mode so you may continue altering VBA code and testing the macro.

To take the VBA programming environment out of break mode, click on the square *Reset* button on the *Standard* VBA toolbar.

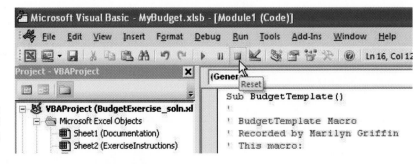

Figure 13-31: Use the *Reset* button to take the VBA program out of break mode after a runtime error is encountered.

9. Add VBA code to the macro that performs the following actions:
   a. Be sure the line of code used to add a new worksheet reads:

   Sheets.Add After:=Sheets(Sheets.Count)

   This instruction ensures that the new worksheet is added to the end the worksheet collection.
   b. The macro should check the name of the previous worksheet and name the new worksheet with the next month and same year if the previous worksheet name is not "Dec . . .". In the case the previous month is December, the year will need to be incremented by one. The order of the instructions that are added is important to the correct performance of macro. Begin at the beginning of the macro and add the instructions in the order that they are specified.

      i. Declare variables to handle the task of naming the worksheet appropriately. The keyword for declaring a variable in VBA is "Dim." The variable data type must follow the keyword "As" after the variable identifier (name).

      Dim prevTitle As String
      Dim newTitle As String
      Dim prevMonth As String
      Dim newMonth As String
      Dim year As Integer

      ii. Capture the name of the previous month's worksheet. Count the worksheets in the workbook then subtract one to locate the one just before the last one. You will be capturing the Count property of the Sheets collection.

      Sheets(Sheets.Count − 1).Select

      iii. Capture the name of the selected worksheet. While the worksheet is selected, copy all cells on the worksheet.

      prevTitle = ActiveSheet.Name
      Cells.Select
      Selection.Copy

      iv. Parse out the first three characters of the previous worksheet name to isolate the month part of the name. The VBA LEFT function works much the same way as the comparable Excel function. The second argument specifies the number of characters to parse.

      prevMonth = Left(ActiveSheet.Name,3)

      v. Parse out the last four characters of the previous worksheet name to isolate the year part of the name. The VBA RIGHT function works much the same way as the comparable Excel function. The second argument specifies the number of characters to parse.

      year = Right(ActiveSheet.Name,4)

      vi. Write a VBA CASE structure that tests the value of "prevMonth and assigns a new value based on the previous value. In the case that the previous month is December, the CASE structure should also increment the year variable by one. The correct syntax for the VBA CASE structure is shown below. The LCase VBA function is used to reduce the actual case of the worksheet name to lower case for an accurate comparison of characters of any case.

```
Select Case LCase(prevMonth)
    Case "jan": newMonth = "Feb"
    Case "feb": newMonth = "Mar"
    Case "mar": newMonth = "Apr"
    Case "apr": newMonth = "May"
    Case "may": newMonth = "Jun"
    Case "jun": newMonth = "Jul"
    Case "jul": newMonth = "Aug"
    Case "aug": newMonth = "Sep"
    Case "sep": newMonth = "Oct"
    Case "oct": newMonth = "Nov"
    Case "nov": newMonth = "Dec"
    Case "dec": newMonth = "Jan"
    year = year + 1
End Select
```

vii. After the Case "dec" instructions, add a CASE ELSE statement to the case structure so that is the month is not recognized, the macro will end and not encounter a runtime error. (More error-handling techniques will be discussed in future chapters.)

```
. . .
Case "nov": newMonth = "Dec"
Case "dec"
    newMnth = "Jan"
    year = year + 1
Case Else
    Exit Sub
End Select
```

Test the case structure by changing the month name of the previous worksheet to something other than a month and year abbreviation before running the macro. When the macro is ended with the "Exit Sub" statement, you will need to delete the new worksheet added by the macro before attempting to run the macro again.

viii. Wrap an IF structure around the assignment statement for year so that if the last four characters are not numeric, the program will not encounter a runtime error. Use the ISNUMERIC VBA function to test the value of the parsed year value before assigning it to the year variable. Without some error handling, if the parsed value is not numeric, a type mismatch run-time error will occur when trying to assign a character value to an integer type variable.

```
If IsNumeric(Right(ActiveSheet.Name, 4)) Then
    year = Right(ActiveSheet.Name, 4)
Else
    Exit Sub
End If
```

Test the macro by changing a number in the year value on the previous worksheet to an alpha character. When the macro is ended with the "Exit Sub" statement, you will need to delete the new worksheet added by the macro before attempting to run the macro again.

ix. Concatenate the "newMonth" and "year" to form the new worksheet name. Assign the new worksheet name to the new worksheet. While the worksheet is selected, paste the copied contents (from an earlier macro step) from the previous worksheet.

```
        newTitle = newMonth & year
        Sheets(Sheets.Count).Select
        ActiveSheet.Name = newTitle
        ActiveSheet.Paste
```

c. If you used the *Ctrl* key (held it down) to select all cells to clear at once, you may delete all except the final Range selection code. Each time a new worksheet range is selected while holding down the *Ctrl* key, the previous range selections are repeated in the VBA statement.

d. Allow the existing macro code to clear the appropriate cells and select the first input cell at the end of the macro. Use apostrophes to comment out the code that is no longer needed or has been replaced by your VBA code. (Use the *Comment Block* command from the VBA *Edit* toolbar to comment multiple lines of code at once.)

When testing the revised macro, be sure to remove any incomplete worksheets that were added by the macro before running the macro each time. (More information about troubleshooting VBA code will be provided in Chapters 14 and 16.) The complete VBA code for the revised macro is shown in Figure 13-32.

Quick Tip!

To quickly figure out the VBA code for interacting with a worksheet object, record a short macro that does just the one thing and view the code generated by the macro recorder to see how to copy the code instruction(s) and paste it into your current module. Modify as the code as needed. To view an explanation of an object, property, or method used in the recorded macro, select the VBA syntax in the code editor and press the *F1* key.

Quick Tip Example

If you do not know the VBA code for setting the background color of a cell, record a macro that sets the background color for a cell. Use the color you wish to use in your module code and the macro recorder will show you the code to specify that color. The following VBA code was generated when setting a selected cell's background color to solid yellow.

```
With Selection.Interior
        .Pattern = xlSolid
        .PatternColorIndex = xlAutomatic
        .color = 65535
        .TintAndShade = 0
        .PatternTintAndShade = 0
End With
```

Note that the property that represents the background color is *Interior* and the color "65535" represents the shade of yellow selected by the user. Now when you wish to set a background color for selected cells in VBA, you can use the line of code:

Selection.Interior.color = <your selected color>

The WITH Block

A WITH block is used frequently in VBA macro syntax when multiple properties of the same object are set and/or multiple methods are invoked. The shortcut syntax prevents the programmer from having to state the object before each property or action coded. The general syntax for the WITH block:

```
Sub BudgetTemplate()
'
' BudgetTemplate Macro
' Recorded by Marilyn Griffin
' This macro:
'   1. Copies the budget template from the selected worksheet.
'   2. Inserts a new worksheet after the last ws in the project.
'   3. Pastes the contents from the previous worksheet to the new worksheet.
'   4. Removes budget values from previous month.
'   5. Names the new worksheet an appropriate name for the upcoming month.
'   6. Selects the first cell for new data entry.

' Some macro generated statemetns have been moved to create the correct sequence of actions.

'Declare variables to manipulate worksheet names.
    Dim prevTitle As String
    Dim newTitle As String
    Dim prevMonth As String
    Dim newMonth As String
    Dim year As Integer

    'Add a new worksheet to the end of the worksheet collection.
    Sheets.Add After:=Sheets(Sheets.Count)

    'Select the second worksheet from the end.
    Sheets(Sheets.Count - 1).Select

    'Capture the name of the selected worksheet.
    prevTitle = ActiveSheet.Name

    'The next two lines were generated by the macro recorder.
    Cells.Select
    Selection.Copy

    'Parse the previous worksheet name into month and year.
    prevMonth = Left(ActiveSheet.Name, 3)

    'Test the value in the last 4 positions of the worksheet name
    'to make sure the characters are numeric.
    If IsNumeric(Right(ActiveSheet.Name, 4)) Then
        year = Right(ActiveSheet.Name, 4)
    Else
        'Stop the macro without completing it.
        Exit Sub
    End If

    'Assign the new worksheet month (and possibly year).
    Select Case LCase(prevMonth)
        Case "jan": newMonth = "Feb"
        Case "feb": newMonth = "Mar"
        Case "mar": newMonth = "Apr"
        Case "apr": newMonth = "May"
        Case "may": newMonth = "Jun"
        Case "jun": newMonth = "Jul"
        Case "jul": newMonth = "Aug"
        Case "aug": newMonth = "Sep"
        Case "sep": newMonth = "Oct"
        Case "oct": newMonth = "Nov"
        Case "nov": newMonth = "Dec"
        Case "dec"
        newMonth = "Jan"
        year = year + 1
        Case Else
            'Stop the macro without completing it.
            Exit Sub
    End Select

    'Assign the name for the new worksheet.  The & is used to concatenate
    'the two string variable values.
    newTitle = newMonth & year

    'Select the last worksheet to name.
    Sheets(Sheets.Count).Select

    'Name the selected worksheet.
    ActiveSheet.Name = newTitle

    'This line was generated by the macro recorder and pastes the copied
    'cells into the new worksheet.
    ActiveSheet.Paste

    'Range("E6:E7, E10:E11").Select
    'Range("E10").Activate

    'Range("E6:E7, E10:E11,C15:D24,H15:I23").Select
    'Range("H15").Activate

    'Range("E6:E7, E10:E11,C15:D24,H15:I23,C28:D34,H27:I32,C38:D41,H36:I39,H43:I45,C45:D47").Select
    'Range("C45").Activate

    'Only the last total range specification is required when
    'using the Ctrl key to select non-contiguous ranges.
    Range( _
        "E6:E7, E10:E11,C15:D24,H15:I23,C28:D34,H27:I32,C38:D41,H36:I39,H43:I45,C45:D47,C51:D55,C59:D65,H
        ).Select
    Range("H55").Activate
    Application.CutCopyMode = False
    Selection.ClearContents
    'Sheets("Sheet2").Select
    'Sheets("Sheet2").Name = "Feb2008"
    'Range("L48").Select
    Range("E6").Select
End Sub
```

Figure 13-32: The complete macro code revised.

```
With object
        .property1 = someValue
        .property2 = someValue
        .method1
        .method2
        . . .
End With
```

In the recorded macro example above, a WITH block is used to set the properties for the cell background. In VBA the object-oriented syntax is often varied such that different sub-properties of a property are set by adding an additional period to the standard syntax "object.property" and naming a sub-property to follow the period. Without the WITH block structure, the recorded macro code would read:

```
Selection.Interior.Pattern = xlSolid
Selection.Interior.PatternColorIndex = xlAutomatic
Selection.Interior.color = 65535
Selection.Interior.TintAndShade = 0
Selection.Interior.PatternTintAndShade = 0
```

The Excel Integrated Development Environment

This chapter has explored some very basic features of the VBA programming environment in Excel and has introduced some sample VBA syntax for manipulating worksheet and workbook objects. By recording and altering macros, a great deal of functionality and automation can be added to an Excel project with very little knowledge of programming required. The user-friendly interface and the many tools to assist the novice programmer make VBA a relatively unintimidating programming environment. With the addition of VBA to the Excel application, the capability of Excel has been escalated to the level at which complete software applications can be developed on the Excel/VBA platform. Excel now supports the three major components of a standalone software application.

1. *User Interface:* Provided by user forms and worksheet controls with which the user can interact.

2. *Data Storage:* The Excel worksheets provide data storage in such a way that the data can be sorted, queried, summarized, and analyzed in the same way as data stored in more powerful database applications.

3. *Programming Language:* VBA provides a programming language that allows the developer not only to develop modular programs, but also to develop graphical user interfaces, user-defined classes, and custom functions and procedures for complex data processing. VBA also supports the interaction of Excel projects with third-party software applications.

Review Questions

1. What is a macro in Excel?

   _____

   _____

   _____

2. What is a macro in VBA?

   _____

   _____

   _____

3. What does it mean to "record a macro"?

   _____

   _____

   _____

4. List at least four examples of how macros might add functionality to an Excel project.

   _____

   _____

   _____

5. List at least six ways a macro can be executed.

   _____

   _____

   _____

6. What is the Personal Macro Workbook and how is it used?

   _____

   _____

   _____

7. What makes the Personal Macro Workbook open each time Excel starts?

8. How can the Excel *Trust Center* help protect the system from harmful macros?

9. In terms of Excel macro security what is a *digital signature*?

10. When a digital signature is applied to a macro project, what is actually "signed"?

11. In terms of Excel macro security what is a *trusted publisher*?

12. In terms of Excel macro security what is a *trusted location*?

13. What does it mean to "self-sign" a macro project?

_____

_____

_____

14. What is the difference between ActiveX form controls and non-ActiveX controls for an Excel worksheet?

_____

_____

_____

15. What is VBA and how is it related to Excel?

_____

_____

_____

16. Explain why *VBA* is said to be *event-driven*.

_____

_____

_____

17. Explain how VBA is *object-oriented*.

_____

_____

_____

18. Why is VBA considered a *procedural* programming language?

_____

_____

_____

19. What is the general object-oriented syntax for accessing an object's property?

_____

_____

_____

20. What is the general object-oriented syntax for invoking an object's method?

_____

_____

_____

Practice Problems

1. Download a budget template from Microsoft's gallery of Office templates. Record a new macro named "BudgetTemplate2" that behaves similarly to the "BudgetTemplate" exercise in this chapter. Use VBA code to modify the template as you did in the practice problem.

2. For the macro you recorded in Problem 1, open the VBA application and locate the macro code in the *Visual Basic Editor*. Insert a comment preceding each line of VBA code to indicate what each line of code does with respect to the Excel worksheet. (Use the debugging tools if needed to execute one line at a time to see its functionality.)

3. Open the workbook "Employees_ch13.xlsx." Save a copy of the workbook using the Excel extension ".xlsm."

   a. Record a macro that applies subtotals to the salary column. Group the salaries by department and sum salaries for each department. Use the *Subtotal* ribbon command for applying the subtotals.
   b. Insert two blank rows at the top of the Employees worksheet. In the new rows add a button form control (non-ActiveX control) to the worksheet. Format the button with the caption "Add Subtotals." Assign the macro you recorded in the previous part of the problem to the worksheet button. Test the macro. (You will need to remove the subtotals using the Subtotal command before running the macro each time.)
   c. Record a second macro that removes the subtotals from the worksheet and sorts the worksheet by employee's last name, then employee's first name.
   d. Add a second button to the worksheet. Format the button with the caption "Remove Subtotals." Assign the macro you created in the previous step to the button. Test the two macros to toggle subtotals on and off in the list.

CHAPTER FOURTEEN

Writing Custom Functions in VBA

1. Use pre-defined VBA functions in VBA functions and procedures
2. Use selected Excel worksheet functions in VBA
3. Identify the steps in creating a custom function
4. Use VBA data types to declare variables and constants in VBA
5. Declare and initialize constants in VBA
6. Select the appropriate variable scope for custom functions and procedures
7. Distinguish among the three types of programming errors and understand the general actions required to resolve each type
8. Use the VBA code editor to test and troubleshoot a custom function
9. Practice using the VBA debugging tools
10. Understand how a Variant data type behaves in VBA
11. Create a custom function that can be used in Excel worksheet formulas
12. Store a custom function in a global VBA workbook that can be accessed from any Excel VBA project
13. Understand how variables behave that are passed to other modules *byRef* and *byVal* in VBA

An Overview of VBA Functions

In any context a function is a pre-defined formula that has a specific ordered list of inputs and produces exactly one output. Excel has a vast number of worksheet functions already available to all Excel workbooks. These functions may be called from worksheet formulas. A function's output is returned back to the worksheet formula from which it was called.

Since VBA is a separate application from Excel, it has its own set of functions available for use in the programming language. For example, pre-defined functions perform such actions as converting data of one type to another type such as text to date, and formatting data for output. Table 14-1 includes selected VBA functions commonly used in business applications.

In addition to using VBA functions in the programming code, some, but not all, of the Excel worksheet functions may be accessed using VBA. In order to use a worksheet function in VBA, special syntax is used to access the Excel application, then the worksheet function. The general syntax for accessing an Excel worksheet function from VBA:

returnValue = Application.WorksheetFunction.*FunctionName(argument list)*

The name of the function will replace *FunctionName* in the syntax, and the function arguments will be listed inside the parentheses separated by commas. Below is a sample of VBA code that calls the COUNTA function to count the number of non-blank rows of a worksheet column.

numRows = Application.WorksheetFunction.CountA(Range ("A:A"))

Table 14-2 lists Excel worksheet functions that are available to VBA code.

In spite of all the functions already available to VBA from its own function library and that of Excel, developers often wish to create custom functions for a particular business application or business discipline. For example, if a tax calculation for a retail sale routinely requires more manipulation that a typical calculation of taxable amount multiplied by tax rate, it may benefit the developer to take the time to write a custom function in VBA that will perform all the actions required and return a simple tax value back to a worksheet cell. One advantage of putting complex calculations into custom functions is that less experienced Excel users can utilize the function when they may not be comfortable managing the complex calculation. Another advantage of custom functions is to simplify interactions with cell formulas when automating worksheet

Table 14-1: Common VBA functions used in business applications

Function Name	Return Value
Abs	Returns an expression's absolute value
CBool	Converts a string ("true," "false") or integer value (1, 0) to a Boolean value
C . . .	Converts a value to the type specified (Byte, Cur, Date, Dbl, Dec, Int, Sng, Str, Var)
Choose	Uses an index number (first argument) to return a value from a list (remaining arguments)
Chr	Converts an ANSI value to a string
Date	Returns the current system date
DateAdd	Returns a date to which a specified time interval has been added—for example, one month from a particular date
DateDiff	Returns an integer showing the number of specified time intervals between two dates, for example, the number of months between now and your birthday
DatePart	Returns an integer containing the specified part of a given date—for example, a date's day of the year
DateSerial	Converts a date to a serial number
DateValue	Converts a formatted string to a date
Day, Month, Year, Second	Returns the day of the month from a date value (also Month, Year, Hour, Minute, Second)
Erl	Returns the line number that caused an error
Err	Returns the error number of an error condition
Error	Returns the error message that corresponds to an error number
Fix, Int	Returns a number's integer portion
Format . . .	Displays an expression in a particular format (Currency, DateTime, Number, Percent)
InputBox	Displays a box to prompt a user for input
InStr	Returns the position of one string within another string
IPmt	Returns the interest payment for an annuity or loan
Is . . .	Returns TRUE if a variable meets the criteria (Array, Date, Empty, Error, Missing (for optional argument passed to a procedure), Null, Numeric, Object)

(continued)

Table 14-1: Common VBA functions used in business applications (*continued*)

Function Name	Return Value
LBound, UBound	Returns the smallest (or largest) subscript for a dimension of an array
LCase, UCase	Returns a string converted to lowercase (or uppercase)
Left, Right	Returns a specified number of characters from the left (or right) of a string
Len	Returns the number of characters in a string
Mid	Returns a specified number of characters from a string
MsgBox	Displays a message box and (optionally) returns a value
Now	Returns the current system date and time
RGB	Returns a numeric RGB value representing a color
RND	Returns a random number between 0 and 1
Space	Returns a string with a specified number of spaces
Str	Returns a string representation of a number
StrComp	Returns a value indicating the result of a string comparison
String	Returns a repeating character or string
Time	Returns the current system time
Timer	Returns the number of seconds since midnight
TimeSerial	Returns the time for a specified hour, minute, and second
TimeValue	Converts a string to a time serial number
Trim	Returns a string without leading or trailing spaces (also LTRIM and RTRIM to remove left or right spaces)
TypeName	Returns a string that describes a variable's data type
Val	Returns the numbers contained in a string
VarType	Returns a value indicating a variable's subtype
Weekday	Returns a number representing a day of the week

updates. Entering a return value from a VBA custom function is much easier than writing a worksheet formula into cells using VBA.

While many custom functions arise from the need for simplification of worksheet formulas, others result from the practice of modular program design (the topic of Chapter 10). In modular program design, the goal is to break the program into manageable pieces

Table 14-2: Excel worksheet functions available to VBA

Worksheet Functions Available to VBA				
Acos	Ddb	HypGeomDist	NormSDist	Sinh
Acosh	Degrees	Index	NormSInv	Skew
And	DevSq	Intercept	NPer	Sln
Asc	DGet	Ipmt	Npv	Slope
Asin	DMax	Irr	Odd	Small
Asinh	DMin	IsErr	Or	Standardize
Atan2	Dollar	IsError	Pearson	StDev
Atanh	DProduct	IsLogical	Percentile	StDevP
AveDev	DStDev	IsNA	PercentRank	StEyx
Average	DStDevP	IsNonText	Permut	Substitute
BahtText	DSum	IsNumber	Phonetic	Subtotal
BetaDist	DVar	Ispmt	Pi	Sum
BetaInv	DVarP	IsText	Pmt	SumIf
BinomDist	Even	Kurt	Poisson	SumProduct
Ceiling	ExponDist	Large	Power	SumSq
ChiDist	Fact	LinEst	Ppmt	SumX2MY2
ChiInv	FDist	Ln	Prob	SumX2PY2
ChiTest	Find	Log	Product	SumXMY2
Choose	FindB	Log10	Proper	Syd
Clean	FInv	LogEst	Pv	Tanh
Combin	Fisher	LogInv	Quartile	TDist
Confidence	FisherInv	LogNormDist	Radians	Text
Correl	Fixed	Lookup	Rank	TInv
Cosh	Floor	Match	Rate	Transpose
Count	Forecast	Max	Replace	Trend
CountA	Frequency	MDeterm	ReplaceB	Trim

(continued)

Table 14-2: Excel worksheet functions available to VBA (*continued*)

Worksheet Functions Available to VBA				
CountBlank	FTest	Median	Rept	TrimMean
CountIf	Fv	Min	Roman	TTest
Covar	GammaDist	MInverse	Round	USDollar
CritBinom	GammaInv	MIrr	RoundDown	Var
DAverage	GammaLn	MMult	RoundUp	VarP
Days360	GeoMean	Mode	RSq	Vdb
Db	Growth	NegBinomDist	RTD	VLookup
DCount	HarMean	NormDist	Search	Weekday
DCountA	HLookup	NormInv	SearchB	Weibull
				ZTest

that can be easily designed and programmed. Functions tend to be the lowest level modules, the ones that do the actual business processing in the program. In the payroll program introduced in Chapter 10, the modules on the lower two levels are actually functions that perform the various calculations required in the payroll program. The structure chart in Figure 14-1 (repeated from Figure 10-3) shows a partial breakdown of the btnPrintChecks_Click event procedure module. Note the functions on the lower two levels have one or more input values and return exactly one value to the calling module.

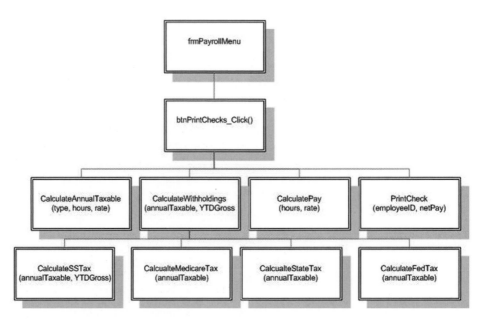

Figure 14-1: Structure chart model for modules related to the "PrintPayrollChecks" use case.

Other custom functions in VBA arise from calculations steps that are repeated in multiple Excel formulas or in VBA procedures and functions. If these frequently used steps are factored out into a separate custom function, the same function may be called from both Excel worksheet formulas and from other VBA procedures and function.

Steps to Create a Custom Function

Before beginning to write the custom function in VBA code, think about what will be needed to perform the functions and exactly what the function needs to do. These steps offer some guidelines for creating a custom function.

1. Identify what the function should return and its data type.
2. Identify the required inputs and their data types.
3. Identify optional inputs and their data types.
   (When optional inputs are identified, a different function will need to be defined for using each group of inputs that may be used. All the functions may have the same name, but each has a different parameter list.)
4. Design the internal logic of the function with pseudocode or flowchart.
5. Test the design logic.
6. Write the function in program code.
   a. Create function header
      - Function name
      - Parameter list, including types
      - Return type
   b. Declare variables and constants needed beyond inputs and return.
   c. Write function instructions in VBA code.
   d. Test the function execution.
   e. Add a function description.
   f. Debug as needed.

In order to write custom functions directly into the Visual Basic Editor some knowledge of basic VBA syntax and structure is required. Many functions involve decisions so the developer will need to use VBA IF and CASE structures for many functions. All functions will require the manipulation of data by way of parameters and arguments, and variables and/or constants.

Variables and Constants in VBA

In order to handle any additional data items inside the function, variables and/or constants may be needed. (See Chapter 9 for general programming use of variables and constants.) Table 14-3 lists data types for variables and constants that are available in VBA.

To declare variables in VBA use the keyword "Dim" followed by the variable identifier and its data type. The following VBA code is an example of a variable declaration for a variable called rate that is a decimal data type. Decimal data in VBA are represented by the Single, Double, and Currency types. The currency type may be used for general decimal data. Its use is not restricted to monetary data.

```
Dim rate As Currency
```

Multiple variables may be declared in one declaration statement. The declaration keyword ("Dim" or "Private") begins the line and the declarations are separated by commas. In order for each variable declared to be assigned a specific data type (other than the default Variant), the data type must also be specified along with the identifier.

```
Dim price As Currency, subtotal As Currency, taxable As Boolean
```

Constants should be used to represent values within the function will not change during function execution. An example of a value that may remain constant is a state sales tax rate. Whenever the state tax rate changes, the programmer will change the initial

Table 14-3: VBA data types

Data Type	Storage Space (in Bytes)	Range of Values
Boolean	2	TRUE, FALSE
Integer	2	−32,768 to 32,767
Long	4	−2,147,483,648 to 2,147,483,647
Single	4	−3.402823E38 to −1.401298E-45 for negative numbers 1.401298E-48 to 3.402823E38 for positive numbers
Double	8	−1.79769313486231E308 to −4.94065645841247E-324 for negative numbers; 4.94065645841247E-324 to 1.79769313486232E308 to for positive numbers
Currency	8	−922,337,203,685,477.5808 to 922,337,203,685,477.5807
Date	8	January 1, 1900 to December 31, 9999
Object	4	Any object
String (variable length)	10 + string length	0 to approximately 2,000,000,000
String (fixed length)	String length	0 to approximately 65,400
Variant (numeric)	16	Same range as Double
Variant (String)	22 + string length	Same range as variable length String

value of the constant at design time. Other examples of data that remains constant while a program executes are, fee schedules, multipliers, and color definitions. To declare a constant in VBA use the keyword "Const" followed by the identifier, data type and initial value. Below is a VBA statement that declares a constant for the state sales tax rate. The common naming convention for constants is all upper case letters to make their declaration and initialization statements easier to locate in the program code to ease code maintenance. VBA requires that constants be initialized when declared.

Const STATE_RATE As Currency = .045

Programming languages are very strict about how variables and constants are named. These are rules for assigning identifiers to VBA variables and constants.

- The name must be one word with no spaces. Underscores or camel casing may be used to make longer variable identifiers more readable.
- No special characters (@, #, $, %, ^, &, *) are permitted in the name except for the underscore (_).
- The name must not begin with an underscore or a numeric character.

- The maximum length is 255 characters.
- VBA is not case sensitive. The identifier "num" is the same as "NUM" or "Num" to VBA.

Variable and Constant Scope

In modular program design a variable or constant may be used for one function or procedure or for all procedures in the entire module. The level of its use is called the scope of the variable or constant. *Local* variables and constants are recognized inside one low-level module only, such as one function or procedure. *Module level* variables are recognized in and shared by every lower level module of a larger program module. *Public* variables are recognized in all program modules, but are not used in modern programming techniques because they further complicate coding, troubleshooting, and maintenance of programs.

The scope of a variable or constant is determined by the location of the declaration statement. They are recognized inside just the module in which they are declared and all its lower level modules. A module level variable is declared inside a program module that contains other modules and is recognized inside all functions and procedures contained in the module. A local variable is declared inside of a function or procedure and is recognized inside that one small module only.

When the variable declaration statement executes, computer memory space is allocated to store the variable's value. The memory location is assigned the name of the variable (its identifier). The variable is also automatically initialized with a default value. Numeric type variables are assigned the value of zero and text type values are assigned a value of " " (a blank string). Although we say that the first value assigned to the variable at design time (by the programmer) or at runtime (by the program) is its initial value, it is actually the second value assigned to it.

The default option in VBA is that variable declarations are not required before a variable can be used. When a variable is not declared before use, VBA implicitly declares it the first time it is encountered in the program and assigns it the value indicated by the program context. An undeclared variable is assigned the Variant data type. The Variant type in VBA is a flexible data type whose actual type changes as different types of values are assigned to it. If a text value is assigned to a Variant variable, the data type is String. If an integer value is assigned, the type becomes Integer.

In general, using loosely typed variables whose data type is not consistent throughout the program makes the program code more difficult to troubleshoot because variables are being declared and data types changed behind the scene where it is difficult for the programmer to follow. It is best to declare all VBA variables and constants before you use them. To enforce the explicit declaration of variables and constants before they are used, the phrase *Option Explicit* must be entered as the first line of a VBA program module (the whole module, not just one procedure or function). You can set *Option Explicit* to be the default option by selecting **Tools→Options→Editor(tab)→check** *Require Variable Declaration*. When the box is checked, "Option Explicit" will appear at the top of each new module that is added to the project. The option setting affects all programming modules in the VBA environment, not just those in a single project.

The keyword "Dim" can be used for all local and module level variable declaration. Any variables of module level scope may use the optional keyword "Private" instead of "Dim." Module level constants may include the optional keyword "Private" before the keyword "Const" for constant declarations. Whether or not the "Private" keyword is used for module level declarations, the declaration statement must be located in the appropriate place (outside of all inner modules) for a module level variable. Any variables of global scope use the keyword "Public" instead of "Dim" for variables, and in front of "Const" for constant declarations.

Testing Code in VBA

In order to test VBA code as we create functions and procedures, you can execute the module code directly in the VBA programming environment. Although all VBA commands can be accessed via the menu bar, the most frequently used commands can be accessed via their toolbar icons. The VBA application opens with the *Standard* toolbar visible. It contains icons for the most common programming related activities. Other toolbars which may be added include the *Debug, Edit,* and *UserForm* toolbars.

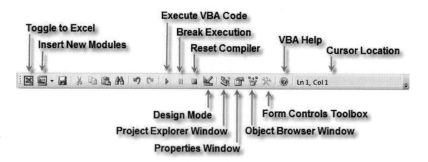

Figure 14-2: *Standard* VBA toolbar.

Procedures can be executed directly by placing the cursor inside the procedure and click the icon to execute the VBA code. The execute icon is commonly called the *Run* icon. Since functions return values and some accept input values, they are best tested by calling them from a procedure set up specifically for testing the function.

Debugging VBA Program Code

To debug program code means to troubleshoot or get rid of program "bugs" or program errors that cause the program not to work as it should. Program errors are categorized into three types:

- Syntax Errors
- Logic Errors
- Runtime Errors

Syntax errors are problems with the way the program code is structured or written that causes the compiler not to compile the program. Some syntax errors may be as simple as typographical errors in keywords or incorrect line breaks. Syntax errors also occur from violation of the programming code rules such as missing variable declarations or assigning a value to a variable that does not match its data type. Some syntax errors are identified in the VBA code editor prior to compiling the module. Others are identified by the compiler. When the compiler encounters a syntax error, the code execution will stop and the program will go into *break* mode. In break mode, the program highlights the line of code that caused the error and displays an error message indicating the kind of error encountered. To edit or re-execute the program code, you must first take the project out of break mode by using the "Reset" icon on the toolbar.

The compiler is the primary tool for troubleshooting syntax errors. It will locate one error at a time and provide an error message to indicate the syntax rule that is violated. The compiler also includes an auto-complete tool that assists with the insertion of property and method names of objects. When the period is typed after the object name, a list drops from the line of code and lists all properties and methods that are available for that object type. Begin typing or use the cursor to locate the property or method to insert into the code and use the *Tab* key or *Shift+Spacebar* to complete the entry.

Logic errors are more difficult to find and correct. The logic should be tested at design time and should be retested after it is programmed. Some logic such as incorrect output display is easy to detect and correct. Incorrect results from such things as using the wrong variable or incrementing a variable in the wrong location require more extensive testing to correct once they are discovered. VBA includes several debugging tools that are helpful in troubleshooting logic errors.

Runtime errors are program errors that are not encountered until the program executes. If runtime errors are not avoided or mitigated, the program will cease to run and will require a complete restart to resume operation. Runtime errors can cause loss of valuable time and data if not properly handled in the program code. Writing VBA code to handle runtime errors is a topic in Chapter 16 of this text.

Debugging Tools

To assist developers with testing and troubleshooting program code, the VBA application has an assortment of debugging tools.

- *Locals Window:* Displays all local variable types and values as the code executes. Good tool to use for troubleshooting logic errors and such errors as data type mismatches.

- *Immediate Window:* Displays printed output from the program code. To print output to the *Immediate* window, use the statement *Debug.Print* followed by the variable name or literal value to print. To print literal text strings, the text must be enclosed with double quotes. Useful for providing feedback from the code as it executes. For example, a feedback statement may be printed when the end of a case structure is executed to indicate the selected case.

- *Watch Window:* Displays selected project variables from any module, procedure, or function whose values and data types can be monitored any time the project is in break mode. The variable of interest is added to the watch list by the developer. A *Watch* window variable can be set to cause a program to go into break mode when its value changes.

- *Breakpoint:* Allows the developer to set a point in the program code for the program to halt execution and execute one statement at a time controlled by the developer. Set the break point by clicking on the left border of the code window beside the line of code for the break. With the cursor on the line of code, you may also toggle the break point on and off using the "hand" icon 🖐 on the Debug toolbar. Once the break point is set, the line of code is highlighted in brown and a large dot appears in the code editor margin beside the code statement.

- *Line-by-Line Code Execution:* The debug toolbar has three options for executing code during break mode.

  - *Step Into:* Each time the toolbar icon is pressed, the next line of code executes. When other modules are called, it steps into those also line-by-line.

  - *Step Over:* Works like *Step Into* unless the call is to another module. In that case, it executes the called module without stepping into it. Execution stops at the next line of code after the procedure or function call.

  - *Step Out:* Executes the remaining function or procedure instructions without stopping.

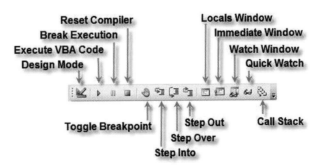

Figure 14-3: VBA *Debug* Toolbar.

As its name implies, the *Edit* toolbar includes icons for commands that help with writing or editing VBA code. Two very useful tools for code editing are the *Comment Block,* and the *Uncomment Block* commands. The *Comment Block* command adds an apostrophe in front of each line of selected code text which causes the compiler to ignore the lines of code. The *Uncomment Block* command removes an apostrophe from in front of each line of code in the selected block. When editing multiple lines of code, it is helpful to be able to comment or uncomment the lines all at once instead of having to insert and remove each line's apostrophe manually. Commenting lines and blocks of code instead of deleting them can significantly increase programming productivity.

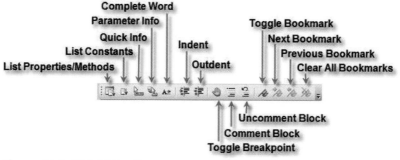

Figure 14-4: VBA *Edit* toolbar.

Quick Tip!

In addition to toolbar shortcuts, VBA has many keyboard shortcuts too. View the keyboard shortcuts for common VBA commands by moving the mouse over the toolbar icons. The code editor uses the same shortcut keys used in other Microsoft products. In addition to the text editing shortcuts, here are a few shortcuts that will significantly increase you productivity in the VBA environment.

Table 14-4: Keyboard shortcuts for common VBA debugging commands

Keyboard Shortcut	Command
F5	Execute the module
F9	Toggle breakpoint on and off
Ctrl+Shift+F9	Remove all breakpoints
Ctrl+G	Opens the *Immediate* window
F8	*Step Into* (execute next line of code)
Ctrl+F8	Execute to cursor
Shift+F8	*Step Over*
Ctrl+Shift+F8	*Step Out*
Ctrl+F9	Skip to cursor and execute next line
Shift+F2	With cursor inside function or procedure name in calling module, jumps to function or procedure definition for the called module
Ctrl+Shift+F2	Reverses the last Shift+F2 action

Practice 14-1: Test a Variant Variable

Objective: To watch as an undeclared Variant type variable changes its data type as data of different types are assigned to it.

1. Open a new file in Excel. Name it "Practice_ch4-1.xlsm."

2. Open the VBA application. Insert a new module into the project. Name the new module "Module_ch14."

3. Type the VBA code that is shown below into the module. If "Option Explicit" appears at the top of the module, comment it out so it will be ignored by the compiler.

```
Sub testVariant( )
    varVariable = "Hello"
    varVariable = 1
    varVariable = Date
End Sub
```

4. Open the *Locals* window. Note the three columns in the window, *Expression* (variable), *Value,* and *Type.*

5. Click in the left margin beside the first line of the procedure. The line of code will be highlighted in brown and will have a brown dot beside it in the left margin.

6. Place the cursor on a line of code within the procedure (including its header code and "End Sub" line). Execute the procedure by clicking the *Run* toolbar icon.

7. Using the *Step Into* icon on the *Debug* toolbar, execute one line of the procedure at a time until all lines have been executed. After each line of code has executed, note the types change in the *Locals* window.

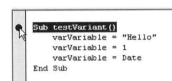

Figure 14-5: Click in the margin of the code editor to set a breakpoint.

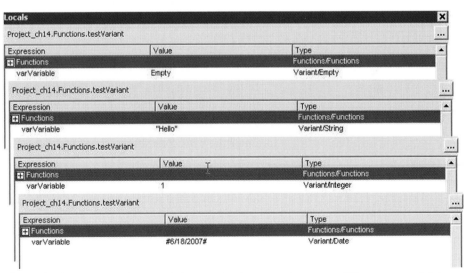

Figure 14-6: *Locals* window serial views as the data type changes as different types of data are assigned to a Variant type variable.

Practice 14-2: Test Variable Scope

Objective: Observe the results of executing procedures with local versus module level variables.

Examine the following examples of local and module level variable use. The procedure "AddTwoNumbers1" uses local variables. The procedures "InitNumbers", "AddTwoNumbers2" and "MultiplyTwoNumbers" share module level variables. (In the code examples, the green text is non-executable code comments.)

Local Variable Examples

```
Sub AddTwoNumbers1( )
    Dim num1 As Integer
    Dim num2 As Integer
    Dim sum As Integer
    sum = num1 + num2
    num1 = num1 + 1
    num2 = num2 + 2
End Sub
```

Module Level Variable Examples

```
'These variables are declared inside a module but outside of all inner module functions
'and procedures.
    Private num1 As Integer
    Private num2 As Integer
    Private result As Integer
    Private Const MULTIPLIER As Integer = 5

Sub InitNumbers( )
    num1 = 1
    num2 = 2
End Sub

Sub AddTwoNumbers2( )
    result = num1 + num2
    num1 = num1 + 1
    num2 = num2 + 2
End Sub

Sub MultiplyTwoNumbers2( )
    result = num1 * MULTIPLIER
    num1 = num1 + 3
End Sub
```

1. Continue with the VBA project, "Practice_ch14-1.xlsm" from the previous practice.

2. In the "Module_ch14" module enter the module level variable declaration immediately under the "Option Explicit" phrase at the top of the module. This area is called the *variables declaration* area of the module.

3. Enter the VBA code shown above for each of the four procedures.

4. Open the *Immediate* window. Add *Debug.Print* statements after each variable value change statement. The *Debug.Print* statements are shown below for the first module. Use the same pattern to add *Debug.Print* statements to remaining modules.

```
Sub AddTwoNumbers1()
    Dim num1 As Integer
    Dim num2 As Integer
    Dim sum As Integer
    num1 = 1
    num2 = 2
    Debug.Print num1
    Debut.Print num2
    sum = num1 + num2
    Debug.Print sum
    num1 = num1 + 1
    num2 = num2 + 2
    Debug.Print num1
    Debug.Print num2
End Sub
```

5. Place the cursor inside the "AddTwoNumbers1" module. Execute the code using the *Run* toolbar icon. Note the printed values in the *Immediate* window.

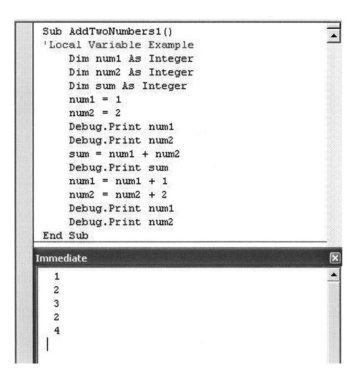

Figure 14-7: The print statements of the procedure can be viewed in the *Immediate* window.

6. Execute the procedure again and observe the results in the *Immediate* window.

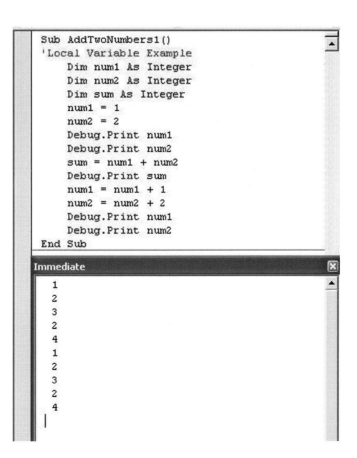

Figure 14-8: Subsequent executions of procedures with local variables produce the same result.

Note that the results are the same. Each time the procedure executes, the variables are declared anew and initialized back to the same initial values. No values are held from one execution of the procedure to another. Contrast the behavior of these variables with those in the next Practice exercise. Keep in mind that the variables are declared in the outer module and outside of the inner three procedures that use the variables. One procedure initializes the variables and the others alter the variable values. When one procedure alters the module level variable value, it retains its altered value even when accessed by a different procedure.

7. Be sure *Debug.Print* statements have been added to the remaining three procedures to show each variable value after it has been altered.

8. Now place the cursor inside the "InitVariables" procedure. Execute the code and observe the results in the *Immediate* window.

9. In the same way, execute the other procedures in the order they appear in the example code. Observe the variable values after each procedure is executed. Note how the variable values are carried over from one procedure to another.

Module level variables must be used very carefully for variables that may be shared by multiple modules. In most cases, the program can be designed to eliminate module level variables entirely by passing local variable values to other functions or procedures by way of arguments. Procedures typically follow one after another in the flow of program logic, so one procedure may pass its local variable values to another procedure when it is called.

Writing the Custom Function

To get ready to code a custom function, open the VBA programming application and insert a new module. Name the new module something that will indicate its purpose. Use the *Properties* window to rename the module. If you put all the custom functions for one application into one module, you might name it "Functions." You may want to put procedures and functions together in a module that support a particular task, such as the payroll calculation. In that case you may name it something like "PayrollProcessing." Use the module folders and module names to help you organize your VBA macro, procedure, and function code.

The first step in coding a custom function is writing the function header. The function header includes the function name, its parameter list, and the data type of its return value. The general syntax for a function header:

> Funtion *functionName* (*parameter1* As *dataType1*, *parameter1* As *dataType2*, . . .)
>   As *functionReturnDataType*

The italicized words in the general syntax are replaced by those specific to the function. An example of a function header for a function that calculates tax:

> Function SalesTax (taxableAmount As Currency, taxRate As Single) As Currency

The "SalesTax" function accepts two arguments, both decimal values, and returns a decimal value. When the function header is created, variables are created automatically to be used within the function. Each parameter identifier can be used in the function body to reference the argument values. The VBA function header also creates the return variable automatically. The return variable is the same name as the function and of the data type specified in the function header as the return value data type. To return the function's output value back to the calling environment, the final result of the function is assigned to the return variable.

There are two ways that VBA can pass arguments called modules, *byVal* (by value) or *byRef* (by reference). If a variable value is passed *by value* as an argument, logically a copy of the argument variable is passed to the memory location allocated to hold its matching parameter. If the variable is altered in the called module, the original variable value is not altered.

Passing *by reference* means that the actual memory reference to the variable is passed to the called module. The parameter in the called module is like an alias to the original variable. Any alteration to the argument in the called module alters the original variable value.

When given a choice, passing by value is considered the safer practice because it minimizes the exposure of the arguments to permanent change. Passing by reference is more efficient than passing by value because only a small pointer (the reference) is passed which takes very little memory to define. The pointer "points" directly to the variable data without duplications in memory requirements. In some cases where complex data structures are used, such as arrays or objects, passing by reference is required in some programming languages. When passing values in VBA, passing *byRef* is the default when a passing reference is not specified. When a passing reference is specified, it is entered in front of the variable to which it applies as in the following example. Since a passing reference is not supplied for "taxableAmount" it will be passed *byRef*.

Function SalesTax (taxableAmount As Currency, byVal taxRate As Single) As Currency

The next step in creating the custom function is identifying any local variables and constants needed to process the function data other than the input parameters and the return variable which have already been defined in the function header. Declare these variables and constants inside the function module immediately after the function header. Declare the constants first so they will be easy to locate in case changes in those values are needed later.

Once the variables and constants are defined, you are ready to write the code body. Below is an example of a function to calculate sales tax that accepts three arguments, the taxable amount (decimal value), the state tax rate (decimal value), and whether or not the city tax rate applies (Boolean value). When the Boolean argument value is TRUE, the city rate is applied, otherwise only the state rate is used to calculate the tax.

```
'The function header
Function Tax(amt As Currency, sRate As Single, city As Boolean) As Currency
    'Declare a variable to hold total tax rate when the city tax also applies.
    Dim rate As Single
    'Declare a constant to hold the city tax rate.
    Const CITY_RATE As Single = .02
    'If the city value is TRUE add the two rates together before calculating tax.
    If city Then
        rate = sRate + CITY_RATE
    Else
        rate = sRate
    End If
    'Calculate the tax
    Tax = amt * rate
End Function
```

When the tax calculation is performed the result is assigned to the "tax" variable so it will be returned from the function. The "tax" variable is the output variable and is declared automatically to match the function name and return type when the function header executes. In order for a value to be returned from the function, it must be assigned to the variable that bears the same name as the function.

Practice 14-3: Create a Custom Function

Objective: To follow the steps outlined in this chapter to write a custom function for the following business case.

Leisure Time Pools & Spas is a company that sells products and installation and repair services to customers in a very broad geographic area. Since the supplies and products they sell are delivered to customers' homes, the company is required to charge sales tax on supplies based on where the customer lives. They provide service in 10 different tax localities and each with a different sales tax rate. A few customers actually live in different states. In those cases, the pool company is not required to collect any sales tax. The company keeps its sales and service records in an Excel workbook. The formula for calculating the tax rate is somewhat complex.

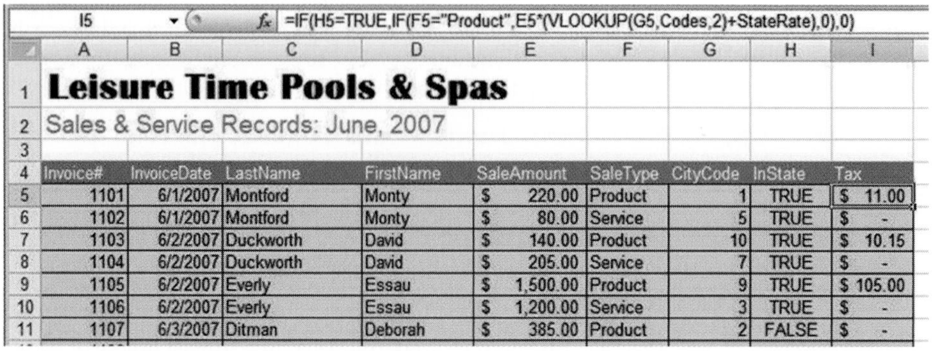

Invoice#	InvoiceDate	LastName	FirstName	SaleAmount	SaleType	CityCode	InState	Tax
1101	6/1/2007	Montford	Monty	$ 220.00	Product	1	TRUE	$ 11.00
1102	6/1/2007	Montford	Monty	$ 80.00	Service	5	TRUE	$ -
1103	6/2/2007	Duckworth	David	$ 140.00	Product	10	TRUE	$ 10.15
1104	6/2/2007	Duckworth	David	$ 205.00	Service	7	TRUE	$ -
1105	6/2/2007	Everly	Essau	$ 1,500.00	Product	9	TRUE	$ 105.00
1106	6/2/2007	Everly	Essau	$ 1,200.00	Service	3	TRUE	$ -
1107	6/3/2007	Ditman	Deborah	$ 385.00	Product	2	FALSE	$ -

Figure 14-9: Monthly sales data for products and service. Note the tax formula in column I.

The lookup table for city tax code and rate is a named range called "Codes" and the state tax rate is a single cell named "StateRate." The state sales tax rate is 4.5%.

Table 14-5: Table of city codes and tax rates for Leisure Time Pools & Spas

City Code	Tax Rate(%)
1	0.5
2	0.75
3	1
4	1.25
5	1.5
6	1.75
7	2
8	2.25
9	2.5
10	2.75

Custom functions can greatly simplify complex worksheet formulas such as the tax calculation in column I of the Leisure Time worksheet. We can use VBA code to create a custom function that performs the tax calculation by simply entering a call to the function into the "Tax" column cells and sending the arguments "SaleAmount," "SaleType," "CityCode," and "InState."

1. Open the practice file "LeisureTime_ch14-3.xlsm." Save the file as "LeisureTime_ch14-3_S.xlsm." Open the VBA application. Add a new module. Name it "TaxFunction."
2. Design the logic of the function before beginning to write the function.
   a. The function should perform the following actions:
      (i)   Check to see if the sale was a product or service. Sales tax is collected only on product sales. If the product sale was to an out-of-state customer, no state sales tax is collected.
      (ii) If the sale was a product, get the tax rate. If the sale is a service, the tax is zero.
      (iii) Use the city code to get the city sales tax rate from a table.
      (iv) Check the value of "InState." If it is TRUE, add the state sales tax rate to the city rate.
      (v)   Calculate the tax for the product sale.

3. Create the function header, including input parameters and function return data type. (The VBA code will automatically insert the "End Function" line when the function header is added.)

```
Function tax(amt As Currency, servType As String, code As Integer, inState As Boolean) As Currency
```

4. Declare a variable to hole the cumulative rate when both city and state rates apply.

```
Dim rate As Currency
```

5. Write the VBA code for the function logic. Use the worksheet lookup table for the city tax rate and the "stateRate" named cell reference for the state sales tax rate.

```
If servType = "Product" Then
    rate = Application.WorksheetFunction.VLookup(code, Range("Codes"), 2)
    If inState Then
        rate = rate + Range("stateRAte")
    End If
    tax = amt * rate
Else
    tax = 0
End If
```

"Tax" Function Explained

The "tax" function uses a VBA IF statement to test the value of "servType" for "Product" or "Service" to see if tax should be calculated or if it should be zero. If the sale is a product it looks up the city tax rate by calling the worksheet VLOOKUP function to look up the function input value "code" in a worksheet cell range named "Codes." A *Debug.Print* statement has been added to verify the value of rate when the function is tested. A nested IF statement checks the Boolean value of "instate." If "inState" is TRUE, the state rate is referenced from a worksheet cell named "stateRate" and added to the city rate that was returned from the VLOOKUP worksheet function and the tax is calculated. The "tax" variable is the return value and was declared automatically to match the function name and return type.

```
Function tax(amt As Currency, servType As String, _
            code As Integer, inState As Boolean) As Currency
Dim rate As Currency
    If servType = "Product" Then
        rate = Application.WorksheetFunction.VLookup(code, Range("Codes"), 2)
        'Print statement added to verify the value of rate when
        'the function is tested.
        Debug.Print rate
        If inState Then
            rate = rate + Range("stateRAte")
        End If
        tax = amt * rate
    Else
        tax = 0
    End If
End Function
```

Figure 14-10: The completed VBA code for the sales tax function.

6. Add a function description that will display when a user inserts the function into an Excel formula.

   a. In Excel select **Developer(tab)→Code(group)→Macros** from the ribbon. The *Macro* dialog box will appear.
   b. Type the function name into the *Macro* name text box.
   c. Click the *Options* button. The *Macro Options* dialog box will appear.
   d. Type a function description into the *Description* text box. Click the *OK* button to save the description and close the *Macro Options* dialog box. Click the *Cancel* button to close the *Macro* dialog box.

7. Test the function in Excel. On the "LeisureTime" sales list, select the first formula cell in the tax column. Delete the formula, then use the *Shift+F3* keyboard shortcut (or other technique) to access the *Insert Function* dialog box. Select the *User-Defined* function category, the select the "tax" function.

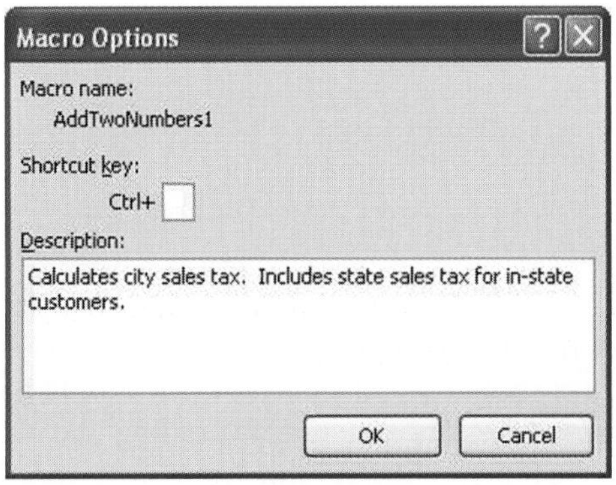

Figure 14-11: The function description entered in the *Macro Options* dialog box will appear in the *Insert Function* and *Function Arguments* dialog boxes.

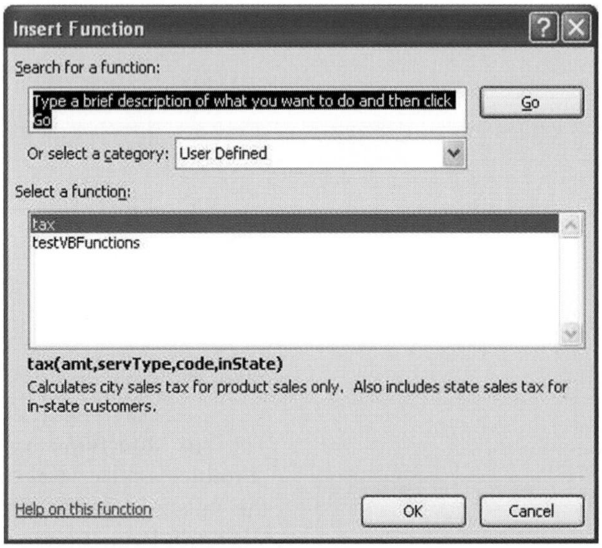

Figure 14-12: The "tax" function is listed in the *User-Defined* category. The function description added by the developer is displayed when the function is selected.

8. Complete the function call as you would for any Excel function. The function result should be the same as the previous formula result.

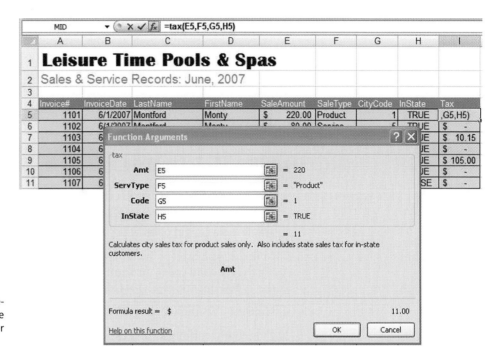

Figure 14-13: The function description is also displayed in the *Function Argument* dialog box for the custom function.

9. Practice calling the function from another VBA module.
   a. Enter the following procedure code into the same VBA module as the function you created. It is simple to create such a "test" procedure to test the behavior of a function from the VBA environment.

```
Sub testTaxFxn( )
        Dim taxtotal As Currency
        Dim amt As Currency
        Dim rate As Currency
        Dim code As Integer
        Dim inState As Boolean
        'Assign hard-coded values to variables for test purposes.
        amt = 100
        rate = 0.045
        code = 2
        inState = True
        'Call to the "tax" function.
        taxtotal = tax(amt, rate, code, inState)
        'Print statement to test value of return value.
        Debug.Print taxtotal
End Sub
```

   b. With the *Immediate* window open, execute the procedure to see that the correct function value is returned back to the procedure.

Store Custom Function in a Global Workbook

In practice exercises in Chapter 13, you stored macros in a global workbook called the Personal Macro Workbook. The Personal Macro Workbook is stored as personal.xlsb (or personal.xls) in a folder named XLSTART so it will open every time Excel opens. Storing a macro workbook or a workbook containing user-defined functions in an XLSTART folder will enable all Excel VBA projects to access the worksheet and VBA code it contains just as it can access the Personal Macro Workbook.

All workbooks containing custom VBA code should be hidden from users' view. The Personal Macro Workbook is hidden from Excel but is visible in the VBA application as a VBA project because it contains VBA code. To hide the active open Excel workbook from users' view, select **View(tab)→Window(group)→Hide** from the Excel ribbon. The workbook will be instantly hidden. To unhide, select the Unhide command from the same task group. The Unhide command will prompt the user to select the workbook to unhide from a list of all hidden workbooks.

Practice 14-4: Creating a Custom VBA Workbook

1. Open a new Excel workbook. Name the workbook "VBAFunctions_14-4.xlsm."

2. Make sure the "LeisureTime_ch14-3.xlsm" workbook you used in the previous example is saved and open.

3. In the *Project Explorer* window of VBA, select the "TaxFunction" module containing the function code you wrote in the previous Practice and drag and drop it onto the "VBAFuncntions_ch14-4.xlsm" project name.

4. Hide the "VBAFunctions_ch14-4.xlsm" workbook.

5. Close both workbooks and close Excel.

6. Move the "VBAFunctions_ch14-4.xlsm" workbook to one of the XLSTART folders (see Chapter 13 for XLSTART locations).

7. Reopen Excel. Open the VBA Project Explorer window. Note that both the "personal.xlsb" (or "personal.xls") file and the "VBAFunctions_ch14-4.xlsm" are visible but neither is visible from Excel.

8. Open the "LeisureTime_ch14-3.xlsm" workbook.

9. Update the formula in the tax column of the sales list to call the function from the global VBA workbook. Note that the function name now includes the name of the global workbook project since the function code is outside the current VBA project.

Review Questions

1. How are Excel worksheet functions used in the VBA environment? Can all worksheet functions be used in VBA?

_____

_____

_____

2. What are two advantages of creating custom VBA functions?

_____

_____

_____

3. List at least two ways the need for custom functions is identified.

_____

_____

_____

4. List the six general steps for creating a custom function.

_____

_____

_____

5. How does the declaration of constants in VBA differ from the declaration of variables?

_____

_____

_____

6. What variable types in VBA are used to represent decimal values?

_____

_____

_____

7. List four strict rules (not just conventions) that must be applied to the declaration of variables in VBA.

_____

_____

_____

8. What is meant by the scope of a variable?

_____

_____

_____

9. Why is it a good idea to explicitly declare variables before they are used?

_____

_____

_____

10. What happens with a variable that is not declared in VBA in the default mode ("Option Explicit" not present) of the program environment?

_____

_____

_____

11. What type of data does a VBA Variant data type hold?

_____

_____

_____

12. How can the developer be assured every variable is explicitly declared before it is used?

_____

_____

13. List the three types of programming errors and at least one cause of each type.

_____

_____

_____

14. What is meant by *break* mode in VBA?

_____

_____

_____

15. How is the *Locals* window used for troubleshooting program code? When can it be viewed?

_____

_____

_____

16. What is displayed in the *Immediate* window during program execution?

_____

_____

_____

17. What is a *breakpoint* in VBA code?

_____

_____

_____

18. Describe what each of the three line-by-line code execution features do; *Step Into*, *Step Over*, and *Step Out*.

_____

_____

_____

19. What does the *Comment Block* command do?

_____

_____

_____

20. What is meant by a global function workbook? What are the options for storing the global workbook (review from Chapter 13)?

_____

_____

_____

Practice Problems

1. Create a custom function in VBA that accepts a retail sales order subtotal and a zip code, and calculates sales tax based on the sales tax rate for the given zip code. After the sales tax is computed, the system displays the order subtotal, the tax rate applied, and the function's return value in the *Immediate* window in VBA. (Use a CASE structure to assign tax rates based on zip codes.)

    For zip code 27409 the sales tax rate is 6.5%.
    For zip code 24060 the sales tax rate is 5.0%.
    For zip code 24343 the sales tax rate is 4.5%.
    For zip code 28149 the sales tax rate is 5.5%.

2. In return for handling the legal matters for settling estates, a legal practice charges according to the following schedule:

    *   10% of the first $500,000 of the estate value
    *   8% of the next $700,000 of the estate value
    *   5% of the remaining estate value

    Create a custom function that accepts the estate value and returns a value for the legal fee. Have the legal fee print in a message box.

3. Create a custom function that accepts the current gross income and year-to-date gross income for an employee and returns the amount of social security tax to withhold for the current pay period. The following rules apply to calculating the social security tax owed for 2007.

    a. The portion of tax paid by the employee (withheld from pay) is 6.2% of gross wages.
    b. Social security tax is paid on only the first $97,500 earned in 2007.

4. Create a custom function that accepts the date and time an employee clocked in to work and the date and time he clocked out and returns the number of hours worked as a decimal value. Have the return value of the function print in the *Immediate* window.

5. Open the workbook "Employees_Prob14-5.xlsm." Add a new module to the project and name it "VestedFunction." Create a custom function in the module that accepts the hire date of an employee and returns a value of "Yes" or "No" if the employee is vested in the company retirement system. The employee must have worked at least 5 years to be vested. Enter a formula in the Vested column of the employee worksheet that calls the function and supplies the hire date argument.

6. Open the workbook "HealthClub_Prob14-6.xlsm." Insert a new module and name it "CalcFeeFunction." Create a custom function in the module that calculates a health club membership fee based on the following input factors:

   a. Family size

      • The health club charges a base rate of $500/year for one person.
      • For two family members the rate is 1.5 times the base rate.
      • For three or more family members the fee is 2 times the base rate.

   b. Age group

      • If the primary member of the family is of 60 years or older the total family membership fee is reduced by 10%.
      • If the primary member of the family is of 70 or over the total family membership fee is reduced by 70%.

   c. Corporate affiliation

      • If the primary membership subscriber is affiliated with a company that subsidized employee membership, the total family membership fee is reduced by 10%.

   Enter a formula into the "Fee" column of the "Members" worksheet that calls the function and supplies arguments of number of members, age group, and corporate affiliation from the worksheet.

7. Open the workbook "Grades_Prob14-7.xlsm." Insert a new module into the workbook and name it "GradesAverageFxn." Create a custom function in the module that accepts four exam grades and returns the average of the highest three scores. Exam scores represent a percentage score and are entered as mixed numbers. Enter a formula into the FinalAverage column that calls the function and supplies the four exam scores as arguments.

8. Create a new version of the function you created in the previous problem that assigns a letter grade to each set of exam scores based on the average of the highest three scores. The revised function should return the letter grade for each set of exam grades. The letter grade is assigned based on the following scale.

   a. A: 90 and above
   b. B: 80 and above, but less than 90
   c. C: 70 and above, but less than 80
   d. D: 60 and above, but less than 70
   e. F: Less than 60

Enter a formula into the "FinalGrade" column of the Grades worksheet that calls the function and supplies the four exam scores as arguments.

9. Create a custom function that accepts a value for estimated taxable income and returns the annual state income tax owed according to the following tax schedule.

   a. 2% of the first $3000 of taxable income
   b. 3% on income over $3000 but not over $5000
   c. 5% on income over $5000 but not over $17,000
   d. 5.75% on income over $17,000

10. Create a function that calculates an employee's state (for paying state income taxes) estimated annual taxable income based on the current gross pay, pay frequency, and number of dependents. (Use a constant to specify the pay frequency.) Tax payers are not taxed on the first $3000 of annual income. Annual taxable income is reduced $800 for each dependent. If a dependent is over 65 years of age or blind, the reduction for that dependent is $900 instead of $800.

11. Revise the function you created in Problem 9 so that it accepts the current gross pay, number of regular dependents, and number of dependents over 65 or blind. The revised function should call the function you created in Problem 10 and use its return value to calculate estimated annual tax. The estimated annual tax liability should be used to determine the amount to withhold for the current pay period (this function's return value).

CHAPTER FIFTEEN

Using Forms to Enhance Excel Applications

Learning Objectives

1. Design and create a custom user form using the VBA programming environment
2. Use the VBA MsgBox function to display information to the user
3. Use the VBA InputBox function to capture a single input from the user
4. Set form and form control properties at design time using the *Properties* window
5. Set form and form control properties at run time using VBA code
6. Display a form by clicking on a worksheet button
7. Display a form in response to a workbook event
8. Display or show a form from another form
9. Use VBA decision structures to validate input data
10. Use selected form controls to validate input data
11. Create a splash screen that displays when the workbook opens
12. Write custom event procedures in VBA to respond to form control events
13. Insert form data into worksheet cells

Introduction to Custom Forms in VBA

Creating custom dialog boxes for your Excel project can add functionality, create a more professional interface for the project, and provide users a friendly way to interact with the workbook application. Excel's VBA programming environment offers several options for adding custom dialog boxes. Each type of dialog box can be customized to fit the needs of the Excel project.

The message box can be used to display a message to the user and take some action based on the user's interaction with the message box. The message box is a pre-defined dialog box in the VBA programming environment that is created by using the MsgBox function in VBA.

The input box provides a simple interface for capturing one item of input at a time from the user. The input box is a pre-defined dialog box that can be created by using either the InputBox function or the InputBox method in VBA. An input box created with the InputBox method differs from one created using the InputBox function in that it allows validation of the user's input for the most common data types.

A VBA custom form provides a blank palette for creating a custom form for collecting and processing many types of data entered by the user. The custom form is created by inserting a *UserForm* module into the Excel/VBA project and adding the desired form controls which are used for capturing various types of input data. Each UserForm module is an instance (object) of the UserForm class in VBA. VBA code can be written to process form data in response to a user's interactions with the form.

The benefits of creating custom dialog boxes and forms are very similar to those of creating a custom function. Both tools serve to simplify, clarify, and improve the speed at which a user can accomplish a given task in an Excel workbook. Some uses of custom dialog boxes in Excel include:

- Efficiently capture input data from a user and perform some manipulation or calculation outside the Excel worksheet environment.
- Provide a way for the user to enter data into an Excel worksheet that may not be entered using a typical Excel *Data Form*.
- Display a title page (called a "splash screen") for an Excel workbook.
- Display a message to the user about what the program is doing or about errors encountered.
- Provide a menu for navigating worksheets and other interfaces in the customized Excel application.

VBA Message Boxes and Input Boxes

VBA Message Box

A message box is used to display information to the user. It is typically used to provide feedback to the user such as displaying error messages or the status of some program object. A message box is created by using the MsgBox function rather than creating an instance (object) of the UserForm class. The MsgBox function takes one mandatory argument, and three optional arguments. We will be concerned with only the first three arguments; the mandatory argument and the first two optional arguments.

Mandatory argument: *Prompt* is the message to be displayed on the dialog box. The message may be a variable value or a literal text string. If the message is a text string, it must be specified inside a set of double quotes.

Optional arguments:

1. *Buttons:* Type of buttons to display. The most common types of button combinations are:

   0 = vbOKOnly
   1 = vbOKCancel
   2 = vbAbortRetryIgnore
   3 = vbYesNoCancel
   4 = vbYesNo
   5 = vbRetryCancel

2. *Title:* Text to display in the title bar of the message box. This is a text string so it must be specified inside double quotes.

Message Box Return Value

The user responds to a message box by clicking on a button on the message box. Each message box has at least one button, the *OK* button which closes the message box when clicked by the user. When multiple buttons are used on a message box, it is necessary to determine which button the user clicked in order for the program to execute the appropriate response. Each button has an associated integer value that can be captured by the program when it is selected by the user. The integer value of the selected button is called the "return" value from the message box. The return value is an integer, so the data type of the return variable must be a numeric type. Below are the return values for each type of message box button.

   1 = vbOk
   2 = vbCancel
   3 = vbAbort
   4 = vbRetry
   5 = vbIgnore
   6 = vbYes
   7 = vbNo

Practice 15-1: Message Box 1

Objective: When the Excel workbook opens, show a message box that greets the user and asks him if he would like to continue. The message box will look similar to the one pictured below. If the user clicks the *Yes* button, the message box will close and the user may begin using the workbook. If the user clicks the *No* button, the workbook will close.

1. Open the practice file "Employees_ch15-1.xlsm."

2. In the Visual Basic Project Explorer, double click on the *ThisWorkbook* object to open that program module for writing the VBA code.

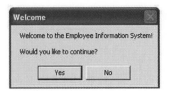

Figure 15-1: The welcome screen can be created using the MsgBox function.

3. From the drop list on the left above the code window, select the *Workbook* object.

4. From the drop list on the right above the code window, select the *Open* procedure. The VBA procedure header "Sub Workbook_Open( )" and "End Sub" will be added automatically to the module.

5. Between the procedure header and "End Sub" add the VBA code that allows a message box to appear when the workbook opens. The message box should have a welcome message. It should ask the user if he wants to continue. Provide the argument that places the *Yes* and *No* buttons on the message box.

    a. Declare a variable named "result" to capture the return value of the message box. What type should it be to accept the result? (Make it a numeric data type since the return value of a button is an integer.)

    Dim result As Integer

    b. Assign the result of the message box to the return variable. Use the concatenation operator (&) to insert two "line feeds" (ANSI character #10) for friendlier formatting. (The ANSI character for a "tabbed" space is character #9 and is also useful in formatting dialog boxes. Insert it the same way as the line feed character using the Chr(9) syntax.)

    result = MsgBox("Welcome to the Employee Information System!" & _
    Chr(10) & Chr(10) & "Would you like to continue?", vbYesNo, "Welcome")

    The underscore at the end of the first line of code is used as a line-continuation character to note that the line of VBA code is continued on an additional new line. There must be a space in front of the underscore when used in this context.

    c. Code the actions for the return values. Use an IF-THEN-ELSE structure to test to see which button was clicked by the user. If the *Yes* button is clicked by the user, 6 is the value returned from the MsgBox function. If the *No* button is clicked the value 7 is returned.

    If result = 6 Then
        ThisWorkbook.Activate
    Else
        ThisWorkbook.Close
    End If

    Since there are only two options available to the user, there is no need to test for a *No* button value (7). If the return value is not 6, then it will be 7.

6. Test the procedure with the workbook open, then close the workbook and reopen it to see that it executes correctly when the workbook opens. Debug and correct the code as needed.

Practice 15-2: Message Box 2

Objective: To add functionality to the "BudgetTemplate" macro we recorded and edited in Chapter 13, add a message box to the CASE statement (Case Else) that notifies the user if the macro does not find a match for the month of the previous worksheet. The message box should have only one button, the *Yes* button. When the user clicks the *Yes* button, the macro should end without allowing the program to crash.

1. Open the Excel file "MyBudget_ch15-2.xlsm".

2. Open the macro "BudgetTemplate" in the Visual Basic Editor.

3. Locate the CASE ELSE statement in the macro.

4. Before the "Exit Sub" statement in the case structure, insert a statement that will display a message box that will inform the user that the previous month cannot be

identified and that the task to add an addition worksheet for the new budget will be terminated.

MsgBox ("The previous worksheet Month cannot be identified. Correct the previous worksheet's Month to a 3-character abbreviation and restart the task.")

5. Test the revised macro and debug as needed. Be sure to change a final worksheet name to be incorrect in order to test the error handling code.

VBA Input Box

The VBA input box is used to capture simple input from the user, one input item at a time. An input box is created by using the InputBox function. The InputBox function takes one mandatory argument, and five optional arguments. We will be concerned with only the first two arguments; the mandatory argument and the first optional argument.

<u>Mandatory argument</u>: *Prompt* which is the instruction to the user regarding the input.

<u>Optional argument</u> (first one only): *Title* which is the text displayed in the title bar of the input box.

Input Box Return Value

The return value of the input box is the input entered by the user into its text box. The input captured from an InputBox function is a text string. The programmer declares a String variable to hold the return value.

Practice 15-3: Input Boxes

Objective: To add functionality to the "BudgetTemplate" macro we recorded and edited in Chapter 13, add an input box to the CASE statement (Case Else) so that the user can enter the correct month and year in case the previous worksheet month abbreviation is not recognized by the CASE statement. It will enable the macro to keep running correctly instead of exiting with a runtime error. The input boxes will be similar to those pictured below. When no string value is entered for the *Title* argument the default "Title" is used (which in this case is "Microsoft Excel").

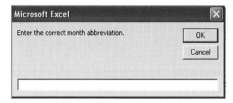

Figure 15-2: Create an input box to accept the correct month abbreviation.

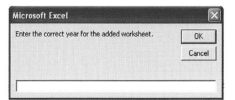

Figure 15-3: Create a second input box to accept the correct year abbreviation.

1. Open the Excel file "MyBudget_ch15-3.xlsm".

2. Open the macro "BudgetTemplate" in the Visual Basic Editor.

3. Locate the CASE ELSE statement in the macro.

4. After the MsgBox statement (entered during the previous practice exercise), and before the statement that concatenates the month and year into a new worksheet

name, enter the code to create an input box that asks the user to enter the correct new month abbreviation. Assign the user's input to the "newMonth" variable.

newMonth = InputBox("Enter the correct month abbreviation.")

5. Create a second input box that asks the user to enter the correct year. Assign the user's input to the "year" variable.

year = InputBox("Enter the correct year for the added worksheet.")

6. Test the macro and debug as needed. Be sure to change the final worksheet name to be incorrect in order to test the error handling code.

7. Insert the same VBA statements before the "Exit Sub" line of code in the IF structure used to validate the year as numeric. Test the macro and debug as needed.

Creating VBA User Forms

A VBA custom form may be designed and created from the ground up by adding a UserForm module to the Excel/VBA project and adding the desired form controls to the new form. The UserForm module is an instance (object) of the VBA UserForm class. To insert the UserForm module, select the Excel/VBA project in the Project Explorer window then select **Insert→UserForm** from the VBA menu bar. A new UserForm palette will appear in the main window.

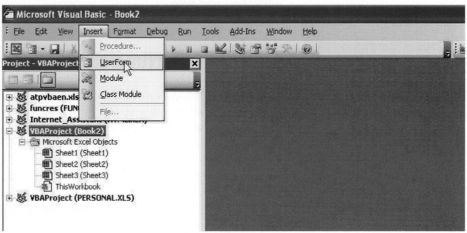

Figure 15-4: Insert a new UserForm from the *Insert* menu.

Quick Tip!

Quickly insert a new module using the second icon from the left on the VBA *Standard* toolbar. A drop list reveals the three module types. When the icon is simply clicked, a module of the last type added will be added without accessing it from the drop list.

The default name for the new form is "UserForm1" (for the fist form inserted). The name of the form can be modified in the *Properties* window (lower left of VBA window) along with many other form properties. By convention, form names should begin with the "frm" prefix. An appropriate name for a form that calculates a membership fee might be "frmMemberFee".

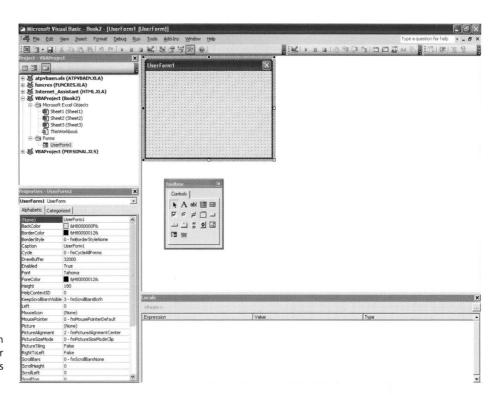

Figure 15-5: The new UserForm palette and form control toolbar appears when a new UserForm is added.

Form Controls

When the UserForm module is added to the VBA project, it provides the container to which form "controls" can be added. The form controls are the actual items on the form with which the user interacts. Forms allow the user to input data, display data, or select defined options. Each type of control is used for a specific type of user input. Form controls are selected from the floating *Toolbox* window that appears when the form is the selected module. (Note the *Toolbox* in Figure 15-5.) Place the mouse pointer over each control in the *Toolbox* to view the name of the type of control. To add a control to the form, drag the control from the *Toolbox* to the form using the left mouse button. The control can be resized and formatted once it is on the form palette.

Naming Form and Control Objects

Names and many other properties for form controls can be set in the *Properties* window while the control is selected on the form design palette. Just as the UserForm class in VBA is used to create UserForm objects, each control class is used to create an actual control object. For example, many text boxes can be created for each form object. Each text box is an instance of the TextBox class so each text box must be assigned a unique name.

The VBA programming environment assigns a default name to each control object created. Examples of default names are "TextBox1", "TextBox2", "Label1", "Label2", etc. When we create a new UserForm or form control object, it should be named using a common convention to help identify each particular object in the VBA code. A default name is assigned by the VBA application, but the name has no meaning with regard to its functionality or its role in the Excel/VBA project. A name assigned by the developer is able to reflect more information about the purpose of the form control. For example, a TextBox named "txtFirstName" gives the developer information about the data that is collected from the particular control. It not only indicates that the last name will be entered into the TextBox, but it also indicates that the control is a TextBox which is helpful when processing the captured data in VBA code. Table 15-1 that shows the *Toolbox* icon and standard naming convention prefix for the most common VBA form control objects.

Table 15-1: Form controls available for VBA user forms

Toolbox Icon	Control Type	Naming Prefix	Description and Use
A	Label	lbl	For displaying information. Used to label textboxes and other controls. Used to display formatted output on the form. The label is not used for data input.
ab|	TextBox	txt	Box in which users usually type text of numeric input. Is also used in association with a SpinButton to display its value.
	ListBox	lst	Displays a list of items from which users can select one.
	ComboBox	cbo	Combination of a TextBox and a ListBox. Users may select from the list or type input into the TextBox. Is also called a drop-down list or drop-down box.
	CheckBox	chk	Displays a square box and a label for the box that allows users to make a choice of "Yes" (box checked) or 'No' (box unchecked).
	OptionButton	opt	Displays a small circle with an associated label. Used in a group to allow the user to choose only one option from the group of OptionButtons. OptionButtons for one group are placed inside a frame. More than one group of OptionButtons can be used on one form by using a different frame for each group. Also called radio button.
	ToggleButton	tgl	A button that can appear pressed or not pressed. Allows users to make a choice of "Yes" (button pressed) or "No" (button not pressed).
	Frame	fra	A container in which OptionButtons or other controls can be grouped for functionality of formatting.
	CommandButton	btn or cmd	More commonly called simply "button." Events (most commonly the click event) associated with a button are typically programmed to run event procedures or macros.
	TabStrip	tab	Contains a collection of tabs used to organize controls on one form.

(continued)

Table 15-1: Form controls available for VBA user forms (*continued*)

Toolbox Icon	Control Type	Naming Prefix	Description and Use
	MultiPage	mul	Uses tabs to access a separate page of a form which is actually a separate form.
	ScrollBar	scr	A bar that can be placed vertically or horizontally that enables you to change a value by dragging slider along the bar.
	SpinButton	spn	A control that contains an up and a down button that is used to change the value of the SpinButton. To view the value of a SpinButton on a form, a Label or TextBox must be associated with the SpinButton using VBA code. To associate the TextBox or Label with a SpinButton, the Text or Value property of a TextBox, or the Caption property of a Label is assigned the value of the SpinButton. The SpinButton can be changed from vertical to horizontal by dragging a size handle to one side. Change it back to a vertical position by dragging a size handle toward the top or bottom of the form.
	Image	img or pic	Displays a graphic image.
	RefEdit	ref	Button used to select a range in a worksheet.

Building a Custom Form

The first step in designing a custom UserForm is deciding what controls are needed on the form and the arrangement of the controls on the form.

General steps involved with creating a new custom form are these:

1. Plan what you want the user to do with the custom form. It may be helpful to sketch the layout of the form on paper before beginning to create the form.

2. In the Visual Basic Editor, insert a new UserForm module and modify its properties as desired.

3. In the Visual Basic Editor, add form controls to the form design palette, and modify each form control's properties as needed.

4. Check and modify the tab order of the form as needed.

5. Decide how the form should be launched. For example, Welcome screens can be launched when the workbook opens, whereby other forms can be launched from a related worksheet. Forms can even be launched from other forms such as in a menu hierarchy.

6. In the proper module, write the VBA code to launch the form.

7. In the Visual Basic Editor, write VBA event procedures for form or control events of interest. These event procedures should be written in the code window of the UserForm object module

Event Programming Revisited

Program procedures (or macros) are recorded or written in VBA to respond to user events as the user interacts with a UserForm object. For example, you might write a "Calculate" procedure to execute when a button labeled "Calculate" is clicked by the user. You might write a procedure that clears and resets all the controls on a UserForm object when a button labeled "Clear Form" is clicked. You would write a procedure that removes the form from view when a button labeled "Cancel" is clicked. There are several events possible for each type of form control, but only a few event procedures are typically needed for each UserForm object. Event procedures need not be written for all form controls or for all events of a single control. Write only the procedures that are needed by the program.

Practice 15-4: VBA Custom Form—Part 1

Objective: To create the form interface for a game that an elementary school student may play to help him improve his basic math skills. He will enter two numbers on which a mathematical operation will be performed. He will select the operation to perform; addition, subtraction, multiplication, or division. He will also enter his answer to the calculation. When he clicks the *Check Answer* button, the program will calculate the correct answer and compare it to the user's answer. If the user's answer is correct, a "thumbs up" image will be displayed on the form. If the user's answer is incorrect, the program will display a "thumbs down" image on the form. When the user clicks the *Clear* button, the text boxes and math operator options will be reset to the way they were when the form opened and the images will disappear from the form.

1. Open a new Excel workbook. Name the workbook "MathGame_ch15-4.xlsm".

2. Open the VBA application by selecting **Developer(tab)→Code→Visual Basic** from the Excel ribbon.

3. Insert a new UserForm module into the project by selecting the project name then select **Insert→UserForm** from the menu bar.

4. In the *Properties* window:
   a. Set the Name property to "frmMath."
   b. Set the Caption property to "Math Game."

5. Add a Label control to the top of the form.

6. With the Label control selected, set the Caption property in the *Properties* window to "Welcome to the Math Game."

7. Add three TextBox controls to the form. Set the Name property for each of them "txtNum1", "txtNum2", and "txtAnswer", respectively.

8. Add a Frame to the form. Set the Caption property of the Frame to "Math Operation".

9. Add four OptionButtons to inside of the frame. Set the Name property of the four OptionButtons "optPlus", "optMinus", "optMul", "optDiv", respectively. Set the Caption property for the four options to "+", "−", "*", and "/" respectively.

10. Arrange the form controls as shown in Figure 15-6.

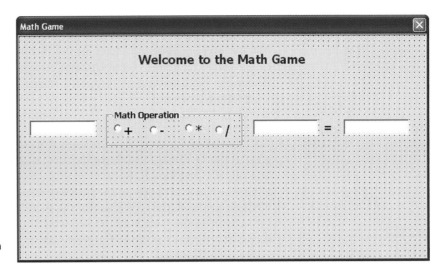

Figure 15-6: Layout for the form controls for the Math Game form.

Add a Label that extends across the top of the TextBoxes and OptionButtons that tells the user what to enter with each of the controls. Include the instructions in the Caption property for the label. You will need to include spaces between the text to align each instruction with each form control. (Optionally, you may add four separate Label controls above the four controls. Set the Caption property for each with the user instruction for the associated control.)

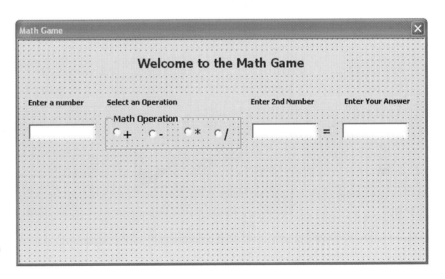

Figure 15-7: Add labels to the form controls.

11. Add a button (a CommandButton control) to the form.
    a. Set the Name property to "btnCheck".
    b. Set the Caption property to "Check Answer."

12. Add another button to the form.
    a. Set the Name property to "btnClear."
    b. Set the Caption property to "Clear."

13. Add two more labels to the form.
    a. For the first label, set the Caption property to "Correct Answer."
    b. For the second label:
      • Remove the default value for the Caption property so that there is nothing displayed in the Label.
      • Set the Name property of the Label to "lblAnswer,"

14. Add an image control to the form.
    a. Set the Name property of the image control to "imgCorrect."
    b. Click on the ellipse (. . .) icon for the Picture property.
    c. Navigate to the "oneThumbUp.wmf" image file. Select the file.
    d. For the PictureSizeMode property, select *1—fmPictureSizeModeStretch* from the drop-down list.
    e. Set the Visible property to *FALSE* using the drop-down list.

15. Add another image control to the form that overlays the first image. Leave only an edge of the first image visible on the form design so that each image control may be easily selected for editing.
    a. Set the Name property of the image control to "imgIncorrect."
    b. Click on the ellipse (. . .) icon for the Picture property.
    c. Navigate to the "oneThumbDown.wmf" image file. Select the file.
    d. For the PictureSizeMode property, select *1—fmPictureSizeModeStretch* from the drop-down list.
    e. For the Visible property, select *FALSE* from the drop-down list.

The completed form layout should look similar to the one in Figure 15-8.

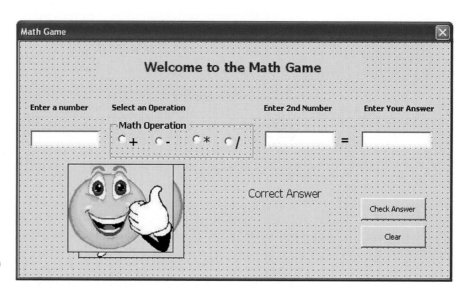

Figure 15-8: The completed Math Game form design.

Navigating the Form with the Tab Key

The *tab order* of form refers to the order in which the cursor (control focus) will move from one control to another when the user presses the *Tab* key. After all controls are on the form and the layout is complete, set the tab order to allow the user to navigate the form controls in the order that supports the functionality of the form. For example, the user will want to enter the first number, then the sign, then the second number, and finally their answer. The user will then check the answer using the "Check Answer" button. After that, the "Clear" button will be used to clear the form for another math problem. Setting the tab order of the form controls permits the user to use the keyboard *Tab* key to more about the form in the order customary for typical use of the form.

For each form control two properties are involved in setting its tab order. The first property, *TabStop*, must be set to TRUE for the control to accept focus. All form controls have a default value for *TabStop*. For example, the TabStop is automatically set to TRUE for a text box, but set to FALSE for a label because users enter data into a text box, but typically do not interact with a label.

The second property used for tab control is the *TabIndex* property. That is the index number that represents the relative order in which the controls are accessed by the *Tab* key. The first control that accepts focus has a *TabIndex* of zero (0), the second is one (1), etc. The default value of *TabIndex* is set by the order in which the controls are added to the form. The default values are set for all controls, even those whose default value of *TabStop* is FALSE. As long as the *TabIndex* of one control is lower than another, it will accept the focus before the control with the higher index value. For example, the form controls that accept focus may be represented by tax indexes of 3, 5, 8, 10, and 13. In this example form, the controls with indices of 1, 2, 4, 6, 7, 9, 11, and 12 have the *TabStop* property set to FALSE.

The tab order of the form controls may be set by setting the TabIndex value for each control individually in the *Properties* window, or by using the special tab order tool in VBA. The tab order tool allows the developer to set the tab order by arranging the control names in the order in which you wish them to set focus. To use the tab order tool, select the form and select **View→Tab Order** from the VBA menu bar. The *Tab Order* dialog box will appear listing all the form control names in the default tab order. To change the order, select a control name and use the *Move Up* and *Move Down* buttons to reposition it in the tab order list.

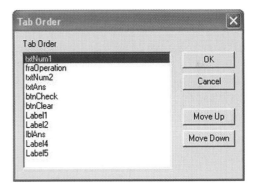

Figure 15-9:   Select *View→Tab Order* from the VBA toolbar to view and change the tab order of form controls.

Note that the option buttons do not appear in the tab order list for the form. The frame containing the option buttons is listed and is set to accept focus after the text box for the first number. The tab order for the option buttons within each frame is separate from the form controls as a group. To set the tab order of option buttons, select just the option button frame and a separate tab order list will be visible for just the option buttons. Alternately, you may set each option button TabIndex property in the *Properties* window. The indices for each option button group (within one frame) will start with zero (0).

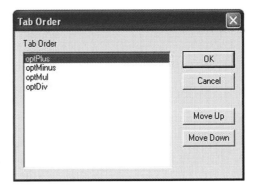

Figure 15-10:   Select the option button frame to set the tab order of an option button group.

Setting a Default Button

CommandButtton controls have a *Default* property that may be set to TRUE or FALSE. When the *Default* property is set to TRUE, that particular button's Click event will be executed when the user presses the *Enter* key. Only one button on each form may have a TRUE value. Whenever one button's *Default* value is set to TRUE, the other buttons are automatically reset to FALSE.

Handling Custom Form Data

Now that you have the custom form created, you should plan the logic needed to collect and process data the user enters using the form controls. Consider which controls will need to trigger an action.

1. When the "Check Answer" button is clicked the program will need to:

   a. Validate user input to make sure he has entered numbers that can be used in a mathematical calculation.
   b. Calculate and display the correct answer in the appropriate Label.
   c. Compare the user's answer with the correct answer, and then show the correct image for whether the answer is correct or incorrect.

2. When the "Clear" button is clicked:

   a. All the text boxes should be cleared.
   b. The output Label for the correct answer should be cleared.
   c. The cursor should be reset to the first text box.

3. Other tasks that are needed:

   The form should clear when it opens or reopens. In Excel and VBA a form may be shown and hidden rather than re-created each time it is called upon to display. If there is data in the form when it is hidden or closed, the data may still be there when it is reopened. Clearing the form either when it activates or when it closes will eliminate the problem of left-over data populating the form when it opens.

Capturing User Input from Custom Forms

In order to process user input from custom forms, the input must be captured from the form controls. Table 15-2 summarizes the usual property that is captured and the actual VBA syntax for capturing the user input or selection depending on the type of form control. In each case the input is captured into a variable of the appropriate data type for the control property value. For example, a TextBox input is captured into a String type variable whereas the input for a CheckBox (checked = True, not checked = False) is captured into a Boolean type variable. Each property listed below is also the default property for the particular type of form control. *The default property of a form control is the property that is captured if a property is not specified.* The first VBA code example for each control type is the syntax for capturing the input specifying the property to capture. The second VBA code example for each control type is the syntax for capturing the default property when that property is not specified.

Converting from One Data Type to Another

When capturing form data into variables it is sometimes necessary to convert data from one type to another. For example, text boxes only accept text data. Properties of forms and controls are really variables that hold some item of data related to its object so they each have an assigned data type just as other program variables. The Text property of the text box is a text data type. Even when numeric characters are entered into a text box, it is still regarded as text. To assign the contents of a text box to a numeric

Table 15-2: VBA syntax for capture form input from each type of from control

Control Type	Naming Prefix	Property to Capture (default)	VBA Syntax to Capture
TextBox	txt	Text or Value	custCity = txtCity.Text custCity = txtCity
ListBox	lst	Text	itemType = lstItemType.Text itemType = lstItemType
ComboBox	cbo	Text	custState = cboState.Text custState = cboState
CheckBox	chk	Value	isReg = chkReg.Value isReg = chkReg
OptionButton	opt	Value	isRed = optRed.Value isRed = optRed
ToggleButton	tgl	Value	isCelsius = tglCelsius.Value isCelsius = tglCelsius
SpinButton	spn	Value	quantity = spnQty.Value quantity = spnQty
RefEdit	ref	Value	range1 = refRange1.Value range1 = refRange1

variable, the data should be converted from a character data type to a numeric data type. VBA has a group of pre-defined functions that can be used to perform that operation. Each of these functions begins with a C (for "convert") followed by an abbreviation to represent the new data type.

Table 15-3: Type conversion functions in VBA

Function Name	Return Value	Example
CBool	Converts a string ("true", "false") or integer value (1, 0) to a Boolean value	isSame= CBool(strName = "Heidi")
CByte	Converts a value to a byte value	num = CByte(dblNum)
Ccur	Converts a value to a Currency value	tax = CCur(txtTax.Text)
CDate	Converts a value to a Date/Time value	dtBirthdate = CDate(txtBirthdate.Text)
CDbl	Converts a value to a Double decimal value	dblFactor = CDbl(sngNum1/sngNum2)
CDec	Converts a value to a Decimal value	decNum = CDec(varNum)

(continued)

Table 15-3: Type conversion functions in VBA (*continued*)

Function Name	Return Value	Example
CInt	Converts a value to a Integer value	intAge = CInt(txtAge.Text)
CSng	Converts a value to a Single decimal value	price = CSng(txtPrice.Text)
CStr	Converts a value to a String value	lblNum1.Caption = CStr(intNum1)
CVar	Converts a value to a Variant value	CVar(txtAddInfo.Text)

The Caption property of a label is also a text data type. In order to display formatted numbers or dates, the data must be converted from numeric types to a text type of data. VBA has a group of pre-defined format functions that can be used to perform that operation. Each of these functions begins with the word "Format" followed by the type of format. These format functions include special characters and decimals as indicated by the type, such as dollar and percent signs. The FormatCurrency, FormatNumber, and FormatPercent have a default number of decimal places of two. To change the default number or decimal places, enter the desired number of places as the second argument which is optional. The FormatDateTime has five options for displaying the formatted date/time value.

Table 15-4: Pre-defined number formatting functions in VBA

Function Name	Example	Displays
FormatCurrency	lblDisplay.Caption = FormatCurrency(expression)	$39,456.26
	lblDisplay.Caption = FormatCurrency(expression, 0)	$39,456
FormatDateTime	lblDisplay.Caption = FormatDateTime(expression) [Default format is "vbGeneralDate"]	1/9/2008 6:12:40 AM
	lblDisplay.Caption = FormatDateTime(expression, vbLongDate)	Wednesday, January 09, 2008
	lblDisplay.Caption = FormatDateTime(expression, vbLongTime)	6:12:40 AM
	lblDisplay.Caption = FormatDateTime(expression, vbShortDate)	1/9/2008
	lblDisplay.Caption = FormatDateTime(expression, vbShortTime)	06:12
FormatNumber	lblDisplay.Caption = FormatCurrency(expression)	39,456.26
	lblDisplay.Caption = FormatCurrency(expression, 4)	39,456.2588
FormatPercent	lblDisplay.Caption = FormatCurrency(expression)	45.25%
	lblDisplay.Caption = FormatCurrency(expression, 4)	45.2498

In addition to the pre-defined format functions, VBA also offers a general FORMAT function that may be used to add a pre-defined format or a custom format designed by the user. To use a pre-defined format, specify the name of the format in the second argument of the function. There are many format names in VBA that reference pre-defined functions such as "Currency," "Long Date," "Scientific," "Yes/No," and "Fixed." The general syntax for the FORMAT function:

Format(*expression, formatName*)
Example: Format(num1 = num2, "Yes/No") 'Returns "Yes" or "No"

In addition to the fixed formats, the developer may define custom formats using system symbols and place holders.

Custom Format Examples:

strVariable = Format(factor, "0.00%")	'Returns "85.45%"
strVariable = Format(time1, "hh:mm:ss AMPM")	'Returns "06:30:00 AM"
strVariable = Format("Hello", "<")	'Returns "hello"
strVariable = Format("Hello", ">")	'Returns "HELLO"

Validating User Input for Custom Forms

When the program requires numeric data to perform its operations, the program will cease to run when non-numeric data is supplied. Fields left blank can also cause problems when the program refers to the control input data that does not exist. To ensure that the program encounters only valid input values from a form, the programmer writes VBA code that validates the data as it is collected from the form. Data can be validated to prevent blank fields, to ensure that text or numeric data has been entered, that data entered is within a range of values or is from a finite list of values.

The most common program structure for validating input data is the decision structure. The decision structure is implemented in VBA using the IF-THEN-ELSE structure. VBA provides some functions that can be used for testing the type of data and other characteristics of the user input. For example, the ISNUMERIC function tests an input value to see if it is a numeric value. The ISDATE function tests an input value to see if it is in a date format that VBA recognizes.

After input data has been validated, the user should be notified if any data entered is not valid. The most common way of notifying the user of entry errors is with a message box created with the MsgBox function. Once the message box is displayed, the user should be directed back to the control that contained the invalid data. The invalid data should be cleared from the control so the user can enter valid data.

Practice 15-5: VBA Custom Form—Part 2

Objective: To validate and process data entered by the user for the Math Game. The program must check each of the three TextBoxes for valid numeric data. If any of the three TextBoxes contain invalid data, the user should be notified and the TextBox containing the invalid data should be cleared and selected so that the user can enter valid data.

The data validation is performed when the *Check Answer* button is clicked. The VBA code for validating the data is written in the click event procedure (macro) for the *Check Answer* button. All data entry must be validated before the procedure attempts to calculate the correct answer so the data validation must be performed in nested decision structures.

1. Continue with the Math Game form you built in the previous practice session.

2. In the Visual Basic Editor, select the frmMathGame object. Double-click the *Check Answer* button on the form design palette. The VBA code window for the form will appear and the event procedure header ("Sub btnCheck_Click(()") and "End Sub" will automatically be added to the code window.

3. Immediately following the procedure header, write VBA code to declare variables to hold form data for processing.

   a. A string variable to hold the sign the user selects:

   Dim sign As String

b. A string variable to hold the formula that is concatenated using the input from the first text box, the math operator, and the second text box.

Dim formula As String

c. A numeric variable to hold the calculated answer.

Dim answer As Single

Use decision structures to figure out which math operator the user selected. (Note that a CASE structure cannot be used for this operation because the values of numerous expressions (the different option buttons) are being evaluated. A CASE structure may only be used when one variable or expression is tested against multiple values.) Include a message to the user in the case that no option button has been selected.

```
If optPlus.Value = True Then
    sign = "+"
ElseIf optMinus.Value = True Then
    sign = "-"
ElseIf optMul.Value = True Then
    sign = "*"
ElseIf optDiv.Value = True Then
    sign = "/"
Else
    MsgBox ("Please select a math operation.")
End If
```

4. Validate the data input in each of the TextBoxes. For each invalid entry, display a message to the user, clear the TextBox and select the TextBox for new entry by the user. If all data input is valid, calculate, and compare the answer with the user's answer. Display the answer in the control lblAns. Text following an apostrophe is a comment added to explain the VBA code, and are not executable statements.

```
'Test each TextBox to make sure none are blank or non-numeric
If txtNum1.Text <> "" And IsNumeric(txtNum1.Text) = True Then
    If txtNum2.Text <> "" And IsNumeric(txtNum2.Text) = True Then
        If txtAns.Text <> "" And IsNumeric(txtAns.Text) = True Then
            'Concatenate the elements of the formula into a string
            formula = txtNum1.Text & sign & txtNum2.Text
            'The Evaluate function will return a value from the formula string.
            answer = Evaluate(formula)
            'Show the appropriate image for correct or incorrect answers.
            lblAns.Caption = answer
            'Compare the calculated answer and the user's answer.
            'Show the appropriate image for correct or incorrect answer.
            If answer = txtAns.Text Then
                imgCorrect.Visible = True
                imgIncorrect.Visible = False
            Else
                imgIncorrect.Visible = True
                imgCorrect.Visible = False
            End If
        Else
            'Message displays when answer TextBox is empty or non-numeric.
            MsgBox "Enter a numeric value for your answer."
            'The TextBox is reset for new input.
            txtAns.Text = ""
            txtAns.SetFocus
        End If
```

```
            Else
                    'Message displays when answer TextBox is empty or non-numeric.
                    MsgBox "Enter a numeric value for the second number."
                    'The TextBox is reset for new input.
                    txtNum2.Text = ""
                    txtNum2.SetFocus
            End If
    Else
            'Message displays when answer TextBox is empty or non-numeric.
            MsgBox "Enter a numeric value for the first number.
            'The TextBox is reset for new input.
            txtNum1.Text = ""
            txtNum1.SetFocus
    End If
```

5. Run the form and test it. Be sure to test it with various types of input to make sure the appropriate error messages display at the proper time.

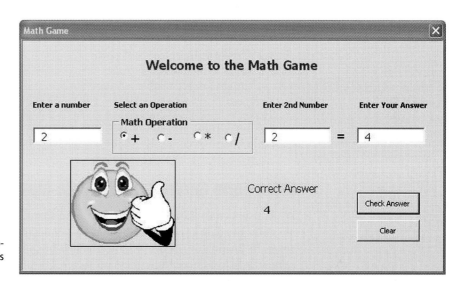

Figure 15-11: Executed form appearance when correct answer is entered.

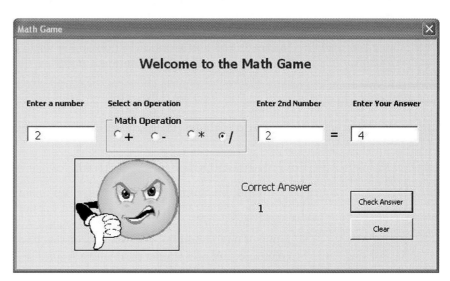

Figure 15-12: Executed form appearance when incorrect answer is entered.

6. Write code to clear the form when the *Clear* button is clicked. Double-click on the Clear button on the form design palette. The VBA code window for the form will appear and the event procedure header ("Sub btnClear_Click(()") and "End Sub" will automatically be added to the code window. Write the VBA

code between the procedure header and the 'End Sub' statement to clear all form controls.

```
Private Sub btnClear_Click()
    'Set the Caption property of the answer Label to an empty string.
    lblAns.Caption = ""
    'Set the text property of the first TextBox to an empty string.
    With txtNum1
        .Text = ""
        'Set the cursor to the first TextBox.
        .SetFocus
    End With
    'Clear remaining TextBoxes.
    txtNum2.Text = ""
    txtAns.Text = ""
    'Reset all option buttons to the unselected state.
    optPlus.Value = False
    optMinus.Value = False
    optMul.Value = False
    optDiv.Value = False
    'Make both images invisible.
    imgCorrect.Visible = False
    imgIncorrect.Visible = False
End Sub
```

7. Test the form to make sure all controls are cleared and reset when the Clear button is clicked. (See Figure 15-13 for completed VBA code for this Practice.)

Using Form Controls to Validate Input

When users enter data into text boxes on a form, there are chances that a user may not enter the data correctly or he may not enter the correct data into the correct text boxes. In the previous VBA practice the text box input must be validated for numeric values if it is to be used in mathematical calculations. To help prevent data entry errors, VBA offers form controls that help the developer control the quality of data that is entered into the form. You have already seen how option buttons provide a way to permit the use to select from a finite list of values rather than enter values in free text format. In addition to option buttons, other forms controls are available to aid in input data validation. The OptionButton, CheckBox, ComboBox, ListBox, and SpinButton form controls eliminate the necessity of text boxes in which users would otherwise need to type the data. These controls limit the user's choice of selections, therefore limiting the chances of user entry error. Once the developer sets up the controls with the desired parameters, little additional data validation is required for their inputs.

OptionButtton Form Controls

OptionButton controls are used in a group to allow the user to select only one item from the group. Option buttons are used for options such as color, age group, and gender for which only one selection is valid. A form may contain more than one group of option buttons. For example, one set of option buttons may be used for item color selection on an order form and a second set of option buttons may be used for size selection. A Frame form control is used for grouping option buttons on user forms. The Frame object should be added to the form, after which the option buttons are added to the Frame. The Frame around the option buttons is the indicator that those option buttons inside are a group of which only one can be selected. If a second option button is selected, the one that was previously selected become unselected. Each individual option button is named with a prefix of "opt."

```
Option Explicit
Private Sub btnCheck_Click()
    'Declare a string variable to hold the sign the user selects.
    Dim sign As String

    'Declare a string variable to hold the formula that is concatenated.
    Dim formula As String

    'Declare a string variable to hold the calcualtion result.
    Dim answer As String

    'Assign a symbol to sign based on the option button selected.
    If optPlus.Value = True Then
        sign = "+"
    ElseIf optMinus.Value = True Then
        sign = "-"
    ElseIf optMul.Value = True Then
        sign = "*"
    ElseIf optDiv.Value = True Then
        sign = "/"
    Else
        'In case no operator is selected, a message to user.
        MsgBox ("Please select a math operation.")
    End If

    'Test each TextBox to make sure none are blank or non-numeric
    If txtNum1.Text <> "" And IsNumeric(txtNum1.Text) = True Then
        If txtNum2.Text <> "" And IsNumeric(txtNum2.Text) = True Then
            If txtAns.Text <> "" And IsNumeric(txtAns.Text) = True Then
                'Concatenate the elements of the formula into a string
                formula = txtNum1.Text & sign & txtNum2.Text
                'The Evaluate function will return a value from the formula string.
                answer = Evaluate(formula)
                'Show the appropriate image for correct or incorrect answers.
                lblAns.Caption = answer
                'Compare the calculated answer and the user's answer.
                'Show the appropriate image for correct or incorrect answer.
                If answer = txtAns.Text Then
                    imgCorrect.Visible = True
                    imgIncorrect.Visible = False
                Else
                    imgIncorrect.Visible = True
                    imgCorrect.Visible = False
                End If
            Else
                'Message displays when answer TextBox is empty or non-numeric.
                MsgBox "Enter a numeric value for your answer."
                'The TextBox is reset for new input.
                txtAns.Text = ""
                txtAns.SetFocus
            End If
        Else
            'Message displays when answer TextBox is empty or non-numeric.
            MsgBox "Enter a numeric value for the second number."
            'The TextBox is reset for new input.
            txtNum2.Text = ""
            txtNum2.SetFocus
        End If
    Else
        'Message displays when answer TextBox is empty or non-numeric.
        MsgBox "Enter a numeric value for the first number."
        'The TextBox is reset for new input.
        txtNum1.Text = ""
        txtNum1.SetFocus
    End If
End Sub
Private Sub btnClear_Click()
    'Set the Caption property of the answer Label to an empty string.
    lblAns.Caption = ""

    'Set the text property of the first TextBox to an empty string.
    With txtNum1
        .Text = ""
        'Set the cursor to the first TextBox.
        .SetFocus
    End With
    'Clear remaining TextBoxes.
    txtNum2.Text = ""
    txtAns.Text = ""
    'Reset all option buttons to the unselected state.
    optPlus.Value = False
    optMinus.Value = False
    optMul.Value = False
    optDiv.Value = False
    'Make both images invisible.
    imgCorrect.Visible = False
    imgIncorrect.Visible = False
End Sub
```

Figure 15-13: Complete VBA code for the two button Click events of the Math Game form.

The Value property of an option button is set to TRUE or FALSE to indicate that the option button is either selected (TRUE) or not selected (FALSE). When the option button is added to the form, the Value property is FALSE by default. To capture the value of the selected option button, all the button values in a group must be tested. The best programming structure for testing option buttons is nested IF statements or an IF statement that uses an ESLEIF pattern. Since each test is for a different object's value, a CASE structure would not be an appropriate structure for testing option buttons. Consider the example below where the user selects the color of a text message to display on a form. In the example, the colors are standard colors in VBA.

```
Dim fontColor As String
If optRed.Value = True Then          OR      If optRed.Value Then
    fontColor = vbRed                              . . . . . .
ElseIf optBlue.Value = True Then              ("=True" may be omitted)
    fontColor = vbBlue
ElseIf optGreen.Value = True Then
    fontColor = vbGreen
Else:
    fontColor = vbBlack
End If
```

In the following example, a group of option buttons is used to select the color of the text to be displayed in the "Hello" message in a label on a form. The combo box is used to select the font type for the message. The user selections for the option buttons and combo boxes are captured using VBA code similar to the previous example for option buttons. Declare variable for the font type and font color.

```
Dim fontColor As String
Dim fontType As String
```

Set the font type and color of the message label using the following VBA code:

```
lblMessage.Font.Name = fontType
lblMessage.ForeColor = fontColor
```

Figure 15-14: Use the option buttons to select one font color for the "Hello" message.

Practice 15-6: OptionButton Form Controls

Objective: Create a form like the form in Figure 15-14 that permits the user to select the font color for the "Hello" message by selecting one of the option buttons.

1. Open a new Excel file. Name the file "OptionButtons_ch15-6.xlsm".

2. Open the VBA application. Insert a new user form into the project file you just created.

3. Name the user form "frmOptionButtons."

4. Set the form caption to "OptionButtons Example."

5. Add a label to the form. Set the caption of the label to "Hello." Name the label lblMessage. Set the label font size to 16.

6. Add a frame control to the form. You do not need to change the default name of the frame.

7. Add four options buttons to the frame. Name each one 'opt' plus the color it represents, for example, optRed, optBlue, etc.

8. Set the captions for the option buttons to represent the colors Red, Blue, Green, Black.

9. In the *Properties* window set the option button for "Black" to be the default value selected by setting the Value property to TRUE.

10. Add a button to the form. Name the button 'btnShow.' Set the caption of the button to "Show Message."

11. Double click on the button you just added to insert a default event procedure. Enter the VBA code into the procedure that performs the following actions:

   a. Declare a text variable to accept the font color as the option buttons are processed.

   Dim fontColor As String

   b. Use a decision structure to test the values of each option button to see if it is selected. You will need to use a nested ELSEIF pattern for the decision structure. Since option buttons represent mutually exclusive options, you need not check the last option button value. You can use the last ELSE instruction to set the font to black. (If you do not set a default button to be selected, the ELSE instruction prevents the situation in which no option button is selected. For each option button tested, set the fontColor variable to the appropriate Visual Basic color constant (vbRed, vbBlue, etc.).

   ```
   If optRed.Value Then
       fontColor = vbRed
   ElseIf optBlue.Value Then
       fontColor = vbBlue
   ElseIf optGreen.Value Then
       fontColor = vbGreen
   Else
       fontColor = vbBlack
   End If
   ```

   c. Set the color of the message box text to the color selected using the option buttons. The font color is the ForeColor property. (The background color is the BackColor property.)

   lblMessage.ForeColor = fontColor

   d. Test the form and debug the code as needed.

```
(General)                                        ▼   (Declaratio

    Option Explicit|

 Private Sub btnShow_Click()
     'Declare a variable to assign the vb color
     'constant based on the option button selected.
     Dim fontColor As String

     'Test the value of each option button to see
     'which on is selected (TRUE).
     If optRed.Value Then
         fontColor = vbRed
     ElseIf optBlue.Value Then
         fontColor = vbBlue
     ElseIf optGreen.Value Then
         fontColor = vbGreen
     Else  'no need to check the last option
         fontColor = vbBlack
     End If

     'Set the color of the font for the message label.
     lblMessage.ForeColor = fontColor
 End Sub
```

Figure 15-15: Completed VBA code for the "btnShow" click event.

CheckBox Form Controls

A CheckBox control consists of a small empty square box with a caption. When the box or caption is clicked by the user, a check is displayed in the small square. A check box may be used alone or several may be grouped into a set. In contrast to option buttons, a user may select any or all check boxes in a group. Consider the example that uses check boxes to allow employees to select the benefits for which they want to enroll. An employee may elect to enroll in any or all of the following benefits: medical insurance, dental insurance, vision plan, and long-term disability.

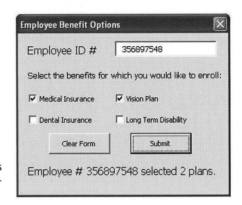

Figure 15-16: Check box controls offer the user a way to select multiple options.

Since each of the check boxes are separate items and not related to a group, each input is captured in a separate code structure so that some action can be taken for each check box rather than just one action for the entire group (as in option buttons). Like the option buttons, it is the Value property that is captured when the check box is checked. If the check box is checked, the Value property = True. Like the option buttons, the "= True" may be omitted since referring to a Boolean property (the Value property) by name implies its TRUE value. The VBA code to capture the selected check boxes is:

```
If chkMed.Value = True Then
   medical = 1
End If

If chkDental.Value = True Then
   dental = 1
End If

If chkVis.Value = True Then
   vision = 1
End If

If chkLtd.Value = True Then
   ltd = 1
End If
```

In the code above, the integer value of 1 is assigned to the plan variable so the number of plans can be counted and displayed on the form in order to test the operation of the check boxes. Note that each check box value is evaluated in a separate (single alternative) IF statement.

Practice 15-7: CheckBox Form Controls

Objective: Practice capturing check box values using separate IF structures and taking some action based on whether the check box is checked or unchecked.

1. Open a new Excel file. Name the file "CheckBoxes_ch15-7.xlsm".

2. Open the VBA application. Insert a new user form into the project file you just created.

3. Name the user form "frmCheckBoxes."

4. Set the form caption to "Employee Benefit Options."

5. Add a label to the form for the "Employee ID #" label. Set the caption to "Employee ID #" and the font size to 12.

6. Add a text box for the user to enter the employee identification number. In the *Properties* window set the maximum length of the entry to 9 characters. (MaxLength property)

7. Add a second label to the form to display user instructions for selecting the check boxes. You do not need to change the default name or font size of the label. Set the label caption to "Select the benefit for which you would like to enroll."

8. Add four check boxes to the form to represent the benefit options. Name the check boxes chkMed, chkDental, chkVision, chkLtd, respectively. Format the captions to match those in Figure 15-16.

9. Add two button controls to the form. Name the two buttons "btnClear" and "btnSubmit," respectively. Set the caption for the "btnClear" button to "Clear Form." Set the caption of the "btnSubmit" button to "Submit."

10. Add a third label to the form to display the results of the employee's selection. Name the label "lblDisplay." Set the label font size to 12.

11. Double-click the "btnClear" control to add VBA code for its Click event.

    a. Clear the text from the employee ID text box.

       txtEmpID.Text = ""

    b. Set all the check box values to FALSE.

       chkMed.Value = False
       chkDental.Value = False
       chkVision.Value = False
       chkLtd.Value = False

    c. Clear the text from the lblDisplay control.

       lblDisplay.Caption = ""

```
Private Sub btnclear_Click()
    chkMed.Value = False
    chkDental.Value = False
    chkVision.Value = False
    chkLtd.Value = False
    txtEmpID.Text = ""
    lblDisplay.Caption = ""
End Sub
Private Sub btnSubmit_Click()

    Dim plans As Integer
    Dim empid As String

    empid = txtEmpID.Text

    If chkMed.Value = True Then
        plans = plans + 1
    End If

    If chkDental.Value = True Then
        plans = plans + 1
    End If

    If chkVision.Value = True Then
        plans = plans + 1
    End If

    If chkLtd.Value = True Then
        plans = plans + 1
    End If

    If plans = 1 Then
        lblDisplay.Caption = "Employee # " & empid & " selected " & plans & " plan."
    Else
        lblDisplay.Caption = "Employee # " & empid & " selected " & plans & " plans."
    End If

End Sub
```

Figure 15-17: Completed VBA code for the two button click events of the "frmCheckBoxes."

ListBox and ComboBox Controls

A ListBox control is somewhat like a large text box except that it initially holds a list of items from which the user can select one item. The list of text items that is displayed may be set ahead of time, or items may be added to the list at runtime. A list box or combo box can be populated ahead of runtime with a named range of cell values in Excel. In the properties window for the list box or combo box control, enter the assignment operator (=) followed by the range name in the cell beside the RowSource property. For a list of font types whose range name in Excel is "fontTypes" enter "=fontTypes" in the cell beside the RowSource property.

A ComboBox control is much like a list box that is attached to a text box. In the default style of combo box, the list box drops down from the text box. The developer may include instructions or a default value to display in the text box. The text box text is not a part of the actual list of values to display. A ComboBox object is named with a prefix of "cbo".

Figure 15-18: List box (left) and combo box (top right) controls validate input by limiting users' choices.

A ListBox object is named using the prefix "lst". The string value that the user highlights in the list box is the Text property of the ListBox object. The Text property is the default property that is captured from the list box selection. Alternate properties that may be captured are the Value property which captures the same values as the Text property, and the ListIndex property which is an index number that represents the item's position in the list that is selected. The first item in the list has an index number of zero. For a list box that allows the user to select the font for a message, the user's selection would be captured using the following VBA code:

```
Dim fontType As String
fontType = lstFont.Text (the selected text from the list box)
Or
fontType = lstFont.Value
Or
Dim fontIndex As Integer
fontIndex = lstFont.ListIndex (ListIndex in the index number of the item that is
currently selected. The first item has an index number of zero.)
```

Items may be added to or removed from list boxes at runtime if the list of items is not bound to a data source that is specified as the RowSource property value. To add an item to a list box at run time, use the AddItem method. To add a new font type "Courier" to the list box, the following VBA code is used:

```
lstFont.AddItem "Courier"
```

If you wish to allow the user to specify an item to add, the item must first be captured from the user by using another control or dialog box then assigned to the list box as a new list item.

```
Dim newItem As String
newItem = InputBox("Enter an item to add to the list box.")
```

To remove an item from a list box use the RemoveItem method of the ListBox object. The integer following the method name represents the index number of the item (its position in the list) to be removed. The following VBA code removes the fourth item in the list box. (The first item has an index number of zero.)

```
lstFont.RemoveItem 3
lstFont.RemoveItem lstFont.ListIndex (Removes the item that is currently high-
    lighted.)
lstFont.Clear (Removes all items from the list box.)
```

Most of the commonly used properties and methods of the ListBox objects are the same for ComboBox objects. Like the ListBox, the ComboBox user selection is captured by capturing the Text property value by default. The Value and ListIndex properties may also be captured from the user selection.

```
Dim fontType As String
fontType = cboFont.Text
Or
fontType = cboFont.Value
Or
Dim fontIndex As Integer
fontIndex =cboFont.ListIndex
```

To permit a user to add a list item to the combo box at runtime, capture the user input from the text box and add it to the combo box list.

```
cboFont.AddItem cboFont.Text
```

Processing ComboBox and ListBox Selections

When trying to figure out which programming structure(s) to use to process the selections from list boxes and combo boxes, think about the nature of the selections and how they fit into the programming structures. CASE structures are generally used for evaluating values of a variable or expression when the values (cases) are mutually exclusive. Recall that the option button selections represent mutually exclusive options, but each option evaluated is a different expression (each individual option button's value) therefore could not be processed using a CASE statement. In most cases the list box and combo box are used to represent different values for one expression (the Text, Value, or ListIndex property). When used in this way, a CASE structure is the most efficient way to process list box and combo box selections. However, list boxes and combo boxes may be set to permit the selections of multiple options. In that case each option would need to be handled separately, each item tested with its own IF structure.

Practice 15-8: ListBox and ComboBox Form Controls

Objective: Practice capturing check box values using separate IF structures and taking some action based on whether the check box is checked or unchecked.

1. Open a new Excel file. Name the file "ListComboBoxes_ch15-8.xlsm".

2. On any worksheet list the colors "Red", "Blue", "Green", "Black" in a column in four consecutive rows. Name the cell range "colors."

3. On any worksheet list the font styles "Arial", "Broadway", "Courier New" in a column in four consecutive rows. Name the cell range "fonts."

4. Open the VBA application. Insert a new user form into the project file you just created.

5. Name the user form "frmComboList."

6. Set the form caption to "ListBox and ComboBox Examples."

7. Add a list box to the form. In the *Properties* window set the:

   a. Name the list box "lstColor."
   b. RowSource property "=colors" (without quotes).

8. Add a label above the list box you added in the previous step. Set the caption of the label to "Select a Font Color." Set the font size to 10 and the font effects to bold.

9. Add a combo box to the form. In the *Properties* window set the:

   a. Name property to "cboFont."
   b. RowSource property "=fonts" (without quotes).
   c. Text property of the combo box to "Select Font Style."

10. Add a label to display the "Hello" message. In the *Properties* window set the:

    a. Name property to "lblMessage."
    b. Caption property to "Hello."
    c. Font to size 16 and bold effect.

11. Add a button to the form. Name the button "btnShow." Set the caption to "Show Message."

12. Double-click the btnShow to add VBA code to its Click event.

    a. Declare string variables to hold values for font style and font color.

    ```
    Dim fontType As String
    Dim fontColor As String
    ```

    b. Use a decision structure to check to see which color option was selected in the list box. Since the same property is tested each time (lstColor.Text), a CASE structure is appropriate. The color names preceded by "vb" are Visual Basic color constants whose color is already defined by the programming language.

    ```
    Select Case lstColor.Text
        Case "Red": fontColor = vbRed
        Case "Blue": fontColor = vbBlue
        Case "Green": fontColor = vbGreen
        Case Else: fontColor = vbBlack
    End Select
    ```

    c. Since the font style is an actual string value when it is applied in VBA code, the combo box selection can be used directly to set the font style.

    ```
    fontType = cboFont.Text
    ```

    d. Set the font color and font style for the message label.

    ```
    lblMessage.Font.Name = fontType
    lblMessage.ForeColor = fontColor
    ```

13. Run the form and debug as needed.

```
Private Sub btnShow_Click()

    Dim fontType As String
    Dim fontColor As String

    Select Case lstColor.Text
        Case "Red": fontColor = vbRed
        Case "Blue": fontColor = vbBlue
        Case "Green": fontColor = vbGreen
        Case Else: fontColor = vbBlack
    End Select

    fontType = cboFont.Text

    lblMessage.Font.Name = fontType
    lblMessage.ForeColor = fontColor
End Sub
```

Figure 15-19: Completed VBA code for the "btnShow" Click event.

ComboBox MatchRequired Property

The default value for the MatchRequired property of a combo box is FALSE. With the value set to FALSE, the user is not required to select an item from the list. If the user types into the text box, the typed text will be captured as the combo box selection. In the previous practice exercise, the MatchRequried property was not changed from the default FALSE value. Run the form and type a font style into the text box that is not included in the list (i.e., Tahoma, Times New Roman, Freestyle Script). Note that the typed value is applied to the "Hello" text.

Now change the MatchRequired property for the combo box to TRUE. Try to type text into the combo box. The program does not permit any free text entries. It requires the user to select an item from the list.

SpinButton Form Controls

The SpinButton form control allows a user to select a number by scrolling an up or down arrow that increases or decreases the number. The spin button itself does not provide a way for the user to see what he has selected, so the developer must add a text box to the form to show the value of the spin button.

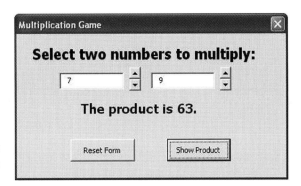

Figure 15-20: A text box must be added to the form for displaying the spin button value.

The text box's Value property is set to match the Value property of the spin button when the user changes the value of the spin button by clicking on one of the up or down arrows. In the following example, the spin button is used to select the quantity for an order item. The VBA code for showing the value of the spin button in the text box is written for the Change event of the spin button.

```
Sub spnQty_Change()
    txtQty.Value = spnQty.Value
End Sub
```

Once the Value property of the spin button is assigned to the text box Value property, either object's Value may be captured for use in other subsequent operations. In the example above, either Value can be captured in a variable that may be used in the calculation of an extended price for the ordered item.

```
Dim quantity As Integer
quantity = spnQty.Value        OR        quantity = txtQty.Value
```

Practice 15-9: SpinButton Form Controls

Objective: Use spin buttons together with text boxes to display the spin button value. Write the VBA code that will update the text box with the spin button value when the form opens and whenever the spin button value changes. Capture the spin button values and use them in a calculation.

1. Open a new Excel file. Name the file "SpinButtons_ch15-9.xlsm".

2. Open the VBA application. Insert a new user form into the project file you just created.

3. Name the user form "frmSpinButton."

4. Set the form caption to "Multiplication Game."

5. Add a label to the top of the form that provides user instructions. You do not need to change the default name of the label. Set the label caption to "Select two numbers to multiply:". Set the font size to 16 and the font effect to bold.

6. Add two spin buttons and a text box for each. Name the spin buttons "spn1" and "spn2" and the text boxes "txt1" and "txt2", respectively.

7. Double-click on each spin button to set the value of the spin button to display in the text box each time the spin button's value is changed. The spin button's Value property is assigned to the text box's Text property. The VBA code is written in the Change event of each spin button. The event procedure in automatically inserted when the spin button control is double-clicked since the Change event is the default event for a spin button.

```
Private Sub spn1_Change()
    txt1.Value = spn1.Value
End Sub

Private Sub spn2_Change()
    txt2.Value = spn2.Value
End Sub
```

8. Add a label to the form that displays the calculation result. Name the label "lblProduct." Set the font size to 14 and the font effect to bold.

9. Add two buttons controls to the form. Name them "btnReset" and "btnCalc", respectively. Set the caption for the "btnReset" to "Reset Form" and the caption for the "btnCalc" to "Show Product."

10. Double-click on the "btnReset" to add the VBA code in its Click event. In the VBA code:

   a. Set the values of both spin buttons back to zero
   b. Clear the product display label.
   c. Set the cursor to the first spin button.

```
Private Sub btnReset_Click()
    spn1.Value = 0
    spn1.SetFocus
    spn2.Value = 0
    lblProduct.Caption = ""
End Sub
```

11. Double-click the "btnCalc" to add VBA code to its Click event. The event procedure should:

   a. Capture both spin button values into separate variables.
   b. Multiply the two spin button values.
   c. Display the product in the product display label.

```
Private Sub btnCalc_click()
    Dim num1 As Integer
    Dim num2 As Integer
    num1 = spn1.Value
    num2 = spn2.Value
    lblProduct.Caption = "The product is " & num1 * num2 & "."
End Sub
```

12. Set each spin button value to display in its respective text box when the form opens. In the Visual Basic Editor, select UserForm from the drop list on the top left of the code editor window and select Activate from the drop list on the right side. The UserForm_Activate event procedure will be added to the form code module. Have the cursor set to the first spin button when the form opens.

```
Private Sub UserForm_Activate()
    txt1.Value = spn1.Value
    txt2.Value = spn2.Value
    spn1.SetFocus
End Sub
```

```
'Sets the spin button value to appear in the text
'box whenever the spin button value changes.
Private Sub spn1_Change()
    txt1.Value = spn1.Value
End Sub
'Change event for second spin button.
Private Sub spn2_Change()
    txt2.Value = spn2.Value
End Sub
'Captures spin button values, performs the
'calcuation and displays the product.
Private Sub btnCalc_click()
    Dim num1 As Integer
    Dim num2 As Integer
    num1 = spn1.Value
    num2 = spn2.Value
    lblProduct.Caption = "The product is " & num1 * num2 & "."
End Sub
'Resets the spin buttons back to zero to reset
'the form for a new calculation.
Private Sub btnReset_Click()
    spn1.Value = 0
    spn2.Value = 0

    'Sets teh cursor to the first spin button
    spn1.SetFocus
    'Clears the display label.
    lblProduct.Caption = ""
End Sub
```

Figure 15-21: Completed VBA code for the event procedures of the frmSpinButton user form.

Integrating User Forms into the Excel Project

Splash Screens

Integrating forms into an Excel project can have a big impact on the project's functionality and appearance. Forms can be used as navigation tools for the project. A form used as an opening screen, or "splash" screen can add a professional appearance to the project and can serve as a main menu for the project. Figure 15-22 is an example of a splash screen for a health club membership management application developed with Excel and VBA. The form consists mostly of formatted labels. The "Continue" button has no other functionality other than to close the form. It takes very little VBA programming skill to set up a splash screen that opens when the workbook opens.

Figure 15-22: A splash screen for an Excel project.

To make the form appear when the workbook opens, the form must be activated from the Workbook_Open event. To add VBA code to the Workbook_Open event:

1. Select the ThisWorkbook object in the Project Explorer window.

2. Open the code window for the object by clicking on the *Code View* icon at the top left of *the Project Explorer* window. (If you double-click on the ThisWorkbook object in the *Project Explorer* this step is not needed. The code window will already be open.)

3. Locate the object in the drop list at the top left of the code editor window and select Open from the event list at the top right area of the same window. The Workbook_ Open event procedure will be added to the project.

4. Add one line of VBA code in the Workbook_Open procedure:

   frmWelcome.Show

5. To close the form, enter the one line of VBA code in the "Close" button Click event:

   Unload frmWelcome

   Forms may be closed using the ActiveX window close icon in the top right margin of the form, but closing the form using this method hides the form but does not actually destroy the form.

Use Custom Functions to Handle Form Data

Not only can user-defined VBA functions be used in formulas on Excel worksheets, but custom function can also be used to process form data. Recall the function in Chapter 14 that calculates the sales tax for Leisure Time Pools & Spas product sales. Its four input parameters represent sale amount, type of service, city code, and customer's in-state status. When the function is called from a worksheet formula, the four arguments were provided by cell references to four columns in the sale record and the calculated tax was returned back to the worksheet cell formula.

Just as functions are used to process worksheet data, they may also be used to process form data. Once data is captured from form controls, it may be sent to a function for processing. The return value from the function may be manipulated further or displayed as form output.

For new installations and expensive replacements such as pool liners and covers, customer frequently ask Leisure Time to provide a written estimate for them that includes the product, service and sales tax since taxes can be significant on a large purchase. Leisure Time can benefit from a simple form that calculates the sales tax that can be added to an estimate. To use the form, the sales associate may enter the estimated sale price, the type of sale (product or service), city code, and whether or not the customer lives in the state. Once the four data items are captured from the form, the data may be sent to the function as arguments (inputs) and the function will return the function output (sales tax) back to the form for display.

Practice 15-10: Use a Custom Function to Process Form Data

Objective: To create a form that allows a sales associate to enter the sale amount, type of service, city code and customer's in-state status. The form captures the data with an event procedure and sends the data to the tax function created in Practice 14-3. The function's return value is displayed on the form.

1. Open the file 'LeisureForm_ch15-10.xlsm.' The form contains one module named "TaxFunction." The "tax" function created in Practice 14-3 is inside the module.

2. In the VBA application, add a user form to the project. Name the user form "frmEstimateTax."

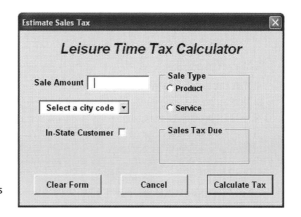

Figure 15-23: Form layout for sales tax estimator form.

3. Add controls to the form in a layout similar to the form in Figure 15-23.

4. Name the controls:

    a. Label to display form heading "Leisure Time Tax Calculator", leave name as the default name

    b. "txtAmt": TextBox to enter sale amount

    c. "cboCity": ComboBox to select customer city code

    d. "chkInState": CheckBox for in-state status

    e. "fraServType": Frame for option buttons

         • "optProduct"
         • "optService"

    f. "fraTax": Frame that holds the label for displaying tax result

         • "lblTax": Label that actually displays the tax

    g. "btnClear": Button that resets all form controls

    h. "btnCancel": Button that resets all form controls and closes the form

    i. "btnCalc": Button that captures input, calculates tax, displays tax

5. Set other form and control properties so that your form's appearance resembles the form in the example in Figure 15-23. Set the "btnCalc" *Default* property to TRUE.

6. Populate the combo box with the worksheet range "Codes" by setting the *RowSource* property "=Codes". Edit the named range to include a zero range at the top. The city code should be zero and the tax rate in the second column should also be zero. (When the combo box is disabled, the value captured for city code will be zero because the city code variable will be initialized automatically to zero when it is declared.)

7. Write a procedure for the Change event of the "optService" option button that disables the "cboCity" and "chkInState" controls when the "Service" option is selected and re-enables them if the "Service" option is not selected.

```
Private Sub optService_Change()
    If optService.Value = True Then
        cboCity.Enabled = False
        chkInState.Enabled = False
    Else
        cboCity.Enabled = True
        chkInState.Enabled = True
    End If
End Sub
```

8. Double-click the "Calculate Tax" button to enter VBA code into its Click event.

   a. Declare variables for tax (Currency), sale amount (Currency), city code (Integer), in-state status (Boolean), service type (String).

   ```
   Dim tax As Currency
   Dim amt As Currency
   Dim citycode As Integer
   Dim instate As Boolean
   Dim serviceType As String
   ```

   b. Capture the value of "chkInState" into the in-state variable.

   ```
   If chkInState.Value = True Then
       instate = True
   Else
       instate = False
   End If
   ```

   c. Test the sale amount field to make sure it is numeric, then capture its input. (The IF statement will be nested, so the ELSE and END IF will not immediately follow the THEN instruction.)

   ```
   If IsNumeric(txtAmt.Text) Then
       amt = txtAmt.Value

       . . .

   Else: MsgBox "Please enter a numeric value for the sale amount."
       txtAmt.SetFocus
   End If
   ```

   d. Capture the option button that was checked.

   ```
   If optProduct.Value = True Then
       serviceType = "Product"

       . . .

   ElseIf optService.Value = True Then
       serviceType = "Service"
       cboCity.Enabled = False
       chkInState.Enabled = False
       tax = 0
       lblTax.Caption = FormatCurrency(tax)
   Else: MsgBox "Please select the type of sale."
       optProduct.SetFocus
   End If
   ```

   e. Check to make sure the city code is selected, then capture the city code selection. (This is the final nested IF statement so the processing code will be included in the THEN instructions.)

   ```
   If IsNumeric(cboCity.Text) Then
       citycode = CInt(cboCity.Text)

       . . .

   Else: MsgBox "Please select a city code."
   End If
   ```

   f. Calculate the tax by calling the tax function. Send as arguments data captured from the form. Be sure arguments are in the same order as specified in the function definition. Assign the function output to the "tax" variable (also goes inside the final nested IF statement).

   ```
   tax = TaxFunction.tax(amt, serviceType, citycode, instate)
   ```

   g. Display the tax in the "lblTax" control (also goes inside the final nested IF statement).

   ```
   lblTax.Caption = FormatCurrency(tax)
   ```

9. Double-click the "Clear" button to enter VBA code to reset all form controls back to their original settings and set the cursor at the first control.

```
txtAmt.Text = ""
txtAmt.SetFocus
lblTax.Caption = ""
optService.Value = False
optProduct.Value = False
chkInState.Value = False
cboCity.Text = "Select a city code"
```

10. Double-click the "Cancel" button to enter VBA code to clear the form controls and hide the form. To reset the form controls, call the click event of the "Clear" button.

```
btnClear_Click
frmPractice15.Hide
```

11. To set the tab order of the form controls select **View→Tab Order** from the VBA menu bar. Put the controls in the proper tab order.

12. Test the form and debug as needed. (See the completed VBA code in Figure 15-24.)

Launch a Form from a Worksheet

In many cases with Excel VBA projects, it is helpful to be able to launch a user form from a worksheet. To open a form from a worksheet, a form control must be added to the worksheet from the form control toolbox. When the form control is added to the worksheet, the worksheet enters *design* mode. While in *design* mode, double-click the form control to add the event procedure. The only instruction in the procedure is to launch the user form. The Show method is used to display the form.

```
frmEstimateTax.Show
```

Launch One Form from Another

To launch one user form from another, include a form control such as a button on the first form that will launch the second form. The instruction (*FormName*.Show) is written in the desired event (like the button Click event) procedure for the form control.

When two or more forms are used together frequently, the second form responds more quickly to the display command if it is already loaded. When the first form is displayed, other forms may also be "loaded" in the same event procedure using the *Load* command. To display UserForm1 and load UserForm2 so it is ready to show when called, use the following syntax:

```
Load UserForm2
UserForm1.Show
```

When UserForm2 is displayed, UserForm1 may be hidden in the same event procedure.

```
UserForm1.Hide
UserForm2.Show
```

Inserting Worksheet Data from a Custom Form

Although the Excel *Data Form* is commonly used to add, modify, or delete data in an Excel list, there are occasions when a developer may want to create a custom

```
Option Explicit
Private Sub btncalc_Click()
Dim tax As Currency
Dim amt As Currency
Dim citycode As Integer
Dim instate As Boolean
Dim serviceType As String
    'Capture input from check box
    If chkInState.Value = True Then
        instate = True
    Else
        instate = False
    End If

    'Check the sale amount text box for numeric value.
    'If there is no data in the text box, the isnumeric function
    'will return false just as it will if there is text in the box
    'instead of numbers.
    If IsNumeric(txtAmt.Text) Then
        amt = txtAmt.Value
        'Capture which option button is selected.
        'This is done here instead of outside the nested IF statements
        'because further processing of the form is determined by which
        'option is selected.
        If optProduct.Value = True Then
            serviceType = "Product"
                'Check to see if a city code was selected.  If not, a text value
                'will be present (the text box default content.
            If IsNumeric(cboCity.Text) Then
                citycode = CInt(cboCity.Text)
                'Call the tax function in the TaxFunction module.
                tax = TaxFunction.tax(amt, serviceType, citycode, instate)
                'Display the calculated tax in the display label.
                lblTax.Caption = FormatCurrency(tax)
            Else: MsgBox "Please select a city code."
            End If
        ElseIf optService.Value = True Then
            serviceType = "Service"
            cboCity.Enabled = False
            chkInState.Enabled = False
            tax = 0
            lblTax.Caption = FormatCurrency(tax)
        Else: MsgBox "Please select the type of sale."
            optProduct.SetFocus
        End If
    Else: MsgBox "Please enter a numeric value for the sale amount."
        txtAmt.SetFocus
    End If
End Sub
Private Sub btnCancel_Click()
    'Call the Click event of the Clear button
    btnClear_Click
    'Hide the form.
    frmPractice15.Hide
End Sub
Private Sub btnClear_Click()
    'Clear the text box
    txtAmt.Text = ""
    'Set the cursor to the text box
    txtAmt.SetFocus
    'Clear the display label
    lblTax.Caption = ""
    'Reset the option buttons to unselected
    optService.Value = False
    optProduct.Value = False
    'Reset the check box
    chkInState.Value = False
    'Reset the combo box
    cboCity.Text = "Select a city code"
End Sub
Private Sub optService_Change()
    'Anytime the Service option is selected or unselected
    'by selecting the other option, the city code and in-state
    'form controls are disabled because they are not needed.
    If optService.Value = True Then
        cboCity.Enabled = False
        chkInState.Enabled = False
    Else
        cboCity.Enabled = True
        chkInState.Enabled = True
    End If
End Sub
```

Figure 15-24: Completed VBA code for the "Leisure Time Tax Calculator" form.

form that adds data to a worksheet. To interact with an Excel worksheet, objects associated with the workbook and worksheets must be referenced in VBA code. Common workbook and worksheet objects include single objects and collections of objects. The object collections are plural, such as "Sheets." Single items in a collection are referenced using an index number or other identifier in parentheses following the collection name. For example, the worksheet named "Employees" may be referenced using:

Sheets("Employees").Select   Or
Sheets(2).Select   'the worksheet in the second position

Common workbook and worksheet objects:
- ActiveCell object
- Range object
- Worksheets (use an index number or name to access a single worksheet.)
- Sheets collection
- Cells collection
- Rows collection
- Columns collection

Common methods used to manipulate workbook and worksheet objects include:
- Select
- Activate
- Offset (to locate cells relative to a selected cell)

Typically when custom forms are used to manipulate data on a worksheet, the worksheet is arranged in a list and data is captured from or written to records in the list. The most common interaction with a worksheet is to add records to a list. In the process of adding a new record, the program may need to access data in other cells related to the new record. For example, if the records are numbered sequentially using an identification number, the previous identification number may be assessed so it can be incremented to make the new identification number.

To add a new row of data to an Excel worksheet, the first empty row must be located. One of the easiest ways to locate the first empty row in a list is to count the filled cells in a column of the list. The number of filled cells can be adjusted to represent the row number of the new record. The cell location can be adjusted using the VBA Offset function. The Offset function specifies a location relative to the current cell which is the ActiveCell object. The relative location is specified in the two arguments, number of rows and number of columns. The general syntax of the Offset function:

ActiveCell.Offset(rows, columns).Method (or .Property)

Examples Using the Offset Function
To enter a value in the cell three rows down and two column to the right:

ActiveCell.Offset(3, 2).Value = 250

To select a cell that is one row up and 2 columns to the left:

ActiveCell.Offset(-1, -2).Select

Practice 15-11: Insert Worksheet Data from a Form

Objective: To capture worksheet data and write worksheet data using VBA. Make a form to enter new team members' names and jersey numbers to an Excel worksheet list. Before writing the new member's record, the program should check the previous member's unique identification number so that it can assign a new sequential identification number for the new record.

1. Open the Excel file "TeamRoster_ch15-11.xlsm".

2. Open the VBA application. Insert a new user form module. Name the form "frmAddMember."

Figure 15-25: Custom form to add team members to a worksheet list.

3. Add three text boxes and one button in a layout similar to the one pictured in Figure 15-25. Add a label for the form heading "Enter New Team Members."

4. Name the controls:

   a. "txtFirst": To enter first name
   b. "txtLast": To enter last name
   c. "txtJersey": To enter a jersey number
   d. "btnAdd": To capture form data and write to worksheet.

5. Set other form and control properties so that your form resembles the one in Figure 15-25.

6. Set the *Default* property of the button to TRUE.

7. Set the *Left* property of the form to 200 and the *Top* property to 200. Change the *StartUpPositon* property to *Manual*. (This displays the form in a position that is more comfortable for most users.)

8. Double-click the "Add Member" button to enter VBA code into its Click event.

   a. Declare variables first name (String), last name (String), jersey number (Integer), player ID number (Integer), and row number (Integer).

   ```
   Dim firstname As String
   Dim lastname As String
   Dim jersey As Integer
   Dim id As Integer
   Dim rowNum As Integer
   ```

   b. Add VBA code to capture the first name into the variable declared in the previous step. Check first to see that it is not blank or has numbers included. Capture last name in the same manner. (The IF statement will be nested, so the ELSE and END IF will not immediately follow the THEN instruction.)

   ```
   If txtFirst.Text <> "" Then
       If Not IsNumeric(txtFirst.Text) Then
           firstname = txtFirst.Text
           If txtLast.Text <> "" Then
               If Not IsNumeric(txtLast.Text) Then
                   lastname = txtLast.Text

                   . . .

               Else: MsgBox "Numbers are not permitted in player's last name."
                   txtLast.Text = ""
                   txtLast.SetFocus
               End If
   ```

```
            Else: MsgBox "Please enter player's last name."
                txtLast.Text = ""
                txtLast.SetFocus
            End If
        Else: MsgBox "Numbers are not permitted in player's first name."
            txtFirst.Text = ""
            txtFirst.SetFocus
        End If
    Else: MsgBox "Please enter player's first name."
        txtFirst.Text = ""
        txtFirst.SetFocus
    End If
```

c. Add VBA code to capture jersey number. Check first to make sure the entry is numeric and not blank. The ISNUMERIC function will also return FALSE if the cell is blank as well as when it contains non-numeric characters. (The IF statement will be nested, so the ELSE and END IF will not immediately follow the THEN instruction.)

```
If IsNumeric(txtJersey.Text) Then
    jersey = txtJersey.Text
    . . .
Else: MsgBox "Please enter a numeric value for jersey number."
    txtJersey.Text = ""
    txtJersey.SetFocus
End If
```

d. Add VBA code to count the filled rows in the worksheet.

```
Sheets("Roster").Select
rowNum = _ Application.WorksheetFunction.CountA(Range("A:A"))
```

e. Add VBA code to capture the previous ID number from the worksheet in the last filled row.

```
Range("A1").Select
ActiveCell.Offset(rowNum, 0).Select
id = Selection.Value
```

f. Increment the ID number by one and add it to the next row, same column of the team member list.

```
ActiveCell.Offset(1, 0).Value = id + 1
```

g. Write the first name, last name, and jersey number into the appropriate columns for the new record.

```
ActiveCell.Offset(1, 1).Value = firstname
ActiveCell.Offset(1, 2).Value = lastname
ActiveCell.Offset(1, 3).Value = jersey
```

9. Set the tab order of the form controls.

10. Test the form and debug as needed.

In this chapter you have seen how pre-formatted dialog boxes can be used to display messages to the user or capture simple input from the user. Custom user forms may be developed for specialized input or output to add additional functionality to the Excel VBA project. Advanced form controls, such as list boxes, combo boxes, option buttons, check boxes, and spin buttons can validate user input for user forms. The VBA user form has vast options available for enhancing an Excel

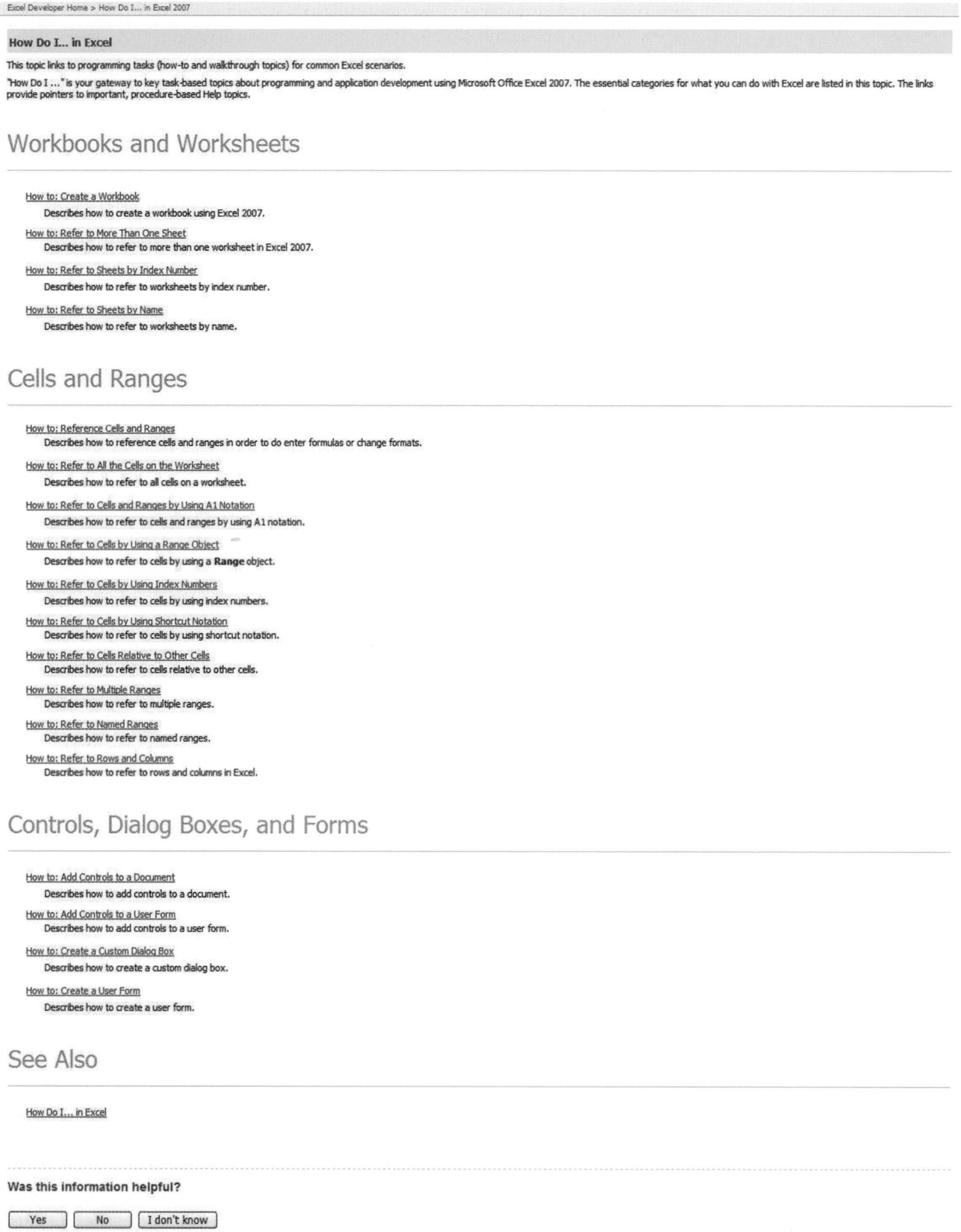

How Do I... in Excel

This topic links to programming tasks (how-to and walkthrough topics) for common Excel scenarios.

"How Do I ..." is your gateway to key task-based topics about programming and application development using Microsoft Office Excel 2007. The essential categories for what you can do with Excel are listed in this topic. The links provide pointers to important, procedure-based Help topics.

Workbooks and Worksheets

How to: Create a Workbook
  Describes how to create a workbook using Excel 2007.

How to: Refer to More Than One Sheet
  Describes how to refer to more than one worksheet in Excel 2007.

How to: Refer to Sheets by Index Number
  Describes how to refer to worksheets by index number.

How to: Refer to Sheets by Name
  Describes how to refer to worksheets by name.

Cells and Ranges

How to: Reference Cells and Ranges
  Describes how to reference cells and ranges in order to do enter formulas or change formats.

How to: Refer to All the Cells on the Worksheet
  Describes how to refer to all cells on a worksheet.

How to: Refer to Cells and Ranges by Using A1 Notation
  Describes how to refer to cells and ranges by using A1 notation.

How to: Refer to Cells by Using a Range Object
  Describes how to refer to cells by using a **Range** object.

How to: Refer to Cells by Using Index Numbers
  Describes how to refer to cells by using index numbers.

How to: Refer to Cells by Using Shortcut Notation
  Describes how to refer to cells by using shortcut notation.

How to: Refer to Cells Relative to Other Cells
  Describes how to refer to cells relative to other cells.

How to: Refer to Multiple Ranges
  Describes how to refer to multiple ranges.

How to: Refer to Named Ranges
  Describes how to refer to named ranges.

How to: Refer to Rows and Columns
  Describes how to refer to rows and columns in Excel.

Controls, Dialog Boxes, and Forms

How to: Add Controls to a Document
  Describes how to add controls to a document.

How to: Add Controls to a User Form
  Describes how to add controls to a user form.

How to: Create a Custom Dialog Box
  Describes how to create a custom dialog box.

How to: Create a User Form
  Describes how to create a user form.

See Also

How Do I... in Excel

Was this information helpful?

[Yes]   [No]   [I don't know]

Figure 15-26: VBA's How Do I . . . help feature.

project when launched from a worksheet, from a splash screen or from other user forms. To help you develop further skills in form development consult the "How Do I . . ." help features in VBA. The help menu offers syntax and code examples for the most common ways that VBA can be used to interact with Excel worksheets and their users.

Review Questions

1. What is a VBA message box? What is its purpose? How is it created?

_____

_____

_____

2. What is a VBA input box? What is its purpose? How is it created?

_____

_____

_____

3. What is the "return value" from the VBA MsgBox function? Why is the return value not always captured from the MsgBox function?

_____

_____

_____

4. What is the "return value" from the VBA InputBox function?

_____

_____

_____

5. What is the main advantage of including an ELSE statement in a CASE statement?

_____

_____

_____

6. How are TextBox form controls typically used on custom forms?

_____

_____

_____

7. How are Label form controls typically used on custom forms?

_____

_____

_____

8. How is the value of a SpinButton control viewed on a user form?

_____

_____

_____

9. What type of programming control structure is used most often for validating form input data?

_____

_____

_____

10. Give three examples of how form controls can be used to validate form input data.

_____

_____

_____

11. What is meant by the *Tab Order* of a form?

_____

_____

_____

12. What is the "default" button on a user form?

_____

_____

_____

13. How do the appropriate uses of CheckBox controls and OptionButton controls differ?

_____

_____

_____

14. What is a common cause of a type mismatch error?

_____

_____

_____

15. What are the basic steps for using a custom function to process form data?

_____

_____

_____

Practice Problems

1. Using a VBA user form design a splash screen for any new workbook of your choice. The form should display the name of the project, the project developer and date developed. The splash screen should have one button that closes the form and allows the user to continue using the worksheet project.

2. Create a user form that has two text boxes that allow the user to enter a taxable subtotal and a zip code for a retail customer. When the "Calculate" button is clicked, an event procedure should:

   a. Determine the correct tax rate based on the zip code
   b. Calculate the sales tax
   c. Display the sales tax in a label.

   Add a button for clearing the text boxes and resetting the control focus and a button that closes the form. The tax rates are effective for the following zip codes. Only these zip codes are valid in the sales region so the user must only be able to enter these zip code values. Apply applicable data validation to the form data as it is captured.

   For zip code 27409 the sales tax rate is 6.5%.
   For zip code 24060 the sales tax rate is 5.0%.
   For zip code 24343 the sales tax rate is 4.5%.
   For zip code 28149 the sales tax rate is 5.5%.

3. For the form you created in the previous problem, revise the event procedure so that the form data is captured and sent as arguments to the function you created in Problem 1 of Chapter 14. The function should return the sales tax to the form. The form will display the sales tax.

4. Create a user form that will allow a student to enter his four exam grades for the term and have the form calculate an average of the highest three scores and display a letter grade for the term. Exam grades represent a percentage score and may be entered as mixed numbers. The letter grade is assigned based on the following scale.

   A: 90 and above
   B: 80 and above, but less than 90
   C: 70 and above, but less than 80
   D: 60 and above, but less than 70
   F: Less than 60

5. Revise the previous problem solution so that it captures input from the form and sends it as arguments to the function you created in Problem 7 of Chapter 14. The function should return the letter grade to display on the form.

6. *Challenge Problem:* At a local health club prospective members frequently call to inquire about membership fees for new members. The associates of the club who speak with prospective members would like to have a form that they could launch from the Excel worksheet that contains their current member list. The form would allow them to enter the pertinent data and have it calculate and display an annual and monthly membership fee. The form should provide a way the associates can quickly enter the member data and provide data validation so that the estimated fee will be accurate. Membership fees are calculated based on the following input factors:

   a. Family size

      - The health club charges a base rate of $500/year for one person.
      - For two family members the rate is 1.5 times the base rate.
      - For three or more family members the fee is 2 times the base rate.

   b. Age group

      - If the primary membership subscriber is aged 60 years or older the total family membership fee is reduced by 10%.
      - If the primary membership subscriber is aged 70 or over the total family membership fee is reduced by 70%

   c. Corporate affiliation

      - If the primary membership subscriber is affiliated with a company that subsidized employee membership, the total family membership fee is reduced by 10%.

7. For the form you created in the previous problem, revise the event procedure so that the form data is captured and sent as arguments to the function you created in Problem 6 of Chapter 14. The function should return the annual membership fee. Be sure to display both the annual and monthly membership fee estimates on the form.

8. *Challenge Problem:* Create a user form that helps a payroll clerk calculate the hours worked for each employee in a pay period. The form should:

   a. Prompt the user to enter the date and time an employee clocked in to work. The date and time should be entered into separate text boxes. The date and time they clocked out should be entered in a similar manner.
   b. Prompt the user to enter the date and time in the proper format that the event program will recognize and handle appropriately.
   c. Provide a way the clerk can indicate whether or not the employee took a lunch break. If the employee took a lunch break, one-half hour is deducted from the hours worked that day.
   d. Have a button that allows the user to continue to add hours for one employee until all hours for that employee are entered.
   e. Display a running total of hours worked as each day's hours are entered.

f. Have a button (like "New Employee") for clearing the running total of hours for one employee and resetting the form for the next employee's set of hours worked.

g. Have labels to display the results. The following form layout is one example of how the form might be designed.

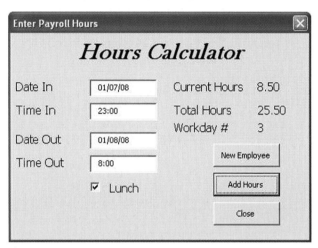

Figure 15-27: Layout ideas for the payroll entry form.

CHAPTER SIXTEEN

Controlling Code Execution with Loops and Error Handling

Learning Objectives

1. Determine which loop structure to use for a specific project requirement
2. Use the VBA FOR NEXT loop for a known number of iterations
3. Use the VBA FOR EACH loop to process a collection of objects
4. Use one- and two-dimensional arrays to manipulate collections of data
5. Use the ARRAY function to store arrays of elements in simple variables
6. Use VBA loops to process array elements
7. Use VBA WHILE and UNTIL loops with leading and trailing loop decisions
8. Use VBA loops to access and update Excel worksheet data
9. Call VBA functions, worksheet functions, and user-defined functions from loops
10. Reference worksheet cells in VBA using R1C1 reference style
11. Create nested loops
12. Write VBA code to handle runtime errors
13. Lock VBA code from user viewing and editing

Loop Structure Review

A loop in VBA is a set of programming instructions that can be written once and repeated any number of times. In Chapter 12 you saw that there are a number of ways a loop can be structured depending on how it should perform to solve the business problem. There are three main questions to answer that will help determine which loop structure is the best solution for a particular project requirement.

1. Does the loop need to iterate a fixed number of times, determined either at design time or at runtime?

2. Does the loop need to iterate at least once? If so the loop condition should be tested at the end of the loop. If not, the loop condition should be tested at the beginning of the loop.

3. Should the loop enter/exit based on a TRUE value or FALSE value for the loop condition?

VBA "Fixed" Loops

Loops that iterate a fixed number of times are called *definite* loops because the number of times they will loop is defined before the loop begins, either at design time or at runtime. The general FOR loop is designed as an efficient alternate to the WHILE loop for count controlled loops. When looping a fixed number of times using a WHILE loop, the loop control variable must be declared and initialized outside the loop, then tested inside the loop body, and finally altered inside the loop body. With the general FOR loop, the three steps in managing the loop control variable are automatic. The loop control variable (also called the counter) must still be declared outside the loop, but it is initialized, tested, and altered automatically by the FOR loop.

FOR NEXT Loop

VBA has two versions of the FOR loop. The FOR NEXT loop is the general FOR loop for VBA. The loop begins with the keyword FOR and ends with the keyword NEXT indicating advancement to the next counter value. The following FOR NEXT loop iterates five times and displays the value of the loop control variable in a VBA message box on each iteration. The effective range for the loop control variable is inclusive of both the upper and lower bounds.

FOR NEXT Loop Examples

VBA Loop Example 1:

```
Sub ForLoop()
    Dim a As Integer
    For a = 4 To 8
        AMsgBox ("a = " & a)
    Next
End Sub
```

VBA has as a special version of the FOR loop that is designed to loop through a collection of things, such as worksheets or cells. It is called a FOR EACH loop since it performs some action on each item in the collection. The FOR EACH loop is considered a definite loop because its number of iterations is known by the program before the loop executes. The program knows the upper and lower bounds of the collection. For example, the program knows how many worksheets are in the project, or how many cells in a specified range. The following procedure contains FOR EACH loop that processes all worksheets of a workbook and assigns a new name to each worksheet. Note that the counter (i) used in the example is not the loop control variable, but is the counter to increment the number concatenated to "Grades" which composes the worksheet name. Keep in mind that the loop counter is initialized, tested, and altered automatically so we will not need to add those steps in the VBA code.

VBA Loop Example 2:

```
Sub EachGrades()
    Dim page As Worksheet
    Dim i As Integer   'used to add a number to the "Grades" sheet name
    i = 1              'first sheet name is "Grades1"

    For Each page In ThisWorkbook.Worksheets
        page.Name = "Grades" & i
        i = i + 1      'not the loop counter, increments the sheet name only
    Next
End Sub
```

A Note about the VBA Loop Examples in This Chapter

The loop examples in this chapter use actual VBA syntax. All loop examples are included inside a VBA procedure so that the reader may enter the example code into the VBA code editor and execute the procedure on his own machine. If you would like to try the sample code in "VBA Loop Example 2," use the following VBA procedure code to rename the worksheet back to "Sheet1," "Sheet2," etc. before executing the example procedure each time. Otherwise, the example will cause runtime errors when it attempts to name worksheets the same name that is assigned to another sheet as a result of the first execution of the example code.

```
Sub ReverseEachGrades()
    'Use this procedure to undo the name assignment of the previous loop procedure
        'so the "EachGrades" macro will run again without conflicting worksheet
        'names.
    'This procedure does the same thing as the previous one except it substitutes
        '"Sheet" for "Grades" in the worksheet name.
    Dim page As Worksheet
    Dim i As Integer
    i = 1
    For Each page In ThisWorkbook.Worksheets
        page.Name = "Sheet" & i
        i = i + 1
    Next
End Sub
```

Collections and Arrays

You have certainly noticed by now that many Excel objects manipulated in VBA are pleural such as *Worksheets* and *Cells*. The pleural object name indicates that the object is actually a collection of like objects. We usually refer to the Worksheets object the worksheet collection. In VBA code, we can process the entire collection by calling its name as we did in the previous example. "ThisWorkbook.Worksheets" refers to all sheets in ThisWorkbook object. We can also process one item of the collection by using its index number (that represents its relative position in the collection) in parentheses after the collection name. In the case of the Worksheets collection, we can also call an individual worksheet by name expressed as a String value inside the parentheses instead of its index number.

Example References to Worksheets

```
Worksheets.Add       'adds a new worksheet to the workbook
Worksheets(5).Name = "Grades Fall 2007"    'names the fifth worksheet
```

The Worksheets object (collection) is a member of the Sheets object. The difference between Worksheets and Sheets collections is that Sheets includes both Worksheets and Charts (sheets) collections.

Other VBA collection objects include Cells, PivotTables, Ranges, Scenarios, Shapes, Watches, Windows, Workbooks, and many, many more. For more information about managing Excel objects, visit the Microsoft Developers' Network (MSDN) at http://msdn2.microsoft.com/en-us/library/bb149081.aspx.

VBA Arrays

Collection objects in VBA are actually arrays of like objects. An *array* is a collection of related data items of the same data type. The Worksheets collection is an array of worksheets in one workbook. The array structure provides a way of referring to a collection of data by one variable name. The data collection may be simple data items such as Integer or String values, or they may be complex data items such as worksheets or cells.

When accessing one item in the array, the index number (also called subscript) is used to indicate the item to reference based on its relative position in the array. User-declared arrays in VBA begin with an index number of zero (0) such that the index of the upper bound of the array is one less than the actual number of items contained in the array. The Excel collection objects that are manipulated in VBA work a little differently in that their first index number is one (1) such that the index number of the last worksheet is the same as the number of worksheets contained in the collection. The first worksheet object in a worksheet would be referenced by Worksheets(1).

All modern programming languages provide an array as a type of data structure. Many languages permit the creation of both static and dynamic arrays. Static arrays are declared with a fixed number of item positions. Dynamic arrays are declared using a slightly different syntax, usually leaving the "size" part of the declaration statement empty. The program allocates size (memory space) to the dynamic array in increments as more items are added and the array reaches its capacity. Some developers refer to "dynamic" arrays in VBA, but there are no purely dynamic arrays in VBA. VBA will permit the developer to declare an array without a size (which in many languages indicates a dynamic array), but the array must be re-declared with a fixed size before array items can be added. The special keyword "ReDim" is used to set the size of an array that has already been declared.

Arrays are declared in VBA using the same syntax, naming rules and conventions as other variable declarations except that a set of parentheses follows the array identifier. The data type specified is the type of data of each array item. If no data type is specified, the array is a Variant type.

```
Dim days(6) As String          'one-dimensional array of text items
Dim table(6, 3) As Integer     'two-dimensional array of 4 by 7 positions
Dim days() As String           'one-dimensional un-sized array
ReDim days(3) As String        'a size of 4 is assigned to the un-sized array
```

When the array is re-declared, its current data is deleted because a whole new array is created overwriting the previous one with the same name. VBA includes the keyword "Preserve" to move the current array data to the newly dimensioned array.

```
ReDim Preserve days(6) as String    'A new array is declared and the contents of
                                    'the old array with the same name is entered
                                    'into the new array.
```

Adding Items to an Array

The positions in an array are referenced by index numbers called *subscripts*. The index numbers begin at 0 for the first position in the array. For example, our String type "days(6)" array will hold seven String data items. To add an item to the array, indicate the position to fill using its subscript (position index) in parentheses following the array name in the assignment statement. The actual VBA syntax is exactly like the pseudocode syntax used in Chapter 9 for adding array items.

```
days(0) = "Sunday"
```

VBA arrays do not require us to fill the positions in order. We can add an item to any index by referencing its subscript.

```
days(3) = "Wednesday"
```

Figure 16-1: Logical representation of writing to positions (2, 2) and (3, 2).

When adding data to a multi-dimensional array subscripts of each dimension must be included.

```
table(2, 2) = "Virginia"
table(3, 2) = "Tech"
```

Accessing Items in an Array

Items in an array are accessed just as they are added, by referencing the item's position.

```
Dim days(6) As String
Dim firstDay As String
Dim fourthDay As String

firstDay = days(0)
fourthDay = days(4)
```

Referencing the Whole Array

The biggest advantage in using the array structure is being able to pass the entire array through the program as one named package instead of having to reference each item individually. Consider the array declared earlier to hold the days of the week. To reference all the days in the week, we need only to reference the array name, "days." The following example is repeated from Chapter 9, but uses actual VBA syntax for filling and accessing array elements.

```
Sub DaysArray()
    Dim days(6) As String
    days(0) = "Sunday"
    days(1) = "Monday"
    days(2) = "Tuesday"
    days(3) = "Wednesday"
    days(4) = "Thursday"
    days(5) = "Friday"
    days(6) = "Saturday"
    Call PrintDays(days)        'the Call keyword must be included
End Sub

Sub PrintDays(d() As String)   'array parameters pass byRef which is VBA default
    Debug.Print d(0)
    Debug.Print d(1)
    Debug.Print d(2)
    Debug.Print d(3)
    Debug.Print d(4)
    Debug.Print d(5)
    Debug.Print d(6)
End Sub
```

A big part of the array advantage is being able to process entire arrays using a loop. Since each array item differs only by its subscript, program code can be written once to process every item in the array. In many loops the array subscript doubles as the loop counter. The following VBA loop produces exactly the same results as the previous procedure "PrintDays".

```
Sub PrintDaysLoop(d() As String)      'bounds are hardcoded
    Dim i As Integer
    For i = 0 To 6
        Debug.Print d(i)
    Next
End Sub
```

Since we knew the exact size of the previous loop, we could "hard-code" the lower and upper subscripts for the loop condition (0 to 6). A better and more flexible design could accommodate any size array. The LBOUND and UBOUND functions allow us to refer to the lowest and highest array subscript using the returns from each of these two functions. The following VBA code example is a much more flexible design and produces exactly the same result as the previous hard-coded loop.

```
Sub PrintDaysLoop2(d() As String)
    Dim i As Integer
    For i = LBound(d) To UBound(d)
        Debug.Print d(i)
    Next
End Sub
```

The VBA ARRAY Function

In the earlier example where we assigned days of the week to an array, we could not load that array very efficiently. It required a separate statement to assign each array element. Even using a loop would not make loading that particular array easier. The VBA ARRAY function provides a way to load a (non-array) variable with an array of values at design time. Arrays cannot be declared as constants in VBA, only as variables using the "Dim" keyword. A Variant variable (not an array) may be declared and then loaded with an array of values that may be accessed within the module as constants (values that do not change during program execution). In order to use an array of values in this way, the variable must be declared as a Variant. (If the type is not specified, it will be Variant since that is the default variable type in VBA.) Once the (non-array) variable is declared, it can be loaded with an array of any variable type using the ARRAY function. Below is an example of VBA code to declare the non-array variable, load it with an array of values then use a loop to access all elements of the array.

```
Sub DaysArrayFxn()
        Dim days As Variant        'the type must be Variant
        Dim i As Integer           'used for the test loop only
        'The Array function creates an array of String values and assigns the array to
            'the Variant (non array) variable.
        days = Array("Sunday", "Monday", "Tuesday", "Wednesday", _
            "Thursday", "Friday", "Saturday")
        'FOR loop used only to test the array contents
        For i = LBound(days) To UBound(days)
            'Print each element of the array
            Debug.Print days(i)
        Next
End Sub
```

Once the variable is loaded with the array of values, an individual value may be accessed individually by using its subscript, just as if the "days" variable was a true array. The subscripts begin at zero (0).

```
firstDay = days(0)
```

The ARRAY function may be used to assign an array of values of any data type. The days of the week assigned to the "days" variable are String values, but an array of numeric or Boolean values may be loaded into the variable as well. No matter what type of data has been added to the Variant variable, it is still handled in the program like a non-array variable. To enable the "PrintDaysLoop2" procedure to print the days of the week from the Variant non-array variable "days" loaded with the array of days, we simply pass the variable without any reference to the fact that it contains an array of values. The "PrintDaysLoop2" procedure's input parameter is redefined so that it accepts a simple Variant variable instead of a String array. The references to each element within the argument passed to the procedure use the same syntax as it did for accessing a true array element.

```
Sub PrintDaysLoop3(d As Variant)  'parameter was (d() As Sting)
        'This sub receives a non-array variable which has been assigned an array of values
        Dim i As Integer
        For i = LBound(d) To UBound(d)
            Debug.Print d(i)
        Next
End Sub
```

Important points to remember when using the ARRAY function:

1. The variable that contains the array of values must be a Variant type.

2. The Variant variable may be assigned an array of values of any data type.

3. When the variable is passed to other modules, it must be passed as a non-array Variant variable, not as an array. The called procedure parameter must be defined as a non-array Variant.

4. The variable which contains an array of values may be passed byVal or byRef (VBA default) whereas a true array of any type may only be passed byRef.

Process Arrays with FOR EACH Loops

VBA views an array as a user-defined collection. The FOR EACH loop is designed to process items in a collection. In order for the FOR EACH loop to process items in a user-defined array, the array must be a Variant type or a user-defined type (a class). This is a very strict requirement. Other types of arrays may be processed using other loop structures in VBA, but only Variant arrays may be processed with the FOR EACH loop. To adapt our previous example for processing with the "days" array with a FOR EACH loop, we need only to change the "days" array from a String type to a Variant type.

```
Sub DaysArrayForEach()
    Dim days(6) As Variant       'must be Variant type
    days(0) = "Sunday"
    days(1) = "Monday"
    days(2) = "Tuesday"
    days(3) = "Wednesday"
    days(4) = "Thursday"
    days(5) = "Friday"
    days(6) = "Saturday"
    Call PrintEachDay(days)
End Sub

Sub PrintEachDay(d() As Variant) 'array parameter must be Variant
    Dim i As Variant       'array element must be Variant
    For Each i In d
        Debug.Print i
    Next
End Sub
```

All along we emphasize that array subscripts begin with zero (0) whereas Excel object collection subscripts begin with one (1). If you prefer to have the subscripts for all your user-defined arrays to begin with one instead of zero, you may set that option in each VBA module by adding the statement "Option Base 1" at the top of the module in the variable declaration area. Beware that if VBA code is already written using the base 0 subscripts, a "subscript out of range" error will occur when the program tries to process any array elements referenced by the index of zero. The compiler displays the same error any time the program code references an array or collection subscript that is outside the bounds defined for the array or collection. In essence, the program is referencing something that does not exist which always causes a runtime error.

VBA Indefinite Loops

The two VBA FOR loops are likely the most popular loops used in Excel projects because of the nature of the project environment. There are many requirements for processing collection of objects and data in Excel. VBA also supports a wide variety of other loop structures that will fit other loop requirements in Excel VBA projects. At the beginning of this chapter, you were presented with three questions to serve as a guide in selecting the correct loop structure for the project requirement. The VBA FOR loops are used when the loop will iterate a fixed number of times which is defined at design time or is determined at runtime. When the number of iterations is unknown to the developer or program until runtime, other loop structures provide additional flexibility to the project solution.

After asking the first loop design question and determining that a count controlled loop will not meet the project requirement, the second question must be considered: Does the loop need to iterate at least once? If so the loop condition should be tested at the end of the loop (a trailing loop decision). If not, the loop condition should be tested at the beginning of the loop (a leading loop decision). The following examples do exactly the same thing, but use different loop structures depending on where the loop condition is tested. In the remaining VBA loop examples, note the keywords used to begin and end each type of loop.

Leading Decision Loops

Each of the next three procedures includes a loop that tests the loop condition at the top of the loop. The loop condition is an *entrance* condition for the loop. If the condition test is met, the loop will be entered. In addition to these examples, both of the VBA FOR loops use leading loop decisions.

VBA Loop Example 3:

```
Sub DoUntilTop()
    Dim a As Integer
    a = 1
    Do Until a = 5
        MsgBox ("a = " & a)
        a = a + 1
    Loop
End Sub
```

VBA Loop Example 4:

```
Sub WhileTop()
    Dim a As Integer
    a = 1
    While a < 5
        MsgBox ("a = " & a)
        a = a + 1
    Wend
End Sub
```

VBA Loop Example 5:

```
Sub DoWhileTop()
    Dim a As Integer
    a = 1
    Do While a < 5
        MsgBox ("a = " & a)
        a = a + 1
    Loop
End Sub
```

Trailing Decision Loops

Each of the following procedures includes a loop that tests the loop condition at the bottom of the loop. The loop condition is an *exit* condition for the loop. The loop will always be entered and execute at least once. When the condition test is met, the loop will be exited.

VBA Loop Example 6:

```
Sub WhileBottom()
    Dim a As Integer
    a = 1
    Do
        MsgBox ("a = " & a)
        a = a + 1
    Loop While a < 5
End Sub
```

VBA Loop Example 7:

```
Sub DoUntilBottom()
    Dim a As Integer
    a = 1
    Do
        MsgBox ("a = " & a)
        a = a + 1
    Loop Until a = 5
End Sub
```

The third loop design question addresses whether the loop condition should be expressed using positive or negative logic. There are very few cases in which the logic must be expressed as only positive or negative logic. Almost every loop condition used in VBA can be reversed to represent positive or negative logic. For example, a loop may continue to iterate as long as "rowNum < numRows" or it may iterate until "rowNum = numRows" or until "NOT (rowNum < numRows)." The WHILE loop structures use positive logic to continue the loop and the UNTIL loop structures use negative logic to continue the loop.

VBA loop examples 4, 5, and 6 (repeated below) all use WHILE loops which use positive logic for loop iteration. The two VBA FOR loops also use positive logic for the loop condition.

VBA Loop Example 4:

```
Sub WhileTop()
    Dim a As Integer
    a = 1
    While a < 5
        MsgBox ("a = " & a)
        a = a + 1
    Wend
End Sub
```

VBA Loop Example 5:

```
Sub DoWhileTop()
    Dim a As Integer
    a = 1
    Do While a < 5
        MsgBox ("a = " & a)
        a = a + 1
    Loop
End Sub
```

VBA Loop Example 6:

```
Sub WhileBottom()
    Dim a As Integer
    a = 1
    Do
        MsgBox ("a = " & a)
        a = a + 1
    Loop While a < 5
End Sub
```

VBA loop examples 3 and 7 (repeated below) all use UNTIL loops which use negative logic for loop iteration.

VBA Loop Example 3:

```
Sub DoUntilTop()
    Dim a As Integer
    a = 1
    Do Until a = 5
        MsgBox ("a = " & a)
        a = a + 1
    Loop
End Sub
```

VBA Loop Example 7:

```
Sub DoUntilBottom()
    Dim a As Integer
    a = 1
    Do
        MsgBox ("a = " & a)
        a = a + 1
    Loop Until a = 5
End Sub
```

VBA Indefinite Loop in Action

Consider the following worksheet that contains the results of employee evaluations. The employees are each evaluated by their manager and are also evaluated by two of their peers. The evaluation results are entered into a worksheet called "Evaluations."

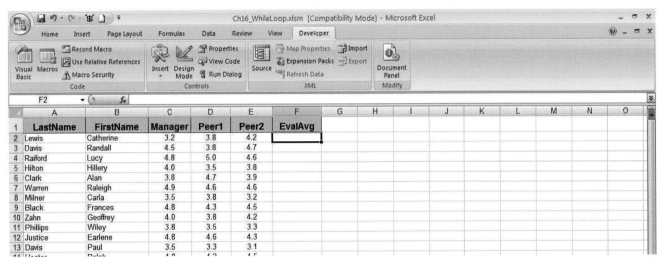

Figure 16-2: Partial worksheet for employee evaluations.

A VBA procedure is used to update all employee records with an average evaluation rating for each employee.

```
Sub UpdateAvg()
    Sheets("Evaluations").Range("a2").Select 'first employee last name
    Do While Not IsEmpty(Selection) 'tests the selected cell
        'moves to the cell 5 columns to the right and in the same row
        ActiveCell.Offset(0, 5).select
        Enters the formula into the selected cell
        ActiveCell.FormulaR1C1 = "=Average(RC[-1]:RC[-4])"
        ActiveCell.Offset(1, 0).Select 'the new selected cell
    Loop
End Sub
```

In the example above the loop condition is the selected cell not being empty. The "IS . . ." group of functions in VBA are useful for setting up loop conditions when interacting with worksheets in VBA. (Other IS . . . functions include IsArray, IsDate, IsError, IsNull, IsNumeric, and IsObject.) When the selected cell is empty, the loop terminates. Note the selected cell in Figure 16-3 is empty.

R1C1 Cell References

Excel uses two styles for referencing worksheet cells in Excel and VBA. The conventional (and default) type is called "A1" reference style. Worksheet columns are labeled with consecutive letters and rows are labeled with numbers. Each cell is referenced by its column letter and row number. An alternate style of cell reference is called "R1C1" reference style. In R1C1 reference style, columns on the Excel worksheet are labeled with numbers instead of letters. The rows are still labeled with numbers. When using the reference style, the row number is always referenced first usually preceded by an R, then the column number is referenced preceded by a C. To change the cell reference style for the Excel worksheets from A1 to R1C1, select the **Office Button→ Excel Options→Formulas→Working with Formulas** and check the box beside **R1C1 reference style**.

	A	B	C	D	E	F	G
1	**LastName**	**FirstName**	**Manager**	**Peer1**	**Peer2**	**EvalAvg**	
2	Lewis	Catherine	3.2	3.8	4.2	3.73	
3	Davis	Randall	4.5	3.8	4.7	4.33	
4	Raiford	Lucy	4.8	5.0	4.6	4.80	
5	Hilton	Hillery	4.0	3.5	3.8	3.77	
6	Clark	Alan	3.8	4.7	3.9	4.13	
7	Warren	Raleigh	4.9	4.6	4.6	4.70	
8	Milner	Carla	3.5	3.8	3.2	3.50	
9	Black	Frances	4.8	4.3	4.5	4.53	
10	Zahn	Geoffrey	4.0	3.8	4.2	4.00	
11	Phillips	Wiley	3.8	3.5	3.3	3.53	
12	Justice	Earlene	4.8	4.6	4.3	4.57	
13	Davis	Paul	3.5	3.3	3.1	3.30	
14	Hester	Ralph	4.0	4.2	4.5	4.23	
15	Crockett	Carol	4.0	3.9	4.2	4.02	
16	Richardson	Samatha	3.9	3.8	4.7	4.15	
17	Horne	Mickey	4.3	5.0	4.6	4.63	
18	Conrad	Michael	3.9	3.5	3.8	3.73	
19	Bateman	Matthew	3.9	3.6	3.8	3.75	
20	Brown	Rebecca	3.8	3.8	4.2	3.94	
21	Harris	Magan	3.8	3.5	3.7	3.66	
22	Singleton	Marc	3.8	4.2	3.9	3.95	
23	Norris	Kacey	4.8	4.6	4.5	4.63	
24	Livingston	Nadine	3.5	3.8	3.9	3.73	
25	Walker	Vance	4.1	4.0	4.3	4.13	
26	Schnider	Elizabeth	4.4	4.0	4.1	4.17	
27	Rogers	Timothy	4.0	3.8	4.7	4.17	
28	Ross	Kevin	4.2	5.0	4.6	4.61	
29	Jameson	Jennifer	3.9	3.5	3.8	3.73	
30	Edwards	Minnie	4.1	3.3	3.6	3.67	
31							
32							
33							

Evaluations

Figure 16-3: The procedure fills formulas in the "EvalAvg" column for each row. Note the selected cell is empty so the loop terminates.

	1	2	3	4	5	6	7
1	**LastName**	**FirstName**	**Manager**	**Peer1**	**Peer2**	**EvalAvg**	
2	Lewis	Catherine	3.2	3.8	4.2	3.73	
3	Davis	Randall	4.5	3.8	4.7	4.33	
4	Raiford	Lucy	4.8	5.0	4.6	4.80	
5	Hilton	Hillery	4.0	3.5	3.8	3.77	
6	Clark	Alan	3.8	4.7	3.9	4.13	
7	Warren	Raleigh	4.9	4.6	4.6	4.70	
8	Milner	Carla	3.5	3.8	3.2	3.50	
9	Black	Frances	4.8	4.3	4.5	4.53	
10	Zahn	Geoffrey	4.0	3.8	4.2	4.00	
11	Phillips	Wiley	3.8	3.5	3.3	3.53	

Figure 16-4: Column labels are numbers in the R1C1 reference style.

The advantage of using the R1C1 cell reference style is the ease in which column offsets can be determined by the developer. Instead of having to count offset columns, the developer can quickly subtract the source column number from the target column number to get the number of columns to offset. A positive value indicates offset to the right and a negative number means offset to the left. Row numbers can also be used in the same way to calculate row offsets. In the previous procedure, the source column at the beginning of the procedure is column number 1 and the target column, the one in which the formula is written, is number 6, so the offset is 6-1, or 5 columns. The result is positive, so the column offset is to the right.

The reference style as it is set in Excel has no effect on the way cells are referenced in VBA. When a macro is recorded, the reference style for selected cells is the A1 style. Cell selections are recorded by default using absolute references. When cell C3 is selected, the VBA code is *Range("C3").Select*. Cell ranges may also be captured in recorded macros as relative references from the current cell by toggling on the *Use Relative References* icon in the *Macro* task group of the *Developer* ribbon in Excel. When the feature is on, cell ranges are captured using the Offset property of the ActiveCell object. The VBA code "ActiveCell.Offset(2, 1).Select" resulted from recording a macro step with the relative reference option turned on.

In VBA, the A1 reference style can be used only as an absolute reference in the programming code. The R1C1 reference style is the way VBA handles dynamic cell references. Being able to reference cells dynamically can be a tremendous advantage with moving through a worksheet range of cells. The ability to reference cells in a specified range of cells using a relative reference enables a procedure to enter formulas into worksheet cells and use cells in positions relative to the formula cell as references for the formula or function being entered. Note the formula entered using VBA code uses R1C1 notation to reference adjoining cells as inputs to the AVERAGE worksheet function.

```
ActiveCell.FormulaR1C1 = "=Average(RC[-1]:RC[-4])"
```

The R1C1 reference style may also be used indirectly for referencing absolute cell ranges in VBA. To reference a range using A1 notation, the cell reference included as a qualifier for the VBA Range object in the following format "Range("C3")" or "Range("A2:E2")" for a range of cells. To reference a cell range using R1C1 notation, a Cells object is used. The first index provided in the object qualifier is the row number and the second argument is the column number in the following format "Cells(3, 1)". A range is specified using the Cells objects as qualifiers for a Range object in the following format "Range(Cells(2, 1), Cells(2, 5))".

The FormulaR1C1 property of a Range object (single or multi-cell) represents the formula of the range object in R1C1 style. The property may be used to capture the cell formula or to enter a cell formula. It is the property that is set when anything is entered into a cell in a recorded macro. The user's entry into the cell is recorded as a text string. Content captured from the FormulaR1C1 property is also a String value. When a formula is entered into a cell via the FormulaR1C1 property the equal sign (=) should also be included inside the double quotes since it must be written to the cell to indicate that a formula follows. Square brackets around row or column numbers indicate a relative reference. If there is no number following the R or C in the relative reference, the row or column without the number will not change. The FormulaR1C1 accepts only the R1C1 notation style for its formulas.

```
Cells(7, 7).FormulaR1C1 = "=RC[-1]+RC[-2]"    'uses a relative reference
Cells(8, 7).FormulaR1C1 = "=R3C3+R3C4"        'uses an absolute reference
```

The Formula property of a Range object parallels the FormulaR1C1 property and can be used to capture cell content and write cell content to the worksheet. It represents the A1 style of cell reference in VBA. Unlike the FormulaR1C1 property, the Formula property accepts both A1 style and R1C1 style references in its formulas. Use only the R1C1 notation in the Formula property for formulas that require relative references.

```
Cells(2, 7).Formula = "=D3 + D3"        'uses an absolute reference
Cells(3, 7).Formula = "=$D$3 + $D$3"    'uses an absolute reference
Cells(4, 7).Formula = "=R3C3 + R3C4"    'uses an absolute reference
Cells(6, 7).Formula = "=RC[-1]+RC[-2]"  'uses a relative reference
```

Nesting VBA Loops

The VBA FOR loops are ideal for processing array data since loop counters can easily increment to match array element subscripts in one dimension. In Excel we commonly work with cell ranges which are by nature two-dimensional arrays. For each row of a range that is processed, there may be multiple cells within the row to be processed. Two-dimensional arrays logically, and in many cases physically, represent an array whose elements are other arrays. An array of worksheet cells is a set of rows of which each contains a set of cells.

The most efficient way to process two-dimensional arrays is with nested loops. The outer loop will advance through one dimension of the array, and the inner loop will advance through the other array dimension just as if it was an array element of the outer array. When loops are nested, the loop control conditions for the two loops are managed separately although both loop exit condition values may be captured before either loop begins. (Remember that FOR loops always iterate at least once.) The following examples are simple VBA code examples used to demonstrate:

1. Capturing worksheet data from a range of cells.
2. Assigning the worksheet data to a two-dimensional array that matches the structure of the worksheet cell range.
3. Accessing elements of the two-dimensional array and writing each element back to a worksheet cell in a new contiguous range.

Nested Loop Example 1

The following VBA procedure captures data from each cell in a worksheet range and prints the cell data to the *Immediate* window. If you wish to execute the nested loop examples, open the "NestedLoops_ch16.xlsm" workbook and navigate to the "NestedLoops" module.

```
Sub GetWsData()
    Dim r As Integer            'row loop counter
    Dim numRows As Integer      'upper bound of row loop counter
    Dim c As Integer            'column loop counter
    Dim numCols As Integer      'upper bound of column loop counter
    Dim n As String             'the text string captured from the cell

    Sheets("Ladies").Activate
    'CurrentRegion is used for specifying a filled worksheet range.
    'Subtract one to get the correct array upper bound index.
    numRows = Range("A1").CurrentRegion.Rows.Count - 1
    numCols = Range("A1").CurrentRegion.Columns.Count - 1
    Range("A1").Select 'set a starting point

    'Two FOR NEXT loop, r and c are loop control variables (counters)
    For r = 0 To numRows
        For c = 0 To numCols
            n = ActiveCell.Offset(r, c).FormulaR1C1
            Debug.Print n
        Next
    Next
End Sub
```

Nested Loop Example 2

The following VBA procedure builds on the previous example. It captures data from each cell in a worksheet range and adds each cell's content to a two-dimensional array. It prints the value captured from the worksheet and also accesses each array element and prints it in the *Immediate* window. The two print statements should print the same name. The example also illustrates the concept of declaring an empty array, then re-declaring it so it may be filled. When an array size is determined by a program variable, VBA will not permit it to be declared initially using the variable indices. It must be declared empty first, then re-declared to set the size using variables.

```
Sub GetWsDataToArray()
    Dim r As Integer              'row loop counter & array index counter for
                                  '1st dimension
    Dim numRows As Integer        'upper bound of loop & array's 1st dimension
    Dim c As Integer              'column column counter & array index for
                                  '2nd dimension
    Dim numCols As Integer        'upper bound of column loop & array's 2nd
                                  'dimension
    Dim n As String               'the text string captured from the cell
    Dim arrName() As String       'the empty array

    Sheets("Ladies").Activate
    numRows = Range("A1").CurrentRegion.Rows.Count - 1
    numCols = Range("A1").CurrentRegion.Columns.Count - 1
    Range("A1").Select
    'Re-declare the array and assign a size using variables representing the row
        'and column count.
    ReDim arrName(numRows, numCols) As String

    For r = 0 To numRows
        For c = 0 To numCols
            n = ActiveCell.Offset(r, c).FormulaR1C1
            'Assign the captured cell value to the two-dimensional array
            arrName(r, c) = n
            'Print the variable captured from the worksheet.
            Debug.Print n & "is from the worksheet."
            'Print the value from the array, should be same as previous print result
            Debug.Print arrName(r, c) & "is from the array."
        Next
    Next
End Sub
```

Nested Loop Example 3

This example continues to build on the previous nested loop example. It goes one step further by performing the following actions.

1. Captures data from each cell in a worksheet cell range.
2. Assigns the data value to an array element in a two-dimensional array,
3. Accesses each element from the two-dimensional array and writes it to a new cell in the worksheet.

The procedure defines two ranges, one for the source range and one for the target range for the new data entries.

```
Sub GetWriteWsDataArray
    'These variables are the same as for the previous nested loop examples.
    Dim r As Integer, numRows As Integer
    Dim c As Integer, numCols As Integer
    Dim n As String
    Dim arrName() As String

    'Declare two ranges to define the source range and the target range
    Dim range1 As Range
    Dim range2 As Range
    'We know that the source range includes cell A1.
    Set range1 = Range("A1")
    'The starting cell for the new range
    Set range2 = Range("A6")
```

```
Sheets("Ladies").Activate
numRows = Range("A1").CurrentRegion.Rows.Count - 1
numCols = Range("A1").CurrentRegion.Columns.Count - 1
Range("A1").Select

ReDim arrName(numRows, numCols) As String

For r = 0 To numRows
    For c = 0 To numCols
        n = range1.Offset(r, c).FormulaR1C1
        'Assigns the captured value to a two-dimensional array
        arrName(r, c) = n
        Debug.Print n
        Debug.Print arrName(r, c) & "From the array"
            'Write the array element value back to the new worksheet range.
        range2.Offset(r, c).FormulaR1C1 = arrName(r, c)
    Next
Next
End Sub
```

Named workbook ranges may also be used to select a worksheet range. Since each named range is unique within a workbook, it is not necessary to activate the worksheet before referencing the named range. Once the range is selected, the rows and columns may be counted directly. To implement the named range "names" for the source data for the nested loop examples, replace this block of code:

```
Sheets("Ladies").Activate
numRows = Range("A1").CurrentRegion.Rows.Count - 1
numCols = Range("A1").CurrentRegion.Columns.Count - 1
Range("A1").Select
```

With this block of code:

```
Range("names").Select       'select the range named "names"
numRows = Selection.Rows.Count - 1
numCols = Selection.Columns.Count - 1
'select the first cell in the 2-D named cell range
Range("names").Cells(1, 1).Select
```

Managing Runtime Errors in VBA

You cannot assume users will always enter appropriate data and use the program as the developer intended. When a user performs some action that the program does not expect, a runtime error may occur. A runtime error will produce an error message to the user and cause the program to behave unpredictably at best, and most often causes the program to halt or shut down. Managing runtime errors is a time-consuming but essential part of programming. The goal of managing runtime errors is to prevent fatal program errors and keep the program running, or to control its shutdown in the event of an unavoidable fatal error.

There are two main strategies for managing runtime errors; avoiding them and handling them when they occur. As you have studied the examples and performed the practice exercises in this book, you have already seen the first error management strategy in action. Decision structures were often used to validate form data to prevent data of the wrong type or range to enter the project. Message boxes were used to instruct users to correct their input, and input boxes were used to give users a chance to provide new input to avert potential runtime errors.

Developers can predict many runtime errors, but rarely can they think of every user scenario that might occur. Discovery of the likely runtime errors results from extensive testing of the program in ways the users are likely to use it, including using it incorrectly. When runtime errors become evident as the program is tested, the developer writes code to manage each one to keep the program running. The VBA language includes error management commands that the developer can use to efficiently redirect the program in the case of a runtime error.

On Error Command

One solution to a runtime error is to exit the function or procedure using an exit statement, such as "Exit Sub" or "Exit Function." The exit statement may prevent the program from crashing, but it does nothing to support the program instructions in the remainder of the module. A better technique is to use a statement that will redirect the program to its recovery. The *On Error* statement directs the program flow to statements or modules written specifically to handle the particular program error encountered. The *On Error* statement may include the *GoTo* command that directs the program to a specific line of code that is specified after the *GoTo* keyword either by way of a line number or a line label. A line label is a word that follows the naming rules for variables and is followed by a colon. The error handling instructions are written beginning on the line immediately following the line label.

In most cases, it is best to place the error handling routines at the end of the function or procedure. Place an exit statement immediately preceding the error handler's label that ends the function or procedure. If the exit statement is omitted, the function or procedure will process the error handler routinely each time the module executes. Below is the basic framework in VBA for the placement of the *On Error* statement and the error handler routine. The actual instructions for processing the error would be written following the "Label:" line.

```
Sub MyProcedure()
    . . .
    On Error GoTo Label
    . . .
    Exit Sub
    Label:
    . . .
End Sub
```

If you wish to disable the error handler for a particular *On Error* statement, set the *GoTo* target to zero(0), for example, "On Error GoTo 0." The following procedure is a short example of how error handling may be used to redirect the program execution to help the application recover from a runtime error. The procedure attempts to assign a String value to a numeric variable. If the string contains no numeric characters, the conversion functions cannot convert the String to a numeric value. Only the Val function can extract a numeric value from a text string (value is zero (0) if no numeric characters are present). The error handling routine simply displays a message box to tell the user why nothing is printing. It may not be the most eloquent way of handling the error, but it does keep the program running.

```
Sub TestErrorHandling1()
    Dim stringVar As String
    Dim numVar As Single

    stringVar = "Hi"
    On Error GoTo ErrorHelp
    numVar = CSng(stringVar) 'produces runtime for original String value
    Debug.Print numVar
    Exit Sub
ErrorHelp:
    MsgBox "The variable cannot be converted to a numeric value."
End Sub
```

Resume Command

The *Resume* command can be used to redirect the program execution to a specific line of code within the module. The module will continue execution from that point forward, even though the *Resume* command may move the point of execution back to previous statements in the module. The *Resume* statement may be used immediately following and on the same line as the *On Error* command, or it may be used as a stand-alone statement in the error handling routine. When used in the error handling routine, it is the last statement at the end of the routine. The *Resume* command should be used in this context rather than the *GoTo* command to redirect program execution to another location within the module. The *GoTo* command should be reserved for directing the program to the error handling routine. The following options are available for using the *Resume* command.

- **On Error Resume Next:** When a runtime error occurs the program goes to the next line of code following the line that produced the error thereby continuing with the execution of the module.

- **Resume 0:** Resumes execution with the line of code that caused the error. The 0 is optional. This allows the program to retry executing the line that caused the error after some corrective action has been taken.

- **Resume <line or label>:** Directs the program execution to a specific line of code indicated by the line number or line label. A line label is followed by a colon.

If a separate error handling procedure is used to handle the runtime error, the procedure call should be placed after the error handling line label. The *GoTo* statement should direct the program execution to the error handling routine and the procedure call should be a part of the error handling routine. Do not attempt to call a procedure directly using the *GoTo* statement. Below is a revision of the previous example that shows additional functionality of the error handling routine. The user is notified of the error then is asked for new input using an input box. The result from the input box is assigned to the String variable. The program is then redirected to the point at which the error occurred. The *On Error* statement will continue to apply to each new attempt to process the line of code that follows it.

```
Sub TestErrorHandling2()
    Dim stringVar As String
    Dim numVar As Single

    stringVar = "Hi"
    On Error GoTo ErrorHelp
    numVar = CSng(stringVar)        'produces runtime error when no numeric
                                    'characters are present
    Debug.Print numVar
    Exit Sub
ErrorHelp:
    MsgBox "The variable cannot be converted to a numeric value."
    stringVar = InputBox("Please enter a numeric string.")
    Resume
End Sub
```

Err Object

Error handling can be more effective when the exact cause of the error is known. It is especially helpful if the program can give the user feedback on the cause of a runtime error. Each type of VBA program runtime error has an error number associate with it.

The *Err* object includes properties that assist with error identification. Properties of the *Err* object include *Number*, *Description*, and *Source*. *Number* is the number associated with the particular type of error. *Description* is the textual description of the error. *Source* is the file in which the error occurred. If multiple VBA projects are interacting, the *Source* will indicate which project file caused the error.

```
Sub TestErrorHandling3()
    Dim stringVar As String
    Dim numVar As Single

    stringVar = "Hi"
    On Error GoTo ErrorHelp
    numVar = CSng(stringVar)        'produces runtime error when no numeric
                                    'characters are present

    Debug.Print numVar
    Exit Sub
ErrorHelp:
    MsgBox "Runtime error number" & Err.Number & ":" & Err.Description
    stringVar = InputBox("Please enter a numeric string.")
    Resume
End Sub
```

After a *Resume* or *On Error* statement, the properties of the *Err* object are reset to the original values of zero (0) for the *Number* property and empty strings for *Description* and *Source* properties. If you wish to reset the properties in the VBA code, call the *Clear* method of the *Err* object in the following statement "Err.Clear."

It is very time-consuming for a developer to try to create all the potential runtime error types when writing error handling routines for a module. To help predict how the program will behave when a particular error type is encountered, the *Raise* method of the *Err* object can be used to simulate a specific error type by including the error number argument in the method call. Care must be taken to handle the simulated error as well as an actual runtime error to keep the program from crashing or entering an interminable cycle while error handling routines are developed. The following example procedure raises the "Internal Error" error then jumps back to the labeled line after the *Err.Raise* statement so that it does not enter into a cycle that the program or user cannot resolve.

```
Sub TestErrorHandling5()
    Dim stringVar As String
    Dim numVar As Single

    stringVar = "Hi"

    On Error GoTo ErrorHelp
    Err.Raise (51)
AfterSimulatedError: 'resume the program after the Err.Raise statement
    numVar = Val(stringVar) 'works, does not product runtime error
    Debug.Print numVar
    Exit Sub
ErrorHelp:
    MsgBox "Runtime error number " & Err.Number & ":" & Err.Description
    Resume AfterSimulatedError
End Sub
```

Protecting VBA Code

If others will be using the VBA projects you develop, you may wish to add protection to the VBA code so that it cannot be edited. If you are developing Excel projects for clients, you may wish to hide your proprietary code so it cannot be viewed or copied. You can secure your VBA code so that a password is required to view or edit the code modules. When code protection is enabled, the user cannot expand the project in the Project Explorer window so that the project objects cannot be viewed in the VBA application. Take the following steps to secure you VBA code.

1. In the VBA application, select **Tools→Project Properties→General (tab)** from the VBA menu bar.

2. It is a good idea to assign a name to the VBA project. Enter other project properties as desired. (This step is not required to secure the code.)

3. Select the *Protection Tab*.

4. Check the box beside *Lock project for viewing*.

5. Enter a password and confirm the password.

6. Click the OK button to save the settings.

7. Save the project and close the project. The VBA code protection will be enabled the next time the project file is opened.

When the VBA file is opened each time, the user may navigate to the VBA application and may view project file names in the *Project Explorer* window. When the user tried to expand a VBA project file to view its objects or modules, he will be prompted to enter the password.

Review Questions

1. What three questions should be answered to determine the best loop structure for a particular project requirement?

    _____

    _____

    _____

2. What characteristic differentiates the FOR NEXT and FOR EACH loops from other VBA loops?

    _____

    _____

    _____

3. What is special about the FOR EACH loop as it differs from the FOR NEXT loop?

    _____

    _____

    _____

4. What is a collection object?

    _____

    _____

    _____

5. What is an array?

    _____

    _____

    _____

6. What do collection objects and arrays have in common?

    _____

    _____

    _____

7. List two advantages in using arrays to handle program data?

_____

_____

_____

8. Explain the purpose of the VBA ARRAY function. How does using the ARRAY function differ from using a true array variable?

_____

_____

_____

9. List a specific requirement when processing a user-defined array with the FOR EACH loop.

_____

_____

_____

10. Which VBA loop type(s) can be used for negative logic loop decisions (the loop iterates when the loop condition evaluates to FALSE)?

_____

_____

_____

11. Which VBA loop type(s) can be used for positive logic loop decisions (the loop iterates when the loop condition evaluates to TRUE)?

_____

_____

_____

12. How does the R1C1 reference style differ from the A1 reference style on Excel worksheets?

_____

_____

_____

13. What is a runtime error?

_____

_____

_____

14. What two VBA commands are used to redirect program flow after a runtime error is encountered?

_____

_____

_____

15. How is the Err object used to manage runtime errors?

_____

_____

_____

16. How can a developer lock VBA code for viewing or editing by the user?

_____

_____

_____

Practice Problems

1. Open the "Grades_Prob16-1.xlsm" workbook. Insert a new VBA module. Write a VBA procedure that loops through the grade records and inserts the AVERAGE worksheet function into the last column. The AVERAGE function will average all four scores in each grade records.

2. Revise the previous loop to capture all the grade items for each grade record and average just the highest three scores. The average should be written to the last column of the list.

3. Revise the previous loop to capture all the grade items for each grade record, average just the highest three scores and assign a letter grade based on the average of the top three scores. The letter grade should be written into the last column of the list. Letter grades are based on the following scale.

   a. A: 90 and above
   b. B: 80 and above, but less than 90
   c. C: 70 and above, but less than 80
   d. D: 60 and above, but less than 70
   e. F: Less than 60

4. Open the "HealthClub_Prob16-4.xlsm" workbook. Insert a new VBA module. Write a VBA loop that loops through the member records and updates the membership fees based on the family size, age group of the primary subscriber, and whether or not the member receives a corporate subsidy for his membership. The following factors are considered when calculating the membership fee.

   a. Family size

   - The health club charges a base rate of $500/year for one person.
   - For two family members the rate is 1.5 times the base rate.
   - For three or more family members the fee is 2 times the base rate.

   b. Age group

   - If the primary member of the family is aged 60 years or older the total family membership fee is reduced by 10%.
   - If the primary member of the family is aged 70 or over the total family membership fee is reduced by 70%

   c. Corporate affiliation

   - If the primary membership subscriber is affiliated with a company that subsidized employee membership, the total family membership fee is reduced by 10%.

5. Revise the procedure you created in the previous problem so that the procedure will capture the input from the worksheet list and send it to the function you created in Problem 6 of Chapter 14. Write the function's return value into the annual membership fee column. The procedure should calculate a monthly fee and write it to the monthly fee column.

6. Open the "Inventory_Prob16-6.xlsm" workbook. Insert a new VBA module. Write a procedure that updates each inventory record by capturing the item cost and quantity on hand for each item and multiplying the two values to calculate the current inventory value for each inventory product. Write the new inventory value to the "CurrentValue" column. Add a button to the worksheet that that the user can click to execute the update procedure.

7. Open the "Employees_Prob16-7.xlsm" workbook. Insert a new VBA module. Write a VBA procedure that calculates a year-end bonus for each employee and writes it into the "Bonus" column of the "Employees" worksheet. The bonus calculation is based on the following rules:

   a. Hourly employees are assumed to work 2080 hours a year.
   b. Employees who earn more than $100,000/year receive a 3% bonus.
   c. Employees who earn less than $100,000/year receive a 5% bonus.

8. Open the "Employee_Prob16-8.xlsm" workbook. Insert a new VBA module. Write a procedure that captures the hire date for each employee, determines whether or not the employee is vested in the company retirement program and writes "Yes" or "No" to the "Vested" column. The employee must have worked for the company for at least 5 years to be vested.

9. Revise the procedure you created in the previous problem so that the hire date is captured and sent to the function you created in Problem 5 of Chapter 14. Write the function's return value to the cell in the "Vested" column for each employee.

10. **Challenge Problem:** In a new Excel workbook, insert a new VBA module and write a procedure that prints an amortization table to an Excel worksheet for the following problem.

    A friend needs to borrow $1500 to purchase a new laptop. She can afford to make payments of $75 each month. She would like your help in creating a solution that will print an amortization table in Excel that shows her payment number, payment amount, interest paid each month, and current balance after each payment. The interest rate is 1% a month. Create a procedure that will:

a. Print column headers Payment Number, Payment Amount, Interest, and Balance in the first row of a worksheet.
b. Print each payment number, payment amount, interest paid, and current balance for each payment on the next row each time.
c. Adjust the balance and last payment amount so that the last payment will be the exact balance and the ending balance will be zero. (Hint: test the balance inside the loop for a negative value each time.)

INDEX